THIRD EDITION

MANAGEMENT ACCOUNTING FOR BUSINESS

COLIN DRURY

SOUTH-WESTERN
CENGAGE Learning™

Australia • Brazil • Japan • Korea • Mexico • Singapore • Spain • United Kingdom • United States

SOUTH-WESTERN
CENGAGE Learning™

Management Accounting for Business
3rd Edition
Colin Drury

Publishing Director: John Yates

Publisher: Patrick Bond

Development Editor: Anna Carter

Production Editor: Alissa Chappell

Manufacturing Manager: Helen Mason

Senior Production Controller: Maeve Healy

Marketing Manager: Anne-Marie Scoones

Typesetter: Saxon Graphics, Derby

Cover design: Jackie Wrout

Text design: Design Deluxe, Bath, UK

For product information and technology assistance, contact **emea.info@cengage.com**.

For permission to use material from this text or product, and for permission queries, email **clsuk.permissions@cengage.com**

British Library Cataloguing-in-Publication Data
A catalogue record for this book is available from the British Library.

ISBN: 978-1-84480-152-7

Cengage Learning EMEA
High Holborn House, 50-51 Bedford Row
London WC1R 4LR

Cengage Learning products are represented in Canada by Nelson Education Ltd.

For your lifelong learning solutions, visit
www.cengage.co.uk

Purchase e-books or e-chapters at:
http://estore.bized.co.uk

Printed by C &C Offset, China
4 5 6 7 8 9 10 – 10 09 08

MANAGEMENT ACCOUNTING FOR BUSINESS

ABBREVIATED CONTENTS

CONTENTS

PART 2
Information for Decision-making   46

PART 3
Information for Planning, Control and Performance Measurement 260

PART 4
Cost Management and Strategic Management Accounting   426

PREFACE AND WALK THROUGH TOUR

The aim of this book is to provide an introduction to the theory and practice of management accounting and emphasize its role in making business decisions. It is intended primarily for students who are pursuing a one or two semester basic management accounting course. The more advanced technical aspects are not covered. These topics are covered in the author's successful *Management and Cost Accounting*, the sixth edition of which is also published by Cengage Learning.

Feedback from teachers in a large number of universities indicated that they had found the content, structure and presentation of *Management and Cost Accounting* extremely satisfactory and most appropriate for accounting students pursuing a two year management accounting course. They also indicated that there was a need for a book (based on *Management and Cost Accounting*) for students on shorter courses. This book is particularly suitable for accounting students on the following courses:

- A first-level course for undergraduate students
- Higher national diploma in business and finance
- Post-graduate introductory management accounting courses

An introductory course in financial accounting is not a prerequisite, although many students will have undertaken such a course.

Structure and plan of the book

In writing this book I have adopted the same structure and included much of the introductory content of *Management and Cost Accounting*. The major theme is that different information is required for different purposes. The framework is based on the principle that there are three ways of constructing accounting information. One is conventional cost accounting with its emphasis on producing product costs for allocating costs between cost of goods sold and inventories to meet external and internal financial accounting inventory valuation and profit measurement requirements. The second is the notion of decision relevant costs with the emphasis on providing information to help managers make good decisions. The third is responsibility accounting, cost control and performance measurement which focuses on both financial and non-financial information, in particular the assignment of cost and revenues to responsibility centres. This book focuses on the second and third of the above purposes. Conventional cost accounting is not emphasized because an understanding of this topic is not essential for those students who are not specializing in accounting.

This book consists of 16 chapters divided into four parts. The first part (Part One) consists of two chapters and provides an introduction to management and cost accounting and a framework for studying the remaining chapters. Part Two consists of seven chapters and is entitled 'Information for Decision-making'. Here the focus is on measuring and identifying those costs which are relevant for different types of decisions. The title of Part Three is

'Information for Planning, Control and Performance Measurement'. It consists of five chapters and concentrates on the process of translating organizational goals and objectives into specific activities and the resources that are required, via the short-term (budgeting) and long-term panning processes, to achieve the goals and objectives. In addition, the management control systems that organizations use are described and the role that management accounting control systems play within the overall control process is examined. The emphasis here is on the accounting process as a means of providing information to help managers control the activities for which they are responsible. Performance measurement and evaluation within different segments of the organization is also examined. Part Four consists of two chapters and is entitled 'Cost Management and Strategic Management Accounting.' The first chapter focuses on cost management and the second on strategic management accounting.

Major changes in the content of the third edition

To accommodate the enormous changes that occurred in the theory and practice of management accounting during the 1990s the previous edition incorporated an extensive rewrite of the text. Although significant changes in the content have been made to the sixth edition the major focus has been on pedagogical changes. The most notable alterations are:

1 New text has been added to Chapter 1 relating to the impact of information technology and the international convergence of management accounting practices.

2 New material relating to basing transfer prices on marginal cost plus opportunity cost has been added to Chapter 14 (Transfer pricing in divisionalized companies).

3 In Chapter 15 (Cost management) a new section has been added entitled 'Environmental cost management.'

4 The content relating to strategic management accounting and the balanced scorecard in Chapter 16 (Strategic management accounting) has been rewritten and new material has been added.

5 The introduction of illustrative boxed examples (entitled 'Real World Views') throughout the text highlighting the practical application of management accounting concepts and techniques by real companies operating in a range of industry sectors in various countries throughout the world.

6 The end-of-chapter summaries for all of the chapters have been rewritten and replaced with a comprehensive summary of the learning objectives listed at the beginning of each chapter. This will enable readers to test their knowledge of key concepts and evaluate their ability to achieve chapter learning objectives.

7 Revision of end-of-chapter assessment material. The assessment material consists of review questions and review problems. The review questions are short introductory questions that enable readers to assess their understanding of the main topics included in the text. Each question is followed by page numbers within parentheses that indicate where in the text the answers to specific questions can be found. The review problems are more complex and require readers to relate and apply the chapter content to various business problems. The problems normally begin with multiple-choice questions that generally take about 10 minutes to complete. The multiple-choice questions are followed by questions that generally progress according to their level of difficulty. Fully worked solutions to the review problems are provided in a separate section at the end of the book. A major feature of the third edition is that the number of solutions to the review problems provided in the separate section at the end of the book has been substantially increased.

8 Previous editions of the book contained end-of-chapter questions where the answers were only available to lecturers in the *Instructors' Manual* that was available to download from the website supporting the second edition. Seven case studies were also included in a separate section at the end of the book. These questions and case studies have now been removed from the text and are available for students and lecturers to access on the accompanying website www.drury-online.com. In addition, the number of case studies has been increased from seven to over thirty. Solutions to the questions and case study teaching notes are only available to lecturers on the lecturer's password protected section of the website.

Case studies

Details relating to the case studies that are available on the dedicated website for this book are provided in a separate section immediately following the final chapter. Both lecturers and students can download these case studies from the open access section of the website. Teaching notes for the case studies can be downloaded only by lecturers from the password protected lecturer's section of the website. The cases generally cover the content of several chapters and contain questions to which there is no ideal answer. They are intended to encourage independent thought and initiative and to relate and apply your understanding of the content of this book in more uncertain situations. They are also intended to develop your critical thinking and analytical skills.

Highlighting of advanced reading sections

ADVANCED READING

Some readers will not require a comprehensive treatment of all of the topics that are contained in the book. To meet the different requirements of the readers, the more advanced material that is not essential for those readers not requiring an in-depth knowledge of a particular topic has been highlighted. As shown here, the start of each advanced reading section is marked with a symbol and a blue line is used to highlight the full section. If you do require an in-depth knowledge of a topic you may find it helpful to initially omit the advanced reading sections, or skim them, on your first reading. You should read them in detail only when you fully understand the content of the remaining parts of the chapter. The advanced reading sections are not normally an essential requirement of an introductory course.

International focus

The book has now become an established text in many different countries throughout the world. Because of this a more international focus has been adopted. A major feature is the presentation of boxed exhibits of surveys and practical applications of management accounting in companies in many different countries, particularly the European mainland. To simplify the presentation, however, the UK pound monetary unit has been used throughout the book. Most of the assessment material has incorporated questions set within a UK context. These questions, however, are appropriate for world-wide use and contain the beneficial features described above for case study assignments.

Assessment material

Throughout this book I have kept the illustrations simple. You can check your understanding of each chapter by answering the review questions. Each question is followed by page numbers within parentheses that indicate where in the text the answers to specific questions can be found. More complex review problems are also set at the end of each chapter to enable students to pursue certain topics in more depth. Fully worked solutions to the review problems are provided in a separate section at the end of the book.

This book is part of an integrated educational package. Additional questions and case studies are available for students and lecturers to access on the accompanying website www.drury-online.com. Solutions to the questions and case study teaching notes are only available to lecturers on the lecturer's password protected section of the website.

Supplementary material

Dedicated website

The dedicated website can be found at www.drury-online.com The lecturer section is password protected and the password is available free to lecturers who confirm their adoption of the third edition - lecturers should complete the registration form on the website to apply for their password, which will then be sent to them by e-mail.

The following range of material is available:

For students and lecturers (open access)

Case studies

Internationally focused case studies. (NB Teaching notes to accompany the cases are available in the password protected lecturer area of the site).

Instructors' questions

Solutions are available on the password protected lecturer area of the site

Testbank *(compiled by Wayne Fiddler of Huddersfield University)*

Interactive multiple choice questions to accompany each chapter. The student takes the test online to check their grasp of the key points in each chapter. Detailed feedback is provided for each question if the student chooses the wrong answer.

Links to accounting and finance sites on the web

Including links to the main accounting firms, accounting magazines and journals and careers and job search pages.

For lecturers only (password protected)

Instructors' manual

Available to download free from the site in PDF (Portable Document Format), the manual includes answers to the instructors' questions on the open access website.

Teaching notes to the case studies

To accompany the case studies available in the student area of the website.

Powerpoint(TM) slides

Powerpoint(TM) presentations to accompany each chapter.

Overhead transparencies

Available to download as pdf files

Alternative course sequences

Although conceived and developed as a unified whole for a one year introductory course, the book can be tailored to the individual requirements of two separate modular semester courses. All or selected chapters from Parts One and Two can be assigned to the first module and Parts Three and Four to the second module. Alternatively, Part One and selected chapters from Parts Two and Three can be assigned to the first module and the remaining chapters to the second module. For example, topics selected from Chapters 1-5 and Chapters 10-12 may be assigned to the first module and the remaining content to the second module.

Acknowledgements

I am indebted to many individuals for their ideas and assistance in preparing this and previous editions of the book. In particular, I would like to thank the following who have provided material for inclusion in the text and the dedicated website or who have commented on this and earlier editions of the book:

Anthony Atkinson, University of Waterloo
Stan Brignall, Aston Business School
Jose Manuel de Matos Carvalho, ISCA de Coimbra, Portugal
Peter Clarke, University College Dublin
Jayne Ducker, Sheffield Hallam University
Ian G Fisher, John Moores University
Lin Fitzgerald, Loughborough University Business School
Wayne Fiddler, University of Huddersfield
Richard Grey, University of Strathclyde
Alicia Gazely, Nottingham Trent University
Antony Head, Sheffield Hallam University
Mike Johnson, University of Dundee

Michel Lebas, Groupe HEC
Peter Nordgaard, Copenhagen Business School
Deryl Northcott, University of Manchester
Dan Otzen, Copenhagen Business School
Rona O'Brien , Sheffield Hallam University
Graham Parker, Kingston University
Tony Rayman, University of Bradford
Carsten Rohde, Copenhagen Business School
Robin Roslender, University of Stirling
John Shank, The Amos Tuck School of Business, Dartmouth College
Helen Smith, Abertay University
Mike Tayles, University of Hull
Eric Tonner, Glasgow Caledonian Univeristy
Richard M.S. Wilson, Loughborough University Business School
Magdy Abdel-Kader, University of Essex
Keith Gainsley, Sheffield Hallam University
Phillip McCosker, University College Worcester
David Grinton, University of Brighton
Bhaguoan Moorjani, University of Westminster
Ben Ukaegbu, London Metropolitan University
Olive Gardiner, Fife College
Gin Chong, Southampton Institute
University of Ulster
Chandres Tejura, University of North London

I am also indebted to Patrick Bond and Anna Carter at Cengage Learning for their valuable publishing advice, support and assistance. My appreciation goes also to the Chartered Institute of Management Accountants, the Chartered Association of Certified Accountants, the Institute of Chartered Accountants in England and Wales, and the Association of Accounting Technicians for permission to reproduce examination questions. The answers in the text and accompanying instructors' manual to this book are my own and are in no way the approved solutions of the above professional bodies. Finally, and most importantly I would like to thank my wife, Bronwen, for converting the original manuscript of the earlier editions into final type-written form and for her continued help and support throughout the six editions of this book.

Walk through tour

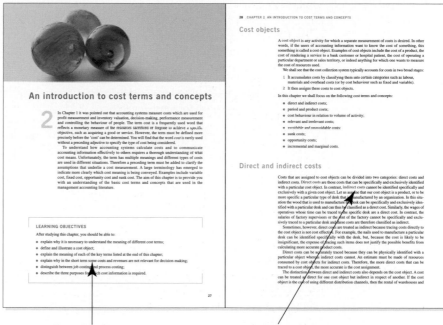

Learning Objectives
Listed at the start of each chapter, highlighting the core coverage that you should acquire after studying each chapter.

Key Terms and Concepts
Highlighted throughout the text where they first appear alerting the student to the core concepts and techniques. Also listed at the end of each chapter with page references.

Real World View
Real-world cases are provided throughout the text, they help to demonstrate the theory in practice and practical application of accounting in real-companies internationally.

Exhibits
Illustrations of accounting techniques and information are presented throughout the text.

Advanced Reading

The more advanced material that is not essential for those readers not requiring an in-depth knowledge of a topic has been highlighted. These should be read when you have fully understood the remaining content of the chapter.

---

430   CHAPTER 15 COST MANAGEMENT

Whereas traditional cost control systems are routinely applied on a continuous basis, cost management tends to be applied on an *ad hoc* basis when an opportunity for cost reduction is identified. Also many of the approaches that are incorporated within the area of cost management do not necessarily involve the use of accounting techniques. In contrast, cost control relies heavily on accounting techniques.

Cost management consists of those actions that are taken by managers to reduce costs, some of which are prioritized on the basis of information extracted from the accounting system. Other actions, however, are undertaken without the use of accounting information. They involve process improvements, where an opportunity has been identified to perform processes more effectively and efficiently, and which have obvious cost reduction outcomes. It is important that you are aware of all the approaches that can be used to reduce costs even if these methods do not rely on accounting information. You should also note that although cost management seeks to reduce costs, it should not be at the expense of customer satisfaction. Ideally, the aim is to take actions that will both reduce costs and enhance customer satisfaction.

Life-cycle costing

Traditional management accounting control procedures have focused primarily on the manufacturing stage of a product's life cycle. Pre-manufacturing costs, such as research and development and design and post-manufacturing abandonment and disposal costs are treated as period costs. Therefore they are not incorporated in the product cost calculations, nor are they subject to the conventional management accounting control procedures.

Life-cycle costing estimates and accumulates costs over a product's entire life cycle in order to determine whether the profits earned during the manufacturing phase will cover the costs incurred during the pre- and post-manufacturing stages. Identifying the costs incurred during the different stages of a product's life cycle provides an insight into understanding and managing the total costs incurred throughout its life cycle. In particular, life-cycle costing helps management to understand the cost consequences of developing and making a product and to identify areas in which cost reduction efforts are likely to be most effective.

Figure 15.1 illustrates a typical pattern of cost commitment and cost incurrence during the three stages of a product's life cycle – the planning and design stage, the manufacturing stage and the service and abandonment stage. Committed or locked-in costs are those costs that have not been incurred but that will be incurred in the future on the basis of decisions that have already been made. It is difficult to significantly alter costs after they have been committed. For example, the product design specifications determine a product's material and labour inputs and the production process. At this stage costs become committed and broadly determine the future costs that will be incurred during the manufacturing stage.

You will see from Figure 15.1 that approximately 80% of a product's costs are *committed* during the planning and design stage. At this stage product designers determine the product's design and the production process. In contrast, the majority of costs are *incurred* at the manufacturing stage, but they have already become locked-in at the planning and design stage and are difficult to alter.

It is apparent from Figure 15.1 that cost management can be most effectively exercised during the planning and design stage and not at the manufacturing stage when the product design and processes have already been determined and costs have been committed. At this latter stage the focus is more on cost containment than cost management. An understanding of life-cycle costs and how they are committed and incurred at different stages throughout a product's life cycle led to the emergence of target costing, a technique that focuses on managing costs during a product's planning and design phase.

Examples

Worked accounting examples are shown throughout the text.

---

350   CHAPTER 12 STANDARD COSTING AND VARIANCE ANALYSIS

EXAMPLE 12.1

Alpha manufacturing company produces a single product, which is known as sigma. The product requires a single operation, and the standard cost for this operation is presented in the following standard cost card:

Standard cost card for product sigma	(£)
Direct materials:	
2 kg of A at £10 per kg	20.00
1 kg of B at £15 per kg	15.00
Direct labour (3 hours at £9 per hour)	27.00
Variable overhead (3 hours at £2 per direct labour hour)	6.00
Total standard variable cost	68.00
Standard contribution margin	20.00
Standard selling price	88.00

Alpha Ltd plan to produce 10 000 units of sigma in the month of April, and the budgeted costs based on the information contained in the standard cost card are as follows:

Budget based on the above standard costs and an output of 10 000 units	(£)	(£)	(£)
Sales (10 000 units of sigma at £88 per unit)			880 000
Direct materials:			
A: 20 000 kg at £10 per kg	200 000		
B: 10 000 kg at £15 per kg	150 000	350 000	
Direct labour (30 000 hours at £9 per hour)		270 000	
Variable overheads (30 000 hours at £2 per direct labour hour)		60 000	680 000
Budgeted contribution			200 000
Fixed overheads			120 000
Budgeted profit			80 000

Annual budgeted fixed overheads are £1 440 000 and are assumed to be incurred evenly throughout the year. The company uses a variable costing system for internal profit measurement purposes.

The actual results for April are:

	(£)	(£)
Sales (9000 units at £90)		810 000
Direct materials:		
A: 19 000 kg at £11 per kg	209 000	
B: 10 100 kg at £14 per kg	141 400	
Direct labour (28 500 hours at £9.60 per hour)	273 600	
Variable overheads	52 000	676 000
Contribution		134 000
Fixed overheads		116 000
Profit		18 000

Manufacturing overheads are charged to production on the basis of direct labour hours. Actual production and sales for the period were 9000 units.

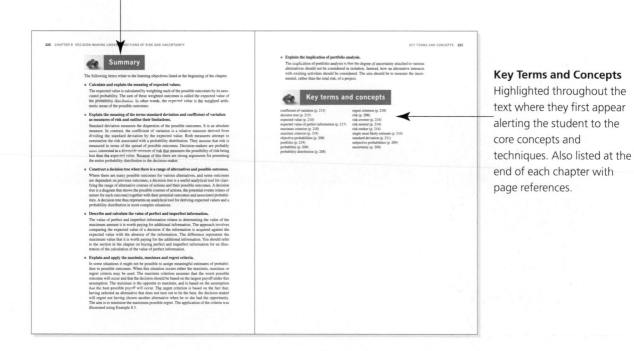

Review Questions

Review Questions allow revision of the main issues and concepts learnt within the chapter. Page numbers next to the questions show where the answers can be found.

Review Problems

Review Problems allow you to relate and apply the chapter content to various business problems. Fully worked solutions are found in the back of the text.

Summary

Bulleted list at the end of each chapter reviewing briefly the main concepts and key points covered in each chapter, linked back to the Learning Objectives.

Key Terms and Concepts

Highlighted throughout the text where they first appear alerting the student to the core concepts and techniques. Also listed at the end of each chapter with page references.

Accompanying Website

Visit the *Management Accounting for Business* 3/e accompanying website at www.drury-online.com to find further teaching and learning material including:

For Students

- Multiple Choice Questions for each chapter
- Case studies with accompanying questions
- Related weblinks
- Instructor Manual Questions

For Lecturers

- Instructors Manual – including model answers to Instructor Questions found on the students side of the site
- Downloadable PowerPoint slides and overhead transparencies
- Case Study Teaching Notes to accompany the case studies on the website and within the text

MANAGEMENT ACCOUNTING FOR BUSINESS

PART 1

Introduction to Management and Cost Accounting

1	Introduction to management accounting
2	An introduction to cost terms and concepts

The objective of this section is to provide an introduction to management and cost accounting. In Chapter 1 we define accounting and distinguish between financial, management and cost accounting. This is followed by an examination of the role of management accounting in providing information to managers for decision-making, planning, control and performance measurement. In addition, the important changes that are taking place in the business environment are considered. Progression through the book will reveal how these changes are influencing management accounting systems. In Chapter 2 the basic cost terms and concepts that are used in the management accounting literature are described.

Introduction to management accounting

1

There are many definitions of accounting, but the one that captures the theme of this book is the definition formulated by the American Accounting Association. It describes accounting as

the process of identifying, measuring and communicating economic information to permit informed judgements and decisions by users of the information.

In other words, accounting is concerned with providing both financial and non-financial information that will help decision-makers to make good decisions. An understanding of accounting therefore requires an understanding of the decision-making process and an awareness of the users of accounting information.

During the past two decades many organizations in both the manufacturing and service sectors have faced dramatic changes in their business environment. Deregulation combined with extensive competition from overseas companies in domestic markets has resulted in a situation where most companies are now competing in a highly competitive global market. At the same time there has been a significant reduction in product life cycles arising from technological innovations and the need to

LEARNING OBJECTIVES

After studying this chapter, you should be able to:

- distinguish between management accounting and financial accounting;
- identify and describe the elements involved in the decision-making, planning and control process;
- justify the view that a major objective of commercial organizations is to broadly seek to maximize the present value of future cash flows;
- explain the factors that have influenced the changes in the competitive environment;
- outline and describe the key success factors that directly affect customer satisfaction;
- identify and describe the functions of a management accounting system;
- provide a brief historical description of managment accounting.

meet increasingly discriminating customer demands. To compete successfully in today's highly competitive global environment companies have made customer satisfaction an overriding priority. They have also adopted new management approaches, changed their manufacturing systems and invested in new technologies. These changes have had a significant influence on management accounting systems. Progression through the book will reveal how these changes have influenced management accounting systems, but first of all it is important that you have a good background knowledge of some of the important changes that have occurred in the business environment. This chapter aims to provide such knowledge.

The objective of this first chapter is to provide the background knowledge that will enable you to achieve a more meaningful insight into the issues and problems of management accounting that are discussed in the book. We begin by looking at the users of accounting information and identifying their requirements. This is followed by a description of the decision-making process and the changing business and manufacturing environment. Finally, the different functions of management accounting are described.

The users of accounting information

Accounting is a language that communicates economic information to people who have an interest in an organization: managers, shareholders and potential investors, employees, creditors and the government. Managers require information that will assist them in their decision-making and control activities; for example, information is needed on the estimated selling prices, costs, demand, competitive position and profitability of various products/services that are provided by the organization. Shareholders require information on the value of their investment and the income that is derived from their shareholding. Employees require information on the ability of the firm to meet wage demands and avoid redundancies. Creditors and the providers of loan capital require information on a firm's ability to meet its financial obligations. Government agencies like the Central Statistical Office collect accounting information and require such information as the details of sales activity, profits, investments, stocks, dividends paid, the proportion of profits absorbed by taxation and so on. In addition the Inland Revenue needs information on the amount of profits that are subject to taxation. All this information is important for determining policies to manage the economy.

Accounting information is not confined to business organizations. Accounting information about individuals is also important and is used by other individuals; for example, credit may only be extended to an individual after the prospective borrower has furnished a reasonable accounting of his private financial affairs. Non-profit-making organizations such as churches, charitable organizations, clubs and government units such as local authorities, also require accounting information for decision-making, and for reporting the results of their activities. For example, a tennis club will require information on the cost of undertaking its various activities so that a decision can be made as to the amount of the annual subscription that it will charge to its members. Similarly, local authorities need information on the costs of undertaking specific activities so that decisions can be made as to which activities will be undertaken and the resources that must be raised to finance them.

The foregoing discussion has indicated that there are many users of accounting information who require information for decision-making. The objective of accounting is to provide sufficient information to meet the needs of the various users at the lowest possible cost. Obviously, the benefit derived from using an information system for decision-making must be greater than the cost of operating the system.

An examination of the various users of accounting information indicates that they can be divided into two categories:

1 internal parties within the organization;

2 external parties such as shareholders, creditors and regulatory agencies, outside the organization.

It is possible to distinguish between two branches of accounting, that reflect the internal and external users of accounting information. Management accounting is concerned with the provision of information to people within the organization to help them make better decisions and improve the efficiency and effectiveness of existing operations, whereas financial accounting is concerned with the provision of information to external parties outside the organization. Thus, management accounting could be called internal accounting and financial accounting could be called external accounting. This book concentrates on management accounting.

Differences between management accounting and financial accounting

The major differences between these two branches of accounting are:

- *Legal requirements.* There is a statutory requirement for public limited companies to produce annual financial accounts regardless of whether or not management regards this information as useful. Management accounting, by contrast, is entirely optional and information should be produced only if it is considered that the benefits from the use of the information by management exceed the cost of collecting it.

- *Focus on individual parts or segments of the business.* Financial accounting reports describe the whole of the business whereas management accounting focuses on small parts of the organization, for example the cost and profitability of products, services, customers and activities. In addition, management accounting information measures the economic performance of decentralized operating units, such as divisions and departments.

- *Generally accepted accounting principles.* Financial accounting statements must be prepared to conform with the legal requirements and the generally accepted accounting principles established by the regulatory bodies such as the Financial Accounting Standards Board (FASB) in the USA and the Accounting Standards Board (ASB) in the UK. These requirements are essential to ensure the uniformity and consistency that is needed for external financial statements. Outside users need assurance that external statements are prepared in accordance with generally accepted accounting principles so that the inter-company and historical comparisons are possible. In contrast, management accountants are not required to adhere to generally accepted accounting principles when providing managerial information for internal purposes. Instead, the focus is on the serving management's needs and providing information that is useful to managers relating to their decision-making, planning and control functions.

- *Time dimension.* Financial accounting reports what has happened in the past in an organization, whereas management accounting is concerned with *future* information as well as past information. Decisions are concerned with *future* events and management therefore requires details of expected *future* costs and revenues.

- *Report frequency.* A detailed set of financial accounts is published annually and less detailed accounts are published semi-annually. Management requires information quickly if it is to act on it. Consequently management accounting reports on various activities may be prepared at daily, weekly or monthly intervals.

The decision-making process

Because information produced by management accountants must be judged in the light of its ultimate effect on the outcome of decisions, a necessary precedent to an understanding of management accounting is an understanding of the *decision-making process*.

Figure 1.1 presents a diagram of a decision-making model. The first five stages represent the decision-making or the planning process. **Planning** involves making choices between alternatives and is primarily a decision-making activity. The final two stages represent the *control process*, which is the process of measuring and correcting actual performance to ensure that the alternatives that are chosen and the plans for implementing them are carried out. Let us now examine each of the items listed in Figure 1.1.

Identifying objectives

Before good decisions can be made there must be some guiding aim or direction that will enable the decision-makers to assess the desirability of favouring one course of action over another. Hence, the first stage in the decision-making process should be to specify the **goals** or **objectives of the organization**.

Considerable controversy exists as to what the objectives of firms are or should be. Economic theory normally assumes that firms seek to maximize profits for the owners of the firm (the ordinary shareholders in a limited company) or, more precisely, the maximization of shareholders' wealth. Various arguments have been used to support the profit maximization objective. There is the legal argument that the ordinary shareholders are the owners of the firm, which therefore should be run for their benefit by trustee managers. Another argument supporting the profit objective is that profit maximization leads to the maximization of overall economic welfare. That is, by doing the best for yourself, you are unconsciously doing the best for society. Moreover, it seems a reasonable belief that the interests of firms will be better served by a larger profit than by a smaller profit, so that maximization is at least a useful approximation.

Some writers (e.g. Simon, 1959) believe that businessmen are content to find a plan that provides satisfactory profits rather than to maximize profits. Because people have limited powers of understanding and can deal with only a limited amount of information at a time (Simon uses the term **bounded rationality** to describe these constraints), they tend to search for solutions only until the first acceptable solution is found. No further attempt is made to find an even better solution or to continue the search until the best solution is discovered. Such behaviour, where the search is terminated on finding a satisfactory, rather than optimal solution, is known as **satisficing**.

Cyert and March (1969) have argued that the firm is a coalition of various different groups – shareholders, employees, customers, suppliers and the government – each of whom must be paid a minimum to participate in the coalition. Any excess benefits after meeting these minimum constraints are seen as being the object of bargaining between the various groups. In addition, a firm is subject to constraints of a societal nature. Maintaining a clean environment, employing disabled workers and providing social and recreation facilities are all examples of social goals that a firm may pursue.

FIGURE 1.1 *The decision-making, planning and control process*

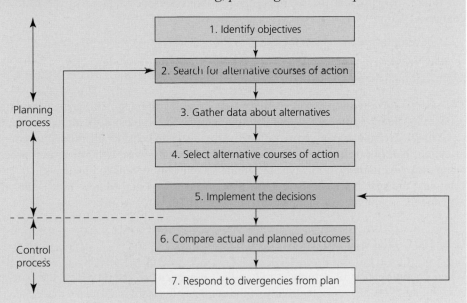

Clearly it is too simplistic to say that the only objective of a business firm is to maximize profits. Some managers seek to establish a power base and build an empire; another goal is security; the removal of uncertainty regarding the future may override the pure profit motive. Nevertheless, the view adopted in this book is that, broadly, firms seek to maximize the value of future net cash inflows (that is, future cash receipts less cash payments) or to be more precise the present value of future net cash inflows.[1] This is equivalent to maximizing shareholder value. (The concept of present value is explained in Chapter 9.) The reasons for choosing this objective are as follows:

1 It is unlikely that any other objective is as widely applicable in measuring the ability of the organization to survive in the future.

2 It is unlikely that maximizing the present value of future cash flows can be realized in practice, but by establishing the principles necessary to achieve this objective you will learn how to increase the present value of future cash flows.

3 It enables shareholders as a group in the bargaining coalition to know how much the pursuit of other goals is costing them by indicating the amount of cash distributed among the members of the coalition.

The search for alternative courses of action

The second stage in the decision-making model is a search for a range of possible courses of action (or **strategies**) that might enable the objectives to be achieved. If the management of a company concentrates entirely on its present product range and markets, and market shares and cash flows are allowed to decline, there is a danger that the company will be unable to generate sufficient cash flows to survive in the future. To maximize future cash flows, it is essential that management identifies potential opportunities and threats in its current environment and takes specific steps immediately so that the organization will not be taken by surprise by any developments which may occur in the future. In particular, the company should consider one or more of the following courses of action:

1 developing *new* products for sale in *existing* markets;
2 developing *new* products for *new* markets;
3 developing *new* markets for *existing* products.

The search for alternative courses of action involves the acquisition of information concerning future opportunities and environments; it is the most difficult and important stage of the decision-making process. Ideally, firms should consider all alternative courses of action, but, in practice they consider only a few alternatives, with the search process being localized initially. If this type of routine search activity fails to produce satisfactory solutions, the search will become more widespread (Cyert and March, 1969). We shall examine the search process in more detail in Chapter 10.

Gather data about alternatives

When potential areas of activity are identified, management should assess the potential growth rate of the activities, the ability of the company to establish adequate market shares, and the cash flows for each alternative activity for various **states of nature**. Because decision problems exist in an uncertain environment, it is necessary to consider certain factors that are outside the decision-maker's control, which may occur for each alternative course of action. These uncontrollable factors are called states of nature. Some examples of possible states of nature are economic boom, high inflation, recession, the strength of competition and so on.

The course of action selected by a firm using the information presented above will commit its resources for a lengthy period of time, and how the overall place of the firm will be affected within its environment; that is, the products it makes, the markets it operates in and its ability to meet future changes. Such decisions dictate the firm's long-run possibilities and hence the type of decisions it can make in the future. These decisions are normally referred to as **long-run** or **strategic decisions**. Strategic decisions have a profound effect on the firm's future position, and it is therefore essential that adequate data are gathered about the firm's capabilities and the environment in which it operates. We shall discuss this topic in Chapters 9 and 10. Because of their importance, strategic decisions should be the concern of top management.

Besides strategic or long-term decisions, management must also make decisions that do not commit the firm's resources for a lengthy period of time. Such decisions are known as **short-term** or **operating decisions** and are normally the concern of lower-level managers. Short-term decisions are based on the environment of today, and the physical, human and financial resources presently available to the firm. These are, to a considerable extent, determined by the quality of the firm's long-term decisions. Examples of short-term decisions include the following.

1 What selling prices should be set for the firm's products?
2 How many units should be produced of each product?
3 What media shall we use for advertising the firm's products?
4 What level of service shall we offer customers in terms of the number of days required to deliver an order and the after-sales service?

Data must also be gathered for short-term decisions; for example, data on the selling prices of competitors' products, estimated demand at alternative selling prices, and predicted costs for different activity levels must be assembled for pricing and output decisions. When the data have been gathered, management must decide which courses of action to take.

Select appropriate alternative courses of action

In practice, decision-making involves choosing between competing alternative courses of action and selecting the alternative that best satisfies the objectives of an organization. Assuming that our objective is to maximize future net cash inflows, the alternative selected should be based on a comparison of the differences between the cash flows. Consequently, an incremental analysis of the net cash benefits for each alternative should be applied. The alternatives are ranked in terms of net cash benefits, and those showing the greatest benefits are chosen subject to taking into account any qualitative factors. We shall discuss how incremental cash flows are measured for short-term and long-term decisions and the impact of qualitative factors in Chapters 4–9.

Implementation of the decisions

Once alternative courses of action have been selected, they should be implemented as part of the budgeting process. The **budget** is a financial plan for implementing the various decisions that management has made. The budgets for all of the various decisions are expressed in terms of cash inflows and outflows, and sales revenues and expenses. These budgets are merged together into a single unifying statement of the organization's expectations for future periods. This statement is known as a **master budget**. The master budget consists of a budgeted profit and loss account, cash flow statement and balance sheet. The budgeting process communicates to everyone in the organization the part that they are expected to play in implementing management's decisions. Chapter 10 focuses on the budgeting process.

Comparing actual and planned outcomes and responding to divergencies from plan

The final stages in the process outlined in Figure 1.1 of comparing actual and planned outcomes and responses to divergencies from plan represent the firm's control process. The managerial function of **control** consists of the measurement, reporting and subsequent correction of performance in an attempt to ensure that the firm's objectives and plans are achieved. In other words, the objective of the control process is to ensure that the work is done so as to fulfil the original intentions.

To monitor performance, the accountant produces **performance reports** and presents them to the appropriate managers who are responsible for implementing the various decisions. Performance reports consisting of a comparison of actual outcomes (actual costs and revenues) and planned outcomes (budgeted costs and revenues) should be issued at regular intervals. Performance reports provide **feedback** information by comparing planned and actual outcomes. Such reports should highlight those activities that do not conform to plans, so that managers can devote their scarce time to focusing on these items. This process represents the application of **management by exception**. Effective control requires that corrective action is taken so that actual outcomes conform to planned outcomes. Alternatively, the plans may require modification if the comparisons indicate that the plans are no longer attainable.

The process of taking corrective action so that actual outcomes conform to planned outcomes, or the modification of the plans if the comparisons indicate that actual outcomes do not conform to planned outcomes, is indicated by the arrowed lines in Figure 1.1 linking stages 7 and 5 and 7 and 2. These arrowed lines represent **'feedback loops'**. They signify that the process is dynamic and stress the interdependencies between the various stages in the process. The feedback loop between stages 7 and 2 indicates that the plans should be regularly reviewed, and if they are no longer attainable then alternative courses of action must be considered for achieving the organization's objectives. The second loop stresses the corrective action taken so that actual outcomes conform to planned outcomes. Chapters 10–13 focus on the planning and control process.

Changing competitive environment

Prior to the 1980s many organizations in Western countries operated in a protected competitive environment. Barriers of communication and geographical distance, and sometimes protected markets, limited the ability of overseas companies to compete in domestic markets. There was little incentive for firms to maximize efficiency and improve management practices, or to minimize costs, as cost increases could often be passed on to customers. During the 1980s, however, manufacturing organizations began to encounter severe competition from overseas competitors that offered high-quality products at low prices. By establishing global networks for acquiring raw materials and distributing goods overseas, competitors were able to gain access to domestic markets throughout the world. To be successful companies now have to compete not only against domestic competitors but also against the best companies in the world.

Excellence in manufacturing can provide a competitive weapon to compete in sophisticated world-wide markets. In order to compete effectively companies must be capable of manufacturing innovative products of high quality at a low cost, and also provide a first-class customer service. At the same time, they must have the flexibility to cope with short product life cycles, demands for greater product variety from more discriminating customers and increasing international competition. World-class manufacturing companies have responded to these competitive demands by replacing traditional production systems with new just-in-time production systems and investing in advanced manufacturing technologies (AMTs). The major features of these new systems and their implications for management accounting will be described throughout the book.

Virtually all types of service organization have also faced major changes in their competitive environment. Before the 1980s many service organizations, such as those operating in the airlines, utilities and financial service industries, were either government-owned monopolies or operated in a highly regulated, protected and non-competitive environment. These organizations were not subject to any great pressure to improve the quality and efficiency of their operations or to improve profitability by eliminating services or products that were making losses. Furthermore, more efficient competitors were often prevented from entering the markets in which the regulated companies operated. Prices were set to cover operating costs and provide a predetermined return on capital. Hence cost increases could often be absorbed by increasing the prices of the services. Little attention was therefore given to developing cost systems that accurately measured the costs and profitability of individual services.

Privatization of government-controlled companies and deregulation in the 1980s completely changed the competitive environment in which service companies operated. Pricing and competitive restrictions were virtually eliminated. Deregulation, intensive competition and an expanding product range created the need for service organizations to focus on cost management and develop management accounting information systems that enabled them to understand their cost base and determine the sources of profitability for their products, customers and markets. Many service organizations have only recently turned their attention to management accounting.

Changing product life cycles

A **product's life cycle** is the period of time from initial expenditure on research and development to the time at which support to customers is withdrawn. Intensive global competition and technological innovation combined with increasingly discrimating and sophisticated customer demands have resulted in a dramatic decline in product life cycles. To be successful companies must now speed up the rate at which they introduce new products to the market. Being later to the market than the competitors can have a dramatic effect on product profitability.

In many industries a large fraction of a product's life-cycle costs are determined by decisions made early in its life cycle. This has created a need for management accounting to place greater emphasis on providing information at the design stage because many of the costs are committed or locked in at this time. Therefore to compete successfully companies must be able to manage their costs effectively at the design stage, have the capability to adapt to new, different and changing customer requirements and reduce the time to market of new and modified products.

Focus on customer satisfaction and new management approaches

In order to compete in today's competitive environment companies have had to become more customer-driven and make customer satisfaction an overriding priority. Customers are demanding ever-improving levels of service in cost, quality, reliability, delivery, and the choice of innovative new products. Figure 1.2 illustrates this focus on customer satisfaction as the overriding priority. In order to provide customer satisfaction organizations must concentrate on those key success factors that directly affect it. Figure 1.2 identifies cost efficiency, quality, time and innovation as the key success factors. In addition to concentrating on these factors organizations are adopting new management approaches in their quest to achieve customer satisfaction. These new approaches are illustrated in Figure 1.2. They are continuous improvement, employee empowerment and total value-chain analysis. Let us now examine each of the items shown in Figure 1.2 in more detail.

The first item listed in Figure 1.2 refers to key success factors; which includes cost efficiency, quality, time and innovation. Since customers will buy the product with the lowest price, all other things being equal, keeping costs low and being **cost efficient** provides an organization with a strong competitive advantage. Increased competition has also made decision errors due to poor cost information more probable and more costly. If the cost system results in distorted product costs being reported, then overcosted products will lead to higher bid prices and business lost to those competitors who are able to quote lower prices purely because their cost systems produce more accurate cost information. Alternatively, there is a danger that undercosted products will result in the acceptance of unprofitable business.

These developments have made many companies aware of the need to improve their cost systems so that they can produce more accurate cost information to determine the cost of their products, pinpoint loss-making activities and analyse profits by products, sales outlets, customers and markets.

In addition to demanding low cost products customers are demanding high quality products and services. Most companies are responding to this by focusing on **total quality management** (TQM). The goal of TQM is customer satisfaction. TQM is a term used to describe a situation where *all* business functions are involved in a process of continuous quality improvement. TQM has broadened from its early concentration on the

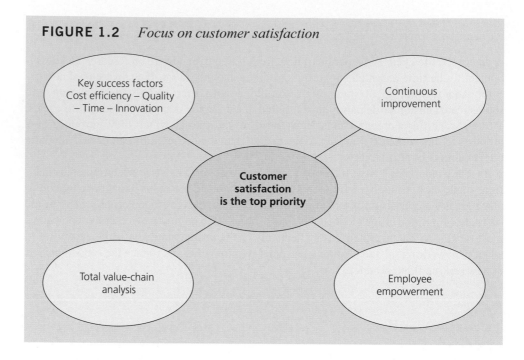

FIGURE 1.2 *Focus on customer satisfaction*

statistical monitoring of manufacturing processes, to a customer-oriented process of continuous improvement that focuses on delivering products or services of consistently high quality in a timely fashion.

Most European and American companies had always considered quality an additional cost of manufacturing, but by the end of the 1980s they began to realize that quality saved money. The philosophy had been to emphasize production volume over quality; but this resulted in high levels of stocks at each production stage in order to protect against shortages caused by inferior quality at previous stages and excessive expenditure on inspection, rework, scrap and warranty repairs. Companies discovered that it was cheaper to produce the items correctly the first time rather than to waste resources making substandard items that had to be detected, reworked, scrapped or returned by customers. In other words, the emphasis in TQM is to design and build quality in rather than trying to inspect and repair it after the event. The emphasis on TQM has created fresh demands on the management accounting function to expand its role by becoming involved in measuring and evaluating the quality of products and services and the activities that produce them.

Organizations are also seeking to increase customer satisfaction by providing a speedier response to customer requests, ensuring 100% on-time delivery and reducing the time taken to develop and bring new products to market. For these reasons management accounting systems now place more emphasis on **time-based measures**, which have beome an important competitive variable. **Cycle time** is one measure that management accounting systems have begun to focus on. It is the length of time from start to completion of a product or service. It consists of the sum of processing time, move time, wait time and inspection time. Move time is the amount of time it takes to transfer the product during the production process from one location to another. Wait time is the amount of time that the product sits around waiting for processing, moving, inspecting, reworking or the amount of time it spends in finished goods stock waiting to be sold and despatched. Inspection time is the amount of time making sure that the product is defect free or the amount of time actually spent reworking the product to remedy identified defects in quality. Only processing time adds value to the product, and the remaining activities are **non-value added activities** in the sense that they can be reduced or eliminated without altering the product's service potential to the customer. Organizations are therefore focusing on minimizing cycle time by reducing the time spent on such activities. The management accounting system has an important role to play in this process by identifying and reporting on the time devoted to value added and non-value added activities.

The final key success factor shown in Figure 1.2 relates to **innovation**. To be successful companies must develop a steady stream of innovative new products and services and have the capability to adapt to changing customer requirements. It has already been stressed earlier in this chapter that being later to the market than competitors can have a dramatic effect on product profitability. Companies have therefore begun to incorporate performance measures that focus on flexibility and innovation into their management accounting systems. Flexibility relates to the responsiveness in meeting customer requirements. Flexibility measures include the total launch time for new products, the length of development cycles and the ability to change the production mix quickly. Innovation measures include an assessment of the key characteristics of new products relative to those of competitors, feedback on customer satisfaction with the new features and characteristics of newly introduced products, and the number of new products launched and their launch time.

You can see by referring to Figure 1.2 that organizations are attempting to achieve customer satisfaction by adopting a philosophy of **continuous improvement**. Traditionally, organizations have sought to study activities and establish standard operating procedures and materials requirements based on observing and establishing optimum input/output relationships. Operators were expected to follow the standard procedures and management accountants developed systems and measurements that compared actual results with predetermined standards. This process created a climate whereby the predetermined standards represented a target to be achieved and maintained rather than a policy of continuous improvement. In today's competitive environment performance against static historical standards is no longer appropriate. To compete successfully companies must adopt a philosophy of continuous improvement, an ongoing process that involves a continuous search to reduce costs, eliminate waste, and improve the quality and performance of activities that increase customer value or satisfaction.

Benchmarking is a technique that is increasingly being adopted as a mechanism for achieving continuous improvement. It is a continuous process of measuring a firm's products, services or activities against the other best performing organizations, either internal or external to the firm. The objective is to ascertain how the processes and activities can be improved. Ideally, benchmarking should involve an external focus on the latest developments, best practice and model examples that can be incorporated within various operations of business organizations. It therefore represents the ideal way of moving forward and achieving high competitive standards.

In their quest for the continuous improvement of organizational activities managers have found that they have had to rely more on the people closest to the operating processes and customers to develop new approaches to performing activities. This has led to employees being provided with relevant information to enable them to make continuous improvements to the output of processes. Allowing employees to take such actions without authorization by superiors has come to be known as **employee empowerment**. It is argued that by empowering employees and giving them relevant information they will be able to respond faster to customers, increase process flexibility, reduce cycle time and improve morale. Management accounting is therefore moving from its traditional emphasis on providing information to managers to monitor the activities of employees to providing information to employees to empower them to focus on the continuous improvement of activities.

Increasing attention is now being given to **value-chain analysis** as a means of increasing customer satisfaction and managing costs more effectively. The value chain is illustrated in Figure 1.3. It is the linked set of value-creating activities all the way from basic raw material sources for component suppliers through to the ultimate end-use product or service

FIGURE 1.3 *The value chain*

delivered to the customer. Coordinating the individual parts of the value chain together to work as a team creates the conditions to improve customer satisfaction, particularly in terms of cost efficiency, quality and delivery. It is also appropriate to view the value chain from the customer's perspective, with each link being seen as the customer of the previous link. If each link in the value chain is designed to meet the needs of its customers, then end-customer satisfaction should ensue. Furthermore, by viewing each link in the value chain as a supplier–customer relationship, the opinions of the customers can be used to provide useful feedback information on assessing the quality of service provided by the supplier. Opportunities are thus identified for improving activities throughout the entire value chain. The aim is to manage the linkages in the value chain better than competitors and thus create a competitive advantage.

Finally, there are other aspects of customer satisfaction that are not specified in Figure 1.2 – namely, **social responsibility** and **corporate ethics**. Customers are no longer satisfied if companies simply comply with the legal requirements of undertaking their activities. They expect company managers to be more proactive in terms of their social responsibility. Company stakeholders are now giving high priority to social responsibility, safety and environmental issues, besides corporate ethics. In response to these pressures many companies are now introducing mechanisms for measuring, reporting and monitoring their environmental costs and activities. A code of ethics has also become an essential part of corporate culture. In addition, professional accounting organizations play an important role in promoting a high standard of ethical behaviour by their members. Both of the professional bodies representing management accountants in the UK (Chartered Institute of Management Accountants) and the USA (Institute of Management Accountants) have issued a code of ethical guidelines for their members and established mechanisms for monitoring and enforcing professional ethics. The guidelines are concerned with ensuring that accountants follow fundamental principles relating to integrity (not being a party to any falsification), objectivity (not being biased or prejudiced), confidentiality and professional competence and due care (maintaining the skills required to ensure a competent professional service).

The impact of information technology

During the past decade the use of information technology (IT) to support business activities has increased dramatically with the development of electronic business communication technologies known as **e-business, e-commerce** or **internet commerce**. These developments are having a big impact on businesses. For example, consumers are becoming more discerning when purchasing products or services because they are able to derive more information from the internet on the relative merits of the different product offerings. E-commerce has provided

A look at a key feature of easyJet's business

As one of the pioneers in the low cost airline market, easyJet bases its business on a number of principles:

- Minimize distribution costs by using the internet to take bookings. About 90% of all easyJet tickets are sold via the Web. This makes the company one of Europe's largest internet retailers.
- Maximize efficient use of assets, by increasing turn-around time at airports.
- A 'simple-service model' means the end of free on-board catering.
- Ticketless travel, where passengers receive an e-mail confirming their booking, cuts the cost of issuing, distributing and processing tickets.
- Intensive use of IT in administration and management, aiming to run a paperless office.

Source: easyJet website (www.easyjet.com)

the potential to develop new ways of doing things that have enabled considerable cost savings to be made from streamlining business processes and generating extra revenues from the adept use of on-line sales facilities (e.g. ticketless airline bookings and internet banking). The ability to use e-commerce more proficiently than competitors provides the potential for companies to establish a competitive advantage.

One advanced IT application that has had a considerable impact on business information systems is **enterprise resource planning systems** (ERPS). The number of adopters of ERPS has increased rapidly throughout the world since they were first introduced in the mid-1990s. An ERPS comprises a set of integrated software applications modules that aim to control all information flows within a company. They cover most business functions (including accounting). Standard ERPS accounting modules incorporate many menus including bookkeeping, product profitability analysis and budgeting. All the modules are fully integrated in a common database and users can access real-time information on all aspects of the business. A major feature of ERPS systems is that all data are entered only once, typically where the data originate. There are a number of ERPS packages on the market provided by companies such as SAP, Baan, Oracle and J.D. Edwards. SAP is the market leader with more than 7500 users in 90 countries (Scapens *et al.*, 1998).

The introduction of ERPS has the potential to have a significant impact on the work of management accountants. In particular, ERPS substantially reduce routine information gathering and the processing of information by management accountants. Instead of managers asking management accountants for information, they can access the system to derive the information they require directly by PC. Because ERPS integrate separate business functions in one system for the whole company coordination is usually undertaken centrally by information specialists who are responsible for both the implementation and operation of the system. In multinational companies this has standardized the global flow of information, but it has also limited the ability to generate locally relevant information.

Because ERPS perform the routine tasks that were once part of the accountants' daily routines, accountants must expand their roles or risk possible redundancy. ERPS provide the potential for accountants to use the time freed up from routine information-gathering to adopt the role of advisers and internal consultants to the business. This role will require management accountants to be involved in interpreting the information generated from the ERPS and to provide business support for managers.

International convergence of management accounting practices

This book has become an established text in many different countries throughout the world. It is therefore assumed that the content is appropriate for use in different countries. This assumption is based on the premise that management accounting practices generally do not differ across countries. Granlund and Lukka (1998) provide support for this assumption. They argue that there is a strong current tendency towards global homogenization of management accounting practices within the industrialized parts of the world.

Granlund and Lukka distinguish between management accounting practices at the macro and micro levels. The macro level relates to concepts and techniques; in other words, it relates mainly to the content of this book. In contrast, the micro level is concerned with the behavioural patterns relating to how management accounting information is actually used. Granlund and Lukka argue that, at the macro level, the forces of convergence have started to dominate those of divergence. They identify various drivers of convergence but the most important relate to the intensified global competition, developments in information technology, the increasing tendency of transnational companies to standardize their practices, the global consultancy industry and the use of globally applied textbooks and teaching.

Firms throughout the world are adopting similar integrated enterprise resource planning systems or standardized software packages that have resulted in the standardization of data collection formats and reporting patterns of accounting information. In multinational companies this process has resulted in the standardization of the global flow of information, but it has also limited the ability to generate locally relevant information. Besides the impact of integrated IT systems, it is common for the headquarters/parent company of a transnational enterprise to force foreign divisions to adopt similar accounting practices to those of the headquarters/parent company. A large global consultancy industry has recently emerged that tends to promote the same standard solutions globally. The consultancy industry also enthusiastically supports mimetic processes. Granlund and Lukka describe mimetic processes as processes by which companies, under conditions of uncertainty, copy publicly known and appreciated models of operation from each other, especially from successful companies that have a good reputation. Finally, the same textbooks are used globally and university and professional accounting syllabuses tend to be similar in different countries.

At the micro level Granlund and Lukka acknowledge that differences in national and corporate culture can result in management accounting practices differing across countries. For example, national cultures have been categorized as the extent to which: (1) the inequality between people is considered to be normal and acceptable; (2) the culture is assertive and competitive as opposed to being modest and caring; (3) the culture feels comfortable with uncertainty and ambiguity; and (4) the culture focuses on long-term or short-term outcomes. There is evidence to suggest that accounting information is used in different ways in different national cultures, such as being used in a rigorous/rigid manner for managerial performance evaluation in cultures exhibiting certain national traits and in a more flexible way in cultures exhibiting different national traits. At the macro level Granlund and Lukka argue that the impact of national culture is diminishing because of the increasing emerging pressures to follow national trends to secure national competitiveness.

Functions of management accounting

A cost and management accounting system should generate information to meet the following requirements. It should:

1 allocate costs between cost of goods sold and inventories for internal and external profit reporting;
2 provide relevant information to help managers make better decisions;
3 provide information for planning, control and performance measurement.

Financial accounting rules require that we match costs with revenues to calculate profit. Consequently any unsold finished goods stock or partly completed stock (work in progress) will *not* be included in the cost of goods sold, which is matched against sales revenue during a given period. In an organization that produces a wide range of different products it will be necessary, for stock (inventory) valuation purposes, to charge the costs to each individual product. The total value of the stocks of completed products and work in progress plus any unused raw materials forms the basis for determining the inventory valuation to be deducted from the current period's costs when calculating profit. This total is also the basis for determining the stock valuation for inclusion in the balance sheet. Costs are therefore traced to each individual job or product for financial accounting requirements in order to allocate the costs incurred during a period between cost of goods sold and inventories. This information is required for meeting *external* financial accounting requirements, but most organizations also produce *internal* profit reports at monthly intervals. Thus product costs are also required for periodic internal profit reporting. Many service organizations, however, do not carry any stocks and product costs are therefore not required by these organizations for valuing inventories.

The second requirement of a cost and management accounting system is to provide relevant financial information to managers to help them make better decisions. This involves both routine and non-routine reporting. Routine information is required relating to the profitability of various segments of the business such as products, services, customers and distribution channels in order to ensure that only profitable activities are undertaken. Information is also required for making resource allocation and product mix and discontinuation decisions. In some situations cost information extracted from the costing system also plays a crucial role in determining selling prices, particularly in markets where customized products and services are provided that do not have readily available market prices. Non-routine information is required for strategic decisions. These decisions are made at infrequent intervals and include decisions relating to the development and introduction of new products and services, investment in new plant and equipment and the negotiation of long-term contracts with customers and suppliers.

Accurate cost information is required in decision-making for distinguishing between profitable and unprofitable activities. If the cost system does not capture accurately enough the consumption of resources by products, the reported product (or service) costs will be distorted, and there is a danger that managers may drop profitable products or continue the production of unprofitable products. Where cost information is used to determine selling prices the undercosting of products can result in the acceptance of unprofitable business whereas overcosting can result in bids being rejected and the loss of profitable business.

Management accounting systems should also provide information for planning, control and performance measurement. Planning involves translating goals and objectives into the specific activities and resources that are required to achieve the goals and objectives. Companies develop both long-term and short-term plans and the management accounting function plays a critical role in this process. Short-term plans, in the form of the budgeting process, are prepared in more detail than the longer-term plans and are one of the mechanisms used by managers as a basis for control and performance evaluation. Control is the process of ensuring that the actual outcomes conform with the planned outcomes. The control process involves the setting of targets or standards (often derived from the budgeting process) against which actual results are measured. Performance is then measured and compared with the targets on a periodic basis. The management accountant's role is to provide managers with feedback information in the form of periodic reports, suitably analysed, to enable them to determine if operations are proceeding according to plan and identify those activities where corrective action is necessary. In particular, the management accounting function should provide economic feedback to managers to assist them in controlling costs and improving the efficiency and effectiveness of operations.

It is appropriate at this point to distinguish between cost accounting and management accounting. **Cost accounting** is concerned with cost accumulation for inventory valuation to meet the requirements of external reporting and internal profit measurement, whereas **management accounting** relates to the provision of appropriate information for decision-making, planning, control and performance evaluation. It is apparent from an examination of the literature that the distinction between cost accounting and management accounting is extremely vague with some writers referring to the decision-making aspects in terms of cost accounting and other writers using the term management accounting; the two terms are often used synonymously. In this book no attempt will be made to distinguish between these two terms.

You should now be aware from the above discussion that a management accounting system serves multiple purposes. The emphasis throughout the book is that costs must be assembled in different ways for different purposes. A firm can choose to have multiple accounting systems (i.e. a separate system for each purpose) or one basic accounting system and set of accounts that serve inventory valuation and profit measurement, decision-making and performance evaluation requirements. Most firms choose, on the basis of costs versus benefits criteria, to operate a single accounting system. A single database is maintained with costs appropriately coded and classified so that relevant cost information can be extracted to meet each of the above requirements. We shall examine in the next chapter how relevant cost information can be extracted from a single database and adjusted to meet different user requirements.

A brief historical review of management accounting

The origins of today's management accounting can be traced back to the industrial revolution of the nineteenth century. According to Johnson and Kaplan (1987), most of the management accounting practices that were in use in the mid-1980s had been developed by 1925, and for the next 60 years there was a slow-down, or even a halt, in management accounting innovation. They argue that this stagnation can be attributed mainly to the demand for product cost information for external financial accounting reports. The separation of the ownership and management of organizations created a need for the owners of a business to monitor the effective stewardship of their investment. This need led to the development of financial accounting, which generated a published report for investors and creditors summarizing the financial position of the company. Statutory obligations were established requiring companies to publish audited annual financial statements. In addition, there was a requirement for these published statements to conform to a set of rules known as Generally Accepted Accounting Principles (GAAP), which were developed by regulators.

The preparation of published external financial accounting statements required that costs be allocated between cost of goods sold and inventories. Cost accounting emerged to meet this requirement. Simple procedures were established to allocate costs to products that were objective and verifiable for financial accounting purposes. Such costs, however, were not sufficiently accurate for decision-making purposes and for distinguishing between profitable and unprofitable products and services. Johnson and Kaplan argue that the product costs derived for financial accounting purposes were also being used for management accounting purposes. They conclude that managers did not have to yield the design of management accounting systems to financial accountants and auditors. Separate systems could have been maintained for managerial and financial accounting purposes, but the high cost of information collection meant that the costs of maintaining two systems exceeded the additional benefits. Thus, companies relied primarily on the same information as that used for external financial reporting to manage their internal operations.

Johnson and Kaplan claim that, over the years, organizations had become fixated on the cost systems of the 1920s. Furthermore, when the information systems were automated in the 1960s, the system designers merely automated the manual systems that were developed in the 1920s. Johnson and Kaplan conclude that the lack of management accounting innovation over the decades and the failure to respond to its changing environment resulted in a situation in the mid-1980s where firms were using management accounting systems that were obsolete and no longer relevant to the changing competitive and manufacturing environment.

During the late 1980s, criticisms of current management accounting practices were widely publicized in the professional and academic accounting literature. In 1987 Johnson and Kaplan's book entitled *Relevance Lost: The Rise and Fall of Management Accounting*, was published. An enormous amount of publicity was generated by this book as a result of the authors' criticisms of management accounting. Many other commentators also concluded that management accounting was in a crisis and that fundamental changes in practice were required.

Since the mid-1980s management accounting practitioners and academics have sought to modify and implement new techniques that are relevant to today's environment and that will ensure that management accounting regains its relevance. By the mid-1990s Kaplan (1994) stated that:

> *The past 10 years have seen a revolution in management accounting theory and practice. The seeds of the revolution can be seen in publications in the early to mid 1980s that identified the failings and obsolescence of existing cost and performance measurement systems. Since that time we have seen remarkable innovations in management accounting; even more remarkable has been the speed with which the new concepts have become widely known, accepted and implemented in practice and integrated into a large number of educational programmes.*

Summary of the contents of this book

This book is divided into five parts. The first part (Part One) consists of two chapters and provides an introduction to management and cost accounting and a framework for studying the remaining chapters. Part Two consists of seven chapters and is entitled 'Information for Decision-making'. Here the focus is on measuring and identifying those costs which are relevant for different types of decisions.

The title of Part Three is 'Information for Planning, Control and Performance Measurement'. It consists of five chapters and concentrates on the process of translating goals and objectives into specific activities and the resources that are required, via the short-term (budgeting) and long-term planning processes, to achieve the goals and objectives. In addition, the management control systems that organizations use are described and the role that management accounting control systems play within the overall control process is examined. The emphasis here is on the accounting process as a means of providing information to help managers control the activities for which they are responsible. Performance measurement and evaluation within different segments of the organization is also examined.

Part Four consists of two chapters and is entitled 'Cost Management and Strategic Management Accounting.' The first chapter focuses on cost management and the second on strategic management accounting. The final part provides details of the case studies that are available on the accompanying website.

Guidelines for using this book

A comprehensive treatment of all of the topics that are contained in this book will not be essential for all readers. To meet the different requirements of the readers, the more advanced material that is not essential for those readers not requiring an in-depth knowledge of a particular topic has been highlighted. The start of each advanced reading section has a clearly identifiable heading and a vertical blue line is used to highlight the full section. If you do require an in-depth knowledge of a topic you may find it helpful initially to omit the advanced reading sections, or skim them, on your first reading. You should read them in detail only when you fully understand the content of the remaining parts of the chapter. The advanced reading sections are more appropriate for an advanced course and may normally be omitted if you are pursuing an introductory course.

Summary

The following items relate to the learning objectives listed at the beginning of the chapter.

- **Distinguish between management accounting and financial accounting.**

  Management accounting differs from financial accounting in several ways. Management accounting is concerned with the provision of information to internal users to help them make better decisions and improve the efficiency and effectiveness of operations. Financial accounting is concerned with the provision of information to external parties outside the organization. Unlike financial accounting there is no statutory requirement for management accounting to produce financial statements or follow externally imposed rules. Furthermore, management accounting provides information relating to different parts of the business whereas financial accounting reports focus on the whole business. Management accounting also tends to be more future oriented and reports are often published on a daily basis whereas financial accounting reports are published semi-annually.

- **Identify and describe the elements involved in the decision-making, planning and control process.**

  The following elements are involved in the decision-making, planning and control process: (a) identify the objectives that will guide the business; (b) search for a range of possible courses of action that might enable the objectives to be achieved; (c) gather data about the alternatives; (d) select appropriate alternative courses of action that will enable the objectives to be achieved; (e) implement the decisions as part of the planning and budgeting process; (f) compare actual and planned outcomes; and (g) respond to divergencies from plan by taking corrective action so that actual outcomes conform to planned outcomes or modify the plans if the comparisons indicate that the plans are no longer attainable.

● **Justify the view that a major objective of commercial organizations is to broadly seek to maximize the present value of future cash flows.**

The reasons for identifying maximizing the present value of future cash flows as a major objective are: (a) it is equivalent to maximizing shareholder value; (b) it is unlikely that any other objective is as widely applicable in measuring the ability of the organization to survive in the future; (c) although it is unlikely that maximizing the present value of future cash flows can be realized in practice it is still important to establish the principles necessary to achieve this objective; and (d) it enables shareholders as a group in the bargaining coalition to know how much the pursuit of other goals is costing them by indicating the amount of cash distributed among the members of the coalition.

● **Explain the factors that have influenced the changes in the competitive environment.**

The factors influencing the change in the competitive environment are (a) globalization of world trade; (b) privatization of government-controlled companies and deregulation in various industries; (c) changing product life cycles; (d) changing customer tastes that demand ever-improving levels of service in cost, quality, reliability, delivery and the choice of new products; and (e) the emergence of e-business.

● **Outline and describe the key success factors that directly affect customer satisfaction.**

The key success factors are cost efficiency, quality, time and innovation. Since customers will generally prefer to buy the product or service at the lowest price, all other things being equal, keeping costs low and being cost efficient provides an organization with a strong competitive advantage. Customers also demand high quality products and services and this has resulted in companies making quality a key competitive variable. Organizations are also seeking to increase customer satisfaction by providing a speedier response to customer requests, ensuring 100 per cent on-time delivery and reducing the time taken to bring new products to the market. To be successful companies must be innovative and develop a steady stream of new products and services and have the capability to adapt rapidly to changing customer requirements.

● **Identify and describe the functions of a management accounting system.**

A cost and management accounting system should generate information to meet the following requirements: (a) allocate costs between cost of goods sold and inventories for internal and external profit reporting and inventory valuation; (b) provide relevant information to help managers make better decisions; and (c) provide information for planning, control and performance measurement.

● **Provide a brief historical description of management accounting.**

Most of the management accounting practices that were in use in the mid-1980s had been developed by 1925, and for the next 60 years there was virtually a halt in management accounting innovation. By the mid-1980s firms were using management accounting systems that were obsolete and no longer relevant to the changing competitive and manufacturing environment. During the late 1980s, criticisms of current management accounting practices were widely publicized in the professional and academic accounting literature. In response to the criticisms considerable progress has been made in modifying and implementing new techniques that are relevant to today's environment and that will ensure that management accounting regains its relevance.

Note

1 The total profits over the life of a business are identical with total net cash inflows. However, the profits calculated for a particular accounting period will be different from the net cash flows for that period. The difference arises because of the accruals concept in financial accounting. For most situations in this book, decisions that will lead to changes in profits are also assumed to lead to identical changes in net cash flows.

Key terms and concepts

Each chapter includes a section like this. You should make sure that you understand each of the terms listed below before you proceed to the next chapter. Their meanings are explained on the page numbers indicated.

benchmarking (p. 15)
bounded rationality (p. 8)
budget (p. 11)
continuous improvement (p. 15)
control (p. 11)
corporate ethics (p. 16)
cost accounting (p. 20)
cost efficient (p. 13)
cycle time (p. 24)
e-business (p. 16)
e-commerce (p. 16)
employee empowerment (p. 15)
enterprise resource planning systems (p. 17)
feedback (p. 11)
feedback loop (p. 11)
financial accounting (p. 7)
goals of the organization (p. 8)
innovation (p. 15)
internet commerce (p. 16)

long-run decisions (p. 10)
management accounting (p. 7)
management by exception (p. 11)
master budget (p. 11)
non-value added activities (p. 14)
objectives of the organization (p. 8)
operating decisions (p. 10)
performance reports (p. 11)
planning (p. 8)
product life cycle (p. 13)
satisficing (p. 8)
short-term decisions (p. 10)
social responsibility (p. 15)
states of nature (p. 10)
strategic decisions (p. 10)
strategies (p. 9)
time-based measures (p. 14)
total quality management (p. 13)
value-chain analysis (p. 15)

Assessment material

Review questions

The review questions are short questions that enable you to assess your understanding of the main topics included in the chapter. The numbers in parentheses provide you with the page numbers to refer to if you cannot answer a specific question.

Review problems

The remaining chapters also contain review problems. These are more complex and require you to relate and apply the chapter content to various business problems. Fully worked solutions to the review problems are provided in a separate section at the end of the book.

Case studies

The website also includes over 30 case study problems. A list of these cases is provided on pages 491–493. The Electronic Boards case is a case study that is relevant to the introductory stages of a management accounting course.

Review questions

1.1 Identify and describe the different users of accounting information. *(pp. 6–7)*

1.2 Describe the differences between management accounting and financial accounting. *(pp. 7–8)*

1.3 Explain each of the elements of the decision-making, planning and control process. *(pp. 8–12)*

1.4 Describe what is meant by management by exception. *(p. 11)*

1.5 What is a product's life cycle? *(p. 13)*

1.6 Describe what is meant by continuous improvement, benchmarking and employee empowerment. *(p. 15)*

1.7 Describe the different activities in the value chain. *(pp. 15–16)*

1.8 Explain why firms are beginning to concentrate on social responsibility and corporate ethics. *(p. 16)*

1.9 Describe the different functions of management accounting. *(pp. 18–20)*

1.10 Describe enterprise resource planning systems and their impact on management accountants. *(p. 17)*

1.11 Provide a brief historical description of management accounting. *(pp. 20–21)*

An introduction to cost terms and concepts

2 In Chapter 1 it was pointed out that accounting systems measure costs which are used for profit measurement and inventory valuation, decision-making, performance measurement and controlling the behaviour of people. The term cost is a frequently used word that reflects a monetary measure of the resources sacrificed or forgone to achieve a specific objective, such as acquiring a good or service. However, the term must be defined more precisely before the 'cost' can be determined. You will find that the word *cost* is rarely used without a preceding adjective to specify the type of cost being considered.

To understand how accounting systems calculate costs and to communicate accounting information effectively to others requires a thorough understanding of what cost means. Unfortunately, the term has multiple meanings and different types of costs are used in different situations. Therefore a preceding term must be added to clarify the assumptions that underlie a cost measurement. A large terminology has emerged to indicate more clearly which cost meaning is being conveyed. Examples include variable cost, fixed cost, opportunity cost and sunk cost. The aim of this chapter is to provide you with an understanding of the basic cost terms and concepts that are used in the management accounting literature.

LEARNING OBJECTIVES

After studying this chapter, you should be able to:

- explain why it is necessary to understand the meaning of different cost terms;
- define and illustrate a cost object;
- explain the meaning of each of the key terms listed at the end of this chapter;
- explain why in the short term some costs and revenues are not relevant for decision-making;
- distinguish between job costing and process costing;
- describe the three purposes for which cost information is required.

Cost objects

A **cost object** is any activity for which a separate measurement of costs is desired. In other words, if the users of accounting information want to know the cost of something, this something is called a cost object. Examples of cost objects include the cost of a product, the cost of rendering a service to a bank customer or hospital patient, the cost of operating a particular department or sales territory, or indeed anything for which one wants to measure the cost of resources used.

We shall see that the cost collection system typically accounts for costs in two broad stages:

1 It accumulates costs by classifying them into certain categories such as labour, materials and overhead costs (or by cost behaviour such as fixed and variable).

2 It then assigns these costs to cost objects.

In this chapter we shall focus on the following cost terms and concepts:

- direct and indirect costs;
- period and product costs;
- cost behaviour in relation to volume of activity;
- relevant and irrelevant costs;
- avoidable and unavoidable costs;
- sunk costs;
- opportunity costs;
- incremental and marginal costs.

Direct and indirect costs

Costs that are assigned to cost objects can be divided into two categories: direct costs and indirect costs. **Direct costs** are those costs that can be specifically and exclusively identified with a particular cost object. In contrast, **indirect costs** cannot be identified specifically and exclusively with a given cost object. Let us assume that our cost object is a product, or to be more specific a particular type of desk that is manufactured by an organization. In this situation the wood that is used to manufacture the desk can be specifically and exclusively identified with a particular desk and can thus be classified as a direct cost. Similarly, the wages of operatives whose time can be traced to the specific desk are a direct cost. In contrast, the salaries of factory supervisors or the rent of the factory cannot be specifically and exclusively traced to a particular desk and these costs are therefore classified as indirect.

Sometimes, however, direct costs are treated as indirect because tracing costs directly to the cost object is not cost effective. For example, the nails used to manufacture a particular desk can be identified specifically with the desk, but, because the cost is likely to be insignificant, the expense of tracing such items does not justify the possible benefits from calculating more accurate product costs.

Direct costs can be accurately traced because they can be physically identified with a particular object whereas indirect costs cannot. An estimate must be made of resources consumed by cost objects for indirect costs. Therefore, the more direct costs that can be traced to a cost object, the more accurate is the cost assignment.

The distinction between direct and indirect costs also depends on the cost object. A cost can be treated as direct for one cost object but indirect in respect of another. If the cost object is the cost of using different distribution channels, then the rental of warehouses and the salaries of storekeepers will be regarded as direct for each distribution channel. Also consider a supervisor's salary in a maintenance department of a manufacturing company. If the cost object is the maintenance department, then the salary is a direct cost. However, if the cost object is the product, both the warehouse rental and the salaries of the storekeepers and the supervisor will be an indirect cost because these costs cannot be specifically identified with the product.

Categories of manufacturing costs

In manufacturing organizations products are frequently the cost object. Traditionally, cost accounting systems in manufacturing organizations have reflected the need to assign costs to products to value stocks and measure profits based on imposed external financial accounting requirements. Cost accounting systems typically accumulate product costs as follows:

Direct materials	xxx
Direct labour	xxx
Prime cost	xxx
Manufacturing overhead	xxx
Total manufacturing cost	xxx

Direct materials consist of all those materials that can be identified with a specific product. For example, wood that is used to manufacture a desk can easily be identified as part of the product, and can thus be classified as direct materials. Alternatively, materials used for the repair of a machine that is used for the manufacture of many different desks are classified as **indirect materials**. These items of materials cannot be identified with any one product, because they are used for the benefit of all products rather than for any one specific product. Note that indirect materials form part of the manufacturing overhead cost.

   Direct labour consists of those labour costs that can be specifically traced to or identified with a particular product. Examples of direct labour costs include the wages of operatives who assemble parts into the finished product, or machine operatives engaged in the production process. By contrast, the salaries of factory supervisors or the wages paid to the staff in the stores department cannot be specifically identified with the product, and thus form part of the **indirect labour costs**. The wages of all employees who do not work on the product itself but who assist in the manufacturing operation are thus classified as part of the indirect labour costs. As with indirect materials, indirect labour is classified as part of the manufacturing overhead cost.

   Prime cost refers to the direct costs of the product and consists of direct labour costs plus direct material costs plus any direct expenses. The cost of hiring a machine for producing a specific product is an example of a direct expense.

   Manufacturing overhead consists of all manufacturing costs other than direct labour, direct materials and direct expenses. It therefore includes all indirect manufacturing labour and materials costs plus indirect manufacturing expenses. Examples of indirect manufacturing expenses in a multi-product company include rent of the factory and depreciation of machinery.

   To ascertain the total manufacturing cost of a product, all that is required for the direct cost items is to record the amount of resources used on the appropriate documents. The specific product or order (i.e. the cost object) to which the costs should be assigned should be entered on the document. For example, the units of materials used in making a particular product are recorded on a stores requisition, and the hours of direct labour used are recorded on job cards. Having obtained the quantity of resources used for the direct items, it is necessary to ascertain the price paid for these resources. The total of the resources used multiplied by the price paid per unit of resources used provides us with the total of the direct costs or the prime cost for a product.

Manufacturing overheads cannot be directly traced to products. Instead they are assigned to products using **cost allocations**. A cost allocation is the process of estimating the cost of resources consumed by products that involves the use of surrogate, rather than direct measures. The process of assigning indirect costs (overheads) to cost objects will be explained in the next chapter.

Period and product costs

External financial accounting rules in most countries require that for inventory valuation, only manufacturing costs should be included in the calculation of product costs (see United Kingdom Statement of Standard Accounting Practice (SSAP 9), published by the Accounting Standards Committee). Accountants therefore classify costs as product costs and period costs. **Product costs** are those costs that are identified with goods purchased or produced for resale. In a manufacturing organization they are costs that the accountant attaches to the product and that are included in the inventory valuation for finished goods, or for partly completed goods (work in progress), until they are sold; they are then recorded as expenses and matched against sales for calculating profit. **Period costs** are those costs that are not included in the inventory valuation and as a result are treated as expenses in the period in which they are incurred. *Hence no attempt is made to attach period costs to products for inventory valuation purposes.*

In a manufacturing organization all manufacturing costs are regarded as product costs and non-manufacturing costs are regarded as period costs. Companies operating in the merchandising sector, such as retailing or wholesaling organizations, purchase goods for resale without changing their basic form. The cost of the goods purchased is regarded as a product cost and all other costs such as administration and selling and distribution expenses are considered to be period costs. The treatment of period and product costs for a manufacturing organization is illustrated in Figure 2.1. You will see that both product and period costs are eventually classified as expenses. The major difference is the point in time at which they are so classified.

Why are non-manufacturing costs treated as period costs and not included in the inventory valuation? There are two reasons. First, inventories are assets (unsold production) and assets represent resources that have been acquired that are expected to contribute to future revenue. Manufacturing costs incurred in making a product can be expected to generate future revenues to cover the cost of production. There is no guarantee, however, that non-manufacturing costs will generate future revenue, because they do not represent value added to any specific product. Therefore, they are not included in the inventory valuation. Second, many non-manufacturing costs (e.g. distribution costs) are not incurred when the product is being stored. Hence it is inappropriate to include such costs within the inventory valuation.

Cost behaviour

A knowledge of how costs and revenues will vary with different levels of activity (or volume) is essential for decision-making. Activity or volume may be measured in terms of units of production or sales, hours worked, miles travelled, patients seen, students enrolled

FIGURE 2.1   *Treatment of period and product costs*

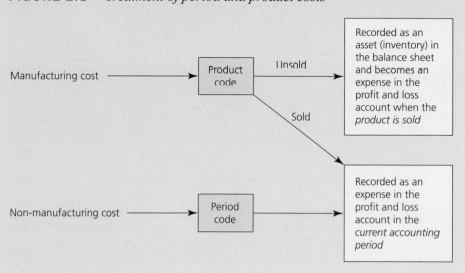

or any other appropriate measure of the activity of an organization. Examples of decisions that require information on how costs and revenues vary with different levels of activity include the following:

1 What should the planned level of activity be for the next year?

2 Should we reduce the selling price to sell more units?

3 Would it be wiser to pay our sales staff by a straight commission, a straight salary, or by some combination of the two?

4 How do the costs and revenues of a hospital change if one more patient is admitted for a seven-day stay?

5 How do the costs and revenues of a hotel change if a room and meals are provided for two guests for a seven-day stay?

6 How will costs and revenues change if output is increased (or decreased) by 15%?

For each of the above decisions management requires estimates of costs and revenues at different levels of activity for the alternative courses of action.

The terms 'variable', 'fixed', 'semi-variable' and 'semi-fixed' have been traditionally used in the management accounting literature to describe how a cost reacts to changes in activity. Short-term **variable costs** vary in direct proportion to the volume of activity; that is, doubling the level of activity will double the total variable cost. Consequently, *total* variable costs are linear and *unit* variable cost is constant. Figure 2.2 illustrates a variable cost where the variable cost per unit of activity is £10. It is unlikely that variable cost per unit will be constant for all levels of activity. We shall discuss the reasons why accountants normally assume that variable costs are constant per unit of activity in the next chapter. Examples of short-term variable manufacturing costs include piecework labour, direct materials and energy to operate the machines. These costs are assumed to fluctuate directly in proportion to operating activity within a certain range of activity. Examples of non-manufacturing variable costs include sales commissions, which fluctuate with sales value, and petrol, which fluctuates with the number of miles travelled.

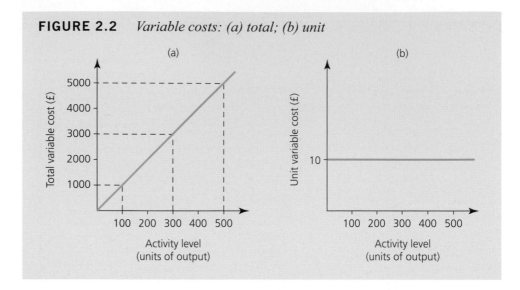

FIGURE 2.2 *Variable costs: (a) total; (b) unit*

Fixed costs remain constant over wide ranges of activity for a specified time period. Examples of fixed costs include depreciation of the factory building, supervisors' salaries and leasing charges for cars used by the salesforce. Figure 2.3 illustrates fixed costs.

You will see that the *total* fixed costs are constant for all levels of activity whereas *unit* fixed costs decrease proportionally with the level of activity. For example, if the total of the fixed costs is £5000 for a month the fixed costs per unit will be as follows:

Units produced	Fixed cost per unit (£)
1	5000
10	500
100	50
1000	5

Because unit fixed costs are not constant per unit they must be interpreted with caution. For decision-making, it is better to work with total fixed costs rather than unit costs.

In practice it is unlikely that fixed costs will be constant over the full range of activity. They may increase in steps in the manner depicted in Figure 2.4. We shall discuss the justification for assuming that fixed costs are constant over a wide range of activity in the next chapter.

The distinction between fixed and variable costs must be made relative to the time period under consideration. Over a sufficiently long time period of several years, virtually all costs are variable. During such a long period of time, contraction in demand will be accompanied by reductions in virtually all categories of costs. For example, senior managers can be released, machinery need not be replaced and even buildings and land can be sold. Similarly, large expansions in activity will eventually cause all categories of costs to increase.

Within shorter time periods, costs will be fixed or variable in relation to changes in activity. The shorter the time period, the greater the probability that a particular cost will be fixed. Consider a time period of one year. The costs of providing the firm's operating capacity such as depreciation and the salaries of senior plant managers are likely to be fixed

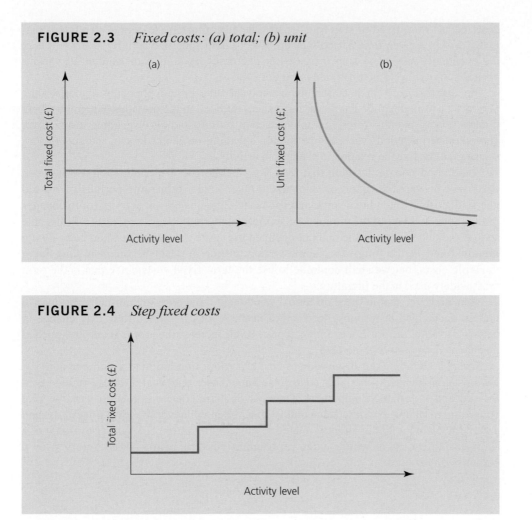

FIGURE 2.3   *Fixed costs: (a) total; (b) unit*

FIGURE 2.4   *Step fixed costs*

in relation to changes in activity. Decisions on the firm's intended future potential level of operating capacity will determine the amount of capacity costs to be incurred. These decisions will have been made previously as part of the long-term planning process. Once these decisions have been made, they cannot easily be reversed in the short term. Plant investment and abandonment decisions should not be based on short-term fluctuations in demand within a particular year. Instead, they should be reviewed periodically as part of the long-term planning process and decisions made based on long-run demand over several years. Thus capacity costs will tend to be fixed in relation to changes of activity within short-term periods such as one year. However, over long-term periods of several years, significant changes in demand will cause capacity costs to change.

Spending on some fixed costs, such as direct labour and supervisory salaries, can be adjusted in the short term to reflect changes in activity. For example, if production activity declines significantly then direct workers and supervisors might continue to be employed in the hope that the decline in demand will be temporary; but if there is no upsurge in demand then staff might eventually be made redundant. If, on the other hand, production capacity expands to some critical level, additional workers might be employed, but the process of recruiting such workers may take several months. Thus within a short-term period, such as one year, labour costs can change in response to changes in demand in a manner similar to that depicted in Figure 2.4. Costs that behave in this manner are described as **semi-fixed** or **step fixed costs**. The distinguishing feature of step fixed costs is that within a given time period they are fixed within specified activity levels, but they are eventually subject to step increases or decreases by a constant amount at various critical activity levels as illustrated in Figure 2.4.

Our discussion so far has assumed a one-year time period. Consider a shorter time period such as one month and the circumstances outlined in the previous paragraph where it takes several months to respond to changes in activity and alter spending levels. Over very short-term periods such as one month, spending on direct labour and supervisory salaries will be fixed in relation to changes in activity.

You should now understand that over a given short-term period, such as one year, costs will be variable, fixed or semi-fixed. Over longer-term time periods of several years, all costs will tend to change in response to large changes in activity (or to changes in the range and variety of products or services marketed), and fixed costs will become semi-fixed and change in the manner depicted in Figure 2.4. Because fixed costs do not remain fixed in the long-term, some writers prefer to describe them as **long-term variable costs**, but we shall continue to use the term fixed costs since this is the term most widely used in the literature.

Note, however, that in the short term, even though fixed costs are normally assumed to remain unchanged in response to changes in the level of activity, they may change in response to other factors. For example, if price levels increase then some fixed costs such as management salaries will increase.

Before concluding our discussion of cost behaviour in relation to volume of activity, we must consider **semi-variable costs** (also known as **mixed costs**). These include both a fixed and a variable component. The cost of maintenance is a semi-variable cost consisting of planned maintenance that is undertaken whatever the level of activity, and a variable element that is directly related to the level of activity. A further example of a semi-variable cost is where sales representatives are paid a fixed salary plus a commission on sales.

REAL WORLD VIEWS 2.1

The impact of cost structure on airline costs

Once a flight is scheduled, airlines are faced with a cost structure where the variable cost of filling a seat is minimal but the fixed costs per aircraft relating to the number of passengers taking a particular flight are extremely high. The costs of taking a meal represent the main variable costs. The costs of the cabin flight crew are a step-fixed cost and the fixed costs include aircraft depreciation, gate rentals, fuel and mainte-nance. Adding one more passenger to an aircraft therefore results in additional revenue but has little impact on total cost. How much? One industry study indicated that yanking just four of the 141 seats from one MD-80 jet would mean an $87,603 annual revenue loss for an airline but almost inconsequential savings in total costs. Removing only two of 127 seats in a different aircraft would sacrifice annual revenue of $51,903. Therefore, every seat counts and this has resulted in the major airlines stuffing more and more seats into aircrafts. Giant 747s, once configured with nine seats across, now frequently have ten. USAir Group Inc. has packed 163 seats into 727–200 narrow-body jets that 10 years ago seated only 145. United Airlines added five rows of seats to its big DC-10–30 planes in the past decade, raising the number of seats to nearly 300 from 232.

Source: McCarthy, Michael J. (1994) Airline squeeze play: more seats, less legroom, *The Wall Street Journal,* 18 April, pp. B1 and B6.

Relevant and irrelevant costs and revenues

For decision-making, costs and revenues can be classified according to whether they are relevant to a particular decision. **Relevant costs and revenues** are those *future* costs and revenues that will be changed by a decision, whereas **irrelevant costs and revenues** are those that will not be affected by the decision. For example, if you are faced with a choice of making a journey using your own car or by public transport, the car tax and insurance costs are irrelevant, since they will remain the same whatever alternative is chosen. However, petrol costs for the car will differ depending on which alternative is chosen, and this cost will be relevant for decision-making.

Let us now consider a further illustration of the classification of relevant and irrelevant costs. Assume a company purchased raw materials a few years ago for £100 and that there appears to be no possibility of selling these materials or using them in future production apart from in connection with an enquiry from a former customer. This customer is prepared to purchase a product that will require the use of all these materials, but he is not prepared to pay more than £250 per unit. The additional costs of converting these materials into the required product are £200. Should the company accept the order for £250? It appears that the cost of the order is £300, consisting of £100 material cost and £200 conversion cost, but this is incorrect because the £100 material cost will remain the same whether the order is accepted or rejected. The material cost is therefore irrelevant for the decision, but if the order is accepted the conversion costs will change by £200, and this conversion cost is a relevant cost. If we compare the revenue of £250 with the relevant cost for the order of £200, it means that the order should be accepted, assuming of course that no higher-priced orders can be obtained elsewhere. The following calculation shows that this is the correct decision.

	Do not accept order (£)	Accept order (£)
Materials	100	100
Conversion costs	—	200
Revenue	—	(250)
Net costs	100	50

The net costs of the company are £50 less, or alternatively the company is £50 better off as a result of accepting the order. This agrees with the £50 advantage which was suggested by the relevant cost method.

In this illustration the sales revenue was relevant to the decision because future revenue changed depending on which alternative was selected; but sales revenue may also be irrelevant for decision-making. Consider a situation where a company can meet its sales demand by purchasing either machine A or machine B. The output of both machines is identical, but the operating costs and purchase costs of the machines are different. In this situation the sales revenue will remain unchanged irrespective of which machine is purchased (assuming of course that the quality of output is identical for both machines). Consequently, sales revenue is irrelevant for this decision; the relevant items are the operating costs and the cost of the machines. We have now established an important principle regarding the classification of cost and revenues for decision-making; namely, that in the short term not all costs and revenues are relevant for decision-making.

Avoidable and unavoidable costs

Sometimes the terms **avoidable** and **unavoidable costs** are used instead of relevant and irrelevant cost. Avoidable costs are those costs that may be saved by not adopting a given alternative, whereas unavoidable costs cannot be saved. Therefore, only avoidable costs are relevant for decision-making purposes. Consider the example that we used to illustrate relevant and irrelevant costs. The material costs of £100 are unavoidable and irrelevant, but the conversion costs of £200 are avoidable and hence relevant. The decision rule is to accept those alternatives that generate revenues in excess of the avoidable costs.

Sunk costs

These costs are the cost of resources already acquired where the total will be unaffected by the choice between various alternatives. They are costs that have been created by a decision made in the past and that cannot be changed by any decision that will be made in the future. The expenditure of £100 on materials that were no longer required, referred to in the preceding section, is an example of a **sunk cost**. Similarly, the written down values of assets previously purchased are sunk costs. For example, if a machine was purchased four years ago for £100 000 with an expected life of five years and nil scrap value then the written down value will be £20 000 if straight line depreciation is used. This written down value will have to be written off, no matter what possible alternative future action might be chosen. If the machine was scrapped, the £20 000 would be written off; if the machine was used for productive purposes, the £20 000 would still have to be written off. This cost cannot be changed by any future decision and is therefore classified as a sunk cost.

Sunk costs are irrelevant for decision-making, but they are distinguished from irrelevant costs because not all irrelevant costs are sunk costs. For example, a comparison of two alternative production methods may result in identical direct material expenditure for both alternatives, so the direct material cost is irrelevant because it will remain the same whichever alternative is chosen, but the material cost is not sunk cost since it will be incurred in the future.

Opportunity costs

Some costs for decision-making cannot normally be collected within the accounting system. Costs that are collected within the accounting system are based on past payments or commitments to pay at some time in the future. Sometimes it is necessary for decision-making to impute costs that will not require cash outlays, and these imputed costs are called opportunity costs. An **opportunity cost** is a cost that measures the opportunity that is lost or sacrificed when the choice of one course of action requires that an alternative course of action be given up. Consider the information presented in Example 2.1.

It is important to note that opportunity costs only apply to the use of scarce resources. Where resources are not scarce, no sacrifice exists from using these resources. In Example 2.1 if machine X was operating at 80% of its potential capacity then the decision to accept the contract would not have resulted in reduced production of product A. Consequently, there would have been no loss of revenue, and the opportunity cost would be zero.

You should now be aware that opportunity costs are of vital importance for decision-making. If no alternative use of resources exist then the opportunity cost is zero, but if resources have an alternative use, and are scarce, then an opportunity cost does exist.

EXAMPLE 2.1

A company has an opportunity to obtain a contract for the production of a special component. This component will require 100 hours of processing on machine X. Machine X is working at full capacity on the production of product A, and the only way in which the contract can be fulfilled is by reducing the output of product A. This will result in a lost profit contribution of £200. The contract will also result in *additional* variable costs of £1000.

If the company takes on the contract, it will sacrifice a profit contribution of £200 from the lost output of product A. This represents an opportunity cost, and should be included as part of the cost when negotiating for the contract. The contract price should at least cover the additional costs of £1000 plus the £200 opportunity cost to ensure that the company will be better off in the short term by accepting the contract.

Incremental and marginal costs

Incremental (also called **differential**) **costs** and revenues are the difference between costs and revenues for the corresponding items under each alternative being considered. For example, the incremental costs of increasing output from 1000 to 1100 units per week are the additional costs of producing an extra 100 units per week. Incremental costs may or may not include fixed costs. If fixed costs change as a result of a decision, the increase in costs represents an incremental cost. If fixed costs do not change as a result of a decision, the incremental costs will be zero.

Incremental costs and revenues are similar in principle to the economist's concept of **marginal cost** and **marginal revenue**. The main difference is that marginal cost/revenue represents the additional cost/revenue of one extra unit of output whereas incremental cost/revenue represents the additional cost/revenue resulting from a group of additional units of output. The economist normally represents the theoretical relationship between cost/revenue and output in terms of the marginal cost/revenue of single additional units of output. We shall see that the accountant is normally more interested in the incremental cost/revenue of increasing production and sales to whatever extent is contemplated, and this is most unlikely to be a single unit of output.

Job costing and process costing systems

There are two basic types of systems that companies can adopt – job costing and process costing systems. **Job costing** relates to a costing system that is required in organizations where each unit or batch of output of a product or service is unique. This creates the need for the cost of each unit to be calculated separately. The term 'job' thus relates to each unique unit or batch of output. Job costing systems are used in industries that provide customized products or services. For example, accounting firms provide customized services to clients with each client requiring services that consume different quantities of resources. Engineering companies often make machines to meet individual customer specifications. The contracts undertaken by construction and civil engineering companies differ greatly for each customer. In all of these organizations costs must be traced to each individual customer's order.

In contrast, **process costing** relates to those situations where masses of identical units are produced and it is unnecessary to assign costs to individual units of output. Products are produced in the same manner and consume the same amount of direct costs and overheads.

It is therefore unnecessary to assign costs to individual units of output. Instead, the average cost per unit of output is calculated by dividing the total costs assigned to a product or service for a period by the number of units of output for that period. Industries where process costing is widely used include chemical processing, oil refining, food processing and brewing.

In practice these two costing systems represent extreme ends of a continuum. The output of many organizations requires a combination of the elements of both job costing and process costing.

Maintaining a cost database

In the previous chapter we noted that a cost and management accounting system should generate information to meet the following requirements:

1 to allocate costs between cost of goods sold and inventories for internal and external profit measurement and inventory valuation;

2 to provide relevant information to help managers make better decisions;

3 to provide information for planning, control and performance measurement.

A database should be maintained, with costs appropriately coded and classified, so that relevant cost information can be extracted to meet each of the above requirements.

A suitable coding system enables costs to be accumulated by the required cost objects (such as products or services, departments, responsibility centres, distribution channels, etc.) and also to be classified by appropriate categories. Typical cost classifications, within the database are by categories of expense (direct materials, direct labour and overheads) and by cost behaviour (fixed and variable). In practice, direct materials will be accumulated by each individual type of material, direct labour by different grades of labour and overhead costs by different categories of indirect expenses (e.g. rent, depreciation, supervision, etc.).

For *inventory valuation* the costs of all partly completed products (work in progress) and unsold finished products can be extracted from the database to ascertain the total cost assigned to inventories. The cost of goods sold that is deducted from sales revenues to compute the profit for the period can also be extracted by summing the manufacturing costs of all those products that have been sold during the period.

The allocation of costs to products is inappropriate for *cost control and performance measurement*, as the manufacture of the product may consist of several different operations, all of which are the responsibility of different individuals. To overcome this problem, costs and revenues must be traced to the individuals who are responsible for incurring them. This system is known as **responsibility accounting**.

Responsibility accounting involves the creation of responsibility centres. A **responsibility centre** may be defined as an organization unit for whose performance a manager is held accountable. Responsibility accounting enables accountability for financial results and outcomes to be allocated to individuals throughout the organization. The objective of responsibility accounting is to measure the results of each responsibility centre. It involves accumulating costs and revenues for each responsibility centre so that deviations from a performance target (typically the budget) can be attributed to the individual who is accountable for the responsibility centre.

For *cost control and performance measurement* the accountant produces performance reports at regular intervals for each responsibility centre. The reports are generated by extracting from the database costs analysed by responsibility centres and categories of expenses. Actual costs for each item of expense listed on the performance report should be compared with budgeted costs so that those costs that do not conform to plan can be pinpointed and investigated.

Future costs, rather than past costs, are required for *decision-making*. Therefore costs extracted from the database should be adjusted for anticipated price changes. We have noted that classification of costs by cost behaviour is important for evaluating the financial impact of expansion or contraction decisions. Costs, however, are not classified as relevant or irrelevant within the database because relevance depends on the circumstances. Consider a situation where a company is negotiating a contract for the sale of one of its products with a customer in an overseas country which is not part of its normal market. If the company has temporary excess capacity and the contract is for 100 units for one month only, then the direct labour cost will remain the same irrespective of whether or not the contract is undertaken. The direct labour cost will therefore be irrelevant. Let us now assume that the contract is for 100 units per month for three years and the company has excess capacity. For long-term decisions direct labour will be a relevant cost because if the contract is not undertaken direct labour can be redeployed or made redundant. Undertaking the contract will result in additional direct labour costs.

The above example shows that the classification of costs as relevant or irrelevant depends on the circumstances. In one situation a cost may be relevant, but in another the same cost may not be relevant. Costs can only be classified as relevant or irrelevant when the circumstances have been identified relating to a particular decision.

Where a company sells many products or services their profitability should be monitored at regular intervals so that potentially unprofitable products can be highlighted for a more detailed study of their future viability. This information is extracted from the database with costs reported by categories of expenses and divided into their fixed and variable elements. In Chapter 4 we shall focus in more detail on product/segmented profitability analysis. Finally, you should note that when the activities of an organization consist of a series of common or repetitive operations, targets or standard product costs, rather than actual costs, may be recorded in the database. Standard costs are predetermined costs; they are target costs that should be incurred under efficient operating conditions. They should be reviewed and updated at periodic intervals. If product standard costs are recorded in the database there is no need continuously to trace costs to products and therefore a considerable amount of data processing time can be saved. Actual costs, however, will still be traced to responsibility centres for cost control and performance evaluation.

 **Summary**

The following items relate to the learning objectives listed at the beginning of the chapter.

- **Explain why it is necessary to understand the meaning of different cost terms.**

   The term 'cost' has multiple meanings and different types of costs are used in different situations. Therefore, a preceding term must be added to clarify the assumptions that underlie a measurement.

- **Define and illustrate a cost object.**

   A cost object is any activity for which a separate measurement of cost is required. In other words managers often want to know the cost of something and the 'thing' that they want to know the cost of is a cost object. Examples of cost objects include the cost of a new product, the cost of operating a sales outlet and the cost of operating a specific machine.

- **Explain the meaning of each of the key terms listed at the end of this chapter.**

   You should check your understanding of each of the terms listed in the key terms and concepts section shown on the next page by referring to the page numbers that are shown in the parentheses following each key term.

● **Explain why in the short term some costs and revenues are not relevant for decision-making.**

In the short term some costs and revenues may remain unchanged for all alternatives under consideration. For example, if you wish to determine the costs of driving to work in your own car or using public transport, the cost of the road fund taxation licence and insurance will remain the same for both alternatives, assuming that you intend to keep your car for leisure purposes. Therefore the costs of these items are not relevant for assisting you in your decision to travel to work by public transport or using your own car. Costs that remain unchanged for all alternatives under consideration are not relevant for decision-making.

● **Distinguish between job costing and process costing.**

A job costing system relates to a costing system where each unit or batch of output of product(s) or service(s) is unique. This creates the need for the cost of each unit or batch to be calculated separately. In contrast a process costing system relates to situations where masses of identical units or batches are produced thus making it unnecessary to assign costs to individual units or batches of output. Instead, the average cost per unit or batch of output is calculated by dividing the total costs assigned to a product or service for the period by the number of units or batches of output for that period.

● **Describe the three purposes for which cost information is required.**

A cost and management accounting system should generate information to meet the following requirements:

(a) to allocate costs between cost of goods sold and inventories for internal and external profit reporting and inventory valuation;
(b) to provide relevant information to help managers make better decisions;
(c) to provide information for planning, control and performance measurement.

A database should be maintained with costs appropriately coded or classified, so that relevant information can be extracted for meeting each of the above requirements.

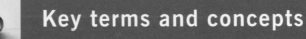

Key terms and concepts

avoidable costs (p. 36)
cost allocations (p. 30)
cost object (p. 28)
differential costs (p. 37)
direct costs (p. 28)
direct labour (p. 29)
direct materials (p. 29)
fixed costs (p. 32)
incremental costs (p. 37)
indirect cost (p. 28)
indirect labour costs (p. 29)
indirect materials (p. 29)
irrelevant costs and revenues (p. 35)
job costing (p. 37)
long-term variable costs (p. 34)
manufacturing overhead (p. 29)

marginal cost/revenue (p. 37)
mixed costs (p. 34)
opportunity cost (p. 36)
period costs (p. 30)
prime cost (p. 29)
process costing (p. 37)
product costs (p. 30)
relevant costs and revenues (p. 35)
responsibility accounting (p. 38)
responsibility centre (p. 38)
semi-fixed costs (p. 34)
semi-variable costs (p. 34)
step fixed costs (p. 34)
sunk cost (p. 36)
unavoidable costs (p. 36)
variable costs (p. 31)

Assessment material

Review questions

The review questions are short questions that enable you to assess your understanding of the main topics included in the chapter. The numbers in parentheses provide you with the page numbers to refer to if you cannot answer a specific question.

Review problems

The review problems are more complex and require you to relate and apply the chapter content to various business problems. The multiple-choice questions are the least demanding and normally take less than 10 minutes to complete. Fully worked solutions to the review problems are provided in a separate section at the end of the book. Further review problems for this chapter are available on the accompanying website, www.drury-online.com. The answers to these problems are available for lecturers on the lecturer's password-protected section of the website.

Case studies

The website also includes over 30 case study problems. A list of these cases is provided on pages 491–93. The Electronic Boards case is a case study that is relevant to the introductory stages of a management accounting course.

Review questions

2.1 Define the meaning of the term 'cost object' and provide three examples of cost objects. *(p. 28)*

2.2 Distinguish between a direct and indirect cost. *(p. 28)*

2.3 Describe how a given direct cost item can be both a direct and indirect cost. *(pp. 28–29)*

2.4 Provide examples of each of the following: (a) direct labour, (b) indirect labour, (c) direct materials, (d) indirect materials, and (e) indirect expenses. *(p. 29)*

2.5 Explain the meaning of the terms: (a) prime cost, (b) overheads, and (c) cost allocations. *(pp. 29–30)*

2.6 Distinguish between product costs and period costs. *(p. 30)*

2.7 Provide examples of decisions that require knowledge of how costs and revenues vary with different levels of activity. *(pp. 31–34)*

2.8 Explain the meaning of each of the following terms: (a) variable costs, (b) fixed costs, (c) semi-fixed costs, and (d) semi-variable costs. Provide examples of costs for each of the four categories. *(pp. 31–34)*

2.9 Distinguish between relevant (avoidable) and irrelevant (unavoidable) costs and provide examples of each type of cost. *(pp. 35–36)*

2.10 Explain the meaning of the term 'sunk cost'. *(p. 36)*

2.11 Distinguish between incremental and marginal costs. *(p. 37)*

2.12 What is an opportunity cost? Give some examples. *(p. 36)*

2.13 Distinguish between job costing and process costing. *(p. 37–38)*

2.14 Explain responsibility accounting. *(p. 38)*

Review problems

2.15 Classify each of the following as being usually fixed (F), variable (V), semi-fixed (SF) or semi-variable (SV):
   (a) direct labour;
   (b) depreciation of machinery;
   (c) factory rental;
   (d) supplies and other indirect materials;
   (e) advertising;
   (f) maintenance of machinery;
   (g) factory manager's salary;
   (h) supervisory personnel;
   (i) royalty payments.

2.16 Which of the following costs are likely to be controllable by the head of the production department?
   (a) price paid for materials;
   (b) charge for floor space;
   (c) raw materials used;
   (d) electricity used for machinery;
   (e) machinery depreciation;
   (f) direct labour;
   (g) insurance on machinery;
   (h) share of cost of industrial relations department.

2.17 A direct cost is a cost which:

    A   is incurred as a direct consequence of a decision;

    B   can be economically identified with the item being costed;

    C   cannot be economically identified with the item being costed;

    D   is immediately controllable;

    E   is the responsibility of the board of directors.

2.18 Which of the following would be classed as indirect labour?

    A   assembly workers in a company manufacturing televisions;

    B   a stores assistant in a factory store;

    C   plasterers in a construction company;

    D   an audit clerk in a firm of auditors.

2.19 Fixed costs are conventionally deemed to be:

    A   constant per unit of output;

    B   constant in total when production volume changes;

    C   outside the control of management;

    D   those unaffected by inflation.

2.20 **Data**

	(£)
Cost of motor car	5500
Trade-in price after 2 years or 60 000 miles is expected to be	1500
Maintenance – 6-monthly service costing	60
Spares/replacement parts, per 1000 miles	20
Vehicle licence, per annum	80
Insurance, per annum	150
Tyre replacements after 25 000 miles, four at £37.50 each	
Petrol, per gallon	1.90
Average mileage from one gallon is 25 miles.	

(a) From the above data you are required:

    (i)   to prepare a schedule to be presented to management showing for the mileages of 5000, 10 000, 15 000 and 30 000 miles per annum:

        (1) total variable cost

        (2) total fixed cost

        (3) total cost

        (4) variable cost per mile (in pence to nearest penny)

        (5) fixed cost per mile (in pence to nearest penny)

        (6) total cost per mile (in pence to nearest penny)

        If, in classifying the costs, you consider that some can be treated as either variable or fixed, state the assumption(s) on which your answer is based together with brief supporting reason(s).

    (ii) on graph paper plot the information given in your answer to (i) above for the costs listed against (1), (2), (3) and (6).

    (iii) to read off from your graph(s) in (ii) and state the approximate total costs applicable to 18 000 miles and 25 000 miles and the total cost per mile at these two mileages.

(b) 'The more miles you travel, the cheaper it becomes.' Comment briefly on this statement.

(25 marks)

2.21 Sunk and opportunity costs for decision-making

Mrs Johnston has taken out a lease on a shop for a down payment of £5000. Additionally, the rent under the lease amounts to £5000 per annum. If the lease is cancelled, the initial payment of £5000 is forfeit. Mrs Johnston plans to use the shop for the sale of clothing, and has estimated operations for the next twelve months as follows:

	(£)	(£)
Sales	115 000	
Less Value-added tax (VAT)	15 000	
Sales Less VAT		100 000
Cost of goods sold	50 000	
Wages and wage related costs	12 000	
Rent including the down payment	10 000	
Rates, heating, lighting and insurance	13 000	
Audit, legal and general expenses	2 000	
		87 000
Net profit before tax		13 000

In the figures no provision has been made for the cost of Mrs Johnston but it is estimated that one half of her time will be devoted to the business. She is undecided whether to continue with her plans, because she knows that she can sublet the shop to a friend for a monthly rent of £550 if she does not use the shop herself.

You are required to:

(a) (i) explain and identify the 'sunk' and 'opportunity' costs in the situation depicted above;

(ii) state what decision Mrs Johnston should make according to the information given, supporting your conclusion with a financial statement;

(11 marks)

(b) explain the meaning and use of 'notional' (or 'imputed') costs and quote *two* supporting examples.

(4 marks)
(Total 15 marks)

PART 2

Information for Decision-making

The objective of this Part, which contains seven chapters, is to consider the provision of financial information that will help managers to make better decisions. Chapters 3–8 are concerned mainly with short-term decisions based on the environment of today, and the physical, human and financial resources that are presently available to a firm; these decisions are determined to a considerable extent by the quality of the firm's long-term decisions. An important distinction between the long-term and short-term decisions is that the former cannot easily be reversed whereas the latter can often be changed. The actions that follow short-term decisions are frequently repeated, and it is possible for different actions to be taken in the future. For example, the setting of a particular selling price or product mix can often be changed fairly quickly. With regard to long-term decisions, such as capital investment, which involves, for example, the purchase of new plant and machinery, it is not easy to change a decision in the short term. Resources may only be available for major investments in plant and machinery at lengthy intervals, and it is unlikely that plant replacement decisions will be repeated in the short term.

Chapters 3–8 concentrate mainly on how accounting information can be applied to different forms of short-term decisions. Chapter 3 focuses on what will happen to the financial results if a specific level of activity or volume fluctuates. This information is required for making optimal short-term output decisions. Chapter 4 examines how costs and revenues should be measured for a range of non-routine short-term and long-term decisions.

Chapters 5 and 6 focus on alternative approaches for measuring resources consumed by cost objects. In Chapter 5 traditional product costing systems that were designed primarily for meeting financial accounting and stock valuation and profit measurement requirements are described. The cost information generated by traditional systems may not be sufficiently accurate for decision-making purposes. In Chapter 6 a more refined approach for measuring resources consumed by cost objects is described. This approach is called activity-based costing. Chapter 7 is concerned with profitability analysis and the provision of financial information for pricing decisions. Chapters 3–7 do not deal with uncertainty, whereas Chapter 8 introduces methods of incorporating uncertainty into the analysis, and the topics covered in Chapters 3–7 are re-examined under conditions of uncertainty.

The final chapter in this part is concerned with long-term decisions. Chapter 9 looks at the techniques that are used for evaluating capital investment decisions, and introduces the concept of the time value of money.

Cost–volume–profit analysis

3 In this chapter we consider how management accounting information can be of assistance in providing answers to questions about the consequences of following particular courses of action. Such questions might include 'How many units must be sold to break-even?' 'What would be the effect on profits if we reduce our selling price and sell more units?' 'What sales volume is required to meet the additional fixed charges arising from an advertising campaign?' 'Should we pay our sales people on the basis of a salary only, or on the basis of a commission only, or by a combination of the two?' These and other questions can be answered using cost–volume–profit (CVP) analysis.

This is a systematic method of examining the relationship between changes in activity (i.e. output) and changes in total sales revenue, expenses and net profit. As a model of these relationships CVP analysis simplifies the real-world conditions that a firm will face. Like most models, which are abstractions from reality, CVP analysis is subject to a number of underlying assumptions and limitations, which will be discussed later in this chapter; nevertheless, it is a powerful tool for decision-making in certain situations.

The objective of CVP analysis is to establish what will happen to the financial results if a specified level of activity or volume fluctuates. This information is vital to management, since one of the most important variables influencing total sales revenue,

---

LEARNING OBJECTIVES

After studying this chapter, you should be able to:

- describe the differences between the accountant's and the economist's model of cost–volume–profit analysis;
- justify the use of linear cost and revenue functions in the accountant's model;
- apply the mathematical approach to answer questions similar to those listed in Example 3.1;
- construct break-even, contribution and profit–volume graphs;
- identify and explain the assumptions on which cost–volume–profit analysis is based;
- apply cost–volume–profit analysis in a multi-product setting.

total costs and profits is output or volume. For this reason output is given special attention, since knowledge of this relationship will enable management to identify the critical output levels, such as the level at which neither a profit nor a loss will occur (i.e. the break-even point).

CVP analysis is based on the relationship between volume and sales revenue, costs and profit in the short run, the short run normally being a period of one year, or less, in which the output of a firm is restricted to that available from the current operating capacity. In the short run, some inputs can be increased, but others cannot. For example, additional supplies of materials and unskilled labour may be obtained at short notice, but it takes time to expand the capacity of plant and machinery. Thus output is limited in the short run because plant facilities cannot be expanded. It also takes time to reduce capacity, and therefore in the short run a firm must operate on a relatively constant stock of production resources. Furthermore, most of the costs and prices of a firm's products will have already been determined, and the major area of uncertainty will be sales volume. Short-run profitability will therefore be most sensitive to sales volume. CVP analysis thus highlights the effects of changes in sales volume on the level of profits in the short run.

The theoretical relationship between total sales revenue, costs and profits with volume has been developed by economists. In order to provide a theoretical basis for examining the accountant's approach to CVP analysis this chapter begins by describing the economist's model of CVP analysis.

The economist's model

An economist's model of CVP behaviour is presented in Figure 3.1. You will see that the total-revenue line is assumed to be curvilinear, which indicates that the firm is only able to sell increasing quantities of output by reducing the selling price per unit; thus the total revenue line does not increase proportionately with output. To increase the quantity of sales, it is necessary to reduce the unit selling price, which results in the total revenue line rising less steeply, and eventually beginning to decline. This is because the adverse effect of price reductions outweighs the benefits of increased sales volume.

The total cost line AD shows that, between points A and B, total costs rise steeply at first as the firm operates at the lower levels of the volume range. This reflects the difficulties of efficiently operating a plant designed for much larger volume levels. Between points B and C, the total cost line begins to level out and rise less steeply because the firm is now able to operate the plant within the efficient operating range and can take advantage of specialization of labour, and smooth production schedules. In the upper portion of the volume range the total cost line between points C and D rises more and more steeply as the cost per unit increases. This is because the output per direct labour hour declines when the plant is operated beyond the activity level for which it was designed: bottlenecks develop, production schedules become more complex, and plant breakdowns begin to occur. The overall effect is that the cost per unit of output increases and causes the total cost line to rise steeply.

The dashed horizontal line from point A represents the cost of providing the basic operating capacity, and is the economist's interpretation of the total fixed costs of the firm. Note also from Figure 3.1 that the shape of the total revenue line is such that it crosses the total cost line at two points. In other words, there are two output levels at which the total costs are equal to the total revenues; or more simply, there are two break-even points.

FIGURE 3.1   *Economist's cost–volume graph*

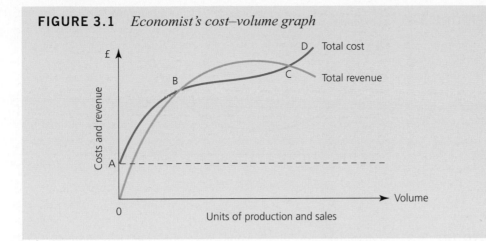

It is the shape of the variable cost function in the economist's model that has the most significant influence on the total cost function; this is illustrated in Figure 3.2. The economist assumes that the average *unit* variable cost declines initially, reflecting the fact that, as output expands, a firm is able to obtain bulk discounts on the purchase of raw materials and can benefit from the division of labour; this results in the labour cost per unit being reduced. The economist refers to this situation as **increasing returns to scale**. The fact that *unit* variable cost is higher at lower levels of activity causes the total cost line between points A and B in Figure 3.1 to rise steeply. From Figure 3.2 you can see that the *unit* variable cost levels out between output levels Q_1 and Q_2 and then gradually begins to rise. This is because the firm is operating at its most efficient output level, and further economies of scale are not possible in the short term. However, beyond output level Q_2, the plant is being operated at a higher level than that for which it was intended, and bottlenecks and plant breakdowns occur. The effect of this is that output per direct labour hour declines, and causes the variable cost per unit to increase. The economist describes this situation as **decreasing returns to scale**.

It is the shape of the variable cost function that causes the total cost line to behave in the manner indicated in Figure 3.1. Between points B and C, the total cost line rises less steeply, indicating that the firm is operating in the range where unit variable cost is at its lowest. Between points C and D, the total cost line rises more steeply, since the variable cost per unit is increasing owing to decreasing returns to scale.

Marginal revenue and marginal cost presentation

The normal presentation of the economist's model is in terms of the marginal revenue and marginal cost curves. Marginal revenue represents the increase in total revenue from the sale of one additional unit. Figure 3.3 is in two parts, with the lower diagram presenting the traditional marginal revenue and marginal cost diagram; the top diagram repeats Figure 3.1. A comparison of the two diagrams in Figure 3.3 enables us to reconcile the traditional marginal revenue and marginal cost diagram with the total cost and total revenue presentation. Economic theory states that the profit maximizing output level is the point at which marginal cost equals marginal revenue. This occurs at Point A on the lower diagram, at output level Q_p. Note that in the top diagram this is the point at which the difference between the total revenue and total cost lines is the greatest. The point where

FIGURE 3.2 *Economist's variable cost function*

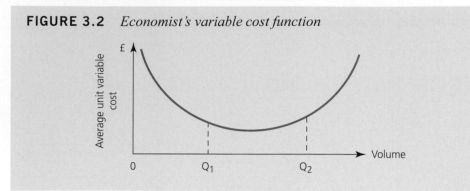

FIGURE 3.3 *Economist's marginal revenue and marginal costs diagrams, and total revenue and total costs diagrams*

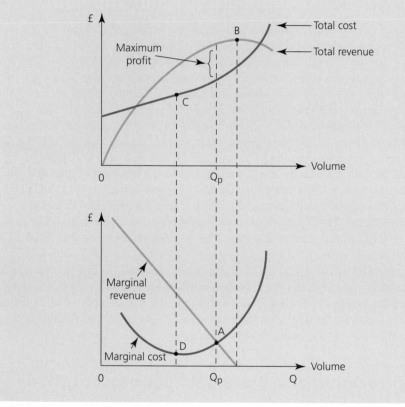

total revenue reaches a maximum, point B, is where marginal revenue is equal to zero. Also note that the marginal cost curve reaches a minimum at point D, where the total cost curve (at point C) changes from concave downwards to concave upwards. Let us now compare the accountant's CVP diagram, or break-even model as it is sometimes called, with the economist's model.

The accountant's cost–volume–profit model

The diagram for the accountant's model is presented in Figure 3.4. Note that the dashed line represents the economist's total cost function, which enables a comparison to be made with the accountant's total cost function. The accountant's diagram assumes a variable cost and a selling price that are constant per unit; this results in a linear relationship (i.e. a straight line) for total revenue and total cost as volume changes. The effect is that there is only one **break-even point** in the diagram, and the profit area widens as volume increases. The most profitable output is therefore at maximum practical capacity. Clearly, the economist's model appears to be more realistic, since it assumes that the total cost curve is non-linear.

Relevant range

How can we justify the accountant's assumption of linear cost and linear revenue functions? The answer is that the accountants' diagram is not intended to provide an accurate representation of total cost and total revenue throughout all ranges of output. The objective is to represent the behaviour of total cost and revenue over the range of output at which a firm expects to be operating within a short-term planning horizon. This range of output is represented by the output range between points X and Y in Figure 3.4. The term **relevant range** is used to refer to the output range at which the firm expects to be operating within a short-term planning horizon. This relevant range also broadly represents the output levels which the firm has had experience of operating in the past and for which cost information is available.

You can see from Figure 3.4 that, between points X and Y, the shape of the accountant's total cost line is very similar to that of the economist's. This is because the total cost line is only intended to provide a good approximation within the relevant range. Within this range, the accountant assumes that the variable cost per unit is the same throughout the entire range of output, and the total cost line is therefore linear. Note that the cost function is approximately linear within this range. It would be unwise, however, to make this assumption for production levels outside the relevant range. It would be more appropriate if the accountant's total cost line was presented for the relevant range of output only, and not extended to the vertical axis or to the output levels beyond Y in Figure 3.4.

Fixed cost function

Note also that the accountant's fixed cost function in Figure 3.4 meets the vertical axis at a different point to that at which the economist's total cost line meets the vertical axis. The reason for this can be explained from Figure 3.5. The fixed cost level of 0A may be applicable to, say, activity level Q_2 to Q_3, but if there were to be a prolonged economic recession then output might fall below Q_1, and this could result in redundancies and shutdowns. Therefore fixed costs may be reduced to 0B if there is a prolonged and a significant decline in sales demand. Alternatively, additional fixed costs will be incurred if long-term sales volume is expected to be greater than Q_3. Over a longer-term time horizon, the fixed cost line will consist of a series of step functions rather than the horizontal straight line depicted in Figure 3.4. However, since within its short-term planning horizon the firm expects to be operating between output levels Q_2 and Q_3, it will be committed, in the short term, to fixed costs of 0A; but you should remember that if there was a prolonged economic recession then in the longer term fixed costs may be reduced to 0B.

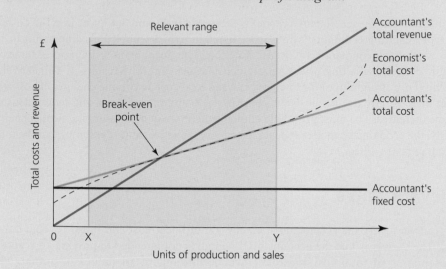

FIGURE 3.4 *Accountant's cost–volume–profit diagram*

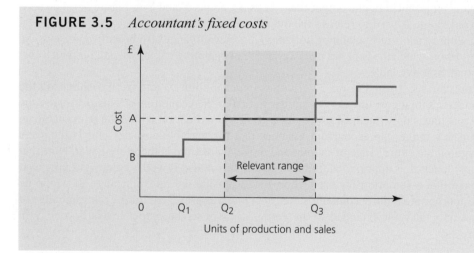

FIGURE 3.5 *Accountant's fixed costs*

The fixed cost line for output levels below Q_1 (i.e. 0B) represents the cost of providing the basic operating capacity, and this line is the equivalent to the point where the economist's total cost line meets the vertical axis in Figure 3.4. Because the accountant assumes that in the short term the firm will operate in the relevant range between Q_2 and Q_3, the accountant's fixed cost line 0A in Figure 3.5 represents the fixed costs for the relevant output range only, which the firm is committed to in the current period, and does not represent the fixed costs that would be incurred at the extreme levels of output beyond the shaded area in Figure 3.5.

Total revenue function

Let us now compare the total revenue line for the accountant and the economist. We have seen that the accountant assumes that selling price is constant over the relevant range of output, and therefore the total revenue line is a straight line. The accountant's assumption about the revenue line is a realistic one in those firms that operate in industries where selling prices tend to be fixed in the short term. A further factor reinforcing the assumption of a fixed selling price is that competition may take the form of non-price rather than price competition. Moreover, beyond the relevant range, increases in output may only be possible by offering substantial reductions in price. As it is not the intention of firms to operate outside the relevant range, the accountant makes no attempt to produce accurate revenue functions outside this range. It might be more meaningful in Figure 3.4 if the total revenue line was presented for output levels X and Y within the relevant range, instead of being extended to the left and right of these points.

Application to longer-term time horizons

CVP analysis becomes more complex and questionable if we extend our application to a longer-term time horizon. Consider a capacity expansion decision. The expansion of output beyond certain points may require increments of fixed costs such as additional supervision and machinery, the appointment of additional sales persons and the expansion of the firm's distribution facilities. Such increases are incorporated in Figure 3.6. Note from this figure that if the current output level is OQ_1 then additional facilities are required, thus increasing fixed costs, if output is to be increased beyond this level. Similarly, additional fixed costs must be incurred to expand output beyond OQ_2.

At this point, for a capacity expansion decision, we are moving from beyond the short term to a longer term application of CVP analysis. In the longer term, other factors besides volume are likely to be important. For example, to utilize the additional capacity reductions in selling prices and alternative advertising strategies may be considered. Also consideration may be given to expanding the product range and mix. Therefore, for longer-term decisions other variables besides volume are likely to have an impact on total costs, total revenues and profits. These additional variables cannot be easily incorporated into the CVP analysis. Hence, the CVP analysis presented in Figure 3.6 is unlikely to be appropriate for long-term decisions because other variables, that are not captured by the CVP analysis, are unlikely to remain unchanged. CVP analysis is only appropriate if all variables, other than volume, remain unchanged.

Let us now assume that management has undertaken a detailed analysis, without using CVP analysis, that incorporates all of these other variables and has concluded that extra fixed costs should be incurred to expand output to a maximum level of OQ_2 as shown in Figure 3.6. For simplicity we shall also assume that the total cost functions are the same as those described in Figure 3.6.

Once a decision has been made to provide productive capacity equal to a maximum of OQ_2, a separate graph may be presented with a total cost function represented by line AB and maximum output of OQ_2. In this revised graph the step increases in fixed costs will not be included, since management has already made a decision to aim to operate within the output range Q_1 to Q_2. Assuming that the total revenue is the same as that depicted in Figure 3.6 the revised graph can now be used as a short-term planning tool to demonstrate the impact that short-term output decisions have on profits. It is this revised graph that was used as a basis for comparing the accountant's and the economist's CVP presentation earlier in this chapter.

A mathematical approach to cost–volume–profit analysis

Instead of using a diagram to present CVP information, we can use mathematical relationships. The mathematical approach is a quicker and more flexible method of producing the appropriate information than the graphical approach, and is a particularly appropriate form of input to a computer financial model.

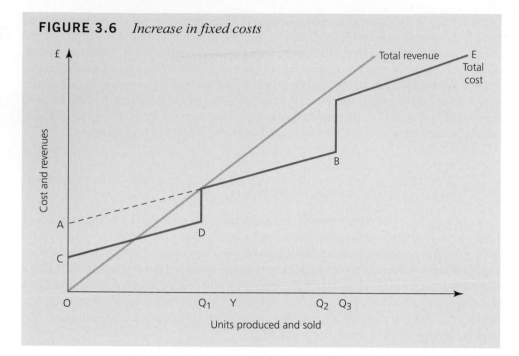

FIGURE 3.6 *Increase in fixed costs*

When developing a mathematical formula for producing CVP information, you should note that one is assuming that selling price and costs remain constant per unit of output. Such an assumption may be valid for unit selling price and variable cost, but remember that in Chapter 2 we noted that in the short run fixed costs are a constant *total* amount whereas *unit* cost changes with output levels. As a result, profit per *unit* also changes with volume. For example, if fixed costs are £10 000 for a period and output is 10 000 units, the fixed cost will be £1 per unit. Alternatively, if output is 5000 units, the fixed cost will be £2 per unit. Profit per unit will not therefore be constant over varying output levels and it is incorrect to unitize fixed costs for CVP decisions.

We can develop a mathematical formula from the following relationship:

$$\text{net profit} = (\text{units sold} \times \text{unit selling price})$$
$$- [(\text{units sold} \times \text{unit variable cost}) + \text{total fixed costs}]$$

The following symbols can be used to represent the various items in the above equation:

NP = net profit

x = units sold

P = selling price

b = unit variable cost

a = total fixed costs

The equation can now be expressed in mathematical terms as

$$NP = Px - (a + bx) \tag{3.1}$$

You should now refer to Example 3.1. This example will be used to illustrate the application of the mathematical approach to CVP analysis.

EXAMPLE 3.1

Norvik Enterprises operate in the leisure and entertainment industry and one of its activities is to promote concerts at locations throughout Europe. The company is examining the viability of a concert in Stockholm. Estimated fixed costs are £60 000. These include the fees paid to performers, the hire of the venue and advertising costs. Variable costs consist of the cost of a pre-packed buffet which will be provided by a firm of caterers at a price, which is currently being negotiated, but it is likely to be in the region of £10 per ticket sold. The proposed price for the sale of a ticket is £20. The management of Norvik have requested the following information:

1 The number of tickets that must be sold to break-even (that is, the point at which there is neither a profit or loss).
2 How many tickets must be sold to earn £30 000 target profit?
3 What profit would result if 8000 tickets were sold?
4 What selling price would have to be charged to give a profit of £30 000 on sales of 8000 tickets, fixed costs of £60 000 and variable costs of £10 per ticket?
5 How many additional tickets must be sold to cover the extra cost of television advertising of £8000?

Let us now provide the information requested in Example 3.1.

1 Break-even point in units (i.e. number of tickets sold)

Since $NP = Px - (a + bx)$, the break-even point is at a level of output (x) where

$$a + bx = Px - NP$$

Substituting the information in Example 3.1, we have

$$60\,000 + 10x = 20x - 0$$
$$60\,000 = 10x$$

and so $x = 6000$ tickets (or £120 000 total sales at £20 per ticket).

An alternative method, called the **contribution margin** approach, can also be used. Contribution margin is equal to sales minus variable expenses. Because the variable cost per unit and the selling price per unit are assumed to be constant the contribution margin per unit is also assumed to be constant. In Example 3.1 note that each ticket sold generates a contribution of £10, which is available to cover fixed costs and, after they are covered, to contribute to profit. When we have obtained sufficient total contribution to cover fixed costs, the break-even point is achieved, and the alternative formula is

$$\text{break-even point in units} = \frac{\text{fixed costs}}{\text{contribution per unit}}$$

The contribution margin approach can be related to the mathematical formula approach. Consider the penultimate line of the formula approach; it reads

$$£60\,000 = 10x$$

and so
$$x = \frac{£60\,000}{£10}$$

giving the contribution margin formula

$$\frac{\text{fixed costs}}{\text{contribution per unit}}$$

The contribution margin approach is therefore a restatement of the mathematical formula, and either technique can be used; it is a matter of personal preference.

2 Units to be sold to obtain a £30 000 profit

Using the equation $NP = Px - (a + bx)$ and substituting the information in Example 3.1, we have

$$£30\,000 = £20x - (£60\,000 + £10x)$$
$$£90\,000 = £10x$$

and so
$$x = 9000 \text{ tickets}$$

If we apply the contribution margin approach and wish to achieve the desired profit, we must obtain sufficient contribution to cover the fixed costs (i.e. the break-even point) plus a further contribution to cover the target profit. Hence we simply add the target profit to the fixed costs so that the equation using the contribution margin approach is

$$\text{units sold for target profit} = \frac{\text{fixed costs + target profit}}{\text{contribution per unit}}$$

This is merely a restatement of the penultimate line of the mathematical formula, which reads

$$£90\,000 = £10x$$

and so
$$x = \frac{£90\,000}{£10}$$

3 Profit from the sale of 8000 tickets

Substituting in the equation $NP = Px - (a + bx)$, we have

$$NP = £20 \times 8000 - (£60\,000 + £10 \times 8000)$$
$$= £160\,000 - (£60\,000 + £80\,000)$$

and so
$$NP = £20\,000$$

Let us now assume that we wish to ascertain the impact on profit if a further 1000 tickets are sold so that sales volume increases from 8000 to 9000 tickets. Assuming that fixed costs remain unchanged, the impact on a firm's profits resulting from a change in the number of units sold can be determined by multiplying the unit contribution margin by the change in units sold. Therefore the increase in profits will be £10 000 (1000 units times a unit contribution margin of £10).

4 Selling price to be charged to show a profit of £30 000 on sales of 8000 units

Applying the formula for net profit (i.e. Equation 3.1)

$$£30\ 000 = 8000P - (60\ 000 + (£10 \times 8000))$$
$$= 8000P - £140\ 000$$

giving $\qquad 8000P = £170\ 000$

and $\qquad\qquad P = £21.25$ (i.e. an increase of £1.25 per ticket)

5 Additional sales volume to meet £8000 additional fixed advertising charges

The contribution per unit is £10 and fixed costs will increase by £8000. Therefore an extra 800 tickets must be sold to cover the additional fixed costs of £8000.

The profit–volume ratio

The **profit–volume ratio** (also known as the **contribution margin ratio**) is the contribution divided by sales. It represents the proportion of each £1 sales available to cover fixed costs and provide for profit. In Example 3.1 the contribution is £10 per unit and the selling price is £20 per unit; the profit–volume ratio is 0.5. This means that for each £1 sale a contribution of £0.50 is earned. Because we assume that selling price and contribution per unit are constant, the profit–volume ratio is also assumed to be constant. Therefore the profit–volume ratio can be computed using either unit figures or total figures. Given an estimate of total sales revenue, it is possible to use the profit–volume ratio to estimate total contribution. For example, if total sales revenue is estimated to be £200 000, the total contribution will be £100 000 (£200 000 × 0.5). To calculate the profit, we deduct fixed costs of £60 000; thus a profit of £40 000 will be obtained from total sales revenue of £200 000.

Expressing the above computations in mathematical terms:

$$NP = (Sales\ revenue \times PV\ ratio) - Fixed\ costs$$
$$NP + Fixed\ costs = Sales\ revenue \times PV\ ratio$$

Therefore the break-even sales revenue (where NP = 0) = Fixed costs/PV ratio.

Relevant range

It is vital to remember that, as with the mathematical approach, the formulae method can only be used for decisions that result in outcomes within the relevant range. Outside this range the unit selling price and the variable cost are no longer deemed to be constant per unit, and any results obtained from the formulae that fall outside the relevant range will be incorrect. The concept of the relevant range is more appropriate for production settings but it can apply within non-production settings. Returning to Norvik Enterprises in Example 3.1, let us assume that the caterers' charges will be higher per ticket if ticket sales are below 4000 but lower if sales exceed 12 000 tickets. Thus, the £10 variable cost relates only to a sales volume within a range of 4000–12 000 tickets. Outside this range other costs apply. Also the number of seats made available at the venue is flexible and the hire cost will be reduced for sales of less than 4000 tickets and increased for sales beyond 12 000 tickets. In other words, we will assume that the relevant range is a sales volume of 4000–12 000 tickets and outside this range the results of our CVP analysis do not apply.

Margin of safety

The **margin of safety** indicates by how much sales may decrease before a loss occurs. Using Example 3.1, where unit selling price and variable cost were £20 and £10 respectively and fixed costs were £60 000, we noted that the break-even point was 6000 tickets or £120 000 sales value. If sales are expected to be 8000 tickets or £160 000, the margin of safety will be 2000 tickets or £40 000. Alternatively, we can express the margin of safety in a percentage form based on the following ratio:

$$\text{percentage margin of safety} = \frac{\text{expected sales} - \text{break-even sales}}{\text{expected sales}}$$

$$= \frac{\text{£160 000} - \text{£120 000}}{\text{£160 000}} = 25\%$$

Constructing the break-even chart

Managers may obtain a clearer understanding of CVP behaviour if the information is presented in graphical format. Using the data in Example 3.1, we can construct the **break-even chart** for Norvik Enterprises (Figure 3.7). In constructing the graph, the fixed costs are plotted as a single horizontal line at the £60 000 level. Variable costs at the rate of £10 per unit of volume are added to the fixed costs to enable the total cost line to be plotted. Two points are required to insert the total cost line. At zero sales volume total cost will be equal to the fixed costs of £60 000. At 12 000 units sales volume total costs will be £180 000 consisting of £120 000 variable cost plus £60 000 fixed costs. The total revenue line is plotted at the rate of £20 per unit of volume. The constraints of the relevant range consisting of two vertical lines are then added to the graph: beyond these lines we have little assurance that the CVP relationships are valid.

The point at which the total sales revenue line cuts the total cost line is the point where the concert makes neither a profit nor a loss. This is the break-even point and is 6000 tickets or £120 000 total sales revenue. The distance between the total sales revenue line and the total cost line at a volume below the break-even point represents losses that will occur for various sales levels below 6000 tickets. Similarly, if the company operates at a sales volume above the break-even point, the difference between the total revenue and the total cost lines represents the profit that results from sales levels above 6000 tickets.

The impact of Volkswagen's high break-even point on profitability

In the early 1990s, Volkswagen AG of Germany reported a large continuing decline in earnings even though in 1992 it sold a record 3.5 million vehicles world-wide. One of the reasons for the declining profitability was that its break-even point was above 90 per cent. Consequently, sales had to exceed 90 per cent capacity before profits  were reported. The company had to run its factory on overtime just to make a small profit. In contrast, European competitors already had break-even points below 70 per cent of capacity. To overcome this problem, steps were taken to reduce fixed capacity costs that would enable it in the short term to rapidly head to a break-even below 90 per cent.

Source: Aeppel, T. (1993) VW Chief declares a crisis and prescribes bold action, *The Wall Street Journal,* 1 April, p. B4.

FIGURE 3.7   *Break-even chart for Example 3.1*

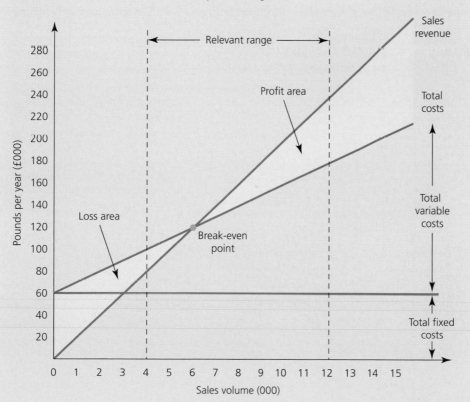

Alternative presentation of cost–volume–profit analysis

Contribution graph

In Figure 3.7 the fixed cost line is drawn parallel to the horizontal axis, and the variable cost is the difference between the total cost line and the fixed cost line. An alternative to Figure 3.7 for the data contained in Example 3.1 is illustrated in Figure 3.8. This alternative presentation is called a **contribution graph**. In Figure 3.8 the variable cost line is drawn first at £10 per unit of volume. The fixed costs are represented by the difference between the total cost line and the variable cost line. Because fixed costs are assumed to be a constant sum throughout the entire output range, a constant sum of £60 000 for fixed costs is added to the variable cost line, which results in the total cost line being drawn parallel to the variable cost line. The advantage of this form of presentation is that the total contribution is emphasized in the graph, and is represented by the difference between the total sales revenue line and the total variable cost line.

Profit–volume graph

The break-even and contribution charts do not highlight the profit or loss at different volume levels. To ascertain the profit or loss figures from a break-even chart, it is necessary to determine the difference between the total-cost and total-revenue lines. The **profit–volume graph** is a more convenient method of showing the impact of changes in volume on profit. Such a graph is illustrated in Figure 3.9. The horizontal axis represents

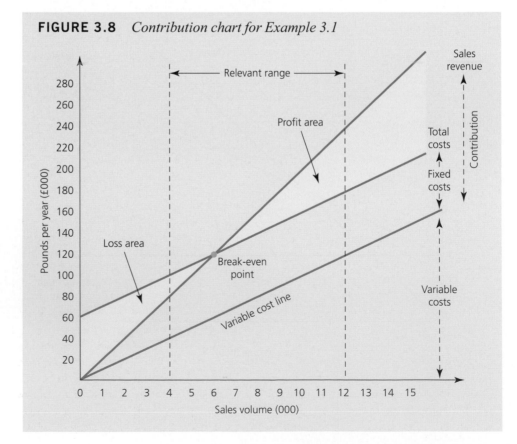

FIGURE 3.8 *Contribution chart for Example 3.1*

FIGURE 3.9   *Profit–volume graph for Example 3.1*

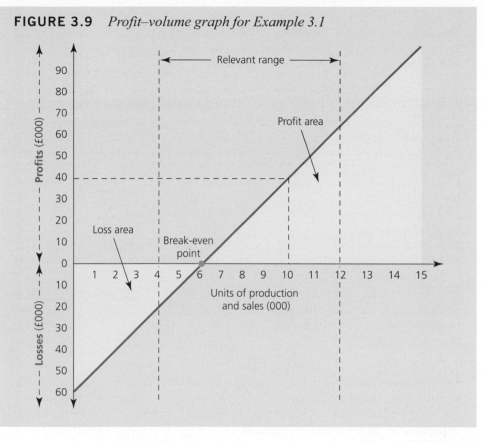

the various levels of sales volume, and the profits and losses for the period are recorded on the vertical scale. You will see from Figure 3.9 that profits or losses are plotted for each of the various sales levels, and these points are connected by a profit line. Two points are required to plot the profit line. When units sold are zero a loss equal to the amount of fixed costs (£60 000) will be reported. At the break-even point (zero profits) sales volume is 6000 units. Therefore the break-even point is plotted at the point where the profit line intersects the horizontal line at a sales volume of 6000 tickets. The profit line is drawn between the two points. With each unit sold, a contribution of £10 is obtained towards the fixed costs, and the break-even point is at 6000 tickets, when the total contribution exactly equals the total of the fixed costs. With each additional unit sold beyond 6000 tickets, a surplus of £10 per ticket is obtained. If 10 000 tickets are sold, the profit will be £40 000 (4000 tickets at £10 contribution). You can see this relationship between sales and profit at 10 000 tickets from the dotted lines in Figure 3.9.

Multi-product cost–volume–profit analysis

Our analysis so far has assumed a single-product setting. However, most firms produce and sell many products or services. In this section we shall consider how we can adapt the analysis used for a single-product setting to a multi-product setting. Consider the situation presented in Example 3.2. You will see that the company sells two products so that there are two unit contribution margins. We can apply the same approach as that used for a single product if all of the fixed costs are directly attributable to products (i.e. there are no common

EXAMPLE 3.2

The Super Bright Company sells two types of washing machines – a de-luxe model and a standard model. The financial controller has prepared the following information based on the sales forecast for the period:

Sales volume (units)	De-luxe machine 1200 (£)	Standard machine 600 (£)	Total (£)
Unit selling price	300	200	
Unit variable cost	150	110	
Unit contribution	150	90	
Total sales revenues	360 000	120 000	480 000
Less: Total variable cost	180 000	66 000	246 000
Contribution to direct and common fixed costs[a]	180 000	54 000	234 000
Less: Direct avoidable fixed costs	90 000	27 000	117 000
Contribution to common fixed costs[a]	90 000	27 000	117 000
Less common (indirect) fixed costs			39 000
Operating profit			78 000

The common fixed costs relate to the costs of common facilities and can only be avoided if neither of the products is sold. The managing director is concerned that sales may be less than forecast and has requested information relating to the break-even point for the activities for the period.

Note
[a]Contribution was defined earlier in this chapter as sales less variable costs. Where fixed costs are divided into direct and common (indirect) fixed costs it is possible to identify two separate contribution categories. The first is described as contribution to direct and common fixed costs and this is identical to the conventional definition, being equivalent to sales less variable costs. The second is after a further deduction of direct fixed costs and is described as 'Contribution to common or indirect fixed costs'.

fixed costs) or our analysis focuses only on the contribution to common fixed costs, rather than operating profit. We simply apply the analysis separately to each product as follows:

De-luxe washing machine break-even point

= Direct fixed costs (£90 000)/Unit contribution (£150)

= 600 units

Standard washing machine break-even point

= Direct fixed costs (£27 000)/Unit contribution (£90)

= 300 units

However, selling 600 de-luxe and 300 standard washing machines will generate a contribution that only covers direct fixed costs; the common fixed costs of £39,000 will not be covered. A loss equal to the common fixed costs will be reported. The break-even point for the firm as a whole has not been ascertained.

You may think that the break-even point for the firm as a whole can be derived if we allocate the common fixed costs to each individual product but this approach is inappropriate because the allocation will be arbitrary. The common fixed costs cannot be specifically identified with either of the products since they can only be avoided if *both* products are not sold. The solution to our problem is to convert the sales volume measure of the individual products into standard batches of products based on the planned sales mix. You will from see from Example 3.2 that Super Bright plans to sell 1200 de-luxe and 600 standard machines giving a sales mix of 1200:600. Reducing this sales mix to the smallest whole number gives a mix of 2:1. In other words, for the sale of every two deluxe machines one standard machine is expected to be sold. We therefore define our standard batch of products as comprising two de-luxe and one standard machine giving a contribution of £390 per batch (two de-luxe machines at a contribution of £150 per unit sold plus and one standard machine at a contribution of £90).

The break-even point in standard batches can be calculated by using the same break-even equation that we used for a single product so that:

$$\text{Break-even number of batches} = \text{Total fixed costs (£156 000)/Contribution margin per batch (£390)}$$

$$= 400 \text{ batches}$$

The sales mix used to define a standard batch (2:1) can be now be used to convert the break-even point (measured in standard batches) into a break-even point expressed in terms of the required combination of individual products sold. Thus, 800 de-luxe machines (2 × 400) and 400 (1 × 400) standard machines must be sold to break-even. The following profit statement verifies this outcome:

Units sold	De-luxe machine 800	Standard machine 400	Total
	(£)	(£)	(£)
Unit contribution margin	150	90	
Contribution to direct and common fixed costs	120 000	36 000	156 000
Less: Direct fixed costs	90 000	27 000	117 000
Contribution to common fixed costs	30 000	9 000	39 000
Less: Common fixed costs			39 000
Operating profit			0

Let us now assume that the actual sales volume for the period was 1200 units, the same total volume as the break-even volume, but consisting of a sales mix of 600 units of each machine. Thus, the actual sales mix is 1:1 compared with a planned sales mix of 2:1. The total contribution to direct and common fixed costs will be £144 000 ([150 × 600] + [£90 × 600]) and a loss of £12 000 (£144 000 contribution – £156 000 total fixed costs) will occur. It should now be apparent to you that the break-even point (or the sales volumes required to achieve a target profit) is not a unique number: it varies depending upon the composition of the sales mix. Because the actual sales mix differs from the planned sales mix, the sales mix used to define a standard batch has changed from 2:1 to 1:1 so that the contribution per batch changes from £390 to £240 ([1 × £150] + [1 × £90]). Therefore the revised break-even point will be 650 batches (£156 000 total fixed costs/£240 contribution per batch) which converts to a sales volume of 650 units of each machine based on a 1:1 sales mix. Generally, an increase in the proportion of sales of higher contribution margin products will decrease the break-even point whereas increases in sales of the lower margin products will increase the break-even point.

Cost–volume–profit analysis assumptions

It is essential that anyone preparing or interpreting CVP information is aware of the underlying assumptions on which the information has been prepared. If these assumptions are not recognized, serious errors may result and incorrect conclusions may be drawn from the analysis. We shall now consider these important assumptions. They are as follows:

1   All other variables remain constant.
2   A single product or constant sales mix.
3   Total costs and total revenue are linear functions of output.
4   The analysis applies to the relevant range only.
5   Costs can be accurately divided into their fixed and variable elements.
6   The analysis applies only to a short-term time horizon.
7   Complexity-related fixed costs do not change.

1 All other variables remain constant

It has been assumed that all variables other than the particular one under consideration have remained constant throughout the analysis. In other words, it is assumed that volume is the only factor that will cause costs and revenues to change. However, changes in other variables such as production efficiency, sales mix, price levels and production methods can have an important influence on sales revenue and costs. If significant changes in these other variables occur the CVP analysis presentation will be incorrect.

2 Single product or constant sales mix

CVP analysis assumes that either a single product is sold or, if a range of products is sold, that sales will be in accordance with a predetermined sales mix. When a predetermined sales mix is used, it can be depicted in the CVP analysis by measuring sales volume using standard batch sizes based on a planned sales mix. Any CVP analysis must be interpreted carefully if the initial product mix assumptions do not hold.

3 Total costs and total revenue are linear functions of output

The analysis assumes that unit variable cost and selling price are constant. This assumption is only likely to be valid within the relevant range of production described on page 53.

4 Analysis applies to relevant range only

Earlier in this chapter we noted that CVP analysis is appropriate only for decisions taken within the relevant production range, and that it is incorrect to project cost and revenue figures beyond the relevant range.

5 Costs can be accurately divided into their fixed and variable elements

CVP analysis assumes that costs can be accurately analysed into their fixed and variable elements. The separation of semi-variable costs into their fixed and variable elements is extremely difficult in practice. Nevertheless a reasonably accurate analysis is necessary if CVP analysis is to provide relevant information for decision-making.

6 The analysis applies only to a short-term time horizon

At the beginning of this chapter we noted that CVP analysis is based on the relationship between volume and sales revenue, costs and profits in the short-term, the short-term being typically a period of one year. In the short-term the costs of providing a firm's operating capacity, such as property taxes and the salaries of senior managers, are likely to be fixed in relation to changes in activity. Decisions on the firm's intended future potential level of operating capacity will determine the amount of capacity costs to be incurred. These decisions will have been made previously as part of the long-term planning process. Once these decisions have been made, they cannot easily be reversed in the short-term. It takes time to significantly expand the capacity of plant and machinery or reduce capacity. Furthermore, plant investment and abandonment decisions should not be based on short-term fluctuations in demand within a particular year. Instead, they should be reviewed periodically as part of the long-term planning process and decisions based on predictions of long-run demand over several years. Thus capacity costs will tend to be fixed in relation to changes of activity within short-term periods such as one year. However, over long-term periods significant changes in volume or product complexity will cause fixed costs to change.

It is therefore assumed that in the short term some costs will be fixed and unaffected by changes in volume whereas other (variable) costs will vary with changes in volume. In the short-run volume is the most important variable influencing total revenue, costs and profit. For this reason volume is given special attention in the form of CVP analysis. You should note, however, that in the long-term other variables, besides volume, will cause costs to change. Therefore, the long-term analysis should incorporate other variables, besides volume, and recognize that fixed costs will increase or decrease in steps in response to changes in the explanatory variables.

7 Complexity-related fixed costs do not change

CVP analysis assumes that **complexity-related costs** will remain unchanged. Cooper and Kaplan (1987) illustrate how complexity-related fixed costs can increase as a result of changes in the range of items produced, even though volume remains unchanged. They illustrate the relationship with an example of two identical plants. One plant produces one million units of product A. The second plant produces 100 000 units of A and 900 000 similar units of 199 similar products. The first plant has a simple production environment and requires limited manufacturing support facilities. Set-ups, expediting, inventory movements and schedule activities are minimal. The other plant has a much more complex production management environment. The 200 products must be scheduled through the plant, and this requires frequent set-ups, inventory movements, purchase receipts and inspections. To handle this complexity, the support departments' fixed costs must be larger.

Cooper and Kaplan use the above example to illustrate that many so-called fixed costs vary not with the volume of items manufactured but with the range of items produced (i.e. the complexity of the production process). Complexity-related costs do not normally vary significantly in the short-term with the volume of production. If a change in volume does not alter the range of products then it is likely that complexity-related fixed costs will not alter, but if volume stays constant and the range of items produced changes then support department fixed costs will eventually change because of the increase or decrease to product complexity.

CVP analysis assumptions will be violated if a firm seeks to enhance profitability by product proliferation: that is, by introducing new variants of products based on short-term contribution margins. The CVP analysis will show that profits will increase as sales volume increases and fixed costs remain constant in the short-term. The increased product diversity, however, will cause complexity-related fixed costs to increase in future periods, and there is a danger that long-term profits may decline as a result of product proliferation. The CVP analysis incorporates the fixed costs required to handle the diversity and complexity within the current product range, but the costs will remain fixed only if diversity and complexity are not increased further. Thus CVP analysis will not capture the changes in complexity-related costs arising from changes in the range of items produced.

Cost–volume–profit analysis and computer applications

The output from a CVP model is only as good as the input. The analysis will include assumptions about sales mix, production efficiency, price levels, total fixed costs, variable costs and selling price per unit. Obviously, estimates regarding these variables will be subject to varying degrees of uncertainty.

Sensitivity analysis is one approach for coping with changes in the values of the variables. Sensitivity analysis focuses on how a result will be changed if the original estimates or the underlying assumptions change. With regard to CVP analysis, sensitivity analysis answers questions such as the following:

1 What will the profit be if the sales mix changes from that originally predicted?
2 What will the profit be if fixed costs increase by 10% and variable costs decline by 5%?

The widespread use of spreadsheet packages has enabled management accountants to develop CVP computerized models. Managers can now consider alternative plans by keying the information into a computer, which can quickly show changes both graphically and numerically. Thus managers can study various combinations of changes in selling prices, fixed costs, variable costs and product mix, and can react quickly without waiting for formal reports from the management accountant.

Separation of semi-variable costs

CVP analysis assumes that costs can be accurately analysed into their fixed and variable elements. Direct material is generally presumed to be a variable cost, whereas depreciation, which is related to time and not usage, is a fixed cost. Semi-variable costs, however, include both a fixed and variable component. The cost of maintenance is a semi-variable cost consisting of planned maintenance which is undertaken whatever the level of activity, and a variable element which is directly related to activity. The separation of semi-variable costs into their fixed and variable elements is extremely difficult in practice, but an accurate analysis is necessary for CVP analysis.

Mathematical techniques should be used to separate costs accurately into fixed and variable elements. For a discussion of these techniques you should refer to Chapter 24 of Drury (2004). However, first-year cost and management accounting examinations sometimes require you to separate fixed and variable costs using a non-mathematical technique called the high–low method.

The high–low method consists of examining past costs and activity, selecting the highest and lowest activity levels and comparing the changes in costs which result from the two levels. Assume that the following activity levels and costs are extracted:

	Volume of production (units)	Indirect costs (£)
Lowest activity	5 000	22 000
Highest activity	10 000	32 000

If variable costs are constant per unit and the fixed costs remain unchanged the increase in costs will be due entirely to an increase in variable costs. The variable cost per unit is therefore calculated as follows:

$$\frac{\text{Difference in cost}}{\text{Difference in activity}} = \frac{£10\,000}{5000 \text{ units}}$$

$$= £2 \text{ variable cost per unit of activity}$$

The fixed cost can be estimated at any level of activity by subtracting the variable cost portion from the total cost. At an activity level of 5000 units the total cost is £22 000 and the total variable cost is £10 000 (5000 units at 2 per unit). The balance of £12 000 is assumed to represent the fixed cost.

 # Summary

The following items relate to the learning objectives listed at the beginning of the chapter.

- **Describe the differences between the accountant's and the economist's model of cost–volume–profit analysis.**

  The major differences are that the total cost and total revenue functions are curvilinear in the economist's model whereas the accountant's model assumes linear relationships. However, the accountant's model is intended to predict CVP behaviour only within the relevant range, where a firm is likely to be operating on constant returns to scale. A comparison of the two models suggested that, within the relevant range of activity, the total costs and revenue functions are fairly similar.

- **Justify the use of linear cost and revenue functions in the accountant's model.**

  Within the relevant range it is generally assumed that cost and revenue functions are approximately linear. Outside the relevant range linearity is unlikely to apply. Care is therefore required in interpreting CVP relationships outside the relevant range.

- **Apply the mathematical approach to answer questions similar to those listed in Example 3.1.**

  In Example 3.1, the break-even point was derived by dividing fixed costs by the contribution per unit. To ascertain the number of units sold to achieve a target profit the sum of the fixed costs and the target profit is divided by the contribution per unit.

- **Construct break-even, contribution and profit–volume graphs.**

  Managers may obtain a clearer understanding of CVP behaviour if the information is presented in graphical format. With the break-even chart the fixed costs are plotted as a single horizontal line. The total cost line is plotted by adding variable costs to fixed costs. The reverse situation applies with a contribution graph. The variable costs are plotted first and the fixed costs are added to variable costs to plot the total cost line. Because fixed costs are assumed to be a constant sum throughout the output range, the total cost line is drawn parallel to the variable cost line. The break-even and contribution graphs do not highlight the profit or loss at different output levels and must be ascertained by comparing the differences between the total cost and total revenue lines. The profit–volume graph shows the impact of changes in volume on profits. The profits and losses are plotted for each of the various sales levels and these are connected by a profit line. You should refer to Figures 3.7–3.9 for an illustration of the graphs.

- **Identify and explain the assumptions on which cost–volume–profit analysis is based.**

  Cost–volume–profit analysis is based on the following assumptions: (a) all variables, other than volume, remain constant; (b) the sales mix remains constant; (c) total costs and revenues are linear functions of output; (d) the analysis applies only to the relevant range; (e) costs can be accurately divided into their fixed and variable elements; (f) the analysis applies only to a short-term horizon, and (g) complexity-related fixed costs do not change.

- **Apply cost–volume–profit analysis in a multi-product setting.**

  Multi-product CVP analysis requires that an assumption is made concerning the expected sales mix. The approach that is used is to convert the multi-product CVP analysis into a single product analysis based on the assumption that output consists of standard batches of the multiple products based on the expected sales mix. However, you should note that the answers change as the sales mix changes.

Key terms and concepts

break-even chart (p. 60)
break-even point (p. 53)
complexity-related costs (p. 67)
contribution graph (p. 62)
contribution margin (p. 57)
contribution margin ratio (p. 59)
decreasing returns to scale (p. 51)

high–low method (p. 69)
increasing returns to scale (p. 51)
margin of safety (p. 60)
profit–volume graph (p. 62)
profit–volume ratio (p. 59)
relevant range (p. 53)
sensitivity analysis (p. 68)

Assessment material

Review questions

The review questions are short questions that enable you to assess your understanding of the main topics included in the chapter. The numbers in parentheses provide you with the page numbers to refer to if you cannot answer a specific question.

Review problems

The review problems are more complex and require you to relate and apply the chapter content to various business problems. The multiple-choice questions are the least demanding and normally take less than 10 minutes to complete. Fully worked solutions to the review problems are provided in a separate section at the end of the book. Further review problems for this chapter are available on the accompanying website, www.drury-online.com. The answers to these problems are available for lecturers on the lecturer's password-protected section of the website.

Case studies

The website also includes over 30 case study problems. A list of these cases is provided on pages 491–93. Several cases are relevant to the content of this chapter. Examples include Dunbellow Ltd, Hardhat Ltd and Merrion Products Ltd.

Review questions

3.1 Provide examples of how cost–volume–profit analysis can be used for decision-making. (*p. 49*)

3.2 Distinguish between the economist's and the accountant's approach to cost–volume–profit analysis. (*pp. 53–55*)

3.3 Explain what is meant by the term 'relevant range'. (*p. 53*)

3.4 Define the term 'contribution margin'. (*p. 57*)

3.5   Define the term 'profit–volume ratio' and explain how it can be used for cost–volume–profit analysis. (*p. 59*)

3.6   Describe and distinguish between the three different approaches of presenting cost–volume–profit relationships in graphical format. (*pp. 60–62*)

3.7   Describe the assumptions underlying cost–volume–profit analysis. (*pp. 66–68*)

3.8   How can a company with multiple products use cost–volume–profit analysis? (*pp. 62–65*)

3.9   Explain why the break-even point changes when there is a change in sales mix. (*p. 65*)

3.10 How can sensitivity analysis be used in conjunction with cost–volume–profit analysis? (*p. 68*)

Review problems

3.11 A company manufactures and sells two products, X and Y. Forecast data for a year are:

	Product X	Product Y
Sales (units)	80 000	20 000
Sales price (per unit)	£12	£8
Variable cost (per unit)	£8	£3

Annual fixed costs are estimated at £273 000.

What is the break-even point in sales revenue with the current sales mix?

A   £570 000

B   £606 667

C   £679 467

D   £728 000

3.12 H Limited manufactures and sells two products, J and K. Annual sales are expected to be in the ratio of J:1, K:3. Total annual sales are planned to be £420 000. Product J has a contribution to sales ratio of 40%, whereas that of product K is 50%. Annual fixed costs are estimated to be £120 000.

The budgeted break-even sales value (to the nearest £1000):

A   £196 000

B   £200 000

C   £253 000

D   £255 000

E   cannot be determined from the above data.

3.13 The following details relate to product R:

Level of activity (units)	1000 (£/unit)	2000 (£/unit)
Direct materials	4.00	4.00
Direct labour	3.00	3.00
Production overhead	3.50	2.50
Selling overhead	1.00	0.50
	11.50	10.00

The total fixed cost and variable cost per unit are:

	Total fixed cost (£)	Variable cost per unit (£)
A	2000	1.50
B	2000	7.00
C	2000	8.50
D	3000	7.00
E	3000	8.50

3.14 Z plc currently sells products Aye, Bee and Cee in equal quantities and at the same selling price per unit. The contribution to sales ratio for product Aye is 40%; for product Bee it is 50% and the total is 48%. If fixed costs are unaffected by mix and are currently 20% of sales, the effect of changing the product mix to:

Aye	40%
Bee	25%
Cee	35%

is that the total contribution/total sales ratio changes to:

A 27.4%

B 45.3%

C 47.4%

D 48.4%

E 68.4%

3.15 E plc operates a marginal costing system. For the forthcoming year, variable costs are budgeted to be 60% of sales value and fixed costs are budgeted to be 10% of sales value.

If E plc increases its selling prices by 10%, but if fixed costs, variable costs per unit and sales volume remain unchanged, the effect on E plc's contribution would be:

A a decrease of 2%

B an increase of 5%

C an increase of 10%

D an increase of 25%

E an increase of $66^2/_3$%

3.16   A Limited has fixed costs of £60 000 per annum. It manufactures a single product which it sells for £20 per unit. Its contribution to sales ratio is 40%.

A Limited's break-even point in units is:

A   1200
B   1800
C   3000
D   5000
E   7500

3.17   Z plc makes a single product which it sells for £16 per unit. Fixed costs are £76 800 per month and the product has a contribution to sales ratio of 40%.

In a period when actual sales were £224 000, Z plc's margin of safety, in units, was

A   2 000
B   6 000
C   8 000
D   12 000
E   14 000

3.18   A break-even chart is shown below for Windhurst Ltd.

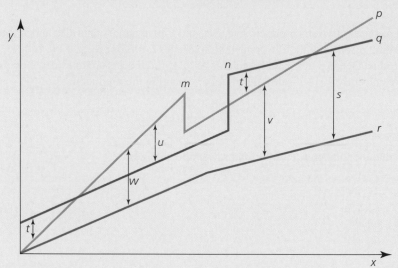

You are required:

(i)   to identify the components of the break-even chart labelled $p, q, r, s, t, u, v, w,$ x and y;

(5 marks)

(ii) to suggest what events are represented at the values of x that are labelled m and n on the chart;

(3 marks)

(iii) to assess the usefulness of break-even analysis to senior management of a small company.

(7 marks)

3.19 **Preparation of break-even and profit–volume graphs**

ZED plc manufactures one standard product, which sells at £10. You are required to:

(a) prepare from the data given below, a break-even and profit–volume graph showing the results for the six months ending 30 April and to determine:

    (i) the fixed costs;

    (ii) the variable cost per unit;

    (iii) the profit–volume ratio;

    (iv) the break-even point;

    (v) the margin of safety;

Month	Sales (units)	Profit/(loss) (£)
November	30 000	40 000
December	35 000	60 000
January	15 000	(20 000)
February	24 000	16 000
March	26 000	24 000
April	18 000	(8 000)

(b) discuss the limitations of such a graph;

(c) explain the use of the relevant range in such a graph.

(20 marks)

3.20 **Changes in sales mix**

XYZ Ltd produces two products and the following budget applies for 20 × 2:

	Product X (£)	Product Y (£)
Selling price	6	12
Variable costs	2	4
Contribution margin	4	8
Fixed costs apportioned	£100 000	£200 000
Units sold	70 000	30 000

You are required to calculate the break-even points for each product and the company as a whole and comment on your findings.

3.21 **Non-graphical CVP analysis**

The summarized profit and loss statement for Exewye plc for the last year is as follows:

	(£000)	(£000)
Sale (50 000 units)		1000
Direct materials	350	
Direct wages	200	
Fixed production overhead	200	
Variable production overhead	50	
Administration overhead	180	
Selling and distribution overhead	120	
		1100
Profit/(loss)		(100)

At a recent board meeting the directors discussed the year's results, following which the chairman asked for suggestions to improve the situation.

You are required as management accountant, to evaluate the following alternative proposals and to comment briefly on each:

(a) Pay salesmen a commission of 10% of sales and thus increase sales to achieve break-even point.

(5 marks)

(b) Reduce selling price by 10%, which it is estimated would increase sales volume by 30%.

(3 marks)

(c) Increase direct wage rates from £4 to £5 per hour, as part of a productivity/pay deal. It is hoped that this would increase production and sales by 20%, but advertising costs would increase by £50 000.

(4 marks)

(d) Increase sales by additional advertising of £300 000, with an increased selling price of 20%, setting a profit margin of 10%.

(8 marks)
(Total 20 marks)

3.22 Advanced: Non-graphical CVP behaviour

Tweed Ltd is a company engaged solely in the manufacture of jumpers, which are bought mainly for sporting activities. Present sales are direct to retailers, but in recent years there has been a steady decline in output because of increased foreign competition. In the last trading year (2001) the accounting report indicated that the company produced the lowest profit for 10 years. The forecast for 2002 indicates that the present deterioration in profits is likely to continue. The company considers that a profit of £80 000 should be achieved to provide an adequate return on capital. The managing director has asked that a review be made of the present pricing and marketing policies. The marketing director has completed this review, and passes the proposals on to you for evaluation and recommendation, together with the profit and loss account for year ending 31 December 2001.

Tweed Ltd profit and loss account for year ending 31 December 2001

	(£)	(£)	(£)
Sales revenue			
(100 000 jumpers at £10)			1 000 000
Factory cost of goods sold:			
Direct materials	100 000		
Direct labour	350 000		
Variable factory overheads	60 000		
Fixed factory overheads	220 000	730 000	
Administration overhead		140 000	
Selling and distribution overhead			
Sales commission (2% of sales)	20 000		
Delivery costs (variable per unit sold)	50 000		
Fixed costs	40 000	110 000	980 000
Profit			20 000

The information to be submitted to the managing director includes the following three proposals:

(i)   To proceed on the basis of analyses of market research studies which indicate that the demand for the jumpers is such that 10% reduction in selling price would increase demand by 40%.

(ii) To proceed with an enquiry that the marketing director has had from a mail order company about the possibility of purchasing 50 000 units annually if the selling price is right. The mail order company would transport the jumpers from Tweed Ltd to its own warehouse, and no sales commission would be paid on these sales by Tweed Ltd. However, if an acceptable price can be negotiated, Tweed Ltd would be expected to contribute £60 000 per annum towards the cost of producing the mail order catalogue. It would also be necessary for Tweed Ltd to provide special additional packaging at a cost of £0.50 per jumper. The marketing director considers that in 2002 the sales from existing business would remain unchanged at 100 000 units, based on a selling price of £10 if the mail order contract is undertaken.

(iii) To proceed on the basis of a view by the marketing director that a 10% price reduction, together with a national advertising campaign costing £30 000 may increase sales to the maximum capacity of 160 000 jumpers.

Required:

(a)   The calculation of break-even sales value based on the 2001 accounts.

(b)   A financial evaluation of proposal (i) and a calculation of the number of units Tweed Ltd would require to sell at £9 each to earn the target profit of £80 000.

(c)   A calculation of the minimum prices that would have to be quoted to the mail order company, first, to ensure that Tweed Ltd would, at least, break even on the mail order contract, secondly, to ensure that the same overall profit is earned as proposal (i) and, thirdly, to ensure that the overall target profit is earned.

(d)   A financial evaluation of proposal (iii).

Measuring relevant costs and revenues for decision-making

4 In this chapter we are going to focus on measuring costs and benefits for non-routine decisions. The term **'special studies'** is sometimes used to refer to decisions that are not routinely made at frequent intervals. In other words, special studies are undertaken whenever a decision needs to be taken; such as discontinuing a product or a channel of distribution, making a component within the company or buying from an outside supplier, introducing a new product and replacing existing equipment. Special studies require only those costs and revenues that are relevant to the specific alternative courses of action to be reported. The term **'decision-relevant approach'** is used to describe the specific costs and benefits that should be reported for special studies. We shall assume that the objective when examining alternative courses of action is to maximize the present value of future net cash inflows. The calculations of present values will be explained in Chapter 9. We also assume for this chapter that future costs and benefits

---

LEARNING OBJECTIVES

After studying this chapter, you should be able to:

- distinguish between relevant and irrelevant costs and revenues;
- explain the importance of qualitative factors;
- distinguish between the relevant and irrelevant costs and revenues for the five decision-making problems described;
- describe the key concept that should be applied for presenting information for product-mix decisions when capacity constraints apply;
- explain why the book value of equipment is irrelevant when making equipment replacement decisions;
- describe the opportunity cost concept.

are known with certainty; decision-making under conditions of uncertainty will be considered in Chapter 8. In Chapter 9 we shall concentrate on the special studies required for capital investment decisions.

It is important that you note at this stage that a decision-relevant approach adopts whichever planning time horizon the decision maker considers appropriate for a given situation. However, it is important not to focus excessively on the short term, since the objective is to maximize long-term net cash inflows. We begin by introducing the concept of relevant cost and applying this principle to special studies relating to the following:

1 special selling price decisions;
2 product-mix decisions when capacity constraints exist;
3 decisions on replacement of equipment;
4 outsourcing (make or buy) decisions;
5 discontinuation decisions.

We shall then consider in more detail the specific problems that arise in assessing the relevant costs of materials and labour.

The aim of this chapter is to provide you with an understanding of the principles that should be used to identify relevant costs and revenues. It is assumed that relevant costs can be easily measured but, in reality, some indirect relevant costs can be difficult to measure. The measurement of indirect relevant costs for decision-making using activity-based-costing techniques will be examined in Chapter 6.

The meaning of relevance

The **relevant costs** and benefits required for decision-making are only those that will be affected by the decision. Costs and benefits that are independent of a decision are obviously not relevant and need not be considered when making that decision. The relevant financial inputs for decision-making purposes are therefore *future* cash flows, which will differ between the various alternatives being considered. In other words, only **differential** (or **incremental**) **cash flows** should be taken into account, and cash flows that will be the same for all alternatives are irrelevant. Since decision-making is concerned with choosing between future alternative courses of action, and nothing can be done to alter the past, then past costs (also known as sunk costs) are not relevant for decision-making. Consider a situation where an individual is uncertain as to whether he or she should purchase a monthly rail ticket to travel to work or use their car. Assuming that the individual will keep the car, whether or not he or she travels to work by train, the cost of the road fund licence and insurance will be irrelevant, since these costs remain the same irrespective of the mode of travel. The cost of petrol will, however, be relevant, since this cost will vary depending on which method of transport is chosen.

You will see that both depreciation and the allocation of common fixed costs are irrelevant for decision-making. Both are sunk costs. Depreciation represents the allocation of past costs to future periods. The original cost is unavoidable and common to all alternatives. Therefore it is irrelevant. Similarly, any allocation of common fixed costs will be irrelevant for decision-making since the choice of allocation method does not affect the level of cost to the company. It merely results in a redistribution of the same sunk cost between cost objects (e.g. products or locations within the organization).

Importance of qualitative factors

In many situations it is difficult to quantify in monetary terms all the important elements of a decision. Those factors that cannot be expressed in monetary terms are classified as **qualitative factors**. A decline in employee morale that results from redundancies arising from a closure decision is an example of a qualitative factor. It is essential that qualitative factors be brought to the attention of management during the decision-making process, since otherwise there may be a danger that a wrong decision will be made. For example, the cost of manufacturing a component internally may be more expensive than purchasing from an outside supplier. However, the decision to purchase from an outside supplier could result in the closing down of the company's facilities for manufacturing the component. The effect of such a decision might lead to redundancies and a decline in employees' morale, which could affect future output. In addition, the company will now be at the mercy of the supplier who might seek to increase prices on subsequent contracts and/or may not always deliver on time. The company may not then be in a position to meet customers' requirements. In turn, this could result in a loss of customer goodwill and a decline in future sales.

It may not be possible to quantify in monetary terms the effect of a decline in employees' morale or loss of customer goodwill, but the accountant in such circumstances should present the relevant quantifiable financial information and draw attention to those qualitative items that may have an impact on future profitability. In circumstances such as those given in the above example management must estimate the likelihood of the supplier failing to meet the company's demand for future supplies and the likely effect on customer goodwill if there is a delay in meeting orders. If the component can be obtained from many suppliers and repeat orders for the company's products are unlikely then the company may give little weighting to these qualitative factors. Alternatively, if the component can be obtained from only one supplier and the company relies heavily on repeat sales to existing customers then the qualitative factors will be of considerable importance. In the latter situation the company may consider that the quantifiable cost savings from purchasing the component from an outside supplier are insufficient to cover the risk of the qualitative factors occurring.

If it is possible qualitative factors should be expressed in quantitative non-financial terms. For example, the increase in percentage of on-time deliveries from a new production process, the reduction in customer waiting time from a decision to invest in additional cash dispensing machines and the reduction in the number of units of defective output delivered to customers arising from an investment in quality inspection are all examples of qualitative factors that can be expressed in non-financial numerical terms.

Let us now move on to apply the relevant cost approach to a variety of decision-making problems. We shall concentrate on measuring the financial outcomes but do remember that they do not always provide the full story. Qualitative factors should also be taken into account in the decision-making process.

Special pricing decisions

Special pricing decisions relate to pricing decisions outside the main market. Typically they involve one-time only orders or orders at a price below the prevailing market price. Consider the information presented in Example 4.1.

At first glance it looks as if the order should be rejected since the proposed selling price is less than the total cost of £33. A study of the cost estimates, however, indicates that during the next quarter, the direct labour, manufacturing (i.e. non-variable) fixed

EXAMPLE 4.1

The Caledonian Company is a manufacturer of clothing that sells its output directly to clothing retailers. One of its departments manufactures jumpers. The department has a production capacity of 50 000 jumpers per month. Because of the liquidation of one of its major customers the company has excess capacity. For the next quarter current monthly production and sales volume is expected to be 35 000 jumpers at a selling price of £40 per jumper. Expected costs and revenues for the next month at an activity level of 35 000 jumpers are as follows:

	(£)	(£)
Direct labour	420 000	12
Direct materials	280 000	8
Variable manufacturing overheads	70 000	2
Manufacturing non-variable overheads	280 000	8
Marketing and distribution costs	105 000	3
Total costs	1 155 000	33
Sales	1 400 000	40
Profit	245 000	7

Caledonian is expecting an upsurge in demand and considers that the excess capacity is temporary. A company in the leisure industry has offered to buy for its staff 3000 jumpers each month for the next three months at a price of £20 per jumper. The company would collect the jumpers from Caledonian's factory and thus no marketing and distribution costs will be incurred. No subsequent sales to this customer are anticipated. The company would require its company logo inserting on the jumper and Caledonian has predicted that this will cost £1 per jumper. Should Caledonian accept the offer from the company?

overheads and the marketing and distribution costs will remain the same irrespective of whether or not the order is accepted. These costs are therefore irrelevant for this decision. The direct material costs, variable manufacturing overheads and the cost of adding the leisure company's logo will be different if the order is accepted. Hence they are relevant for making the decision. The financial information required for the decision is shown in Exhibit 4.1.

You can see from Exhibit 4.1 that different approaches can be used for presenting relevant cost and revenue information. Information can be presented that includes both relevant and irrelevant costs or revenues for all alternatives under consideration. If this approach is adopted the *same* amount for the irrelevant items (i.e. those items that remain unchanged as a result of the decision which are direct labour, manufacturing non-variable overheads and the marketing and distribution costs in our example) are included for all alternatives, thus making them irrelevant to the decision. This information is presented in columns (1) and (2) in Exhibit 4.1. Alternatively, you can present cost information in columns (1) and (2) that excludes the irrelevant costs and revenues because they are identical for both alternatives. A third alternative is to present only the relevant (differential) costs. This approach is shown in column (3) of Exhibit 4.1. Note that column (3) represents the difference between columns (1) and (2). All of the methods show that the company is better off by £27 000 *per month* if the order is accepted.

	(1) Do not accept order (£ per month)	(2) Accept order (£ per month)	(3) Difference (relevant costs) (£ per month)
Direct labour	420 000	420 000	
Direct materials	280 000	304 000	24 000
Variable manufacturing overheads	70 000	76 000	6 000
Manufacturing non-variable overheads	280 000	280 000	
Inserting company logo		3 000	3 000
Marketing and distribution costs	105 000	105 000	
Total costs	1 155 000	1 188 000	33 000
Sales	1 400 000	1 460 000	60 000
Profit per month	245 000	272 000	27 000

EXHIBIT 4.1

Evaluation of three month order from the company in the leisure industry

Four important factors must be considered before recommending acceptance of the order. Most of these relate to the assumption that there are no long-run implications from accepting the offer at a selling price of £20 per jumper. First, it is assumed that the future selling price will not be affected by selling some of the output at a price below the going market price. If this assumption is incorrect then competitors may engage in similar practices of reducing their selling prices in an attempt to unload spare capacity. This may lead to a fall in the market price, which in turn would lead to a fall in profits from future sales. The loss of future profits may be greater than the short-term gain obtained from accepting special orders at prices below the existing market price. Given that Caledonian has found a customer in a different market from its normal market it is unlikely that the market price would be affected. However, if the customer had been within Caledonian's normal retail market there would be a real danger that the market price would be affected. Secondly, the decision to accept the order prevents the company from accepting other orders that may be obtained during the period at the going price. In other words, it is assumed that no better opportunities will present themselves during the period. Thirdly, it is assumed that the company has unused resources that have no alternative uses that will yield a contribution to profits in excess of £27 000 *per month*. Finally, it is assumed that the fixed costs are unavoidable for the period under consideration. In other words, we assume that the direct labour force and the fixed overheads cannot be reduced in the short term, or that they are to be retained for an upsurge in demand, which is expected to occur in the longer term.

It is important that great care is taken in presenting financial information for decision-making. For stock valuation, external financial regulations require that the jumpers must be valued at their manufacturing cost of £30. Using this cost would lead to the incorrect decision being taken. For decision-making purposes only future costs that will be relevant to the decision should be included. Costs that have been computed for meeting stock valuation requirements must not therefore be used for decision-making purposes.

When you are trying to establish which costs are relevant to a particular decision you may find that some costs will be relevant in one situation but irrelevant in another. In Example 4.1 we assumed that direct labour was not a relevant cost. The company wishes to retain the direct labour for an expected upsurge in demand and therefore the direct labour cost will be same whether or not the offer is accepted. Alternatively, Caledonian may have had an agreement with its workforce that entitled them to at least three months' notice in the event of any redundancies. Therefore, even if Caledonian was not expecting an upsurge in demand direct labour would have been a fixed cost within the three month time horizon. But now let us consider what the relevant cost would be if direct labour consisted of casual labour who are hired on a daily basis. In this situation direct labour will be a relevant cost, since the labour costs will not be incurred if the order is not accepted.

The identification of relevant costs depends on the circumstances. In one situation a cost may be relevant, but in another the same cost may not be relevant. It is not therefore possible to provide a list of costs that would be relevant in particular situations. In each situation you should follow the principle that the relevant costs are future costs that differ among alternatives. The important question to ask when determining the relevant cost is: What difference will it make? The accountant must be aware of all the issues relating to a decision and ascertain full details of the changes that will result, and then proceed to select the relevant financial information to present to management.

Evaluation of a longer-term order

In Example 4.1 we focused on a short-term time horizon of three months. Capacity cannot easily be altered in the short term and therefore direct labour and fixed costs are likely to be irrelevant costs with respect to short-term decisions. In the longer-term, however, it may be possible to reduce capacity and spending on fixed costs and direct labour. Let us now assume for Example 4.1 that Caledonian's assumption about an expected upsurge in the market proved to be incorrect and that it estimates that demand in the foreseeable future will remain at 35 000 jumpers *per month*. Given that it has a productive capacity of 50 000 jumpers it has sought to develop a long-term market for the unutilized capacity of 15 000 jumpers. As a result of its experience with the one-time special order with the company in the leisure industry, Caledonian has sought to develop a market with other companies operating in the leisure industry. Assume that this process has resulted in potential customers that are prepared to enter into a contractual agreement for a three year period for a supply of 15 000 jumpers *per month* at an agreed price of £25 per jumper. The cost of inserting the insignia required by each customer would remain unchanged at £1 per jumper. No marketing and distribution costs would be incurred with any of the orders. Caledonian considers that it has investigated all other possibilities to develop a market for the excess capacity. Should it enter into contractual agreements with the suppliers at £25 per jumper?

If Caledonian does not enter into contractual agreement with the suppliers the direct labour required will be made redundant. No redundancy costs will be involved. Further investigations indicate that manufacturing non-variable costs of £70 000 *per month* could be saved if a decision was made to reduce capacity by 15 000 jumpers per month. For example, the rental contracts for some of the machinery will not be renewed. Also some savings will be made in supervisory labour and support costs. Savings in marketing and distribution costs would be £20 000 *per month*. Assume also that if the capacity was reduced factory rearrangements would result in part of the facilities being rented out at £25 000 *per month*. Note that because variable costs vary directly with changes in volume, direct materials and variable manufacturing overheads will decline by 30% if capacity is reduced by 30% from 50 000 to 35 000 jumpers.

We are now faced with a longer-term decision where some of the costs that were fixed in the short term can be changed in the longer term. The appropriate financial data for the analysis is shown in Exhibit 4.2. Note that in Exhibit 4.2 the information for an activity of 35 000 jumpers incorporates the changes arising from the capacity reduction whereas the information presented for the same activity level in Exhibit 4.1 is based on the assumption that capacity will be maintained at 50 000 jumpers. Therefore the direct labour cost in

Exhibit 4.1 is £420 000 because it represents the labour required to meet demand at full capacity. If capacity is permanently reduced from 50 000 to 35 000 jumpers (i.e. a 30% reduction) it is assumed that direct labour costs will be reduced by 30% from £420 000 to £294 000. This is the amount shown in Exhibit 4.2.

A comparison of the monthly outcomes reported in columns (1) and (2) of Exhibit 4.2 indicates that the company is better off by £31 000 *per month* if it reduces capacity to 35 000 jumpers, assuming that there are no qualitative factors. Instead of presenting the data in columns (1) and (2) you can present only the differential (relevant) costs and revenues shown in column (3). This approach also indicates that the company is better off by £31 000 per month. Note that the entry in column (3) of £25 000 is the lost revenues from the rent of the unutilized capacity if the company accepts the orders. This represents the opportunity cost of accepting the orders.

Where the choice of one course of action requires that an alternative course of action is given up, the financial benefits that are forgone or sacrificed are known as **opportunity costs**. In other words, opportunity costs represent the lost contribution to profits arising from the best use of the alternative forgone. Opportunity costs only arise when resources are scarce and have alternative uses. Thus, in our illustration the capacity allocated to producing 15 000 jumpers results in an opportunity cost (i.e. the lost revenues from the rent of the capacity) of £25 000 per month.

In Exhibit 4.2 all of the costs and revenues are relevant to the decision because some of the costs that were fixed in the short term could be changed in the longer term. Therefore whether or not a cost is relevant often depends on the time horizon under consideration. Thus it is important that the information presented for decision-making relates to the appropriate time horizon. If inappropriate time horizons are selected there is a danger that misleading information will be presented. Remember that our aim should always be to maximize *long-term* net cash inflows.

Dangers of focusing excessively on a short-run time horizon

The problems arising from not taking into account the long-term consequences of accepting business that covers short-term incremental costs have been discussed by Kaplan (1990). He illustrates a situation where a company that makes pens has excess capacity, and a salesperson negotiates an order for 20 000 purple pens (a variation to the pens that are currently being made) at a price in excess of the incremental cost. In response to the question 'Should the order be accepted?' Kaplan states:

> *Take the order. The economics of making the purple pen with the excess capacity are overwhelming. There's no question that if you have excess capacity, the workers are all hired, the technology exists, and you have the product designed, and someone says, let's get an order for 20 000 purple pens, then the relevant consideration is price less the material cost of the purple pens. Don't even worry about the labour cost because you're going to pay them anyway. The second thing we tell them, however, is that they are never to ask us this question again ... Suppose that every month managers see that they have excess capacity to make 20 000 more pens, and salespeople are calling in special orders for turquoise pens, for purple pens with red caps, and other such customised products. Why not accept all these orders based on short-run contribution margin? The answer is that if they do, then costs that appear fixed in the short-term will start to increase, or expenses currently being incurred will be incapable of being reduced (p. 14).*

Kaplan stresses that by utilizing the unused capacity to increase the range of products produced (i.e. different variations of pens in the above example), the production process

EXHIBIT 4.2

Evaluation of orders for the unutilized capacity over a three year time horizon

Monthly sales and production in units	(1) Do not accept orders 35 000 (£)	(2) Accept the orders 50 000 (£)	(3) Difference (relevant costs) 15 000 (£)
Direct labour	294 000	420 000	126 000
Direct materials	280 000	400 000	120 000
Variable manufacturing overheads	70 000	100 000	30 000
Manufacturing non-variable overheads	210 000	280 000	70 000
Inserting company logo		15 000	15 000
Marketing and distribution costs	85 000	105 000	20 000
Total costs	939 000	1 320 000	381 000
Revenues from rental of facilities	25 000		25 000
Sales revenues	1 400 000	1 775 000	(375 000)
Profit per month	486 000	455 000	31 000

becomes more complex and consequently the fixed costs of managing the additional complexity will eventually increase. Long-term considerations should therefore always be taken into account when special pricing decisions are being evaluated. In particular, there is a danger that a series of special orders will be evaluated independently as short-term decisions. Consequently, those resources that cannot be adjusted in the short term will be treated as irrelevant for each decision. However, the effect of accepting a series of consecutive special orders over several periods constitutes a long-term decision. If special orders are always evaluated as short-term decisions a situation can arise whereby the decision to reduce capacity is continually deferred. If demand from normal business is considered to be permanently insufficient to utilize existing capacity then a long-term capacity decision is required. This should be based on the long-term approach as illustrated in Exhibit 4.2 and not the short-term approach illustrated in Exhibit 4.1. In other words, this decision should be based on a comparison of the relevant revenues and costs arising from using the excess capacity for special orders with the capacity costs that can be eliminated if the capacity is reduced.

Product-mix decisions when capacity constraints exist

In the short term sales demand may be in excess of current productivity capacity. For example, output may be restricted by a shortage of skilled labour, materials, equipment or space. When sales demand is in excess of a company's productive capacity, the resources responsible for limiting the output should be identified. These scarce resources are known as **limiting factors**. Within a short-term time period it is unlikely that production constraints can be removed and additional resources acquired. Where limiting factors apply, profit is maximized when the greatest possible contribution to profit is obtained each time the scarce or limiting factor is used. Consider Example 4.2.

In this situation the company's ability to increase its output and profits/net cash inflows is limited in the short term by the availability of machine capacity. You may think, when first looking at the available information, that the company should give top priority to

EXAMPLE 4.2

Rhine Autos is a major European producer of automobiles. A department within one of its divisions supplies component parts to firms operating within the automobile industry. The following information is provided relating to the anticipated demand and the productive capacity for the next quarter in respect of three components that are manufactured within the department:

	Component X	Component Y	Component Z
Contribution per unit of output	£12	£10	£6
Machine hours required			
per unit of output	6 hours	2 hours	1 hour
Estimated sales demand	2 000 units	2000 units	2000 units
Required machine hours			
for the quarter	12 000 hours	4000 hours	2000 hours

Because of the breakdown of one of its special purpose machines capacity is limited to 12 000 machine hours for the period, and this is insufficient to meet total sales demand. You have been asked to advise on the mix of products that should be produced during the period.

producing component X, since this yields the highest contribution per unit sold, but this assumption would be incorrect. To produce each unit of component X, 6 scarce machine hours are required, whereas components Y and Z use only 2 hours and 1 hour respectively of scarce machine hours. By concentrating on producing components Y and Z, the company can sell 2000 units of each component and still have some machine capacity left to make component X. If the company concentrates on producing component X it will only be able to meet the maximum sales demand of component X, and will have no machine capacity left to make components Y or Z. The way in which you should determine the optimum production plan is to calculate the contribution per limiting factor for each component and then to rank the components in order of profitability based on this calculation.

Using the figures in the present example the result would be as follows:

	Component X	Component Y	Component Z
Contribution per unit	£12	£10	£6
Machine hours required	6 hours	2 hours	1 hour
Contribution per machine hour	£2	£5	£6
Ranking	3	2	1

The company can now allocate the 12 000 scarce machine hours in accordance with the above rankings. The first choice should be to produce as much as possible of component Z. The maximum sales are 2000 units, and production of this quantity will result in the use of 2000 machine hours, thus leaving 10 000 unused hours. The second choice should be to produce as much of component Y as possible. The maximum sales of 2000 units will result in the use of 4000 machine hours. Production of both components Z and Y require 6000 machine hours, leaving a balance of 6000 hours for the production of component X, which will enable 1000 units of component X to be produced.

**REAL WORLD
VIEWS 4.1**

Assumed irrelevance of fixed overheads

A survey of approximately 250 UK manufacturing companies by Brealey (2005) indicated that approximately 70 per cent used costs incorporating the assignment of a share of fixed overheads for decision-making (e.g. make or buy and cost reduction decisions) and the remaining 30 per cent relied on using direct costs (excluding a share of the fixed overheads). Fifty-four of the respondents were interviewed and the major reasons for relying only on direct costs related to them representing the majority of the costs and the fact that indirect costs were not considered relevant for decision-making. These respondents appeared to adopt a short-term focus in determining the relevant costs for decision-making. The following represent the responses from two interviewees relating to make or buy decisions:

It's really what you're going to save. If you send something out you're not going to save fixed overhead at all, you'd be foolish to put fixed overhead into something. So if you're comparing it with another plant you need to look at the variable cost.

Any fixed overhead is irrelevant to that decision. It will remain regardless of whether we make or buy a product in. Therefore we look at the direct costs, the labour and material costs when we're doing that comparison. It simply would be incorrect to include costs that are not going to change.

Source: Brealey, J. A. (2005) The calculation of product costs and their use in decision-making in the British Manufacturing Industry, PhD dissertation, University of Huddersfield.

We can now summarize the allocation of the scarce machine hours:

Production	Machine hours used	Balance of machine hours available
2000 units of Z	2000	10 000
2000 units of Y	4000	6 000
1000 units of X	6000	—

This production programme results in the following total contribution:

	(£)
2000 units of Z at £6 per unit contribution	12 000
2000 units of Y at £10 per unit contribution	20 000
1000 units of X at £12 per unit contribution	12 000
Total contribution	44 000

Always remember that it is necessary to consider other qualitative factors before the production programme is determined. For example, customer goodwill may be lost causing a fall in future sales if the company is unable to supply all three products to, say, 150 of its regular customers. Difficulties may arise in applying this procedure when there is more than one scarce resource. It could not be applied if, for example, labour hours were also scarce and the contribution per labour hour resulted in component Y being ranked first, followed by components X and Z. In this type of situation, where more than one resource is scarce, it is necessary to resort to linear programming methods in order to determine the optimal production programme. For an explanation of how linear programming can be applied to decision-making, where there are several scarce resources, you should refer to Drury (2004, Ch. 26).

The approach described above can also be applied in non-manufacturing organizations. For example, in a major UK retail store display space is the limiting factor. The store maximizes its short-term profits by allocating shelving space on the basis of contribution per metre of shelving space. For an illustration of a product-mix decision with a capacity constraint within an agricultural setting you should refer to the solution to Review Problem 4.23 at the end of this chapter.

Finally, it is important that you remember that the approach outlined in this section applies only to those situations where capacity constraints cannot be removed in the short term. In the longer term additional resources should be acquired if the contribution from the extra capacity exceeds the cost of acquisition.

Replacement of equipment – the irrelevance of past costs

Replacement of equipment is a capital investment or long-term decision that requires the use of discounted cash flow procedures. These procedures are discussed in detail in Chapter 9, but one aspect of asset replacement decisions which we will consider at this stage is how to deal with the book value (i.e. the written-down value) of old equipment. This is a problem that has been known to cause difficulty, but the correct approach is to apply relevant cost principles (i.e. past or sunk costs are irrelevant for decision-making). We shall now use Example 4.3 to illustrate the irrelevance of the book value of old equipment in a replacement decision. To avoid any possible confusion, it will be assumed here that £1 of cash inflow or outflow in year 1 is equivalent to £1 of cash inflow or outflow in, say, year 3. Such an assumption would in reality be incorrect and you will see why this is so in Chapter 9, but by adopting this assumption at this stage, the replacement problem can be simplified and we can focus our attention on the treatment of the book value of the old equipment in the replacement decision.

You can see from an examination of Example 4.3 that the total costs over a period of three years for each of the alternatives are as follows:

	(1) Retain present machine (£)	(2) Buy replacement machine (£)	(3) Difference (relevant costs/ revenues) (£)
Variable/incremental operating costs:			
20 000 units at £3 per unit for 3 years	180 000		
20 000 units at £2 per unit for 3 years		120 000	(60 000)
Old machine book value:			
3-year annual depreciation charge	90 000		
Lump sum write-off		90 000	
Old machine disposal value		(40 000)	(40 000)
Initial purchase price of new machine		70 000	70 000
Total cost	270 000	240 000	30 000

EXAMPLE 4.3

A division within Rhine Autos purchased a machine three years ago for £180 000. Depreciation using the straight line basis, assuming a life of six years and with no salvage value, has been recorded each year in the financial accounts. The present written-down value of the equipment is £90 000 and it has a remaining life of three years. Management is considering replacing this machine with a new machine that will reduce the variable operating costs. The new machine will cost £70 000 and will have an expected life of three years with no scrap value. The variable operating costs are £3 per unit of output for the old machine and £2 per unit for the new machine. It is expected that both machines will be operated at a capacity of 20 000 units per annum. The sales revenues from the output of both machines will therefore be identical. The current disposal or sale value of the old machine is £40 000 and it will be zero in three years time.

You can see from the above analysis that the £90 000 book value of the old machine is irrelevant to the decision. Book values are not relevant costs because they are past or sunk costs and are therefore the same for all potential courses of action. If the present machine is retained, three years' depreciation at £30 000 per annum will be written off annually whereas if the new machine is purchased the £90 000 will be written off as a lump sum if it is replaced. Note that depreciation charges for the new machine are not included in the analysis since the cost of purchasing the machine is already included in the analysis. The sum of the annual depreciation charges are equivalent to the purchase cost. Thus, including both items would amount to double counting.

The above analysis shows that the costs of operating the replacement machine are £30 000 less than the costs of operating the existing machine over the three year period. Again there are several different methods of presenting the information. They all show a £30 000 advantage in favour of replacing the machine. You can present the information shown in columns (1) and (2) above, as long as you ensure that the same amount for the irrelevant items is included for all alternatives. Instead, you can present columns (1) and (2) with the irrelevant item (i.e. the £90 000) omitted or you can present the differential items listed in column (3). However, if you adopt the latter approach you will probably find it more meaningful to restate column (3) as follows:

	(£)
Savings on variable operating costs (3 years)	60 000
Sale proceeds of existing machine	40 000
	100 000
Less purchase cost of replacement machine	70 000
Savings on purchasing replacement machine	30 000

Outsourcing and make or buy decisions

Outsourcing is the process of obtaining goods or services from outside suppliers instead of producing the same goods or providing the same services within the organization. Decisions on whether to produce components or provide services within the organization or to acquire them from outside suppliers are called outsourcing or make or buy decisions. Many organizations outsource some of their activities such as their payroll and purchasing functions or the purchase of speciality components. Increasingly municipal local services such as waste disposal, highways and property maintenance are being outsourced. Consider the information presented in Example 4.4 (Case A).

EXAMPLE 4.4

Case A

One of the divisions within Rhine Autos is currently negotiating with another supplier regarding outsourcing component A that it manufactures. The division currently manufactures 10 000 units per annum of the component. The costs currently assigned to the components are as follows:

	Total costs of producing 10 000 components (£)	Unit cost (£)
Direct materials	120 000	12
Direct labour	100 000	10
Variable manufacturing overhead costs (power and utilities)	10 000	1
Fixed manufacturing overhead costs	80 000	8
Share of non-manufacturing overheads	50 000	5
Total costs	360 000	36

The above costs are expected to remain unchanged in the foreseeable future if the Rhine Autos division continues to manufacture the components. The supplier has offered to supply 10 000 components per annum at price of £30 per unit guaranteed for a minimum of three years. If Rhine Autos outsources component A the direct labour force currently employed in producing the components will be made redundant. No redundancy costs will be incurred. Direct materials and variable overheads are avoidable if component A is outsourced. Fixed manufacturing overhead costs would be reduced by £10 000 per annum but non-manufacturing costs would remain unchanged. Assume initially that the capacity that is required for component A has no alternative use. Should the Division of Rhine Autos make or buy the component?

Case B

Assume now that the extra capacity that will be made available from outsourcing component A can be used to manufacture and sell 10 000 units of part B at a price of £34 per unit. All of the labour force required to manufacture component A would be used to make part B. The variable manufacturing overheads, the fixed manufacturing overheads and non-manufacturing overheads would be the same as the costs incurred for manufacturing component A. The materials required to manufacture component A would not be required but additional materials required for making part B would cost £13 per unit. Should Rhine Autos outsource component A?

At first glance it appears that the component should be outsourced since the purchase price of £30 is less than the current total unit cost of manufacturing. However, the unit costs include some costs that will be unchanged whether or not the components are outsourced. These costs are therefore not relevant to the decision. Assume also that there are no alternative uses of the

REAL WORLD
VIEWS 4.2

Measures of product attractiveness in retail operations

Shelf space limits the quantity and variety of products offered by a retail operation. The visibility of a particular stock-keeping unit (SKU) and probability of a stock-out are related to the space allocated to the SKU. Total contribution for the retail operation is influenced by how shelf space is allocated to the SKUs. For retailers, shelf space 'is their life blood – and it's very limited and expensive'. Shelf space, accordingly, can be treated as a constraint in retailing operations. The most attractive SKU is the SKU that generates the greatest contribution per unit of space (square foot or cubic foot). To calculate contribution, all incremental expenses are deducted from incremental revenue. Incremental revenues include retail price and other direct revenue such as deals, allowances, forward-buy and prompt-payment discounts. Incremental expenses include any money paid out as a result of selling one unit of a particular item. Included in the incremental expenses would be the invoice unit cost and other invoiced amounts (shipping charges, for example) that can be traced directly to the sale of the particular item. Incremental revenues and expenses are found by dividing case values by the number of units per case.

If capacity is not changed, then the relevant costs are the incremental costs rather than full costs. If the costs of capacity are fixed, then using less capacity will not save money. Like the product mix problem, the answer to the space management problem is how to allocate existing capacity so that profit is maximized. To maximize profits where profits are constrained by space limitations, capacity should be allocated on the basis of the SKU that generates the greatest contribution per unit of space.

Source: © J Sainsbury plc 2003

Source: Adapted from Gardiner, S.C. (1993) Measures of product attractiveness and the theory of constraints, *International Journal of Retail and Distribution*, **21**(7), 37–40. http://www.emeraldinsight.com/ijrdm.htm

released capacity if the components are outsourced. The appropriate cost information is presented in Exhibit 4.3 (Section A). Alternative approaches to presenting relevant cost and revenue information are presented. In columns (1) and (2) of Exhibit 4.3 cost information is presented that includes both relevant and irrelevant costs for both alternatives under consideration. The same amount for non-manufacturing overheads, which are irrelevant, is included for both alternatives. By including the same amount in both columns the cost is made irrelevant. Alternatively, you can present cost information in columns (1) and (2) that excludes any irrelevant costs and revenues because they are identical for both alternatives. Adopting either approach will result in a difference of £60 000 in favour of making component A.

The third approach is to list only the relevant costs, cost savings and any relevant revenues. This approach is shown in column (3) of Exhibit 4.3 (Section A). This column represents the differential costs or revenues and it is derived from the differences between columns (1) and (2). In column (3) only the information that is relevant to the decision is presented. You will see that this approach compares the relevant costs of making directly against outsourcing. It indicates that the additional costs of making component A are £240 000 but this enables purchasing costs of £300 000 to be saved. Therefore the company makes a net saving of £60 000 from making the components compared with outsourcing.

EXHIBIT 4.3

Evaluating a make or buy decision

Section A – Assuming there is no alternative use of the released capacity

	Total cost of continuing to make 10 000 components (1) (£ per annum)	Total cost of buying 10 000 components (2) (£ per annum)	Difference (relevant) (cost) (3) (£ per annum)
Direct materials	120 000		120 000
Direct labour	100 000		100 000
Variable manufacturing overhead costs (power and utilities)	10 000		10 000
Fixed manufacturing overhead costs	80 000	70 000	10 000
Non-manufacturing overheads	50 000	50 000	
Outside purchase cost incurred/(saved)		300 000	(300 000)
Total costs incurred/(saved) per annum	360 000	420 000	(60 000)

Column 3 is easier to interpret if it is restated as two separate alternatives as follows:

	Relevant cost of making component A (£ per annum)	Relevant cost of outsourcing component A (£ per annum)
Direct materials	120 000	
Direct labour	100 000	
Variable manufacturing overhead costs	10 000	
Fixed manufacturing overhead costs	10 000	
Outside purchase cost incurred		300 000
	240 000	300 000

Section B – Assuming the released capacity has alternative uses

	(1) Make component A and do not make part B (£ per annum)	(2) Buy component A and do not make part B (£ per annum)	(3) Buy component A and make part B (£ per annum)
Direct materials	120 000		130 000
Direct labour	100 000		100 000
Variable manufacturing overhead costs	10 000		10 000
Fixed manufacturing overhead costs	80 000	70 000	80 000
Non-manufacturing overheads	50 000	50 000	50 000
Outside purchase cost incurred		300 000	300 000
Revenues from sales of part B			(340 000)
Total net costs	360 000	420 000	330 000

However, you will probably find column (3) easier to interpret if it is restated as two separate alternatives as shown in Exhibit 4.3. All of the approaches described in this and the preceding paragraph yield identical results. You can adopt any of them. It is a matter of personal preference.

Let us now re-examine the situation when the extra capacity created from not producing component A has an alternative use. Consider the information presented in Example 4.4 (Case B). The management of Rhine Autos now have three alternatives. They are:

1 Make component A and do not make part B.

2 Outsource component A and do not make part B.

3 Outsource component A and make and sell part B.

It is assumed there is insufficient capacity to make both component A and part B. The appropriate financial information is presented in Exhibit 4.3 (Section B). You will see that, with the exception of non-manufacturing costs, all of the items differ between the alternatives and are therefore relevant to the decision. Again we can omit the non-manufacturing costs from the analysis or include the same amount for all alternatives. Either approach makes them irrelevant. The first two alternatives that do not involve making and selling part B are identical to the alternatives considered in Case A so the information presented in columns (1) and (2) in sections A and B of Exhibit 4.3 are identical. In column 3 of section B the costs incurred in making part B in respect of direct labour, variable and fixed manufacturing overheads and non-manufacturing overheads are identical to the costs incurred in making component A. Therefore the same costs for these items are entered in column 3. However, different materials are required to make part B and the cost of these (10 000 units at £13) are entered in column 3. In addition, the revenues from the sales of part B are entered in column 3. Comparing the three columns in Section B of Exhibit 4.3 indicates that buying component A and using the extra capacity that is created to make part B is the preferred alternative.

The incremental costs of outsourcing are £60 000 more than making component B (see Section A of Exhibit 4.3) but the extra capacity released from outsourcing component A enables Rhine Autos to obtain a profit contribution of £90 000 (£340 000 incremental sales from part B less £250 000 incremental/relevant costs of making part B). The overall outcome is a £30 000 net benefit from outsourcing. Note that the relevant costs of making part B are the same as those of making component A, apart from direct materials, which cost £130 000. In other words, the relevant (incremental) costs of making part B (compared with outsourcing) are as follows:

	(£)
Direct materials	130 000
Direct labour	100 000
Variable manufacturing overhead costs	10 000
Fixed manufacturing overhead costs	10 000
	250 000

Discontinuation decisions

Most organizations periodically analyse profits by one or more cost objects, such as products or services, customers and locations. Periodic profitability analysis provides attention-directing information that highlights those unprofitable activities that require a more detailed appraisal (sometimes referred to as a special study) to ascertain whether or not they should be discontinued. In this section we shall illustrate how the principle of relevant costs can be applied to discontinuation decisions. Consider Example 4.5. You will see that it focuses on a decision whether to discontinue operating a sales territory, but the same principles can also be applied to discontinuing products, services or customers.

In Example 4.5 Euro Company analyses profits by locations. Profits are analysed by regions which are then further analysed by sales territories within each region. It is apparent from Example 4.5 that the Scandinavian region is profitable but the profitability analysis suggests that the Helsinki sales territory is unprofitable. A more detailed study is required to ascertain whether it should be discontinued. Let us assume that this study indicates that:

1 Discontinuing the Helsinki sales territory will eliminate cost of goods sold, salespersons salaries, sales office rent and regional and headquarters expenses arising from cause-and-effect cost allocations.

2 Discontinuing the Helsinki sales territory will have no effect on depreciation of sales office equipment, warehouse rent, depreciation of warehouse equipment and regional and headquarters expenses arising from arbitrary cost allocations. The same costs will be incurred by the company for all of these items even if the sales territory is discontinued.

Note that in the event of discontinuation the sales office will not be required and the rental will be eliminated whereas the warehouse rent relates to the warehouse for the region as a whole and, unless the company moves to a smaller warehouse, the rental will remain unchanged. It is therefore not a relevant cost. Discontinuation will result in the creation of additional space and if the extra space remains unused there are no financial consequences to take into account. However, if the additional space can be sub-let to generate rental income the income would be incorporated as an opportunity cost for the alternative of keeping the Helsinki territory.

Exhibit 4.4 shows the relevant cost computations. Column (1) shows the costs incurred by the company if the sales territory is kept open and column (2) shows the costs that would be incurred if a decision was taken to drop the sales territory. Therefore in column (2) only those costs that would be eliminated (i.e. those items listed in item (1) above) are deducted from column (1). You can see that the company will continue to incur some of the costs (i.e. those items listed in item (2) above) even if the Helsinki territory is closed and these costs are therefore irrelevant to the decision. Again you can either include, or exclude, the irrelevant costs in columns (1) and (2) as long as you ensure that the same amount of irrelevant costs is included for both alternatives if you adopt the first approach. Both approaches will show that future profits will decline by £154 000 if the Helsinki territory is closed. Alternatively, you can present just the relevant costs and revenues shown in column (3). This approach indicates that keeping the sales territory open results in additional sales revenues of £1 700 000 but additional costs of £1 546 000 are incurred giving a contribution of £154 000 towards fixed costs and profits.

You will have noted that we have assumed that the regional and headquarters costs assigned to the sales territories on the basis of cause-and-effect allocations can be eliminated if the Helsinki territory is discontinued. These are indirect costs that fluctuate in the longer term according to the demand for them and it is assumed that the selected allocation base (ie. the cost driver), provides a reasonably accurate measure of resources consumed by the sales territories. Cause-and-effect allocation bases assume that if the cause is eliminated or reduced, the effect (i.e. the costs) will be eliminated or reduced. If cost drivers are selected that result in allocations that are inaccurate measures of resources consumed by cost objects (i.e. sales territories) the relevant costs derived from these allocations will be

EXAMPLE 4.5

The Euro Company is a wholesaler who sells its products to retailers throughout Europe. Euro's headquarters is in Brussels. The company has adopted a regional structure with each region consisting of 3–5 sales territories. Each region has its own regional office and a warehouse which distributes the goods directly to the customers. Each sales territory also has an office where the marketing staff are located. The Scandinavian region consists of three sales territories with offices located in Stockholm, Oslo and Helsinki. The budgeted results for the next quarter are as follows:

	Stockholm (£000s)	Oslo (£000s)	Helsinki (£000s)	Total (£000s)
Cost of goods sold	800	850	1000	2650
Salespersons salaries	160	200	240	600
Sales office rent	60	90	120	270
Depreciation of sales office equipment	20	30	40	90
Apportionment of warehouse rent	24	24	24	72
Depreciation of warehouse equipment	20	16	22	58
Regional and headquarters costs				
Cause-and-effect allocations	120	152	186	458
Arbitrary apportionments	360	400	340	1100
Total costs assigned to each location	1564	1762	1972	5298
Reported profit/(loss)	236	238	(272)	202
Sales	1800	2000	1700	5500

Assuming that the above results are likely to be typical of future quarterly performance should the Helsinki territory be discontinued?

incorrect and incorrect decisions may be made. We shall explore this issue in some detail in Chapter 6 when we look at activity-based costing.

Determining the relevant costs of direct materials

So far in this chapter we have assumed, when considering various decisions, that any materials required would not be taken from existing stocks but would be purchased at a later date, and so the estimated purchase price would be the relevant material cost. Where materials are taken from existing stock do remember that the original purchase price represents a past or sunk cost and is therefore irrelevant for decision-making. If the materials are to be replaced then using the materials for a particular activity will necessitate their replacement. Thus, the decision to use the materials on an activity will result in additional acquisition costs compared with the situation if the materials were not used on that particular activity. Therefore the future replacement cost represents the relevant cost of the materials.

Consider now the situation where the materials have no further use apart from being used on a particular activity. If the materials have some realizable value, the use of the materials will result in lost sales revenues, and this lost sales revenue will represent an

	Total costs and revenues to be assigned			
	(1) Keep Helsinki territory open (£000s)	(2) Discontinue Helsinki territory (£000s)	(3) Difference incremental costs and revenues (£000s)	
Cost of goods sold	2650	1650	1000	
Salespersons salaries	600	360	240	
Sales office rent	270	150	120	
Depreciation of sales office equipment	90	90		
Apportionment of warehouse rent	72	72		
Depreciation of warehouse equipment	58	58		
Regional and headquarters costs				
Cause-and-effect allocations	458	272	186	
Arbitrary apportionments	1100	1100		
Total costs to be assigned	5298	3752	1546	
Reported profit	202	48	154	
Sales	5500	3800	1700	

EXHIBIT 4.4

Relevant cost analysis relating to the discontinuation of the Helsinki territory

opportunity cost that must be assigned to the activity. Alternatively, if the materials have no realizable value the relevant cost of the materials will be zero.

Determining the relevant costs of direct labour

Determining the direct labour costs that are relevant to short-term decisions depends on the circumstances. Where a company has temporary spare capacity and the labour force is to be maintained in the short term, the direct labour cost incurred will remain the same for all alternative decisions. The direct labour cost will therefore be irrelevant for short-term decision-making purposes. Consider now a situation where casual labour is used and where workers can be hired on a daily basis; a company may then adjust the employment of labour to exactly the amount required to meet the production requirements. The labour cost will increase if the company accepts additional work, and will decrease if production is reduced. In this situation the labour cost will be a relevant cost for decision-making purposes.

In a situation where full capacity exists and additional labour supplies are unavailable in the short term, and where no further overtime working is possible, the only way that labour resources could then be obtained for a specific order would be to reduce existing production. This would release labour for the order, but the reduced production would result in a lost contribution, and this lost contribution must be taken into account when ascertaining the relevant cost for the specific order. The relevant labour cost per hour where full capacity exists is therefore the hourly labour rate plus an opportunity cost consisting of the contribution per hour that is lost by accepting the order.

Summary

The following items relate to the learning objectives listed at the beginning of the chapter.

● **Distinguish between relevant and irrelevant costs and revenues.**

Relevant costs/revenues represent those future costs/revenues that will be changed by a particular decision, whereas irrelevant costs/revenues will not be affected by that decision. In the short-term total profits will be increased (or total losses decreased) if a course of action is chosen where relevant revenues are in excess of relevant costs.

● **Explain the importance of qualitative factors.**

Quantitative factors refer to outcomes that can be measured in numerical terms. In many situations it is difficult to quantify all the important elements of a decision. Those factors that cannot be expressed in numerical terms are called qualitative factors. Examples of qualitative factors include changes in employee morale and the impact of being at the mercy of a supplier when a decision is made to close a company's facilities and sub-contract components. Although qualitative factors cannot be quantified it is essential that they are taken into account in the decision-making process.

● **Distinguish between the relevant and irrelevant costs and revenues for the five decision-making problems described.**

The five decision-making problems described were: (a) special selling price decisions; (b) product-mix decisions when capacity constraints apply; (c) decisions on the replacement of equipment; (d) outsourcing (make or buy) decisions; and (e) discontinuation decisions. Different approaches can be used for presenting relevant cost and revenue information. Information can be presented that includes both relevant and irrelevant items for all alternatives under consideration. If this approach is adopted the same amount for the irrelevant items (i.e. those items that remain unchanged as a result of the decision) are included for all alternatives thus making them irrelevant for the decision. Alternatively, information can be presented that lists only the relevant costs for the alternatives under consideration. Where only two alternatives are being considered a third approach is to present only the relevant (differential) items. You can adopt either approach. It is a matter of personal preference. All three approaches were illustrated for the five decision-making problems.

● **Describe the key concept that should be applied for presenting information for product-mix decisions when capacity constraints apply.**

The information presented should rank the products by the contribution per unit of the constraining or limiting factor (i.e. the scarce resource). The capacity of the scarce resource should allocated according to this ranking.

● **Explain why the book value of equipment is irrelevant when making equipment replacement decisions.**

The book value of equipment is a past (sunk) cost that cannot be changed for any alternative under consideration. Only future costs or revenues that will differ between alternatives are relevant for replacement decisions.

● **Describe the opportunity cost concept.**

Where the choice of one course of action requires that an alternative course of action be given up the financial benefits that are forgone or sacrificed are known as opportunity costs. Opportunity costs thus represent the lost contribution to profits arising from the best alternative forgone. They arise only when the resources are scarce and have alternative uses. Opportunity costs must therefore be included in the analysis when presenting relevant information for decision-making.

Key terms and concepts

decision-relevant approach (p. 79)
differential cash flow (p. 80)
incremental cash flow (p. 80)
limiting factor (p. 86)
opportunity cost (p. 85)
outsourcing (p. 90)

qualitative factors (p. 81)
relevant cost (p. 80)
replacement cost (p. 96)
special studies (p. 79)
written-down value (p. 89)

Assessment material

Review questions

The review questions are short questions that enable you to assess your understanding of the main topics included in the chapter. The numbers in parentheses provide you with the page numbers to refer to if you cannot answer a specific question.

Review problems

The review problems are more complex and require you to relate and apply the chapter content to various business problems. The multiple-choice questions are the least demanding and normally take less than 10 minutes to complete. Fully worked solutions to the review problems are provided in a separate section at the end of the book. Further review problems for this chapter are available on the accompanying website, www.drury-online.com. The answers to these problems are available for lecturers on the lecturer's password-protected section of the website.

Case studies

The website also includes over 30 case study problems. A list of these cases is provided on pages 491–93. Several cases are relevant to the content of this chapter. Examples include Fleet Ltd and High Street Reproduction Furniture Ltd.

Review questions

4.1 What is a relevant cost? (*p. 80*)

4.2 Why is it important to recognize qualitative factors when presenting information for decision-making? Provide examples of qualitative factors. (*p. 81*)

4.3 What underlying principle should be followed in determining relevant costs for decision-making? (*p. 84*)

4.4 Explain what is meant by special pricing decisions. (*p. 81*)

4.5 Describe the important factors that must be taken into account when making special pricing decisions. (*p. 83*)

4.6 Describe the dangers involved in focusing excessively on a short-run decision-making time horizon. (*pp. 85–86*)

4.7 Define limiting factors. (*p. 86*)

4.8 How should a company determine its optimal product mix when a limiting factor exists? (*p. 87*)

4.9 Why is the written down value and depreciation of an asset being considered for replacement irrelevant when making replacement decisions? (*p. 90*)

4.10 Explain the importance of opportunity costs for decision-making. (*p. 85*)

4.11 Explain the circumstances when the original purchase price of materials are irrelevant for decision-making. (*pp. 96–97*)

4.12 Why does the relevant cost of labour differ depending upon the circumstances? (*p. 97*)

Review problems

4.13 Z Limited manufactures three products, the selling price and cost details of which are given below:

	Product X (£)	Product Y (£)	Product Z (£)
Selling price per unit	75	95	95
Direct materials (£5/kg)	10	5	15
Direct labour (£4/hour)	16	24	20
Variable overhead	8	12	10
Fixed overhead	24	36	30

In a period when direct materials are restricted in supply, the most and the least profitable uses of direct materials are

	Most profitable	Least profitable
A	X	Z
B	Y	Z
C	X	Y
D	Z	Y
E	Y	X

4.14 Your company regularly uses material X and currently has in stock 600 kg, for which it paid £1500 two weeks ago. It this were to be sold as raw material it could be sold today for £2.00 per kg. You are aware that the material can be bought on the open market for £3.25 per kg, but it must be purchased in quantities of 1000 kg.

You have been asked to determine the relevant cost of 600 kg of material X to be used in a job for a customer. The relevant cost of the 600 kg is:

(a) £1200
(b) £1325
(c) £1825
(d) £1950
(e) £3250

4.15 Q plc makes two products – Quone and Qutwo – from the same raw material. The selling price and cost details of these products are as shown below:

	Quone (£)	Qutwo (£)
Selling price	20.00	18.00
Direct material (£2.00/kg)	6.00	5.00
Direct labour	4.00	3.00
Variable overhead unit	2.00	1.50
	12.00	9.50
Contribution per unit	8.00	8.50

The maximum demand for these products is:

Quone   500 units per week
Qutwo   unlimited number of units per week

If materials were limited to 2000 kg per week, the shadow price (opportunity cost) of these materials would be:

(a) nil;
(b) £2.00 per kg;
(c) £2.66 per kg;
(d) £3.40 per kg;
(e) none of these.

4.16 BB Limited makes three components: S, T and U. The following costs have been recorded:

	Component S Unit cost (£)	Component T Unit cost (£)	Component U Unit cost (£)
Variable cost	2.50	8.00	5.00
Fixed cost	2.00	8.30	3.75
Total cost	4.50	16.30	8.75

Another company has offered to supply the components to BB Limited at the following prices:

	Component S	Component T	Component U
Price each	£4	£7	£5.50

Which component(s), if any, should BB Limited consider buying in?

(a) Buy in all three components.
(b) Do not buy any.
(c) Buy in S and U.
(d) Buy in T only.

4.17 A company is considering accepting a one-year contract which will require four skilled employees. The four skilled employees could be recruited on a one-year contract at a cost of £40 000 per employee. The employees would be supervised by an existing manager who earns £60 000 per annum. It is expected that supervision of the contract would take 10% of the manager's time.

Instead of recruiting new employees, the company could retrain some existing employees who currently earn £30 000 per year. The training would cost £15 000 in total. If these employees were used they would need to be replaced at a total cost of £100 000.

The relevant labour cost of the contract is:

A £100 000
B £115 000
C £135 000
D £141 000
E £166 000

4.18 A company is considering the costs for a special order. The order would require 1250 kg of material D. This material is readily available and regularly used by the company. There are 265 kg of material D in stock which cost £795 last week. The current market price is £3.24 per kg.

Material D is normally used to make product X. Each unit of X requires 3 kg of material D and, if material D is costed at £3 per kg, each unit of X yields a contribution of £15.

The cost of material D to be included in the costing of the special order is nearest to

A £3990　　　B £4050　　　C £10 000　　　D £10 300

4.19 Camden has three divisions. Information for the year ended 30 September is as follows:

	Division A £'000	Division B £'000	Division C £'000	Total £'000
Sales	350	420	150	920
Variable costs	280	210	120	610
Contribution	70	210	30	310
Fixed costs				262.5
Net profit				47.5

General fixed overheads are allocated to each division on the basis of sales revenue; 60% of the total fixed costs incurred by the company are specific to each division being split equally between them.

Using relevant costing techniques, which divisions should remain open if Camden wishes to maximize profits?

A   A, B and C
B   A and B only
C   B only
D   B and C only.

4.20   **Decision on which of two mutually exclusive contracts to accept**

A company in the civil engineering industry with headquarters located 22 miles from London undertakes contracts anywhere in the United Kingdom.

The company has had its tender for a job in north-east England accepted at £288 000 and work is due to begin in March. However, the company has also been asked to undertake a contract on the south coast of England. The price offered for this contract is £352 000. Both of the contracts cannot be taken simultaneously because of constraints on staff site management personnel and on plant available. An escape clause enables the company to withdraw from the contract in the north-east, provided notice is given before the end of November and an agreed penalty of £28 000 is paid.

The following estimates have been submitted by the company's quantity surveyor:

Cost estimates	North-east (£)	South coast (£)
Materials:		
In stock at original cost, Material X	21 600	
In stock at original cost, Material Y		24 800
Firm orders placed at original cost, Material X	30 400	
Not yet ordered – current cost, Material X	60 000	
Not yet ordered – current cost, Material Z		71 200
Labour – hired locally	86 000	110 000
Site management	34 000	34 000
Staff accommodation and travel for site management	6 800	5 600
Plant on site – depreciation	9 600	12 800
Interest on capital, 8%	5 120	6 400
Total local contract costs	253 520	264 800
Headquarters costs allocated at rate of 5% on total contract costs	12 676	13 240
	266 196	278 040
Contract price	288 000	352 000
Estimated profit	21 804	73 960

Notes:

1.   X, Y and Z are three building materials. Material X is not in common use and would not realize much money if re-sold; however, it could be used on other contracts but only as a substitute for another material currently quoted at 10% less than the original cost of X. The price of Y, a material in common use, has doubled since it was purchased; its net realizable value if re-sold would be its

new price less 15% to cover disposal costs. Alternatively it could be kept for use on other contracts in the following financial year.

2. With the construction industry not yet recovered from the recent recession, the company is confident that manual labour, both skilled and unskilled, could be hired locally on a subcontracting basis to meet the needs of each of the contracts.

3. The plant which would be needed for the south coast contract has been owned for some years and £12 800 is the year's depreciation on a straight-line basis. If the north-east contract is undertaken, less plant will be required but the surplus plant will be hired out for the period of the contract at a rental of £6000.

4. It is the company's policy to charge all contracts with notional interest at 8% on estimated working capital involved in contracts. Progress payments would be receivable from the contractee.

5. Salaries and general costs of operating the small headquarters amount to about £108 000 each year. There are usually ten contracts being supervised at the same time.

6. Each of the two contracts is expected to last from March to February which, coincidentally, is the company's financial year.

7. Site management is treated as a fixed cost.

You are required, as the management accountant to the company,

(a) to present comparative statements to show the net benefit to the company of undertaking the more advantageous of the two contracts;

(12 marks)

(b) to explain the reasoning behind the inclusion in (or omission from) your comparative financial statements, of each item given in the cost estimates and the notes relating thereto.

(13 marks)
(Total 25 marks)

4.21 Deletion of a product

Blackarm Ltd makes three products and is reviewing the profitability of its product line. You are given the following budgeted data about the firm for the coming year.

Product	A	B	C
Sales (in units)	100 000	120 000	80 000
	(£)	(£)	(£)
Revenue	1 500 000	1 440 000	880 000
Costs:			
Material	500 000	480 000	240 000
Labour	400 000	320 000	160 000
Overhead	650 000	600 000	360 000
	1 550 000	1 400 000	760 000
Profit/(Loss)	(50 000)	40 000	120 000

The company is concerned about the loss on product A. It is considering ceasing production of it and switching the spare capacity of 100 000 units to Product C.

You are told:

(i) All production is sold.

(ii) 25% of the labour cost for each product is fixed in nature.

(iii) Fixed administration overheads of £900 000 in total have been apportioned to each product on the basis of units sold and are included in the overhead costs above. All other overhead costs are variable in nature.

(iv) Ceasing production of product A would eliminate the fixed labour charge associated with it and one-sixth of the fixed administration overhead apportioned to product A.

(v) Increasing the production of product C by 100 000 units would mean that the fixed labour cost associated with product C would double, the variable labour cost would rise by 20% and its selling price would have to be decreased by £1.50 in order to achieve the increased sales.

Required:

(a) Prepare a marginal cost statement for a unit of each product on the basis of:
   (i) the original budget;
   (ii) if product A is deleted.

(12 marks)

(b) Prepare a statement showing the total contribution and profit for each product group on the basis of:
   (i) the original budget;
   (ii) if product A is deleted.

(8 marks)

(c) Using your results from (a) and (b) advise whether product A should be deleted from the product range, giving reasons for your decision.

(5 marks)
(Total 25 marks)

4.22 Alternative uses of obsolete materials

Brown Ltd is a company that has in stock some materials of type XY that cost £75 000 but that are now obsolete and have a scrap value of only £21 000. Other than selling the material for scrap, there are only two alternative uses for them.

Alternative 1: Converting the obsolete materials into a specialized product, which would require the following additional work and materials:

Material A	600 units
Material B	1 000 units
Direct labour:	
5000 hours unskilled	
5000 hours semi-skilled	
5000 hours highly skilled	15 000 hours
Extra selling and delivery expenses	£27 000
Extra advertising	£18 000

The conversion would produce 900 units of saleable product, and these could be sold for £400 per unit.

Material A is already in stock and is widely used within the firm. Although present stocks together with orders already planned will be sufficient to facilitate normal activity, any extra material used by adopting this alternative will necessitate such materials being replaced immediately. Material B is also in stock, but it is unlikely that any additional supplies can be obtained for some considerable time because of an industrial dispute. At the present time material B is normally used in the production of product Z, which sells at £390 per unit and incurs total variable cost (excluding material B) of £210 per unit. Each unit of product Z uses four units of material B.

The details of materials A and B are as follows:

	Material A (£)	Material B (£)
Acquisition cost at time of purchase	100 per unit	10 per unit
Net realizable value	85 per unit	18 per unit
Replacement cost	90 per unit	—

Alternative 2: Adapting the obsolete materials for use as a substitute for a sub-assembly that is regularly used within the firm. Details of the extra work and materials required are as follows:

Material C	1000 units
Direct labour:	
4000 hours unskilled	
1000 hours semi-skilled	
4000 hours highly skilled	9000 hours

1200 units of the sub-assembly are regularly used per quarter, at a cost of £900 per unit. The adaptation of material XY would reduce the quantity of the sub-assembly purchased from outside the firm to 900 units for the next quarter only. However, since the volume purchased would be reduced, some discount would be lost, and the price of those purchased from outside would increase to £950 per unit for that quarter.

Material C is not available externally, but is manufactured by Brown Ltd. The 1000 units required would be available from stocks, but would be produced as extra production. The standard cost per unit of material C would be as follows:

	(£)
Direct labour, 6 hours unskilled labour	36
Raw materials	13
Variable overhead, 6 hours at £1	6
Fixed overhead, 6 hours at £3	18
	73

The wage rates and overhead recovery rates for Brown Ltd are:

Variable overhead	£1 per direct labour hour
Fixed overhead	£3 per direct labour hour
Unskilled labour	£6 per direct labour hour
Semi-skilled labour	£8 per direct labour hour
Highly skilled labour	£10 per direct labour hour

The unskilled labour is employed on a casual basis and sufficient labour can be acquired to exactly meet the production requirements. Semi-skilled labour is part of the permanent labour force, but the company has temporary excess supply of this type of labour at the present time. Highly skilled labour is in short supply and cannot be increased significantly in the short term; this labour is presently engaged in meeting the demand for product L, which requires 4 hours of highly skilled labour. The contribution (sales less direct labour and material costs and variable overheads) from the sale of one unit of product L is £24.

Given this information, you are required to present cost information advising whether the stocks of material XY should be sold, converted into a specialized product (alternative 1) or adapted for use as a substitute for a sub-assembly (alternative 2).

4.23 Limiting factors and optimal production programme

A market gardener is planning his production for next season, and he has asked you as a cost accountant, to recommend the optimal mix of vegetable production for the coming year. He has given you the following data relating to the current year.

	Potatoes	Turnips	Parsnips	Carrots
Area occupied (acres)	25	20	30	25
Yield per acre (tonnes)	10	8	9	12
Selling price per tonne (£)	100	125	150	135
Variable cost per acre (£):				
Fertilizers	30	25	45	40
Seeds	15	20	30	25
Pesticides	25	15	20	25
Direct wages	400	450	500	570

Fixed overhead per annum £54 000

The land that is being used for the production of carrots and parsnips can be used for either crop, but not for potatoes or turnips. The land being used for potatoes and turnips can be used for either crop, but not for carrots or parsnips. In order to provide an adequate market service, the gardener must produce each year at least 40 tonnes each of potatoes and turnips and 36 tonnes each of parsnips and carrots.

(a) You are required to present a statement to show:

(i)   the profit for the current year;

(ii) the profit for the production mix that you would recommend.

(b) Assuming that the land could be cultivated in such a way that any of the above crops could be produced and there was no market commitment, you are required to:

(i)   advise the market gardener on which crop he should concentrate his production;

(ii) calculate the profit if he were to do so;

(iii) calculate in sterling the break-even point of sales.

(25 marks)

Cost assignment

5 In Chapters 1 and 2 it was pointed out that companies need cost and management accounting systems to perform a number of different functions. In this chapter we are going to concentrate on two of these functions – they are (i) allocating costs between cost of goods sold and inventories for internal and external profit reporting and (ii) providing relevant decision-making information for distinguishing between profitable and unprofitable activities.

In order to perform the above functions a cost accumulation system is required that assigns costs to cost objects. The aim of this chapter is to provide you with an understanding of how costs are accumulated and assigned to cost objects. You should have remembered from Chapter 2 that a cost object is anything for which a separate measurement of cost is desired. Typical cost objects include products, services, customers and locations. In this chapter we shall either use the term cost object as a generic term or assume that products are the cost object. However, the same cost assignment principles can be applied to all cost objects.

In the previous chapter we concentrated on identifying the relevant costs that should be extracted from the costing system for making non-routine decisions. This chapter focuses on the costing system and explains the process of how costs are accumulated and assigned

LEARNING OBJECTIVES

After studying this chapter, you should be able to:

- distinguish between cause-and-effect and arbitrary cost allocations;
- explain why different cost information is required for different purposes;
- describe how cost systems differ in terms of their level of sophistication;
- understand the factors influencing the choice of an optimal cost system;
- explain why departmental overhead rates should be used in preference to a single blanket overhead rate;
- construct an overhead analysis sheet and calculate cost centre allocation rates;
- justify why budgeted overhead rates should be used in preference to actual overhead rates;
- calculate and explain the accounting treatment of the under/over recovery of overheads.

to cost objects. You should note at this stage the monetary amounts accumulated within the costing system may consist of past actual costs or estimated future costs. If the former approach is adopted past costs that are extracted for decision-making should be adjusted to represent estimated future costs.

Besides providing a database from which relevant costs can be extracted for non-routine decisions, information is extracted from the costing system for routine periodic profitability analysis relating to various segments of the business (e.g. products, services, customers, distribution channels). Profits should be analysed periodically to ensure that only profitable activities are undertaken. In some situations cost information is also routinely extracted from the costing system for determing selling prices, particularly in markets where customized products and services are provided that do not have readily availalbe selling prices.

We begin by explaining how the cost assignment process differs for direct and indirect costs.

Assignment of direct and indirect costs

Costs that are assigned to cost objects can be divided into two categories – direct costs and indirect costs. Sometimes the term **overheads** is used instead of indirect costs. Direct costs can be accurately traced to cost objects because they can be specifically and exclusively traced to a particular cost object whereas indirect costs cannot. Where a cost can be directly assigned to a cost object the term **cost tracing** is used. In contrast, indirect costs cannot be traced directly to a cost object because they are usually common to several cost objects. Indirect costs are therefore assigned to cost objects using cost allocations.

A **cost allocation** is the process of assigning costs when a direct measure does not exist for the quantity of resources consumed by a particular cost object. Cost allocations involve the use of surrogate rather than direct measures. For example, consider an activity such as receiving incoming materials. Assuming that the cost of receiving materials is strongly influenced by the number of receipts then costs can be allocated to products (i.e. the cost object) based on the number of material receipts each product requires. The basis that is used to allocate costs to cost objects (i.e. the number of material receipts in our example) is called an **allocation base** or **cost driver**. If 20% of the total number of receipts for a period were required for a particular product then 20% of the total costs of receiving incoming materials would be allocated to that product. Assuming that the product was discontinued, and not replaced, we would expect action to be taken to reduce the resources required for receiving materials by 20%.

In the above illustration the allocation base is assumed to be a significant determinant of the cost of receiving incoming materials. Where allocation bases are significant determinants of the costs we shall describe them as **cause-and-effect allocations**. Where a cost allocation base is used that is not a significant determinant of its cost the term **arbitrary allocation** will be used. An example of an arbitrary allocation would be if direct labour hours were used as the allocation base to allocate the costs of materials receiving. If a labour intensive product required a large proportion of direct labour hours (say 30%) but few material receipts it would be allocated with a large proportion of the costs of material receiving. The allocation would be an inaccurate assignment of the resources consumed by the product. Furthermore, if the product were discontinued, and not replaced, the cost of the material receiving activity would not decline by 30% because the allocation base is not a significant determinant of the costs of the materials receiving activity. Arbitrary allocations are therefore likely to result in inaccurate allocations of indirect costs to cost objects.

Figure 5.1 provides a summary of the assignment process. You can see that direct costs are assigned to cost objects using cost tracing whereas indirect cost are assigned using cost allocations. For accurate assignment of indirect costs to cost objects cause-and-effect allocations should be used. Two types of systems can be used to assign indirect costs to cost

FIGURE 5.1   *Cost allocations and cost tracing*

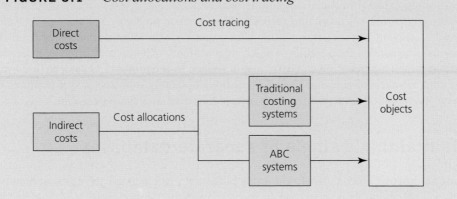

objects. They are **traditional costing systems** and **activity-based-costing (ABC)** systems. Traditional costing systems were developed in the early 1900s and are still widely used today. They rely extensively on arbitrary cost allocations. ABC systems only emerged in the late 1980s. One of the major aims of ABC systems is to use only cause-and-effect cost allocations. Both cost systems adopt identical approaches to assigning direct costs to cost objects. In this chapter we shall concentrate on traditional costing systems and ABC systems will be examined in the next chapter.

Different costs for different purposes

Manufacturing organizations assign costs to products for two purposes: first, for internal profit measurement and external financial accounting requirements in order to allocate the manufacturing costs incurred during a period between cost of goods sold and inventories; secondly, to provide useful information for managerial decision-making requirements. In order to meet financial accounting requirements, it may not be necessary to accurately trace costs to *individual* products. Consider a situation where a firm produces 1000 different products and the costs incurred during a period are £10 million. A well-designed product costing system should accurately analyse the £10 million costs incurred between cost of sales and inventories. Let us assume the true figures are £7 million and £3 million. Approximate but inaccurate *individual* product costs may provide a reasonable approximation of how much of the £10 million should be attributed to cost of sales and inventories. Some product costs may be overstated and others may be understated, but this would not matter for financial accounting purposes as long as the *total* of the individual product costs assigned to cost of sales and inventories was approximately £7 million and £3 million.

For decision-making purposes, however, more accurate product costs are required so that we can distinguish between profitable and unprofitable products. By more accurately measuring the resources consumed by products, or other cost objects, a firm can identify its sources of profits and losses. If the cost system does not capture sufficiently accurately the consumption of resources by products, the reported product costs will be distorted, and there is a danger that managers may drop profitable products or continue production of unprofitable products.

Besides different levels of accuracy, different cost information is required for different purposes. For meeting external financial accounting requirements, financial accounting regulations and legal requirements in most countries require that inventories should be valued at manufacturing cost. Therefore only manufacturing costs are assigned to products for meeting external financial accounting requirements. For decision-making non-manufacturing costs must be taken into account and assigned to products. Not all costs, however may be relevant for decision-making. For example, you should remember from the previous chapter that depreciation of plant and machinery will not be affected by a decision to discontinue a product. Such costs were described in the previous chapter as irrelevant and sunk for decision-making. Thus depreciation of plant must be assigned to products for inventory valuation but it should not be assigned for discontinuation decisions.

Maintaining a single or separate databases

Because different costs and different levels of accuracy are required for different purposes some organizations maintain two separate costing systems, one for decision-making and the other for inventory valuation and profit measurement. In a survey of 187 UK companies Drury and Tayles (2000) reported that 9% of the companies maintained two cost accumulation systems, one for decision-making and the other for inventory valuation. The remaining 91% of organizations maintained a costing system on a single database from which appropriate cost information was extracted to provide the required information for both decision-making and inventory valuation. When a single database is maintained only costs that must be assigned for inventory valuation are extracted for meeting financial accounting requirements, whereas for decision-making only costs which are relevant for the decision are extracted. Inventory valuation is not an issue for many service organizations. They do not carry inventories and therefore a costing system is not required for meeting inventory valuation requirements.

Where a single database is maintained cost assignments cannot be at different levels of accuracy for different purposes. In the late 1980s, according to Johnson and Kaplan (1987), most organizations were relying on costing systems that had been designed primarily for meeting external financial accounting requirements. These systems were designed decades ago when information processing costs were high and precluded the use of more sophisticated methods of assigning indirect costs to products. Such systems are still widely used today. They rely extensively on arbitrary cost allocations which may be sufficiently accurate for meeting external financial accounting requirements but not for meeting decision-making requirements. Johnson and Kaplan concluded that management accounting practices have followed and become subservient to meeting financial accounting requirements.

Cost–benefit issues and cost systems design

These criticisms resulted in the emergence of ABC in the late 1980s. Surveys in many countries suggest that between 20 and 30% of the surveyed organizations have implemented ABC systems. The majority of organizations therefore continue to operate traditional systems. Both traditional and ABC systems vary in their level of sophistication but, as a general rule, traditional systems tend to be simplistic whereas ABC systems tend to be more sophisticated. What determines the chosen level of sophistication of a costing system? The answer is that the choice should be made on costs versus benefits criteria. Simplistic systems are inexpensive to operate, but they are likely to result in inaccurate cost assignments and the reporting of inaccurate costs. Managers using cost information extracted from simplistic systems are more likely to make important mistakes arising from using inaccurate cost information. The end result may be a high cost of errors. Conversely, sophisticated systems are more expensive to operate but they minimize the cost of errors. However, the aim should not be to have the most accurate cost system. Improvements

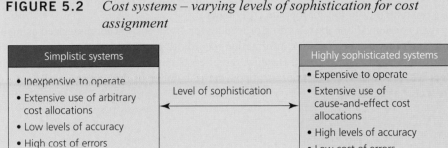

FIGURE 5.2   *Cost systems – varying levels of sophistication for cost assignment*

should be made in the level of sophistication of the costing system up to the point where the marginal cost of improvement equals the marginal benefit from the improvement.

Figure 5.2 illustrates the above points with costing systems ranging from simplistic to sophisticated. Highly simplistic costing systems are located on the extreme left. Common features of such systems are that they are inexpensive to operate, make extensive use of arbitrary allocations of indirect costs and normally result in low levels of accuracy and a high cost of errors. On the extreme right are highly sophisticated systems. These systems use only cause-and-effect allocations, are more expensive to operate, have high levels of accuracy and minimize the cost of errors. Cost systems in most organizations are not located at either of these extreme points. Instead, they are located at different points within the range shown in Figure 5.2.

The optimal cost system is different for different organizations. For example, the optimal costing system will be located towards the extreme left for an organization whose indirect costs are a low percentage of total costs and which also has a fairly standardized product range, all consuming organizational resources in similar proportions. In these circumstances simplistic systems may not result in the reporting of inaccurate costs. In contrast, the optimal costing system for organizations with a high proportion of indirect costs, whose products consume organizational resources in different proportions, will be located towards the extreme right. More sophisticated costing systems are required to capture the diversity of consumption of organizational resources and accurately assign the high level of indirect costs to different cost objects.

Assigning direct costs to cost objects

Both simplistic and sophisticated systems accurately assign direct costs to cost objects. Cost assignment merely involves the implementation of suitable clerical procedures to identify and record the resources consumed by cost objects. Consider direct labour. The time spent on providing a service to a specific customer, or manufacturing a specific product, is recorded on source documents, such as **time sheets** or **job cards**. Details of the customer's account number, job number or the product's code are also entered on these documents. The employee's hourly rate of pay is then entered so that the direct labour cost for the employee can be assigned to the appropriate cost object.

For direct materials the source document is a **materials requisition**. Details of the materials issued for manufacturing a product, or providing a specific service, are recorded on the materials requisition. The customer's account number, job number or product code is also entered and the items listed on the requisition are priced at their cost of acquisition. The details on the material requisition thus represent the source information for assigning the cost of the materials to the appropriate cost object.

In many organizations the recording procedure for direct costs is computerized using bar coding and other forms of on-line information recording. The source documents only exist in the form of computer records. Because direct costs can be accurately assigned to cost objects whereas many indirect costs cannot, the remainder of this chapter will focus on indirect cost assignment.

Plant-wide (blanket) overhead rates

The most simplistic traditional costing system assigns indirect costs to cost objects using a single overhead rate for the organization as a whole. You will recall at the start of this chapter that it was pointed out that indirect costs are also called overheads. The terms **blanket overhead rate** or **plant-wide rate** are used to describe a single overhead rate that is established for the organization as a whole. Let us assume that the total manufacturing overheads for the manufacturing plant of Arcadia are £900 000 and that the company has selected direct labour hours as the allocation base for assigning overheads to products. Assuming that the total number of direct labour hours are 60 000 for the period the plant-wide overhead rate for Arcadia is £15 per direct labour hour (£900 000/60 000 direct labour hours). This calculation consists of two stages. First, overheads are accumulated in one single plant-wide pool for a period. Second, a plant-wide rate is computed by dividing the total amount of overheads accumulated (£900 000) by the selected allocation base (60 000 direct labour hours). The overhead costs are assigned to products by multiplying the plant-wide rate by the units of the selected allocation base (direct labour hours) used by each product.

Assume now that Arcadia is considering establishing separate overheads for each of its three production departments. Further investigations reveal that the products made by the company require different operations and some products do not pass through all three departments. These investigations also indicate that the £900 000 total manufacturing overheads and 60 000 direct labour hours can be analysed as follows:

	Department A	Department B	Department C	Total
Overheads	£200 000	£600 000	£100 000	£900 000
Direct labour hours	20 000	20 000	20 000	60 000
Overhead rate per direct labour hour	£10	£30	£5	£15

Consider now a situation where product Z requires 20 direct labour hours in department C but does not pass through departments A and B. If a plant-wide overhead rate is used then overheads of £300 (20 hours at £15 per hour) will be allocated to product Z. On the other hand, if a departmental overhead rate is used, only £100 (20 hours at £5 per hour) would be allocated to product Z. Which method should be used? The logical answer must be to establish separate departmental overhead rates, since product Z only consumes overheads in department C. If the plant-wide overhead rate were applied, all the factory overhead rates would be averaged out and product Z would be indirectly allocated with some of the overheads of department B. This would not be satisfactory, since product Z does not consume any of the resources and this department incurs a large amount of the overhead expenditure.

Where some departments are more 'overhead-intensive' than others, products spending more time in the overhead-intensive departments should be assigned more overhead costs than those spending less time. Departmental rates capture these possible effects but plant-wide rates do not, because of the averaging process. We can conclude that a plant-wide rate will generally result in the reporting of inaccurate product costs. A plant-wide rate can only be justified when all products consume departmental overheads in approximately the same proportions. In the above illustration each department accounts for one-third of the total direct labour hours. If all products spend approximately one-third of their time in each department, a plant-wide overhead rate can be used. Consider a situation where product X spends one hour in each department and product Y spends five hours in each department. Overheads of £45 and £225 respectively would be allocated to products X and Y using either a plant-wide rate (3 hours at £15 and 15 hours at £15) or separate departmental overhead rates. If a diverse product range is produced with products spending different proportions of time in each department, separate departmental overhead rates should be established.

However, significant usage of plant-wide overhead rates have been reported in surveys undertaken in many different countries. For example, the percentage usages vary from 20–30% in the UK (Drury and Tayles, 1994), USA (Emore and Ness, 1991), Australian (Joye and Blayney, 1990, 1991) and Indian (Joshi, 1998) surveys. In contrast, in Scandinavia only 5% of the Finnish companies (Lukka and Granlund, 1996), one Norwegian company (Bjornenak, 1997b) and none of the Swedish companies sampled (Ask et al., 1996) used a single plant-wide rate. Zero usage of plant-wide rates was also reported from a survey of Greek companies (Ballas and Venieris, 1996). In a more recent study of UK organizations Drury and Tayles (2000) reported that a plant-wide rate was used by 3% of surveyed organizations possibly suggesting a move towards more sophisticated costing systems.

The two-stage allocation process

A framework, known as the two-stage allocation process, can be used to summarize the different approaches we have looked at for Arcadia to assign overhead costs to products. The process applies to assigning costs to other cost objects, besides products, and is applicable to all organizations that assign indirect costs to cost objects. The framework applies to both traditional and ABC systems.

The framework is illustrated in Figure 5.3. You can see that in the first stage overheads are assigned to cost centres (also called cost pools). The terms **cost centre** or **cost pool** are used to describe a location to which overhead costs are initially assigned. Normally cost centres consist of departments, but in some cases they consist of smaller segments such as groups of machines. In the second stage the costs accumulated in the cost centres are allocated to cost objects using selected allocation bases (you should remember from our discussion earlier that allocation bases are also called cost drivers). Traditional costing systems tend to use a small number of second stage allocation bases, typically direct labour hours or machine hours. In other words, traditional systems assume that direct labour or machine hours have a significant influence in the long term on the level of overhead expenditure. Other allocation bases used to a lesser extent by traditional systems are direct labour cost, direct materials cost and units of output. Let us now apply the framework to our discussion in the previous stage relating to Arcadia. With the plant-wide rate overheads (£9000 000) are collected in a single cost pool for the plant, or the whole organization if non-manufacturing overheads are to be incorporated in the overhead rate. In the second stage a single plant-wide overhead rate (£15 per hour) is allocated to products based on the number of direct labour hours used by each product.

We concluded that, because some departments were more 'overhead intensive' than others, it was preferable to establish separate cost centre overhead rates based on departments. With this approach the total overheads of £900 000 were assigned to the three

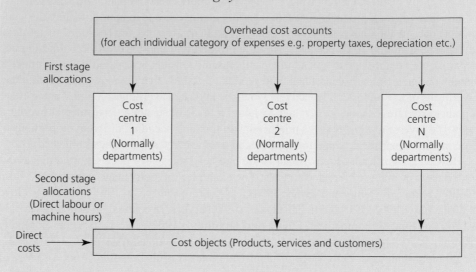

FIGURE 5.3 *An illustration of the two-stage allocation process for a traditional costing system*

production departments in the first stage. Separate departmental overhead rates were computed for each department in the second stage (i.e. £10 per direct labour hour department A, £30 for B and £5 for C). Finally, departmental overheads were assigned to products by multiplying the hours spent by a product in each department by the hourly overhead rate. The total overhead assigned to a product is simply the sum of the amounts applied in each department.

How many cost centres should a firm establish? If only a small number of cost centres are established it is likely that activities within a cost centre will not be homogeneous and, if the consumption of the activities by products/services within the cost centres varies, activity resource consumption will not be accurately measured. Therefore, in most situations, increasing the number of cost centres increases the accuracy of measuring the indirect costs consumed by cost objects. The choice of the number of cost centres should be based on cost–benefit criteria using the principles described on pages 114–15. Exhibit 5.1 (Section A) shows the number of cost centres and second stage cost allocation bases reported by Drury *et al.* (1993) in a survey of 187 UK organizations. It can be seen that 35% of the organizations used less than 11 cost centres whereas 23% used more than 30 cost centres. In terms of the number of different types of second stage cost drivers/allocation bases 69% of the responding organizations used less than four.

An illustration of the two-stage process for a traditional costing system

We shall now use Example 5.1 to provide a more detailed illustration of the two-stage allocation process for a traditional costing system. To keep the illustration manageable it is assumed that the company has only five cost centres – machine departments X and Y, an assembly department, and materials handling and general factory support cost centres. The

Views on the treatment of manufacturing overheads

A questionnaire survey by Brealey (2005) reported the following results in respect of UK manufacturing companies:

	N	%
Blanket (plant-wide rates)	31	13
Production department rates	150	63
Activity-based costing rates	8	4
Variable costing rates (i.e. overheads not assigned to products)	45	19
Other	3	1
	237	100

Nine of the thirty-one respondents who used a blanket rate were interviewed to ascertain the reasons for using such a rate. Five interviewees were happy with the product costs derived from using this rate and four acknowledged its limitations. The following is a response from one of the respondents who argued that the improved accuracy of the product costs derived from a blanket overhead rate could not be justified on cost–benefit criteria:

> *The added value ... for breaking [the overhead] down any further would be minimal. ... I think if I go down any further within separate areas in the manufacturing operations to split down production, purchasing and quality departments, I don't think it would make much difference to the blanket overhead rate that we've got.*

One of the four interviewees who acknowledged the limitations of blanket overhead rates argued that it was reasonable to use a blanket rate because overheads were a small proportion of total costs. The second interviewee argued that the rate was used because it was simple to calculate and the third cited the lack of resources. The final interviewee intended to change from a blanket rate to multiple departmental rates.

Forty of the respondents who used separate production department rates were interviewed. Reasons cited for using these rates included: the factory was divided into different production processes; cost centres use different resources in different proportions; and the fact that the factory was organized so that each production department was responsible for a product group. One respondent justified the use of separate overhead rates throughout the factory as follows:

> *We actually have manufacturing cells which are cost centres in their own right, so it's best if we have a cost centre which is trying to recover those costs against what it's manufacturing. So rather than saying we have lots of manufacturing cells but only one cost centre, it seems more straightforward to say here's a cell of cost which manufactures and fills something and does some sort of service. It's easier to allocate the costs so that a particular cost centre can recover the costs of that cost centre and certainly you can see overall whether it's over or under recovering.*

Five interviews were conducted with units that only assigned variable costs to products. They justified this approach on the grounds that fixed overheads would remain unchanged irrespective of the decisions that were made so they were irrelevant for decision-making.

Source: Brealey, J. A. (2005) The calculation of product costs and their use in decision-making in the British Manufacturing Industry, PhD dissertation, University of Huddersfield.

EXHIBIT 5.1

Surveys of practice

(a) Cost centres used in the first stage of the two-stage allocation process

- A survey of Australian organizations by Joye and Blayney (1990):
  36% of the responding organizations used a single plant-wide rate
  24% used overhead rates for groups of work centres
  31% used overhead rates for each work centre
  9% used overhead rates for each machine

- A survey of Swedish organizations by Ask and Ax (1992)[a]:
  70% indicated that cost centres consisted of departments
  32% consisted of work cells
  22% consisted of groups of machines
  15% consisted of single machines

- A Norwegian study by Bjornenak (1997b) reported an average of 38.3 cost centres used by the respondents

- A survey of UK organizations by Drury and Tayles (2000):
  14% used less than 6 cost centres
  21% used 6–10 cost centres
  29% used 11–20 cost centres
  36% used more than 20 cost centres

(b) Number of different second stage allocation bases/cost drivers used

- A survey of UK organizations by Drury and Tayles (2000):
  34% used 1 cost driver
  25% used 2 drivers
  10% used 3 drivers
  21% used 3–10 drivers
  10% used more than 10 drivers

- A Norwegian study by Bjornenak (1997a) reported an average usage of 1.79 cost drivers

(c) Second stage cost allocation bases/cost drivers used[a]

	Norway[b]	Holland[c]	Ireland[d]	Australia[e]	Japan[e]	UK[f]	UK[f]
Direct labour hours/cost	65%	20%	52%	57%	57%	68%	73%
Machine hours	29	9	19	19	12	49	26
Direct materials costs	26	6	10	12	11	30	19
Units of output	40	30	28	20	16	42	31
Prime cost				1	21		
Other	23	35	9				
ABC cost drivers						9	7

A survey of Finnish companies by Lukka and Granlund (1996) reported that direct labour costs, direct labour hours, machine hours, materials use and production quantity were the most widely used allocation bases. Usage rates were not reported.

Notes
[a] The reported percentages exceed 100% because many companies used more than one type of cost centre or allocation base.
[b] Bjornenak (1997b).
[c] Boons *et al.* (1994).
[d] Clarke (1995).
[e] Blayney and Yokoyama (1991).
[f] Drury *et al.* (1993) – The first column relates to the responses for automated and the second to non-automated production centres.

EXAMPLE 5.1

The annual overhead costs for the Enterprise Company which has three production centres (two machine centres and one assembly centre) and two service centres (materials procurement and general factory support) are as follows:

	(£)	(£)
Indirect wages and supervision		
Machine centres: X	1 000 000	
Y	1 000 000	
Assembly	1 500 000	
Materials procurement	1 100 000	
General factory support	1 480 000	6 080 000
Indirect materials		
Machine centres: X	500 000	
Y	805 000	
Assembly	105 000	
Materials procurement	0	
General factory support	10 000	1 420 000
Lighting and heating	500 000	
Property taxes	1 000 000	
Insurance of machinery	150 000	
Depreciation of machinery	1 500 000	
Insurance of buildings	250 000	
Salaries of works management	800 000	4 200 000
		11 700 000

The following information is also available:

	Book value of machinery (£)	Area occupied (sq. metres)	Number of employees	Direct labour hours	Machine hours
Machine shop: X	8 000 000	10 000	300	1 000 000	2 000 000
Y	5 000 000	5 000	200	1 000 000	1 000 000
Assembly	1 000 000	15 000	300	2 000 000	
Stores	500 000	15 000	100		
Maintenance	500 000	5 000	100		
	15 000 000	50 000	1000		

Details of total materials issues (i.e. direct and indirect materials) to the production centres are as follows:

	£
Machine shop X	4 000 000
Machine shop Y	3 000 000
Assembly	1 000 000
	8 000 000

To allocate the overheads listed above to the production and service centres we must prepare an overhead analysis sheet, as shown in Exhibit 5.2.

illustration focuses on manufacturing costs but we shall look at non-manufacturing costs later in the chapter. Applying the two-stage allocation process requires the following four steps:

1 assigning all manufacturing overheads to production and service cost centres;

2 reallocating the costs assigned to service cost centres to production cost centres;

3 computing separate overhead rates for each production cost centre;

4 assigning cost centre overheads to products or other chosen cost objects.

Steps 1 and 2 comprise stage one and steps 3 and 4 relate to the second stage of the two-stage allocation process. Let us now consider each of these steps in detail.

Step 1 – Assigning all manufacturing overheads to production and service cost centres

Using the information given in Example 5.1 our initial objective is to assign all manufacturing overheads to production and service cost centres. To do this requires the preparation of an **overhead analysis sheet**. This document is shown in Exhibit 5.2. In many organizations it will consist only in computer form.

If you look at Example 5.1 you will see that the indirect labour and indirect material costs have been directly traced to cost centres. Although these items cannot be directly assigned to products they can be directly assigned to the cost centres. In other words, they are indirect costs when products are the cost objects and direct costs when cost centres are the cost object. Therefore they are traced directly to the cost centres shown in the overhead analysis sheet in Exhibit 5.2. The remaining costs shown in Example 5.1 cannot be traced directly to the cost centres and must be allocated to the cost centre using appropriate allocation bases. The term **first stage allocation bases** is used to describe allocations at this point. The following list summarizes commonly used first stage allocation bases:

Cost	Basis of allocation
Property taxes, lighting and heating	Area
Employee-related expenditure:	
works management, works canteen, payroll office	Number of employees
Depreciation and insurance of plant and machinery	Value of items of plant and machinery

EXHIBIT 5.2

Overhead analysis sheet

Item of expenditure	Basis of allocation	Total (£)	Machine centre X (£)	Machine centre Y (£)	Assembly (£)	Materials procurement (£)	General factory support (£)
			Production centres			**Service centres**	
Indirect wages and supervision	Direct	6 080 000	1 000 000	1 000 000	1 500 000	1 100 000	1 480 000
Indirect materials	Direct	1 420 000	500 000	805 000	105 000		10 000
Lighting and heating	Area	500 000	100 000	50 000	150 000	150 000	50 000
Property taxes	Area	1 000 000	200 000	100 000	300 000	300 000	100 000
Insurance of machinery	Book value of machinery	150 000	80 000	50 000	10 000	5 000	5 000
Depreciation of machinery	Book value of machinery	1 500 000	800 000	500 000	100 000	50 000	50 000
Insurance of buildings	Area	250 000	50 000	25 000	75 000	75 000	25 000
Salaries of works management	Number of employees (1)	800 000	240 000	160 000	240 000	80 000	80 000
		11 700 000	2 970 000	2 690 000	2 480 000	1 760 000	1 800 000
Reallocation of service centre costs							
Materials procurement	Value of materials issued	—	880 000	660 000	220 000	1 760 000	
General factory support	Direct labour hours (2)	—	450 000	450 000	900 000		1 800 000
		11 700 000	4 300 000	3 800 000	3 600 000	—	—
Machine hours and direct labour hours		2 000 000	1 000 000	2 000 000			
Machine hour overhead rate			£2.15	£3.80			
Direct labour hour overhead rate					£1.80		

Applying the allocation bases to the data given in respect of the Enterprise Company in Example 5.1 it is assumed that property taxes, lighting and heating, and insurance of buildings are related to the total floor area of the buildings, and the benefit obtained by each cost centre can therefore be ascertained according to the proportion of floor area which it occupies. The total floor area of the factory shown in Example 5.1 is 50 000 square metres; machine centre X occupies 20% of this and machine centre Y a further 10%. Therefore, if you refer to the overhead analysis sheet in Exhibit 5.2 you will see that 20% of property taxes, lighting and heating and insurance of buildings are allocated to machine centre X, and 10% are allocated to machine centre Y.

The insurance premium paid and depreciation of machinery are generally regarded as being related to the book value of the machinery. Because the book value of machinery for machine centre X is 8/15 of the total book value and machine centre Y is 5/15 of the total book value then 8/15 and 5/15 of the insurance and depreciation of machinery is allocated to machine centres X and Y.

It is assumed that the amount of time that works management devotes to each cost centre is related to the number of employees in each centre; since 30% of the total employees are employed in machine centre X, 30% of the salaries of works management will be allocated to this centre.

If you now look at the overhead analysis sheet shown in Exhibit 5.2, you will see in the row labelled '(1)' that all manufacturing overheads for the Enterprise Company have been assigned to the three production and two service cost centres.

Step 2 – Reallocating the costs assigned to service cost centres to production cost centres

The next step is to reallocate the costs that have been assigned to service cost centres to production cost centres. Service departments (i.e. service cost centres) are those departments that exist to provide services of various kinds to other units within the organization. They are sometimes called support departments. The Enterprise Company has two service centres. They are materials procurement and general factory support, which includes activities such as production scheduling and machine maintenance. These service centres render essential services that support the production process, but they do not deal directly with the products. Therefore it is not possible to allocate service centre costs to products passing through these centres. To assign costs to products traditional costing systems reallocate service centre costs to production centres that actually work on the product. The method that is chosen to allocate service centre costs to production centre should be related to the benefits that the production centres derive from the service rendered.

We shall assume that the value of materials issued (shown in Example 5.1) provides a suitable approximation of the benefit that each of the production centres receives from materials procurement. Therefore 50% of the value of materials is issued to machine centre X, resulting in 50% of the total costs of materials procurement being allocated to this centre. If you refer to Exhibit 5.2 you will see that £880 000 (50% of material procurement costs of £1 760 000) has been reallocated to machine centre X. It is also assumed that direct labour hours provides an approximation of the benefits received by the production centres from general factory support resulting in the total costs for this centre being reallocated to the production centres proportionate to direct labour hours. Therefore since machine centre X consumes 25% of the direct labour hours £450 000 (25% of the total costs of £1 800 000 assigned to general factory support) has been reallocated to machine centre X. You will see in the row labelled '(2)' in Exhibit 5.2 that all manufacturing costs have now been assigned to the three production centres. This completes the first stage of the two-stage allocation process.

Step 3 – Computing separate overhead rates for each production cost centre

The second stage of the two-stage process is to allocate overheads of each production centre to overheads passing through that centre. The most frequently used allocation bases in traditional costing systems are based on the amount of time products spend in each production centre – normally direct labour hours and machine hours. In respect of non-machine centres, direct labour hours is the most frequently used allocation base. This implies that the overheads incurred by a production centre are closely related to direct labour hours worked. In the case of machine centres a machine hour overhead rate is preferable since most of the overheads (e.g. depreciation) are likely to be more closely related to machine hours. We shall assume that the Enterprise Company uses a **machine hour rate** for the machine production centres and a **direct labour hour rate** for the assembly centre. The overhead rates are calculated by applying the following formula:

$$\frac{\text{cost centre overheads}}{\text{cost centre direct labour hours or machine hours}}$$

The calculations using the information given in Example 5.1 are as follows:

$$\text{Machine centre X} = \frac{£4\,300\,000}{2\,000\,000 \text{ machine hours}} = £2.15 \text{ per machine hour}$$

$$\text{Machine centre Y} = \frac{£3\,800\,000}{1\,000\,000 \text{ machine hours}} = £3.80 \text{ per machine hour}$$

$$\text{Assembly department} = \frac{£3\,600\,000}{2\,000\,000 \text{ direct labour hours}} = £1.80 \text{ per direct labour hour}$$

Step 4 – Assigning cost centre overheads to products or other chosen cost objects

The final step is to allocate the overheads to products passing through the production centres. Therefore if a product spends 10 hours in machine cost centre A overheads of £21.50 (10 × £2.15) will be allocated to the product. We shall compute the manufacturing costs of two products. Product A is a low sales volume product with direct costs of £100. It is manufactured in batches of 100 units and each unit requires 5 hours in machine centre A, 10 hours in machine centre B and 10 hours in the assembly centre. Product B is a high sales volume product thus enabling it to be manufactured in larger batches. It is manufactured in batches of 200 units and each unit requires 10 hours in machine centre A, 20 hours in machine centre B and 20 hours in the assembly centre. Direct costs of £200 have been assigned to product B. The calculations of the manufacturing costs assigned to the products are as follows:

Product A	£
Direct costs (100 units × £100)	10 000
Overhead allocations	
Machine centre A (100 units × 5 machine hours × £2.15)	1 075
Machine centre B (100 units × 10 machine hours × £3.80)	3 800
Assembly (100 units × 10 direct labour hours × £1.80)	1 800
Total cost	16 675

Cost per unit (£16 675/100 units) = £166.75

Product B	£
Direct costs (200 units × £200)	40 000
Overhead allocations	
Machine centre A (200 units × 10 machine hours × £2.15)	4 300
Machine centre B (200 units × 20 machine hours × £3.80)	15 200
Assembly (200 units × 20 direct labour hours × £1.80)	7 200
Total cost	66 700
Cost per unit (£66 700/200 units) = £333.50	

The overhead allocation procedure is more complicated where service cost centres serve each other. In Example 5.1 it was assumed that materials procurement does not provide any services for general factory support and that general factory support does not provide any services for materials procurement. An understanding of situations where service cost centres do serve each other is not, however, necessary for a general understanding of the overhead procedure, and the problem of service centre reciprocal cost allocations is therefore not dealt with in this book. For an explanation of how to deal with the problem of service centre reciprocal cost allocations you should refer to Drury (2004, Chapter 3).

Extracting relevant costs for decision-making

The cost computations relating to the Enterprise Company for products A and B represent the costs that should be generated for meeting stock valuation and profit measurement requirements. For decision-making non-manufacturing costs should also be taken into account. In addition, some of the costs that have been assigned to the products may not be relevant for certain decisions. For example, if you look at the overhead analysis sheet in Exhibit 5.2 you will see that property taxes, depreciation of machinery and insurance of buildings and machinery have been assigned to cost centres, and thus included in the costs assigned to products, for both traditional and ABC systems. If these cost are unaffected by a decision to discontinue a product they should not be assigned to products when undertaking product discontinuation reviews. However, if cost information is used to determine selling prices such costs may need to be assigned to products to ensure that the selling price of a customer's order covers a fair share of all organizational costs. It is therefore necessary to ensure that the costs incorporated in the overhead analysis are suitably coded so that different overhead rates can be extracted for different combinations of costs. This will enable relevant cost information to be extracted from the database for meeting different requirements. For an illustration of this approach you should refer to the answer to Review problem 5.20.

Our objective in this chapter has not been to focus on the cost information that should be extracted from the costing system for meeting decision-making requirements. Instead, it is to provide you with an understanding of how cost systems assign costs to cost objects. In the previous chapter, and also in Chapter 7, the rationale for determining the cost information that should be extracted for decision-making is explained.

Budgeted overhead rates

Our discussion in this chapter has assumed that the *actual* overheads for an accounting period have been allocated to the products. However, the calculation of overhead rates based on the *actual* overheads incurred during an accounting period causes a number of problems.

First, the product cost calculations have to be delayed until the end of the accounting period, since the overhead rate calculations cannot be obtained before this date, but information on product costs is required quickly if it is to be used for monthly profit calculations and inventory valuations or as a basis for setting selling prices. Secondly, one may argue that the timing problem can be resolved by calculating actual overhead rates at more frequent intervals, say on a monthly basis, but the objection to this proposal is that a large amount of overhead expenditure is fixed in the short term whereas activity will vary from month to month, giving large fluctuations in the overhead rates. Consider Example 5.2.

Such fluctuating overhead rates are not representative of typical, normal production conditions. Management has committed itself to a specific level of fixed costs in the light of foreseeable needs for beyond one month. Thus, where production fluctuates, monthly overhead rates may be volatile. Furthermore, some costs such as repairs, maintenance and heating are not incurred evenly throughout the year. Therefore, if monthly overhead rates are used, these costs will not be allocated fairly to units of output. For example, heating costs would be charged only to winter production so that products produced in winter would be more expensive than those produced in summer.

An average, annualized rate based on the relationship of total annual overhead to total annual activity is more representative of typical relationships between total costs and volume than a monthly rate. What is required is a normal product cost based on average long-term production rather than an actual product cost, which is affected by month-to-month fluctuations in production volume. Taking these factors into consideration, it is preferable to establish a **budgeted overhead rate** based on annual *estimated* overhead expenditure and activity. Consequently the procedure outlined in the previous sections for calculating cost centre overhead rates for traditional and ABC systems should be based on *standard* activity levels and not *actual* activity levels. Surveys of product costing practices indicate that most organizations use annual budgeted activity as a measure of standard activity.

Under- and over-recovery of overheads

The effect of calculating overhead rates based on budgeted annual overhead expenditure and activity is that it will be most unlikely that the overhead allocated to products manufactured during the period will be the same as the actual overhead incurred. Consider a situation where the estimated annual fixed overheads are £2 000 000 and the estimated annual activity is 1 000 000 direct labour hours. The estimated fixed overhead rate will be £2 per hour. Assume that actual overheads are £2 000 000 and are therefore identical with the estimate, but that actual activity is 900 000 direct labour hours instead of the estimated 1 000 000 hours. In this situation only £1 800 000 will be charged to production. This calculation is based on 900 000 direct labour hours at £2 per hour, giving an under-recovery of overheads of £200 000.

Consider an alternative situation where the actual overheads are £1 950 000 instead of the estimated £2 000 000, and actual activity is 1 000 000 direct labour hours, which is identical to the original estimate. In this situation 1 000 000 direct labour hours at £2 per hour will be charged to production giving an over-recovery of £50 000. This example illustrates that there will be an **under- or over-recovery of overheads** whenever actual activity or overhead expenditure is different from the budgeted overheads and activity used to estimate the budgeted overhead rate. This under- or over-recovery of fixed overheads is also called a **volume variance**.

Accounting regulations in most countries recommend that the under- or over-recovery of overheads should be regarded as a period cost adjustment. For example, the UK Statement of Standard Accounting Practice on Stocks and Work in Progress (SSAP 9) recommends the allocation of overheads in the valuation of inventories and work in

EXAMPLE 5.2

The fixed overheads for Euro are £24 000 000 per annum, and monthly production varies from 400 000 to 1 000 000 hours. The monthly overhead rate for fixed overhead will therefore fluctuate as follows:

Monthly overhead	£2 000 000	£2 000 000
Monthly production	400 000 hours	1 000 000 hours
Monthly overhead rate	£5 per hour	£2 per hour

Overhead expenditure that is fixed in the short term remains constant each month, but monthly production fluctuates because of holiday periods and seasonal variations in demand. Consequently the overhead rate varies from £2 to £5 per hour. It would be unreasonable for a product worked on in one month to be allocated overheads at a rate of £5 per hour and an identical product worked on in another month allocated at a rate of only £2 per hour.

progress needs to be based on the company's normal level of activity and that any under- or over-recovery should be written off in the current year. This procedure is illustrated in Figure 5.4. Note that any under- or over-recovery of overhead is not allocated to products. Also note that the under-recovery is recorded as an expense in the current accounting period whereas an over-recovery is recorded as a reduction in the expenses for the period. Finally you should note that our discussion here is concerned with how to treat any under- or over-recovery for the purpose of financial accounting and its impact on inventory valuation and profit measurement.

Maintaining the database at standard costs

Most organizations whose activities consist of a series of common or repetitive operations maintain their database at standard, rather than actual cost, for both traditional and ABC systems. Standard costs are predetermined target costs that should be incurred under efficient operating conditions. For example, assume that the standard direct labour cost for performing a particular operation is £40 (consisting of 5 hours at £8 per hour) and the standard cost of a purchased component (say component Z) is £50. The direct costs for a product requiring only this operation and the purchased component Z would be recorded in the database at a standard cost of £90. Assuming that the product only passed through a single cost centre with a budgeted overhead rate of £20 per direct labour hour the overhead cost for the product would be recorded in the database at £100 standard cost (5 standard direct labour hours at £20 per hour). Instead of a product being recorded in the database at its standard *unit* cost the database may consist of the standard costs of a batch of output, such as normal batch sizes of say 100 or 200 units output of the product.

When a standard costing system is used the database is maintained at standard cost and actual output is costed at the standard cost. Actual costs are recorded, but not at the individual product level, and an adjustment is made at the end of the accounting period by recording as a period cost the difference between standard cost and actual cost for the actual output. This adjustment ensures that the standard costs are converted to actual costs in the profit statement for meeting external financial accounting reporting requirements.

FIGURE 5.4   *Illustration of under-recovery of factory overheads*

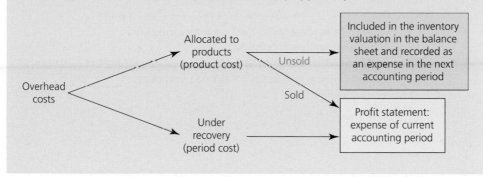

It is not important at this point that you have a detailed understanding of a standard costing system. However, it is important that you are aware that a database may consist of standard (estimated) costs rather than actual costs. We shall look at standard costing in detail in Chapter 12.

Non-manufacturing overheads

In respect of financial accounting, only manufacturing costs are allocated to products. Non-manufacturing overheads are regarded as period costs and are disposed of in exactly the same way as the under- or over-recovery of manufacturing overheads outlined in Figure 5.4. For external reporting it is therefore unnecessary to allocate non-manufacturing overheads to products. However, for decision-making non-manufacturing costs should be assigned to products. For example, in many organizations it is not uncommon for selling prices to be based on estimates of total cost or even actual cost. Housing contractors and garages often charge for their services by adding a percentage profit margin to actual cost.

Some non-manufacturing costs may be a direct cost of the product. Delivery costs, salesmen's salaries and travelling expenses may be directly identifiable with the product, but it is likely that many non-manufacturing overheads cannot be allocated directly to specific products. On what basis should we allocate non-manufacturing overheads? The answer is that we should select an allocation base/cost driver that corresponds most closely to non-manufacturing overheads. The problem is that allocation bases that are widely used by traditional costing systems, such as direct labour hours and machine hours, are not necessarily those that are closely related to non-manufacturing overheads. Therefore traditional systems tend to use arbitrary, rather than cause-and-effect allocation bases, to allocate non-manufacturing overheads to products. The most widely used approach (see Exhibit 5.3) is to allocate non-manufacturing overheads on the ability of the products to bear such costs. This approach can be implemented by allocating non-manufacturing costs to products on the basis of their manufacturing costs. This procedure is illustrated in Example 5.3.

Because of the arbitrary nature of the cost allocations, some organizations that use traditional costing systems as a basis for setting selling prices do not use them to allocate non-manufacturing overheads to products. Instead, they add a percentage profit margin to each product so that it provides a profit contribution and a contribution to non-manufacturing overheads. We shall consider in more detail how cost information can be used in determining selling prices in Chapter 7. Recent developments in ABC have provided a mechanism for more accurately assigning non-manufacturing overheads to products. These developments will be explained in the next chapter.

EXHIBIT 5.3

Methods used by UK organizations to allocate non-manufacturing overheads to products

	(%)
Allocation as a percentage of total manufacturing cost	32
Direct labour hours/cost methods	25
Percentage of total selling price	12
Non-manufacturing overheads not traced to products	23
Other method	8
	100

SOURCE: Drury *et al.* (1993).

EXAMPLE 5.3

The estimated non-manufacturing and manufacturing costs of a company for the year ending 31 December are £500 000 and £1 million respectively. The non-manufacturing overhead absorption rate is calculated as follows:

$$\frac{\text{estimated non-manufacturing overhead}}{\text{estimated manufacturing cost}}$$

In percentage terms each product will be allocated with non-manufacturing overheads at a rate of 50% of its total manufacturing cost.

 **Summary**

The following items relate to the learning objectives listed at the beginning of the chapter.

- **Distinguish between cause-and-effect and arbitrary allocations.**

  Direct costs can be directly traced to cost objects whereas indirect costs cannot. Therefore, indirect costs must be assigned using cost allocation bases. Allocation bases which are significant determinants of costs that are being allocated are described as cause-and-effect allocations whereas arbitrary allocations refer to allocation bases that are not the significant determinants of the costs. To accurately measure the cost of resources used by cost objects cause-and-effect allocations should be used.

- **Explain why different cost information is required for different purposes.**

  Manufacturing organizations assign costs to products for two purposes: first for external (financial accounting) profit measurement and inventory valuation purposes in order to allocate manufacturing costs incurred during a period to cost of goods sold and inventories; secondly to provide useful information for managerial decision-making requirements. Financial accounting regulations specify that only manufacturing costs should be assigned to products for meeting inventory and profit measurement requirements. Both manufacturing and non-manufacturing costs, however, may be relevant for decision-making. In addition, not all costs that are assigned to products for inventory valuation and profit measurement are relevant for decision-making. For example, costs that will not be affected by a decision (e.g. depreciation) are normally not relevant for decision-making.

- **Describe how cost systems differ in terms of their level of sophistication.**

  Cost systems range from simplistic to sophisticated. Simplistic systems are inexpensive to operate, involve extensive use of arbitrary allocations, have a high likelihood of reporting inaccurate product costs and generally result in a high cost of errors. Sophisticated costing systems are more expensive to operate, rely more extensively on cause-and-effect allocations, generally report more accurate product costs and have a low cost of errors. Further distinguishing features are that simplistic costing systems have a small number of first-stage cost centres/pools and use a single second-stage cost driver. In contrast, sophisticated costing systems use many first-stage cost centres/pools and many different types of second-stage drivers.

- **Understand the factors influencing the choice of an optimal costing system.**

  The optimal costing system is different for different organizations and should be determined on a costs versus benefits basis. Simplistic costing systems are appropriate in organizations whose indirect costs are a low percentage of total costs and which also have a fairly standardized product range, all consuming organizational resources in similar proportions. Under these circumstances simplistic costing systems may report costs that are sufficiently accurate for decision-making purposes. Conversely, organizations with a high proportion of indirect costs, whose products consume organizational resources in different proportions, are likely to require sophisticated costing systems. Relying on sophisticated costing systems under these circumstances is likely to result in the additional benefits from reporting more accurate costs exceeding the costs of operating more sophisticated systems.

- **Explain why departmental overhead rates should be used in preference to a single blanket overhead rate.**

  A blanket (also known as plant-wide) overhead rate establishes a single overhead rate for the organization as a whole whereas departmental rates involve indirect costs being accumulated by different departments and a separate overhead rate being established for each department. A blanket overhead rate can only be justified when all products or services consume departmental overheads in approximately the same proportions. Such circumstances are unlikely to be applicable to most organizations resulting in blanket overheads generally reporting inaccurate product/service costs.

- **Construct an overhead analysis sheet and calculate cost centre allocation rates.**

  Cost centre overhead allocation rates are established and assigned to cost objects using the two-stage allocation overhead procedure. In the first stage, an overhead analysis sheet is used to (a) allocate overheads to production and service centres or departments and (b) to reallocate the total service department overheads to production departments. The second stage involves (a) the calculation of appropriate departmental overhead rates and (b) the allocation of overheads to products passing through each department. These steps were illustrated using data presented in Example 5.1.

- **Justify why budgeted overhead rates should be used in preference to actual overhead rates.**

  Because the uses of actual overhead rates causes a delay in the calculation of product or service costs, and the use of monthly rates causes fluctuations in the overhead rates throughout the year, it is recommended that annual budgeted overhead rates should be used.

- **Calculate and explain the treatment of the under/over recovery of overheads.**

  The use of annual budgeted overhead rates gives an under- or over-recovery of overheads whenever actual overhead expenditure or activity is different from budget. Any under- or over-recovery is generally regarded as a period cost adjustment and written off to the profit and loss statement and thus not allocated to products.

Key terms and concepts

activity-based-costing (ABC) (p. 113)
allocation base (p. 112)
arbitrary allocation (p. 112)
blanket overhead rate (p. 116)
budgeted overhead rate (p. 127)
cause-and-effect allocations (p. 112)
cost allocation (p. 112)
cost centre (p. 117)
cost driver (p. 112)
cost pool (p. 117)
cost tracing (p. 112)
direct labour hour rate (p. 125)
first stage allocation bases (p. 122)

job cards (p. 115)
machine hour rate (p. 125)
materials requisition (p. 115)
overhead analysis sheet (p. 122)
overheads (p. 112)
plant-wide rate (p. 116)
service departments (p. 124)
standard costs (p. 128)
support departments (p. 124)
time sheets (p. 115)
traditional costing systems (p. 113)
under- or over-recovery of overheads (p. 127)
volume variance (p. 127)

Assessment material

Review questions

The review questions are short questions that enable you to assess your understanding of the main topics included in the chapter. The numbers in parentheses provide you with the page numbers to refer to if you cannot answer a specific question.

Review problems

The review problems are more complex and require you to relate and apply the chapter content to various business problems. The multiple-choice questions are the least demanding and normally take less than 10 minutes to complete. Fully worked solutions to the review problems are provided in a separate section at the end of the book. Further review problems for this chapter are available on the accompanying website, www.drury-online.com. The answers to these problems are available for lecturers on the lecturer's password-protected section of the website.

Case studies

The website also includes over 30 case study problems. A list of these cases is provided on pages 491–93. Cases that are relevant to the content of this chapter include Oak City and Gustavsson, AB.

Review questions

5.1   Why are indirect costs not directly traced to cost objects in the same way as direct costs? *(p. 112)*

5.2   Define cost tracing, cost allocation, allocation base and cost driver. *(p. 112)*

5.3   Distinguish between arbitrary and cause-and-effect allocations. *(p. 112)*

5.4   Explain how cost information differs for profit measurement/inventory valuation requirements compared with decision-making requirements. *(pp. 113–14)*

5.5   Explain why cost systems should differ in terms of their level of sophistication. *(pp. 114–15)*

5.6   Describe the process of assigning direct labour and direct materials to cost objects. *(p. 115)*

5.7   Why are separate departmental or cost centre overhead rates preferred to a plant-wide (blanket) overhead rate? *(pp. 116–17)*

5.8   Describe the two-stage overhead allocation procedure. *(p. 117)*

5.9   Why are some overhead costs sometimes not relevant for decision-making purposes? *(p. 126)*

5.10   Why are budgeted overhead rates preferred to actual overhead rates? *(pp. 126–27)*

5.11   Give two reasons for the under or over-recovery of overheads at the end of the accounting period. *(pp. 127–28)*

Review problems

5.12   A company uses a predetermined overhead recovery rate based on machine hours. Budgeted factory overhead for a year amounted to £720 000, but actual factory overhead incurred was £738 000. During the year, the company absorbed £714 000 of factory overhead on 119 000 actual machine hours.

What was the company's budgeted level of machine hours for the year?

A   116 098
B   119 000
C   120 000
D   123 000

5.13   A company absorbs overheads on machine hours which were budgeted at 11 250 with overheads of £258 750. Actual results were 10 980 hours with overheads of £254 692.

Overheads were:

A   under-absorbed by £2152
B   over-absorbed by £4058
C   under-absorbed by £4058
D   over-absorbed by £2152

5.14   The following data are to be used for sub-questions (i) and (ii) below:

Budgeted labour hours   8500
Budgeted overheads   £148 750
Actual labour hours   7928
Actual overheads   £146 200

(i)   Based on the data given above, what is the labour hour overhead absorption rate?

A   £17.50 per hour
B   £17.20 per hour
C   £18.44 per hour
D   £18.76 per hour

(ii) Based on the data given above, what is the amount of overhead under/over-absorbed?

    A   £2550 under-absorbed

    B   £2529 over-absorbed

    C   £2550 over-absorbed

    D   £7460 under-absorbed

5.15 A firm makes special assemblies to customers' orders and uses job costing. The data for a period are:

	Job no. AA10 (£)	Job no. BB15 (£)	Job no. CC20 (£)
Opening WIP	26 800	42 790	—
Material added in period	17 275	—	18 500
Labour for period	14 500	3 500	24 600

The budgeted overheads for the period were £126 000.

(i)   What overhead should be added to job number CC20 for the period?

    A   £24 600

    B   £65 157

    C   £72 761

    D   £126 000

(ii) Job no. BB15 was completed and delivered during the period and the firm wishes to earn $33^{1}/_{3}\%$ profit on sales.

    What is the selling price of job number BB15?

    A   £69 435

    B   £75 521

    C   £84 963

    D   £138 870

(iii) What was the approximate value of closing work in progress at the end of the period?

    A   £58 575

    B   £101 675

    C   £147 965

    D   £217 323

5.16 A company absorbs overheads on machine hours. In a period, actual machine hours were 17 285, actual overheads were £496 500 and there was under-absorption of £12 520.

What was the budgeted level of overheads?

    A   £483 980

    B   £496 500

    C   £509 020

    D   It cannot be calculated from the information provided.

5.17   Canberra has established the following information regarding fixed overheads for the coming month:

Budgeted information:

Fixed overheads	£180 000
Labour hours	3 000
Machine hours	10 000
Units of production	5 000

Actual fixed costs for the last month were £160 000.

Canberra produces many different products using highly automated manufacturing processes and absorbs overheads on the most appropriate basis.

What will be the predetermined overhead absorption rate?

A   £16
B   £18
C   £36
D   £60

5.18   **Overhead analysis and calculation of product costs**

A furniture-making business manufactures quality furniture to customers' orders. It has three production departments and two service departments. Budgeted overhead costs for the coming year are as follows:

	Total (£)
Rent and Rates	12 800
Machine insurance	6 000
Telephone charges	3 200
Depreciation	18 000
Production Supervisor's salaries	24 000
Heating/Lighting	6 400
	70 400

The three production departments – A, B and C, and the two service departments – X and Y, are housed in the new premises, the details of which, together with other statistics and information, are given below.

	Departments				
	A	B	C	X	Y
Floor area occupied (sq. metres)	3000	1800	600	600	400
Machine value (£000)	24	10	8	4	2
Direct labour hrs budgeted	3200	1800	1000		
Labour rates per hour	£3.80	£3.50	£3.40	£3.00	£3.00
Allocated overheads:					
Specific to each department (£000)	2.8	1.7	1.2	0.8	0.6
Service Department X's costs apportioned	50%	25%	25%		
Service Department Y's costs apportioned	20%	30%	50%		

Required:

(a) Prepare a statement showing the overhead cost budgeted for each department, showing the basis of apportionment used. Also calculate suitable overhead absorption rates.

(9 marks)

(b) Two pieces of furniture are to be manufactured for customers. Direct costs are as follows:

	Job 123	Job 124
Direct material	£154	£108
Direct labour	20 hours Dept A	16 hours Dept A
	12 hours Dept B	10 hours Dept B
	10 hours Dept C	14 hours Dept C

Calculate the total costs of each job.

(5 marks)

(c) If the firm quotes prices to customers that reflect a required profit of 25% on selling price, calculate the quoted selling price for each job.

(2 marks)

(Total 16 marks)

5.19 Calculation of product overhead costs

Bookdon Public Limited Company manufactures three products in two production departments, a machine shop and a fitting section; it also has two service departments, a canteen and a machine maintenance section. Shown below are next year's budgeted production data and manufacturing costs for the company.

	Product X	Product Y	Product Z
Production	4200 units	6900 units	1700 units
Prime cost:			
Direct materials	£11 per unit	£14 per unit	£17 per unit
Direct labour:			
Machine shop	£6 per unit	£4 per unit	£2 per unit
Fitting section	£12 per unit	£3 per unit	£21 per unit
Machine hours per unit	6 hours per unit	3 hours per unit	4 hours per unit

	Machine shop	Fitting section	Canteen	Machine maintenance section	Total
Budgeted overheads (£):					
Allocated overheads	27 660	19 470	16 600	26 650	90 380
Rent, rates, heat and light					17 000
Depreciation and					
insurance of equipment					25 000
Additional data:					
Gross book value of					
equipment (£)	150 000	75 000	30 000	45 000	
Number of employees	18	14	4	4	
Floor space occupied					
(square metres)	3 600	1 400	1 000	800	

It has been estimated that approximately 70% of the machine maintenance section's costs are incurred servicing the machine shop and the remainder incurred servicing the fitting section.

Required:

(a) (i) Calculate the following budgeted overhead absorption rates:

        A machine hour rate for the machine shop.

        A rate expressed as a percentage of direct wages for the fitting section.

      All workings and assumptions should be clearly shown.

(12 marks)

    (ii) Calculate the budgeted manufacturing overhead cost per unit of product X.

(2 marks)

(b) The production director of Bookdon PLC has suggested that 'as the actual overheads incurred and units produced are usually different from the budgeted and as a consequence profits of each month end are distorted by over-/under-absorbed overheads, it would be more accurate to calculate the actual overhead cost per unit each month end by dividing the total number of all units actually produced during the month into the actual overheads incurred.'

    Critically examine the production director's suggestion.

(8 marks)
(Total 22 marks)

5.20 Make or buy decision

Shown below is next year's budget for the forming and finishing departments of Tooton Ltd. The departments manufacture three different types of component, which are incorporated into the output of the firm's finished products.

		Component	
	A	B	C
Production (units)	14 000	10 000	6 000
Prime cost (£ per unit):			
Direct materials			
Forming dept	8	7	9
Direct labour			
Forming dept	6	9	12
Finishing dept	10	15	8
	24	31	29
Manufacturing times (hours per unit):			
Machining			
Forming dept	4	3	2
Direct labour			
Forming dept	2	3	4
Finishing dept	3	10	2

	Forming department (£)	Finishing department (£)
Variable overheads	200 900	115 500
Fixed overheads	401 800	231 000
	£602 700	£346 500
Machine time required and available	98 000 hours	—
Labour hours required and available	82 000 hours	154 000 hours

The forming department is mechanized and employs only one grade of labour, the finishing department employs several grades of labour with differing hourly rates of pay.

Required:

(a) Calculate suitable overhead absorption rates for the forming and finishing departments for next year and include a brief explanation for your choice of rates.

(6 marks)

(b) Another firm has offered to supply next year's budgeted quantities of the above components at the following prices:

Component A   £30   Component B   £65
Component C   £60

Advise management whether it would be more economical to purchase any of the above components from the outside supplier. You must show your workings and, considering cost criteria only, clearly state any assumptions made or any aspects that may require further investigation.

(8 marks)

(c) Critically consider the purpose of calculating production overheads absorption rates.

(8 marks)
(Total 22 marks)

Activity-based costing

6 In the previous chapter the cost assignment process for a traditional costing system was described. During the 1980s the limitations of traditional product costing systems began to be widely publicized. These systems were designed decades ago when most companies marketed a narrow range of products. Indirect costs were relatively small, and the distortions arising from inappropriate overhead allocations were not significant. Information processing costs were high and it was therefore difficult to justify more sophisticated methods of assigning indirect costs to cost objects.

By the 1980s companies were marketing a wide range of products, indirect costs were no longer relatively unimportant and information costs had ceased to be a barrier to introducing more sophisticated systems. Furthermore, the intense global competition of the 1980s resulted in decision errors from poor cost information becoming more probable and more costly. It is against this background that a new, and more sophisticated costing system, called activity-based costing (ABC) emerged in the late 1980s.

In this chapter we shall focus on ABC systems. In particular, the measurement of indirect costs for decision-making using ABC techniques will be examined. The major aims of the

---

LEARNING OBJECTIVES

After studying this chapter you should be able to:

- explain why a cost accumulation system is required for generating relevant cost information for decision-making;
- describe the differences between activity-based and traditional costing systems;
- explain why traditional costing systems can provide misleading information for decision-making;
- compute product costs using an activity-based costing system;
- identify and explain each of the four stages involved in designing ABC systems;
- describe the ABC cost hierarchy;
- describe the ABC profitability analysis hierarchy;
- describe the ABC resource consumption model.

chapter are to explain how an ABC system operates and provide you with a conceptual understanding of ABC. You should note that ABC can also be used for managing and controlling costs. These aspects are considered in Chapter 15.

Some of the issues explored in the chapter are complex and may not be appropriate for readers pursuing an introductory management accounting course. The sections that relate to the more advanced reading material are highlighted. If you are pursuing an introductory course you may prefer to omit the advanced reading sections, or skim them, on your first reading. You should read them only when you fully understand the remaining content of the chapter.

Unless otherwise stated, we shall assume that products are the cost objects but the techniques used and the principles established can be applied to other cost objects such as customers, services and locations. We begin with an examination of the role that a cost accumulation system plays in generating relevant cost information for decision-making.

The need for a cost accumulation system in generating relevant cost information for decision-making

There are three main reasons why a cost accumulation system is required to generate relevant cost information for decision-making. They are:

1 many indirect costs are relevant for decision-making;
2 an attention-directing information system is required that periodically identifies those potentially unprofitable products that require more detailed special studies;
3 product decisions are not independent.

There is a danger that only those incremental costs that are uniquely attributable to individual products will be classified as relevant and indirect costs will be classified as irrelevant for decision-making. Direct costs are transparent and how they will be affected by decisions is clearly observable. In contrast, how indirect costs will be affected by decisions is not clearly observable. There has been a tendency in the past to assume that these costs are fixed and irrelevant for decision-making. In many organizations, however, these are costs that have escalated over the years. The message is clear – they cannot be assumed to be fixed and irrelevant for decision-making.

The costs of many joint resources fluctuate in the long term according to the demand for them. The cost of support functions falls within this category. They include activities such as materials procurement, materials handling, production scheduling, warehousing, expediting and customer order processing. The costs of these activities are either not directly traceable to products, or would involve such detailed tracing that the costs of doing so would far exceed their benefits. Product introduction, discontinuation, redesign and mix decisions determine the demand for support function resources. For example, if a decision results in a 10% reduction in the demand for the resources of a support activity then we would expect, in the long term, some of the costs of that support activity to decline by 10%. Therefore, to estimate the impact that decisions will have on the support activities (and their future costs) a cost accumulation system is required that assigns those indirect costs, using cause-and-effect allocations, to products.

The second reason relates to the need for a periodic attention-directing reporting system. For decision-making it could be argued that relevant/incremental costs need only be ascertained when the need arises. For example, why not undertake special studies involving incremental cost/revenue analysis at periodic intervals to make sure that each product is still profitable? Estimates could be made only when undertaking a special study of those relevant costs that would be avoided if a product was discontinued. This approach is fine for highly simplified situations where an organization only produces a few products and where all relevant costs are uniquely attributable to individual products. However, most organizations produce hundreds of products and the range of potential decisions to explore undertaking special studies is enormous and unmanageable. For example, Kaplan (1990) considers a situation where a company has 100 products and outlines the difficulties of determining which product, or product combinations, should be selected for undertaking special studies. Kaplan states:

> *First how do you think about which product you should even think about making a decision on? There are 100 different products to consider. But think about all the combinations of these products: which two products, three products or groupings of 10 or 20 products should be analyzed? It's a simple exercise to calculate that there are 2^{100} different combinations of the 100 products ... so there is no way to do an incremental revenue/incremental analysis on all relevant combinations (p. 13).*

To cope with the vast number of potential product combinations organizations need attention-directing information to highlight those specific products, or combination of products, that appear to be questionable and which require further detailed special studies to ascertain their viability. Periodic product profitability analysis meets this requirement. A cost accumulation system is therefore required to assign costs to products for periodic profitability analysis.

The third reason for using a cost accumulation system is that many product-related decisions are not independent. Consider again those joint resources shared by most products and that fluctuate in the longer term according to the demand for them. If we focus only on individual products and assume that they are independent, decisions will be taken in isolation of decisions made on other products. For joint resources the incremental/avoidable costs relating to a decision to add or drop a *single* product may be zero. Assuming that 20 products are viewed in this manner then the sum of the incremental costs will be zero. However, if the 20 products are viewed as a *whole* there may be a significant change in resource usage and incremental costs for those joint resources that fluctuate according to the demand for them.

Cooper (1990b) also argues that decisions should not be viewed independently. He states:

> *The decision to drop one product will typically not change 'fixed' overhead spending. In contrast, dropping 50 products might allow considerable changes to be made. Stated somewhat tritely, the sum of the parts (the decision to drop individual products) is not equal to the sum of the whole (the realisable savings from having dropped 50 products). To help them make effective decisions, managers require cost systems that provide insights into the whole, not just isolated individual parts (p. 58).*

Thus, where product decisions are not independent the multiplication of product costs, that include the cost of joint resources, by the units lost from ceasing production (or additional units from introducing a new product) may provide an approximation of the change in the long term of total company costs arising from the decisions. The rationale for this is that the change in resource consumption will ultimately be followed by a change in the cash flow pattern of the organization because organizations make product introduction or abandonment decisions for many products rather than just a single product. These issues are complex and will be explained in more detail later in the chapter.

Types of cost systems

Costing systems can vary in terms of which costs are assigned to cost objects and their level of sophistication. Typically cost systems are classified as follows:

1 direct costing systems;

2 traditional absorption costing systems;

3 activity-based costing systems.

Direct costing systems only assign direct costs to cost objects. Because they do not assign indirect costs to cost objects they report contributions to indirect costs. Direct costing systems can therefore be classified as partial costing systems. They are appropriate for decision-making where the cost of those joint resources that fluctuate according to the demand for them are insignificant. Negative or low contribution items should then be highlighted for special studies. An estimate of those indirect costs that are relevant to the decision should be incorporated within the analysis at the special study stage. The disadvantage of direct costing systems is that systems are not in place to measure and assign indirect costs to cost objects. Thus any attempt to incorporate indirect costs into the analysis at the special studies stage must be based on guesswork and arbitrary estimates. Direct costing systems can therefore only be recommended where indirect costs are a low proportion of an organization's total costs.

Both traditional and ABC systems assign indirect costs to cost objects. The major features of traditional systems were described in the previous chapter. In this chapter we shall concentrate on ABC systems.

A comparison of traditional and ABC systems

Figure 6.1 illustrates the major differences between traditional costing and ABC systems. The upper panel of this diagram is identical to Figure 5.3, used in the previous chapter to describe a traditional costing system. In the first stage a traditional system allocates overheads to production and service departments and then reallocates service department costs to the production departments. An ABC system assigns overheads to each major activity (rather than departments). With ABC systems, many **activity-based cost centres** (alternatively known as **activity cost pools**) are established, whereas with traditional systems overheads tend to be pooled by departments, although they are normally described as cost centres.

Activities consist of the aggregation of many different tasks and are described by verbs associated with objects. Typical support activities include: schedule production, set-up machines, move materials, purchase materials, inspect items, process supplier records, expedite and process customer orders. Production process activities include machine products and assembling products. Within the production process, activity cost centres are often identical to the cost centres used by traditional cost systems. Support activities are also sometimes identical to cost centres used by traditional systems, such as when the purchasing department and activity are both treated as cost centres. Overall, however, ABC systems will normally have a greater number of cost centres.

The second stage of the two-stage allocation process allocates costs from cost centres (pools) to products or other chosen cost objects. Traditional costing systems trace overheads to products using a small number of second stage allocation bases (normally described as overhead allocation rates), which vary directly with the volume produced. Instead of using the terms 'allocation bases' or 'overhead allocation rates' the term **'cost driver'** is used by ABC systems. Direct labour and machine hours are the allocation bases that are normally used by

FIGURE 6.1   *An illustration of the two-stage allocation process for traditional and activity-based costing systems*

(a) Traditional costing systems

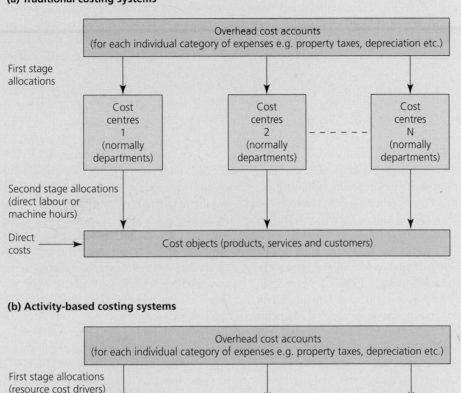

(b) Activity-based costing systems

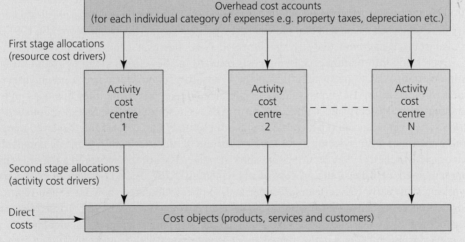

traditional costing systems. In contrast, ABC systems use many different types of second-stage cost drivers, including non-volume-based drivers, such as the number of production runs for production scheduling and the number of purchase orders for the purchasing activity. A further distinguishing feature is that traditional systems normally allocate service/support costs to production centres. Their costs are merged with the production cost centre costs and thus included within the production centre overhead rates. In contrast, ABC systems tend to establish separate cost driver rates for support centres, and assign the cost of support activities directly to cost objects without any reallocation to production centres.

Therefore the major distinguishing features of ABC systems are that within the two-stage allocation process they rely on:

1 a greater number of cost centres;

2 a greater number and variety of second stage cost drivers.

By using a greater number of cost centres and different types of cost drivers that cause activity resource consumption, and assigning activity costs to cost objects on the basis of cost driver usage, 'ABC systems can more accurately measure the resources consumed by cost objects.' Traditional cost systems report less accurate costs because they use cost drivers where no cause-and-effect relationships exist to assign support costs to cost objects.

The emergence of ABC systems

During the 1980s the limitations of traditional product costing systems began to be widely publicized. These systems were designed decades ago when most companies manufactured a narrow range of products, and direct labour and materials were the dominant factory costs. Overhead costs were relatively small, and the distortions arising from inappropriate overhead allocations were not significant. Information processing costs were high, and it was therefore difficult to justify more sophisticated overhead allocation methods.

Today companies produce a wide range of products; direct labour represents only a small fraction of total costs, and overhead costs are of considerable importance. Simplistic overhead allocations using a declining direct labour base cannot be justified, particularly when information processing costs are no longer a barrier to introducing more sophisticated cost systems. Furthermore, the intense global competition of the 1980s has made decision errors due to poor cost information more probable and more costly. Over the years the increased opportunity cost of having poor cost information, and the decreased cost of operating more sophisticated cost systems, increased the demand for more accurate product costs (Holzer and Norreklit, 1991). It is against this background that ABC has emerged. ABC, however, is not a recent innovation.

Decreasing information processing costs resulted in a few firms in the USA and Europe implementing ABC-type systems during the 1980s. In a series of articles based on observations of innovative ABC-type systems Cooper and Kaplan conceptualized the ideas underpinning these systems and coined the term ABC. These articles were first published in 1988. They generated a considerable amount of publicity and consultants began to market and implement ABC systems before the end of the decade. In a survey of UK companies Innes and Mitchell (1991) reported that approximately 10% of the surveyed companies had implemented, or were in the process of implementing ABC. Based on their experience of working with early US adopters, Cooper and Kaplan articulated their ideas and reported further theoretical advances in articles published between 1990 and 1992. These ideas and the theoretical advances are described in the remainder of this chapter. ABC ideas have now become firmly embedded in the management accounting literature and educational courses and many practitioners have attended courses and conferences on the topic.

Volume-based and non-volume-based cost drivers

Our comparison of ABC systems with traditional costing systems indicated that ABC systems rely on a greater number and variety of second stage cost drivers. The term 'variety of cost drivers' refers to the fact that ABC systems use both volume-based and non-volume-based cost drivers. In contrast, traditional systems use only volume-based cost drivers. **Volume-based cost drivers** assume that a product's consumption of overhead resources is directly related to units produced. In other words, they assume that the overhead consumed by products is highly correlated with the number of units produced. Typical volume-based cost drivers used by traditional systems are units of output, direct labour hours and machine hours. These cost drivers are appropriate for measuring the consumption of expenses such as machine energy costs, depreciation related to machine usage, indirect labour employed in production centres and inspection costs where each item produced is subject to final inspection. For example, machine hours are an appropriate cost driver for energy costs since if volume is increased by 10%, machine hours are likely to increase by 10%, thus causing 10% more energy costs to be consumed. Similarly, an increase in volume of 10% is likely to increase the consumption of direct labour hours by 10% and, assuming that indirect labour hours are correlated with direct labour hours, 10% more indirect labour costs will be consumed.

Volume-based drivers are appropriate in the above circumstances because activities are performed each time a unit of the product or service is produced. In contrast, non-volume related activities are not performed each time a unit of the product or service is produced. Consider, for example, two activities – setting up a machine and re-engineering products. Set-up resources are consumed each time a machine is changed from one product to another. It costs the same to set-up a machine for 10 or 5000 items. As more set-ups are done more set-up resources are consumed. The number of set-ups, rather than the number of units produced, is a more appropriate measure of the consumption of the set-up activity. Similarly, product re-engineering costs may depend upon the number of different engineering works orders and not the number of units produced. For both of these activities, **non-volume-based cost drivers** such as number of set-ups and engineering orders are needed for the accurate assignment of the costs of these activities.

Using only volume-based cost drivers to assign non-volume related overhead costs can result in the reporting of distorted product costs. The extent of distortion depends on what proportion of total overhead costs the non-volume based overheads represent and the level of product diversity. If a large proportion of an organization's costs are unrelated to volume there is a danger that inaccurate product costs will be reported. Conversely, if non-volume related overhead costs are only a small proportion of total overhead costs, the distortion of product costs will not be significant. In these circumstances traditional product costing systems are likely to be acceptable.

Product diversity applies when products consume different overhead activities in dissimilar proportions. Differences in product size, product complexity, sizes of batches and set-up times cause product diversity. If all products consume overhead resources in similar proportions product diversity will be low and products will consume non-volume related activities in the same proportion as volume-related activities. Hence, product cost distortion will not occur with traditional product costing systems. Two conditions are therefore necessary for product cost distortion – non-volume-related overhead costs are a large proportion of total overhead costs and product diversity applies. Where these two conditions exist traditional product costing systems can result in the overcosting of high volume products and undercosting of low volume products. Consider the information presented in Example 6.1.

The reported product costs and profits for the two products are as follows:

| | Traditional system | | ABC system | |
	Product HV (£)	Product LV (£)	Product HV (£)	Product LV (£)
Direct costs	310 000	40 000	310 000	40 000
Overheads allocated[a]	300 000 (30%)	50 000 (5%)	150 000 (15%)	150 000 (15%)
Reported profits/(losses)	(10 000)	60 000	140 000	(40 000)
Sales revenues	600 000	150 000	600 000	150 000

Note

[a]Allocation of £1 million overheads using direct labour hours as the allocation base for the traditional system and number of batches processed as the cost driver for the ABC system.

EXAMPLE 6.1

Assume that the Balearic company has only one overhead cost centre or cost pool. It currently operates a traditional costing system using direct labour hours to allocate overheads to products. The company produces several products, two of which are products HV and LV. Product HV is made in high volumes whereas product LV is made in low volumes. Product HV consumes 30% of the direct labour hours and product LV consumes only 5%. Because of the high volume production product HV can be made in large production batches but the irregular and low level of demand for product LV requires it to be made in small batches. A detailed investigation indicates that the number of batches processed causes the demand for overhead resources. The traditional system is therefore replaced with an ABC system using the number of batches processed as the cost driver. You ascertain that each product accounts for 15% of the batches processed during the period and the overheads assigned to the cost centre that fluctuate in the long term according to the demand for them amount to £1 million. The direct costs and sales revenues assigned to the products are as follows:

	Product HV (£)	Product LV (£)
Direct costs	310 000	40 000
Sales revenues	600 000	150 000

Show the product profitability analysis for products HV and LV using the traditional and ABC systems.

Because product HV is a high volume product that consumes 30% of the direct labour hours whereas product LV, the low volume product consumes only 5%, the traditional system that uses direct labour hours as the allocation base allocates six times more overheads to product HV. However, ABC systems recognize that overheads are caused by other factors, besides volume. In our example, all of the overheads are assumed to be volume unrelated. They are caused by the number of batches processed and the ABC system establishes a cause-and-effect allocation relationship by using the number of batches processed as the cost driver. Both products require 15% of the total number of batches so they are allocated with an equal amount of overheads.

It is apparent from the consumption ratios of the two products that the traditional system based on direct labour hours will overcost high volume products. Consumption ratios represent the proportion of each activity consumed by a product. The consumption ratios if direct labour hours are used as the cost driver are 0.30 for product HV and 0.05 for product LV so that six times more overheads will be assigned to product HV. When the number of batches processed are used as the cost driver the consumption ratios are 0.15 for each product and an equal amount of overhead will be assigned to each product. Distorted product costs are reported with the traditional costing system that uses the volume-based cost driver because the two conditions specified above apply. First, non-volume related overheads are a large proportion of total overheads, being 100% in our example. Second, product diversity exists because the product consumption ratios for the two identified cost drivers are significantly different. Our illustration shows that if the consumption ratios for batches processed had been the same as the ratios for direct labour the traditional and ABC systems would report identical product costs.

With the traditional costing system misleading information is reported. A small loss is reported for product HV and if it were discontinued the costing system mistakenly gives the impression that overheads will decline in the longer term by £300 000. Furthermore, the message from the costing system is to concentrate on the more profitable speciality products like product LV. In reality this strategy would be disastrous because low volume products like product LV are made in small batches and require more people for scheduling production, performing set-ups, inspection of the batches and handling a large number of customer requests for small orders. The long-term effect would be escalating overhead costs.

In contrast, the ABC system allocates overheads on a cause-and-effect basis and more accurately measures the relatively high level of overhead resources consumed by product LV. The message from the profitability analysis is the opposite from the traditional system; that is, product HV is profitable and product LV is unprofitable. If product LV is discontinued, and assuming that the cost driver is the cause of all the overheads then a decision to discontinue product LV should result in the reduction in resource spending on overheads by £150 000.

Example 6.1 is very simplistic. It is assumed that the organization has established only a single cost centre or cost pool, when in reality many will be established with a traditional system, and even more with an ABC system. Furthermore, the data have been deliberately biased to show the superiority of ABC. The aim of the illustration has been to highlight the potential cost of errors that can occur when information extracted from simplistic and inaccurate cost systems is used for decision-making.

An illustration of the two-stage process for an ABC system

We shall now use the data presented in Example 5.1 (the Enterprise Company) from the previous chapter to illustrate ABC in more detail. This example was used to provide the relevant information to compute the product costs shown in Exhibit 5.2 for a traditional costing system. To refresh your memory you should now refer back to Example 5.1 and Exhibit 5.2 in the previous chapter and also read pages 122–126 relating to steps 1–4 of the two-stage process.

With the ABC system it is assumed in Example 5.1 that the activity cost centres for machining and assembling products are identical to the production cost centres used by the traditional costing system. We shall also assume that three activity cost centres have been established for each of the support functions. They are purchasing components, receiving components and disbursing materials for materials procurement and production scheduling, setting-up machines and a quality inspection of the completed products for general factory support. Exhibit 6.1 provides the additional information required for an ABC system and also shows the activity-based product cost calculations.

Both ABC and traditional systems use the same approach to assign costs to cost centres in the first stage of the two-stage allocation process. If you refer to column 2 in the upper section of Exhibit 6.1 you will see that the costs assigned to the production activities have been extracted from row 1 in the overhead analysis sheet shown in Exhibit 5.2, which was used for the traditional costing system. In the overhead analysis sheet we only assigned costs with the traditional costing system to materials procurement and general factory support, and not to the activities within these support functions. However, the costs for the activities within these functions would be derived adopting the same approach as that used in Exhibit 5.2, but to simplify the presentation the cost assignments to the materials procurement and general factory support activity cost centres are not shown.

REAL WORLD VIEWS 6.1

The shift in the assignment of overhead costs at Hewlett-Packard

A division of Hewlett-Packard that manufactures electronic circuit boards faced an environment that conformed closely to the conditions for which ABC is recommended:

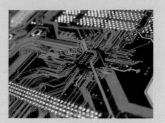

- diverse products,
- relatively high overhead costs and, for some products, higher than the direct costs,
- production volumes that vary significantly among products,
- the belief by the operating managers that the old traditional system did not give meaningful product costs.

An ABC system was introduced consisting of ten different cost pools and drivers. The composition of the cost pools and selection of the most appropriate drivers resulted from an intense analysis of the production process and cost behaviour patterns. When the company implemented ABC, the costs of the old and new system were compared. One circuit board that would have been assigned with overheads of $5 with the old system had a reported total cost of $25 with ABC – an increase of 400 per cent. Another circuit board that would have been assigned an overhead of $123 with the old system was assigned $45 with ABC.

During a six-month forecast and budget cycle, the ABC system resulted in shifting millions of dollars of costs between customers and products and thus had a dramatic impact on product design and pricing decisions.

Source: Merz, M. and Hardy, A. (1993) ABC puts accountants on the design team at HP, *Management Accounting (USA)*, September, pp. 24–26.

Exhibit 6.1 shows the product cost calculations for an ABC system. By referring to the second column in the upper section of this exhibit you will see that the costs assigned to the purchasing, receiving and disbursement of materials activities total £1 760 000, the same as the total allocated to the materials procurement function by the traditional system shown in Exhibit 5.2. Similarly, the total costs assigned to the production scheduling, set-up and quality inspection activities in column 2 of the upper section of Exhibit 6.1 total £1 800 000, the same as the total costs allocated to the general factory support function in Exhibit 5.2.

Now look at columns 1 and 3 in the upper section of Exhibit 6.1. You will see that with the ABC system The Enterprise Company has established nine activity cost centres and seven different second-stage cost drivers. Note also that the cost drivers for the production activities are the same of those used for the traditional costing system. Based on their observations of ABC systems Kaplan and Cooper (1998) suggest that relatively simple ABC systems having 30–50 activity cost centres and many cost drivers ought to report reasonably accurate costs.

To emphasize the point that ABC systems use cause-and-effect second stage allocations the term cost driver tends to be used instead of allocation base. Cost drivers should be significant determinants of the cost of activities. For example, if the cost of processing purchase orders is determined by the number of purchase orders that each product generates, then the number of purchase orders would represent the cost driver for the cost of processing purchase orders. Other cost drivers used by the Enterprise Company are shown in column 3 of Exhibit 6.1. They are the number of receipts for receiving components, number of production runs for disbursing materials and scheduling production, number of

EXHIBIT 6.1

An illustration of cost assignment with an ABC system

(1) Activity	(2) Activity cost £	(3) Activity cost driver	(4) Quantity of activity cost driver	(5) Activity cost driver rate (Col. 2/Col.4)
Production activities:				
Machining: activity centre A	2 970 000	Number of machine hours	2 000 000 machine hours	£1.485 per hour
Machining: activity centre B	2 690 000	Number of machine hours	1 000 000 machine hours	£2.69 per hour
Assembly	2 480 000	Number of direct labour hours	2 000 000 direct lab. hours	£1.24 per hour
	8 140 000			
Materials procurement activities:				
Purchasing components	960 000	Number of purchase orders	10 000 purchase orders	£96 per order
Receiving components	600 000	Number of material receipts	5 000 receipts	£120 per receipt
Disburse materials	200 000	Number of production runs	2 000 production runs	£100 per production run
	1 760 000			
General factory support activities:				
Production scheduling	1 000 000	Number of production runs	2 000 production runs	£500 per production run
Set-up machines	600 000	Number of set-up hours	12 000 set-up hours	£50 per set-up hour
Quality inspection	200 000	Number of first item inspections	1 000 inspections	£200 per inspection
	1 800 000			
Total cost of all manufacturing activities	11 700 000			

Computation of product costs

(1) Activity	(2) Activity cost driver rate	(3) Quantity of cost driver used by 100 units of product A	(4) Quantity of cost driver used by 200 units of product B	(5) Activity cost assigned to product A (Col. 2 × Col. 3)	(6) Activity cost assigned to product B (Col. 2 × Col. 4)
Machining: activity centre A	£1.485 per hour	500 hours	2 000 hours	742.50	2 970.00
Machining: activity centre B	£2.69 per hour	1 000 hours	4 000 hours	2 690.00	10 760.00
Assembly	£1.24 per hour	1 000 hours	4 000 hours	1 240.00	4 960.00
Purchasing components	£96 per order	1 component	1 component	96.00	96.00
Receiving components	£120 per receipt	1 component	1 component	120.00	120.00
Disburse materials	£100 per production run	5 production runs[a]	1 production run	500.00	100.00
Production scheduling	£500 per production run	5 production runs[a]	1 production run	2 500.00	500.00
Set-up machines	£50 per set-up hour	50 set-up hours	10 set-up hours	2 500.00	500.00
Quality inspection	£200 per inspection	1 inspection	1 inspection	200.00	200.00
Total overhead cost				10 588.50	20 206.00
Units produced				100 units	200 units
Overhead cost *per unit*				£105.88	£101.03
Direct costs *per unit*				100.00	200.00
Total cost *per unit* of output				205.88	301.03

Note

[a] Five production runs are required to machine several unique components before they can be assembled into a final product.

set-up hours for setting up the machines and the number of first item inspections for quality inspection of a batch of completed products. You will see from column 5 in the first section of Exhibit 6.1 that cost driver rates are computed by dividing the activity centre cost by the quantity of the cost driver used.

Activity centre costs are assigned to products by multiplying the cost driver rate by the quantity of the cost driver used by products. These calculations are shown in the second section of Exhibit 6.1. You will see from the first section in Exhibit 6.1 that the costs assigned to the purchasing activity are £960 000 for processing 10 000 purchasing orders resulting in a cost driver rate of £96 per purchasing order. The second section (line 4) shows that a batch of 100 units of product A, and 200 units of product B, each require one purchased component and thus one purchase order. Therefore purchase order costs of £96 are allocated to each batch. The same approach is used to allocate the costs of the remaining activities shown in Exhibit 6.1. You should now work through Exhibit 6.1 and study the product cost calculations.

The costs assigned to products using each costing system are as follows:

	Traditional costing system £	ABC system £
Product A	166.75	205.88
Product B	333.50	301.03

Compared with the ABC system the traditional system undercosts product A and overcosts product B. By reallocating the service centre costs to the production centres and allocating the costs to products on the basis of either machine hours or direct labour hours the traditional system incorrectly assumes that these allocation bases are the cause of the costs of the support activities. Compared with product A, product B consumes twice as many machine and direct labour hours per unit of output. Therefore, relative to Product A, the traditional costing system allocates twice the amount of support costs to product B.

In contrast, ABC systems create separate cost centres for each major support activity and allocate cost to products using cost drivers that are the significant determinants of the cost of the activities. The ABC system recognizes that a batch of both products consume the same quantity of purchasing, receiving and inspection activities and, for these activities, allocates the same costs to both products. Because product B is manufactured in batches of 200 units, and product A in batches of 100 units, the cost per unit of output for product B is half the amount of Product A for these activities. Product A also has five unique machined components, whereas product B has only one, resulting in a batch of Product A requiring five production runs whereas a batch of Product B only requires one. Therefore, relative to product B, the ABC system assigns five times more costs to product A for the production scheduling and disbursement of materials activities (see columns 5 and 6 in the lower part of Exhibit 6.1). Because product A is a more complex product, it requires relatively more support activity resources and the cost of this complexity is captured by the ABC system.

Designing ABC systems

The discussion so far has provided a broad overview of ABC. We shall now examine ABC in more detail by looking at the design of ABC systems. Four steps are involved. They are:

1 identifying the major activities that take place in an organization;

2 assigning costs to cost pools/cost centres for each activity;

3 determining the cost driver for each major activity;

4 assigning the cost of activities to products according to the product's demand for activities.

The first two steps relate to the first stage, and the final two steps to the second stage, of the two-stage allocation process shown in Figure 6.1. Let us now consider each of these stages in more detail.

Step 1: Identifying activities

Activities are composed of the aggregation of units of work or tasks and are described by verbs associated with tasks. For example, purchasing of materials might be identified as a separate activity. This activity consists of the aggregation of many different tasks, such as receiving a purchase request, identifying suppliers, preparing purchase orders, mailing purchase orders and performing follow-ups.

Activities are identified by carrying out an activity analysis. Innes and Mitchell (1995b) suggest that a useful starting point is to examine a physical plan of the workplace (to identify how all work space is being used) and the payroll listings (to ensure all relevant personnel have been taken into account). This examination normally has to be supplemented by a series of interviews with the staff involved, or having staff complete a time sheet for a specific time period explaining how their time is spent. Interviewers will ask managers and employees questions such as what staff work at the location and what tasks are performed by the persons employed at the location.

Many detailed tasks are likely to be identified in the first instance, but after further interviews, the main activities will emerge. The activities chosen should be at a reasonable level of aggregation based on costs versus benefits criteria. For example, rather than classifying purchasing of materials as an activity, each of its constituent tasks could be classified as separate activities. However, this level of decomposition would involve the collection of a vast amount of data and is likely to be too costly for product costing purposes. Alternatively, the purchasing activity might be merged with the materials receiving, storage and issuing activities to form a single materials procurement and handling activity. This is likely to represent too high a level of aggregation because a single cost driver is unlikely to provide a satisfactory determinant of the cost of the activity. For example, selecting the number of purchase orders as a cost driver may provide a good explanation of purchasing costs but may be entirely inappropriate for explaining costs relating to receiving and issuing. Therefore, instead of establishing materials procurement and handling as a single activity it may be preferable to decompose it into three separate activities; namely purchasing, receiving and issuing activities, and establish separate cost drivers for each activity.

In some of the early ABC systems hundreds of separate activity cost centres were established but recent studies suggest that between twenty and thirty activity centres tend to be the norm. The final choice of activities must be a matter of judgement but it is likely to be influenced by factors such as the total cost of the activity centre (it must be of significance to justify separate treatment) and the ability of a single driver to provide a satisfactory determinant of the cost of the activity. Activities with the same product consumption ratios can use the same cost driver to assign costs to products. Thus, all activities that have the same cost driver can be merged to form a single activity cost centre. However, if there are significant differences in activity product consumption ratios products will consume activities in dissimilar proportions and the activities should not be aggregated.

Step 2: Assigning costs to activity cost centres

After the activities have been identified the cost of resources consumed over a specified period must be assigned to each activity. The aim is to determine how much the organization is spending on each of its activities. Many of the resources will be directly attributable to specific activity centres but others (such as labour and lighting and heating costs) may be indirect and jointly shared by several activities. These costs should be assigned to activities on the basis of cause-and-effect cost drivers, or interviews with staff who can provide reasonable estimates of the resources consumed by different activities. Arbitrary allocations should not be used. The greater the amount of costs traced to activity centres by cost apportionments at this stage the more arbitrary and less reliable will be the product cost information generated by ABC systems. Cause-and-effect cost drivers used at this stage to allocate shared resources to individual activities are called **resource cost drivers**.

Step 3: Selecting appropriate cost drivers for assigning the cost of activities to cost objects

In order to assign the costs attached to each activity cost centre to products a cost driver must be selected for each activity centre. Cost drivers used at this stage are called **activity cost drivers**. Several factors must be borne in mind when selecting a suitable cost driver. First, it should provide a good explanation of costs in each activity cost pool. Second, a cost driver should be easily measurable, the data should be relatively easy to obtain and be identifiable with products. The costs of measurement should therefore be taken into account.

Activity cost drivers consist of transaction and duration drivers. **Transaction drivers**, such as the number of purchase orders processed, number of customer orders processed, number of inspections performed and the number of set-ups undertaken, all count the number of times an activity is performed. Transaction drivers are the least expensive type of cost driver but they are also likely to be the least accurate because they assume that the same quantity of resources is required every time an activity is performed. However, if the variation in the amount of resources required by individual cost objects is not great transaction drivers will provide a reasonably accurate measurement of activity resources consumed. If this condition does not apply then duration cost drivers should be used.

Duration drivers represent the amount of time required to perform an activity. Examples of duration drivers include set-up hours and inspection hours. For example, if one product requires a short set-up time and another requires a long time then using set-up hours as the cost driver will more accurately measure activity resource consumption than the transaction driver (number of set-ups), which assumes that an equal amount of activity resources are consumed by both products. Using the number of set-ups will result in the product that requires a long set-up time being undercosted whereas the product that requires a short set-up will be overcosted. This problem can be overcome by using set-up hours as the cost driver, but this will increase the measurement costs.

In most situations data will not initially be available relating to the past costs of activities or potential cost driver volumes. To ascertain potential cost drivers interviews will be required with the personnel involved with the specific activities. The interviews will seek to ascertain what causes the particular activity to consume resources and incur costs. The final choice of a cost driver is likely to be based on managerial judgement after taking into account the factors outlined above.

Step 4: Assigning the cost of the activities to products

The final stage involves applying the cost driver rates to products. Therefore the cost driver must be measurable in a way that enables it to be identified with individual products. Thus, if set-up hours are selected as a cost driver, there must be a mechanism for measuring the set-up hours consumed by each product. Alternatively, if the number of set-ups is selected as the cost driver measurements by products are not required since all products that require a set-up are charged with a constant set-up cost. The ease and cost of obtaining data on cost driver consumption by products is therefore a factor that must be considered during the third stage when an appropriate cost driver is being selected.

Activity hierarchies

Early ABC systems were subject to a number of criticisms, particularly relating to theoretical aspects. As a response to these criticisms a number of theoretical developments emerged during the 1990s.

The first theoretical development was reported by Cooper (1990a) who classified manufacturing activities along a cost hierarchy dimension consisting of:

1 unit-level activities;
2 batch-level activities;
3 product-sustaining activities;
4 facility-sustaining activities.

Unit-level activities (also known as volume-related activities) are performed each time a unit of the product or service is produced. Expenses in this category include direct labour, direct materials, energy costs and expenses that are consumed in proportion to machine processing time (such as maintenance). Unit-level activities consume resources in proportion to the number of units of production and sales volume. For example, if a firm produces 10% more units it will consume 10% more labour cost, 10% more machine hours and 10% more energy costs. Typical cost drivers for unit level activities include labour hours, machine hours and the quantity of materials processed. These cost drivers are also used by traditional costing systems. Traditional systems are therefore also appropriate for assigning the costs of unit-level activities to cost objects.

Batch-related activities, such as setting up a machine or processing a purchase order, are performed each time a batch of goods is produced. The cost of batch-related activities varies with the number of batches made, but is common (or fixed) for all units within the batch. For example, set-up resources are consumed when a machine is changed from one product to another. As more batches are produced, more set-up resources are consumed. It costs the same to set-up a machine for 10 or 5000 items. Thus the demands for the set-up resources are independent of the number of units produced after completing the set-up. Similarly, purchasing resources are consumed each time a purchasing order is processed, but the resources consumed are independent of the number of units included in the purchase order. Other examples of batch-related costs include resources devoted to production scheduling, first-item inspection and materials movement. Traditional costing systems treat batch-related expenses as fixed costs whereas ABC systems assume that they vary with the number of batches produced.

Product-sustaining activities or **service-sustaining activities** are performed to enable the production and sale of individual products (or services). Examples of product-sustaining activities provided by Kaplan and Cooper (1998) include maintaining and updating product specifications and the technical support provided for individual products and services. Other examples are the resources to prepare and implement engineering change notices (ECNs), to design processes and test routines for individual products, and to perform product enhancements. The costs of product-sustaining activities are incurred irrespective of the number of units of output or the number of batches processed and their expenses will tend to increase as the number of products manufactured is increased. ABC uses product-level bases such as number of active part numbers and number of ECNs to assign these costs to products. Kaplan and Cooper (1998) have extended their ideas to situations where customers are the cost objects with the equivalent term for product-sustaining being **customer-sustaining activities**. Customer market research and support for an individual customer, or groups of customers if they represent the cost object, are examples of customer-sustaining activities.

The final activity category is **facility-sustaining** (or **business-sustaining**) **activities**. They are performed to support the facility's general manufacturing process and include general administrative staff, plant management and property costs. They are incurred to support the organization as a whole and are common and joint to all products manufactured in the plant. There would have to be a dramatic change in activity, resulting in an expansion or contraction in the size of the plant, for facility-sustaining costs to change. Such events are most unlikely in most organizations. Therefore the ABC literature advocates that these costs should not be assigned to products since they are unavoidable and irrelevant for most decisions. Instead, they are regarded as common costs to *all* products made in the plant and deducted as a lump sum from the total of the operating margins from *all* products.

Activity-based costing profitability analysis

ADVANCED READING

The second theoretical development was first highlighted by Kaplan (1990) and Cooper and Kaplan (1991). They apply the ABC hierarchical activity classification to profitability analysis. In addition, they stress that the reported ABC product costs do not provide information that can be used directly for decision-making. Instead, they report attention-directing information by highlighting those potentially unprofitable products or services that require more detailed special studies. Cooper (1997) has stressed that a major role of ABC is to develop profitability maps (i.e. periodic profitability analysis by cost objects) that are used to focus managerial attention. He argues that because the cost of special studies are high the number performed has to be carefully controlled; hence the need for good attention-directing information. He concludes that the primary value of ABC systems lies in the quality of the profitability analysis generated.

Kaplan and Cooper (1998) extended cost hierarchies to develop activity-profitability maps by different cost objects. The general principles of activity profitability maps (or profitability analysis) analysed by different cost objects is illustrated in Figure 6.2. This approach categorizes costs according to the causes of their variability at different hierarchical levels. Hierarchies identify the lowest level to which cost can meaningfully be assigned without relying on arbitrary allocations. In Figure 6.2 the lowest hierarchical levels (shown at the top of the diagram) are product, customer and facility contributions and, ignoring the business unit level the highest levels (shown at the bottom of the diagram) are product lines, distribution channels and country profits.

Let us initially focus on products as the cost object. Look at the column for products as the cost object in Figure 6.2. You will see that a unit-level contribution margin is calculated for each *individual* product. This is derived by deducting the cost of unit-level activities from sales revenues. From this unit-level contribution expenses relating to batch-related activities are deducted. Next the cost of product-sustaining activities is deducted. Thus, three different contribution levels are reported at the *individual* product level. Differentiating contributions at these levels provides a better understanding of the implications of product-mix and discontinuation decisions in terms of cost and profit behaviour.

In Figure 6.2 there are two further levels within the product hierarchy. They are the product brand level and the product line level. Some organizations do not market their products by brands and therefore have only one further level within the product hierarchy. A product line consists of a group of similar products. For example, banks have product lines such as savings accounts, lending services, currency services, insurance services and brokering services. Each product line contains individual product variants. The savings product line would include low balance/low interest savings accounts, high balance/high interest accounts, postal savings accounts and other product variants. The lending services product line would include personal loans, house mortgage loans, business loans and other product variants within the product line.

Some organizations market groupings of products within their product lines as separate brands. A typical example of the difference between product brands and product lines is Procter and Gamble who market some of their products within their detergent product line under the Tide label and others without this label.

Where products are marketed by brands, all expenditure relating to a brand, such as management and brand marketing, is for the benefit of all products within the brand and not for any specific individual product. Therefore, such **brand-sustaining expenses** should be attributed to the brand and not to individual products within the brand.

The same reasoning can be applied to the next level in the hierarchy. For example, marketing, research and development and distribution expenses might be incurred for the benefit of the whole product line and not for any specific brands or products within the line. Therefore these **product line-sustaining expenses** should be attributed to the product line but no attempt should be made to allocate them to individual products or brands. Finally, the profit for the organizational unit as a whole can be determined by deducting facility-sustaining expenses from the sum of the individual product line contributions.

A similar approach to the one described above for products can also be applied to other cost objects. The two final columns shown in Figure 6.2 illustrate how the approach can be applied to customers and locations. The aim of ABC hierarchical profitability analysis is to assign all organizational expenses to a particular hierarchical or organizational level where cause-and-effect cost assignments can be established so that arbitrary allocations are non-existent. The hierarchical approach helps to identify the impact on resource consumption by adding or dropping items at each level of the hierarchy. For example, if a brand is dropped activities at the brand level and below (i.e. above the brand profits row in Figure 6.2) which are uniquely associated with the brand will be affected, but higher level activities (i.e. at the product line level) will be unaffected. Similarly, if a product within a particular brand is dropped then all unit, batch and product-sustaining activities uniquely associated with that product will be affected but higher level brand and product-level activities will be unaffected.

Resource consumption models

The third, and possibly the most important theoretical advance in ABC systems was reported by Cooper and Kaplan (1992) in a paper which emphasized that ABC systems are **models of resource consumption**. The paper showed how ABC systems measure the cost of using resources and not the cost of supplying resources and highlighted the critical role played by unused capacity. To have a good conceptual grasp of ABC it is essential that you understand the content of this section.

FIGURE 6.2 *An illustration of hierarchical profitability analysis*

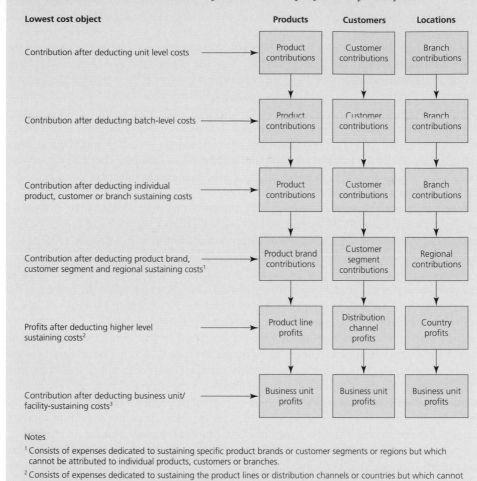

Notes

[1] Consists of expenses dedicated to sustaining specific product brands or customer segments or regions but which cannot be attributed to individual products, customers or branches.

[2] Consists of expenses dedicated to sustaining the product lines or distribution channels or countries but which cannot be attributed to lower items within the hierarchy.

[3] Consists of expenses dedicated to the business as a whole and not attributable to any lower items within the hierarchy.

Kaplan (1994) used the following equation to formalize the relationship between activity resources supplied and activity resources used for each activity:

$$\text{Cost of resources supplied} = \text{Cost of resources used} + \text{Cost of unused capacity} \tag{6.1}$$

To illustrate the application of the above formula we shall use Example 6.2. The left-hand side of the above equation indicates that the amount of expenditure on an activity depends on the cost of resources supplied rather than the cost of resources used. Example 6.2 contains data relating to the processing of purchase orders activity in which the equivalent of ten full-time staff are committed to the activity. You will see that the estimated annual cost is £300 000. This represents the **cost of resources supplied**. This expenditure provides the capacity to process 15 000 purchase orders (i.e. the quantity of resources supplied of the cost driver) per annum. Therefore the estimated cost of processing each purchase order is £20 (£300 000/15 000 orders that can be processed).

EXAMPLE 6.2

The following information relates to the purchasing activity in a division of the Etna Company for the next year:

(1) Resources supplied

10 full-time staff at £30 000 per year (including employment costs)	= £300 000 annual activity cost
Cost driver	= Number of purchase orders processed

Quantity of cost driver supplied per year:

(Each member of staff can process 1500 orders per year)	= 15 000 purchase orders
Estimated cost driver rate	= £20 per purchase order (£300 000/15 000 orders)

(2) Resources used

Estimated number of purchase orders to be processed during the year	= 13 000
Estimated cost of resources used assigned to parts and materials	= £260 000 (13 000 × £20)

(3) Cost of unused capacity

Resources supplied (15 000) – Resources used (13 000) at £20 per order	= £40 000 (2000 × £20)

During any particular period the number of orders processed will vary. In Example 6.2 it is assumed that the Etna Company expects to process 13 000 purchase orders (i.e. the quantity of resources used). The ABC system will therefore assign £260 000 (13 000 orders at £20 per order) to the parts and materials ordered during the year. This represents the **cost of resources used**.

The **cost of unused capacity** represents the difference between the cost of resources supplied and the cost of resources used. Resources have been acquired to enable 15 000 purchase orders to be processed but during the year only 13 000 orders will be processed giving an unused capacity of 2000 purchase orders. Hence the predicted cost of the unused capacity will be £40 000 (2000 orders at £20 per order).

Unused capacity arises because the supply of some resources has to be acquired in discrete amounts in advance of usage such that the supply cannot be continually adjusted in the short run to match exactly the usage of resources. Typical expenses in this category include the acquisition of equipment or the employment of non-piecework employees. The expenses of supplying these resources are incurred independently of usage in the short run and this independence has led to them being categorized as fixed costs. Kaplan and Cooper (1998) describe such resources as **committed resources**. In contrast, there are other types of resources whose supply can be continually adjusted to match exactly the usage of resources. For example, materials, casual labour and the supply of energy for running machinery can be continually adjusted to match the exact demand. Thus the cost of supplying these resources will generally equal the cost of resources used and the resources will have no unused capacity. Kaplan and Cooper classify these resources as **'flexible resources'** although they have traditionally been categorized as variable costs.

The problem of adjusting the supply of resources to match the usage of resources and eliminating unused capacity therefore applies only to committed resources. Where the cost of supplying resources in the short run is fixed, the quantity used will fluctuate each period based on the activities performed for the output produced. Activity-based systems measure the cost of *using* these resources, even though the cost of supplying them will not vary with short-run usage.

Managers make decisions (for example, changes in output volume and mix, process changes and improvements and changes in product and process design) that result in changes in activity resource usage. Assuming that such decisions result in a decline in the demand for activity resources then the first term on the right-hand side of equation 6.1 will decline (the cost of resources used) but the cost of unused capacity (the second term on the right-hand side of the equation) will increase to offset exactly the lower resource usage cost. To translate the benefits of reduced activity demands into cash flow savings management action is required. They must permanently remove the unused capacity by reducing spending on the supply of the resources. Thus to make a resource variable in the downward direction requires two management decisions: first to reduce the demand for the resource and, second, to lower the spending on the resource.

Demands for activity resources can also increase because of decisions to introduce new products, expand output and create greater product variety. Such decisions can lead to situations where activity resource usage exceeds the supply of resources. In the short term the excess demand might be absorbed by people working longer or faster or delaying production. Eventually, however, additional spending will be required to increase the supply of activity resources. Thus, even if permanent changes in activity resource consumption occur that result in either unused or excess capacity there may be a significant time lag before the supply of activity resources is adjusted to match the revised predicted activity usage. Indeed, there is always a danger that managers may not act to reduce the spending on the supply of resources to match a reduction in demand. They may keep existing resources in place even when there has been a substantial decline in demands for the activities consuming the resources. Consequently, there will be no benefits arising from actions to reduce activity usage. However, if decisions are made based on reported ABC costs it is implicitly assumed that predicted changes in activity resource usage will be translated into equivalent cash flow changes for the resources supplied.

A major feature of ABC systems is therefore that reported product, service or customer costs represent estimates of the cost of resources used. In a period, many decisions are made that affect the usage of resources. It is not feasible to link the required changes in the supply of resources with the change in usage predicted by each *individual* decision. The periodic reporting of both the predicted quantity and the cost of unused capacity for each activity signals the need for management to investigate the potential for reducing the activity resources supplied. In the case of flexible resources cash flow changes will soon follow decisions to reduce activity usage, such as dropping a product, but for committed resources performing one less set-up, ordering one less batch of materials or undertaking one fewer engineering change notice will not result in an automatic reduction in spending. It will create additional capacity and changes in spending on the supply of resources will often be the outcome of the totality of many decisions rather than focusing on a one-off product decision. Such ideas are considered to be of such vital importance by Kaplan and Cooper that they conclude that managing used and unused capacity is the central focus of ABC.

Cost versus benefit considerations

In the previous chapter it was pointed out that the design of a cost system should be based on cost versus benefit considerations. A sophisticated ABC system should generate the most accurate product costs. However, the cost of implementing and operating an ABC system is significantly more expensive than operating a direct costing or a traditional costing system. The partial costs reported by direct costing systems, and the distorted costs reported by traditional systems, may result in significant mistakes in decisions (such as selling unprofitable products or dropping profitable products) arising from the use of this information. If the cost of errors arising from using partial or distorted information generated from using these systems exceeds the additional costs of implementing and operating an ABC system then an ABC system ought to be implemented. In other words ABC must meet the cost/benefit criterion and improvements should be made in the level of sophistication of the costing system up to the point where the marginal cost of improvement equals the marginal benefit from improvement.

The optimal costing system is different for different organizations. A simplistic traditional costing system may report reasonably accurate product costs in organizations that have the following characteristics:

1   low levels of competition;

2   non-volume related indirect costs that are a low proportion of total indirect costs;

3   a fairly standardized product range all consuming organizational resources in similar proportions (i.e. low product diversity).

In contrast, a sophisticated ABC system may be optimal for organizations having following characteristics:

1   intensive competition;

2   non-volume related indirect costs that are a high proportion of total indirect costs;

3   a diverse range of products, all consuming organizational resources in significantly different proportions (i.e. high product diversity).

Single product firms and multiple-product firms that have entire facilities dedicated to the production of a single product have few problems with costing accuracy. With the former all costs will be directly attributable to the single product and with the latter only the costs of central facilities, such as central headquarter costs, will be indirect. All of the costs of the dedicated facilities will be directly attributable to products and therefore indirect costs will be a low proportion of total costs.

In Chapter 15 the major features of a just in time (JIT) manufacturing system will be described and we shall also look at how JIT affects management accounting. At this stage, however, you should note that JIT manufacturing systems result in the establishment of production cells that are dedicated to the manufacturing of a single product or a family of similar products. With JIT firms many of the support activities can be directly traced to the product dedicated cells. Thus, a high proportion of costs can be directly assigned to products. We can conclude that the benefits from implementing ABC product costing will be lower for single products or firms that have product dedicated facilities.

Periodic review of an ABC data base

The detailed tracking of costs is unnecessary when ABC information is used for decision-making. A data base should be maintained that is reviewed periodically, say once or twice a year. In addition periodic cost and profitability audits (similar to that illustrated in Figure 6.2) should be undertaken to provide a strategic review of the costs and profitability of a firm's products, customers and sales outlets. The data base and periodic cost and profitability review can be based on either past or future costs. Early adopters, and firms starting off with ABC initially analysed past costs. Besides being historical the disadvantage of this approach is that actual cost driver usage is used as the denominator level to calculate the cost driver rates. Thus cost driver rates and product costs will include the cost of unused capacity. Hence the cost of unused capacity for each activity is not highlighted for management attention. Nevertheless, the information provided for the first time an insight into the resources consumed by products and customers and their profitability based on measuring the resource usage rather than arbitrary allocations.

However, rather than focusing on the past it is preferable to concentrate on the future profitability of products and customers using estimated activity-based costs. It is therefore recommended that an activity-cost database is maintained at estimated standard costs that are updated on an annual or semi-annual basis.

ABC in service organizations

Kaplan and Cooper (1998) suggest that service companies are ideal candidates for ABC, even more than manufacturing companies. Their justification for this statement is that most of the costs in service organizations are indirect. In contrast, manufacturing companies can trace important components (such as direct materials and direct labour) of costs to individual products. Therefore indirect costs are likely to be a much smaller proportion of total costs. Service organizations must also supply most of their resources in advance, and fluctuation in the usage of activity resources by individual services and customers does not influence short-term spending to supply the resources. Such costs are treated by traditional costing systems as fixed and irrelevant for most decisions. This resulted in a situation where profitability analysis was not considered helpful for decision-making. Furthermore, until recently many service organizations were either government owned monopolies or operated in a highly regulated, protected and non-competitive environment. These organizations were not subject to any great pressures to improve profitability by identifying and eliminating non-profit making activities. Cost increases could also be absorbed by increasing the prices of services to customers. Little attention was therefore given to developing cost systems that accurately measured the costs and profitability of individual services.

Privatization of government-owned monopolies, deregulation, intensive competition and an expanding product range created the need for service organizations to develop management accounting systems that enabled them to understand their cost base and determine the sources of profitability for their products/services, customers and markets. Many service organizations have therefore only recently implemented management accounting systems. They have had the advantage of not having to meet some of the constraints imposed on manufacturing organizations, such as having to meet financial accounting stock valuation requirements or the reluctance to scrap or change existing cost systems that might have become embedded in organizations. Furthermore, service organizations have been implementing new costing systems at the same time as the deficiencies of traditional systems were being widely publicized. Also new insights were beginning to emerge on how cost systems could be viewed as resource consumption models which could be used to make decisions on adjusting the spending on the supply of resources to match resource consumption.

A UK survey by Drury and Tayles (2000) suggests that service organizations are more likely to implement ABC systems. They reported that 51% of the financial and service organizations surveyed, compared with 15% of manufacturing organizations, had implemented ABC. Kaplan and Cooper (1998) illustrate how ABC was applied in The Co-operative Bank,

ABC within a service organization

On face value, product costing at British Telecom (BT) should be both simple and uncontroversial. This is not so for two reasons:

- Most products share the use of the same network or support structure and costs do not vary with volume usage. This means that relatively few costs can be directly allocated to individual products and even apportionment poses practical problems.

- Different product costs are subject to different levels of competition. There are few natural markets in which prices can be established; therefore prices tend to be cost-based and subject to the approval of the regulator. BT's cost allocation processes must be open to detailed scrutiny to prove there is no unfair cross-subsidization between competitive and monopoly activities.

The fundamental principle underlying BT's methods, cost causation, states that costs should be apportioned on the basis of what caused them to be incurred. BT's cost apportionments use a variety of non-financial data taken from all parts of the business. For marketing and sales costs, traditional techniques would probably treat these costs as fixed or allocate them based on turnover. The BT approach is to analyse by activity and to seek a cost driver for each. In other words, ABC techniques are used to allocate costs to products via activity analysis.

There has been an increasing drive from the government to break up monopolies and introduce further privatization. This is likely to leave a general network provider who will provide a fixed-cost asset base used jointly by other parties. Problems of how to charge equitably for this usage are likely to result in an even greater pressure for accurate fixed cost analysis. One answer may be a more extended use of ABC techniques in the way that BT has adopted them.

Source: Bussey, B.A. (1993) ABC within a service organization, *Management Accounting (UK)*, pp. 40–41, 65.

a medium sized UK bank. ABC was used for product and customer profitability analysis. The following are some of the activities and cost drivers that were identified:

Activity	Cost driver
Provide ATM services	Number of ATM transactions
Clear debit items	Number of debits processed
Clear credit items	Number of credits processed
Issue chequebooks	Number of chequebooks issued
Computer processing	Number of computer transactions
Prepare statements of account transactions	Number of statements issued
Administer mortgages	Number of mortgages maintained

Activity costs were allocated to the different savings and loans products based on their demand for the activities using the cost drivers as a measure of resource consumption. Some expenses, such as finance and human resource management, were not assigned to products because they were considered to be for the benefit of the organization as a whole and not attributable to individual products. These business sustaining costs represented approximately 15% of total operating expenses. Profitability analysis was extended to customer segments within product groups. The study revealed that approximately half of the current accounts, particularly those with low balances and high transactions, were unprofitable. By identifying the profitable customer segments the marketing function was able to direct its effort to attracting more new customers, and enhancing relationships with those existing customers, whose behaviour would be profitable to the bank.

ABC cost management applications

Our aim in this chapter has been to look at how ABC can be used to provide information for decision-making by more accurately assigning costs to cost objects, such as products, customers and locations. In addition, ABC can be used for a range of cost management applications. They include cost reduction, activity-based budgeting, performance measurement, benchmarking of activities, process management and business process re-engineering. Figure 6.3 illustrates the product costing and cost management applications of ABC. The vertical box relates to product costing where costs are first assigned to activities and then to cost objects. The horizontal box relates to cost management. Here a process approach is adopted and costs are assigned to activities which then represent the basis for cost management applications. Thus, ABC can be adopted for both product costing and cost management or applied only to product costing or cost management. If ABC is only applied to cost management the second stage of assigning costs from activities to cost objects is omitted.

The decision to implement ABC should not, therefore, be based only on its ability to produce more accurate and relevant decision-making information. Indeed, surveys by Innes and Mitchell (1995a) and Innes *et al.* (2000) on ABC applications suggests that the cost management applications tend to outweigh the product costing applications which were central to ABC's initial development. We shall examine ABC applications to cost management in Chapter 15.

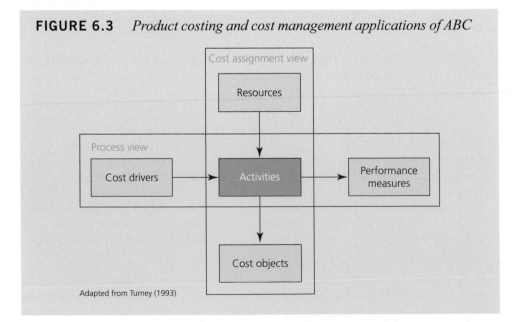

FIGURE 6.3   *Product costing and cost management applications of ABC*

Adapted from Turney (1993)

Summary

The following items relate to the learning objectives listed at the beginning of the chapter.

- **Explain why a cost accumulation system is required for generating relevant cost information for decision-making.**

  There are three main reasons why a cost accumulation system is required for generating relevant cost information. First, many indirect costs are relevant for decision-making and a costing system is therefore required that provides an estimate of resources consumed by cost objects using cause-and-effect allocations to allocate indirect costs. Second, an attention-directing information system is required that periodically identifies those potentially unprofitable products that require more detailed special studies. Third, many product decisions are not independent and to capture product interdependencies those joint resources that fluctuate in the longer term according to the demand for them should be assigned to products.

- **Describe the differences between activity-based and traditional costing systems.**

  The major differences relate to the two-stage allocation process. In the first-stage, traditional systems allocate indirect costs to cost centres (normally departments) whereas activity-based systems allocate indirect costs to cost centres based on activities rather than departments. Since there are many more activities than departments a distinguishing feature is that activity-based systems will have a greater number of cost centres in the first stage of the allocation process. In the second stage, traditional systems use a limited number of different types of second stage volume-based allocation bases (cost drivers) whereas activity-based systems use many different types of volume-based and non-volume-based cause-and-effect second stage drivers.

- **Explain why traditional costing systems can provide misleading information for decision-making.**

  Traditional systems often tend to rely on arbitrary allocations of indirect costs. In particular, they rely extensively on volume-based allocations. Many indirect costs are not volume-based but, if volume-based allocation bases are used, high volume products are likely to be assigned with a greater proportion of indirect costs than they have consumed whereas low volume products will be assigned a lower proportion. In these circumstances traditional systems will overcost high volume products and undercost low volume products. In contrast, ABC systems recognize that many indirect costs vary in proportion to changes other than production volume. By identifying the cost drivers that cause the costs to change and assigning costs to cost objects on the basis of cost driver usage, costs can be more accurately traced. It is claimed that this cause-and-effect relationship provides a superior way of determining relevant costs.

- **Compute product costs using an activity-based costing system.**

  The computation of product costs was illustrated in Exhibit 6.1 using data derived from Exhibit 5.1 in the previous chapter.

- **Identify and explain each of the four stages involved in designing ABC systems.**

  The design of ABC systems involves the following four stages: (a) identify the major activities that take place in the organization; (b) create a cost centre/cost pool for each activity; (c) determine the cost driver for each major activity; and (d) trace the cost of activities to the product according to a product's demand (using cost drivers as a measure of demand) for activities.

EXHIBIT 6.2

*Surveys of
company practice*

Significant variations in the usage of ABC both within the same country and across different countries have been reported. These differences may arise from the difficulty in precisely defining the difference between traditional costing systems and ABC systems and the specific time period when the surveys were actually undertaken.

Survey evidence suggests that over the last decade there has been an increasing interest in ABC. In the UK, surveys in the early 1990s reported adoption rates around 10% (Innes and Mitchell, 1991; Nicholls, 1992; Drury *et al.*, 1993). Similar adoption rates of 10% were found in Ireland (Clarke, 1992) and 14% in Canada (Armitage and Nicholson, 1993). In the USA Green and Amenkhienan (1992) claimed that 45% of firms used ABC to some extent. More recent surveys suggest higher ABC adoption rates. In the UK reported usage was 18% (Innes *et al.*, 2000), 22% (Banerjee and Kane, 1996), 21% (Evans and Ashworth, 1996) and 23% (Drury and Tayles, 2000). In the USA Shim and Stagliano (1997) reported a usage rate of 27%.

Reported usage rates for mainland Europe are 19% in Belgium (Bruggeman *et al.*, 1996) and 6% in Finland in 1992, 11% in 1993 and 24% in 1995 (Virtanen *et al.*, 1996). Low usage rates have been reported in Denmark (Israelsen *et al.*, 1996), Sweden (Ask *et al.*, 1996) and Germany (Scherrer, 1996). Activity-based techniques do not appear to have been adopted in Greece (Ballas and Venieris, 1996), Italy (Barbato *et al.*, 1996) or Spain (Saez-Torrecilla *et al.*, 1996).

Other studies have examined the applications of ABC. Innes and Mitchell (1995a) and Innes *et al.* (2000) found that cost reduction was the most widely used application. Other widely used applications included product/service pricing, cost modelling and performance measurement/improvement. ABC was used for stock valuation by 29% of ABC adopters thus suggesting that the majority of ABC users have separate systems for stock valuation and management accounting applications.

According to Bjornenak (1997a) there has been little research on who adopts ABC and for what reasons. His survey indicated that 40% of the responding Norwegian companies had adopted ABC as an idea (i.e. they had implemented ABC or planned to do so). Different variables relating to cost structure, competition, existing cost systems, size and product diversity were tested as explanatory factors for the adoption of ABC but only cost structure and size were found to be statistically significant. The UK study by Drury and Tayles (2000) indicated that company size and business sector had a significant impact on ABC adoption rates. The adoption rates were 45% for the largest organizations and 51% for financial and service organizations. Although the ABC adopters used significantly more cost pools and cost drivers than the non-adopters, most adopters used fewer cost pools and drivers compared with what is recommended in the literature. Approximately 50% of the ABC adopters used less than 50 cost centres and less than 10 separate types of cost driver rates.

Friedman and Lyne (1995, 1999) used longitudinal case studies to study the factors influencing ABC success and failure in 12 UK companies. They observed that top management support was a significant factor influencing the success or failure of ABC systems. Implementation problems identified by the various studies included the amount of work in setting up the system and data collection, difficulties in identifying activities and selecting cost drivers, lack of resources and inadequate computer software. The benefits reported by the studies included more accurate cost information for product pricing, more accurate profitability analysis, improved cost control and a better understanding of cost causation.

Studies in the USA by Shields (1995) and McGowan and Klammer (1997) indicated that ABC success was linked to six behavioural and organizational variables. They were top management support; integration with competitive strategy initiatives (e.g. total quality management and just in time); performance evaluation and compensation; non-accounting ownership of the ABC project; training provided in designing, implementing and using ABC; and the provision of adequate resourcing. Technical characteristics of the systems had no influence.

● **Describe the ABC cost hierarchy.**

ABC systems classify activities along a cost hierarchy consisting of unit-level, batch-level, product-sustaining and facility-sustaining activities. Unit-level activities are performed each time a unit of the product or service is produced. Examples include direct labour and energy costs. Batch-level activities are performed each time a batch is produced. Examples include setting up a machine or processing a purchase order. Product-sustaining activities are performed to enable the production and sale of individual products. Examples include the technical support provided for individual products and the resources required performing product enhancements. Facility-sustaining activities are performed to support the facility's general manufacturing process. They include general administrative staff and property support costs.

● **Describe the ABC profitability analysis hierarchy.**

The ABC profitability analysis hierarchy categorizes costs according to their variability at different hierarchical levels to report different hierarchical contribution levels. At the final level, facility or business-sustaining costs are deducted from the sum of the product contributions to derive a profit at the business unit level. In other words, facility/business sustaining costs are not allocated to individual products. The aim of hierarchical profitability analysis is to assign all organizational expenses to a particular hierarchical or organizational level where cause-and-effect cost assignments can be established so that arbitrary apportionments are non-existent.

● **Describe the ABC resource consumption model.**

ABC systems are models of resource consumption. They measure the cost of using resources and not the cost of supplying resources. The difference between the cost of resources supplied and the cost of resources used represents the cost of unused capacity. The cost of unused capacity for each activity is the reporting mechanism for identifying the need to adjust the supply of resources to match the usage of resources. However, to translate the benefits of reduced activity demands into cash flow savings, management action is required to remove the unused capacity by reducing the spending on the supply of resources.

Key terms and concepts

activities (p. 144)

activity-based cost centres (p. 144)

activity cost drivers (p. 154)

activity cost pools (p. 144)

batch-related activities (p. 155)

brand-sustaining expenses (p. 157)

business-sustaining activities (p. 156)

committed resources (p. 159)

consumption ratios (p. 148)

cost drivers (p. 144)

cost of resources supplied (p. 158)

cost of resources used (p. 159)

cost of unused capacity (p. 159)

customer-sustaining activities (p. 156)

duration drivers (p. 154)

facility-sustaining activities (p. 156)

flexible resources (p. 159)

models of resource consumption (p. 157)

non-volume-based cost drivers (p. 147)

product line-sustaining activities (p. 157)

product-sustaining activities (p. 155)

resource cost drivers (p. 154)

service-sustaining activities (p. 155)

transaction drivers (p. 154)

unit-level activities (p. 155)

volume-based cost drivers (p. 146)

Review questions

6.1 Explain why a cost accumulation system is required for generating relevant cost information for decision-making. (*pp. 142–43*)

6.2 Describe the three different types of cost systems that can be used to assign costs to cost objects. (*p. 144*)

6.3 What are the fundamental differences between a traditional and an ABC system? (*pp. 144–46*)

6.4 Define activities and cost drivers. (*p. 144*)

6.5 What factors led to the emergence of ABC systems? (*p. 146*)

6.6 Distinguish between volume-based and non-volume-based cost drivers. (*pp. 146–47*)

6.7 Describe the circumstances when traditional costing systems are likely to report distorted costs. (*p. 160–61*)

6.8 Explain how low volume products can be undercosted and high volume products overcosted when traditional costing systems are used. (*pp. 147–49*)

6.9 What is meant by 'product diversity' and why is it important for product costing? (*p. 147*)

6.10 Describe each of the four stages involved in designing ABC systems. (*pp. 152–55*)

6.11 Distinguish between resource cost drivers and activity cost drivers. (*p. 154*)

6.12 Distinguish between transaction and duration cost drivers. (*p. 154*)

6.13 Describe the ABC manufacturing cost hierarchy. (*p. 155–56*)

6.14 Describe the ABC profitability analysis hierarchy. (*pp. 156-57*)

6.15 What is an ABC resource consumption model? (*pp. 157–60*)

6.16 Distinguish between the cost of resources supplied, the cost of resources used and the cost of unused capacity. (*pp. 158–59*)

6.17 Explain the circumstances when ABC is likely to be preferred to traditional costing systems. (*p. 161*)

6.18 Provide examples of how ABC can be used in service organizations. (*pp. 162–64*)

Review problems

6.19 S Ltd manufactures components for the aircraft industry. The following annual information regarding three of its key customers is available:

	W	X	Y
Gross margin	£1 100 000	£1 750 000	£1 200 000
General administration costs	£40 000	£80 000	£30 000
Units sold	1 750	2 000	1 500
Orders placed	1 000	1 000	1 500
Sales visits	110	100	170
Invoices raised	900	1 200	1 500

The company uses an activity-based costing system and the analysis of customer-related costs is as follows:

Sales visits	£500 per visit
Order processing	£100 per order placed
Despatch costs	£100 per order placed
Billing and collections	£175 per invoice raised

Using customer profitability analysis, the ranking of the customers would be:

	W	X	Y
A	1st	2nd	3rd
B	1st	3rd	2nd
C	2nd	1st	3rd
D	2nd	3rd	1st
E	3rd	2nd	1st

(4 marks)

6.20 DRP Limited has recently introduced an Activity-Based Costing system. It manufactures three products, details of which are set out below:

	Product D	Product R	Product P
Budgeted annual production (units)	100 000	100 000	50 000
Batch size (units)	100	50	25
Machine set-ups per batch	3	4	6
Purchase orders per batch	2	1	1
Processing time per unit (minutes)	2	3	3

Three cost pools have been identified. Their budgeted costs for the year ending 30 June 2003 are as follows:

Machine set-up costs	£150 000
Purchasing of materials	£70 000
Processing	£80 000

The budgeted machine set-up cost per unit of product R is nearest to

A   £0.52   B   £0.60   C   £6.52   D   £26.09

(3 marks)

6.21 *It is now fairly widely accepted that conventional cost accounting distorts management's view of business through unrepresentative overhead allocation and inappropriate product costing.*

This is because the traditional approach usually absorbs overhead costs across products and orders solely on the basis of the direct labour involved in their manufacture. And as direct labour as a proportion of total manufacturing cost continues to fall, this leads to more and more distortion and misrepresentation of the impact of particular products on total overhead costs.

(From an article in the *Financial Times*)

You are required to discuss the above and to suggest what approaches are being adopted by management accountants to overcome such criticism.

(15 marks)

6.22   Large service organizations, such as banks and hospitals, used to be noted for their lack of standard costing systems, and their relatively unsophisticated budgeting and control systems compared with large manufacturing organizations. But this is changing and many large service organizations are now revising their use of management accounting techniques.

Requirements:

(a) Explain which features of large-scale service organizations encourage the application of activity-based approaches to the analysis of cost information.

(6 marks)

(b) Explain which features of service organizations may create problems for the application of activity-based costing.

(4 marks)

(c) Explain the uses for activity-based cost information in service industries.

(4 marks)

(d) Many large service organizations were at one time state-owned, but have been privatized. Examples in some countries include electricity supply and telecommunications. They are often regulated. Similar systems of regulation of prices by an independent authority exist in many countries, and are designed to act as a surrogate for market competition in industries where it is difficult to ensure a genuinely competitive market.

Explain which aspects of cost information and systems in service organizations would particularly interest a regulator, and why these features would be of interest.

(6 marks)
(Total 20 marks)

6.23   **Advanced: Computation of product costs for traditional and ABC systems**

The following information provides details of the costs, volume and cost drivers for a particular period in respect of ABC plc, a hypothetical company:

	Product X	Product Y	Product Z	Total
1. Production and sales (units)	30 000	20 000	8 000	
2. Raw material usage (units)	5	5	11	
3. Direct material cost	£25	£20	£11	£1 238 000
4. Direct labour hours	$1\frac{1}{3}$	2	1	88 000
5. Machine hours	$1\frac{1}{3}$	1	2	76 000
6. Direct labour cost	8	£12	£6	
7. Number of production runs	3	7	20	30
8. Number of deliveries	9	3	20	32
9. Number of receipts $(2 \times 7)^a$	15	35	220	270
10. Number of production orders	15	10	25	50
11. Overhead costs:				
Set-up	30 000			
Machines	760 000			
Receiving	435 000			
Packing	250 000			
Engineering	373 000			
	£1 848 000			

^aThe company operates a just in time inventory policy, and receives each component once per production run.

In the past the company has allocated overheads to products on the basis of direct labour hours.

However, the majority of overheads are more closely related to machine hours than direct labour hours.

The company has recently redesigned its cost system by recovering overheads using two volume-related bases: machine hours and a materials handling overhead rate for recovering overheads of the receiving department. Both the current and the previous cost system reported low profit margins for product X, which is the company's highest-selling product. The management accountant has recently attended a conference on activity-based costing, and the overhead costs for the last period have been analysed by the major activities in order to compute activity-based costs.

From the above information you are required to:

(a) Compute the product costs using a traditional volume-related costing system based on the assumptions that:
  (i) all overheads are recovered on the basis of direct labour hours (i.e. the company's past product costing system);
  (ii) the overheads of the receiving department are recovered by a materials handling overhead rate and the remaining overheads are recovered using a machine hour rate (i.e. the company's current costing system).

(b) Compute product costs using an activity-based costing system.

(c) Briefly explain the differences between the product cost computations in (a) and (b).

6.24 **Preparation of conventional costing and ABC profit statements**

The following budgeted information relates to Brunti plc for the forthcoming period:

	Products		
	XYI (000)	YZT (000)	ABW (000)
Sales and production (units)	50	40	30
	(£)	(£)	(£)
Selling price (per unit)	45	95	73
Prime cost (per unit)	32	84	65
	Hours	Hours	Hours
Machine department (machine hours per unit)	2	5	4
Assembly department (direct labour hours per unit)	7	3	2

Overheads allocated and apportioned to production departments (including service cost centre costs) were to be recovered in product costs as follows:

Machine department at
£1.20 per machine hour
Assembly department at
£0.825 per direct labour hour

You ascertain that the above overheads could be re-analysed into 'cost pools' as follows:

Cost pool	£000	Cost driver	Quantity for the period
Machining services	357	Machine hours	420 000
Assembly services	318	Direct labour hours	530 000
Set-up costs	26	Set-ups	520
Order processing	156	Customer orders	32 000
Purchasing	84	Suppliers orders	11 200
	941		

You have also been provided with the following estimates for the period:

	Products		
	XYI	YZT	ABW
Number of set-ups	120	200	200
Customer orders	8000	8000	16 000
Suppliers' orders	3000	4000	4 200

Required:

(a) Prepare and present profit statements using:
   (i) conventional absorption costing;

(5 marks)

   (ii) activity-based costing;

(10 marks)

(b) Comment on why activity-based costing is considered to present a fairer valuation of the product cost per unit.

(5 marks)
(Total 20 marks)

Pricing decisions and profitability analysis

7 Accounting information is often an important input to pricing decisions. Organizations that sell products or services that are highly customized or differentiated from each other by special features, or who are market leaders, have some discretion in setting selling prices. In these organizations the pricing decision will be influenced by the cost of the product. The cost information that is accumulated and presented is therefore important for pricing decisions. In other organizations prices are set by overall market and supply forces and they have little influence over the selling prices of their products and services. Nevertheless, cost information is still of considerable importance in these organizations for determining the relative profitability of different products and services so that management can determine the target product mix to which its marketing effort should be directed.

In this chapter we shall focus on both of the above situations. We shall consider the role that accounting information plays in determining the selling price by a price-setting firm. Where prices are set by the market our emphasis will be on examining the cost information

LEARNING OBJECTIVES:

After studying this chapter, you should be able to:

- describe how the optimum output and selling price is determined using economic theory;
- explain the relevant cost information that should be presented in price setting firms for both short-term and long-term decisions;
- describe product and customer profitability analysis and the information that should be included for managing the product and customer mix;
- describe the target costing approach to pricing;
- describe the different cost-plus pricing methods for deriving selling prices;
- explain the limitations of cost-plus pricing;
- justify why cost-plus pricing is widely used;
- identify and describe the different pricing policies.

that is required for product-mix decisions. In particular, we shall focus on both product and customer profitability analysis.

The theoretical solution to pricing decisions is derived from economic theory, which explains how the optimal selling price is determined. A knowledge of economic theory provides a suitable framework for considering the cost information that is appropriate for pricing decisions. This chapter therefore begins with a description of economic theory.

Economic theory

The central feature of the economic model is the assumption that the firm will attempt to set the selling price at a level where profits are maximized. For **monopolistic/ imperfect competition** the model assumes that the lower the price, the larger will be the volume of sales.[1] This relationship is depicted in Figure 7.1, which is known as a demand curve.

Points A and B represent two of many possible price/quantity combinations. You will see that at a price P_a, the quantity demanded will be Q_a, while at the lower price of P_b the quantity demanded will increase to Q_b. The economist describes the sensitivity of demand to changes in price as the **price elasticity of demand**. Demand is elastic when there are substitutes for a product, or when customers do not value the product very highly; the result is that a small increase/decrease in price causes a large decrease/increase in the quantity demanded. Alternatively, demand is inelastic when customers place a high value on the product, or when no close substitutes exist; the result is that a small increase/decrease in price causes only a small decrease/increase in the quantity demanded (see Figure 7.2).

If you compare the two graphs in Figure 7.2, you will see that in (a) an increase in price from P_A to P_B results in only a small reduction in the quantity demanded, whereas in (b) the same increase in price results in a large reduction in the quantity demanded.

Establishing the optimum selling price

The precise quantification of the relationship between the selling price and the quantity demanded is very difficult in practice, but let us assume here that management has produced an estimate of the sales demand at various selling prices, as shown in Exhibit 7.1.

You will note that if the price is reduced from £40 to £38 the total revenue will increase by £18, and that each successive price reduction causes incremental or marginal revenue to increase by successively smaller amounts. This process eventually results in a decline in total revenue when the price per unit is reduced from £30 to £28.

To determine the optimum selling price (i.e. the price at which total profits are maximized), it is also necessary for management to estimate the total costs for each of the sales levels given in Exhibit 7.1; this cost information is set out in Exhibit 7.2.

The final stage is to calculate the profit for each sales level and select the most profitable price–volume combination. The profit calculations are obtained by combining the information given in Exhibits 7.1 and 7.2 (see Exhibit 7.3).

You can see from Exhibit 7.3 that profits are maximized at a selling price of £34 when 13 units are sold.

FIGURE 7.1   *A demand curve*

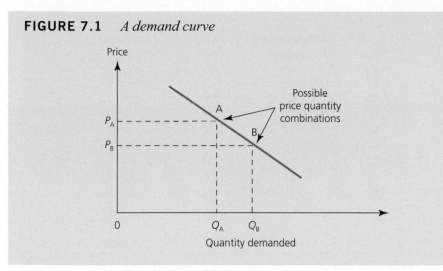

FIGURE 7.2   *Price elasticity of demand: (a) inelastic demand;
(b) elastic demand*

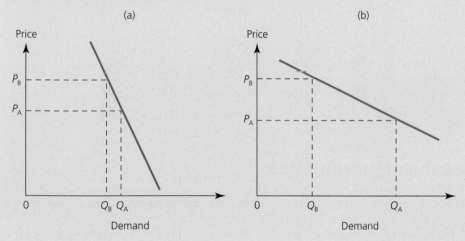

Price (£)	Unit of sales demand	Total revenue (£)	Marginal revenue (£)
40	10	400	
38	11	418	18
36	12	432	14
34	13	442	10
32	14	448	6
30	15	450	2
28	16	448	−2

EXHIBIT 7.1

Estimate of sales demand at different price levels

EXHIBIT 7.2				
Estimate of total costs at different volume levels	Price (£)	Demand and output	Total costs (£)	Marginal cost (£)
	40	10	360	
	38	11	364	4
	36	12	370	6
	34	13	378	8
	32	14	388	10
	30	15	400	12
	28	16	414	14

EXHIBIT 7.3					
Estimate of profits at different output levels	Price (£)	Units sold	Total revenue (£)	Total cost (£)	Profit (£)
	40	10	400	360	40
	38	11	418	364	54
	36	12	432	370	62
	34	13	442	378	64
	32	14	448	388	60
	30	15	450	400	50
	28	16	448	414	34

Graphical presentation

Economic theory would normally present the information contained in Exhibits 7.1 to 7.3 in graphical form as shown in Figure 7.3.

The shape of the graphs for the total revenue and the total cost lines is based on the explanations outlined in Chapter 3. If you refer to the top diagram in Figure 7.3, you will see that it indicates that the difference between total revenue and total cost increases as long as total revenue is climbing more rapidly than total cost. When total cost is climbing more rapidly than total revenue (i.e. unit marginal cost exceeds unit marginal revenue), a decision to increase the number of units sold will actually reduce the total profit. The difference between total cost and total revenue is the greatest at a volume level of 13 units; the price required to generate this demand is £34 and this is the optimum selling price.

The lower part of Figure 7.3 shows the cost and revenue information in terms of marginal revenue and marginal cost. Marginal revenue represents the increase in total revenue from the sale of one additional unit, and marginal cost represents the increase in total cost when output is increased by one additional unit. Note that the marginal revenue line slopes downwards to the right as demand increases, reflecting the fact that the slope of the total revenue line decreases as demand increases. Similarly, the marginal cost line slopes upwards because of the assumption that total cost increases as output increases.

Exhibit 7.1 and the demand/price curve in the lower part of Figure 7.3 indicates that to increase sales demand from 10 units to 11 units it is necessary to reduce the selling price

FIGURE 7.3 *Economist's model for establishing optimum price.*
MC, marginal cost; MR, marginal revenue; TC, total cost;
TR, total revenue

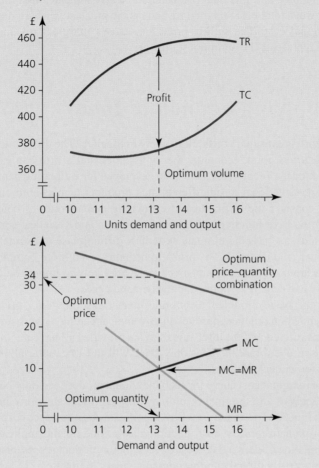

from £40 to £38. This increases total revenue from £400 to £418, the difference of £18 being the marginal revenue of the eleventh unit (shown in the graph as the height of the marginal revenue line at that point). The marginal revenues for the 12th, 13th and 14th units are £14, £10 and £6 respectively. The marginal cost is calculated by assessing the cost of one extra unit (or batch, etc.), and this information is presented in Exhibit 7.2. For example, the marginal cost is £4 for the eleventh unit and £6 for the twelfth unit. The marginal cost is plotted in Figure 7.3, and the optimum price is determined by the intersection of the marginal revenue and marginal cost curves; this is at a price of £34, when sales demand will be 13 units. Note that the intersection of the graphs occurs at a demand just in excess of 13 units. Clearly, we must work in whole units demanded, and therefore the optimal output is 13 units.

The demand curve is also included in the lower part of Figure 7.3, and to obtain the optimum price it is necessary to extend a vertical line upwards from the intersection of the marginal cost and marginal revenue curves. The point where this line cuts the demand curve provides us with the optimum selling price.

Note that if the vertical line at the point of intersection of the marginal cost and marginal revenue curve is extended further upwards into the top part of the graph, it will cut the total cost and the total revenue curves at the point where the difference between these two lines is the greatest. In other words, it cuts the total cost and total revenue curves at the points where the profits are maximized. The graphs in the lower and upper sections of Figure 7.3 are therefore related, and this dual presentation clearly indicates that the point where the difference between total cost and total revenue is the greatest is where marginal revenue is equal to marginal cost. The selling price that causes marginal revenue to be equal to marginal cost represents the optimum selling price.

Difficulties with applying economic theory

Economic theory is extremely difficult to apply in practice. The difficulties can be grouped into three categories. First, economic theory assumes that a firm can estimate a demand curve for its products. Techniques have been developed for estimating demand curves at the industry, or aggregate level for undifferentiated products such as automobiles, coffee and crude oil but consider the difficulties of estimating demand curves below the aggregate level. Most firms have hundreds of different products and varieties, some with complex interrelationships, and it is therefore an extremely difficult task to estimate demand curves at the individual product level. The problem becomes even more complex when competitive reactions are taken into account since these are likely to impact on the price/demand estimates that have been incorporated in the demand curve.

Secondly, the basic model of economic theory assumes only price influences the quantity demanded. In practice, product quality and packaging, advertising and promotion, the credit terms offered and the after-sales service provided all have an important influence on price. Thus a model that includes only price will fail to capture all of the factors that determine customer demand.

Thirdly, the marginal cost curve for each individual product can only be determined after considerable analysis and the final result may only represent an approximation of the true marginal cost function, particularly where significant joint product costs exist. However, whilst an approximation of the cost function may suffice for the application of economic theory the estimation of demand curves for each major product represents the major reason why many firms do not directly apply economic theory in practice.

Nevertheless, economic theory does provide useful insights and stresses the need for managers to think about price/demand relationships, even if the relationships cannot be precisely measured. For example, we shall see that many firms add a profit margin to a product's cost. If managers can identify products or customers where demand is inelastic they can add higher margins to a product's costs. Alternatively, where demand is elastic price changes are likely to be crucial and accurate cost measurement becomes vital. There is a danger where profit margins are reduced to minimal percentage figures that any undercosting of products may result in acceptance of unprofitable business whereas overcosting may result in the loss of profitable business to competitors.

The role of cost information in pricing decisions

Most organizations need to make decisions about setting or accepting selling prices for their products or services. In some firms prices are set by overall market supply and demand forces and the firm has little or no influence over the selling prices of its products or services. This situation is likely to occur where there are many firms in an industry and there is little to distinguish their products from each other. No one firm can influence prices significantly by its own actions. For example, in commodity markets such as wheat, coffee, rice and sugar prices are set for the market as a whole based on the forces of supply and demand. Also, small firms operating in an industry where prices are set by the dominant market leaders will have little influence over the price of their products or services. Firms that have little or no influence over the prices of their products or services are described as **price takers**.

In contrast firms selling products or services which are highly customized or differentiated from each other by special features, or who are market leaders, have some discretion in setting prices. Here the pricing decision will be influenced by the cost of the product, the actions of competitors and the extent to which customers value the product. We shall describe those firms that have some discretion over setting the selling price of their products or services as **price setters**. In practice, firms may be price setters for some of their products and price takers for others.

Where firms are price setters cost information is often an important input into the pricing decision. Cost information is also of vital importance to price takers in deciding on the output and mix of products and services to which their marketing effort should be directed, given their market prices. For both price takers and price setters the decision time horizon determines the cost information that is relevant for product pricing or output-mix decisions. We shall therefore consider the following four different situations:

1 a price setting firm facing short-run pricing decisions;
2 a price setting firm facing long-run pricing decisions;
3 a price taker firm facing short-run product-mix decisions;
4 a price taker firm facing long-run product-mix decisions.

A price setting firm facing short-run pricing decisions

Companies can encounter situations where they are faced with the opportunity of bidding for a one-time special order in competition with other suppliers. In this situation only the incremental costs of undertaking the order should be taken into account. It is likely that most of the resources required to fill the order will have already been acquired and the cost of these resources will be incurred whether or not the bid is accepted by the customer. Typically, the incremental costs are likely to consist of:

- extra materials that are required to fulfil the order;
- any extra part-time labour, overtime or other labour costs;
- the extra energy and maintenance costs for the machinery and equipment required to complete the order.

The incremental costs of one-off special orders in service companies are likely to be minimal. For example, the incremental cost of accepting one-off special business for a hotel may consist of only the cost of additional meals, laundering and bathroom facilities. In most cases, incremental costs are likely to be confined to items within unit-level activities. Resources for batch, product and service-sustaining activities are likely to have already been acquired and in most cases no extra costs on the supply of activities are likely to be incurred.

Bids should be made at prices that exceed incremental costs. Any excess of revenues over incremental costs will provide a contribution to committed fixed costs which would not otherwise have been obtained. Given the short-term nature of the decision long-term considerations are likely to be non-existent and, apart from the consideration of bids by competitors, cost data are likely to be the dominant factor in determining the bid price.

Any bid for one-time special orders that is based on covering only short-term incremental costs must meet all of the following conditions:

- Sufficient capacity is available for all resources that are required to fulfil the order. If some resources are fully utilized, opportunity costs (see Chapter 4 for an illustration) of the scarce resources must be covered by the bid price.

- The bid price will not affect the future selling prices and the customer will not expect repeat business to be priced to cover short-term incremental costs.

- The order will utilize unused capacity for only a short period and capacity will be released for use on more profitable opportunities. If more profitable opportunities do not exist and a short-term focus is always adopted to utilize unused capacity then the effect of pricing a series of special orders over several periods to cover incremental costs constitutes a long-term decision. Thus, the situation arises whereby the decision to reduce capacity is continually deferred and short-term incremental costs are used for long-term decisions.

A price setting firm facing long-run pricing decisions

In this section we shall focus on three approaches that are relevant to a price setting firm facing long-run pricing decisions. They are:

1 Pricing customized products
2 Pricing non-customized products
3 Target costing for pricing non-customized products.

Pricing customized products

In the long run firms can adjust the supply of virtually all of their activity resources. Therefore a product or service should be priced to cover all of the resources that are committed to it. If a firm is unable to generate sufficient revenues to cover the long-run costs of all its products, and its business sustaining costs, then it will make losses and will not be able to survive. Setting prices to cover all of the resources that are committed to each individual product (or service) requires a costing system that accurately measures resources consumed by each product. If inaccurate costs are used under-costing or overcosting will occur. In the former situation there is a danger that prices will be set that fail to cover the long-run resources committed to a product. Conversely, with the latter situation profitable business may be lost because overstated product costs have resulted in excessive prices being set that adversely affect sales volumes and revenues. Where firms are price setters there are stronger grounds for justifying the adoption of ABC systems.

The terms **full cost** or **long-run cost** are used to represent the sum of the cost of all those resources that are committed to a product in the long-term. The term is not precisely defined and may include or exclude facility/business sustaining costs. Let us now consider a full cost computation for a product pricing decision using an ABC system. You should now refer to the data presented in Example 7.1.

EXAMPLE 7.1

The Kalahari Company has received a request for a price quotation from one of its regular customers for an order of 500 units with the following characteristics:

Direct labour per unit produced	2 hours
Direct materials per unit produced	£22
Machine hours per unit produced	1 hour
Number of component and material purchases	6
Number of production runs for the components prior to assembly	4
Average set-up time per production run	3 hours
Number of deliveries	1
Number of customer visits	2
Engineering design and support	50 hours
Customer support	50 hours

Details of the activities required for the order are as follows:

Activity	Activity cost driver rate
Direct labour processing and assembly activities	£10 per labour hour
Machine processing	£30 per machine hour
Purchasing and receiving materials and components	£100 per purchase order
Scheduling production	£250 per production run
Setting-up machines	£120 per set-up hour
Packaging and delivering orders to customers	£400 per delivery
Invoicing and accounts administration	£120 per customer order
Marketing and order negotiation	£300 per customer visit
Customer support activities including after sales service	£50 per customer service hour
Engineering design and support	£80 per engineering hour

The estimate of the cost of the resources required to fulfil the order is as follows:

Unit-level expenses		
Direct materials (500 × £22)	11 000	
Direct labour (500 × 2 hours × £10)	10 000	
Machining (500 × 1 hour × £30)	15 000	36 000
Batch-level expenses		
Purchasing and receiving materials and components (6 × £100)	600	
Scheduling production (4 production runs × £250)	1 000	
Setting-up machines (4 production runs × 3 hours × £120)	1 440	
Packaging and delivering (1 delivery at £400)	400	3 440
Product-sustaining expenses		
Engineering design and support (50 hours × £80)		4 000
Customer-sustaining expenses		
Marketing and order negotiation (2 visits × £300 per visit)	600	
Customer support (50 support hours × £50)	2 500	3 100
Total cost of resources (excluding facility-sustaining costs)		46 540

The full cost (excluding facility-sustaining costs) of the order is £46 540. It was pointed out in the previous chapter that facility-sustaining costs are incurred to support the organization as a whole and not for individual products. Therefore they should not be allocated to products for most decisions. Any allocation will be arbitrary. However, such costs must be covered by sales revenues, and for pricing purposes their allocation can be justified as long as they are separately reported.

What allocation base should be used for facility-sustaining costs? The answer is a base that will influence behaviour that the organization wishes to encourage. For example, if the organization has adopted a strategy of standardizing and reducing the number of separate parts maintained it could choose the number of parts as the allocation base. Thus, the facility-sustaining costs allocated to a product would increase with the number of parts used for an order and product designers would be motivated to use standard parts.

To determine a proposed selling price an appropriate percentage mark-up is added to the estimated cost. In our example facility-sustaining costs have not been allocated to the order. Thus the mark-up that is added should be sufficient to cover a fair share of facility-sustaining costs and provide a profit contribution. Where facility-sustaining costs are allocated a smaller percentage mark-up would be added since the mark-up is required to provide only a profit contribution. Let us assume that the Kalahari Company adds a mark-up of 20%. This would result in a mark-up of £9308 (20% × £46 540) being added to the cost estimate of £46 540, giving a proposed selling price of £55 848. The approach that we have adopted here is called **cost-plus pricing**. We shall discuss cost-plus pricing and the factors influencing the determination of the profit mark-ups later in the chapter.

Note that the activity-based cost information provides a better understanding of cost behaviour. The batch, product and customer-sustaining costs are unrelated to quantity ordered whereas the unit-level costs are volume related. This provides useful information for salespersons in negotiations with the customer relating to the price and size of the order. Assume that the customer considers purchasing 3000 units, instead of the 500 units originally quoted. If the larger order will enable the company to order 3000 components, instead of 500, and each production run for a component processes 3000 units instead of 500, the batch-level expenses will remain unchanged. Also the cost of the product and customer-sustaining activities will be the same for the larger order but the cost of the unit-level activity resources required will increase by a factor of six because six times the amount of resources will be required for the larger order. Thus the cost of the resources used for an order of 3000 units will be:

	(£)
Unit-level expenses (6 × £36 000[a])	216 000
Batch-level expenses	3 440
Product-sustaining expenses	4 000
Customer-sustaining expenses	3 100
Total cost of resources (excluding facility-sustaining costs)	226 540

Note
[a]Unit-level expenses for an order of 500 units multiplied by a factor of 6.

The cost per unit for a 500 unit order size is £93.08 (£46 540/500) compared with £75.51 (£226 540/3000) for a 3000 unit order size and the resulting proposed unit selling prices are £111.70 (£93.08 × 120%) and £90.61 (£75.51 × 120%) respectively.

Pricing non-customized products

In Example 7.1 the Kalahari Company was faced with a pricing decision for the sale of a highly customized product to a single customer. The pricing decision would have been based on direct negotiations with the customer for a known quantity. In contrast, a market leader must make a pricing decision, normally for large and unknown volumes, of a single product that is sold to thousands of different customers. To apply cost-plus pricing in this situation an estimate is required of sales volume to determine a unit cost which will determine the cost-plus selling price. This circular process occurs because we are now faced with two unknowns which have a cause-and-effect relationship, namely selling price and sales volume. In this situation it is recommended that cost-plus selling prices are estimated for a range of potential sales volumes. Consider the information presented in Example 7.2 (Case A).

You will see that the Auckland Company has produced estimates of total costs for a range of activity levels. Ideally, the cost estimates should be built up in a manner similar to the activity-based cost estimates that were used by the Kalahari Company in Example 7.1. However, for brevity the cost build-up is not shown. Instead of adding a percentage profit margin the Auckland Company has added a fixed lump sum target profit contribution of £2 million.

The information presented indicates to management the sales volumes, and their accompanying selling prices, that are required to generate the required profit contribution. The unit cost calculation indicates the break-even selling price at each sales volume that is required to cover the cost of the resources committed at that particular volume. Management must assess the likelihood of selling the specified volumes at the designated prices and choose the price which they consider has the highest probability of generating at least the specified sales volume. If none of the sales volumes are likely to be achieved at the designated selling prices management must consider how demand can be stimulated and/or costs reduced to make the product viable. If neither of these, or other strategies, are successful the product should not be launched. The final decision must be based on management judgement and knowledge of the market.

The situation presented in Example 7.2 represents the most extreme example of the lack of market data for making a pricing decision. If we reconsider the pricing decision faced by the company it is likely that similar products are already marketed and information may be available relating to their market shares and sales volumes. Assuming that Auckland's product is differentiated from other similar products a relative comparison should be possible of its strengths and weaknesses and whether customers would be prepared to pay a price in excess of the prices of similar products. It is therefore possible that Auckland may be able to undertake market research to obtain rough approximations of demand levels at a range of potential selling prices. Let us assume that Auckland adopts this approach, and apart from this, the facts are the same as those given in Example 7.2 (Case A).

Now look at Case B in Example 7.2. The demand estimates are given for a range of selling prices. In addition the projected costs, sales revenues and profit contribution are shown. You can see that profits are maximized at a selling price of £80. The information also shows the effect of pursuing other pricing policies. For example, a lower selling price of £70 might be selected to discourage competition and ensure that a larger share of the market is obtained in the future. Where demand estimates are available ABC cost information should be presented for different potential volume levels and compared with projected sales revenues derived from estimated price/output relationships. Ideally, the cost projections should be based on a life-cycle costing approach to ensure that costs incurred over the whole of a product's life cycle are taken into account in the pricing decision. We shall look at life-cycle costing in Chapter 15.

EXAMPLE 7.2

Case A

The Auckland Company is launching a new product. Sales volume will be dependent on the selling price and customer acceptance but because the product differs substantially from other products within the same product category it has not been possible to obtain any meaningful estimates of price/demand relationships. The best estimate is that demand is likely to range between 100 000 and 200 000 units provided that the selling price is less than £100. Based on this information the company has produced the following cost estimates and selling prices required to generate a target profit contribution of £2 million from the product.

Sales volume (000s)	100	120	140	160	180	200
Total cost (£000s)	10 000	10 800	11 200	11 600	12 600	13 000
Required profit contribution (£000s)	2 000	2 000	2 000	2 000	2 000	2 000
Required sales revenues (£000s)	12 000	12 800	13 200	13 600	14 600	15 000
Required selling price to achieve target profit contribution (£)	120.00	106.67	94.29	85.00	81.11	75.00
Unit cost (£)	100.00	90.00	80.00	72.50	70.00	65.00

Case B

Assume now an alternative scenario for the product in Case A. The same cost schedule applies but the £2 million minimum contribution no longer applies. In addition, Auckland now undertakes market research. Based on this research, and comparisons with similar product types and their current selling prices and sales volumes, estimates of sales demand at different selling prices have been made. These estimates, together with the estimates of total costs obtained in Case A are shown below:

Potential selling price	£100	£90	£80	£70	£60
Estimated sales volume at the potential selling price (000s)	120	140	180	190	200
Estimated total sales revenue (£000s)	12 000	12 600	14 400	13 300	12 000
Estimated total cost (£000s)	10 800	11 200	12 600	12 800	13 000
Estimated profit (loss) contribution (£000s)	1 200	1 400	1 800	500	(1 000)

Pricing non-customized products using target costing

Instead of using cost-plus pricing approach described in Example 7.2 (Case A) whereby cost is used as the starting point to determine the selling price, **target costing** is the reverse of this process. With target costing the starting point is the determination of the target selling price. Next a standard or desired profit margin is deducted to get a target cost for the product. The aim is to ensure that the future cost will not be higher than the target cost. The stages involved in target costing can be summarized as follows:

Stage 1: determine the target price which customers will be prepared to pay for the product;

Stage 2: deduct a target profit margin from the target price to determine the target cost;

Stage 3: estimate the actual cost of the product;

Stage 4: if estimated actual cost exceeds the target cost investigate ways of driving down the actual cost to the target cost.

The first stage requires market research to determine the customers' perceived value of the product, its differentiation value relative to competing products and the price of competing products. The target profit margin depends on the planned return on investment for the organization as a whole and profit as a percentage of sales. This is then decomposed into a target profit for each product which is then deducted from the target price to give the target cost. The target cost is compared with the predicted actual cost. If the predicted actual cost is above the target cost intensive efforts are made to close the gap. Product designers focus on modifying the design of the product so that it becomes cheaper to produce. Manufacturing engineers also concentrate on methods of improving production processes and efficiencies.

The aim is to drive the predicted actual cost down to the target cost, but if the target cost cannot be achieved at the pre-production stage the product may still be launched if management are confident that the process of continuous improvement and learning curve effects will enable the target cost to be achieved early in the product's life. If this is not possible the product will not be launched.

The major attraction of target costing is that marketing factors and customer research provide the basis for determining selling price whereas cost tends to be the dominant factor with cost-plus pricing. A further attraction is that the approach requires the collaboration of product designers, production engineers, marketing and finance staff whose focus is on managing costs at the product design stage. At this stage costs can be most effectively managed because a decision to committing the firm to incur costs will not have been made.

Target costing is most suited for setting prices for non-customized and high sales volume products. It is also an important mechanism for managing the cost of future products. We shall therefore look at target costing in more detail when we focus on cost management in Chapter 15.

A price taker firm facing short-run product-mix decisions

Price-taking firms may be faced with opportunities of taking on short-term business at a market determined selling price. In this situation the cost information that is required is no different from that of a price setting firm making a short-run pricing decision. In other words, accepting short-term business where the incremental sales revenues exceed incremental short-run costs will provide a contribution towards committed fixed costs which would not otherwise have been obtained. However, such business is acceptable only if the same conditions as those specified for a price setting firm apply. You should remember that these conditions are:

- sufficient capacity is available for all resources that are required from undertaking the business (if some resources are fully utilized, opportunity costs of the scarce resources must be covered by the selling price);

● the company will not commit itself to repeat longer-term business that is priced to cover only short-term incremental costs;

● the order will utilize unused capacity for only a short period and capacity will be released for use on more profitable opportunities.

Besides considering new short-term opportunities organizations may, in certain situations, review their existing product-mix over a short-term time horizon. Consider a situation where a firm has excess capacity which is being retained for an expected upsurge in demand. If committed resources are to be maintained then the product profitability analysis of existing products should be based on a comparison of incremental revenues with short-term incremental costs. The same principle applies as that which applied for accepting new short-term business where spare capacity exists. That is, in the short term products should be retained if their incremental revenues exceed their incremental short-term costs.

Where short-term capacity constraints apply, such that the firm has profitable products whose sales demand exceeds its productive capacity, the product-mix should be based on maximizing contribution per limiting production factor as described in Chapter 4. You may wish to refer back to Example 4.2 for an illustration of this approach. Do note, however, that in the longer term capacity constraints can be removed.

A price taker firm facing long-run product-mix decisions

When prices are set by the market a firm has to decide which products to sell given their market prices. In the longer term a firm can adjust the supply of resources committed to a product. Therefore the sales revenue from a service or product should exceed the cost of all the resources that are committed to it. Hence there is a need to undertake periodic profitability analysis to distinguish between profitable and unprofitable products in order to ensure that only profitable products are sold. Activity-based profitability analysis should be used to evaluate each product's long-run profitability. In the previous chapter Figure 6.2 was used to illustrate ABC hierarchical profitability analysis. This diagram is repeated in the form of Figure 7.4. You will see that where products are the cost object four different hierarchical levels have been identified – the individual products, the product brand groupings, the product line and finally the whole business unit. At the individual product level all of the resources required for undertaking the unit, batch and product-sustaining activities that are associated with a product would no longer be required if that product were discontinued. Thus, if the product's sales revenues do not exceed the cost of the resources of these activities it should be subject to a special study for a discontinuation decision.

If product groups are marketed as separate brands the next level within the profitability hierarchy is brand profitability. The sum of the individual product profit contributions (that is, sales revenues less the cost of the unit, batch and product-sustaining activities) within a brand must be sufficient to cover those brand-sustaining expenses that can be attributed to the brand but not the individual products within the brand. Thus it is possible for each individual product within the product brand to generate positive contributions but for the brand grouping to be unprofitable because the brand-sustaining expenses exceed the sum of individual product contributions. In these circumstances a special study is required to consider alternative courses of action that can be undertaken to make the brand profitable.

FIGURE 7.4   *An illustration of hierarchical profitability analysis*

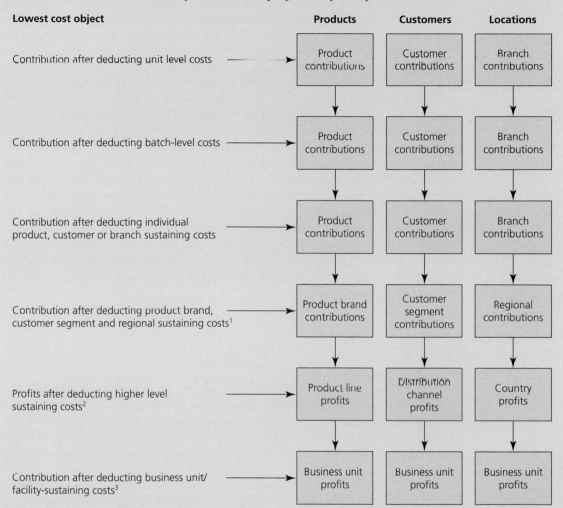

Notes

[1] Consists of expenses dedicated to sustaining specific product brands or customer segments or regions but which cannot be attributed to individual products, customers or branches.

[2] Consists of expenses dedicated to sustaining the product lines or distribution channels or countries but which cannot be attributed to lower items within the hierarchy.

[3] Consists of expenses dedicated to the business as a whole and not attributable to any lower items within the hierarchy.

Product line profitability is the next level in the hierarchy in Figure 7.4. The same principle applies. That is, if the product line consists of a number of separate groupings of branded and non-branded products the sum of their contributions (that is, sales revenues less the cost of the unit, batch, product-sustaining and brand-sustaining activities) should exceed those product-line sustaining expenses that are attributable to the product line as a whole but not the individual groupings of branded and non-branded products within the product line. Here a negative profit contribution would signal the need to undertake a major special study to investigate alternative courses of action relating to how the product line can be made profitable.

The final level in the profitability hierarchy shown in Figure 7.4 relates to the profitability of the business unit as a whole. Here the profit for the business unit can be determined by deducting the facility or business-sustaining expenses that are attributable to the business unit as a whole, but not to lower levels within the hierarchy, from the sum of the product line contributions. Clearly a business must generate profits in the long term if it is to survive.

Most of the decisions are likely to be made at the individual product level. Before discontinuing a product other alternatives or considerations must be taken into account at the special study stage. In some situations it is important to maintain a full product line for marketing reasons. For example, if customers are not offered a full product line to choose from they may migrate to competitors who offer a wider choice. By reporting individual product profitability the cost of maintaining a full product line, being the sum of unprofitable products within the product line, is highlighted. Where maintaining a full product line is not required managers should consider other options before dropping unprofitable products. They should consider re-engineering or redesigning the products to reduce their resource consumption.

The above discussion has concentrated on product profitability analysis. You will see from Figure 7.4 that the same principles can be applied to other cost objects, such as customers or locations. Increasing attention is now being given to customer profitability analysis. Given the importance of this topic we shall consider customer profitability analysis later in the chapter. However, at this stage it is more appropriate to examine cost-plus pricing in more detail.

Cost-plus pricing

Our earlier discussion relating to short-run and long-run pricing suggested that, where it was virtually impossible to estimate demand, cost-plus pricing should be used by a price-setter. Cost-plus pricing was illustrated using the data presented in Examples 7.1 and 7.2. We shall now look at cost-plus pricing in more detail. Companies use different cost bases and mark-ups to determine their selling prices. Consider the information presented below:

Cost base	(£)	Mark-up percentage	Cost-plus selling price (£)
(1) Direct variable costs	200	150	500
(2) Direct non-variable costs	100		
(3) Total direct costs	300	70	510
(4) Indirect costs	80		
(5) Total cost (excluding higher level sustaining costs)	380	40	532
(6) Higher level sustaining costs	60		
(7) Total cost	440	20	528

In the above illustration four different cost bases are used resulting in four different selling prices. In row (1) only direct variable costs are assigned to products for cost-plus pricing and a high percentage mark-up (150%) is added to cover direct non-variable costs, indirect costs and higher level sustaining costs and also to provide a contribution towards profit. Where products are the cost object higher level sustaining costs would include brand, product line and business-sustaining costs. This approach is best suited to short-term pricing decisions.

The second cost base is row (3). Here a smaller percentage margin (70%) is added to cover indirect costs, the higher level sustaining costs and to provide a contribution to profit.

Indirect costs are not therefore assigned to products for cost-plus pricing. This cost base is appropriate if indirect costs are a small percentage of an organization's total costs. The disadvantage of adopting this approach is that the consumption of joint resources by products is not measured. By adding a percentage mark-up to direct costs indirect costs are effectively allocated to products using direct costs as the allocation base. Hence, the approach implicitly uses arbitrary apportionments.

The third cost base is 'Total cost' (excluding higher level sustaining costs). With this base a lower profit margin (40%) is added to cover higher level sustaining costs and a profit contribution. This cost base is recommended for long-run pricing and was the approach illustrated in Examples 7.1 and 7.2. Ideally, ABC systems should be used to compute total (full) costs.

The final cost base is row (7) which includes an allocation of all costs but do remember that higher level sustaining costs cannot be allocated to products on a cause-and-effect basis. Some organizations, however, may wish to allocate all costs to products to ensure that all costs are covered in the cost base. The lowest percentage mark-up (20%) is therefore added since the aim is to provide only a profit contribution.

Some manufacturing organizations also use total manufacturing cost as the cost base and add a mark-up to cover non-manufacturing costs and a contribution to profit. The use of this method reflects the fact that many organizations choose to use the same costs as they use for stock valuation for other purposes, including product pricing. Also traditional costing systems are widely used for stock valuation. These systems were not designed to assign non-manufacturing costs to products. Therefore many organizations do not allocate non-manufacturing costs to products.

Establishing target mark-up percentages

Mark-ups are related to the demand for a product. A firm is able to command a higher mark-up for a product that has a high demand. Mark-ups are also influenced by the elasticity of demand with higher mark-ups being applicable to products which are subject to inelastic demand. Mark-ups are also likely to decrease when competition is intensive. Target mark-up percentages tend to vary from product line to product line to correspond with well-established differences in custom, competitive position and likely demand. For example, luxury goods with a low sales turnover may attract high profit margins whereas non-luxury goods with a high sales turnover may attract low profit margins.

Note that once the target selling price has been calculated, it is rarely adopted without amendment. The price is adjusted upwards or downwards depending on such factors as the future capacity that is available, the extent of competition from other firms, and management's general knowledge of the market. For example, if the price calculation is much lower than that which management considers the customer will be prepared to pay, the price may be increased.

We may ask ourselves the question 'Why should cost-based pricing formulae be used when the final price is likely to be altered by management?' The answer is that cost-based pricing formulae provide an initial approximation of the selling price. It is a target price and is important information, although by no means the only information that should be used when the final pricing decision is made. Management should use this information, together with their knowledge of the market and their intended pricing strategies, before the final price is set.

Limitations of cost-plus pricing

The main criticism that has been made against cost-plus pricing is that demand is ignored. The price is set by adding a mark-up to cost, and this may bear no relationship to the price-demand

The use of cost information in pricing decisions

The following comments were derived from interviews with UK management accountants relating to the use of cost information in pricing decisions:

If we're taking decisions about pricing, generally speaking we would be looking to the market-place to see where our products fit in the market place ..., costing would only be used to see what kind of profit margins we'd get from those prices. The costing system would not be the primary reason for making decisions. (A respondent from a price taking firm)

We have our estimating system, it produces the estimated costs for 1,000 boxes. ... And we then add the haulage cost which is based on where the customer happens to be ... And we then have margins. The system actually calculates a guestimated margin for you based on a number of factors: type of box, type of glue, type of business, etc., and it then says I think your margin should be 25.36%. You then sit there and say ... does that make sense in relation to all the other products that we sell to that customer or does it make sense in relation to another box very similar to that we sell to somebody else. It is initially a cost-plus price, but the percentage is very variable. (An illustration of the use of cost-plus pricing by a price setting firm)

We tend to do the costing with the historic mark-up to set the base price point and then really leave it to the salesmen to negotiate around that. Sometimes they'll get better, sometimes they won't get as much, but what we tend to do is give them a minimum price. We also tend to differentiate between certain of our market sectors. Dress club business, which is less sort of fashion or sporting oriented, we tend to put a lower margin rate on because we know the market will not take that sort of level. In some of the premium sports customers and certainly some of the premium brands that we work with we find that because some of their products have a high price we tend to put a high mark-up on. It's the play in the market to some extent we leave a lot to the sales director and his team to put the best they can on it. ... It gives a little bit of a guide between one market area and another knowing that they will inevitably get better prices in certain areas than in others. Sometimes there will be different prices for exactly the same product with different customers. (The use of cost-plus pricing by a price setting firm)

If we can't meet the retail price that is demanded by the marketing department we'd have to think again. You'd work it back down the other way to see to see how much you could do and then you'd use that product cost. You'd say that's what we were thinking of, if you go for a cheaper bottle, if you go for a cheaper carton, you don't put this in, you don't put that in then you can have what you want and you come to some sort of compromise half way through. (An illustration of simplistic target costing approach)

More and more, certainly with the larger customers it's what they're prepared to pay us. The market drives it. We do our estimate of what we estimate to get from it and all that does is to say that if we accept their price we're going to make a profit or loss. Then we'll look at the price they're prepared to give us. ... We'll look at our estimate and then we'll look at how we can reduce the costs. Then we may work with the customer to substitute materials. (A simplistic form of target costing used by a price taker)

Source: Brealey, J. A. (2005) The calculation of product costs and their use in decision-making in British Manufacturing Industry, PhD dissertation, University of Huddersfield.

relationship. It is assumed that prices should depend solely on costs. For example, a cost-plus formula may suggest a price of £20 for a product where the demand is 100 000 units, whereas at a price of £25 the demand might be 80 000 units. Assuming that the variable cost for each unit sold is £15, the total contribution will be £500 000 at a selling price of £20, compared with a total contribution of £800 000 at a selling price of £25. Thus cost-plus pricing formulae might lead to incorrect decisions. The following statement made over forty years ago by Baxter and Oxenfeldt (1961) highlights the major weakness of cost-plus pricing. They state:

> On the other hand, inability to estimate demand accurately scarcely excuses the substitution of cost information for demand information. Crude estimates of demand may serve instead of careful estimates of demand but cost gives remarkably little insight into demand.

It is often claimed that cost-based pricing formulae serve as a pricing 'floor' shielding the seller from a loss. This argument, however, is incorrect since it is quite possible for a firm to lose money even though every product is priced higher than the estimated unit cost. The reason for this is that if sales demand falls below the activity level that was used to calculate the fixed cost per unit, the total sales revenue may be insufficient to cover the total fixed costs. Cost-plus pricing will only ensure that all the costs will be met, and the target profits earned, if the sales volume is equal to, or more than, the activity level that was used to estimate total unit costs.

Consider a hypothetical situation where all of the costs attributable to a product are fixed in the short-term and amount to £1 million. Assume that the cost per unit is £100 derived from an estimated volume of 10 000 units. The selling price is set at £130 using the cost-plus method and a mark-up of 30%. If actual sales volume is 7000 units, sales revenues will be £910 000 compared with total costs of £1 million. Therefore the product will incur a loss of £90 000 even though it is priced above full cost.

Reasons for using cost-plus pricing

Considering the limitations of cost-plus pricing, why is it that these techniques are frequently used in practice? Baxter and Oxenfeldt (1961) suggest the following reasons:

> They offer a means by which plausible prices can be found with ease and speed, no matter how many products the firm handles. Moreover, its imposing computations look factual and precise, and its prices may well seem more defensible on moral grounds than prices established by other means. Thus a monopolist threatened by a public inquiry might reasonably feel that he is safeguarding his case by cost-plus pricing.

Another major reason for the widespread use of cost-plus pricing methods is that they may help a firm to predict the prices of other firms. For example, if a firm has been operating in an industry where average mark-ups have been 40% in the past, it may be possible to predict that competitors will be adding a 40% mark-up to their costs. Assuming that all the firms in the industry have similar cost structures, it will be possible to predict the price range within which competitors may price their products. If all the firms in an industry price their products in this way, it may encourage price stability.

In response to the main objection that cost-based pricing formulae ignore demand, we have noted that the actual price that is calculated by the formula is rarely adopted without amendments. The price is adjusted upwards or downwards after taking account of the number of sales orders on hand, the extent of competition from other firms, the importance of the customer in terms of future sales, and the policy relating to customer relations. Therefore it is argued that management attempts to adjust the mark-up based on the state of sales demand and other factors which are of vital importance in the pricing decision.

Pricing policies

Cost information is only one of many variables that must be considered in the pricing decision. The final price that is selected will depend upon the pricing policy of the company. A price-skimming or pricing penetration policy might be selected.

A **price-skimming policy** is an attempt to exploit those sections of the market that are relatively insensitive to price changes. For example, high initial prices may be charged to take advantage of the novelty appeal of a new product when demand is initially inelastic. A skimming pricing policy offers a safeguard against unexpected future increases in costs, or a large fall in demand after the novelty appeal has declined. Once the market becomes saturated, the price can be reduced to attract that part of the market that has not yet been exploited. A skimming pricing policy should not be adopted when a number of close substitutes are already being marketed. Here the demand curve is likely to be elastic, and any price in excess of that being charged for a substitute product by a competitor is likely to lead to a large reduction in sales.

A **penetration pricing policy** is based on the concept of charging low prices initially with the intention of gaining rapid acceptance of the product. Such a policy is appropriate when close substitutes are available or when the market is easy to enter. The low price discourages potential competitors from entering the market and enables a company to establish a large share of the market. This can be achieved more easily when the product is new, than later on when buying habits have become established.

Many products have a **product life cycle** consisting of four stages: introductory, growth, maturity and decline. At the introductory stage the product is launched and there is minimal awareness and acceptance of it. Sales begin to expand rapidly at the growth stage because of introductory promotions and greater customer awareness, but this begins to taper off at the maturity stage as potential new customers are exhausted. At the decline stage sales diminish as the product is gradually replaced with new and better versions.

Sizer (1989) suggests that in the introductory stage it may be appropriate to shade upwards or downwards the price found by normal analysis to create a more favourable demand in future years. For example, he suggests that limited production capacity may rule out low prices. Therefore a higher initial price than that suggested by normal analysis may be set and progressively reduced, if and when (a) price elasticity of demand increases or (b) additional capacity becomes available. Alternatively if there is no production capacity constraint, a lower price than that suggested by normal analysis may be preferred. Such a price may result in a higher sales volume and a slow competitive reaction, which will enable the company to establish a large market share and to earn higher profits in the long term.

At the maturity stage a firm will be less concerned with the future effects of current selling prices and should adopt a selling price that maximizes short-run profits.

Customer profitability analysis

In the past, management accounting reports have tended to concentrate on analysing profits by products. Increasing attention is now being given to analysing profits by customers using an activity-based costing approach. **Customer profitability analysis** provides important information that can be used to determine which classes of customers should be emphasized or de-emphasized and the price to charge for customer services. Kaplan and Cooper (1998) use Kanthal – a Harvard Business School case study – to illustrate the benefits of customer profitability analysis. Kanthal is a Swedish company that sells electric heating elements. Customer-related selling costs represent 34% of total costs. Until recently, Kanthal allocated these costs on the basis of sales value when special studies of customer profitability analysis were undertaken. An activity-based costing system was introduced that sought to explain the resources consumed by different customers. A detailed study of the resources used to service different types of customers identified two cost drivers:

1   Number of orders placed: each order had a large fixed cost, which did not vary with the quantity of items purchased. Thus a customer who placed 10 orders of 100 items per order generated 10 times more ordering cost than a customer who placed a single order of 1000 units.

2   Non-standard production items: these items were more costly to produce than standard items.

Kanthal estimated the cost per order and the cost of handling standard and non-standard items. A customer profitability analysis was prepared based on the sales for the previous year. This analysis revealed that only 40% of its customers were profitable and a further 10% lost 120% of the profits. In other words, 10% incurred losses equal to 120% of Kanthal's total profits. Two of the most unprofitable customers turned out to be among the top three in total sales volume. These two companies made many small orders of non-standard items.

Let us now look at an illustration of customer profitability analysis. Consider the information presented in Example 7.3. The profitability analysis in respect of the four customers is as follows:

	A	B	Y	Z
Customer attributable costs:				
Sales order processing	60 000	30 000	15 000	9 000
Sales visits	4 000	2 000	1 000	1 000
Normal deliveries	30 000	10 000	2 500	1 250
Special (urgent) deliveries	10 000	2 500	0	0
Credit collection[a]	24 658	8 220	1 370	5 480
	128 658	52 720	19 870	16 730
Operating profit contribution	90 000	120 000	70 000	200 000
Contribution to higher level				
sustaining expenses	(38 658)	67 280	50 130	183 270

Note
[a](Annual sales revenue × 10%) × (Average collection period/365)

You can see from the above analysis that A and B are high cost to serve whereas Y and Z are low cost to serve customers. Customer A provides a positive operating profit contribution but is unprofitable when customer attributable costs are taken into account. This is because customer A requires more sales orders, sales visits and normal and urgent deliveries than the other customers. In addition, the customer is slow to pay and has higher delivery costs than the other customers. Customer profitability analysis identifies the characteristics of high cost and low cost to serve customers and shows how customer profitability can be increased. The information should be used to persuade high cost to serve customers to modify their buying behaviour away from placing numerous small orders and/or purchasing non-standard items that are costly to make. For example, customer A can be made profitable if action is taken to persuade the customer to place a smaller number of larger quantity orders, avoid special deliveries and reduce the credit period. If unprofitable customers cannot be persuaded to change their buying behaviour selling prices should be increased (or discounts on list prices reduced) to cover the extra resources consumed. Thus ABC is required for customer profitability analysis so that the resources consumed by customers can be accurately measured.

EXAMPLE 7.3

The Darwin Company has recently adopted customer profitability analysis. It has undertaken a customer profitability review for the past 12 months. Details of the activities and the cost driver rates relating to those expenses that can be attributed to customers are as follows:

Activity	Cost driver rate
Sales order processing	£300 per sales order
Sales visits	£200 per sales visit
Normal delivery costs	£1 per delivery kilometre travelled
Special (urgent) deliveries	£500 per special delivery
Credit collection costs	10% per annum on average payment time

Details relating to four of the firm's customers are as follows:

Customer	A	B	Y	Z
Number of sales orders	200	100	50	30
Number of sales visits	20	10	5	5
Kilometres per delivery	300	200	100	50
Number of deliveries	100	50	25	25
Total delivery kilometres	30 000	10 000	2 500	1 250
Special (urgent deliveries)	20	5	0	0
Average collection period (days)	90	30	10	10
Annual sales	£1 million	£1 million	£0.5 million	£2 million
Annual operating profit contribution[a]	£90 000	£120 000	£70 000	£200 000

Note
[a] Consists of sales revenues less cost of unit-level and batch-related activities

The customer profitability analysis can also be used to rank customers by order of profitability based on **Pareto analysis**. This type of analysis is based on observations by Pareto that a very small proportion of items usually account for the majority of the value. For example, the Darwin Company might find that 20% of the customers account for 80% of the profits. Special attention can then be given to enhancing the relationships with the most profitable customers to ensure that they do not migrate to other competitors. In addition greater emphasis can be given to attracting new customers that have the same attributes as the most profitable customers.

Organizations such as banks, often with a large customer base in excess of one million customers, cannot apply customer profitability analysis at the individual customer level. Instead, they concentrate on customer segment profitability analysis by combining groups of customers into meaningful segments. This enables profitable segments to be highlighted where customer retention is particularly important and provides an input for determining the appropriate marketing strategies for attracting the new customers that have the most profit potential. Segment groupings that are used by banks include income classes, age bands, socio-economic categories and family units.

EXHIBIT 7.4
Surveys of practice

A survey of 187 UK organizations by Drury and Tayles (2000) indicated that 60% used cost-plus pricing. Most of the organizations that used cost-plus pricing indicated that it was applied selectively. It accounted for less than 10% of total sales revenues for 26% of the respondents and more than 50% for 39% of the organizations. Most of the firms (85%) used full cost and the remaining 15% used direct cost as the pricing base. The survey also indicated that 74% analysed profits either by customers or customer categories.

An earlier UK study by Innes and Mitchell (1995a) reported that 50% of the respondents had used customer profitability analysis and a further 12% planned to do so in the future. Of those respondents that ranked customer profitability 60% indicated that the Pareto 80/20 rule broadly applied (that, is 20% of the customers were generating 80% of the profits).

Dekker and Smidt (2003) undertook a survey of 32 Dutch firms on the use of costing practices that resembled the Japanese target costing concept. They reported that 19 out of the 32 firms used these practices, although they used different names for them. Adoption was highest among assembling firms and was related to a competitive and unpredictable environment.

Summary

The following items relate to the learning objectives listed at the beginning of the chapter.

- **Describe how the optimum output and selling price is determined using economic theory.**

  Economic theory assumes that demand and costs can be estimated at each potential demand level. The optimum output is determined at the point where marginal cost equals marginal revenue. The selling price at which the optimum output can be sold determines the optimum price. Economic theory is difficult to apply in practice because it is difficult for a firm to estimate demand at different selling prices for all of its products.

- **Explain the relevant cost information that should be presented in price setting firms for both short-term and long-term decisions.**

  For short-term decisions the incremental costs of accepting an order should be presented. Bids should then be made at prices that exceed incremental costs. For short-term decisions many costs are likely to be fixed and irrelevant. Short-term pricing decisions should meet the following conditions: (a) spare capacity should be available for all of the resources that are required to fulfil an order; (b) the bid price should represent a one-off price that will not be repeated for future orders; and (c) the order will utilize unused capacity for only a short period and capacity will be released for use on more profitable opportunities. For long-term decisions a firm can adjust the supply of virtually all of the resources. Therefore, cost information should be presented providing details of all of the resources that are committed to a product or service. Since facility-sustaining costs should be covered in the long-term by sales revenues there are strong arguments for allocating such costs for long-run pricing decisions. To determine an appropriate selling price a mark-up is added to the total cost of the resources assigned to the product/service to provide a contribution to profits. If facility-sustaining costs are not allocated the mark-up must be sufficient to provide a contribution to covering facility-sustaining costs and a contribution to profit.

- **Describe product and customer profitability analysis and the information that should be included for managing the product and customer mix.**

  Price-taking firms have to decide which products to sell, given their market prices. A mechanism is therefore required that ascertains whether or not the sales revenues from a product/service (or customer) exceeds the cost of resources that are committed to it. Periodic profitability analysis meets this requirement. Ideally, ABC hierarchical profitability analysis should be used that categorizes costs according to their variability at different hierarchical levels to report different hierarchical contribution levels. The aim of the hierarchical analysis should be to assign all organizational expenses to a particular hierarchical or organizational level where cause-and-effect cost assignments can be established so that arbitrary apportionments are avoided. The approach is illustrated in Figure 7.4.

- **Describe the target costing approach to pricing.**

  Target costing is the reverse of cost-plus pricing. With target costing the starting point is the determination of the target selling price – the price that customers are willing to pay for the product (or service). Next a target profit margin is deducted to derive a target cost. The target cost represents the estimated long-run cost of the product (or service) that enables the target profit to be achieved. Predicted actual costs are compared with the target cost and, where the predicted actual cost exceeds the target cost, intensive efforts are made through value engineering methods to achieve the target cost. If the target cost is not achieved the product/service is unlikely to be launched.

- **Describe the different cost-plus pricing methods for deriving selling prices.**

  Different cost bases can be used for cost-plus pricing. Bases include direct variable costs, total direct costs, total direct and indirect costs (excluding higher level facility/business sustaining costs) and total cost based on an assignment of a share of all organizational costs to the product or service. Different percentage profit margins are added depending on the cost base that is used. If direct variable cost is used as the cost base, a high percentage margin will be added to provide a contribution to cover a share of all of those costs that are not included in the cost base plus profits. Alternatively if total cost is used as the cost base a lower percentage margin will be added to provide only a contribution to profits.

- **Explain the limitations of cost-plus pricing.**

  Cost-plus pricing has three major limitations. First, demand is ignored. Secondly, the approach requires that some assumption be made about future volume prior to ascertaining the cost and calculating the cost-plus selling prices. This can lead to an increase in the derived cost-plus selling price when demand is falling and vice versa. Thirdly, there is no guarantee that total sales revenue will be in excess of total costs even when each product is priced above 'cost'.

- **Justify why cost-plus pricing is widely used.**

  There are several reasons why cost-plus pricing is widely used. First, it offers a means by which prices can be determined with ease and speed in organizations that produce hundreds of products. Cost-plus pricing is likely to be particularly applicable to those products that generate relatively minor revenues that are not critical to an organization's success. A second justification is that cost-based pricing methods may encourage price stability by enabling firms to predict the prices of their competitors.

Also, target mark-ups can be adjusted upwards or downwards according to expected demand, thus ensuring that demand is indirectly taken into account.

● **Identify and describe the different pricing policies.**

Cost information is only one of the many variables that must be considered in the pricing decision. The final price that is selected will depend upon the pricing policy of a company. A price-skimming policy or a pricing penetration policy might be selected. A price-skimming policy attempts to charge high initial prices to exploit those sections of the market where demand is initially insensitive to pricing changes. In contrast, a penetration pricing policy is based on the concept of charging low prices initially with the intention of gaining rapid acceptance of the product (or service).

Note

1   In a monopolistic competitive market there are many sellers of similar but not necessarily identical products, with no single seller having a large enough share of the market to permit competitors to identify the effect of other individual sellers' pricing decisions on their sales.

Key terms and concepts

cost-plus pricing (p. 184)
customer profitability analysis (p. 194)
full cost (p. 182)
long-run cost (p. 182)
monopolistic/imperfect competition (p. 176)
Pareto analysis (p. 196)
penetration pricing policy (p. 194)

price elasticity of demand (p. 176)
price setters (p. 181)
price-skimming policy (p. 194)
price takers (p. 181)
product life cycle (p. 194)
target costing (p. 186)

Assessment material

Review questions

The review questions are short questions that enable you to assess your understanding of the main topics included in the chapter. The numbers in parentheses provide you with the page numbers to refer to if you cannot answer a specific question.

Review problems

The review problems are more complex and require you to relate and apply the chapter content to various business problems. The multiple-choice questions are the least demanding and normally take less than 10 minutes to complete. Fully worked solutions to the review problems are provided in a separate section at the end of the book. Further review problems for this chapter are available on the accompanying website, www.drury-online.com. The answers to these problems are available for lecturers on the lecturer's password-protected section of the website.

Case studies

The website also includes over 30 case study problems. A list of these cases is provided on pages 491–493. Several cases are relevant to the content of this chapter. Examples include Lynch Printers and Reichard Maschinen.

Review questions

7.1   What does the price elasticity of demand measure? (*p. 176*)

7.2   Distinguish between elastic and inelastic demand. (*p. 176*)

7.3   How can the optimum selling price for a product or service be determined? (*pp. 176–78*)

7.4   Explain why economic theory is difficult to apply in practice. (*p. 180*)

7.5   Distinguish between a price taker and a price setter. (*p. 181*)

7.6 What costs are likely to be relevant for (a) a short-run pricing decision, and (b) a long-run pricing decision? (*pp. 181–82*)

7.7 What is meant by the term 'full cost'? (*p. 182*)

7.8 What is meant by cost-plus pricing? (*p. 184, pp. 190–91*)

7.9 Distinguish between cost-plus pricing and target costing. (*pp. 186–87*)

7.10 Describe the four stages involved with target costing. (*p. 187*)

7.11 What role does cost information play in price taking firms? (*pp. 187–88*)

7.12 Describe the alternative cost bases that can be used with cost-plus pricing. (*pp. 190–91*)

7.13 What are the limitations of cost-plus pricing? (*pp. 191, 193*)

7.14 Why is cost-plus pricing frequently used in practice? (*p. 193*)

7.15 Describe the different kinds of pricing policies that an organization can apply. (*p. 194*)

7.16 Why is customer profitability analysis important? (*pp. 194–96*)

Review problems

7.17 ABC plc is about to launch a new product. Facilities will allow the company to produce up to 20 units per week. The marketing department has estimated that at a price of £8000 no units will be sold, but for each £150 reduction in price one additional unit per week will be sold.

Fixed costs associated with manufacture are expected to be £12 000 per week.

Variable costs are expected to be £4000 per unit for each of the first 10 units; thereafter each unit will cost £400 more than the preceding one.

The most profitable level of output per week for the new product is

A   10 units
B   11 units
C   13 units
D   14 units
E   20 units.

(*3 marks*)

7.18 **Calculation of different cost-plus prices**

Albany has recently spent some time on researching and developing a new product for which they are trying to establish a suitable price. Previously they have used cost plus 20% to set the selling price.

The standard cost per unit has been estimated as follows:

	£	
Direct materials		
Material 1	10	(4 kg at £2.50/kg)
Material 2	7	(1 kg at £7/kg)
Direct labour	13	(2 hours at £6.50/hour)
Fixed overheads	7	(2 hours at £3.50/hour)
	37	

Required:

(a) Using the standard costs calculate two different cost plus prices using two different bases and explain an advantage and disadvantage of each method.

(*6 marks*)

(b) Give two other possible pricing strategies that could be adopted and describe the impact of each one on the price of the product.

(*4 marks*)

(*Total 10 marks*)

7.19 **Calculation of cost-plus selling price and an evaluation of pricing decisions**

A firm manufactures two products EXE and WYE in departments dedicated exclusively to them. There are also three service departments, stores, maintenance and administration. No stocks are held as the products deteriorate rapidly.

Direct costs of the products, which are variable in the context of the whole business, are identified to each department. The step-wise apportionment of service department costs to the manufacturing departments is based on estimates of the usage of the service provided. These are expressed as percentages and assumed to be reliable over the current capacity range. The general factory overheads of £3.6m, which are fixed, are apportioned based on floor space occupied. The company establishes product costs based on budgeted volume and marks up these costs by 25% in order to set target selling prices.

Extracts from the budgets for the forthcoming year are provided below:

	Annual volume (units)	
	EXE	WYE
Max capacity	200 000	100 000
Budget	150 000	70 000

	EXE	WYE	Stores	Maintenance	Admin
Costs (£m)					
Material	1.8	0.7	0.1	0.1	
Other variable	0.8	0.5	0.1	0.2	0.2
Departmental usage (%)					
Maintenance	50	25	25		
Administration	40	30	20	10	
Stores	60	40			
Floor space (sq m)					
	640	480	240	80	160

Required:

Workings may be £000 with unit prices to the nearest penny.

(a) Calculate the budgeted selling price of one unit of EXE and WYE based on the usual mark-up.

(*5 marks*)

(b) Discuss how the company may respond to each of the following independent events, which represent additional business opportunities.

  (i) an enquiry from an overseas customer for 3000 units only of WYE where a price of £35 per unit is offered

  (ii) an enquiry for 50 000 units of WYE to be supplied in full at regular intervals during the forthcoming year at a price which is equivalent to full cost plus 10%

In both cases support your discussion with calculations and comment on any assumptions or matters on which you would seek clarification.

(11 marks)
(Total 16 marks)

7.20 **Preparation of full cost and marginal cost information**

A small company is engaged in the production of plastic tools for the garden. Sub-totals on the spreadsheet of budgeted overheads for a year reveal:

	Moulding Department	Finishing Department	General Factory Overhead
Variable overhead (£000)	1600	500	1050
Fixed overhead (£000)	2500	850	1750
Budgeted activity			
Machine hours (000)	800	600	
Practical capacity			
Machine hours (000)	1200	800	

For the purposes of reallocation of general factory overhead it is agreed that the variable overheads accrue in line with the machine hours worked in each department. General factory fixed overhead is to be reallocated on the basis of the practical machine hour capacity of the two departments.

It has been a long-standing company practice to establish selling prices by applying a mark-up on full manufacturing cost of between 25% and 35%.

A possible price is sought for one new product which is in a final development stage. The total market for this product is estimated at 200 000 units per annum. Market research indicates that the company could expect to obtain and hold about 10% of the market. It is hoped the product will offer some improvement over competitors' products, which are currently marketed at between £90 and £100 each.

The product development department have determined that the direct material content is £9 per unit. Each unit of the product will take two labour hours (four machine hours) in the moulding department and three labour hours (three machine hours) in finishing. Hourly labour rates are £5.00 and £5.50 respectively.

Management estimate that the annual fixed costs which would be specifically incurred in relation to the product are: supervision £20 000, depreciation of a recently acquired machine £120 000 and advertising £27 000. It may be assumed that these costs are included in the budget given above. Given the state of development of this new product, management do not consider it necessary to make revisions to the budgeted activity levels given above, for any possible extra machine hours involved in its manufacture.

Required:

(a) Briefly explain the role of costs in pricing.

(6 marks)

(b) Prepare full cost and marginal cost information which may help with the pricing decision.

(9 marks)

(c) Comment on the cost information and suggest a price range which should be considered.

(5 marks)
(Total 20 marks)

Decision-making under conditions of risk and uncertainty

8

In Chapters 3, 4 and 7 we considered the use of a single representative set of estimates for predicting future costs and revenues when alternative courses of action are followed. For example, in Chapter 7 we used a single representative estimate of demand for each selling price. However, the outcome of a particular decision may be affected by an uncertain environment that cannot be predicted, and a single representative estimate does not therefore convey all the information that might reasonably influence a decision.

Let us now look at a more complicated example; consider a situation where a company has two mutually exclusive potential alternatives, A and B, which each yield receipts of £50 000. The estimated costs of alternative A can be predicted with considerable confidence, and are expected to fall in the range of £40 000–£42 000; £41 000 might be considered a reasonable estimate of cost. The estimate for alternative B is subject to much greater uncertainty, since this alternative requires high-precision work involving operations that are unfamiliar to the company's labour force. The estimated costs are between £35 000 and £45 000, but £40 000 is selected as a representative estimate. If we consider single representative estimates alternative B appears preferable, since the estimated profit is £10 000 compared with an estimated profit of £9000 for alternative A; but a different picture may emerge if we take into account the range of possible outcomes.

Alternative A is expected to yield a profit of between £8000 and £10 000 whereas the range of profits for alternative B is between £5000 and £15 000. Management may consider it preferable to opt for a fairly certain profit of between £8000 and £10 000 for alternative A rather than take the chance of earning a profit of £5000 from alternative B (even though there is the possibility of earning a profit of £15 000 at the other extreme). This example demonstrates that there is a need to incorporate the uncertainty relating to each alternative into the decision-making process, and in this chapter we shall consider the various methods of doing this.

Risk and uncertainty

A distinction is often drawn by decision theorists between risk and uncertainty. Risk is applied to a situation where there are several possible outcomes and there is relevant past experience to enable statistical evidence to be produced for predicting the possible outcomes. Uncertainty exists where there are several possible outcomes, but there is little previous statistical evidence to enable the possible outcomes to be predicted. Most business decisions can be classified in the uncertainty category, but the distinction between risk and uncertainty is not essential for our analysis and we shall use the terms interchangeably.

Probabilities

Because decision problems exist in an uncertain environment, it is necessary to consider those factors that are outside the decision-maker's control and that may occur for alternative courses of action. These uncontrollable factors are called events or states of nature. For example, in a product launch situation these could consist of events such as the launch of a competitor product at a lower price, at the same price, at a higher price or no similar product being launched.

The likelihood that an event or state of nature will occur is known as its probability, and this is normally expressed in decimal form with a value between 0 and 1. A value of 0 denotes a nil likelihood of occurrence whereas a value of 1 signifies absolute certainty – a definite occurrence. A probability of 0.4 means that the event is expected to occur four times out of ten. The total of the probabilities for events that can possibly occur must sum to 1.0. For example, if a tutor indicates that the probability of a student passing an examination is 0.7 then this means that the student has a 70% chance of passing the examination. Given that the pass/fail alternatives represent an exhaustive listing of all possible outcomes of the event, the probability of not passing the examination is 0.3.

The information can be presented in a probability distribution. A probability distribution is a list of all possible outcomes for an event and the probability that each will occur. The probability distribution for the above illustration is as follows:

Outcome	Probability
Pass examination	0.7
Do not pass examination	0.3
Total	1.0

Some probabilities are known as objective probabilities because they can be established mathematically or compiled from historical data. Tossing a coin and throwing a die are examples of objective probabilities. For example, the probability of heads occurring when tossing a coin logically must be 0.5. This can be proved by tossing the coin many times and observing the results. Similarly, the probability of obtaining number 1 when a die is thrown is 0.166 (i.c. one-sixth). This again can be ascertained from logical reasoning or recording the results obtained from repeated throws of the dice.

It is unlikely that objective probabilities can be established for business decisions, since many past observations or repeated experiments for particular decisions are not possible; the probabilities will have to be estimated based on managerial judgement. Probabilities established in this way are known as subjective probabilities because no two individuals will necessarily assign the same probabilities to a particular outcome. Subjective probabilities are based on an individual's expert knowledge, past experience, and observations of current variables which are likely to have an impact on future events. Such probabilities are unlikely to be estimated correctly, but any estimate of a future uncertain event is bound to be subject to error.

The advantage of this approach is that it provides more meaningful information than stating the most likely outcome. Consider, for example, a situation where a tutor is asked to state whether student A and student B will pass an examination. The tutor may reply that both students are expected to pass the examination. This is the tutor's estimate of the most likely outcome. However, the following probability distributions are preferable:

Outcome	Student A probability	Student B probability
Pass examination	0.9	0.6
Do not pass examination	0.1	0.4
Total	1.0	1.0

Such a probability distribution requires the tutor to specify the degree of confidence in his or her estimate of the likely outcome of a future event. This information is clearly more meaningful than a mere estimate of the most likely outcome that both students are expected to pass the examination, because it indicates that it is most unlikely that A will fail, whereas there is a possibility that B will fail. Let us now apply the principles of probability theory to business decision-making.

Probability distributions and expected value

The presentation of a probability distribution for each alternative course of action can provide useful additional information to management, since the distribution indicates the degree of uncertainty that exists for each alternative course of action. Probability distributions enable management to consider not only the possible profits (i.e. the payoff) from each alternative course of action but also the amount of uncertainty that applies to each alternative. Let us now consider the situation presented in Example 8.1.

From the probability distributions shown in Example 8.1 you will see that there is a 1 in 10 chance that profits will be £6000 for product A, but there is also a 4 in 10 chance that profits will be £8000. A more useful way of reading the probability distribution is to state that there is a 7 in 10 chance that profits will be £8000 or less. This is obtained by adding together the probabilities for profits of £6000, £7000 and £8000. Similarly, there is a 3 in 10 chance that profits will be £9000 or more.

EXAMPLE 8.1

A manager is considering whether to make product A or product B, but only one can be produced. The estimated sales demand for each product is uncertain. A detailed investigation of the possible sales demand for each product gives the following probability distribution of the profits for each product.

Product A probability distribution

(1) Outcome	(2) Estimated probability	(3) Weighted (col. 1 amount × col. 2) (£)
Profits of £6000	0.10	600
Profits of £7000	0.20	1400
Profits of £8000	0.40	3200
Profits of £9000	0.20	1800
Profits of £10 000	0.10	1000
	1.00	
	Expected value	8000

Product B probability distribution

(1) Outcome	(2) Estimated probability	(3) Weighted (col. 1 amount × col. 2) (£)
Profits of £4000	0.05	200
Profits of £6000	0.10	600
Profits of £8000	0.40	3200
Profits of £10 000	0.25	2500
Profits of £12 000	0.20	2400
	1.00	
	Expected value	8900

Which product should the company make?

Expected values

The **expected value** (sometimes called expected payoff) is calculated by weighting each of the profit levels (i.e. possible outcomes) in Example 8.1 by its associated probability. The sum of these weighted amounts is called the expected value of the probability distribution. In other words, the expected value is the weighted arithmetic mean of the possible outcomes. The expected values of £8000 and £8900 calculated for products A and B take into account a range of possible outcomes rather than using a **single most likely estimate**. For example, the single most likely estimate is the profit level with the highest probability attached to it. For both products A and B in Example 8.1 the single most likely estimate is £8000, which appears to indicate that we may be indifferent as to which product should be made. However the expected value calculation takes into account the possibility that a range of different profits are possible and weights these profits by the probability of their occurrence. The weighted calculation indicates that product B is expected to produce the highest average profits in the future.

The expected value of a decision represents the long-run average outcome that is expected to occur if a particular course of action is undertaken many times. For example, if the decision to make products A and B is repeated on, say, 100 occasions in the future then product A will be expected to give an average profit of £8000 whereas product B would be expected to give an average profit of £8900. The expected values are the averages of the possible outcomes based on management estimates. There is no guarantee that the actual outcome will equal the expected value. Indeed, the expected value for product B does not appear in the probability distribution.

Measuring the amount of uncertainty

In addition to the expected values of the profits for the various alternatives, management is also interested in the degree of uncertainty of the expected future profits. For example, let us assume that another alternative course of action, say, product C, is added to the alternatives in Example 8.1 and that the probability distribution is as follows:

Product C probability distribution

Outcome	Estimated probability	Weighted amount (£)
Loss of £4000	0.5	(2000)
Profit of £22 000	0.5	11 000
	Expected value	9 000

Product C has a higher expected value than either product A or product B, but it is unlikely that management will prefer product C to product B, because of the greater variability of the possible outcomes. In other words, there is a greater degree of uncertainty attached to product C.

The conventional measure of the dispersion of a probability distribution is the **standard deviation**. The standard deviation (σ) is the square root of the mean of the squared deviations from the expected value and is calculated from the following formula:

$$\sigma = \sqrt{\sum_{x=1}^{n}(A_x - \overline{A})^2 P_x} \qquad (8.1)$$

where A_x are the profit-level observations, $\overline{A}$ is the expected or mean value, P_x is the probability of each outcome, and the summation is over all possible observations, where n is the total number of possibilities.

The square of the standard deviation σ^2 is known as the statistical variance of the distribution, and should not be confused with the variance from budget or standard cost, which will be discussed in subsequent chapters. The calculations of the standard deviations for products A and B in Example 8.1 are set out in Exhibit 8.1.

EXHIBIT 8.1

Calculation of standard deviations

Product A

(1) Profit (£)	(2) Deviation from expected value, $A_x - \bar{A}$ (£)	(3) Squared deviation $(A_x - \bar{A})^2$ (£)	(4) Probability	(5) Weighted amount (col. 3 × col. 4) (£)
6 000	−2000	4 000 000	0.1	400 000
7 000	−1000	1 000 000	0.2	200 000
8 000	0	–	0.4	–
9 000	+1000	1 000 000	0.2	200 000
10 000	+2000	4 000 000	0.1	400 000
		Sum of squared deviations		1 200 000
		Standard deviation		£1095.40
		Expected value		£8000

Product B

(1) Profit (£)	(2) Deviation $A_x - \bar{A}$ (£)	(3) Squared deviation $(A_x - \bar{A})^2$ (£)	(4) Probability	(5) Weighted amount (col. 3 × col. 4) (£)
4 000	−4900	24 010 000	0.05	1 200 500
6 000	−2900	8 410 000	0.10	841 000
8 000	−900	810 000	0.40	324 000
10 000	1100	1 210 000	0.25	302 500
12 000	3100	9 610 000	0.20	1 922 000
		Sum of squared deviations		4 590 000
		Standard deviation		£2142.40
		Expected value		£8900

If we are comparing the standard deviations of two probability distributions with different expected values, we cannot make a direct comparison. Can you see why this should be so? Consider the following probability distribution for another product, say product D.

Product D probability distribution

Outcome	Estimated probability	Weighted amount (£)
Profits of £40 000	0.05	2 000
Profits of £60 000	0.10	6 000
Profits of £80 000	0.40	32 000
Profits of £100 000	0.25	25 000
Profits of £120 000	0.20	24 000
	Expected value	89 000

The standard deviation for product D is £21 424, but all of the possible outcomes are ten times as large as the corresponding outcomes for product B. The outcomes for product D also have the same pattern of probabilities as product B, and we might conclude that the two projects are equally risky. Nevertheless, the standard deviation for product D is ten times as large as that for product B. This scale effect can be removed be replacing the standard deviation with a relative measure of dispersion. The relative amount of dispersion can be expressed by the **coefficient of variation**, which is simply the standard deviation divided by the expected value. The coefficient of variation for product B is 2142.40/8900 = 0.241 (or 24.1%), and for product D it is also 0.241 (21 424/89 000), thus indicating that the relative amount of dispersion is the same for both products.

In our discussion so far we have defined risk in terms of the spread of possible outcomes, so that risk may be large even if all the possible outcomes involve earning high profits. However, the risk attached to possible profits/losses obtained from alternative courses of action is not dispersion *per se* but the possibility of deviations *below* the expected value of the profits. A decision-maker would hardly consider large possible deviations *above* the expected value undesirable. Consider the following probability distributions:

Product X probability distribution

Outcome	Estimated probability	Weighted amount (£)
Profits of £4000	0.1	400
Profits of £6000	0.3	1800
Profits of £8000	0.6	4800
	Expected value	7000

Product Y probability distribution

Outcome	Estimated probability	Weighted amount (£)
Profits of £6000	0.2	1200
Profits of £8000	0.5	4000
Profits of £12 000	0.3	3600
	Expected value	8800

The standard deviations are £1342 for X and £2227 for Y, giving coefficients of variations of 0.19 for X and 0.28 for Y. These measures indicate that the estimates of product Y are subject to a greater variability, but product X appears to be the riskier product since the probability of profits being less than £7000 (the expected value of X) is 0.4 for product X but only 0.2 for product Y. Clearly, the standard deviation and coefficient of variation are not perfect measures of risk, but the mathematical complexities of measuring only those deviations below the expected value are formidable for anything beyond the simplest situation. Measures such as expected values, standard deviations or coefficient of variations are used to summarize the characteristics of alternative courses of action, but they are poor substitutes for representing the probability distributions, since they do not provide the decision-maker with all the relevant information. There is an argument for presenting the entire probability distribution directly to the decision-maker. Such an approach is appropriate when management must select one from a small number of alternatives, but in situations where many alternatives need to be considered the examination of many probability distributions is likely to be difficult and time-consuming. In such situations management may have no alternative but to compare the expected values and coefficients of variation.

Attitudes to risk by individuals

How do we determine whether or not a risky course of action should be undertaken? The answer to this question depends on the decision-maker's attitude to risk. We can identify three possible attitudes: an aversion to risk, a desire for risk and an indifference to risk. Consider two alternatives, A and B, which have the following possible outcomes, depending on the state of the economy (i.e. the state of nature):

	Possible returns	
State of the economy	A (£)	B (£)
Recession	90	0
Normal	100	100
Boom	110	200

If we assume that the three states of the economy are equally likely then the expected value for each alternative is £100. A **risk-seeker** is one who, given a choice between more or less risky alternatives with identical expected values, prefers the riskier alternative (alternative B). Faced with the same choice, a **risk-averter** would select the less risky alternative (alternative A). The person who is indifferent to risk (**risk neutral**) would be indifferent to both alternatives because they have the same expected values. With regard to investors in general, studies of the securities markets provide convincing evidence that the majority of investors are risk-averse.

Let us now reconsider how useful expected value calculations are for choosing between alternative courses of action. Expected values represent a long-run average solution, but decisions should not be made on the basis of expected values alone, since they do not enable the decision-maker's attitude towards risk to be taken into account. Consider for example, a situation where two individuals play a coin-tossing game, with the loser giving the winner £5000. The expected value to the player who calls heads is as follows:

Outcome	Cash flow (£)	Probability	Weighted amount (£)
Heads	+5000	0.5	+2500
Tails	−5000	0.5	−2500
		Expected value	0

The expected value is zero, but this will not be the actual outcome if only one game is played. The expected-value calculation represents the average outcome only if the game is repeated on many occasions. However, because the game is to be played only once, it is unlikely that each player will find the expected value calculation on its own to be a useful calculation for decision-making. In fact, the expected value calculation implies that each player is indifferent to playing the game, but this indifference will only apply if the two players are neutral to risk. However, a risk-averter will find the game most unattractive. As most business managers are unlikely to be neutral towards risk, and business decisions are rarely repeated, it is unwise for decisions to be made solely on the basis of expected values. At the very least, expected values should be supplemented with measures of dispersion and, where possible, decisions should be made after comparing the probability distributions of the various alternative courses of action.

Decision-tree analysis

In the examples earlier in this chapter we have assumed that profits were uncertain because of the uncertainty of sales demand. In practice, more than one variable may be uncertain (e.g. sales and costs), and also the value of some variables may be dependent on the values of other variables. Many outcomes may therefore be possible, and some outcomes may be dependent on previous outcomes. A useful analytical tool for clarifying the range of alternative courses of action and their possible outcomes is a decision tree.

A decision tree is a diagram showing several possible courses of action and possible events (i.e. states of nature) and the potential outcomes for each course of action. Each alternative course of action or event is represented by a branch, which leads to subsidiary branches for further courses of action or possible events. Decision trees are designed to illustrate the full range of alternatives and events that can occur, under all envisaged conditions. The value of a decision tree is that its logical analysis of a problem enables a complete strategy to be drawn up to cover all eventualities before a firm becomes committed to a scheme. Let us now consider Example 8.2. This will be used to illustrate how decision trees can be applied to decision-making under conditions of uncertainty.

The decision tree for Example 8.2 is set out in Figure 8.1. The boxes indicate the point at which decisions have to be taken, and the branches emanating from it indicate the available alternative courses of action. The circles indicate the points at which there are environmental changes that affect the consequences of prior decisions. The branches from these points indicate the possible types of environment (states of nature) that may occur.

Note that the joint probability of two events occurring together is the probability of one event times the probability of the other event. For example, the probability of the development effort succeeding and the product being very successful consists of the products of the probabilities of these two events, i.e. 0.75 times 0.4, giving a probability of 0.30. Similarly, the probability of the development effort being successful and the product being moderately successful is 0.225 (0.75 × 0.3). The total expected value for the decision to develop the product consists of the sum of all the items in the expected value column on the 'Develop product' branch of the decision tree, i.e. £49 500. If we assume that there are no other alternatives available, other than the decision not to develop, the expected value of £49 500 for developing the product can be compared with the expected value of zero for not developing the product. Decision theory would suggest that the product should be developed because a positive expected value occurs. However, this does not mean that an outcome of £49 500 profit is guaranteed. The expected-value calculation indicates that if the probabilities are correct and this decision was repeated on many occasions an average profit of £49 500 would result.

Unfortunately, the decision will not be repeated on many occasions, and a run of repeated losses could force a company out of business before it has the chance to repeat

EXAMPLE 8.2

A company is considering whether to develop and market a new product. Development costs are estimated to be £180 000, and there is a 0.75 probability that the development effort will be successful and a 0.25 probability that the development effort will be unsuccessful. If the development is successful, the product will be marketed, and it is estimated that:

1 if the product is very successful profits will be £540 000;

2 if the product is moderately successful profits will be £100 000;

3 if the product is a failure, there will be a loss of £400 000.

Each of the above profit and loss calculations is after taking into account the development costs of £180 000. The estimated probabilities of each of the above events are as follows:

1 Very successful   0.4

2 Moderately successful   0.3

3 Failure   0.3

FIGURE 8.1   *A simple decision tree*

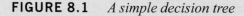

	Possible outcomes (PROFIT)	Probability	Payoff (expected value)
Very successful	£540 000	0.30	£162 000
Moderately successful	£100 000	0.225	£22 500
Failure	–£400 000	0.225	–£90 000
	–£180 000	0.25	–£45 000
		1.00	£49 500
	£0	1.00	£0

Development succeeds (P=0.75) (P=0.4) (P=0.3) (P=0.3)

Develop product

Development fails (P=0.25)

Do not develop product

■ Decision point   ● Possible events

similar decisions. Management may therefore prefer to examine the following probability distribution for developing the product shown in Figure 8.1:

Outcome	Probability
Loss of £400 000	0.225
Loss of £180 000	0.25
Profit of £100 000	0.225
Profit of £540 000	0.30

Management may decide that the project is too risky, since there is nearly a 0.5 probability of a loss occurring.

The decision tree provides a convenient means of identifying all the possible alternative courses of action and their interdependencies. This approach is particularly useful for assisting in the construction of probability distributions when many combinations of events are possible.

Buying perfect and imperfect information

When a decision-maker is faced with a series of uncertain events that might occur, he or she should consider the possibility of obtaining additional information about which event is likely to occur. This section considers how we can calculate the maximum amount it would be worth paying to acquire additional information from a particular source. The approach we shall take is to compare the expected value of a decision if the information is acquired against the expected value with the absence of the information. The difference represents the maximum amount it is worth paying for the additional information. Consider Example 8.3.

Without the additional information, machine A will be purchased using the expected-value decision rule. If the additional information is obtained then this will give a perfect prediction of the level of demand, and the size of the machine can be matched with the level of demand. Therefore if demand is predicted to be low, machine A will be purchased, whereas if demand is predicted to be high, machine B will be purchased. The revised expected value is

$$(0.5 \times \text{£}100\ 000) + (0.5 \times \text{£}200\ 000) = \text{£}150\ 000$$

You can see that the expected value is calculated by taking the highest profit in the case of low and high demand. When the decision to employ the market consultants is being taken, it is not known which level of demand will be predicted. Therefore the best estimate of the outcome from obtaining the additional information is a 0.5 probability that it will predict a low demand and a 0.5 probability that it will predict a high demand. (These are the probabilities that are currently associated with low and high demand.)

The value of the additional information is ascertained by deducting the expected value without the market survey (£130 000) from the expected value with the survey (£150 000). Thus the additional information increases expected value from £130 000 to £150 000 and the **expected value of perfect information** is £20 000. As long as the cost of obtaining the information is less than £20 000, the firm of market consultants should be employed.

In the above illustration it was assumed that the additional information would give a 100% accurate prediction of the expected demand. In practice, it is unlikely that *perfect* information is obtainable, but *imperfect* information (for example, predictions of future demand may be only 80% reliable) may still be worth obtaining. However, the value of imperfect information will always be less than the value of perfect information except when both equal zero. This would occur where the additional information would not change the decision. Note that the principles that are applied for calculating the value of imperfect information are the same as those we applied for calculating the value of perfect information, but the calculations are more complex. For an illustration see Scapens (1991).

Maximin, maximax and regret criteria

In some situations it might not be possible to assign meaningful estimates of probabilities to possible outcomes. Where this situation occurs managers might use any of the following criteria to make decisions: maximin, maximax or the criterion of regret.

EXAMPLE 8.3

The Boston Company must choose between one of two machines – machine A has low fixed costs and high unit variable costs whereas machine B has high fixed costs and low unit variable costs. Consequently, machine A is most suited to low-level demand whereas machine B is suited to high-level demand. For simplicity assume that there are only two possible demand levels – low and high – and the estimated probability of each of these events is 0.5. The estimated profits for each demand level are as follows:

	Low demand (£)	High demand (£)	Expected value (£)
Machine A	100 000	160 000	130 000
Machine B	10 000	200 000	105 000

There is a possibility of employing a firm of market consultants who would be able to provide a perfect prediction of the actual demand. What is the maximum amount the company should be prepared to pay the consultants for the additional information?

The assumption underlying the **maximin criterion** is that the worst possible outcome will always occur and the decision-maker should therefore select the largest payoff under this assumption. Consider the Boston Company in Example 8.3. You can see that the worst outcomes are £100 000 for machine A and £10 000 for machine B. Consequently, machine A should be purchased using the maximin decision rule.

The **maximax criterion** is the opposite of maximin, and is based on the assumption that the best payoff will occur. Referring again to Example 8.3, the highest payoffs are £160 000 for machine A and £200 000 for machine B. Therefore machine B will be selected under the maximax criterion.

The **regret criterion** is based on the fact that, having selected an alternative that does not turn out to be the best, the decision-maker will regret not having chosen another alternative when he or she had the opportunity. Thus if in Example 8.3 machine B has been selected on the assumption that the high level of demand would occur, and the high level of demand actually did occur, there would be no regret. However, if machine A has been selected, the company would lose £40 000 (£200 000 – £160 000). This measures the amount of the regret. Similarly, if machine A was selected on the assumption that demand would be low, and the low level of demand actually did occur, there would be no regret; but if machine B was selected, the amount of the regret would be £90 000 (£100 000 – £10 000). This information is summarized in the following regret matrix:

	State of nature	
	Low demand (£)	High demand (£)
Choose machine A	0	40 000
Choose machine B	90 000	0

The aim of the regret criterion is to minimize the maximum possible regret. The maximum regret for machine A is £40 000 while that for Machine B is £90 000. Machine A would therefore be selected using the regret criterion.

Portfolio analysis

It is unwise for a firm to invest all its funds in a single project, since an unfavourable event may occur that will affect this project and have a dramatic effect on the firm's total financial position. A better approach would be for the firm to invest in a number of different projects. If this strategy is followed, an unfavourable event that affects one project may have relatively less effect on the remaining projects and thus have only a small impact on the firm's overall financial position. That is, a firm should not put all of its eggs in one basket, but should try to minimize risk by spreading its investments over a variety of projects.

The collection of investments held by an individual investor or the collection of projects in which a firm invests is known as a **portfolio**. The objective in selecting a portfolio is to achieve certain desirable characteristics regarding risk and expected return. Let us now consider Example 8.4. From Example 8.4 it can be seen that both the existing activities (umbrella manufacturing) and the proposed new project (ice-cream manufacturing) are risky when considered on their own, but when they are combined, the risk is eliminated because whatever the outcome the cash inflow will be £20 000. Example 8.4 tells us that we should not only consider the risk of individual projects but should also take into account how the risks of potential new projects and existing activities co-vary with each other. Risk is eliminated completely in Example 8.4 because perfect negative correlation (i.e. where the correlation coefficient is –1) exists between the cash flows of the proposed project and the cash flows of the existing activities. When the cash flows are perfectly positively correlated (where the correlation is +1), risk reduction cannot be achieved when the projects are combined. For all other correlation values risk reduction advantages can be obtained by investing in projects that are not perfectly correlated with existing activities.

The important point that emerges from the above discussion is that it is not the risk of individual projects in isolation that is of interest but rather the incremental risk that each project will contribute to the overall risk of the firm.

EXAMPLE 8.4

A firm which currently manufactures umbrellas is considering diversifying and investing in the manufacture of ice cream. The predicted cash flows for the existing activities and the new project are shown below.

States of nature	Existing activities (Umbrella manufacturing) (£)	Proposed project (Ice-cream manufacturing) (£)	Combination of existing activities and the proposed project (£)
Sunshine	–40 000	+60 000	+20 000
Rain	+60 000	–40 000	+20 000

To simplify the illustration it is assumed that only two states of nature exist (rain or sunshine) and each has a probability of 0.5.

Summary

The following items relate to the learning objectives listed at the beginning of the chapter.

- **Calculate and explain the meaning of expected values.**

  The expected value is calculated by weighting each of the possible outcomes by its associated probability. The sum of these weighted outcomes is called the expected value of the probability distribution. In other words, the expected value is the weighted arithmetic mean of the possible outcomes.

- **Explain the meaning of the terms standard deviation and coefficient of variation as measures of risk and outline their limitations.**

  Standard deviation measures the dispersion of the possible outcomes. It is an absolute measure. In contrast, the coefficient of variation is a relative measure derived from dividing the standard deviation by the expected value. Both measures attempt to summarize the risk associated with a probability distribution. They assume that risk is measured in terms of the spread of possible outcomes. Decision-makers are probably more interested in a downside measure of risk that measures the possibility of risk being less than the expected value. Because of this there are strong arguments for presenting the entire probability distribution to the decision-maker.

- **Construct a decision tree when there is a range of alternatives and possible outcomes.**

  Where there are many possible outcomes for various alternatives, and some outcomes are dependent on previous outcomes, a decision tree is a useful analytical tool for clarifying the range of alternative courses of actions and their possible outcomes. A decision tree is a diagram that shows the possible courses of actions, the potential events (states of nature for each outcome) together with their potential outcomes and associated probabilities. A decision tree thus represents an analytical tool for deriving expected values and a probability distribution in more complex situations.

- **Describe and calculate the value of perfect and imperfect information.**

  The value of perfect and imperfect information relates to determining the value of the maximum amount it is worth paying for additional information. The approach involves comparing the expected value of a decision if the information is acquired against the expected value with the absence of the information. The difference represents the maximum value that it is worth paying for the additional information. You should refer to the section in the chapter on buying perfect and imperfect information for an illustration of the calculation of the value of perfect information.

- **Explain and apply the maximin, maximax and regret criteria.**

  In some situations it might not be possible to assign meaningful estimates of probabilities to possible outcomes. When this situation occurs either the maximin, maximax or regret criteria may be used. The maximin criterion assumes that the worst possible outcome will occur and that the decision should be based on the largest payoff under this assumption. The maximax is the opposite to maximin, and is based on the assumption that the best possible payoff will occur. The regret criterion is based on the fact that, having selected an alternative that does not turn out to be the best, the decision-maker will regret not having chosen another alternative when he or she had the opportunity. The aim is to minimize the maximum possible regret. The application of the criteria was illustrated using Example 8.3.

● **Explain the implication of portfolio analysis.**

The implication of portfolio analysis is that the degree of uncertainty attached to various alternatives should not be considered in isolation. Instead, how an alternative interacts with existing activities should be considered. The aim should be to measure the incremental, rather than the total risk, of a project.

Key terms and concepts

coefficient of variation (p. 213)
decision tree (p. 215)
events (p. 208)
expected value (p. 210)
expected value of perfect information (p. 217)
maximax criterion (p. 218)
maximin criterion (p. 218)
objective probabilities (p. 208)
portfolio (p. 219)
probability (p. 208)
probability distribution (p. 208)

regret criterion (p. 218)
risk (p. 208)
risk-averter (p. 214)
risk neutral (p. 214)
risk-seeker (p. 214)
single most likely estimate (p. 210)
standard deviation (p. 211)
states of nature (p.208)
subjective probabilities (p. 209)
uncertainty (p. 208)

Assessment material

Review questions

The review questions are short questions that enable you to assess your understanding of the main topics included in the chapter. The numbers in parentheses provide you with the page numbers to refer to if you cannot answer a specific question.

Review problems

The review problems are more complex and require you to relate and apply the chapter content to various business problems. The multiple-choice questions are the least demanding and normally take less than 10 minutes to complete. Fully worked solutions to the review problems are provided in a separate section at the end of the book. Further review problems for this chapter are available on the accompanying website, www.drury-online.com. The answers to these problems are available for lecturers on the lecturer's password-protected section of the website.

Case studies

The website also includes over 30 case study problems. A list of these cases is provided on pages 491–93.

Review questions

8.1   Distinguish between risk and uncertainty. (*p. 208*)

8.2   What is a probability distribution? (*p. 208*)

8.3   How do subjective probabilities differ from objective probabilities? (*pp. 208–09*)

8.4   Distinguish between expected value and the single most likely estimate. (*p. 210*)

8.5   Distinguish between the standard deviation and the coefficient of variation.
       (*pp. 211, 213*)

8.6   What are the disadvantages of the standard deviation as a measure of risk? (*p. 213*)

8.7   What is a decision tree and what purpose does it serve? (*pp. 215–17*)

8.8   What is the expected value of perfect information and how can it be determined? (*p. 217*)

8.9   Distinguish between maximin, maximax and regret criteria. When might it be appropriate to apply these criteria? (*p. 218*)

8.10   Why is it important to measure risk using a portfolio analysis approach? (*p. 219*)

Review problems

8.11   Which of the following are true with regard to expected values?

Expected values
(i)   represents the single most likely estimate of an outcome.
(ii) take no account of decision-maker's risk.
(iii) are reliant on the accuracy of the probability distribution.

A   (i), (ii) and (iii)
B   (i) and (ii) only
C   (i) and (iii) only
D   (ii) and (iii) only.

8.12   Darwin uses decision tree analysis in order to evaluate potential projects. The company has been looking at the launch of a new product which it believes has a 70% probability of success. The company is, however, considering undertaking an advertising campaign costing £50 000, which would increase the probability of success to 95%.

If successful the product would generate income of £200 000 otherwise £70 000 would be received.

What is the maximum that the company would be prepared to pay for the advertising?

A   £32 500
B   £29 000
C   £17 500
D   £50 000.

8.13 The following data relate to both questions (a) and (b)

X Ltd can choose from five mutually exclusive projects. The projects will each last for one year only and their net cash inflows will be determined by the prevailing market conditions. The forecast annual cash inflows and their associated probabilities are shown below:

Market conditions	Poor	Good	Excellent
Probability	0.20	0.50	0.30
	£000	£000	£000
Project L	500	470	550
Project M	400	550	570
Project N	450	400	475
Project O	360	400	420
Project P	600	500	425

(a) Based on the expected value of the net cash inflows, which project should be undertaken?

A L
B M
C N
D O
E P.

(2 marks)

(b) The value of perfect information about the state of the market is

A Nil
B £5 000
C £26 000
D £40 000
E £128 000.

(3 marks)

8.14 **Decision tree, expected value and maximin criterion**

(a) The Alternative Sustenance Company is considering introducing a new franchised product, Wholefood Waffles.

Existing ovens now used for making some of the present 'Half-Baked' range of products could be used instead for baking the Wholefood Waffles. However, new special batch mixing equipment would be needed. This cannot be purchased, but can be hired from the franchiser in three alternative specifications, for batch sizes of 200, 300 and 600 units respectively. The annual cost of hiring the mixing equipment would be £5000, £15 000 and £21 500 respectively.

The 'Half-Baked' product which would be dropped from the range currently earns a contribution of £90 000 per annum, which it is confidently expected could be continued if the product were retained in the range.

The company's marketing manager considers that, at the market price for Wholefood Waffles of £0.40 per unit, it is equally probable that the demand for this product would be 600 000 or 1 000 000 units per annum.

The company's production manager has estimated the variable costs per unit of making Wholefood Waffles and the probabilities of those costs being incurred, as follows:

Batch size: Cost per unit (pence)	200 units Probability if annual sales are either 600 000 or 1 000 000 units	300 units Probability if annual sales are either 600 000 or 1 000 000 units	600 units Probability if annual sales are 600 000 units	600 units Probability if annual sales are 1 000 000
£0.20	0.1	0.2	0.3	0.5
£0.25	0.1	0.5	0.1	0.2
£0.30	0.8	0.3	0.6	0.3

You are required:

(i) to draw a decision tree setting out the problem faced by the company;

(12 marks)

(ii) to show in each of the following three independent situations which size of mixing machine, if any, the company should hire:

(1) to satisfy a 'maximin' (or 'minimax' criterion),
(2) to maximize the expected value of contribution per annum,
(3) to minimize the probability of earning an annual contribution of less than £100 000.

(7 marks)

(b) You are required to outline briefly the strengths and limitations of the methods of analysis which you have used in part (a) above.

(6 marks)
(Total 25 marks)

8.15 **Pricing decision and the calculation of expected profit and margin of safety**

E Ltd manufactures a hedge-trimming device which has been sold at £16 per unit for a number of years. The selling price is to be reviewed and the following information is available on costs and likely demand.

The standard variable cost of manufacture is £10 per unit and an analysis of the cost variances for the past 20 months show the following pattern which the production manager expects to continue in the future.

Adverse variances of +10% of standard variable cost occurred in ten of the months.

Nil variances occurred in six of the months.

Favourable variances of −5% of standard variable cost occurred in four of the months.

Monthly data

Fixed costs have been £4 per unit on an average sales level of 20 000 units but these costs are expected to rise in the future and the following estimates have been made for the total fixed cost:

	(£)
Optimistic estimate (Probability 0.3)	82 000
Most likely estimate (Probability 0.5)	85 000
Pessimistic estimate (Probability 0.2)	90 000

The demand estimates at the two new selling prices being considered are as follows:

If the selling price/unit is demand would be:	£17	£18
Optimistic estimate (Probability 0.2)	21 000 units	19 000 units
Most likely estimate (Probability 0.5)	19 000 units	17 500 units
Pessimistic estimate (Probability 0.3)	16 500 units	15 500 units

It can be assumed that all estimates and probabilities are independent.

You are required to

(a) advise management, based only on the information given above, whether they should alter the selling price and, if so, the price you would recommend;

(*6 marks*)

(b) calculate the expected profit at the price you recommend and the resulting margin of safety, expressed as a percentage of expected sales;

(*6 marks*)

(c) criticise the method of analysis you have used to deal with the probabilities given in the question;

(*4 marks*)

(d) describe briefly how computer assistance might improve the analysis.

(*4 marks*)

(*Total 20 marks*)

8.16 **Machine hire decision based on uncertain demand and calculation of maximum price to pay for perfect information**

Siteraze Ltd is a company which engages in site clearance and site preparation work. Information concerning its operations is as follows:

(i) It is company policy to hire all plant and machinery required for the implementation of all orders obtained, rather than to purchase its own plant and machinery.

(ii) Siteraze Ltd will enter into an advance hire agreement contract for the coming year at one of three levels – high, medium or low – which correspond to the requirements of a high, medium or low level of orders obtained.

(iii) The level of orders obtained will not be known when the advance hire agreement contract is entered into. A set of probabilities have been estimated by management as to the likelihood of the orders being at a high, medium or low level.

(iv) Where the advance hire agreement entered into is lower than that required for the level of orders actually obtained, a premium rate must be paid to obtain the additional plant and machinery required.

(v) No refund is obtainable where the advance hire agreement for plant and machinery is at a level in excess of that required to satisfy the site clearance and preparation orders actually obtained.

A summary of the information relating to the above points is as follows:

Level of orders	Turnover (£000)	Probability	Plant and machinery hire costs	
			Advance hire (£000)	Conversion premium (£000)
High	15 000	0.25	2300	
Medium	8 500	0.45	1500	
Low	4 000	0.30	1000	
Low to medium				850
Medium to high				1300
Low to high				2150

Variable cost (as percentage of turnover) 70%

Required: Using the information given above:

(a) Prepare a summary which shows the forecast net margin earned by Siteraze Ltd for the coming year for each possible outcome.

(6 marks)

(b) On the basis of maximizing expected value, advise Siteraze whether the advance contract for the hire of plant and machinery should be at the low, medium or high level.

(5 marks)

(c) Explain how the risk preferences of the management members responsible for the choice of advance plant and machinery hire contract may alter the decision reached in (b) above.

(6 marks)

(d) Siteraze Ltd are considering employing a market research consultant who will be able to say with certainty in advance of the placing of the plant and machinery hire contract, which level of site clearance and preparation orders will be obtained. On the basis of expected value, determine the maximum sum which Siteraze Ltd should be willing to pay the consultant for this information.

(5 marks)
(Total 22 marks)

Capital investment decisions

9 Capital investment decisions are those decisions that involve current outlays in return for a stream of benefits in future years. It is true to say that all of the firm's expenditures are made in expectation of realizing future benefits. The distinguishing feature between short-term decisions and capital investment (long-term) decisions is time. Generally, we can classify short-term decisions as those that involve a relatively short time horizon, say less than one year, from the commitment of funds to the receipt of the benefits. On the other hand, capital investment decisions are those decisions where a significant period of time elapses between the outlay and the recoupment of the investment. We shall see that this commitment of funds for a significant period of time involves an interest cost, which must be brought into the analysis. With short-term decisions, funds are committed only for short periods of time, and the interest cost is normally so small that it can be ignored.

Capital investment decisions normally represent the most important decisions that an organization makes, since they commit a substantial proportion of a firm's resources to actions that are likely to be irreversible. Such decisions are applicable to all sectors of society. Business firms' investment decisions include investments in plant and machinery, research and development, advertising and warehouse facilities. Investment decisions in the public sector include new roads, schools and airports. Individuals' investment decisions include house-buying and the purchase of consumer durables. In this and the following chapter we shall examine the economic evaluation of the desirability of investment proposals. We shall concentrate on the investment decisions of business firms, but the same principles, with modifications, apply to individuals, and the public sector.

For most of this chapter we shall assume that the investments appraised are in firms that are all equity financed. In other words, projects are financed by either the issue of new ordinary shares or from retained earnings. Later in this chapter we shall relax this assumption and assume that projects are financed by a combination of debt and equity capital.

The opportunity cost of an investment

You will recall that in Chapter 1 we adopted the view that broadly firms seek to maximize the present value of future net cash inflows. It is therefore important that you acquire an understanding of the terms 'opportunity cost of investment' and 'present value'. Investors can invest in securities traded in financial markets. If you prefer to avoid risk, you can invest in government securities, which will yield a *fixed* return. On the other hand, you may prefer to invest in *risky* securities such as the ordinary shares of companies quoted on the stock exchange. If you invest in the ordinary shares of a company, you will find that the return will vary from year to year, depending on the performance of the company and its future expectations. Investors normally prefer to avoid risk if possible, and will generally invest in risky securities only if they believe that they will obtain a greater return for the increased risk. Suppose that **risk-free gilt-edged securities** issued by the government yield a return of 10%. You will therefore be prepared to invest in ordinary shares only if you expect the return to be greater than 10%; let us assume that you require an *expected* return of 15% to induce you to invest in ordinary shares in preference to a risk-free security.

Suppose you invest in company X ordinary shares. Would you want company X to invest your money in a capital project that gives less than 15%? Surely not, assuming the project has the same risk as the alternative investments in shares of other companies that are yielding a return of 15%. You would prefer company X to invest in other companies' ordinary shares at 15% or, alternatively, to repay your investment so that you could invest yourself at 15%.

The rates of return that are available from investments in securities in financial markets such as ordinary shares and government gilt-edged securities represent the **opportunity cost of an investment** in capital projects; that is, if cash is invested in the capital project, it cannot be invested elsewhere to earn a return. A firm should therefore invest in capital projects only if they yield a return in excess of the opportunity cost of the investment. The opportunity cost of the investment is also known as the **minimum required rate of return, cost of capital**, **discount rate** or **interest rate**.

The return on securities traded in financial markets provides us with the opportunity costs, that is the required rates of return available on securities. The expected returns that investors require from the ordinary shares of different companies vary because some companies' shares are more risky than others. The greater the risk, the greater the expected returns. Consider Figure 9.1. You can see that as the risk of a security increases the return that investors require to compensate for the extra risk increases. Consequently, investors will expect to receive a return in excess of 15% if they invest in securities that have a higher risk than company X ordinary shares. If this return was not forthcoming, investors would not purchase high-risk securities. It is therefore important that companies investing

FIGURE 9.1   *Risk–return trade-off*

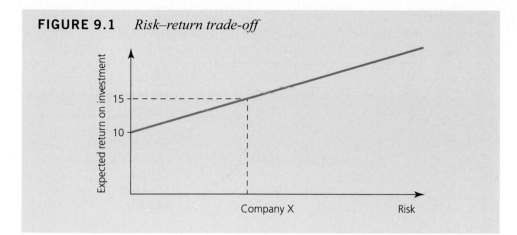

in high-risk capital projects earn higher returns to compensate investors for this risk. You can also see that a risk-free security such as a gilt-edged government security yields the lowest return, i.e. 10%. Consequently, if a firm invests in a project with zero risk, it should earn a return in excess of 10%. If the project does not yield this return and no other projects are available then the funds earmarked for the project should be repaid to the shareholders as dividends. The shareholders could then invest the funds themselves at 10%.

Compounding and discounting

Our objective is to calculate and compare returns on an investment in a capital project with an alternative equal risk investment in securities traded in the financial markets. This comparison is made using a technique called **discounted cash flow (DCF)** analysis. Because a DCF analysis is the opposite of the concept of **compounding interest**, we shall initially focus on compound interest calculations.

Suppose you are investing £100 000 in a risk-free security yielding a return of 10% payable at the end of each year. Exhibit 9.1 shows that if the interest is reinvested, your investment will accumulate to £146 410 by the end of year 4. Period 0 in the first column of Exhibit 9.1 means that no time has elapsed or the time is *now*, period 1 means one year later, and so on. The values in Exhibit 9.1 can also be obtained by using the formula:

$$FV_n = V_0 (1 + K)^n \tag{9.1}$$

where FV_n denotes the future value of an investment in n years, V_0 denotes the amount invested at the beginning of the period (year 0), K denotes the rate of return on the investment and n denotes the number of years for which the money is invested. The calculation for £100 000 invested at 10% for two years is

$$FV_2 = £100\ 000\ (1 + 0.10)^2 = £121\ 000$$

In Exhibit 9.1 all of the year-end values are equal as far as the time value of money is concerned. For example, £121 000 received at the end of year 2 is equivalent to £100 000 received today and invested at 10%. Similarly, £133 100 received at the end of year 3 is equivalent to £121 000 received at the end of year 2, since £121 000 can be invested at the end of year 2 to accumulate to £133 100. Unfortunately, none of the amounts are directly

EXHIBIT 9.1

The value of £100 000 invested at 10%, compounded annually, for four years

End of year	Interest earned (£)	Total investment (£)
0		100 000
	0.10 × 100 000	10 000
1		110 000
	0.10 × 110 000	11 000
2		121 000
	0.10 × 121 000	12 100
3		133 100
	0.10 × 133 100	13 310
4		146 410

comparable at any single moment in time, because each amount is expressed at a different point in time.

When making capital investment decisions, we must convert cash inflows and outflows for different years into a common value. This is achieved by converting the cash flows into their respective values at the same point in time. Mathematically, any point in time can be chosen, since all four figures in Exhibit 9.1 are equal to £100 000 at year 0, £110 000 at year 1, £121 000 at year 2, and so on. However, it is preferable to choose the point in time at which the decision is taken, and this is the present time or year 0. All of the values in Exhibit 9.1 can therefore be expressed in values at the present time (i.e. 'present value') of £100 000.

The process of converting cash to be received in the future into a value at the present time by the use of an interest rate is termed discounting and the resulting present value is the discounted present value. Compounding is the opposite of discounting, since it is the future value of present value cash flows. Equation (9.1) for calculating future values can be rearranged to produce the present value formula:

$$V_0 \text{ (present value)} = \frac{FV_n}{(1 + K)^n} \tag{9.2}$$

By applying this equation, the calculation for £121 000 received at the end of year 2 can be expressed as

$$\text{present value} = \frac{£121\,000}{(1 + 0.10)^2} = £100\,000$$

You should now be aware that £1 received today is not equal to £1 received one year from today. No rational person will be equally satisfied with receiving £1 a year from now as opposed to receiving it today, because money received today can be used to earn interest over the ensuing year. Thus one year from now an investor can have the original £1 plus one year's interest on it. For example, if the interest rate is 10% each £1 invested now will yield £1.10 one year from now. That is, £1 received today is equal to £1.10 one year from today at 10% interest. Alternatively, £1 one year from today is equal to £0.9091 today, its present value because £0.9091, plus 10% interest for one year amounts to £1. The concept that £1 received in the future is not equal to £1 received today is known as the time value of money.

We shall now consider four different methods of appraising capital investments: the net present value, internal rate of return, accounting rate of return and payback methods.

We shall see that the first two methods take into account the time value of money whereas the accounting rate of return and payback methods ignore this factor.

The concept of net present value

By using discounted cash flow techniques and calculating present values, we can compare the return on an investment in capital projects with an alternative equal risk investment in securities traded in the financial market. Suppose a firm is considering four projects (all of which are risk-free) shown in Exhibit 9.2. You can see that each of the projects is identical with the investment in the risk-free security shown in Exhibit 9.1 because you can cash in this investment for £110 000 in year 1, £121 000 in year 2, £133 100 in year 3 and £146 410 in year 4. In other words your potential cash receipts from the risk-free security are identical to the net cash flows for projects A, B, C and D shown in Exhibit 9.2. Consequently, the firm should be indifferent as to whether it uses the funds to invest in the projects or invests the funds in securities of identical risk traded in the financial markets.

The most straightforward way of determining whether a project yields a return in excess of the alternative equal risk investment in traded securities is to calculate the **net present value (NPV)**. This is the present value of the net cash inflows less the project's initial investment outlay. If the rate of return from the project is greater than the return from an equivalent risk investment in securities traded in the financial market, the NPV will be positive. Alternatively, if the rate of return is lower, the NPV will be negative. A positive NPV therefore indicates that an investment should be accepted, while a negative value indicates that it should be rejected. A zero NPV calculation indicates that the firm should be indifferent to whether the project is accepted or rejected.

You can see that the present value of each of the projects shown in Exhibit 9.2 is £100 000. You should now deduct the investment cost of £100 000 to calculate the project's NPV. The NPV for each project is zero. The firm should therefore be indifferent to whether it accepts any of the projects or invests the funds in an equivalent risk-free security. This was our conclusion when we compared the cash flows of the projects with the investments in a risk-free security shown in Exhibit 9.1.

You can see that it is better for the firm to invest in any of the projects shown in Exhibit 9.2 if their initial investment outlays are less than £100 000. This is because we have to pay £100 000 to obtain an equivalent stream of cash flows from a security traded in the financial markets. Conversely, we should reject the investment in the projects if their initial investment outlays are greater than £100 000. You should now see that the NPV rule leads to a direct comparison of a project with an equivalent risk security traded in the financial market. Given that the present value of the net cash inflows for each project is £100 000, their NPVs will be positive (thus signifying acceptance) if the initial investment outlay is less than £100 000 and negative (thus signifying rejection) if the initial outlay is greater than £100 000.

Calculating net present values

You should now have an intuitive understanding of the NPV rule. We shall now learn how to calculate NPVs. The NPV can be expressed as:

$$\text{NPV} = \frac{FV_1}{1+K} + \frac{FV_2}{(1+K)^2} + \frac{FV_3}{(1+K)^3} + \cdots + \frac{FV_n}{(1+K)^n} - I_0 \qquad (9.3)$$

EXHIBIT 9.2

Evaluation of four risk-free projects

	A (£)	B (£)	C (£)	D (£)
Project investment outlay	100 000	100 000	100 000	100 000
End of year cash flows:				
Year 1	110 000	0	0	0
2	0	121 000	0	0
3	0	0	133 100	0
4	0	0	0	146 410
present value =	$\dfrac{110\ 000}{1.10}$	$\dfrac{121\ 000}{(1.10)^2}$	$\dfrac{133\ 000}{(1.10)^3}$	$\dfrac{146\ 410}{(1.10)^4}$
	= 100 000	= 100 000	= 100 000	= 100 000

where I_0 represents the investment outlay and FV represents the future values received in years 1 to n. The rate of return K used is the return available on an equivalent risk security in the financial market. Consider the situation in Example 9.1.

The net present value calculation for Project A is:

$$\text{NPV} = \frac{£300\ 000}{(1.10)} + \frac{£1\ 000\ 000}{(1.10)^2} + \frac{£400\ 000}{(1.10)^3} - £1\ 000\ 000 = +£399\ 700$$

Alternatively, the net present value can be calculated by referring to a published table of present values. You will find examples of such a table if you refer to Appendix A (see pages 500–01). To use the table, simply find the discount factors by referring to each year of the cash flows and the appropriate interest rate.

For example, if you refer to year 1 in Appendix A, and the 10% column, this will show a discount factor of 0.9091. For years 2 and 3 the discount factors are 0.8264 and 0.7513. You then multiply the cash flows by the discount factors to find the present value of the cash flows. The calculation is as follows:

Year	Amount (£000's)	Discount factor	Present value (£)
1	300	0.9091	272 730
2	1000	0.8264	826 400
3	400	0.7513	300 520
			1 399 650
		Less initial outlay	1 000 000
		Net present value	399 650

The difference between the two calculations is due to rounding differences.

Note that the discount factors in the present value table are based on £1 received in n years time calculated according to the present value formula (equation 9.2). For example, £1 received in years 1, 2 and 3 when the interest rate is 10% is calculated as follows:

$$\text{Year } 1 = £1/1.10 = 0.9091$$

$$\text{Year } 2 = £1(1.10)^2 = 0.8264$$

$$\text{Year } 3 = £1(1.10)^3 = 0.7513$$

EXAMPLE 9.1

The Bothnia Company is evaluating two projects with an expected life of three years and an investment outlay of £1 million. The estimated net cash inflows for each project are as follows:

	Project A (£)	Project B (£)
Year 1	300 000	600 000
Year 2	1 000 000	600 000
Year 3	400 000	600 000

The opportunity cost of capital for both projects is 10%. You are required to calculate the net present value for each project.

The positive net present value from the investment indicates the increase in the market value of the shareholders' funds which should occur once the stock market becomes aware of the acceptance of the project. The net present value also represents the potential increase in present consumption that the project makes available to the ordinary shareholders, after any funds used have been repaid with interest. For example, assume that the firm finances the investment of £1 million in Example 9.1 by borrowing £1 399 700 at 10% and repays the loan and interest out of the project's proceeds as they occur. You can see from the repayment schedule in Exhibit 9.3 that £399 700 received from the loan is available for current consumption, and the remaining £1 000 000 can be invested in the project. The cash flows from the project are just sufficient to repay the loan. Therefore acceptance of the project enables the ordinary shareholders' present consumption to be increased by the net present value of £399 700. Hence the acceptance of all available projects with a positive net present value should lead to the maximization of shareholders' wealth.

Let us now calculate the net present value for Project B. When the annual cash flows are constant, the calculation of the net present value is simplified. The discount factors when the cash flows are the same each year (that is, an annuity) are set out in Appendix B (see pages 502–3). We need to find the discount factor for 10% for three years. If you refer to Appendix B, you will see that it is 2.487. The NPV is calculated as follows:

Annual cash inflow	Discount factor	Present value (£)
£600 000	2.487	1 492 200
	Less investment cost	1 000 000
	Net present value	492 200

You will see that the total present value for the period is calculated by multiplying the cash inflow by the discount factor. It is important to note that the annuity tables shown in Appendix B can only be applied when the annual cash flows are the same each year.

The internal rate of return

The **internal rate of return (IRR)** is an alternative technique for use in making capital investment decisions that also takes into account the time value of money. The internal rate

EXHIBIT 9.3

The pattern of cash flows assuming that the loan is repaid out of the proceeds of the project

Year	Loan outstanding at start of year (1) (£)	Interest at 10% (2) (£)	Total amount owed before repayment (3) = (1) + (2) (£)	Proceeds from project (4) (£)	Loan outstanding at year end (5) = (3) − (4) (£)
1	1 399 700	139 970	1 539 670	300 000	1 239 670
2	1 239 670	123 967	1 363 637	1 000 000	363 637
3	363 637	36 363	400 000	400 000	0

of return represents the true interest rate earned on an investment over the course of its economic life. This measure is sometimes referred to as the **discounted rate of return**. The internal rate of return is the interest rate K that when used to discount all cash flows resulting from an investment, will equate the present value of the cash receipts to the present value of the cash outlays. In other words, it is the discount rate that will cause the net present value of an investment to be zero. Alternatively, the internal rate of return can be described as the maximum cost of capital that can be applied to finance a project without causing harm to the shareholders. The internal rate of return is found by solving for the value of K from the following formula:

$$I_0 = \frac{FV_1}{1+K} + \frac{FV_2}{(1+K)^2} + \frac{FV_3}{(1+K)^3} + \cdots + \frac{FV_n}{(1+K)^n}$$ (9.4)

It is easier, however, to use the discount tables. Let us now calculate the internal rate of return for Project A in Example 9.1.

The IRR can be found by trial and error by using a number of discount factors until the NPV equals zero. For example, if we use a 25% discount factor, we get a positive NPV of £84 800. We must therefore try a higher figure. Applying 35% gives a negative NPV of £66 530. We know then that the NPV will be zero somewhere between 25% and 35%. In fact, the IRR is approximately 30%, as indicated in the following calculation:

Year	Net cash flow (£)	Discount factor (30%)	Present value of cash flow (£)
1	300 000	0.7692	230 760
2	1 000 000	0.5917	591 700
3	400 000	0.4552	182 080
		Net present value	1 004 540
		Less initial outlay	1 000 000
		Net present value	4 540

It is claimed that the calculation of the IRR does not require the prior specification of the cost of capital. The decision rule is that if the IRR is greater than the opportunity cost of capital, the investment is profitable and will yield a positive NPV. Alternatively, if the IRR is less than the cost of capital, the investment is unprofitable and will result in a negative

FIGURE 9.2 *Interpretation of the internal rate of return*

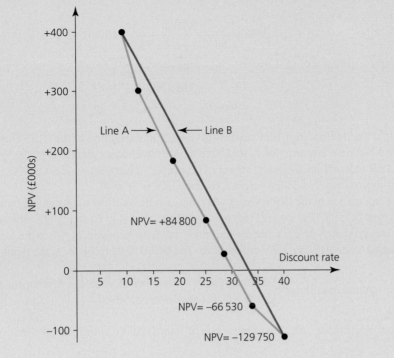

NPV. Therefore any interpretation of the significance of the IRR will still require that we estimate the cost of capital. The calculation of the IRR is illustrated in Figure 9.2.

The dots in the graph represent the NPV at different discount rates. The point where the line joining the dots (ie. Line A) cuts the horizontal axis indicates the IRR (the point at which the NPV is zero). Figure 9.2 indicates that the IRR is 30%, and you can see from this diagram that the interpolation method can be used to calculate the IRR without carrying out trial and error calculations. When we use interpolation, we infer the missing term (in this case the discount rate at which NPV is zero) from a known series of numbers. For example, at a discount rate of 25% the NPV is +£84 800 and for a discount rate of 35% the NPV is –£66 530. The total distance between these points is £151 330 (+£84 800 and –£66 530). The calculation for the approximate IRR is therefore

$$25\% + \frac{84\ 800}{151\ 330} \times (35\% - 25\%) = 30.60\%$$

In other words, if you move down line A in Figure 9.2 from a discount rate of 25% by £84 800, you will reach the point at which NPV is zero. The distance between the two points on line A is £151 330, and we are given the discount rates of 25% and 35% for these points. Therefore 84 800/151 330 represents the distance that we must move between these two points for the NPV to be zero. This distance in terms of the discount rate is 5.60% [(84 800/151 330) × 10%], which, when added to the starting point of 25%, produces an IRR of 30.60%. The formula using the interpolation method is as follows:

$$A + \frac{C}{C - D}(B - A) \qquad (9.5)$$

where A is the discount rate of the low trial, B is the discount rate of the high trial, C is the NPV of cash inflow of the low trial and D is the NPV of cash inflow of the high trial. Thus

$$25\% + \left[\frac{84\,800}{84\,800 - (-66\,530)} \times 10\% \right]$$

$$= 25\% + \left[\frac{84\,800}{151\,330} \times 10\% \right]$$

$$= 30.60\%$$

Note that the interpolation method only gives an approximation of the IRR. The greater the distance between any two points that have a positive and a negative NPV, the less accurate is the IRR calculation. Consider line B in Figure 9.2. The point where it cuts the horizontal axis is approximately 33%, whereas the actual IRR is 30.60%.

The calculation of the IRR is easier when the cash flows are of a constant amount each year. Let us now calculate the internal rate of return for project B in Example 9.1. Because the cash flows are equal each year, we can use the annuity table in Appendix B. When the cash flows are discounted at the IRR, the NPV will be zero. The IRR will therefore be at the point where

$$[\text{annual cash flow}] \times \left[\begin{array}{c} \text{discount factor for number of years} \\ \text{for which cash flow is received} \end{array} \right] - \left[\begin{array}{c} \text{investment} \\ \text{cost} \end{array} \right] = 0$$

Rearranging this formula, the internal rate of return will be at the point where

$$\text{discount factor} = \frac{\text{investment cost}}{\text{annual cash flow}}$$

Substituting the figures for project B in Example 9.1,

$$\text{discount factor} = \frac{£1\,000\,000}{£600\,000} = 1.666$$

We now examine the entries for the year 3 row in Appendix B to find the figures closest to 1.666. They are 1.673 (entered in the 36% column) and 1.652 (entered in the 37% column). We can therefore conclude that the IRR is between 36% and 37%. However, because the cost of capital is 10%, an accurate calculation is unnecessary; the IRR is far in excess of the cost of capital.

The calculation of the IRR can be rather tedious (as the cited examples show), but the trial-and-error approach can be programmed for fast and accurate solution by a computer or calculator. The calculation problems are no longer a justification for preferring the NPV method of investment appraisal. Nevertheless, there are theoretical justifications, which we shall discuss later in this chapter, that support the NPV method.

Relevant cash flows

Investment decisions, like all other decisions, should be analysed in terms of the cash flows that can be directly attributable to them. These cash flows should include the incremental cash flows that will occur in the future following acceptance of the investment. The cash flows will include cash inflows and outflows, or the inflows may be represented by savings in cash outflows. For example, a decision to purchase new machinery may generate cash savings in the form of reduced out-of-pocket operating costs. For all practical purposes such cost savings are equivalent to cash receipts.

It is important to note that depreciation is not included in the cash flow estimates for capital investment decisions, since it is a non-cash expense. This is because the capital investment cost of the asset to be depreciated is included as a cash outflow at the start of the project, and depreciation is merely a financial accounting method for allocating past capital costs to future accounting periods. Any inclusion of depreciation will lead to double counting.

Timing of cash flows

Our calculations have been based on the assumption that any cash flows in future years will occur in one lump sum at the year end. Obviously, this is an unrealistic assumption, since cash flows are likely to occur at various times throughout the year, and a more accurate method is to assume monthly cash flows and use monthly discount rates. However, the use of annual cash flows enables all cash flows which occur in a single year to be combined and discounted in one computation. Even though the calculated results that are obtained are not strictly accurate, they are normally accurate enough for most decisions.

Comparison of net present value and internal rate of return

In many situations the internal rate of return method will result in the same decision as the net present value method. In the case of conventional projects (in which an initial cash outflow is followed by a series of cash inflows) that are independent of each other (i.e. where the selection of a particular project does not preclude the choice of the other), both NPV and IRR rules will lead to the same accept/reject decisions. However, there are also situations where the IRR method may lead to different decisions being made from those that would follow the adoption of the NPV procedure.

Mutually exclusive projects

Where projects are mutually exclusive, it is possible for the NPV and the IRR methods to suggest different rankings as to which project should be given priority. Mutually exclusive projects exist where the acceptance of one project excludes the acceptance of another project, for example the choice of one of several possible factory locations, or the choice of one of many different possible machines. When evaluating mutually exclusive projects, the IRR method can incorrectly rank the projects, because of its reinvestment assumptions, and in these circumstances it is recommended that the NPV method is used.

Percentage returns

Another problem with the IRR rule is that it expresses the result as a percentage rather than in monetary terms. Comparison of percentage returns can be misleading; for example, compare an investment of £10 000 that yields a return of 50% with an investment of £100 000 that yields a return of 25%. If only one of the investments can be undertaken, the first investment will yield £5000 but the second will yield £25 000. If we assume that the cost of capital is 10%, and that no other suitable investments are available, any surplus funds will be invested at the cost of capital (i.e. the returns available from equal risk securities traded in financial markets). Choosing the first investment will leave a further £90 000 to be invested, but this can only be invested at 10%, yielding a return of £9000. Adding this to the return of £5000 from the £10 000 investment gives a total return of £14 000. Clearly, the second investment, which yields a return of £25 000, is preferable. Thus, if the objective is to maximize the shareholders' wealth then NPV provides the correct measure.

Reinvestment assumptions

The assumption concerning the reinvestment of interim cash flows from the acceptance of projects provides another reason for supporting the superiority of the NPV method. The implicit assumption if the NPV method is adopted is that the cash flows generated from an investment will be reinvested at the cost of capital (i.e. the returns available from equal risk securities traded in financial markets). However, the IRR method makes a different implicit assumption about the reinvestment of the cash flows. It assumes that all the proceeds from a project can be reinvested to earn a return equal to the IRR of the original project. In theory, a firm will have accepted all projects which offer a return in excess of the cost of capital, and any other funds that become available can only be reinvested at the cost of capital. This is the assumption that is implicit in the NPV rule.

Unconventional cash flows

Where a project has unconventional cash flows, the IRR has a technical shortcoming. Most projects have conventional cash flows that consist of an initial negative cash flow followed by positive cash inflows in later years. In this situation the algebraic sign changes, being negative at the start and positive in all future periods. If the sign of the net cash flows changes in successive periods, it is possible for the calculations to produce as many internal rates of return as there are sign changes. While multiple rates of return are mathematically possible, only one rate of return is economically significant in determining whether or not the investment is profitable.

Fortunately, the majority of investment decisions consist of conventional cash flows that produce a single IRR calculation. However, the problem cannot be ignored, since unconventional cash flows are possible and, if the decision-maker is unaware of the situation, serious errors may occur at the decision-making stage. Example 9.2 illustrates a situation where two internal rates of return occur.

You will find that the cash flows in Example 9.2 give internal rates of return of 5% and 50%. The effect of multiple rates of return on the NPV calculations is illustrated in Figure 9.3.

When the cost of capital is between 5% and 50%, the NPV is positive and, following the NPV rule, the project should be accepted. However, if the IRR calculation of 5% is used, the project may be incorrectly rejected if the cost of capital is in excess of 5%. You can see that the graph of the NPV in Figure 9.3 indicates that this is an incorrect decision when the cost of capital is between 5% and 50%. Alternatively, if the IRR of 50% is used, this will lead to the same decision being made as if the NPV rule were adopted, provided that the cost of capital is greater than 5%. Note that the NPV is negative if the cost of capital is less than 5%.

The Bothnia Company has the following series of cash flows for a specific project:

Year 0   –£400 000 (Investment outlay)
Year 1   +£1 020 000 (Net cash inflows)
Year 2   –£630 000 (Environmental and disposal costs)

You are required to calculate the internal rate of return.

FIGURE 9.3   *Net present values for unconventional cash flows*

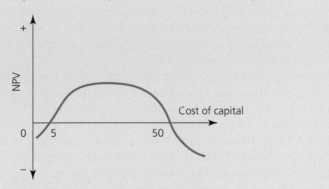

Techniques that ignore the time value of money

In addition to those methods that take into account the time value of money two other methods that ignore this factor are frequently used in practice. These are the payback method and the accounting rate of return method. Methods that ignore the time value of money are theoretically weak, and they will not necessarily lead to the maximization of the market value of ordinary shares. Nevertheless, the fact that they are frequently used in practice means that we should be aware of these techniques and their limitations.

Payback method

The **payback method** is one of the simplest and most frequently used methods of capital investment appraisal. It is defined as the length of time that is required for a stream of cash proceeds from an investment to recover the original cash outlay required by the investment. If the stream of cash flows from the investment is constant each year, the payback period can be calculated by dividing the total initial cash outlay by the amount of the expected annual cash proceeds. Therefore if an investment requires an initial outlay of £60 000 and is expected to produce annual cash inflows of £20 000 per year for five years, the payback period will be £60 000 divided by £20 000, or three years. If the stream of expected proceeds is not constant from year to year, the payback period is determined by adding up the cash inflows expected in successive years until the total is equal to the original outlay. Example 9.3 illustrates two projects, A and B, that require the same initial outlay of £50 000 but that display different time profiles of benefits.

In Example 9.3 project A pays back its initial investment cost in three years, whereas project B pays back its initial cost in four years so that project A would be ranked in preference to project B. However, project B has a higher NPV, and the payback method incorrectly ranks project A in preference to project B. Two obvious deficiencies are apparent from these calculations. First, the payback method does not take into account cash flows that are earned after the payback period and, secondly, it fails to take into account the differences in the timing of the proceeds which are earned before the payback period. Payback computations ignore the important fact that future cash receipts cannot be validly compared with an initial outlay until they are discounted to their present values.

Not only does the payback period incorrectly rank project A in preference to project B, but the method can also result in the acceptance of projects that have a negative NPV. Consider the cash flows for project C in Example 9.4.

The payback period for project C is three years, and if this was within the time limit set by management, the project would be accepted in spite of its negative NPV. Note also that the payback method would rank project C in preference to project B in Example 9.3, despite the fact that B would yield a positive NPV.

The payback period can only be a valid indicator of the time that an investment requires to pay for itself, if all cash flows are first discounted to their present values and the discounted values are then used to calculate the payback period. This adjustment gives rise to what is known as the adjusted or discounted payback method. Even when such an adjustment is made, the adjusted payback method cannot be a complete measure of an investment's profitability. It can estimate whether an investment is likely to be profitable, but it cannot estimate how profitable the investment will be.

Despite the theoretical limitations of the payback method it is the method most widely used in practice (see Exhibit 9.4). Why, then, is payback the most widely applied formal investment appraisal technique? It is a particularly useful approach for ranking projects where a firm faces liquidity constraints and requires a fast repayment of investments. The payback method may also be appropriate in situations where risky investments are made in uncertain markets that are subject to fast design and product changes or where future cash flows are extremely difficult to predict. The payback method assumes that risk is time-related: the longer the period, the greater the chance of failure. By concentrating on the early cash flows, payback uses data in which managers have greater confidence. Thus, the payback period can be used as a rough measure of risk, based on the assumption that the longer it takes for a project to pay for itself, the riskier it is. Managers may also choose projects with quick payback periods because of self-interest. If a manager's performance is measured using short-term criteria, such as net profits, there is a danger that he or she may choose projects with quick paybacks to show improved net profits as soon as possible. The payback method is also frequently used in conjunction with the NPV or IRR methods. It serves as a simple first-level screening device that identifies those projects that should be subject to more rigorous investigation. A further attraction of payback is that it is easily understood by all levels of management and provides an important summary measure: how quickly will the project recover its initial outlay? Ideally, the payback method should be used in conjunction with the NPV method, and the cash flows discounted before the payback period is calculated.

It is apparent from the surveys shown in Exhibit 9.4 that firms use a combination of appraisal methods. The studies by Pike (1996) indicate a trend in the increasing usage of discount rates. The Drury *et al.* (1993) study suggests that larger organizations use net present value and internal rate of return to a greater extent than the smaller organizations. The Drury *et al.* study also asked the respondents to rank the appraisal methods in order of importance for evaluating major projects. The larger organizations ranked internal rate of return first,

EXAMPLE 9.3

The cash flows and NPV calculations for two projects are as follows:

	Project A		Project B	
	(£)	(£)	(£)	(£)
Initial cost				
Net cash inflows		50 000		50 000
Year 1	10 000		10 000	
Year 2	20 000		10 000	
Year 3	20 000		10 000	
Year 4	20 000		20 000	
Year 5	10 000		30 000	
Year 6	–		30 000	
Year 7	–	80 000	30 000	140 000
NPV at a 10% cost capital		10 500		39 460

EXAMPLE 9.4

The cash flows and NPV calculation for project C are as follows:

	(£)	(£)
Initial cost		
Net cash inflows		50 000
Year 1	10 000	
Year 2	20 000	
Year 3	20 000	
Year 4	3 500	
Year 5	3 500	
Year 6	3 500	
Year 7	3 500	64 000
NPV (at 10% cost of capital)		(−1 036)

followed by payback and net present value whereas the smaller organizations ranked payback first, internal rate of return second and intuitive management judgement third.

The use of the accounting rate of return probably reflects the fact that it is a widely used external financial accounting measure by financial markets and managers therefore wish to assess what impact a project will have on the external reporting of this measure. Also it is a widely used measure for evaluating managerial performance.

Accounting rate of return

The **accounting rate of return** (also known as the **return on investment** and **return on capital employed**) is calculated by dividing the average annual profits from a project into the average investment cost. It differs from other methods in that profits rather than cash

EXHIBIT 9.4

Surveys of practice

Surveys conducted by Pike relating to the investment appraisal techniques by 100 large UK companies between 1975 and 1992 provide an indication of the changing trends in practice in large UK companies. Pike's findings relating to the percentage of firms using different appraisal methods are as follows:

	1975 %	1981 %	1986 %	1992 %
Payback	73	81	92	94
Accounting rate of return	51	49	56	50
DCF methods (IRR or NPV)	58	68	84	88
Internal rate of return (IRR)	44	57	75	81
Net present value (NPV)	32	39	68	74

Source: Pike (1996)

A study of 300 UK manufacturing organizations by Drury *et al.* (1993) sought to ascertain the extent to which particular techniques were used. The figures below indicate the percentage of firms that often or always used a particular technique:

	All organizations %	Smallest organizations %	Largest organizations %
Payback (unadjusted)	63	56	55
Discounted payback	42	30	48
Accounting rate of return	41	35	53
Internal rate of return	57	30	85
Net present value	43	23	80

More recently a UK study by Arnold and Hatzopoulos (2000) reported that NPV has overtaken IRR as the most widely used method by larger firms. They reported that 97% of large firms use NPV compared with 84% which employ IRR.

Few studies have been undertaken in mainland Europe. The following usage rates relate to surveys undertaken in the USA and Belgium. For comparative purposes Pike's UK study is also listed:

	UK[a] %	USA[b] %	Belgium[c] %
Payback	94	72	50
Accounting rate of return	50	65	65
Internal rate of return	81	91	77
Net present value	74	88	60
Discounted payback		65	68

[a]Pike (1996)
[b]Trahan and Gitman (1995)
[c]Dardenne (1998)

flows are used. Note that profits are not equal to cash flows because financial accounting profit measurement is based on the accruals concept. Assuming that depreciation represents the only non-cash expense, profit is equivalent to cash flows less depreciation. The use of accounting rate of return can be attributed to the wide use of the return on investment measure in financial statement analysis.

When the average annual net profits are calculated, only additional revenues and costs that follow from the investment are included in the calculation. The average annual net profit is therefore calculated by dividing the difference between incremental revenues and costs by the estimated life of the investment. The incremental costs include either the *net* investment cost or the total depreciation charges, these figures being identical. The average investment figure that is used in the calculation depends on the method employed to calculate depreciation. If straight-line depreciation is used, it is presumed that investment will decline in a linear fashion as the asset ages. The average investment under this assumption is one-half of the amount of the initial investment plus one-half of the scrap value at the end of the project's life.[1]

For example, the three projects described in Examples 9.3 and 9.4 for which the payback period was computed required an initial outlay of £50 000. If we assume that the projects have no scrap values and that straight-line depreciation is used, the average investment for each project will be £25 000. The calculation of the accounting rate of return for each of these projects is as follows:

$$\text{accounting rate of return} = \frac{\text{average annual profits}}{\text{average investment}}$$

$$\text{project A} = \frac{6\,000}{25\,000} = 24\%$$

$$\text{project B} = \frac{12\,857}{25\,000} = 51\%$$

$$\text{project C} = \frac{2\,000}{25\,000} = 8\%$$

For project A the total profit over its five-year life is £30 000 (£80 000 – £50 000), giving an average annual profit of £6000. The average annual profits for projects B and C are calculated in a similar manner.

It follows that the accounting rate of return is superior to the payback method in one respect; that is, it allows for differences in the useful lives of the assets being compared. For example, the calculations set out above reflect the high earnings of project B over the whole life of the project, and consequently it is ranked in preference to project A. Also, projects A and C have the same payback periods, but the accounting rate of return correctly indicates that project A is preferable to project C.

However, the accounting rate of return suffers from the serious defect that it ignores the time value of money. When the method is used in relation to a project where the cash inflows do not occur until near the end of its life, it will show the same accounting rate of return as it would for a project where the cash inflows occur early in its life, providing that the average cash inflows are the same. For this reason the accounting rate of return cannot be recommended. Nevertheless, the accounting rate of return is widely used in practice (see Exhibit 9.4). This is probably due to the fact that the annual accounting rate of return is frequently used to measure the managerial performance of different business units within a company. Therefore, managers are likely to be interested in how any new investment contributes to the business unit's overall accounting rate of return.

Investment appraisal at Cyto Technologies

Cyto Technologies[1] is a rapidly growing biotechnology company in the USA that manufactures and sells hundreds of products. In the past, the project selection process at Cyto lacked a structured approach. Projects were selected with just sketchy ideas about financial numbers and rough ideas of payback periods. Increasing competition and the higher cost of capital have forced Cyto to change its approach. A project approval team was set up to provide structure for the project development and evaluation process. It consists of five constant members (the heads of manufacturing, quality assurance, finance, marketing, and research and development). The team oversees the allocation of resources to new projects in alignment with the company's objectives.

The new project development and evaluation process consists of four phases. Phase 1 consists of two stages: idea generation and investigation. In the generation stage any R&D scientist with an idea for a new product or technique is granted a small sum of money to undertake initial research. The idea is documented in an idea evaluation report and screened by marketing and R&D. If the idea appears promising, it enters the investigation stage, which results in a proposal, and the project is reviewed by members of the project approval team.

Phase 2, product design, consists of a feasibility study. The study results in a report on the final definition of the product – image, specifications, marketing potential and initial estimates of the return on investment and IRR. Once again the report is reviewed by the project appraisal team and a favourable review moves the project to the next phase.

Phase 3, product development, consists of two stages: specifications and final optimization. In the specifications stage production cost estimates are established and marketing personnel determine the final sales forecasts. Final appraisal estimates of the payback period, NPV and IRR are computed. At this point the project evaluation team once again review the project, which if approved, enters the final optimization stage. Financial performance is one of nine criteria used by the project evaluation team to evaluate projects, so a project may be approved even if it performs relatively poorly on that test. Examples of non-financial criteria include the potential for spin-off products, strategic fit within the planned and existing activities and the impact on long-term corporate positioning. During the optimization stage the first batch is made, quality assurance specifications are detailed, regulatory compliances are met, and the final design is demonstrated. The marketing personnel are involved in planning product promotion and advertising campaigns. Finally, in phase 4, the product is launched.

Note:
[1]The company name has been changed at the request of management.

Source: Kalagnanam, S. and Schimdt, S.K. (1996) Analyzing capital investments in new products, *Management Accounting (USA)*, January, pp. 31–36.

The effect of performance measurement on capital investment decisions

The way that the performance of a manager is measured is likely to have a profound effect on the decisions he or she will make. There is a danger that, because of the way performance is measured, a manager may be motivated to take the wrong decision and not follow the NPV rule. Consider the information presented in Exhibit 9.5 in respect of the net cash inflows and the annual reported profits or losses for projects J and K. The figures without the parentheses refer to the cash inflows whereas the figures within the parentheses refer to annual reported profit. You will see that the total cash inflows over the five year lives for projects J and K are £11 million and £5 million respectively. Both projects require an initial outlay of £5 million. Assuming a cost of capital of 10%, without undertaking any calculations it is clear that project J will have a positive NPV and project K will have a negative NPV.

If the straight line method of depreciation is used the annual depreciation for both projects will be £1 million (£5 million investment cost/5 years). Therefore the reported profits are derived from deducting the annual depreciation charge from the annual net cash inflows. For decision-making the focus is on the entire life of the projects. Our objective is to ascertain whether the present value of the cash inflows exceeds the present value of the cash outflows over the entire life of a project, and not allocate the NPV to different accounting periods as indicated by the dashed vertical lines in Exhibit 9.5. In other words we require an answer to the question will the project add value?

In contrast, a company is required to report on its performance externally at annual intervals and managerial performance is also often evaluated on an annual or more frequent basis. Evaluating managerial performance at the end of the five year project lives is clearly too long a time scale since managers are unlikely to remain in the same job for such lengthy periods. Therefore, if a manager's performance is measured using short-term criteria, such as annual profits, he or she may choose projects that have a favourable impact on short-term financial performance. Because Project J will have a negative impact on performance in its early years (i.e. it contributes losses) there is a danger that a manager who is anxious to improve his or her short-term performance might reject project J even though it has a positive impact on the performance measure in the long-term.

The reverse may happen with project K. This has a favourable impact on the short-term profit performance measure in years one and two but a negative impact in the longer-term so the manager might accept the project to improve his or her short-term performance measure.

It is thus important to avoid an excessive focus on short-term profitability measures since this can have a negative impact on long-term profitability. Emphasis should also be given to measuring a manager's contribution to an organization's long-term objectives. These issues are discussed in Chapter 13 when we shall look at performance measurement in more detail. However, at this point you should note that the way in which managerial performance is measured will influence their decisions and may motivate them to work in their own best interests, even when this is not in the best interest of the organization.

Qualitative factors

Not all investment projects can be described completely in terms of monetary costs and benefits (e.g. a new cafeteria for the employees or the installation of safety equipment). Nevertheless, the procedures described in this chapter may be useful by making the value placed by management on quantitative factors explicit. For example, if the present value of the cash outlays for a project is £100 000 and the benefits from the project are difficult to quantify, management must make a value judgement as to whether or not the benefits are in excess of £100 000. In the case of capital expenditure on facilities for employees, or expenditure to avoid unpleasant environmental effects from the company's manufacturing process, one can take the view that the present value of the cash outlays represents the cost

EXHIBIT 9.5

Annual net cash inflows (profits/losses) for two projects each with an initial outlay of £5 million

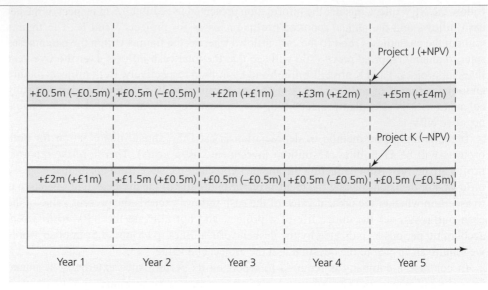

to shareholders of the pursuit of goals other than the maximization of shareholders' funds. In other words, ordinary shareholders, as a group in the bargaining coalition, should know how much the pursuit of other goals is costing them.

Taxation and investment decisions

In our discussions so far we have ignored the impact of taxation. Taxation rules differ between countries but in most countries similar principles tend to apply relating to the taxation allowances available on capital investment expenditure. Companies rarely pay taxes on the profits that are disclosed in their annual published accounts, since certain expenses that are deducted in the published accounts are not allowable deductions for taxation purposes. For example, depreciation is not an allowable deduction; instead, taxation legislation enables **capital allowances** (also known as **writing-down allowances** or **depreciation tax shields**) to be claimed on capital expenditure that is incurred on plant and machinery and other fixed assets. Capital allowances represent standardized depreciation allowances granted by the tax authorities. These allowances vary from country to country but their common aim is to enable the *net* cost of assets to be deducted as an allowable expense, either throughout their economic life or on an accelerated basis which is shorter than an asset's economic life.

Taxation laws in different countries typically specify the amount of capital expenditure that is allowable, the time period over which the capital allowances can be claimed and the depreciation method to be employed. Currently in the UK, larger companies can claim annual capital allowances of 25% on the written-down value of plant and equipment based on the reducing balance method of depreciation. Different percentage capital allowances are also available on other assets such as industrial buildings where an allowance of 4% per annum based on straight line depreciation can be claimed.[2]

Let us now consider how taxation affects the NPV calculations. You will see that the calculation must include the incremental tax cash flows arising from the investment. Consider the information presented in Example 9.5.

The first stage is to calculate the annual writing down allowances (i.e. the capital allowances). The calculations are as follows:

End of year	Annual writing-down allowance (£)	Written-down value (£)
0	0	1 000 000
1	250 000 (25% × £1 000 000)	750 000
2	187 500 (25% × £750 000)	562 500
3	140 630 (25% × £562 500)	421 870
4	105 470 (25% × £421 870)	316 400
	683 600	

Next we calculate the additional taxable profits arising from the project. The calculations are as follows:

	Year 1 (£)	Year 2 (£)	Year 3 (£)	Year 4 (£)
Incremental annual profits	500 000	500 000	500 000	500 000
Less annual writing-down allowance	250 000	187 500	140 630	105 470
Incremental taxable profits	250 000	312 500	359 370	394 530
Incremental tax at 35%	87 500	109 370	125 780	138 090

You can see that for each year the incremental tax payment is calculated as follows:

corporate tax rate × (incremental profits – capital allowance)

Note that depreciation charges should not be included in the calculation of incremental cash flows or taxable profits. We must now consider the timing of the taxation payments. In the UK taxation payments vary depending on the end of the accounting year, but they are generally paid approximately one year after the end of the company's accounting year. We shall apply this rule to our example. This means that the tax payment of £87 500 for year 1 will be paid at the end of year 2, £109 370 tax will be paid at the end of year 3 and so on.

The incremental tax payments are now included in the NPV calculation:

Year	Cash flow (£)	Taxation	Net cash flow (£)	Discount factor	Present value (£)
0	−1 000 000	0	−1 000 000	1.0000	−1 000 000
1	+500 000	0	+500 000	0.9091	+454 550
2	+500 000	−87 500	+412 500	0.8264	+348 090
3	+500 000	−109 370	+390 630	0.7513	+293 480
4	+500 000 ⎱ +316 400[a] ⎰	−125 780	+690 620	0.6830	+471 690
5	0	−138 090	−138 090	0.6209	−85 740
				Net present value	+482 070

[a]Sale of machinery for written down value of £316 400.

The taxation rules in most countries allow capital allowances to be claimed on the *net* cost of the asset. In our example the machine will be purchased for £1 million and the estimated realizable value at the end of its life is its written-down value of £316 400. Therefore the

EXAMPLE 9.5

The Sentosa Company operates in Ruratania where investments in plant and machinery are eligible for 25% annual writing-down allowances on the written-down value using the reducing balance method of depreciation. The corporate tax rate is 35%. The company is considering whether to purchase some machinery which will cost £1 million and which is expected to result in additional net cash inflows and profits of £500 000 per annum for four years. It is anticipated that the machinery will be sold at the end of year 4 for its written-down value for taxation purposes. Assume a one year lag in the payment of taxes. Calculate the net present value assuming a cost of capital of 10%.

estimated net cost of the machine is £683 600. You will see from the above calculations of additional taxable profits that the total of the annual writing-down allowances (Row 2) amount to the net cost. How would the analysis change if the estimated realizable value for the machine was different from its written-down value, say £450 000? The company will have claimed allowances of £683 600 but the estimated net cost of the machine is £550 000 (£1 million – £450 000 estimated net realizable value). Therefore excess allowances of £133 600 (£683 600 – £550 000) will have been claimed and an adjustment must be made at the end of year 4 so that the tax authorities can claim back the excess allowance. This adjustment is called a balancing charge.

Note that the above calculation of taxable profits for year 4 will now be as follows:

Incremental annual profits	500 000
Less annual writing-down allowance	(105 470)
Add balancing charge	133 600
Incremental taxable profits	528 130
Incremental taxation at 35%	184 845

Let us now assume that the estimated disposal value is less than the written-down value for tax purposes, say £250 000. The net investment cost is £750 000 (£100 0000 – £250 000), but you will see that our calculations at the start of this section indicate that estimated taxation capital allowances of £683 600 will have been claimed by the end of year 4. Therefore an adjustment of £66 400 (£750 000 – £683 600) must be made at the end of year 4 to reflect the fact that insufficient capital allowances have been claimed. This adjustment is called a balancing allowance.

Thus in year 4 the total capital allowance will consist of an annual writing-down allowance of £105 470 plus a balancing allowance of £66 400, giving a total of £171 870. Taxable profits for year 4 are now £328 130 (500 000 – £171 870), and tax at the rate of 35% on these profits will be paid at the end of year 5.

Weighted average cost of capital

So far we have assumed that firms are financed only by equity finance (i.e. ordinary share capital and retained earnings). However, most companies are likely to be financed by a combination of debt and equity capital. These companies aim to maintain target proportions of debt and equity.

The cost of *new* debt capital is simply the after tax interest cost of raising new debt. Assume that the after tax cost of new debt capital is 6% and the required rate of return on equity capital is 14% and that the company intends to maintain a capital structure of 50% debt and 50% equity. The overall cost of capital for the company is calculated as follows:

$$= \left(\begin{array}{c} \text{proportion of debt capital} \\ \times \text{ cost of debt capital} \\ (0.5 \times 6\%) \end{array} \right) + \left(\begin{array}{c} \text{proportion of equity capital} \\ \times \text{ cost of equity capital} \\ (0.5 \times 14\%) \end{array} \right) = 10\%$$

The overall cost of capital is also called the **weighted average cost of capital**. Can we use the weighted average cost of capital as the discount rate to calculate a project's NPV? The answer is yes, provided that the project is of equivalent risk to the firm's existing assets and the firm intends to maintain its target capital structure of 50% debt and 50% equity.

We have now established how to calculate the discount rate for projects that are of similar risk to the firm's existing assets and to incorporate the financing aspects. It is the weighted average cost of equity and debt capital.

Summary

The following items relate to the learning objectives listed at the beginning of the chapter.

- **Explain the opportunity cost of an investment.**

  The rates of return that are available from investments in financial markets in securities with different levels of risk (e.g. company shares, company and government bonds) represent the opportunity cost of an investment. In other words, if cash is invested in a capital project it cannot be invested elsewhere to earn a return. A firm should therefore only invest in projects that yield a return in excess of the opportunity cost of investment.

- **Distinguish between compounding and discounting.**

  The process of converting cash invested today at a specific interest rate into a future value is known as compounding. Discounting is the opposite of compounding and refers to the process of converting cash to be received in the future into the value at the present time. The resulting present value is called the discounted present value.

- **Explain the concepts of net present value (NPV), internal rate of return (IRR), payback method and accounting rate of return (ARR).**

  Both NPV and IRR are methods of determining whether a project yields a return in excess of an equal risk investment in traded financial securities. A positive NPV provides an absolute value of the amount by which an investment exceeds the return available from an alternative investment in financial securities of equal risk. Conversely, a negative value indicates the amount by which an investment fails to match an equal risk investment in financial securities. In contrast, the IRR indicates the true percentage return from an investment after taking into account the time value of money. To ascertain whether an investment should be undertaken, the percentage internal rate of return on investment should be compared with the returns available from investing in equal risk in financial securities. Investing in all projects that have positive NPV's or IRR's in excess of the opportunity cost of capital should maximize shareholder value. The payback method is the length of time that is required for a stream of cash proceeds from an investment to recover the original cash outflow required by the investment. The ARR expresses the annual average profits arising from a project as a percentage return on the average investment required for the project.

● **Calculate NPV, IRR, the payback period and ARR.**

The NPV is calculated by discounting the net cash inflows from a project and deducting the investment outlay. The IRR is calculated by ascertaining the discount rate that will cause the NPV of a project to be zero. The payback period is calculated by adding up the cash flows expected in successive years until the total is equal to the original outlay. The ARR is calculated by dividing the average annual profits estimated from a project by the average investment cost. The calculation of NPV and IRR was illustrated using Example 9.1 and Examples 9.3 and 9.4 were used to illustrate the calculations of the payback period and the ARR.

● **Justify the superiority of NPV over the IRR.**

NPV is considered to be theoretically superior to IRR because: (a) unlike the NPV method the IRR method cannot be guaranteed to rank mutually exclusive projects correctly; (b) the percentage returns generated by the IRR method can be misleading when choosing between alternatives; (c) the IRR method makes incorrect reinvestment assumptions by assuming that the interim cash flows can be reinvested at the IRR rather than the cost of capital; and (d) where unconventional cash flows occur multiple IRR's are possible.

● **Explain the limitations of payback and ARR.**

The major limitations of the payback method are that it ignores the time value of money and it does not take into account the cash flows that are earned after the payback period. The ARR also fails to take into account the time value of money and relies on a percentage return rather than an absolute value.

● **Justify why the payback and ARR methods are widely used in practice.**

The payback method is frequently used in practice because (a) it is considered useful when firms face liquidity constraints and require a fast repayment of their investments; (b) it serves as a simple first-level screening device that identifies those projects that should be subject to more rigorous investigations; and (c) it provides a rough measure of risk, based on the assumption that the longer it takes for a project to pay for itself, the riskier it is. The ARR is a widely-used financial accounting measure of managerial and company performance. Therefore, managers are likely to be interested in how any new investment contributes to the business unit's overall accounting rate of return.

● **Describe the effect of performance measurement on capital investment decisions.**

Managerial and company performance is normally evaluated using short-term financial criteria whereas investment appraisal decisions should be based on the cash flows over the whole life of the projects. Thus, the way that performance is evaluated can have a profound influence on investment decisions and there is a danger that managers will make decisions on the basis of an investment's impact on the short-term financial performance evaluation criteria rather than using the NPV decision rule.

● **Calculate the incremental taxation payments arising from a proposed investment.**

The cash flows from a project must be reduced by the amount of taxation payable on these cash flows. However, the taxation savings arising from the capital allowances (i.e. annual writing down allowances) reduce the taxation payments. Because taxation payments do not occur at the same time as the associated cash flows, the precise timing of the taxation payments should be identified to calculate NPV. You should refer to the section headed 'Taxation and investment decisions' for an illustration of the computation of the incremental taxation payment.

Notes

1 Consider a project that costs £10 000 and has a life of four years and an estimated scrap value of £2000. The following diagram illustrates why the project's scrap value is added to the initial outlay to calculate the average capital employed. You can see that at the mid-point of the project's life the capital employed is equal to £6000 (i.e. ½ (10 000 + £2000)).
2 In 2003 the profits of UK companies were subject to a corporate tax rate of 30%. For small companies with annual profits of less than £300 000 the corporate tax rate was 19%.

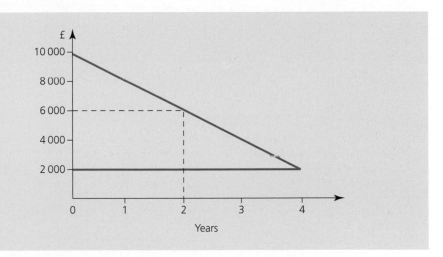

Key terms and concepts

accounting rate of return (p. 243)
balancing allowance (p. 250)
balancing charge (p. 250)
capital allowances (p. 248)
compounding interest (p. 231)
cost of capital (p. 230)
depreciation tax shield (p. 248)
discount rate (p. 230)
discounted rate of return (p. 236)
discounted cash flow (p. 231)
discounted payback method (p. 242)
discounted present value (p. 232)
discounting (p. 232)
interest rate (p. 230)

internal rate of return (p. 235)
minimum required rate of return (p. 230)
mutually exclusive projects (p. 239)
net present value (p. 233)
opportunity cost of an investment (p. 230)
payback method (p. 241)
present value (p. 232)
return on capital employed (p. 243)
return on investment (p. 243)
risk-free gilt-edged securities (p. 230)
time value of money (p. 232)
weighted average cost of capital (p. 251)
writing down allowance (p. 248)

Assessment material

Review questions

The review questions are short questions that enable you to assess your understanding of the main topics included in the chapter. The numbers in parentheses provide you with the page numbers to refer to if you cannot answer a specific question.

Review problems

The review problems are more complex and require you to relate and apply the chapter content to various business problems. The multiple-choice questions are the least demanding and normally take less than 10 minutes to complete. Fully worked solutions to the review problems are provided in a separate section at the end of the book. Further review problems for this chapter are available on the accompanying website, www.drury-online.com. The answers to these problems are available for lecturers on the lecturer's password-protected section of the website.

Case studies

The website also includes over 30 case study problems. A list of these cases is provided on pages 491–93. The Rawhide Development Company is a case study that is relevant to the content of this chapter.

Review questions

9.1 What is meant by the opportunity cost of an investment? What role does it play in capital investment decisions? (*p. 230*)

9.2 Distinguish between compounding and discounting. (*pp. 231–32*)

9.3 Explain what is meant by the term 'time value of money'. (*p. 232*)

9.4 Describe the concept of net present value (NPV). (*p. 233*)

9.5 Explain what is meant by the internal rate of return (IRR). (*pp. 235–36*)

9.6   Distinguish between independent and mutually exclusive projects. (*p. 239*)

9.7   Explain the theoretical arguments for preferring NPV to IRR when choosing among mutually exclusive projects. (*pp. 239–40*)

9.8   Why might managers choose to use IRR in preference to NPV? (*pp. 242–43*)

9.9   Describe the payback method. What are its main strengths and weaknesses? (*pp. 241–42*)

9.10   Describe the accounting rate of return. What are its main strengths and weaknesses? (*pp. 243, 245*)

9.11   Distinguish between the payback method and discounted payback method. (*p. 242*)

9.12   What impact can the way in which a manager's performance is measured have on capital investment decisions? (*pp. 246–47*)

9.13   How does taxation affect the appraisal of capital investments? (*pp. 248–50*)

9.14   Define writing-down-allowances (also known as depreciation tax shields or capital allowances), balancing allowances and balancing charges. (*pp. 248–50*)

Review problems

9.15   Dalby is currently considering an investment that gives a positive net present value of £3664 at 15%. At a discount rate of 20% it has a negative net present value of £21 451.

What is the internal rate of return of this investment?

A   15.7%
B   16.0%
C   19.3%
D   19.9%.

9.16   Ayr is planning on paying £300 into a fund on a monthly basis starting 3 months from now, for 12 months. The interest earned will be at a rate of 3% per month.

What is the present value of these payments?

A   £2816
B   £2733
C   £2541
D   £2986.

9.17   Calculation of payback, ARR and NPV

The following data are supplied relating to two investment projects, only one of which may be selected:

	Project A (£)	Project B (£)
Initial capital expenditure	50 000	50 000
Profit (loss) year 1	25 000	10 000
2	20 000	10 000
3	15 000	14 000
4	10 000	26 000
Estimated resale value at end of year 4	10 000	10 000

Notes

1   Profit is calculated after deducting straight-line depreciation.
2   The cost of capital is 10%.

Required:

(a) Calculate for each project:
  (i)   average annual rate of return on average capital invested;
  (ii) payback period;
  (iii) net present value.

(12 marks)

(b) Briefly discuss the relative merits of the three methods of evaluation mentioned in (a) above.

(10 marks)

(c) Explain which project you would recommend for acceptance.

(3 marks)
(Total 25 marks)

9.18 A machine with a purchase price of £14 000 is estimated to eliminate manual operations costing £4000 per year. The machine will last five years and have no residual value at the end of its life.

You are required to calculate:

(a) the internal rate of return (IRR);
(b) the level of annual saving necessary to achieve a 12% IRR;
(c) the net present value if the cost of capital is 10%.

9.19   Calculation of payback, ARR and NPV

Stadler is an ambitious young executive who has recently been appointed to the position of financial director of Paradis plc, a small listed company. Stadler regards this appointment as a temporary one, enabling him to gain experience before moving to a larger organization. His intention is to leave Paradis plc in three years' time, with its share price standing high. As a consequence, he is particularly concerned that the reported profits of Paradis plc should be as high as possible in his third and final year with the company.

Paradis plc has recently raised £350 000 from a rights issue, and the directors are considering three ways of using these funds. Three projects (A, B and C) are being considered, each involving the immediate purchase of equipment costing £350 000. One project only can be undertaken, and the equipment for each project will have a useful life equal to that of the project, with no scrap value. Stadler favours project C because it is expected to show the highest accounting profit in the third year. However, he does not wish to reveal his real reasons for favouring project C, and so, in his report to the chairman, he recommends project C because it shows the highest internal rate of return. The following summary is taken from his report:

Project	Net cash flows (£000) Years									Internal rate of return (%)
	0	1	2	3	4	5	6	7	8	
A	−350	100	110	104	112	138	160	180	–	27.5
B	−350	40	100	210	260	160	–	–	–	26.4
C	−350	200	150	240	40	–	–	–	–	33.0

The chairman of the company is accustomed to projects being appraised in terms of payback and accounting rate of return, and he is consequently suspicious of the use of internal rate of return as a method of project selection. Accordingly, the chairman has asked for an independent report on the choice of project. The company's cost of capital is 20% and a policy of straight-line depreciation is used to write off the cost of equipment in the financial statements.

Requirements:

(a) Calculate the payback period for each project.

(*3 marks*)

(b) Calculate the accounting rate of return for each project.

(*5 marks*)

(c) Prepare a report for the chairman with supporting calculations indicating which project should be preferred by the ordinary shareholders of Paradis plc.

(*12 marks*)

(d) Discuss the assumptions about the reactions of the stock market that are implicit in Stadler's choice of project C.

(*5 marks*)

Note: ignore taxation.

(*Total 25 marks*)

9.20 **Computation of NPV and tax payable**

Sound Equipment Ltd was formed five years ago to manufacture parts for hi-fi equipment. Most of its customers were individuals wanting to assemble their own systems. Recently, however, the company has embarked on a policy of expansion and has been approached by JBZ plc, a multinational manufacturer of consumer electronics. JBZ has offered Sound Equipment Ltd a contract to build an amplifier for its latest consumer product. If accepted, the contract will increase Sound Equipment's turnover by 20%.

JBZ's offer is a fixed price contract over three years, although it is possible for Sound Equipment to apply for subsequent contracts. The contract will involve Sound Equipment purchasing a specialist machine for £150 000. Although the machine has a 10-year life, it would be written off over the three years of the initial contract as it can only be used in the manufacture of the amplifier for JBZ.

The production director of Sound Equipment has already prepared a financial appraisal of the proposal. This is reproduced below. With a capital cost of £150 000 and total profits of £60 300, the production director has calculated the return on capital employed as 40.2%. As this is greater than Sound Equipment's cost of capital of 18%, the production director is recommending that the board accepts the contract.

	Year 1 (£)	Year 2 (£)	Year 3 (£)	Total
Turnover	180 000	180 000	180 000	540 000
Materials	60 000	60 000	60 000	180 000
Labour	40 000	40 000	40 000	120 000
Depreciation	50 000	50 000	50 000	150 000
Pre-tax profit	30 000	30 000	30 000	90 000
Corporation tax at 33%	9 900	9 900	9 900	29 700
After-tax profit	20 100	20 100	20 100	60 300

You are employed as the assistant accountant to Sound Equipment Ltd and report to John Green, the financial director, who asks you to carry out a full financial appraisal for the proposed contract. He feels that the production director's presentation is inappropriate. He provides you with the following additional information:

● Sound Equipment pays corporation tax at the rate of 33%;

● the machine will qualify for a 25% writing-down allowance on the reducing balance;

● the machine will have no further use other than in manufacturing the amplifier for JBZ;

● on ending the contract with JBZ, any outstanding capital allowances can be claimed as a balancing allowance;

● the company's cost of capital is 18%;

● the cost of materials and labour is forecast to increase by 5% per annum for years 2 and 3.

John Green reminds you that Sound Equipment operates a just in time stock policy and that production will be delivered immediately to JBZ, who will, under the terms of the contract, immediately pay for the deliveries. He also reminds you that suppliers are paid immediately on receipt of goods and that employees are also paid immediately.

Write a report to the financial director. Your report should:

(a) use the net present value technique to identify whether or not the initial three-year contract is worthwhile;

(b) explain your approach to taxation in your appraisal;

(c) identify *one* other factor to be considered before making a final decision.

Notes:
For the purpose of this task, you may assume the following:

● the machine would be purchased at the beginning of the accounting year;

● there is a one-year delay in paying corporation tax;

● all cashflows other than the purchase of the machine occur at the end of each year;

● Sound Equipment has no other assets on which to claim capital allowances.

PART 3

Information for Planning, Control and Performance Measurement

The objective in this section is to consider the implementation of decisions through the planning and control process. Planning involves systematically looking at the future, so that decisions can be made today which will bring the company its desired results. Control can be defined as the process of measuring and correcting actual performance to ensure that plans for implementing the chosen course of action are carried out.

Part Three contains five chapters. Chapter 10 considers the role of budgeting within the planning process and the relationship between the long-range plan and the budgeting process.

Chapters 11 and 12 are concerned with the control process. To fully understand the role that management accounting control systems play in the control process, it is necessary to be aware of how they relate to the entire array of control mechanisms used by organizations. Chapter 11 describes the different types of controls that are used by companies. The elements of management accounting control systems are described within the context of the overall control process. Chapter 12 focuses on the accounting control system. It describes the major features of a standard costing system: a system that enables the differences between the planned and actual outcomes to be analysed in detail. Chapter 12 also describes the operation of a standard costing system and explains the procedure for calculating the variances.

Chapters 13 and 14 examine the special problems of control and measuring performance of divisions and other decentralized units within an organization. Chapter 13 considers how divisional financial performance measures might be devised which will motivate managers to pursue overall organizational goals. Chapter 14 focuses on the transfer pricing problem and examines how transfer prices can be established that will motivate managers to make optimal decisions and also ensure that the performance measures derived from using the transfer prices represent a fair reflection of managerial performance.

The budgeting process

10

In the previous seven chapters we have considered how management accounting can assist managers in making decisions. The actions that follow managerial decisions normally involve several aspects of the business, such as the marketing, production, purchasing and finance functions, and it is important that management should coordinate these various interrelated aspects of decision-making. If they fail to do this, there is a danger that managers may each make decisions that they believe are in the best interests of the organization when, in fact, taken together they are not; for example, the marketing department may introduce a promotional campaign that is designed to increase sales demand to a level beyond that which the production department can handle. The various activities within a company should be coordinated by the preparation of plans of actions for future periods. These detailed plans are usually referred to as **budgets**.

Our objective in this chapter is to focus on the planning process within a business organization and to consider the role of budgeting within this process. What do we mean by planning? Planning is the design of a desired future and of effective ways of bringing it about (Ackoff, 1981). A distinction is normally made between short-term planning

---

LEARNING OBJECTIVES

After studying this chapter, you should be able to:

- explain how budgeting fits into the overall planning and control framework;
- identify and describe the six different purposes of budgeting;
- identify and describe the various stages in the budget process;
- prepare functional and master budgets;
- describe the use of computer-based financial models for budgeting;
- describe the limitations of incremental budgeting;
- describe activity-based budgeting;
- describe zero-base budgeting (ZBB).

(budgeting) and **long-range planning**, alternatively known as **strategic** or **corporate planning**. How is long-range planning distinguished from other forms of planning? Sizer (1989) defines long-range planning as a systematic and formalized process for purposely directing and controlling future operations towards desired objectives for periods extending beyond one year. Short-term planning or budgeting, on the other hand, must accept the environment of today, and the physical, human and financial resources at present available to the firm. These are to a considerable extent determined by the quality of the firm's long-range planning efforts.

Some of the material covered in this chapter relating to activity-based budgeting is complex and may not be appropriate for readers pursuing an introductory management accounting course. The more complex material has been highlighted as an advanced reading section. If you are pursuing an introductory course you may prefer to omit the highlighted section, or skim it on your first reading. You should delay reading this section until you have a good understanding of the principles of activity-based costing described in Chapter 6.

Stages in the planning process

To help you understand the budgetary process we shall begin by looking at how it fits into an overall general framework of planning, decision-making and control. The framework outlined in this model will be used to illustrate the role of long-term and short-term planning within the overall planning and control process (Figure 10.1). The first stage involves establishing the objectives of the organization.

Stage 1: Establishing objectives

Establishing **objectives** is an essential prerequisite of the planning process. In all organizations employees must have a good understanding of what the organization is trying to achieve. Strategic or long-range planning therefore begins with the specification of the objectives towards which future operations should be directed. The attainment of objectives should be measurable in some way and ideally people should be motivated by them. Johnson and Scholes (2002) distinguish between three different objectives, which form a hierarchy: the 'mission' of an organization, corporate objectives and unit objectives.

The **mission** of an organization describes in very general terms the broad purpose and reason for an organization's existence, the nature of the business(es) it is in and the customers it seeks to serve and satisfy. It is a visionary projection of the central and over-riding concepts on which the organization is based. Objectives tend to be more specific, and represent desired states or results to be achieved.

Corporate objectives relate to the organization as a whole. They are normally measurable and are expressed in financial terms such as desired profits or sales levels, return on capital employed, rates of growth or market share. Corporate objectives are normally formulated by members of the board of directors and handed down to senior managers. It is important that senior managers in an organization understand clearly where their company is going and why and how their own role contributes to the attainment of corporate objectives. Once the overall objectives of the organization have been established they must be broken down into subsidiary objectives relating to areas such as product range, market segmentation, customer service and so on. Objectives must also be developed for the different parts of an organization. **Unit objectives** relate to the specific objectives of individual units within the organization, such as a division or one company within a holding company. Corporate objectives are normally set for the organization as a whole and are then translated into unit objectives, which

FIGURE 10.1   *The role of long- and short-term planning within the planning, decision-making and control process*

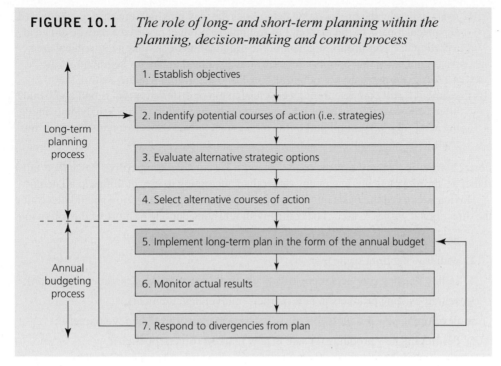

become the targets for the individual units. You should note that the expression **aims** is some-times used as an alternative to mission and the term **goals** is synonymous with objectives.

Stage 2: Identify potential strategies

The next stage shown in Figure 10.1 is to identify a range of possible courses of action (or **strategies**) that might enable the company's objectives to be achieved. The corporate strategy literature advocates that, prior to developing strategies, it is necessary to undertake a **strategic analysis** to become better informed about the organization's present strategic situation. This involves understanding the company's present position, its strengths and weaknesses and its opportunities and risks.

Having undertaken a strategic analysis, the next stage is to identify alternative strategies. The identification of strategies should take into account the following:

1 the generic strategy to be pursued (i.e. the basis on which the organization will compete or sustain excellence).

2 the alternative directions in which the organization may wish to develop.

An organization should determine the basis on which it will compete and/or sustain a superior level of performance (i.e. the generic strategy that it will follow). The purpose is to ensure that deliberate choices are made regarding the type of competitive advantage it wishes to attain. Porter (1985) has identified three **generic strategies** that an organization can follow:

1 *cost leadership*, whereby the organization aims to be the lowest cost producer within the industry;

2 *differentiation*, through which the organization seeks some unique dimension in its product/service that is valued by consumers, and which can command a premium price;

3 *focus*, whereby the organization determines the way in which the strategy is focused at particular parts of the market. For example, a product or service may be aimed at a particular buyer group, segment of the product line or smaller geographical area. An organization that adopts a focused strategy aimed at narrow segments of the market to the exclusion of others also needs to determine whether within the segment it will compete through cost leadership or differentiation. Small companies often follow very focused or *niche* strategies by becoming so specialized in meeting the needs of a very small part of the market that they are secure against competition from large organizations.

Porter's view is that any organization seeking a sustainable competitive advantage must select an appropriate generic strategy rather than attempting to be 'all things to all people'.

Having identified the basis on which it will compete, an organization should determine the directions it wishes to take. The company should consider one or more of the following:

1 doing nothing;
2 withdrawing from some markets;
3 selling existing products more effectively in existing markets (market penetration);
4 selling existing products in new markets (market development);
5 developing new products for sale in existing markets (product development);
6 developing new products for sale in new markets (diversification).

Stage 3: Evaluation of strategic options

The alternative strategies should be examined based on the following criteria:[1]

1 *suitability*, which seeks to ascertain the extent to which the proposed strategies fit the situation identified in the strategic analysis. For example, does the strategy exploit the company strengths and environmental opportunities, avoid the weaknesses and counter the environmental threats?

2 *feasibility*, which focuses on whether the strategy can be implemented in resource terms. For example, can the strategy be funded? Can the necessary market position be achieved? Can the company cope with the competitive reactions?

3 *acceptability*, which is concerned with whether a particular strategy is acceptable. For example, will it be sufficiently profitable? Is the level of risk acceptable?

The above criteria represent a broad framework of general criteria against which strategic options can be judged. The criteria narrow down the options to be considered for a detailed evaluation. The evaluation of the options should be based on the approaches described in Chapter 9 and will not be repeated here. Management should select those strategic options that have the greatest potential for achieving the company's objectives. There could be just one strategy chosen or several.

Stage 4: select course of action

When management has selected those strategic options that have the greatest potential for achieving the company's objectives, long-term plans should be created to implement the strategies. A **long-term plan** is a statement of the preliminary targets and activities required by an organization to achieve its strategic plans together with a broad estimate for each year of the resources required.

Because long-term planning involves 'looking into the future' for several years ahead the plans tend to be uncertain, general in nature, imprecise and subject to change.

Stage 5: implementation of the long-term plans

Budgeting is concerned with the implementation of the long-term plan for the year ahead. Because of the shorter planning horizon budgets are more precise and detailed. Budgets are a clear indication of what is expected to be achieved during the budget period whereas long-term plans represent the broad directions that top management intend to follow.

The budget is not something that originates 'from nothing' each year – it is developed within the context of ongoing business and is ruled by previous decisions that have been taken within the long-term planning process. When the activities are initially approved for inclusion in the long-term plan, they are based on uncertain estimates that are projected for several years. These proposals must be reviewed and revised in the light of more recent information. This review and revision process frequently takes place as part of the annual budgeting process, and it may result in important decisions being taken on possible activity adjustments within the current budget period. The budgeting process cannot therefore be viewed as being purely concerned with the current year – it must be considered as an integrated part of the long-term planning process.

Stages 6 and 7: Monitor actual outcomes and respond to divergencies from planned outcomes

The final stages in the decision-making, planning and control process outlined in Figure 10.1 are to compare the actual and the planned outcomes, and to respond to any divergencies from the plan. These stages represent the control process of budgeting, but a detailed discussion of this process will be deferred until Chapter 11. Let us now consider the short-term budgeting process in more detail.

The multiple functions of budgets

Budgets serve a number of useful purposes. They include:

1 *planning* annual operations;
2 *coordinating* the activities of the various parts of the organization and ensuring that the parts are in harmony with each other;
3 *communicating* plans to the various responsibility centre managers;
4 *motivating* managers to strive to achieve the organizational goals;
5 *controlling* activities;
6 *evaluating* the performance of managers.

Let us now examine each of these six factors.

Planning

The major planning decisions will already have been made as part of the long-term planning process. However, the annual budgeting process leads to the refinement of those plans, since managers must produce detailed plans for the implementation of the long-range plan. Without the annual budgeting process, the pressures of day-to-day operating problems may tempt managers not to plan for future operations. The budgeting process ensures that managers do plan for future operations, and that they consider how conditions in the next year might change and what steps they should take now to respond to these changed conditions. This process encourages managers to anticipate problems before they arise, and hasty decisions that are made on the spur of the moment, based on expediency rather than reasoned judgement, will be minimized.

Coordination

The budget serves as a vehicle through which the actions of the different parts of an organization can be brought together and reconciled into a common plan. Without any guidance, managers may each make their own decisions, believing that they are working in the best interests of the organization. For example, the purchasing manager may prefer to place large orders so as to obtain large discounts; the production manager will be concerned with avoiding high stock levels; and the accountant will be concerned with the impact of the decision on the cash resources of the business. It is the aim of budgeting to reconcile these differences for the good of the organization as a whole, rather than for the benefit of any individual area. Budgeting therefore compels managers to examine the relationship between their own operations and those of other departments, and, in the process, to identify and resolve conflicts.

Communication

If an organization is to function effectively, there must be definite lines of communication so that all the parts will be kept fully informed of the plans and the policies, and constraints, to which the organization is expected to conform. Everyone in the organization should have a clear understanding of the part they are expected to play in achieving the annual budget. This process will ensure that the appropriate individuals are made accountable for implementing the budget. Through the budget, top management communicates its expectations to lower level management, so that all members of the organization may understand these expectations and can coordinate their activities to attain them. It is not just the budget itself that facilitates communication – much vital information is communicated in the actual act of preparing it.

Motivation

The budget can be a useful device for influencing managerial behaviour and motivating managers to perform in line with the organizational objectives. A budget provides a standard that under certain circumstances, a manager may be motivated to strive to achieve. However, budgets can also encourage inefficiency and conflict between managers. If individuals have actively participated in preparing the budget, and it is used as a tool to assist managers in managing their departments, it can act as a strong motivational device by providing a challenge. Alternatively, if the budget is dictated from above, and imposes a threat rather than a challenge, it may be resisted and do more harm than good. We shall discuss the dysfunctional motivational consequence of budgets in Chapter 11.

Control

A budget assists managers in managing and controlling the activities for which they are responsible. By comparing the actual results with the budgeted amounts for different categories of expenses, managers can ascertain which costs do not conform to the original plan and thus require their attention. This process enables management to operate a system of **management by exception** which means that a manager's attention and effort can be concentrated on significant deviations from the expected results. By investigating the reasons for the deviations, managers may be able to identify inefficiencies such as the purchase of inferior quality materials. When the reasons for the inefficiencies have been found, appropriate control action should be taken to remedy the situation.

Performance evaluation

A manager's performance is often evaluated by measuring his or her success in meeting the budgets. In some companies bonuses are awarded on the basis of an employee's ability to achieve the targets specified in the periodic budgets, or promotion may be partly dependent upon a manager's budget record. In addition, the manager may wish to evaluate his or her own performance. The budget thus provides a useful means of informing managers of how well they are performing in meeting targets that they have previously helped to set. The use of budgets as a method of performance evaluation also influences human behaviour, and for this reason we shall consider the behavioural aspects of performance evaluation in Chapter 11.

Conflicting roles of budgets

Because a single budget system is normally used to serve several purposes there is a danger that they may conflict with each other. For instance the planning and motivation roles may be in conflict with each other. Demanding budgets that may not be achieved may be appropriate to motivate maximum performance, but they are unsuitable for planning purposes. For these a budget should be set based on easier targets that are expected to be met.

There is also a conflict between the planning and performance evaluation roles. For planning purposes budgets are set in advance of the budget period based on an anticipated set of circumstances or environment. Performance evaluation should be based on a comparison of actual performance with an adjusted budget to reflect the circumstances under which managers actually operated. In practice, many firms compare actual performance with the original budget (adjusted to the actual level of activity, i.e. a flexible budget), but if the circumstances envisaged when the original budget was set have changed then there will be a planning and evaluation conflict.

The budget period

The conventional approach is that once per year the manager of each budget centre prepares a detailed budget for one year. The budget is divided into either twelve monthly or thirteen four-weekly periods for control purposes. The preparation of budgets on an annual basis has been strongly criticized on the grounds that it is too rigid and ties a company to a twelve month commitment, which can be risky because the budget is based on uncertain forecasts.

An alternative approach is for the annual budget to be broken down by months for the first three months, and by quarters for the remaining nine months. The quarterly budgets are then developed on a monthly basis as the year proceeds. For example, during the first quarter, the monthly budgets for the second quarter will be prepared; and during the second quarter, the monthly budgets for the third quarter will be prepared. The quarterly budgets may also be reviewed as the year unfolds. For example, during the first quarter, the budget for the next three quarters may be changed as new information becomes available. A new budget for a fifth quarter will also be prepared. This process is known as **continuous** or **rolling budgeting**, and ensures that a twelve month budget is always available by adding a quarter in the future as the quarter just ended is dropped. Contrast this with a budget prepared once per year. As the year goes by, the period for which a budget is available will shorten until the budget for next year is prepared. Rolling budgets also ensure that planning is not something that takes place once a year when the budget is being formulated. Instead, budgeting is a continuous process, and managers are encouraged to constantly look ahead and review future plans. Furthermore, it is likely that actual performance will be compared with a more realistic target, because budgets are being constantly reviewed and updated. The main disadvantage of a rolling budget is that it can create uncertainty for managers because the budget is constantly being changed.

Irrespective of whether the budget is prepared on an annual or a continuous basis, it is important that monthly or four-weekly budgets be used for *control* purposes.

Administration of the budgeting process

It is important that suitable administration procedures be introduced to ensure that the budget process works effectively. In practice, the procedures should be tailor-made to the requirements of the organization, but as a general rule a firm should ensure that procedures are established for approving the budgets and that the appropriate staff support is available for assisting managers in preparing their budgets.

The budget committee

The budget committee should consist of high-level executives who represent the major segments of the business. Its major task is to ensure that budgets are realistically established and that they are coordinated satisfactorily. The normal procedure is for the functional heads to present their budget to the committee for approval. If the budget does not reflect a reasonable level of performance, it will not be approved and the functional head will be required to adjust the budget and re-submit it for approval. It is important that the person whose performance is being measured should agree that the revised budget can be achieved; otherwise, if it is considered to be impossible to achieve, it will not act as a motivational device. If budget revisions are made, the budgetees should at least feel that they were given a fair hearing by the committee. We shall discuss budget negotiation in more detail later in this chapter.

The budget committee should appoint a budget officer, who will normally be the accountant. The role of the budget officer is to coordinate the individual budgets into a budget for the whole organization, so that the budget committee and the budgetee can see the impact of an individual budget on the organization as a whole.

Accounting staff

The accounting staff will normally assist managers in the preparation of their budgets; they will, for example, circulate and advise on the instructions about budget preparation, provide past information that may be useful for preparing the present budget, and ensure that managers submit their budgets on time. The accounting staff do not determine the content of the various budgets, but they do provide a valuable advisory and clerical service for the line managers.

Budget manual

A budget manual should be prepared by the accountant. It will describe the objectives and procedures involved in the budgeting process and will provide a useful reference source for managers responsible for budget preparation. In addition, the manual may include a timetable specifying the order in which the budgets should be prepared and the dates when they should be presented to the budget committee. The manual should be circulated to all individuals who are responsible for preparing budgets.

Stages in the budgeting process

The important stages are as follows:

1 communicating details of budget policy and guidelines to those people responsible for the preparation of budgets;
2 determining the factor that restricts output;
3 preparation of the sales budget;
4 initial preparation of various budgets;
5 negotiation of budgets with superiors;
6 coordination and review of budgets;
7 final acceptance of budgets;
8 ongoing review of budgets.

Let us now consider each of these stages in more detail.

Communicating details of the budget policy

Many decisions affecting the budget year will have been taken previously as part of the long-term planning process. The long-range plan is therefore the starting point for the preparation of the annual budget. Thus top management must communicate the policy effects of the long-term plan to those responsible for preparing the current year's budgets. Policy effects might include planned changes in sales mix, or the expansion or contraction of certain activities. In addition, other important guidelines that are to govern the preparation of the budget should be specified – for example the allowances that are to be made for price and wage increases, and the expected changes in productivity. Also, any expected changes in industry demand and output should be communicated by top management to the managers responsible for budget preparation. It is essential that all managers be made aware of the policy of top management for implementing the long-term plan in the current year's budget so that common guidelines can be established. The process also indicates to the managers responsible for preparing the budgets how they should respond to any expected environmental changes.

Determining the factor that restricts performance

In every organization there is some factor that restricts performance for a given period. In the majority of organizations this factor is sales demand. However, it is possible for production capacity to restrict performance when sales demand is in excess of available capacity. Prior to the preparation of the budgets, it is necessary for top management to determine the factor that restricts performance, since this factor determines the point at which the annual budgeting process should begin.

Preparation of the sales budget

The volume of sales and the sales mix determine the level of a company's operations, when sales demand is the factor that restricts output. For this reason, the sales budget is the most important plan in the annual budgeting process. This budget is also the most difficult plan to produce, because total sales revenue depends on the actions of customers. In addition, sales demand may be influenced by the state of the economy or the actions of competitors.

Initial preparation of budgets

The managers who are responsible for meeting the budgeted performance should prepare the budget for those areas for which they are responsible. The preparation of the budget should be a 'bottom-up' process. This means that the budget should originate at the lowest levels of management and be refined and coordinated at higher levels. The justification for this approach is that it enables managers to participate in the preparation of their budgets and increases the probability that they will accept the budget and strive to achieve the budget targets.

There is no single way in which the appropriate quantity for a particular budget item is determined. Past data may be used as the starting point for producing the budgets, but this does not mean that budgeting is based on the assumption that what has happened in the past will occur in the future. Changes in future conditions must be taken into account, but past information may provide useful guidance for the future. In addition, managers may look to the guidelines provided by top management for determining the content of their budgets. For example, the guidelines may provide specific instructions as to the content of their budgets and the permitted changes that can be made in the prices of purchases of materials and services. For production activities standard costs may be used as the basis for costing activity volumes which are planned in the budget.

Negotiation of budgets

To implement a participative approach to budgeting, the budget should be originated at the lowest level of management. The managers at this level should submit their budget to their superiors for approval. The superior should then incorporate this budget with other budgets for which he or she is responsible and then submit this budget for approval to his or her superior. The manager who is the superior then becomes the budgetee at the next higher level. The process is illustrated in Figure 10.2. Sizer (1989) describes this approach as a two-way process of a top-down statement of objectives and strategies, bottom-up budget preparation and top-down approval by senior management.

The lower-level managers are represented by boxes 1–8. Managers 1 and 2 will prepare their budgets in accordance with the budget policy and the guidelines laid down by top management. The managers will submit their budget to their supervisor, who is in charge of the whole department (department A). Once these budgets have been agreed by the manager of

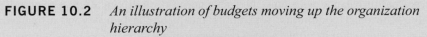

FIGURE 10.2 *An illustration of budgets moving up the organization hierarchy*

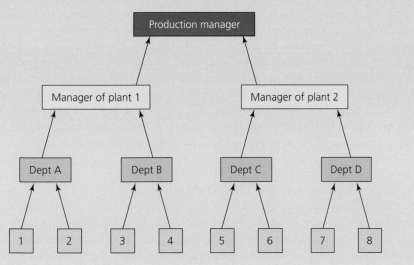

department A, they will be combined by the departmental manager, who will then present this budget to his or her superior (manager of plant 1) for approval. The manager of plant 1 is also responsible for department B, and will combine the agreed budgets for departments A and B before presenting the combined budget to his or her supervisor (the production manager). The production manager will merge the budget for plants 1 and 2, and this final budget will represent the production budget that will be presented to the budget committee for approval.

At each of these stages the budgets will be negotiated between the budgetees and their superiors, and eventually they will be agreed by both parties. Hence the figures that are included in the budget are the result of a bargaining process between a manager and his or her superior. It is important that the budgetees should participate in arriving at the final budget and that the superior does not revise the budget without giving full consideration to the subordinates' arguments for including any of the budgeted items. Otherwise, real participation will not be taking place, and it is unlikely that the subordinate will be motivated to achieve a budget that he or she did not accept.

It is also necessary to be watchful that budgetees do not deliberately attempt to obtain approval for easily attainable budgets, or attempt to deliberately understate budgets in the hope that the budget that is finally agreed will represent an easily attainable target. It is equally unsatisfactory for a superior to impose difficult targets in the hope that an authoritarian approach will produce the desired results. The desired results may be achieved in the short term, but only at the cost of a loss of morale and increased labour turnover in the future.

The negotiation process is of vital importance in the budgeting process, and can determine whether the budget becomes a really effective management tool or just a clerical device. If managers are successful in establishing a position of trust and confidence with their subordinates, the negotiation process will produce a meaningful improvement in the budgetary process and outcomes for the period.

Coordination and review of budgets

As the individual budgets move up the organizational hierarchy in the negotiation process, they must be examined in relation to each other. This examination may indicate that some budgets are out of balance with other budgets and need modifying so that they will be compatible with other conditions, constraints and plans that are beyond a manager's knowledge or control. For example, a plant manager may include equipment replacement in his or her budget when funds are simply not available. The accountant must identify such inconsistencies and bring them to the attention of the appropriate manager. Any changes in the budgets should be made by the responsible managers, and this may require that the budgets be recycled from the bottom to the top for a second or even a third time until all the budgets are coordinated and are acceptable to all the parties involved. During the coordination process, a budgeted profit and loss account, a balance sheet and a cash flow statement should be prepared to ensure that all the parts combine to produce an acceptable whole. Otherwise, further adjustments and budget recycling will be necessary until the budgeted profit and loss account, the balance sheet and the cash flow statement prove to be acceptable.

Final acceptance of the budgets

When all the budgets are in harmony with each other, they are summarized into a **master budget** consisting of a budgeted profit and loss account, a balance sheet and a cash flow statement. After the master budget has been approved, the budgets are then passed down through the organization to the appropriate responsibility centres. The approval of the master budget is the authority for the manager of each responsibility centre to carry out the plans contained in each budget.

Budget review

The budget process should not stop when the budgets have been agreed. Periodically, the actual results should be compared with the budgeted results. These comparisons should normally be made on a monthly basis and a report sent to the appropriate budgetees in the first week of the following month, so that it has the maximum motivational impact. This will enable management to identify the items that are not proceeding according to plan and to investigate the reasons for the differences. If these differences are within the control of management, corrective action can be taken to avoid similar inefficiencies occurring again in the future. However, the differences may be due to the fact that the budget was unrealistic to begin with, or that the actual conditions during the budget year were different from those anticipated; the budget for the remainder of the year would then be invalid.

   During the budget year, the budget committee should periodically evaluate the actual performance and reappraise the company's future plans. If there are any changes in the actual conditions from those originally expected, this will normally mean that the budget plans should be adjusted. This revised budget then represents a revised statement of formal operating plans for the remaining portion of the budget period. The important point to note is that the budgetary process does not end for the current year once the budget has begun; budgeting should be seen as a continuous and dynamic process.

A detailed illustration

Let us now look at an illustration of the procedure for constructing budgets in a manufacturing company, using the information contained in Example 10.1. Note that the level of detail included here is much less than that which would be presented in practice. A truly realistic illustration would fill many pages, with detailed budgets being analysed in various ways. We shall

EXAMPLE 10.1

The Enterprise Company manufactures two products, known as alpha and sigma. Alpha is produced in department 1 and sigma in department 2. The following information is available for 200X.

Standard material and labour costs:

	(£)
Material X	7.20 per unit
Material Y	16.00 per unit
Direct labour	12.00 per hour

Overhead is recovered on a direct labour hour basis.

The standard material and labour usage for each product is as follows:

	Model alpha	Model sigma
Material X	10 units	8 units
Material Y	5 units	9 units
Direct labour	10 hours	15 hours

The balance sheet for the previous year end 200X was as follows:

	(£)	(£)	(£)
Fixed assets:			
Land		170 000	
Buildings and equipment	1 292 000		
Less depreciation	255 000	1 037 000	1 207 000
Current assets:			
Stocks, finished goods	99 076		
raw materials	189 200		
Debtors	289 000		
Cash	34 000		
	611 276		
Less current liabilities			
Creditors	248 800		362 476
Net assets			1 569 476
Represented by shareholder's interest:			
1 200 000 ordinary shares of £1 each		1 200 000	
Reserves		369 476	
			1 569 476

Other relevant data is as follows for the year 200X:

	Finished product	
	Model alpha	Model sigma
Forecast sales (units)	8500	1600
Selling price per unit	£400	£560
Ending inventory required (units)	1870	90
Beginning inventory (units)	170	85

	Direct material	
	Material X	**Material Y**
Beginning inventory (units)	8 500	8 000
Ending inventory required (units)	10 200	1 700

	Department 1 (£)	**Department 2** (£)
Budgeted variable overhead rates (per direct labour hour):		
Indirect materials	1.20	0.80
Indirect labour	1.20	1.20
Power (variable portion)	0.60	0.40
Maintenance (variable portion)	0.20	0.40
Budgeted fixed overheads		
Depreciation	100 000	80 000
Supervision	100 000	40 000
Power (fixed portion)	40 000	2 000
Maintenance (fixed portion)	45 600	3 196

	(£)
Estimated non-manufacturing overheads:	
Stationery etc. (Administration)	4 000
Salaries	
Sales	74 000
Office	28 000
Commissions	60 000
Car expenses (Sales)	22 000
Advertising	80 000
Miscellaneous (Office)	8 000
	276 000

Budgeted cash flows are as follows:

	Quarter 1 (£)	**Quarter 2** (£)	**Quarter 3** (£)	**Quarter 4** (£)
Receipts from customers	1 000 000	1 200 000	1 120 000	985 000
Payments:				
Materials	400 000	480 000	440 000	547 984
Payments for wages	400 000	440 000	480 000	646 188
Other costs and expenses	120 000	100 000	72 016	13 642

You are required to prepare a master budget for the year 200X and the following budgets:

1 sales budget;

2 production budget;

3 direct materials usage budget;

4 direct materials purchase budget;
5 direct labour budget;
6 factory overhead budget;
7 selling and administration budget;
8 cash budget.

consider an annual budget, whereas a realistic illustration would analyse the annual budget into twelve monthly periods. Monthly analysis would considerably increase the size of the illustration, but would not give any further insight into the basic concepts or procedures. In addition, we shall assume in this example that the budgets are prepared for only two responsibility centres (namely departments 1 and 2). In practice, many responsibility centres are likely to exist.

Sales budget

The sales budget shows the quantities of each product that the company plans to sell and the intended selling price. It provides the predictions of total revenue from which cash receipts from customers will be estimated, and it also supplies the basic data for constructing budgets for production costs, and for selling, distribution and administrative expenses. The sales budget is therefore the foundation of all other budgets, since all expenditure is ultimately dependent on the volume of sales. If the sales budget is not accurate, the other budget estimates will be unreliable. We will assume that the Enterprise Company has completed a marketing analysis and that the following annual sales budget is based on the result:

Schedule 1 – Sales budget for year ending 200X

Product	Units sold	Selling price (£)	Total revenue (£)
Alpha	8500	400	3 400 000
Sigma	1600	560	896 000
			4 296 000

Schedule 1 represents the *total* sales budget for the year. In practice, the *total* sales budget will be supported by detailed *subsidiary* sales budgets where sales are analysed by areas of responsibility, such as sales territories, and into monthly periods analysed by products. The detailed *subsidiary* sales budget could be set out as shown on page 278.

Note that with the detailed subsidiary monthly budgets the total budgeted sales of £4 296 000 is analysed by each sales territory for each month of the budget period. The detailed analysis assumes that sales are divided among the four sales territories as follows:

	Alpha	Sigma
North	3000 units	500 units
South	2500 units	600 units
East	1000 units	200 units
West	2000 units	300 units
	8500 units	1600 units

Detailed monthly budgets for North, South, East and West sales territories

		North		South		East		West		Total	
		Units	Value (£)	Units	Value (£)	Units	Value (£)	Units	Value (£)	Units	Value (£)
Month 1	Alpha										
	Sigma	―――	―――	―――	―――	―――	―――	―――	―――	―――	―――
	Total	―――	―――	―――	―――	―――	―――	―――	―――	―――	―――
Month 2											
Month 3											
Month 4											
Month 5											
Month 6											
Month 7											
Month 8											
Month 9											
Month 10											
Month 11											
Month 12											
Total months 1–12											
	Alpha	3000	1 200 000	2500	1 000 000	1000	400 000	2000	800 000	8500	3 400 000
	Sigma	500	280 000	600	336 000	200	112 000	300	168 000	1600	896 000
			1 480 000		1 336 000		512 000		968 000		4 296 000

Production budget and budgeted stock levels

When the sales budget has been completed, the next stage is to prepare the production budget. This budget is expressed in *quantities only* and is the responsibility of the production manager. The objective is to ensure that production is sufficient to meet sales demand and that economic stock levels are maintained. The production budget (schedule 2) for the year will be as follows:

Schedule 2 – Annual production budget

	Department 1 (alpha)	Department 2 (sigma)
Units to be sold	8 500	1600
Planned closing stock	1 870	90
Total units required for sales and stocks	10 370	1690
Less planned opening stocks	170	85
Units to be produced	10 200	1605

The total production for each department should also be analysed on a monthly basis.

Direct materials usage budget

The supervisors of departments 1 and 2 will prepare estimates of the materials which are required to meet the production budget. The materials usage budget for the year will be as follows:

Schedule 3 – Annual direct material usage budget

	Department 1			Department 2			Total units	Total unit price (£)	Total (£)
	Units	Unit price (£)	Total (£)	Units	Unit price (£)	Total (£)			
Material X	102 000[a]	7.20	734 400	12 840[c]	7.20	92 448	114 840	7.20	826 848
Material Y	51 000[b]	16.00	816 000	14 445[d]	16.00	231 120	65 445	16.00	1 047 120
			1 550 400			323 568			1 873 968

[a]10 200 units production at 10 units per unit of production.
[b]10 200 units production at 5 units per unit of production.
[c]1605 units production at 8 units per unit of production.
[d]1605 units production at 9 units per unit of production.

Direct materials purchase budget

The direct materials purchase budget is the responsibility of the purchasing manager, since it will be he or she who is responsible for obtaining the planned quantities of raw materials to meet the production requirements. The objective is to purchase these materials at the right time at the planned purchase price. In addition, it is necessary to take into account the planned raw material stock levels. The annual materials purchase budget for the year will be as follows:

Schedule 4 – Direct materials purchase budget

	Material X (units)	Material Y (units)
Quantity necessary to meet production requirements as per material usage budget	114 840	65 445
Planned closing stock	10 200	1 700
	125 040	67 145
Less planned opening stock	8 500	8 000
Total units to be purchased	116 540	59 145
Planned unit purchase price	£7.20	£16
Total purchases	£839 088	£946 320

Note that this budget is a summary budget for the year, but for detailed planning and control it will be necessary to analyse the annual budget on a monthly basis.

Direct labour budget

The direct labour budget is the responsibility of the respective managers of departments 1 and 2. They will prepare estimates of the departments' labour hours required to meet the planned production. Where different grades of labour exist, these should be specified separately in the budget. The budget rate per hour should be determined by the industrial relations department. The direct labour budget will be as follows:

Schedule 5 – Annual direct labour budget

	Department 1	Department 2	Total
Budgeted production (units)	10 200	1 605	
Hours per unit	10	15	
Total budgeted hours	102 000	24 075	126 075
Budgeted wage rate per hour	£12	£12	
Total wages	£1 224 000	£288 900	£1 512 900

Factory overhead budget

The factory overhead budget is also the responsibility of the respective production department managers. The total of the overhead budget will depend on the behaviour of the costs of the individual overhead items in relation to the anticipated level of production. The overheads must also be analysed according to whether they are controllable or non-controllable for the purpose of cost control. The factory overhead budget will be as follows:

Schedule 6 – Annual factory overhead budget
Anticipated activity – 102 000 direct labour hours (department 1)
24 075 direct labour hours (department 2)

	Variable overhead rate per direct labour hour		Overheads		Total
	Department 1	Department 2	Department 1	Department 2	
	(£)	(£)	(£)	(£)	(£)
Controllable overheads:					
Indirect material	1.20	0.80	122 400	19 260	
Indirect labour	1.20	1.20	122 400	28 890	
Power (variable portion)	0.60	0.40	61 200	9 630	
Maintenance (variable portion)	0.20	0.40	20 400	9 630	
			326 400	67 410	393 810
Non-controllable overheads:					
Depreciation			100 000	80 000	
Supervision			100 000	40 000	
Power (fixed portion)			40 000	2 000	
Maintenance (fixed portion)			45 600	3 196	
			285 600	125 196	410 796
Total overhead			612 000	192 606	804 606
Budgeted departmental overhead rate			£6.00[a]	8.00[b]	

[a]£612 000 total overheads divided by 102 000 direct labour hours.
[b]£192 606 total overheads divided by 24 075 direct labour hours.

The budgeted expenditure for the variable overhead items is determined by multiplying the budgeted direct labour hours for each department by the budgeted variable overhead rate per hour. It is assumed that all variable overheads vary in relation to direct labour hours.

Selling and administration budget

The selling and administration budgets have been combined here to simplify the presentation. In practice, separate budgets should be prepared: the sales manager will be responsible for the selling budget, the distribution manager will be responsible for the distribution expenses and the chief administrative officer will be responsible for the administration budget.

Schedule 7 – Annual selling and administration budget

	(£)	(£)
Selling:		
Salaries	74 000	
Commission	60 000	
Car expenses	22 000	
Advertising	80 000	236 000
Administration:		
Stationery	4 000	
Salaries	28 000	
Miscellaneous	8 000	40 000
		276 000

Departmental budgets

For cost control the direct labour budget, materials usage budget and factory overhead budget are combined into separate departmental budgets. These budgets are normally broken down into twelve separate monthly budgets, and the actual monthly expenditure is compared with the budgeted amounts for each of the items concerned. This comparison is used for judging how effective managers are in controlling the expenditure for which they are responsible. The departmental budget for department 1 will be as follows:

Department 1 – Annual departmental operating budget

	(£)	Budget (£)	Actual (£)
Direct labour (from schedule 5):			
102 000 hours at £12		1 224 000	
Direct materials (from schedule 3):			
102 000 units of material X at £7.20 per unit	734 400		
51 000 units of material Y at £16 per unit	816 000	1 550 400	
Controllable overheads (from schedule 6):			
Indirect materials	122 400		
Indirect labour	122 400		
Power (variable portion)	61 200		
Maintenance (variable portion)	20 400	326 400	

Uncontrollable overheads (from schedule 6):

Depreciation	100 000	
Supervision	100 000	
Power (fixed portion)	40 000	
Maintenance (fixed portion)	45 600	285 600
		3 386 400

Master budget

When all the budgets have been prepared, the budgeted profit and loss account and balance sheet provide the overall picture of the planned performance for the budget period.

Budgeted profit and loss account for the year ending 200X

	(£)	(£)
Sales (schedule 1)		4 296 000
Opening stock of raw materials	189 200	
(from opening balance sheet)		
Purchases (schedule 4)	1 785 408[a]	
	1 974 608	
Less closing stock of raw materials (schedule 4)	100 640[b]	
Cost of raw materials consumed	1 873 968	
Direct labour (schedule 5)	1 512 900	
Factory overheads (schedule 6)	804 606	
Total manufacturing cost	4 191 474	
Add opening stock of finished goods	99 076	
(from opening balance sheet)		
Less closing stock of finished goods	665 984[c]	
	(566 908)	
Cost of sales		3 624 566
Gross profit		671 434
Selling and administration expenses (schedule 7)		276 000
Budgeted operating profit for the year		395 434

[a]£839 088 (X) + £946 320 (Y) from schedule 4.

[b]10 200 units at £7.20 plus 1700 units at £16 from schedule 4.

[c]1870 units of alpha valued at £332 per unit, 90 units of sigma valued at £501.60 per unit. The product unit costs are calculated as follows:

	Alpha		Sigma	
	Units	(£)	Units	(£)
Direct materials				
X	10	72.00	8	57.60
Y	5	80.00	9	144.00
Direct labour	10	120.00	15	180.00
Factory overheads:				
Department 1	10	60.00	—	—
Department 2	—	—	15	120.00
		332.00		501.60

Budgeted balance sheet as at 31 December

	(£)	(£)
Fixed assets:		
Land		170 000
Building and equipment	1 292 000	
Less depreciation[a]	435 000	857 000
		1 027 000
Current assets:		
Raw material stock	100 640	
Finished good stock	665 984	
Debtors[b]	280 000	
Cash[c]	199 170	
	1 245 794	
Current liabilities:		
Creditors[d]	307 884	937 910
		1 964 910
Represented by shareholders' interest:		
1 200 000 ordinary shares of £1 each	1 200 000	
Reserves	369 476	
Profit and loss account	395 434	1 964 910

[a]£255 000 + £180 000 (schedule 6) = £435 000.
[b]£289 000 opening balance + £4 296 000 sales – £4 305 000 cash.
[c]Closing balance as per cash budget.
[d]£248 800 opening balance + £1 785 408 purchases + £141 660 indirect materials – £1 876 984 cash

Cash budgets

The objective of the **cash budget** is to ensure that sufficient cash is available at all times to meet the level of operations that are outlined in the various budgets. The cash budget for Example 10.1 is presented below and is analysed by quarters, but in practice monthly or weekly budgets will be necessary. Because cash budgeting is subject to uncertainty, it is necessary to provide for more than the minimum amount required, to allow for some margin of error in planning. Cash budgets can help a firm to avoid cash balances that are surplus to its requirements by enabling management to take steps in advance to invest the surplus cash in short-term investments. Alternatively, cash deficiencies can be identified in advance, and steps can be taken to ensure that bank loans will be available to meet any temporary cash deficiencies. For example, by looking at the cash budget for the Enterprise Company, management may consider that the cash balances are higher than necessary in the second and third quarters of the year, and they may invest part of the cash balance in short-term investments.

The overall aim should be to manage the cash of the firm to attain maximum cash availability and maximum interest income on any idle funds.

Cash budget for year ending 200X

	Quarter 1 (£)	Quarter 2 (£)	Quarter 3 (£)	Quarter 4 (£)	Total (£)
Opening balance	34 000	114 000	294 000	421 984	34 000
Receipts from debtors	1 000 000	1 200 000	1 120 000	985 000	4 305 000
	1 034 000	1 314 000	1 414 000	1 406 984	4 339 000
Payments:					
Purchase of materials	400 000	480 000	440 000	547 984	1 867 984
Payment of wages	400 000	440 000	480 000	646 188	1 966 188
Other costs and expenses	120 000	100 000	72 016	13 642	305 658
	920 000	1 020 000	992 016	1 207 814	4 139 830
Closing balance	114 000	294 000	421 984	199 170	199 170

Final review

The budgeted profit and loss account, the balance sheet and the cash budget will be submitted by the accountant to the budget committee, together with a number of budgeted financial ratios such as the return on capital employed, working capital, liquidity and gearing ratios. If these ratios prove to be acceptable, the budgets will be approved. In Example 10.1 the return on capital employed is approximately 20%, but the working capital ratio (current assets : current liabilities) is over 4:1, so management should consider alternative ways of reducing investment in working capital before finally approving the budgets.

Computerized budgeting

In the past, budgeting was a task dreaded by many management accountants. You will have noted from Example 10.1 that many numerical manipulations are necessary to prepare the budget. In the real world the process is far more complex, and, as the budget is being formulated, it is altered many times since some budgets are found to be out of balance with each other or the master budget proves to be unacceptable.

In today's world, the budgeting process is computerized instead of being primarily concerned with numerical manipulations, the accounting staff can now become more involved in the real planning process. Computer-based financial models normally consist of mathematical statements of inputs and outputs. By simply altering the mathematical statements budgets can be quickly revised with little effort. However, the major advantage of computerized budgeting is that management can evaluate many different options before the budget is finally agreed. Establishing a model enables 'What-if?' analysis to be employed. For example, answers to the following questions can be displayed in the form of a master budget: What if sales increase or decrease by 10%? What if unit costs increase or decrease by 5%? What if the credit terms for sales were reduced from 30 to 20 days?

In addition, computerized models can incorporate actual results, period by period, and carry out the necessary calculations to produce budgetary *control* reports. It is also possible to adjust the budgets for the remainder of the year when it is clear that the circumstances on which the budget was originally set have changed.

REAL WORLD VIEWS 10.1

Using Web technology for the budget process

An e-budgeting solution completely automates the development of an organization's budget and forecast. From anywhere in the world, at all times, participants in the process can log through the Internet to access their budget and any pertinent related information so they can work on their plans. Web-based enterprise budgeting systems offer a centrally administered system that provides easy-to-use flexible tools for the end users who are responsible for budgeting. The Web functionality of these applications allows constant monitoring, updates and modelling.

E-budgeting provides the flexibility demanded by modern organizations. For example, the finance department can request across-the-board reallocations of expenditures and model the result immediately. No longer do management accountants have to go back and forth with other managers reinputing data and retallying results. E-budgeting can eliminate the cumbersome accounting tasks of pulling numbers from disparate files, cutting and pasting, entering and uploading, and constantly performing reconciliation. Also, a Web-based budgeting application lets managers access data from office or home – wherever they happen to be working. It broadens the system's availability to the user community.

When executives at Toronto-Dominion Bank were searching for a new solution capable of handling the bank's enterprise budgeting and planning function, they turned to the Internet. The company selected Clarus Corporation's Web-deployed, enterprise Clarus™ Budget solution. Its accountant stated 'in the past, we have compiled our business plan using hundreds of spreadsheets, and our analysts have spent a disproportionate amount of their time compiling and verifying data from multiple sources. Implementing a Web-based, enterprise-wide budgeting solution will help us to develop our business plans and allow our analysts to be proactive in monitoring quarterly results.'

Source: Adapted from Hornyak, S. (2000), Budgeting made easy, in Reeve, J.M. (ed.), *Readings and Issues in Cost Management,* South Western College Publishing (USA), pp. 341–346.

Activity-based budgeting

ADVANCED READING

The conventional approach to budgeting works fine for unit level activity costs where the consumption of resources varies proportionately with the volume of the final output of products or services. However, for those indirect costs and support activities where there are no clearly defined input–output relationships, and the consumption of resources does not vary with the final output of products or services, conventional budgets merely serve as authorization levels for certain levels of spending for each budgeted item of expense. Budgets that are not based on well-understood relationships between activities and costs are poor indicators of performance and performance reporting normally implies little more than checking whether the budget has been exceeded. Conventional budgets therefore provide little relevant information for managing the costs of support activities.

With conventional budgeting indirect costs and support activities are prepared on an incremental basis. This means that existing operations and the current budgeted allowance for existing activities are taken as the starting point for preparing the next annual budget. The base is then adjusted for changes (such as changes in product mix, volumes and prices) which are expected to occur during the new budget period. This approach is called **incremental budgeting**, since the budget process is concerned mainly with the increment in operations or expenditure that will occur during the forthcoming budget period. For example, the allowance for budgeted expenses may be based on the previous budgeted allowance plus an increase to cover higher prices caused by inflation. The major disadvantage of the incremental approach is that the majority of expenditure, which is associated with the 'base level' of activity, remains unchanged. Thus, the costs of non-unit level activities become fixed and past inefficiencies and waste inherent in the current way of doing things is perpetuated.

To manage costs more effectively organizations that have implemented activity-based costing (ABC) have also adopted **activity-based budgeting (ABB)**. The aim of ABB is to authorize the supply of only those resources that are needed to perform activities required to meet the budgeted production and sales volume. Whereas ABC assigns resource expenses to activities and then uses activity cost drivers to assign activity costs to cost objects (such as products, services or customers), ABB is the reverse of this process. Cost objects are the starting point. Their budgeted output determines the necessary activities which are then used to estimate the resources that are required for the budget period. ABB involves the following stages:

1 estimate the production and sales volume by individual products and customers;

2 estimate the demand for organizational activities;

3 determine the resources that are required to perform organizational activities;

4 estimate for each resource the quantity that must be supplied to meet the demand;

5 take action to adjust the capacity of resources to match the projected supply.

The first stage is identical to conventional budgeting. Details of budgeted production and sales volumes for individual products and customer types will be contained in the sales and production budgets. Next, ABC extends conventional budgeting to support activities such as ordering, receiving, scheduling production and processing customers' orders. To implement ABB a knowledge of the activities that are necessary to produce and sell the products and services and service customers is essential. Estimates of the quantity of activity cost drivers must be derived for each activity. For example, the number of purchase orders, the number of receipts, the number of set-ups and the number of customer orders processed are estimated using the same approach as that used by conventional budgeting to determine the quantity of direct labour and materials that are incorporated into the direct labour and materials purchase budgets. Standard cost data incorporating a bill of activities is maintained for each product indicating the different activities, and the quantity of activity drivers that are required, to produce a specified number of products. Such documentation provides the basic information for building up the activity-based budgets.

The third stage is to estimate the resources that are required for performing the quantity of activity drivers demanded. In particular, estimates are required of each type of resource, and their quantities required, to meet the demanded quantity of activities. For example, if the number of customer orders to be processed is estimated to be 5000 and each order takes 30 minutes processing time then 2500 labour hours of the customer processing activity must be supplied.

Next, the resources demanded (derived from the third stage) are converted into an estimate of the total resources that must be supplied for each type of resource used by an activity. The quantity of resources supplied depends on the cost behaviour of the resource. For flexible resources where the supply can be matched exactly to meet demand, such as direct materials and energy costs, the quantity of resources supplied will be identical to the quantity demanded. For example, if customer processing were a flexible resource exactly 2500 hours would be purchased. However, a more likely assumption is that customer processing labour will be a step cost function in relation to the volume of the activity (see Chapter 2 for a description of step cost functions). Assuming that each person employed is contracted to work 1500 hours per year then 1.67 persons (2500/1500) represents the quantity of resources required, but because resources must be acquired in uneven amounts, two persons must be employed. For other resources, such as equipment, resources will tend to be fixed and committed over a very wide range of volume for the activity. As long as demand is less than the capacity supplied by the committed resource no additional spending will be required.

The final stage is to compare the estimates of the quantity of resources to be supplied for each resource with the quantity of resources that are currently committed. If the estimated demand for a resource exceeds the current capacity additional spending must be authorized within the budgeting process to acquire additional resources. Alternatively, if the demand for resources is less than the projected supply, the budgeting process should result in management taking action to either redeploy or reduce those resources that are no longer required.

Exhibit 10.1 illustrates an activity-based budget for an order receiving process or department. You will see that the budget is presented in a matrix format with the major activities being shown for each of the columns and the resource inputs are listed by rows. The cost driver activity levels are also highlighted. A major feature of ABB is the enhanced visibility arising from showing the outcomes, in terms of cost drivers, from the budgeted expenditure. This information is particularly useful for planning and estimating future expenditure.

Let us now look at how ABB can be applied using the information presented in Exhibit 10.1. Assume that ABB stages one and two as outlined above result in an estimated annual demand of 2800 orders for the processing of the receipt of the standard customers' order activity (column 6 in Exhibit 10.1). For the staff salaries row (that is, the processing of customers' orders labour resource) assume that each member of staff can process on average 50 orders per month, or 600 per year. Therefore 4.67 (2800 orders/600 orders) persons are required for the supply of this resource (that is, stage three as outlined above). The fourth stage converts the 4.67 staff resources into the amount that must be supplied, that is 5 members of staff. Let us assume that the current capacity or supply of resources committed to the activity is 6 members of staff at £25 000 per annum, giving a total annual cost of £150 000. Management is therefore made aware that staff resources can be reduced by £25 000 per annum by transferring one member of staff to other activities where staff resources need to be expanded or, more drastically, making them redundant.

Some of the other resource expenses (such as office supplies and telephone expenses) listed in Exhibit 10.1 for the processing of customers' order activity represent flexible resources which are likely to vary in the short-term with the number of orders processed. Assuming that the budget for the forthcoming period represents 80% of the number of orders processed during the previous budget period then the budget for those resource expenses that vary in the short-term with the number of orders processed should be reduced by 20%.

With conventional budgeting the budgeted expenses for the forthcoming budget for support activities are normally based on the previous year's budget plus an adjustment for inflation. Support costs are therefore considered to be fixed in relation to activity volume. In contrast, ABB provides a framework for understanding the amount of resources that are required to achieve the budgeted level of activity. By comparing the amount of resources that are required with the amount of resources that are in place, upwards or downwards adjustments can be made during the budget setting phase.

Periodically actual results should be compared with a budget adjusted (flexed) to the actual output for the activities (in terms of cost drivers) to highlight both in financial and non-financial terms those activities with major discrepancies from budget. Assume that practical capacity for salaries for the processing of customers' standard orders activity was set at 3000 orders (5 staff at 600 orders per member of staff), even though budgeted activity was only 2800 orders, and the actual number of orders processed during the period was

EXHIBIT 10.1

Activity-based budget for an order receiving process

Activities →	Handle import goods	Execute express orders	Special Deliveries	Distribution administration	Order receiving (standard products)	Order receiving (non-standard products)	Execute rush orders	Total cost
Resource expense accounts:								
Office supplies								
Telephone expenses								
Salaries								
Travel								
Training								
Total cost								
Activity cost driver → measures	Number of customs documents	Number of customer bills	Number of letters of credit	Number of consignment notes	Number of standard orders	Number of non-standard orders	Number of rush orders	

2500 orders. Also assume that the actual resources committed to the activity in respect of salaries was £125 000 (all fixed in the short term). The following information should be presented in the performance report for salary expenses:

Flexed budget based on the number of orders processed (2500 orders at £41.67)	104 175
Budgeted unused capacity (3000 − 2800) × £41.67	8 334
Actual unplanned unused capacity (2800 − 2500) × £41.67	12 491
	125 000

The cost driver rate of £41.67 per order processed is calculated by dividing the £125 000 budgeted cost of supplying the resources by the capacity supplied (3000 orders). The above activity performance information highlights for management attention the potential reduction in the supply of resources of £20 825 (£8334 expected and £12 491 unexpected) or, alternatively, the additional business that can be accommodated with the existing supply of resources.

A survey of UK organizations by Innes *et al.* (2000) found that 55% of the respondents that had adopted ABC used the activity-based approach for budgeting and 76% of these users rated the ability to set more realistic budgets as the most important benefit from ABB. Other benefits identified by the survey respondents included the better identification of resource needs and the identification of budget slack. In an earlier survey of organizations in the financial services sector Innes and Mitchell (1997) found that these organizations also derived similar benefits from ABB.

Zero-based budgeting

Zero-based budgeting (also known as priority-based budgeting) emerged in the late 1960s as an attempt to overcome the limitations of incremental budgets. This approach requires that all activities are justified and prioritized before decisions are taken relating to the amount of resources allocated to each activity. Besides adopting a 'zero-based' approach zero-base budgeting (ZBB) also focuses on programmes or activities instead of functional departments based on line-items which is a feature of traditional budgeting. Programmes normally relate to various activities undertaken by municipal or government organizations. Examples include extending childcare facilities, improvement of health care for senior citizens and the extension of nursing facilities.

ZBB works from the premise that projected expenditure for existing programmes should start from base zero, with each year's budgets being compiled as if the programmes were being launched for the first time. The budgetees should present their requirements for appropriations in such a fashion that all funds can be allocated on the basis of cost–benefit or some similar kind of evaluative analysis. The cost–benefit approach is an attempt to ensure 'value for money'; it questions long-standing assumptions and serves as a tool for systematically examining and perhaps abandoning any unproductive projects.

ZBB is best suited to discretionary costs and support activities. With discretionary costs management has some discretion as to the amount it will budget for the particular activity in question. Examples of discretionary costs include advertising, research and development and training costs. There is no optimum relationship between inputs (as measured by the costs) and outputs (measured by revenues or some other objective function) for these costs. Furthermore, they are not predetermined by some previous commitment. In effect, management can determine what quantity of service it wishes to purchase and there is no established method for determining the appropriate amount to be spent in particular periods. ZBB has mostly been applied in local and government organizations where the predominant costs are of a discretionary nature. In contrast, direct production and service costs, where input–output relationships exist, are more suited to traditional budgeting using standard costs.

ZBB involves the following three stages:

- a description of each organizational activity in a decision package;
- the evaluation and ranking of decision packages in order of priority;
- allocation of resources based on order of priority up to the spending cut-off level.

Decision packages are identified for each decision unit. Decision units represent separate programmes or groups of activities that an organization undertakes. A decision package represents the operation of a particular programme with incremental packages reflecting different levels of effort that may be expended on a specific function. One package is usually prepared at the 'base' level for each programme. This package represents the minimum level of service or support consistent with the organization's objectives. Service or support higher than the base level is described in one or more incremental packages. For example, managers might be asked to specify the base package in terms of level of service that can be provided at 70% of the current cost level and incremental packages identify higher activity or cost levels.

Once the decision packages have been completed, management is ready to start to review the process. To determine how much to spend and where to spend it, management will rank all packages in order of decreasing benefits to the organization. Theoretically, once management has set the budgeted level of spending, the packages should be accepted down to the spending level based on cost–benefit principles.

The benefits of ZBB over traditional methods of budgeting are claimed to be as follows:

1   Traditional budgeting tends to extrapolate the past by adding a percentage increase to the current year. ZBB avoids the deficiencies of incremental budgeting and represents a move towards the allocation of resources by need or benefit. Thus, unlike traditional budgeting the level of funding is not taken for granted.

2   ZBB creates a questioning attitude rather than one that assumes that current practice represents value for money.

3   ZBB focuses attention on outputs in relation to value for money.

ZBB was first applied in Texas Instruments in 1969. It quickly became one of the fashionable management tools of the 1970s and, according to Phyrr (1976), there were 100 users in the USA in the early 1970s, including the State of Georgia whose governor was ex-president Jimmy Carter. When he became the US President, he directed that all federal agencies adopt ZBB.

During the 1970s many articles on ZBB were published but they declined rapidly towards the end of the decade, and by the 1980s they had become a rarity. ZBB has never achieved the widespread adoption that its proponents envisaged. The major reason for its lack of success would appear to be that it is too costly and time-consuming. The process of identifying decision packages and determining their purpose, cost and benefits is extremely time-consuming. Furthermore, there are often too many decision packages to evaluate and there is frequently insufficient information to enable them to be ranked.

Research suggests that many organizations tend to approximate the principles of ZBB rather than applying the full-scale approach outlined in the literature. For example, it does not have to be applied throughout the organization. It can be applied selectively to those areas about which management is most concerned and used as a one-off cost reduction programme. Some of the benefits of ZBB can be captured by using **priority-based incremental budgets**. Priority incremental budgets require managers to specify what incremental activities or changes would occur if their budgets were increased or decreased by a specified percentage (say 10%). Budget allocations are made by comparing the change in costs with the change in benefits. Priority incremental budgets thus represent an economical compromise between ZBB and incremental budgeting.

Summary

The following items relate to the learning objectives listed at the beginning of the chapter.

- **Explain how budgeting fits into the overall planning and control framework.**

   The annual budget should be set within the context of longer-term plans, which are likely to exist even if they have not been made explicit. A long-term plan is a statement of the preliminary targets and activities required by an organization to achieve its strategic plans together with a broad estimate for each year of the resources required. Because long-term planning involves 'looking into the future' for several years, the plans tend to be uncertain, general in nature, imprecise and subject to change. Annual budgeting is concerned with the detailed implementation of the long-term plan for the year ahead. As the year progresses the control process involves comparing planned and actual outcomes and responding to any deviations by taking appropriate remedial action to ensure that future results will conform to the annual budget. Alternatively, the annual budget may have to be changed if remedial action cannot be taken. Budgeting is therefore a continuous and dynamic process, and should not end once the annual budget has been prepared.

- **Identify and describe the six different purposes of budgeting.**

  Budgets are used for the following purposes: (a) planning annual operations; (b) coordinating the activities of the various parts of the organization and ensuring that the parts are in harmony with each other; (c) communicating the plans to the managers of the various responsibility centres; (d) motivating managers to strive to achieve organizational goals; (e) controlling activities; and (f) evaluating the performance of managers.

- **Identify and describe the various stages in the budget process.**

  The important stages are as follows: (a) communicating details of the budget policy and guidelines to those people responsible for the preparation of the budgets; (b) determining the factor that restricts output (normally sales volume); (c) preparation of the sales budget (assuming that sales demand is the factor that restricts output); (d) initial preparation of the various budgets; (e) negotiation of budgets with superiors; (f) coordination and review of budgets; (g) final acceptance of budgets; and (h) ongoing review of budgets. Each of the above stages is described in the chapter.

- **Prepare functional and master budgets.**

  When all of the budgets have been prepared they are summarized into a master budget consisting in a budgeted profit and loss account, a balance sheet and a cash budget statement. The preparation of functional and master budgets was illustrated using Example 10.1.

- **Describe the use of computer-based financial models for budgeting.**

  Computer-based financial models are mathematical statements of the inputs and output relationships that affect the budget. These models allow management to conduct sensitivity analysis to ascertain the effects on the master budget of changes in the original predicted data or changes in the assumptions that were used to prepare the budgets.

- **Describe the limitations of incremental budgeting.**

  With incremental budgeting indirect costs and support activities are prepared on an incremental basis. This means that existing operations and the current budgeted allowance for existing activities are taken as the starting point for preparing the next annual budget. The base is then adjusted for changes (such as changes in product mix, volumes and prices) which are expected to occur during the new budget period. When this approach is adopted the concern is mainly with the increment in operations or expenditure that will occur during the forthcoming budget period. The major disadvantage of the incremental approach is that the majority of expenditure, which is associated with the 'base level' of activity, remains unchanged. Thus, past inefficiencies and waste inherent in the current way of doing things are perpetuated.

- **Describe activity-based budgeting.**

  With conventional budgeting the budgeted expenses for the forthcoming budget for support activities are normally based on the previous year's budget plus an adjustment for inflation. Support costs are therefore considered to be fixed in relation to activity volume. Activity-based budgeting (ABB) aims to manage costs more effectively by authorizing the supply of only those resources that are needed to perform activities required to meet the budgeted production and sales volume. Whereas ABC assigns resource expenses to activities and then uses activity cost drivers to assign activity costs to cost objects (such as products, services or customers) ABB is the reverse of this process. Cost objects are the starting point. Their budgeted output determines the necessary activities which are then used to estimate the resources that are required for the budget period. ABB involves the following stages: (a) estimate the production and sales volume by individual products and customers; (b) estimate the demand for organizational activities; (c) determine the resources that are required to perform organizational activities; (d) estimate for each resource the quantity that must be supplied to meet the demand; and (e) take action to adjust the capacity of resources to match the projected supply.

● **Describe zero-base budgeting (ZBB).**

ZBB is a method of budgeting that is mainly used in non-profit organizations but it can also be applied to discretionary costs and support activities in profit organizations. It seeks to overcome the deficiencies of incremental budgeting. ZBB works from the premise that projected expenditure for existing programmes should start from base zero, with each year's budgets being compiled as if the programmes were being launched for the first time. The budgetees should present their requirements for appropriations in such a fashion that all funds can be allocated on the basis of cost–benefit or some similar kind of evaluative analysis. The cost–benefit approach is an attempt to ensure 'value for money'; it questions long-standing assumptions and serves as a tool for systematically examining and perhaps abandoning any unproductive projects.

Note

1 The criteria specified are derived from Johnson and Scholes (2002), Chapter 9.

Key terms and concepts

activity-based budgeting (p. 286)
aims (p. 265)
budgeting (p. 267)
budgets (p. 263)
cash budget (p. 283)
continuous budgeting (p. 279)
corporate objectives (p. 264)
corporate planning (p. 264)
decision package (p. 289)
discretionary costs (p. 289)
generic strategies (p. 265)
goals (p. 265)
incremental budgeting (p. 285)
long-range planning (p. 264)

long-term plan (p. 265)
management by exception (p. 269)
master budget (p. 274)
mission (p. 264)
objectives (p. 264)
priority based budgets (p. 289)
priority based incremental budgets (p. 290)
rolling budgeting (p. 270)
strategic analysis (p. 265)
strategic planning (p. 264)
strategies (p. 265)
unit objectives (p. 264)
zero-based budgeting (p. 289)

Assessment material

Review questions

The review questions are short questions that enable you to assess your understanding of the main topics included in the chapter. The numbers in parentheses provide you with the page numbers to refer to if you cannot answer a specific question.

Review problems

The review problems are more complex and require you to relate and apply the chapter content to various business problems. The multiple-choice questions are the least demanding and normally take less than 10 minutes to complete. Fully worked solutions to the review problems are provided in a separate section at the end of the book. Further review problems for this chapter are available on the accompanying website, www.drury-online.com. The answers to these problems are available for lecturers on the lecturer's password-protected section of the website.

Case studies

The website also includes over 30 case study problems. A list of these cases is provided on pages 491–93. Several cases are relevant to the content of this chapter. Examples include Endeavour Toplise Ltd, Global Ltd and Integrated Technology Ltd.

Review questions

10.1   Define the term 'budget'. How are budgets used in planning? (*pp. 263–64*)

10.2   Describe the different stages in the planning and control process. (*pp. 264–67*)

10.3   Distinguish between budgeting and long-range planning. How are they related? (*pp. 264, 267*)

10.4   Describe the different purposes of budgeting. (*pp. 267–69*)

10.5   Explain what is meant by the term 'management by exception'. (*p. 269*)

10.6   Describe how the different roles of budgets can conflict with each other. (*p. 269*)

10.7   Distinguish between continuous and rolling budgets. (*p. 270*)

10.8   Describe the different stages in the budgeting process. (*pp. 271–74*)

10.9   All budgets depend on the sales budget. Do you agree? Explain. (*pp. 277–78*)

10.10   What is a master budget? (*p. 274*)

10.11   Define incremental budgeting. (*pp. 285–86*)

10.12   What are the distinguishing features of activity-based budgeting? (*pp. 285–86*)

10.13   Describe the five different stages that are involved with activity-based budgeting. (*pp. 286–87*)

10.14   How does zero-based budgeting differ from traditional budgeting? (*pp. 289–90*)

10.15   What are discretionary costs? (*p. 289*)

10.16   Distinguish between zero-based budgeting and priority-based incremental budgeting. (*p. 290*)

Review problems

10.17   When preparing a production budget, the quantity to be produced equals

A   sales quantity + opening stock + closing stock
B   sales quantity – opening stock + closing stock
C   sales quantity – opening stock – closing stock
D   sales quantity + opening stock – closing stock
E   sales quantity

10.18   BDL plc is current preparing its cash budget for the year to 31 March 2003. An extract from its sales budget for the same year shows the following sales values:

	£
March	60 000
April	70 000
May	55 000
June	65 000

40% of its sales are expected to be for cash. Of its credit sales, 70% are expected to pay in the month after sale and take a 2% discount; 27% are expected to pay in the second month after the sale, and the remaining 3% are expected to be bad debts.

The value of sales receipts to be shown in the cash budget for May 2002 is:

A   £38 532
B   £39 120
C   £60 532
D   £64 220
E   £65 200

10.19   The following data is to be used to answer questions (a) and (b) below

A division of PLR plc operates a small private aircraft that carries passengers and small parcels for other divisions.

In the year ended 31 March 2002, it carried 1024 passengers and 24 250 kg of small parcels. It incurred costs of £924 400.

The division has found that 70% of its total costs are variable, and that 60% of these vary with the number of passengers and the remainder varies with the weight of the parcels.

The company is now preparing its budget for the 3 months ending 30 September 2002 using an incremental budgeting approach. In this period it expects:

- All prices to be 3% higher than the average paid in the year ended 31 March 2002;
- Efficiency levels to be unchanged;
- Activity levels to be:
  - 209 passengers;
  - 7200 kg of small parcels.

(a) The budgeted passenger related cost (to the nearest £100) for the **three months** ending 30 September 2002 is

A   £81 600
B   £97 100
C   £100 000
D   £138 700.

(2 marks)

(b) The budgeted small parcel related cost (to the nearest £100) for the **three months** ending 30 September 2002 is

A   £64 700
B   £66 600
C   £79 200
D   £95 213.

(2 marks)

10.20   **Preparation of functional budgets**

Wollongong wishes to calculate an operating budget for the forthcoming period. Information regarding products, costs and sales levels is as follows:

Product	A	B
Materials required		
X (kg)	2	3
Y (litres)	1	4
Labour hours required		
Skilled (hours)	4	2
Semi-skilled (hours)	2	5
Sales level (units)	2000	1500
Opening stocks (units)	100	200

Closing stock of materials and finished goods will be sufficient to meet 10% of demand. Opening stocks of material X was 300 kg and for material Y was 1000 litres. Material prices are £10 per kg for material X and £7 per litre for material Y. Labour costs are £12 per hour for the skilled workers and £8 per hour for the semi-skilled workers.

Required:

Produce the following budgets:

(a) production (units);

(b) materials usage (kg and litres);

(c) materials purchases (kg, litres and £); and

(d) labour (hours and £).

(10 marks)

10.21 Budget preparation and comments on sales forecasting methods

You have recently been appointed as the management accountant to Alderley Ltd, a small company manufacturing two products, the Elgar and the Holst. Both products use the same type of material and labour but in different proportions. In the past, the company has had poor control over its working capital. To remedy this, you have recommended to the directors that a budgetary control system be introduced. This proposal has, now, been agreed.

Because Alderley Ltd's production and sales are spread evenly over the year, it was agreed that the annual budget should be broken down into four periods, each of 13 weeks, and commencing with the 13 weeks ending 4 April. To help you in this task, the sales and production directors have provided you with the following information:

1. Marketing and production data

	Elgar	Holst
Budgeted sales for 13 weeks (units)	845	1235
Material content per unit (kilograms)	7	8
Labour per unit (standard hours)	8	5

2. Production labour
    The 24 production employees work a 37-hour, five-day week and are paid £8 per hour. Any hours in excess of this involve Alderley in paying an overtime premium of 25%. Because of technical problems, which will continue over the next 13 weeks, employees are only able to work at 95% efficiency compared to standard.

3. Purchasing and opening stocks
    The production director believes that raw material will cost £12 per kilogram over the budget period. He also plans to revise the amount of stock being kept. He estimates that the stock levels at the commencement of the budget period will be as follows:

Raw materials	Elgar	Holst
2328 kilograms	163 units	361 units

4. Closing stocks

At the end of the 13-week period closing stocks are planned to change. On the assumption that production and sales volumes for the second budget period will be similar to those in the first period:

- raw material stocks should be sufficient for 13 days' production;
- finished stocks of the Elgar should be equivalent to 6 days' sales volume;
- finished stocks of the Holst should be equivalent to 14 days' sales volume.

Task 1

Prepare in the form of a statement the following information for the 13-week period to 4 April:

(a) the production budget in units for the Elgar and Holst;

(b) the purchasing budget for Alderley Ltd in units;

(c) the cost of purchases for the period;

(d) the production labour budget for Alderley Ltd in hours;

(e) the cost of production labour for the period.

Note: Assume a five-day week for both sales and production.

The managing director of Alderley Ltd, Alan Dunn, has also only recently been appointed. He is keen to develop the company and has already agreed to two new products being developed. These will be launched in 18 months' time. While talking to you about the budget, he mentions that the quality of sales forecasting will need to improve if the company is to grow rapidly. Currently, the budgeted sales figure is found by initially adding 5% to the previous year's sales volume and then revising the figure following discussions with the marketing director. He believes this approach is increasingly inadequate and now requires a more systematic approach.

A few days later, Alan Dunn sends you a memo. In that memo, he identifies three possible strategies for increasing sales volume. They are:

- more sales to existing customers;
- the development of new markets;
- the development of new products.

He asks for your help in forecasting likely sales volumes from these sources.

Task 2

Write a brief memo to Alan Dunn. Your memo should:

(a) identify *four* ways of forecasting future sales volume;

(b) show how each of your four ways of forecasting can be applied to *one* of the sales strategies identified by Alan Dunn and justify your choice;

(c) give *two* reasons why forecasting methods might not prove to be accurate.

10.22 Preparation of cash budgets

The management of Beck plc have been informed that the union representing the direct production workers at one of their factories, where a standard product is produced, intends to call a strike. The accountant has been asked to advise the management of the effect the strike will have on cash flow.

The following data has been made available:

	Week 1	Week 2	Week 3
Budgeted sales	400 units	500 units	400 units
Budgeted production	600 units	400 units	Nil

The strike will commence at the beginning of week 3 and it should be assumed that it will continue for at least four weeks. Sales at 400 units per week will continue to be made during the period of the strike until stocks of finished goods are exhausted. Production will stop at the end of week 2. The current stock level of finished goods is 600 units. Stocks of work in progress are not carried.

The selling price of the product is £60 and the budgeted manufacturing cost is made up as follows:

	(£)
Direct materials	15
Direct wages	7
Variable overheads	8
Fixed overheads	18
Total	£48

Direct wages are regarded as a variable cost. The company operates a full absorption costing system and the fixed overhead absorption rate is based upon a budgeted fixed overhead of £9000 per week. Included in the total fixed overheads is £700 per week for depreciation of equipment. During the period of the strike direct wages and variable overheads would not be incurred and the cash expended on fixed overheads would be reduced by £1500 per week.

The current stock of raw materials are worth £7500; it is intended that these stocks should increase to £11 000 by the end of week 1 and then remain at this level during the period of the strike. *All direct materials are paid for one week after they have been received. Direct wages are paid one week in arrears. It should be assumed that all relevant overheads are paid for immediately the expense is incurred.* All sales are on credit, 70% of the sales value is received in cash from the debtors at the end of the first week after the sales have been made and the balance at the end of the second week.

The current amount outstanding to material suppliers is £8000 and direct wage accruals amount to £3200. Both of these will be paid in week 1. The current balance owing from debtors is £31 200, of which £24 000 will be received during week 1 and the remainder during week 2. The current balance of cash at the bank and in hand is £1000.

Required:

(a) (i) Prepare a cash budget for weeks 1 to 6 showing the balance of cash at the end of each week together with a suitable analysis of the receipts and payments during each week.

(13 marks)

(ii) Comment upon any matters arising from the cash budget which you consider should be brought to management's attention.

(4 marks)

(b) Explain why the reported profit figure for a period does not normally represent the amount of cash generated in that period.

(5 marks)
(Total 22 marks)

10.23 **Advanced**

You are the management accountant of a group of companies and your managing director has asked you to explore the possibilities of introducing a zero-base budgeting system experimentally in one of the operating companies in place of its existing orthodox system. You are required to prepare notes for a paper for submission to the board that sets out:

(a) how zero-base budgeting would work within the company chosen;

(6 marks)

(b) what advantages it might offer over the existing system;

(5 marks)

(c) what problems might be faced in introducing a zero-base budgeting scheme;

(5 marks)

(d) the features you would look for in selecting the operating company for the introduction in order to obtain the most beneficial results from the experiment.

(4 marks)
(Total 20 marks)

10.24 Traditional budgeting systems are incremental in nature and tend to focus on cost centres. Activity-based budgeting links strategic planning to overall performance measurement aiming at continuous improvement.

(a) Explain the weaknesses of an incremental budgeting system.

(5 marks)

(b) Describe the main features of an activity-based budgeting system and comment on the advantages claimed for its use.

(10 marks)
(Total 15 marks)

10.25 Budgeting has been criticized as

- a cumbersome process which occupies considerable management time;
- concentrating unduly on short-term financial control;
- having undesirable effects on the motivation of managers;
- emphasizing formal organization structure.

Requirements:

(a) Explain these criticisms.

(8 marks)

(b) Explain what changes can be made in response to these criticisms to improve the budgeting process.

(12 marks)
(Total 20 marks)

Management control systems

11 Control is the process of ensuring that a firm's activities conform to its plan and that its objectives are achieved. There can be no control without objectives and plans, since these predetermine and specify the desirable behaviour and set out the procedures that should be followed by members of the organization to ensure that a firm is operated in a desired manner.

Drucker (1964) distinguishes between 'controls' and 'control'. **Controls** are measurement and information, whereas control means direction. In other words, 'controls' are purely a means to an end; the end is control. **'Control'** is the function that makes sure that actual work is done to fulfil the original intention, and 'controls' are used to provide information to assist in determining the control action to be taken. For example, material costs may be greater than budget. 'Controls' will indicate that costs exceed budget and that this

LEARNING OBJECTIVES:

After studying this chapter you should be able to:

- describe the three different types of controls used in organizations;
- describe a cybernetic control system;
- distinguish between feedback and feed-forward controls;
- explain the potential harmful side-effects of results controls;
- define the four different types of responsibility centres;
- explain the different elements of management accounting control systems;
- describe the controllability principle and the methods of implementing it;
- describe the different approaches that can be used to determine financial performance targets and discuss the impact of their level of difficulty on motivation and performance;
- describe the influence of participation in the budgeting process;
- distinguish between the three different styles of evaluating performance and identify the circumstances when a particular style is most appropriate.

may be because the purchase of inferior quality materials causes excessive wastage. 'Control' is the action that is taken to purchase the correct quality materials in the future to reduce excessive wastage.

'Controls' encompasses all the methods and procedures that direct employees towards achieving the organization objectives. Many different control mechanisms are used in organizations and the management accounting control system represents only one aspect of the various control mechanisms that companies use to control their managers and employees. To fully understand the role that management accounting control systems play in the control process, it is necessary to be aware of how they relate to the entire array of control mechanisms used by organizations.

This chapter begins by describing the different types of controls that are used by companies. The elements of management accounting control systems will then be described within the context of the overall control process.

Control at different organizational levels

Control is applied at different levels within an organization. Merchant (1998) distinguishes between strategic control and management control. Strategic control has an external focus. The emphasis is on how a firm, given its strengths and weaknesses and limitations can compete with other firms in the same industry. We shall explore some of these issues in Chapter 16 within the context of strategic management accounting. In this, and the next three chapters, our emphasis will be on management control systems which consist of a collection of control mechanisms that primarily have an internal focus. The aim of management control systems is to influence employee behaviours in desirable ways in order to increase the probability that an organization's objectives will be achieved.

The terms 'management accounting control systems', 'accounting control systems' and 'management control systems' are often used interchangeably. Both management accounting and accounting control systems refer to the collection of practices such as budgeting, standard costing and periodic performance reporting that are normally administered by the management accounting function. Management control systems represent a broader term that encompasses management accounting/accounting control systems but it also includes other controls such as action, personnel and social controls. These controls are described in the following section.

Different types of controls

Companies use many different control mechanisms to cope with the problem of organizational control. To make sense of the vast number of controls that are used we shall classify them into three categories using approaches that have been adopted by Ouchi (1979) and Merchant (1998). They are:

1 action (or behavioural) controls;
2 personnel and cultural (or clan and social) controls;
3 results (or output) controls.

The terms in parentheses refer to the classification used by Ouchi whereas the other terms refer to the categories specified by Merchant. Because the classifications used by both authors are compatible we shall use the terms interchangeably. You should note that management accounting systems are normally synonymous with output controls whereas management control systems encompass all of the above categories of controls.

Action or behavioural controls

Behavioural controls involve observing the actions of individuals as they go about their work. They are appropriate where cause and effect relationships are well understood, so that if the correct means are followed, the desired outcomes will occur. Under these circumstances effective control can be achieved by having superiors watch and guide the actions of subordinates. For example, if the foreman watches the workers on the assembly line and ensures that the work is done exactly as prescribed then the expected quality and quantity of work should ensue.

Instead of using the term behavioural controls Merchant uses the term action controls. He defines **action controls** as applying to those situations where the actions themselves are the focus of control. They are usable and effective only when managers know what actions are desirable (or undesirable) and have the ability to make sure that the desirable actions occur (or that the undesirable actions do not occur). Forms of action controls described by Merchant include behavioural constraints, preaction reviews and action accountability.

The aim of *behavioural constraints* is to prevent people from doing things that should not be done. They include physical constraints, such as computer passwords that restrict accessing or updating information sources to authorized personnel, and administrative constraints. Imposing ceilings on the amount of capital expenditure that managers may authorize is an example of an administrative constraint. For example, managers at lower levels may be able to authorize capital expenditure below £10 000 within a total annual budget of, say, £100 000. The aim is to ensure that only those personnel with the necessary expertise and authority can authorize major expenditure and that such expenditure remains under their control.

Preaction reviews involve the scrutiny and approval of action plans of the individuals being controlled before they can undertake a course of action. Examples include the approval by municipal authorities of plans for the construction of properties prior to building commencing or the approval by a tutor of a dissertation plan prior to the student being authorized to embark on the dissertation.

Action accountability involves defining actions that are acceptable or unacceptable, observing the actions and rewarding acceptable or punishing unacceptable actions. Examples of action accountability include establishing work rules and procedures and company codes of conduct that employees must follow. Line item budgets are another form of action accountability whereby an upper limit on an expense category is given for the budget period. If managers exceed these limits they are held accountable and are required to justify their actions. The purpose of action accountability is to set limits on employee behaviour. Direct observation of employees' actions by superiors to ensure that they are following prescribed rules represents the main form of ensuring action accountability. Other forms include internal audits which involve checks on transaction records and compliance with pre-set action standards.

Action/behavioural controls can only be used effectively when managers know what actions are desirable (or undesirable). In other words, they are appropriate only when cause-and-effect work relationships are well understood such as when a supervisor can observe the actions of workers on a production line to ensure that work is done exactly as prescribed. In contrast, the application of action controls is limited where the work of employees is complex and uncertain and cause-and-effect relationships cannot be precisely described. For action controls to be effective a second requirement must also be met. Managers must also be able to ensure that desired actions are taken. There must be some means of action tracking so that managers can distinguish between good and bad actions. If both of the above conditions do not apply then action controls are inappropriate.

Action controls that focus on *preventing* undesirable behaviour are the ideal form of control because their aim is to prevent the behaviour from occurring. They are preferable to *detection* controls that are applied after the occurrence of the actions because they avoid the costs of undesirable behaviour. Nevertheless, detection controls can still be useful if they are applied in a timely manner so that they can lead to the early cessation of undesirable actions. Their existence also discourages individuals from engaging in such actions.

Personnel, cultural and social controls

Clan and social controls are the second types of controls described by Ouchi. **Clan controls** are based on the belief that by fostering a strong sense of solidarity and commitment towards organizational goals people can become immersed in the interests of the organization. Macintosh (1985) illustrates an extreme example of clan controls by describing the exploits of the Japanese *kamikaze* pilots during World War II. He describes how each pilot fervently believed his individual interests were served best by complete personal immersion in the needs of Japan and the Emperor. It was understood that each pilot would sacrifice himself and his plane by crashing into an enemy warship. National ruin without resistance represented public disgrace. These beliefs were shared by each pilot.

The main feature of clan controls is the high degree of employee discipline attained through the dedication of each individual to the interests of the whole. At a less extreme level clan controls can be viewed as corporate cultures or a special form of **social control** such as the selection of people who have already been socialized into adopting particular norms and patterns of behaviour to perform particular tasks. For example, if the only staff promoted to managerial level are those who display a high commitment to the firm's objectives then the need for other forms of controls can be reduced, provided that the managers are committed to achieving the 'right' objectives.

Merchant adopts a similar approach to Ouchi and classifies personnel and cultural controls as a second form of control. He defines **personnel controls** as helping employees do a good job by building on employees' natural tendencies to control themselves. In particular, they ensure that the employees have the capabilities (in terms of intelligence, qualifications and experience) and the resources needed to do a good job. Merchant identifies three major methods of implementing personnel controls. They are selection and placement, training and job design and the provision of the necessary resources. Selection and placement involves finding the right people to do a specified job. Training can be used to ensure that employees know how to perform the assigned tasks and to make them fully aware of the results and actions that are expected from them. Job design entails designing jobs in such a way that they enable employees to undertake their tasks with a high degree of success. This requires that jobs are not made too complex, onerous or badly defined so that employees do not know what is expected of them.

Cultural controls represent a set of values, social norms and beliefs that are shared by members of the organization and that influence their actions. Cultural controls are exercised by individuals over one another – for example, procedures used by groups within an organization to regulate performance of their own members and to bring them into line when they deviate from group norms. It is apparent from the above description that cultural controls are virtually the same as social controls.

Merchant suggest that a number of methods can be employed to shape culture and thus effect cultural controls. They include codes of conduct, group-based rewards, and interorganizational transfers. Codes of conduct are formal written documents that incorporate general statements of corporate values and commitments to stakeholders and ways in which top management would like the organization to function. They are designed to indicate to employees what behaviours are expected in the absence of clearly defined rules or controls. Group-based rewards consist of rewards based on collective achievements such as group bonuses and profit sharing schemes. They encourage mutual-monitoring by members of the group and reduce measurement costs because individual performance does not have to be measured. Interorganizational transfers involve moving managers between different functions and divisions in order to give them a better understanding of the organization as a whole. This practice is frequently used by Japanese firms to improve their sense of belonging to an organization rather than to the sub-units and also to ensure that managers are aware of the problems experienced by different parts of the organization.

In recent years working practices have begun to change and managers are now relying on people closest to the operating processes and customers to take actions without authorization from superiors. This approach is known as employee empowerment and places greater emphasis on shared organizational values for ensuring that everyone is acting in the organization's best interests. A strong internal firm culture can decrease the need for other control mechanisms since employee beliefs and norms are more likely to coincide with firm goals. They can also be used to some extent in many different organizational settings and are less costly to operate than other types of controls. They also tend to have less harmful side-effects than other control mechanisms.

Results or output controls

Output or results controls involve collecting and reporting information about the outcomes of work effort. The major advantage of results controls is that senior managers do not have to be knowledgeable about the means required to achieve the desired results or be involved in directly observing the actions of subordinates. They merely rely on output reports to ascertain whether or not the desired outcomes have been achieved. Management accounting control systems can be described as a form of output controls. They are mostly defined in monetary terms such as revenues, costs, profits and ratios such as return on investment. Results measures also include non-accounting measures such as the number of units of defective production, the number of loan applications processed or ratio measures such as the number of customer deliveries on time as a percentage of total deliveries.

Results controls involve the following stages:

1. establishing results (i.e. performance) measures that minimize undesirable behaviour;
2. establishing performance targets;
3. measuring performance;
4. providing rewards or punishment.

Ideally desirable behaviour should improve the performance measure and undesirable behaviour should have a detrimental effect on the measure. A performance measure that is not a good indicator of what is desirable to achieve the organization's objectives might actually encourage employees to take actions that are detrimental to the organization. The term 'What you measure is what you get' can apply whereby employees concentrate on improving the performance measures even when they are aware that their actions are not in the firm's best interests. For example, a divisional manager whose current return on investment (ROI) is 30% might reject a project which yields an ROI of 25% because it will lower the division's average ROI, even though the project has a positive NPV, and acceptance is in the best interests of the organization.

Without the *second-stage* requirement of a pre-set performance target individuals do not know what to aim for. Various research studies suggest that the existence of a clearly defined quantitative target is likely to motivate higher performance than vague statements such as 'do your best'. It is also difficult for employees or their superiors to interpret performance unless actual performance can be compared against predetermined standards.

The *third stage* specified above relates to measuring performance. Ability to measure some outputs effectively constrains the use of results measures. For example measuring the performance of support departments can sometimes be difficult. Consider a personnel department. The accomplishments of the department can be difficult to measure and other forms of control might be preferable.

For results measures to work effectively the individuals whose behaviours are being controlled must be able to control and influence the results. Where factors outside the control of the individuals affect the results measures it is difficult to determine whether the results are the outcome of actions taken or from the impact of uncontrollable factors. If uncontrollable factors cannot be separated from controllable factors results controls measures are unlikely to provide useful information for evaluating the actions taken. Note also that if the outcomes of desirable behaviours are offset by the impact of uncontrollable factors results measures will lose their motivational impact and create the impression that the results measures are unjust. The term **controllability principle** is used to refer to the extent that individuals whose behaviours are being controlled can influence the results controls measures. We shall examine the controllability principle in more detail later in this chapter.

The *final stage* of results controls involves encouraging employees to achieve organizational goals by having rewards (or punishments) linked to their success (or failure) in achieving the results measures. Organizational rewards include salary increases, bonuses, promotions and recognition. Employees can also derive intrinsic rewards through a sense of accomplishment and achievement. Punishments include demotions, failure to obtain the rewards and possibly the loss of one's job.

Cybernetic control systems

The traditional approach in the management control literature has been to view results controls as a simple **cybernetic system**. In describing this process authors often use a mechanical model such as a thermostat that controls a central heating system as a resemblance. This process is illustrated in Figure 11.1. You will see that the control system consists of the following elements:

1 The process (the room's temperature) is continually monitored by an automatic regulator (the thermostat).

2 Deviations from a predetermined level (the desired temperature) are identified by the automatic regulator.

3 Corrective actions are started if the output is not equal to the predetermined level. The automatic regulator causes the input to be adjusted by turning the heater on if the temperature falls below a predetermined level. The heater is turned off when the output (temperature) corresponds with the predetermined level.

The output of the process is monitored, and whenever it varies from the predetermined level, the input is automatically adjusted. Emmanuel *et al.* (1990) state that four conditions must be satisfied before any process can be said to be controlled. First, objectives for the process being controlled must exist. Without an aim or purpose control has no meaning.

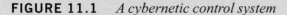

FIGURE 11.1 *A cybernetic control system*

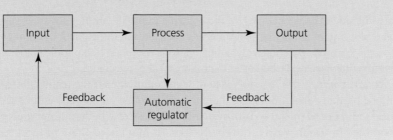

Secondly, the output of the process must be measurable in terms of the dimensions defined by the objectives. In other words, there must be some mechanism for ascertaining whether the process is attaining its objectives. Thirdly, a predictive model of the process being controlled is required so that causes for the non-attainment can be identified and proposed corrective actions evaluated. Finally, there must be a capability for taking action so that deviations from objectives can be reduced. Emmanuel *et al.* stress that if any of these conditions are not met the process cannot be considered to be 'in control'.

Result controls and therefore management accounting controls resemble the thermostat control model. Standards of performance are determined, measurement systems monitor performance, comparisons are made between the standard and actual performance and feedback provides information on the variances. Note that the term **variance** is used to describe the difference the standard and actual performance of the actions that are being measured.

Feedback and feed-forward controls

The cybernetic system of control described in Figure 11.1 is that of feedback control. **Feedback control** involves monitoring outputs achieved against desired outputs and taking whatever corrective action is necessary if a deviation exists. In **feed-forward control** instead of actual outputs being compared against desired outputs, predictions are made of what outputs are expected to be at some future time. If these expectations differ from what is desired, control actions are taken that will minimize these differences. The objective is for control to be achieved before any deviations from desired outputs actually occur. In other words, with feed-forward controls likely errors can be anticipated and steps taken to avoid them, whereas with feedback controls actual errors are identified after the event and corrective action is taken to implement future actions to achieve the desired outputs.

Feed-forward control requires the use of a predictive model that is sufficiently accurate to ensure that control action will improve the situation and not cause it to deteriorate further. A major limitation of feedback control is that errors are allowed to occur. This is not a significant problem when there is a short time lag between the occurrence of an error and the identification and implementation of corrective action. Feed-forward control is therefore preferable when a significant time lag occurs. The budgeting process is a feed-forward control system. To the extent that outcomes fall short of what is desired, alternatives are considered until a budget is produced that is expected to achieve what is desired. The comparison of actual results with budget, in identifying variances and taking remedial action to ensure that future outcomes will conform with budgeted outcomes is an illustration of a feedback control system. Thus accounting control systems consist of both feedback and feed-forward controls.

Harmful side-effects of controls

Harmful side-effects occur when the controls motivate employees to engage in behaviour that is not organizationally desirable. In this situation the control system leads to a lack of goal congruence. Alternatively, when controls motivate behaviour that is organizationally desirable they are described as encouraging goal congruence.

Results controls can lead to a lack of goal congruence if the results that are required can only be partially specified. Here there is a danger that employees will concentrate only on what is monitored by the control system, regardless of whether or not it is organizationally desirable. In other words, they will seek to maximize their individual performance according to the rules of the control system irrespective of whether their actions contribute to the organization's objectives. In addition, they may ignore other important areas, if they are not monitored by the control system. The term 'What you measure is what you get' applies in these circumstances.

Figure 11.2, derived from Otley (1987) illustrates the problems that can arise when the required results can only be partially specified. You will see that those aspects of behaviour on which subordinates are likely to concentrate to achieve their personal goals (circle B) do not necessarily correspond with those necessary for achieving the wider organizational goals (circle A). In an ideal system the measured behaviour (represented by circle C) should completely cover the area of desired behaviour (represented by circle A). Therefore if a manager maximizes the performance measure, he or she will also maximize his or her contribution to the goals of the organization. In other words, the performance measures encourage goal congruence. In practice, it is unlikely that perfect performance measures can be constructed that measure all desirable organizational behaviour, and so it is unlikely that all of circle C will cover circle A. Assuming that managers desire the rewards offered by circle C, their actual behaviour (represented by circle B) will be altered to include more of circle C and, to the extent that C coincides with A, more of circle A.

However, organizational performance will be improved only to the extent that the performance measure is a good indicator of what is desirable to achieve the firm's goals. Unfortunately, performance measures are not perfect and, as an ideal measure of overall performance, is unlikely to exist. Some measures may encourage goal congruence or organizationally desirable behaviour (the part of circle C that coincides with A), but other measures will not encourage goal congruence (the part of circle C that does not coincide with A). Consequently, there is a danger that subordinates will concentrate only on what is measured, regardless of whether or not it is organizationally desirable. Furthermore, actual behaviour may be modified so that desired results appear to be obtained, although they may have been achieved in an undesirable manner which is detrimental to the firm.

The evidence suggests that data manipulation is common with results controls (Merchant, 1990). Data manipulation occurs where individuals try and distort the data in order to improve the performance measure. For example, where individuals have some influence in the setting of performance targets there is a danger that they will seek to obtain easier targets by deliberately underperforming so that their targets will not be increased in the forthcoming period. Merchant (1990) also reported the widespread use of shifting funds between different budget items in order to avoid adverse budget variances.

Another harmful side effect of controls is that they can cause negative attitudes towards the control system. If controls are applied too rigorously they can result in job-related tensions, conflict and a deterioration in relationships with managers. To a certain extent people do not like being subject to controls so that negative attitudes may be unavoidable. Nevertheless, they can be minimized if care is taken in designing control systems. Results controls can cause negative attitudes when targets are set which are considered to be too difficult and unachievable. Negative attitudes can also be exacerbated by a failure to apply

FIGURE 11.2   *The measurement and reward process with imperfect*
measures

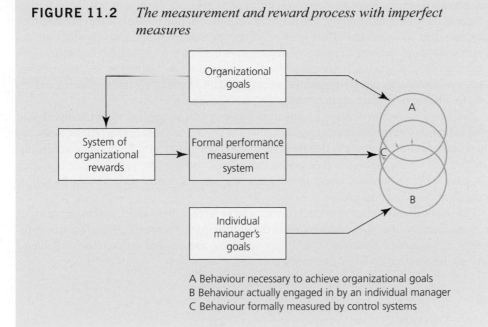

A Behaviour necessary to achieve organizational goals
B Behaviour actually engaged in by an individual manager
C Behaviour formally measured by control systems

the controllability principle. Performance evaluations are likely to be considered unfair
where managers are held accountable for outcomes over which they have little control.
Another potential cause of negative attitudes is the way in which results controls are
applied. If they are applied in an insensitive and rigid manner and used mainly as punitive
devices they are likely to provoke negative reactions. The way that a control system is
applied can be just as important as the design issues in determining the success of a control
system. Negative attitudes are likely to be the cause of many of the harmful side-effects that
have been described above. Thus, if the negative attitudes can be minimized the harmful
side-effects are likely to be minimized.

Advantages and disadvantages of different types of controls

Merchant (1998) suggests that when deciding on the control alternatives managers should
start by considering whether *personnel* or *cultural controls* will be sufficient. He suggests that
they are worthy of first consideration because they have relatively few harmful side effects.
Also in small organizations they may be completely effective without the need to supplement
them with other forms of controls. Merchant concludes that considering personnel/cultural
controls first allows managers to consider how reliable these controls are and the extent to
which it is necessary to supplement them with other forms of control. However, he points out
that these controls are appropriate only if the people in their particular roles understand what
is required, are capable of performing well, and are motivated to perform well without additional rewards or punishments provided by the organization.

Action controls are the most effective form of control because there is a direct link
between the control mechanism and the action and also a high probability that desirable

outcomes will occur. They dispense with the need to measure the results and measurement problems do not therefore apply. The major limitation of action controls is that because they are dependent on cause-and-effect work relationships that are well understood they are not feasible in many situations. These requirements are likely to be applicable only with highly routinized jobs. A second limitation is that they tend to be best suited to stable situations. They can discourage creativity and the ability to adapt to changing circumstances and are therefore likely to be unsuitable in a changing environment.

The major attraction of *results controls* is that they can be applied where knowledge of what actions are desirable is lacking. This situation applies in most organizations. A second attraction of results controls is that their application does not restrict individual autonomy. The focus is on the outcomes thus giving individuals the freedom to determine how they can best achieve the outcomes. Individuals are not burdened with having to follow prescribed rules and procedures.

The major disadvantages of results controls have already been discussed in the previous section. In many cases the results required can only be partially specified, there can be difficulties in separating controllable and uncontrollable factors and measurement problems may inhibit their ability to satisfactorily measure performance.

Management accounting control systems

Although output controls predominantly consist of management accounting controls the latter have not been examined in detail. To enable you to understand the role that management accounting control systems play within the overall control process this chapter has initially adopted a broad approach to describing management control systems. We shall now concentrate on management accounting control systems which represent the predominant controls in most organizations.

Why are accounting controls the predominant controls? There are several reasons. First, all organizations need to express and aggregate the results of a wide range of dissimilar activities using a common measure. The monetary measure meets this requirement. Second, profitability and liquidity are essential to the success of all organizations and financial measures relating to these and other areas are closely monitored by stakeholders. It is therefore natural that managers will wish to monitor performance in monetary terms. Third, financial measures also enable a common decision rule to be applied by all managers when considering alternative courses of action. That is, a course of action will normally benefit a firm only if it results in an improvement in its financial performance. Fourth, measuring results in financial terms enables managers to be given more autonomy. Focusing on the outcomes of managerial actions, summarized in financial terms, gives managers the freedom to take whatever actions they consider to be appropriate to achieve the desired results. Finally, outputs expressed in financial terms continue to be effective in uncertain environments even when it is unclear what course of action should be taken. Financial results provide a mechanism to indicate whether the actions benefited the organization.

Responsibility centres

The complex environment in which most businesses operate today makes it virtually impossible for most firms to be controlled centrally. This is because it is not possible for central management to have all the relevant information and time to determine the detailed plans for all the organization. Some degree of decentralization is essential for all but the smallest firms. Organizations decentralize by creating responsibility centres. A **responsibility centre** may be defined as a unit of a firm where an individual manager is held responsible for the unit's performance. There are four types of responsibility centres. They are:

1 cost or expense centres;
2 revenue centres;
3 profit centres;
4 investment centres.

The creation of responsibility centres is a fundamental part of management accounting control systems. It is therefore important that you can distinguish between the various forms of responsibility centres.

Cost or expense centres

Cost or **expense centres** are responsibility centres whose managers are normally accountable for only those costs that are under their control. We can distinguish between two types of cost centres – standard cost centres and discretionary cost centres. The main features of **standard cost centres** are that output can be measured and the input required to produce each unit of output can be specified. Control is exercised by comparing the standard cost (that is, the cost of the inputs that *should* have been consumed in producing the output) with the cost that was *actually* incurred. The difference between the actual cost and the standard cost is described as the **variance**. Standard cost centres and variance analysis will be discussed extensively in the next chapter.

Discretionary expense centres are those responsibility cost centres where output cannot be measured in financial terms and there are no clearly observable relationships between inputs (the resources consumed) and the outputs (the results achieved). Control normally takes the form of ensuring that actual expenditure adheres to budgeted expenditure for each expense category and also ensuring that the tasks assigned to each centre have been successfully accomplished. Examples of discretionary centres include advertising and publicity and research and development departments. One of the major problems arising in discretionary expense centres is measuring the effectiveness of expenditures. For example, the marketing support department may not have exceeded an advertising budget but this does not mean that the advertising expenditure has been effective. The advertising may have been incorrectly timed, it may have been directed to the wrong audience, or it may have contained the wrong message. Determining the effectiveness and efficiency of discretionary expense centres is one of the most difficult areas of management control.

Revenue centres

Revenue centres are responsibility centres where managers are accountable only for financial outputs in the form of generating sales revenues. Typical examples of revenue centres are where regional sales managers are accountable for sales within their regions. Where managers are evaluated solely on the basis of sales revenues there is a danger that they may concentrate on maximizing sales revenues at the expense of profitability. This can occur when all sales are not equally profitable and managers can achieve higher sales revenues by promoting low-profit products.

Revenue centre managers may also be held accountable for selling expenses, such as salesperson salaries, commissions and order-getting costs. They are not, however, made accountable for the cost of the goods and services that they sell. Revenue centres can be distinguished from profit centres by the fact that revenue centres are accountable for only a small proportion of the total costs of manufacturing and selling products and services, namely selling costs, whereas profit centre managers are responsible for the majority of the costs including both manufacturing and selling costs.

Profit centres

Both cost and revenue centre managers have limited decision-making authority. Cost centre managers are accountable only for managing inputs of their centres and decisions relating to outputs are made by other units within the firm. Revenue centres are accountable for selling the products or services but they have no control over their manufacture. A significant increase in managerial autonomy occurs when unit managers are given responsibility for both production and sales. In this situation managers are normally free to set selling prices, choose which markets to sell in, make product-mix and output decisions and select suppliers. Units within an organization whose managers are accountable for both revenues and costs are called **profit centres**.

Investment centres

Investment centres are responsibility centres whose managers are responsible for both sales revenues and costs and, in addition, have responsibility and authority to make working capital and capital investment decisions. Typical investment centre performance measures include return on investment and economic value added. These measures are influenced by revenues, costs and assets employed and thus reflect the responsibility that managers have for both generating profits and managing the investment base.

Investment centres represent the highest level of managerial autonomy. They include the company as a whole, operating subsidiaries, operating groups and divisions. You will find that many firms are not precise in their terminology and call their investment centres profit centres. Profit and investment centres will be discussed extensively in Chapter 13.

The nature of management accounting control systems

Management accounting control systems have two core elements. The first is the formal planning processes such as budgeting and long-term planning that were described in the previous chapter. These processes are used for establishing performance expectations for evaluating performance. The second is responsibility accounting which involves the creation of responsibility centres. Responsibility centres enable accountability for financial results and outcomes to be allocated to individuals throughout the organization. The objective of **responsibility accounting** is to accumulate costs and revenues for each individual responsibility centre so that the deviations from a performance target (typically the budget) can be attributed to the individual who is accountable for the responsibility centre. For each responsibility centre the process involves setting a performance target, measuring performance, comparing performance against the target, analysing the variances and taking action where significant variances exist between actual and target performance. Financial performance targets for profit or investment centres are typically in terms of profits, return on investment or economic value added whereas performance targets for cost centres are defined in terms of costs.

Responsibility accounting is implemented by issuing performance reports at frequent intervals (normally monthly) that inform responsibility centre managers of the deviations from budgets for which they are accountable and are required to take action. An example of a performance report issued to a cost centre manager is presented in the lower section of Exhibit 11.1. You should note that at successively higher levels of management less detailed information is reported. You can see from the upper sections of Exhibit 11.1 that the information is condensed and summarized as the results relating to the responsibility centre are reported at higher levels. Exhibit 11.1 only includes financial information. In addition non-financial measures such as those relating to quality and timeliness may be reported. We shall look at non-financial measures in more detail in Chapter 16.

Responsibility accounting involves:

- distinguishing between those items which managers can control and for which they should be held accountable and those items over which they have no control and for which they are not held accountable;
- determining how challenging the financial targets should be;
- determining how much influence managers should have in the setting of financial targets.

We shall now examine each of these items in detail.

The controllability principle

Responsibility accounting is based on the application of the controllability principle which means that it is appropriate to charge to an area of responsibility only those costs that are significantly influenced by the manager of that responsibility centre. The controllability principle can be implemented by either eliminating the uncontrollable items from the areas for which managers are held accountable or calculating their effects so that the reports distinguish between controllable and uncontrollable items.

Applying the controllability principle is difficult in practice because many areas do not fit neatly into either controllable and uncontrollable categories. Instead, they are partially controllable. For example, even when outcomes may be affected by occurrences outside a manager's control, such as competitors' actions, price changes and supply shortages, managers can take action to reduce their adverse effects. They can substitute alternative materials where the prices of raw materials change or they can monitor and respond to competitors' actions. If these factors are categorized as uncontrollables managers will be motivated not to try and influence them. A further problem is that even when a factor is clearly uncontrollable, it is difficult to measure in order to highlight its impact on the reported outcomes.

Types of uncontrollable factors

Merchant (1998) identifies three types of uncontrollable factors. They are:

1 economic and competitive factors;
2 acts of nature;
3 interdependencies.

Both revenues and costs are affected by *economic and competitive factors*. Changes in customers' tastes, competitors' actions, business cycles and changing government regulations and foreign exchange rates affect sales revenues. Costs are affected by items such as changes

REAL WORLD
VIEWS 11.1

Responsibility cost control systems in China

Because of the previous lack of effective control of expenditure by the Han Dan Company, a system of responsibility accounting and standard costing was introduced in 1990. The basic principles underlying the responsibility cost control system included: (1) setting cost and profit targets (responsibility standards) that take into account market pressures; (2) assigning target costs to various levels of responsibility centre; (3) evaluating performance based on fulfilment of the responsibility targets; and (4) implementing a reward scheme with built-in incentive mechanisms. In order to facilitate performance measurement and evaluation, non-controllable common costs were excluded from the responsibility costs decomposed within primary production factories. Responsibility contracts between factory managers and managers at lower levels must also be signed. A breakdown of the aggregated responsibility targets to all profit centres and their subordinates is conducted by the Department of Finance and Accounting. In addition, the department is responsible for monthly and yearly reporting of the execution results of the responsibility cost control system. It also reports and analyses the variances between actual outcomes and responsibility targets, and determines the necessary bonus rewards (or penalty) for each responsibility centre in terms of the fulfilment of the cost and profit targets signed by managers. If a responsibility centre or individual worker fails to meet the cost targets specified in the responsibility contracts, all bonus and other benefits relating to the responsibility unit or worker will be forfeited.

Source: Adapted from Z. Jun Lin and Z. Yu (2002) Responsibility cost control system in China: a case of management accounting application, *Management Accounting Research*, **13**(4), pp. 447–467. With permission from Elsevier.

in input prices, interest and foreign exchange rates, government regulations and taxes. Although these items appear to be uncontrollable managers can respond to these changes to relieve their negative impacts. For example, they can respond to changes in customers' tastes by developing new products or redesigning existing products. They can respond to changes in exchange rates by changing their sources of supply and selling in different countries. Responding to such changes is an important part of a manager's job. Therefore most management accounting control systems do not shield managers completely from economic and competitive factors although they may not be required to bear all of the risk.

Acts of nature are usually large, one-time events with effects on performance that are beyond the ability of managers to anticipate. Examples are disasters such as fires, floods, riots, tornadoes, accidents and machine breakdowns. Most organizations protect managers from the adverse consequences of acts of nature by not making them accountable for them provided that the events are considered to be clearly uncontrollable.

The third type of uncontrollable relates to *interdependence* whereby a responsibility centre is not completely self-contained so that the outcomes are affected by other units within the organization. For example, responsibility centres use common/pooled firm resources such as shared administrative activities. Pooled interdependence is low when responsibility centres are relatively self-contained so that use of pooled resources has little impact on a unit's performance. The users of pooled resources should not have to bear any higher costs arising from the bad performance of the shared resource pools. Managers can be protected from inefficiencies of the shared resource pools to a certain extent by negotiations during the annual budgeting process whereby the quantities and amounts of services

EXHIBIT 11.1

Responsibility accounting monthly performance reports

Performance report to managing director

		Budget		Variance[a] F (A)	
		Current month (£)	Year to date (£)	This month (£)	Year to date (£)
Managing director	→ Factory A	453 900	6 386 640	80 000(A)	98 000(A)
	Factory B	X	X	X	X
	Factory C	X	X	X	X
	Administration costs	X	X	X	X
	Selling costs	X	X	X	X
	Distribution costs	X	X	X	X
		2 500 000	30 000 000	400 000(A)	600 000(A)

Performance report to production manager of factory A

Production manager	Works manager's office	X	X	X	X
	→ Machining department 1	165 600	717 600	32 760(A)	89 180(A)
	Machining department 2	X	X	X	X
	Assembly department	X	X	X	X
	Finishing department	X	X	X	X
		453 900	6 386 640	80 000(A)	98 000(A)

Performance report to head of responsibility centre

Head of responsibility centre	Direct materials	X	X	X	X
	Direct labour	X	X	X	X
	Indirect labour	X	X	X	X
	Indirect materials	X	X	X	X
	Power	X	X	X	X
	Maintenance	X	X	X	X
	Idle time	X	X	X	X
	Other	X	X	X	X
		165 600	717 600	32 760(A)	89 180(A)

[a]F indicates a favourable variance (actual cost less than budgeted cost) and (A) indicates an adverse budget (actual cost greater than budget cost). Note that, at the lowest level of reporting, the responsibility centre head's performance report contains detailed information on operating costs. At successively higher levels of management less detail is reported. For example, the managing director's information on the control of activities consists of examining those variances that represent significant departures from the budget for each factory and functional area of the business and requesting explanations from the appropriate managers.

are agreed. Responsibility centre managers are charged with their usage of pooled resources at the budgeted rate and do not bear the cost of any inefficiencies incurred by the pooled resource centres during the current budget period.

Dealing with the distorting effects of uncontrollable factors before the measurement period

Management can attempt to deal with the distorting effects of uncontrollables by making adjustments either before or after the measurement period. Uncontrollable and controllable factors can be determined prior to the measurement period by specifying which budget line items are to be regarded as controllable and uncontrollable. Uncontrollable items can either be excluded from performance reports or shown in a separate section within the performance report so that they are clearly distinguishable from controllable items. The latter approach has the advantage of drawing managerial attention to those costs that a company incurs to support their activities. Managers may be able to indirectly influence these costs if they are made aware of the sums involved.

How do we distinguish between controllable and uncontrollable items? Merchant suggests that the following general rule should be applied to all employees – 'Hold employees accountable for the performance areas you want them to pay attention to.' Applying this rule explains why some organizations assign the costs of shared resource pools, such as administrative costs relating to personnel and data processing departments, to responsibility centres. Assigning these costs authorizes managers of the user responsibility centres to question the amount of the costs and the quantity and quality of services supplied. In addition, responsibility centres are discouraged from making unnecessary requests for the use of these services when they are aware that increases in costs will be assigned to the users of the services.

Care must be taken, however, in making responsibility heads accountable for many areas for which they do not have a significant influence. The additional costs arising from the harmful side-effects described earlier will be incurred and these must be offset against the benefits discussed above.

Dealing with the distorting effects of uncontrollable factors after the measurement period

Merchant identifies four methods of removing the effects of uncontrollable factors from the results measures after the measurement period and before the rewards are assigned. They are:

1 variance analysis;
2 flexible performance standards;
3 relative performance evaluations;
4 subjective performance evaluations.

Variance analysis seeks to analyse the factors that cause the actual results to differ from predetermined budgeted targets. In particular, variance analysis helps to distinguish between controllable and uncontrollable items and identify those individuals who are accountable for the variances. For example, variances analysed by each type of cost, and by their price and quantity effects, enables variances to be traced to accountable individuals and also to isolate those variances that are due to uncontrollable factors. Variance analysis will be discussed extensively in the next chapter.

EXAMPLE 11.1

An item of expense that is included in the budget for a responsibility centre varies directly in relation to activity at an estimated cost of £5 per unit of output. The budgeted monthly level of activity was 20 000 units and the actual level of activity was 24 000 units at a cost of £105 000.

Flexible performance standards apply when targets are adjusted to reflect variations in uncontrollable factors arising from the circumstances not envisaged when the targets were set. The most widely used flexible performance standard is to use **flexible budgets** whereby the uncontrollable volume effects on cost behaviour are removed from the manager's performance reports. Because some costs vary with changes in the level of activity, it is essential when applying the controllability principle to take into account the variability of costs. For example, if the actual level of activity is greater than the budgeted level of activity then those costs that vary with activity will be greater than the budgeted costs purely because of changes in activity. Let us consider the simplified situation presented in Example 11.1.

Assuming that the increase in activity was due to an increase in sales volume greater than that anticipated when the budget was set then the increases in costs arising from the volume change are beyond the control of the responsibility centre manager. It is clearly inappropriate to compare actual *variable* costs of £105 000 from an activity level of 24 000 units with budgeted *variable* costs of £100 000 from an activity level of 20 000 units. This would incorrectly suggest an overspending of £5000. If managers are to be made responsible for their costs, it is essential that they are responsible for performance under the conditions in which they worked, and not for a performance based on conditions when the budget was drawn up. In other words, it is misleading to compare actual costs at one level of activity with budgeted costs at another level of activity. At the end of the period the original budget must be adjusted to the actual level of activity to take into account the impact of the uncontrollable volume change on costs. This procedure is called flexible budgeting. In Example 11.1 the performance report should be as follows:

Budgeted expenditure	Actual expenditure
(flexed to 24 000 units)	(24 000 units)
£120 000	£105 000

The budget is adjusted to reflect what the costs should have been for an actual activity of 24 000 units. This indicates that the manager has incurred £15 000 less expenditure than would have been expected for the actual level of activity, and a favourable variance of £15 000 should be recorded on the performance report, not an adverse variance of £5000, which would have been recorded if the original budget had not been adjusted.

In Example 11.1 it was assumed that there was only one variable item of expense, but in practice the budget will include many different expenses including fixed, semi-variable and variable expenses. You should note that fixed expenses do not vary in the short-term with activity and therefore the budget should remain unchanged for these expenses. The budget should be flexed only for variable and semi-variable expenses.

Budgets may also be adjusted to reflect other uncontrollable factors besides volume changes. Budgets are normally set based on the environment that is anticipated during the budget setting process. If the budget targets are then used throughout the duration of the annual budget period for performance evaluation the managers will be held accountable for uncontrollable factors arising from forecasting errors. To remove the managerial exposure to uncontrollable risks arising from forecasting errors *ex post* **budget adjustments** can be made whereby the budget is adjusted to the environmental and economic conditions that the managers actually faced during the period.

Relative performance evaluation relates to the situations where the performance of a responsibility centre is evaluated relative to the performance of similar centres within the same company or to similar units outside the organization. To be effective responsibility centres must perform similar tasks and face similar environmental and business conditions with the units that they are being benchmarked against. Such relative comparisons with units facing similar environmental conditions neutralizes the uncontrollable factors because they are in effect held constant when making the relative comparisons. The major difficulty relating to relative performance evaluations is finding benchmark units that face similar conditions and uncertainties.

Instead of making the formal and quantitative adjustments that are a feature of the methods that have been described so far **subjective judgements** are made in the evaluation process based on the knowledge of the outcome measures and the circumstances faced by the responsibility centre heads. The major advantage of subjective evaluations is that they can alleviate some of the defects of the measures used by accounting control systems. The disadvantages of subjective evaluations are that they are not objective, they tend not to provide the person being evaluated with a clear indication of how performance has been evaluated, they can create conflict with superiors resulting in a loss of morale and a decline in motivation and they are expensive in terms of management time.

Guidelines for applying the controllability principle

Dealing with uncontrollables represents one of the most difficult areas for the design and operation of management accounting control systems. The following guidelines published by the Report of the Committee of Cost Concepts and Standards in the United States in 1956 still continues to provide useful guidance:

1 If a manager *can control the quantity and price paid* for a service then the manager is responsible for all the expenditure incurred for the service.

2 If the manager *can control the quantity of the service but not the price paid* for the service then only that amount of difference between actual and budgeted expenditure that is due to usage should be identified with the manager.

3 If the manager *cannot control either the quantity or the price paid* for the service then the expenditure is uncontrollable and should not be identified with the manager.

An example of the latter situation is when the costs of an industrial relations department are apportioned to a department on some arbitrary basis; such arbitrary apportionments are likely to result in an allocation of expenses that the managers of responsibility centres may not be able to influence. In addition to the above guidelines Merchants's (1998) general rule should also be used as a guide – 'Hold employees accountable for the performance areas you want them to pay attention to.'

Setting financial performance targets

There is substantial evidence from a large number of studies that the existence of a defined, quantitative goal or target is likely to motivate higher levels of performance than when no such target is stated. People perform better when they have a clearly defined goal to aim for and are aware of the standards that will be used to interpret their performance. There are three approaches that can be used to set financial targets. They are targets derived from engineering studies of input–output relationships, targets derived from historical data and targets derived from negotiations between superiors and subordinates.

Engineered targets can be used when there are clearly defined and stable input–output relationships such that the inputs required can be estimated directly from product specifications. For example, in a fast-food restaurant for a given output of hamburgers it is possible to estimate the inputs required because there is a physical relationship between the ingredients such as meats, buns, condiments and packaging and the number of hamburgers made. Input–output relationships can also be established for labour by closely observing the processes to determine the quantity of labour that will be required for a given output.

Where clearly defined input–output relationships do not exist other approaches must be used to set financial targets. One approach is to use **historical targets** derived directly from the results of previous periods. Previous results plus an increase for expected price changes may form the basis for setting the targets or an improvement factor may be incorporated into the estimate, such as previous period costs less a reduction of 10%. The disadvantage of using historical targets is that they may include past inefficiencies or may encourage employees to underperform if the outcome of efficient performance in a previous period is used as a basis for setting a more demanding target in the next period.

Negotiated targets are set based on negotiations between superiors and subordinates. The major advantage of negotiated targets is that they address the information asymmetry gap that can exist between superior and subordinate. This gap arises because subordinates have more information than their superiors on the relationships between outputs and inputs and the constraints that exist at the operating level, whereas superiors have a broader view of the organization as a whole and the resource constraints that apply. Negotiated targets enable the information asymmetry gap to be reduced so that the targets set incorporate the constraints applying at both the operational level and the firm as a whole. You should refer back to the previous chapter for a more detailed discussion of the negotiation process.

Targets vary in their level of difficulty and the chosen level has a significant effect on motivation and performance. Targets are considered to be moderately difficult (or highly achievable) when they are set at the average level of performance for a given task. According to Merchant (1990) most companies set their annual profit budgets targets at levels that are highly achievable. Their budgets are set to be challenging but achievable 80–90 per cent of the time by an effective management team working at a consistently high level of effort. Targets set at levels above average are labelled as difficult, tight or high, and those set below average are classed as easy, loose or low (Chow, 1983).

The effect of the level of budget difficulty on motivation and performance

The fact that a financial target represents a specific quantitative goal gives it a strong motivational potential, but the targets set must be accepted if managers are to be motivated to achieve higher levels of performance. Unfortunately, it is not possible to specify exactly the optimal degree of difficulty for financial targets, since task uncertainty and cultural, organizational and personality factors all affect an individual manager's reaction to a financial target.

Figure 11.3, derived from Otley (1987), shows the theoretical relationship between budget difficulty, aspiration levels and performance. In Figure 11.3 it is assumed that performance and aspiration levels are identical. Note that the **aspiration level** relates to the personal goal of the budgetee (that is, the person who is responsible for the budget). In other

FIGURE 11.3 *The effect of budget difficulty on performance.*
Source: Otley (1987)

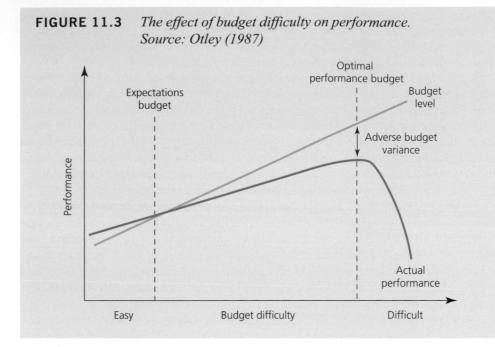

words, it is the level of performance that they hope to attain. You will see from Figure 11.3 that as the level of budget difficulty is increased both the budgetees' aspiration level and performance increases. However, there becomes a point where the budget is perceived as impossible to achieve and the aspiration level and performance decline dramatically. It can be seen from Figure 11.3 that the budget level that motivates the best level of performance may not be achievable. In contrast, the budget that is expected to be achieved (that is, the expectations budget in Figure 11.3) motivates a lower level of performance.

Therefore if budgets are to be set at a level that will motivate individuals to achieve maximum performance, adverse budget variances are to be expected. In such a situation it is essential that adverse budget variances are not used by management as a punitive device, since this is likely to encourage budgetees to attempt to obtain looser budgets by either underperforming or deliberately negotiating easily attainable budgets. This may lead to fewer adverse variances, but also to poorer overall performance.

To motivate the best level of actual performance, demanding budgets should be set and small adverse variances should be regarded as a healthy sign and not as something to be avoided. If budgets are always achieved with no adverse variances, this indicates that the standards are too loose to motivate the best possible results.

Arguments in favour of setting highly achievable budgets

It appears from our previous discussion that tight budgets should be established to motivate maximum performance, although this may mean that the budget has a high probability of not being achieved. Otley (1987) suggests that the optimum point may be at the point where individuals perceive there is significantly less than a 50% chance of target achievement. However, budgets are not used purely as a motivational device to maximize performance. They are also used for planning purposes and it is most unlikely that tight budgets will be suitable for planning purposes. Why? Tight budgets that have a high probability of not being achieved are most unsuitable for cash budgeting and for harmonizing the company plans in the form of a master budget. Because of this conflict, it has been suggested that separate budgets should be used for planning and for motivation purposes. The counter argument to this is that budgetees may react unfavourably to a situation where they believe that one budget is used to evaluate their performance and a second looser budget is used by top management.

Most companies use the same budgets for planning and motivational purposes (Umapathy, 1987). If only one set of budgets is used it is most unlikely that one set can, at the same time, perfectly meet both the planning and the motivational requirements. A compromise is required whereby the targets that can be used for planning purposes are not so easy that they have no motivational impact. Merchant (1990) suggests that highly achievable budgets that are achievable 80–90 per cent of the time require managers to be working consistently at a high level of effort to meet this requirement.

Highly achievable budgets also have a number of other advantages. The theoretical models such as the one illustrated in Figure 11.3 ignores the psychological impact of failure. For example, Merchant (1998) points out that when managers fail to achieve their budget targets they live with that failure for an entire year and that this can result in a prolonged period of discouragement and depression that can be quite costly to the organization. In contrast, highly achievable budgets provide managers with a sense of achievement and self-esteem which can be beneficial to the organization in terms of increased levels of commitment and aspirations. Highly achievable budgets also shield managers from unexpected adverse circumstances which were not anticipated when the budget was set. Hence, they are less likely to look for excuses for failure to achieve the budget. Instead, they promote an increase in commitment to achieving the budgets.

Rewards such as bonuses, promotions and job security are normally linked to budget achievement so that the costs of failing to meet budget targets can be high. The greater the probability of the failure to meet budget targets the greater is the probability that managers will be motivated to distort their performance by engaging in behaviour that will result in the harmful side-effects described earlier in this chapter. You should be able to recall that they include manipulation of data, negative attitudes and deliberately underperforming so that targets will not be increased in the forthcoming periods. Adopting targets that are highly achievable alleviates these harmful side-effects.

The disadvantage of adopting highly achievable budget targets is that aspiration levels and performance may not be maximized. To encourage managers to maximize performance when highly achievable standards are adopted, rewards can be given for achieving the budget, and additional rewards can also be given relating to the extent to which they exceed the budget. Managers therefore have incentives not to merely achieve the budget but to exceed it.

Participation in the budgeting and target setting process

Participation relates to the extent that subordinates or budgetees are able to influence the figures that are incorporated in their budgets or targets. Participation is sometimes referred to as **bottom-up budget setting** whereas a non-participatory approach whereby subordinates have little influence on the target setting process is sometimes called **top-down budget setting**.

Allowing individuals to participate in the setting of performance targets has several advantages. First, individuals are more likely to accept the targets and be committed to achieving them if they have been involved in the target setting process. Second, participation can reduce the information asymmetry gap that applies when standards are imposed from above. Earlier in this chapter it was pointed out that subordinates have more information than their superiors on the relationships between outputs and inputs and the constraints that exist at the operating level whereas the superiors have a broader view of the organization as a whole and the resource constraints that apply. This information sharing process enables more effective targets to be set that attempt to deal with both operational and organizational constraints. Finally, imposed standards can encourage negative attitudes and result in demotivation and alienation. This in turn can lead to a rejection of the targets and poor performance.

Factors influencing the effectiveness of participation

Participation has been advocated by many writers as a means of making tasks more challenging and giving individuals a greater sense of responsibility. For many years participation in decision-making was thought to be a panacea for effective organizational effort but this school of thought was later challenged. The debate has never been resolved. The believers have never been able to demonstrate that participation really does have a positive effect on productivity and the sceptics have never been able to prove the opposite (Macintosh, 1985). The empirical studies have presented conflicting evidence on the usefulness of participation in the management process. For every study indicating that participation leads to better attitudes and improved performance, an alternative frequently exists suggesting the opposite.

Because of the conflicting findings relating to the effectiveness of participation research has tended to concentrate on studying how various factors influence the effectiveness of participation. In a classic study Vroom (1960) demonstrated that personality variables can have an important influence on the effectiveness of participation. He identified authoritarianism as an important factor conditioning the relationship between participation and performance. Vroom found that highly authoritarian people with a low need for independence were unaffected by participative approaches, and that high participation was effective only for individuals who were low on the authoritarianism measure.

Hopwood (1978) identified the importance of the work situation in determining the appropriateness of participation. He states:

> In highly programmed, environmentally and technologically constrained areas, where speed and detailed control are essential for efficiency, participative approaches may have much less to offer from the point of view of the more economic aspects of organizational effectiveness ... In contrast, in areas where flexibility, innovation and the capacity to deal with unanticipated problems are important, participation in decision-making may offer a more immediate and more narrowly economic payoff than more authoritarian styles.

The evidence from the various studies suggests that participative styles of management will not necessarily be more effective than other styles, and that participative methods should be used with care. It is therefore necessary to identify those situations where there is evidence that participative methods are effective, rather than to introduce universal application into organizations. Participation must be used selectively; but if it is used in the right circumstances, it has an enormous potential for encouraging the commitment to organizational goals, improving attitudes towards the budgeting system, and increasing subsequent performance. Note, however, at this stage that there are some limitations on the positive effects of participation in standard setting and circumstances where top-down budget setting is preferable. They are:

1 Performance is measured by precisely the same standard that the budgetee has been involved in setting. This gives the budgetee the opportunity to negotiate lower targets that increase the probability of target achievement and the accompanying rewards. Therefore an improvement in performance – in terms of comparison with the budget – may result merely from a lowering of the standard.

2   Personality traits of the participants may limit the benefits of participation. For example, the evidence appears to indicate that authoritarians and persons of weak independence needs may well perform better on standards set by a higher authority.

3   Participation by itself is not adequate in ensuring commitment to standards. The manager must also believe that he or she can significantly influence the results and be given the necessary feedback about them.

4   A top-down approach to budget setting is likely to be preferable where a process is highly programmable, and there are clear and stable input–output relationships, so that engineered studies can be used to set the targets. Here there is no need to negotiate targets using a bottom-up process.

Side-effects arising from using accounting information for performance evaluation

Earlier in this chapter we discussed some of the harmful side-effects that can arise from the use of results controls. Some of these effects can be due to the ways in which the output measures are used. A number of studies have been undertaken that examine the side-effects arising from the ways that accounting information is used in performance evaluation.

A study on how budgets are used in performance evaluation was undertaken by Hopwood (1976), based on observations in a manufacturing division of a large US company. Three distinct styles of using budget and actual cost information in performance evaluation were observed and were described as follows:

1   **Budget-constrained style**: Despite the many problems in using accounting data as comprehensive measures of managerial performance, the evaluation is based primarily upon the cost centre head's ability continually to meet the budget on a short-term basis. This criterion of performance is stressed at the expense of other valued and important criteria, and a cost centre head will tend to receive an unfavourable evaluation if his or her actual costs exceed the budgeted costs, regardless of other considerations. Budget data are therefore used in a rigid manner in performance evaluation.

2   **Profit-conscious style**: The performance of the cost centre head is evaluated on the basis of his or her ability to increase the general effectiveness of his or her unit's operations in relation to the long-term goals of the organization. One important aspect of this at the cost centre level is the head's concern with the minimization of long-run costs. The accounting data must be used with some care and in a rather flexible manner, with the emphasis for performance evaluation in contributing to long-term profitability.

3   **Non-accounting style**: Accounting data plays a relatively unimportant part in the supervisor's evaluation of the cost centre head's performance.

Emmanuel *et al.* (1990) state that

The three styles of evaluation are distinguished by the way in which extrinsic rewards are associated with budget achievement. In the rigid (budget constrained) style there is a clear-cut relationship; not achieving budget targets results in punishment, whereas achievement results in rewards. In the flexible (profit conscious) style, the relationship depends on other factors; given good reasons for over-spending, non-attainment of the budget can still result in rewards, whereas the attainment of the budget in undesirable ways may result in punishment. In the non-accounting style, the budget is relatively unimportant because rewards and punishment are not directly associated with its attainment (p. 179).

The evidence from Hopwood's study indicated that both the budget-constrained and the profit-conscious styles of evaluation led to a higher degree of involvement with costs than the non-accounting style. Only the profit-conscious style, however, succeeded in attaining this involvement without incurring either emotional costs for the managers in charge of the cost centres or defensive behaviour that was undesirable from the company's point of view.

The budget-constrained style gave rise to a belief that the evaluation was unjust, and caused widespread worry and tension on the job. Hopwood provides evidence of manipulation and undesirable decision behaviour as methods of relieving tension when a budget-constrained style of evaluation is used. In addition, the manager's relationships with the budget-constrained supervisors were allowed to deteriorate, and the rigid emphasis on the short-term budget results also highlighted the interdependent nature of their tasks, so that the immediate instrumental concerns permeated the pattern of social relationships among colleagues. For example, managers went out to improve their own reports, regardless of the detrimental effects on the organization, and then tried to pass on the responsibility by blaming their colleagues. In contrast, Hopwood found that the profit-conscious style avoided these problems, while at the same time it ensured that there was an active involvement with the financial aspects of the operations. A summary of the effect of the three styles of evaluation is given in Exhibit 11.2.

Hopwood's study was based on cost centres having a high degree of interdependence. Rigid measures of performance become less appropriate as the degree of interdependence increases, and therefore the managers used the accounting information in a more flexible manner to ensure that the information remained effective. Otley (1978) replicated Hopwood's study in a British firm that consisted of profit centres with a high degree of independence and where accounting information represented a more adequate basis of performance evaluation. He found no significant differences in the levels of job tension and performance reported by managers evaluated on styles initially used by Hopwood. Three explanations were offered for the differences in results. First, Otley's managers were said to operate more independently of other units within the same organization than Hopwood's managers. Second, Otley's managers were profit centre managers whereas Hopwood's were cost centre managers. Finally, Hopwood's managers operated in a less predictable environment than Otley's.

Otley suggested a style-context framework to reconcile the differences in results between his study and that of Hopwood. The style dimension consisted of a high and low emphasis on budget data in performance evaluation. The context dimension consisted of managerial interdependency[1] (high and low) and task uncertainty[2] (also high and low). Otley's framework suggested that when managers face high levels of interdependency or uncertainty, they may perceive themselves as having less than full control over performance outcomes. Using budget data in a rigid manner in such situations may be dysfunctional for performance, since a rigid use of budget data assumes that most of the factors that have an effect on task outcomes are within the control of the managers being evaluated (Ansari, 1979). On the other hand, Imoisili (1989) suggests that a rigid use of budget data may be more acceptable to managers if they perceive they are able to exercise control over their performance outcomes. This would be the case with tasks characterized by low uncertainty or interdependency. In other words, it is not budget style *per se* that may lead to higher stress or lower performance. Rather, it is the mismatch of budget style and task contexts that may enhance stress or reduce managerial performance (Imoisili, 1989).

	Style of evaluation		
	Budget-constrained	Profit-conscious	Non-accounting
Involvement with costs	High	High	Low
Job-related tension	High	Medium	Medium
Manipulation of accounting information	Extensive	Little	Little
Relations with superior	Poor	Good	Good
Relations with colleagues	Poor	Good	Good

EXHIBIT 11.2

Hopwood's findings on the effect of different styles of evaluating budget performance

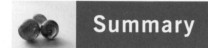

Summary

The following items relate to the learning objectives listed at the beginning of the chapter.

- **Describe the three different types of controls used in organizations.**

  Three different categories of controls are used – action/behavioural controls, personnel and cultural controls and results/output controls. With action controls the actions themselves are the focus of controls. They are usable and effective only when managers know what actions are desirable (or undesirable) and have the ability to make sure that the desirable actions occur (or that the undesirable actions do not occur). Personnel controls help employees do a good job by building on employees' natural tendencies to control themselves. They include selection and placement, training and job design. Cultural controls represent a set of values, social norms and beliefs that are shared by members of the organization and that influence their actions. Output or results controls involve collecting and reporting information about the outcomes of work effort. They involve the following stages – establishing results and performance targets, measuring performance and providing rewards or punishments based on an employee's ability to achieve the performance target.

- **Describe a cybernetic control system.**

  The traditional approach in the management control literature has been to view results controls as a simple cybernetic system. A cybernetic control system resembles the thermostat control model. Standards of performance are determined, measurement systems monitor performance, comparisons are made between the standard and actual performance and feedback provides information on the variances between standard and actual performance of the actions that are being measured.

- **Distinguish between feedback and feed-forward controls.**

  Feedback control involves monitoring outputs achieved against desired outputs and taking whatever corrective action is necessary if a deviation exists. In feed-forward control, instead of actual outputs being compared against desired outputs, predictions are made of what outputs are expected to be at some future time. If these expectations differ from what is desired, control actions are taken that will minimize these differences. The objective is for control to be achieved before any deviations from desired outputs actually occur. The budgeting process is a feed-forward control system. The comparison of actual results with budget, in identifying variances and taking remedial action to ensure future outcomes will conform with budgeted outcomes, is an illustration of a feedback control system.

● **Explain the potential harmful side-effects of results controls.**

Results controls can promote a number of harmful side-effects. They can lead to a lack of goal congruence when employees seek to achieve the performance targets in a way that is not organizationally desirable. They can also lead to data manipulation and negative attitudes, which can result in a decline in morale and a lack of motivation.

● **Define the four different types of responsibility centres.**

A responsibility centre may be defined as a unit of a firm where an individual manager is held accountable for the unit's performance. There are four types of responsibility centres – cost or expense centres, revenue centres, profit centres and investment centres. Cost or expense centres are responsibility centres whose managers are normally accountable for only those costs that are under their control. Revenue centres are responsibility centres where managers are accountable only for financial outputs in the form of generating sales revenues. Both cost and revenue centre managers have limited decision-making authority. A significant increase in managerial autonomy occurs when unit managers are given responsibility for both production and sales. In this situation, managers are normally free to set selling prices, choose which markets to sell in, make product mix and output decisions and select suppliers. Units within an organization whose managers are accountable for both revenues and costs are called profit centres. Investment centres are responsibility centres whose managers are responsible for both sales revenues and costs and, in addition, have responsibility and authority to make working capital and capital investment decisions.

● **Explain the different elements of management accounting control systems.**

Management accounting control systems have two core elements. The first is the formal planning processes such as budgeting and long-term planning. These processes are used for establishing performance expectations for evaluating performance. The second is responsibility accounting, which involves the creation of responsibility centres. Responsibility centres enable accountability for financial results/outcomes to be allocated to individuals throughout the organization. Responsibility accounting involves: (a) distinguishing between those items which managers can control and for which they should be held accountable and those items over which they have no control and for which they are not held accountable; (b) determining how challenging the financial targets should be; and (c) determining how much influence managers should have in the setting of financial targets.

● **Describe the controllability principle and the methods of implementing it.**

The controllability principle states that it is appropriate to charge to an area of responsibility only those costs that are significantly influenced by the manager of that responsibility centre. The controllability principle can be implemented by either eliminating the uncontrollable items from the areas that managers are held accountable for or calculating their effects so that the reports distinguish between controllable and uncontrollable items.

● **Describe the different approaches that can be used to determine financial performance targets and discuss the impact of their level of difficulty on motivation and performance.**

There are three approaches that can be used to set financial targets. They involve targets derived from engineering studies of input–output relationships, targets derived from historical data and targets derived from negotiations between superiors and subordinates. Engineered targets can be used when there are clearly defined and stable input–output relationships such that the inputs required can be estimated directly from product specifications. Where clearly defined input–output relationships do not exist other approaches must be used to set financial targets. One approach is to use historical targets derived directly from the results of previous periods. Previous results plus an increase for expected price changes may form the basis for setting the targets or an improvement factor may be incorporated into the estimate. Negotiated targets are set based on negotiations between superiors and subordinates. Different types of financial performance targets can be set ranging from easily achievable to difficult to achieve. Targets that are considered moderately difficult to achieve (called highly achievable targets) are recommended because they can be used for planning purposes and they also have a motivational impact.

- **Describe the influence of participation in the budgeting process.**

  Participation relates to the extent that budgetees are able to influence the figures that are incorporated in their budgets or targets. Allowing individuals to participate in the setting of performance targets has the following advantages: (a) individuals are more likely to accept the targets and be committed to achieving them if they have been involved in the target setting process; (b) participation can reduce the information asymmetry gap that applies when standards are imposed from above; and (c) imposed standards can encourage negative attitudes and result in demotivation and alienation. Participation, however, is subject to the following limitations: (a) performance is measured by precisely the same standard that the budgetee has been involved in setting; (b) personality traits of the participants may limit the benefits of participation; and (c) a top-down approach to budget setting is likely to be preferable where a process is highly programmable. Participation must be used selectively; but if it is used in the right circumstances, it has an enormous potential for encouraging the commitment to organizational goals.

- **Distinguish between the three different styles of evaluating performance and identify the circumstances when a particular style is most appropriate.**

  Three distinct styles of performance evaluation have been identified – a budget-constrained style, a profit conscious style and a non-accounting style. With a budget-constrained style, evaluation is based primarily upon a budgetee's ability continually to meet the budget on a short-term basis. Budget data are used in a rigid manner in performance evaluation. A profit-conscious style uses accounting data in a more flexible manner, with the emphasis for performance evaluation on a unit's contribution to long-term profitability. With a non-accounting style, accounting data play a relatively unimportant part in performance evaluation. Using a budget-constrained style when managers face high levels of interdependence or uncertainty is likely to be inappropriate because the rigid use of budget data assumes that most of the factors that have an effect on task outcomes are within the control of the managers being evaluated. In contrast, the rigid use of budget data may be more acceptable where managers perceive that they are able to exercise control over their performance outcomes. This applies where low uncertainty or interdependency characterizes tasks.

Notes

1 Managerial interdependency is the extent to which each manager perceives his or her work-related activities to require the joint or cooperative effort of other managers within the organization.

2 Task uncertainty is the extent to which managers can predict confidently the factors that have effects on their work-related activities.

Key terms and concepts

action controls (p. 303)
aspiration level (p. 319)
behavioural controls (p. 303)
bottom-up budget setting (p. 321)
budget-constrained style (p. 323)
clan controls (p. 304)
control (p. 301)
controllability principle (pp. 306, 313)
controls (p. 301)
cost centres (p. 311)
cultural controls (p. 304)
cybernetic system (p. 306)
discretionary expense centres (p. 311)
engineered targets (p. 319)
expense centres (p. 311)
ex post budget adjustments (p. 317)
feedback control (p. 307)
feed-forward control (p. 307)
flexible budgets (p. 317)
goal congruence (p. 308)
historical targets (p. 319)

investment centres (p. 312)
management control systems (p. 302)
negotiated targets (p. 319)
non-accounting style (p. 323)
output controls (p. 305)
participation (p. 321)
personnel controls (p. 304)
profit centres (p. 312)
profit-conscious style (p. 323)
relative performance evaluation (p. 317)
responsibility accounting (p. 312)
responsibility centre (p. 311)
results controls (p. 305)
revenue centres (p. 311)
social control (p. 304)
standard cost centres (p. 311)
strategic control (p. 302)
subjective judgements (p. 318)
top-down budget setting (p. 321)
variance (p. 307)
variance analysis (p. 316)

Assessment material

Review questions

The review questions are short questions that enable you to assess your understanding of the main topics included in the chapter. The numbers in parentheses provide you with the page numbers to refer to if you cannot answer a specific question.

Review problems

The review problems are more complex and require you to relate and apply the chapter content to various business problems. Fully worked solutions to the review problems are provided in a separate section at the end of the book. Further review problems for this chapter are available on the accompanying website, www.drury-online.com. The answers to these problems are available for lecturers on the lecturer's password-protected section of the website.

Case studies

The website also includes over 30 case study problems. A list of these cases is provided on pages 491–93. Cases that are relevant to the content of this chapter include Airport Complex and Integrated Technology Services Ltd.

Review questions

11.1   Distinguish between 'controls' and 'control'. (*p. 301*)

11.2   Identify and describe three different types of control mechanisms used by companies. (*pp. 302–6*)

11.3   Provide examples of behavioural, action, social, personnel and cultural controls. (*pp. 302–6*)

11.4   Describe the different stages that are involved with output/results controls. (*pp. 305–6*)

11.5   Describe the elements of cybernetic control systems. How do they relate to results/output controls? (*pp. 306–07*)

11.6   Distinguish between feedback and feed-forward controls. Provide an example of each type of control. (*p. 307*)

11.7   Describe some of the harmful side-effects that can occur with output/results controls. (*pp. 308–9*)

11.8   Explain the circumstances when it is appropriate or inappropriate to use personnel/cultural, behavioural/action and results/output controls. (*pp. 309–10*)

11.9   Describe the four different types of responsibility centres. (*pp. 310–12*)

11.10   Explain what is meant by the term 'responsibility accounting'. (*pp. 312–13*)

11.11   What factors must be taken into account when operating a responsibility accounting system? (*p. 313*)

11.12   What is the 'controllability principle'? Describe the different ways in which the principle can be applied. (*pp. 313–18*)

11.13   Describe three different types of uncontrollable factors. (*pp. 313–14*)

11.14   What are flexible budgets? Why are they preferred to fixed (static) budgets? (*pp. 317–18*)

11.15   What is meant by the term 'aspiration level'? (*pp. 319–20*)

11.16   Describe the effect of the level of budget difficulty on motivation and performance. (*pp. 319–20*)

11.17   Distinguish between participation and top-down budget setting. (*p. 321*)

11.18   Describe the factors influencing the effectiveness of participation in the budget process. (*pp. 322–23*)

11.19   What are the limitations of participation in the budget process? (*pp. 322–23*)

11.20   Distinguish between budget-constrained, profit-conscious and non-accounting styles of performance evaluation. (*pp. 323–24*)

11.21   Under what circumstances is it considered appropriate to use (a) the budget-constrained and (b) the profit conscious style of performance evaluation? (*p. 324*)

Review problems

11.22   Preparation of a flexible budget performance report

The Viking Smelting Company established a division, called the reclamation division, two years ago, to extract silver from jewellers' waste materials. The waste materials are processed in a furnace, enabling silver to be recovered. The silver is then further processed into finished products by three other divisions within the company.

A performance report is prepared each month for the reclamation division which is then discussed by the management team. Sharon Houghton, the newly appointed financial controller of the reclamation division, has recently prepared her first report for the four weeks to 31 May. This is shown below:

Performance Report Reclamation Division
4 weeks to 31 May

	Actual	Budget	Variance	Comments
Production (tonnes)	200	250	50 (F)[a]	
	(£)	(£)	(£)	
Wages and social security costs	46 133	45 586	547 (A)	Overspend
Fuel	15 500	18 750	3 250 (F)	
Consumables	2 100	2 500	400 (F)	
Power	1 590	1 750	160 (F)	
Divisional overheads	21 000	20 000	1 000 (A)	Overspend
Plant maintenance	6 900	5 950	950 (A)	Overspend
Central services	7 300	6 850	450 (A)	Overspend
Total	100 523	101 386	863 (F)	

[a](A) = adverse, (F) = favourable

In preparing the budgeted figures, the following assumptions were made for May:

- the reclamation division was to employ four teams of six production employees;
- each employee was to work a basic 42-hour week and be paid £7.50 per hour for the four weeks of May;
- social security and other employment costs were estimated at 40% of basic wages;
- a bonus, shared amongst the production employees, was payable if production exceeded 150 tonnes. This varied depending on the output achieved;

1. if output was between 150 and 199 tonnes, the bonus was £3 per tonne produced;
2. if output was between 200 and 249 tonnes, the bonus was £8 per tonne produced;
3. if output exceeded 249 tonnes the bonus was £13 per tonne produced;
   - the cost of fuel was £75 per tonne;
   - consumables were £10 per tonne;
   - power comprised a fixed charge of £500 per four weeks plus £5 per tonne for every tonne produced;
   - overheads directly attributable to the division were £20 000;
   - plant maintenance was to be apportioned to divisions on the basis of the capital values of each division;
   - the cost of Viking's central services was to be shared equally by all four divisions.

You are the deputy financial controller of the reclamation division. After attending her first monthly meeting with the board of the reclamation division, Sharon Houghton arranges a meeting with you. She is concerned about a number of issues, one of them being that the current report does not clearly identify those expenses and variances which are the direct responsibility of the reclamation division.

Task 1

Sharon Houghton asks you to prepare a flexible budget report for the reclamation division for May in a form consistent with responsibility accounting.

On receiving your revised report. Sharon tells you about the other questions raised at the management meeting when the original report was presented. These are summarized below:

(i) Why are the budget figures based on 2-year-old data taken from the proposal recommending the establishment of the reclamation division?

(ii) Should the budget data be based on what we were proposing to do or what we actually did do?

(iii) Is it true that the less we produce the more favourable our variances will be?

(iv) Why is there so much maintenance in a new division with modern equipment and why should we be charged with the actual costs of the maintenance department even when they overspend?

(v) Could the comments, explaining the variances, be improved?

(vi) Should all the variances be investigated?

(vii) Does showing the cost of central services on the divisional performance report help control these costs and motivate the divisional managers?

Task 2

Prepare a memo for the management of the reclamation division. Your memo should answer their queries and justify their comments.

11.23 **Comments on a performance report**

The Victorial Hospital is located in a holiday resort that attracts visitors to such an extent that the population of the area is trebled for the summer months of June, July and August. From past experience, this influx of visitors doubles the activity of the hospital during these months. The annual budget for the hospital's laundry department is broken down into four quarters, namely April–June, July–September, October–December and January–March, by dividing the annual budgeted figures by four. The budgeting work has been done for the current year by the secretary of the hospital using the previous year's figures and adding 3% for inflation. It is realized by the Hospital Authority that management information for control purposes needs to be improved, and you have been recruited to help to introduce a system of responsibility accounting.

You are required, from the information given, to:

(a) comment on the way in which the quarterly budgets have been prepared and to suggest improvements that could be introduced when preparing the budgets for 2001/2002;

(b) state what information you would like to flow from the actual against budget comparison (note that calculated figures are *not* required);

(c) state the amendments that would be needed to the current practice of budgeting and reporting to enable the report shown below to be used as a measure of the efficiency of the laundry manager.

Victorial Hospital – Laundry department
Report for quarter ended 30 September 2000

	Budget	Actual
Patients days	9 000	12 000
Weight processed (kg)	180 000	240 000
	(£)	(£)
Costs:		
Wages	8 800	12 320
Overtime premium	1 400	2 100
Detergents and other supplies	1 800	2 700
Water, water softening and heating	2 000	2 500
Maintenance	1 000	1 500
Depreciation of plant	2 000	2 000
Manager's salary	1 250	1 500
Overhead, apportioned:		
for occupancy	4 000	4 250
for administration	5 000	5 750

(*15 marks*)

11.24 Flexible budgets and the motivational role of budgets

Club Atlantic is an all-weather holiday complex providing holidays throughout the year. The fee charged to guests is fully inclusive of accommodation and all meals. However, because the holiday industry is so competitive, Club Atlantic is only able to generate profits by maintaining strict financial control of all activities.

The club's restaurant is one area where there is a constant need to monitor costs. Susan Green is the manager of the restaurant. At the beginning of each year she is given an annual budget which is then broken down into months. Each month she receives a statement monitoring actual costs against the annual budget and highlighting any variances. The statement for the month ended 31 October is reproduced below along with a list of assumptions:

Club Atlantic Restaurant Performance Statement
Month to 31 October

	Actual	Budget	Variance (over)/ under
Number of guest days	11 160	9 600	(1 560)
	(£)	(£)	(£)
Food	20 500	20 160	(340)
Cleaning materials	2 232	1 920	(312)
Heat, light and power	2 050	2 400	350
Catering wages	8 400	7 200	(1 200)
Rent rates, insurance and depreciation	1 860	1 800	(60)
	35 042	33 480	(1 562)

Assumptions:

(a) The budget has been calculated on the basis of a 30-day calendar month with the cost of rents, insurance and depreciation being an apportionment of the fixed annual charge.

(b) The budgeted catering wages assume that:

   (i) there is one member of the catering staff for every 40 guests staying at the complex;

   (ii) the daily cost of a member of the catering staff is £30.

(c) All other budgeted costs are variable costs based on the number of guest days.

Task 1

Using the data above, prepare a revised performance statement using flexible budgeting. Your statement should show both the revised budget and the revised variances. Club Atlantic uses the existing budgets and performance statements to motivate its managers as well as for financial control. If managers keep expenses below budget they receive a bonus in addition to their salaries. A colleague of Susan is Brian Hilton. Brian is in charge of the swimming pool and golf course, both of which have high levels of fixed costs. Each month he manages to keep expenses below budget and in return enjoys regular bonuses. Under the current reporting system, Susan Green only rarely receives a bonus.

At a recent meeting with Club Atlantic's directors Susan Green expressed concern that the performance statement was not a valid reflection of her management of the restaurant. You are currently employed by Hall and Co., the club's auditors, and the directors of Club Atlantic have asked you to advice them whether there is any justification for Susan Green's concern.

At the meeting with the Club's directors, you were asked the following questions:

(a) Do budgets motivate managers to achieve objectives?

(b) Does motivating managers lead to improved performance?

(c) Does the current method of reporting performance motivate Susan Green and Brian Hilton to be more efficient?

Task 2

Write a *brief* letter to the directors of Club Atlantic addressing their question and justifying your answers.

Note: You should make use of the data given in this task plus your findings in Task 1.

11.25 Recommendations for improvements to a performance report and a review of the management control system

Your firm has been consulted by the managing director of Inzone plc, which owns a chain of retail stores. Each store has departments selling furniture, tableware and kitchenware. Departmental managers are responsible to a store manager, who is in turn responsible to head office (HO).

All goods for sale are ordered centrally and stores sell at prices fixed by HO. Store managers (aided by departmental managers) order stocks from HO and stores are charged interest based on month-end stock levels. HO appoints all permanent staff and sets all pay levels. Store managers can engage or dismiss temporary workers, and are responsible for store running expenses.

The introduction to Inzone plc's management accounting manual states:

'Budgeting starts three months before the budget year, with product sales projections which are developed by HO buyers in consultation with each store's departmental managers. Expense budgets, adjusted for expected inflation, are then prepared by HO for each store. Inzone plc's accounting year is divided into 13 four-weekly control periods, and the budgeted sales and expenses are assigned to periods with due regard to seasonal factors. The budgets are completed one month before the year begins on 1st January.

'All HO expenses are recharged to stores in order to give the clearest indication of the "bottom line" profit of each store. These HO costs are mainly buying expenses, which are recharged to stores according to their square footage.

'Store reports comparing actual results with budgets are on the desks of HO and store management one week after the end of each control period. Significant variations in performance are then investigated, and appropriate action taken.'

Ms Lewis is manager of an Inzone plc store. She is eligible for a bonus equal to 5% of the amount by which her store's 'bottom-line' profit exceeds the year's budget. However, Ms Lewis sees no chance of a bonus this year, because major roadworks near the store are disrupting trade. Her store report for the four weeks ending 21 June is as follows:

	Actual (£)	Budget (£)
Sales	98 850	110 000
Costs:		
Cost of goods (including stock losses)	63 100	70 200
Wages and salaries	5 300	5 500
Rent	11 000	11 000
Depreciation of store fittings	500	500
Distribution costs	4 220	4 500
Other store running expenses	1 970	2 000
Interest charge on stocks	3 410	3 500
Store's share of HO costs	2 050	2 000
Store profit	7 300	10 800
	98 850	110 000
Stocks held at end of period	341 000	350 000
Store fittings at written down value	58 000	58 000

Requirements:

(a) Make recommendations for the improvement of Inzone plc's store report, briefly justifying each recommendation.

(11 marks)

(b) Prepare a report for the managing director of Inzone plc reviewing the company's responsibility delegation, identifying the major strengths and weaknesses of Inzone plc's management control system, and recommending any changes you consider appropriate.

(14 marks)

(Total 25 marks)

11.26 One common approach to organizational control theory is to look at the model of a cybernetic system. This is often illustrated by a diagram of a thermostat mechanism.

You are required:

(a) to explain the limitations of the simple feedback control this model illustrates, as an explanation of the working of organizational control systems;

Note: A diagram is *not* required.

(7 marks)

(b) to explain

(i) the required conditions (prerequisites) for the existence of control in an organization, which are often derived from this approach to control theory;

(5 marks)

(ii) the difficulties of applying control in a not-for-profit organization (NPO).

(8 marks)
(Total 20 marks)

11.27 You are required to:

(i) discuss the factors that are likely to cause managers to submit budget estimates of sales and costs that do not represent their best estimates or expectations of what will actually occur,

(8 marks)

(ii) suggest, as a budget accountant, what procedures you would advise in order to minimize the likelihood of such biased estimates arising.

(4 marks)

11.28 (a) Identify and explain the essential elements of an effective cost control system.

(13 marks)

(b) Outline possible problems which may be encountered as a result of the introduction of a system of cost control into an organization.

(4 marks)
(Total 17 marks)

11.29 You are required, within the context of budgetary control, to:

(a) explain the specific roles of planning, motivation and evaluation;

(7 marks)

(b) describe how these roles may conflict with each other;

(7 marks)

(c) give *three* examples of ways by which the management accountant may resolve the conflict described in (b).

(6 marks)

11.30 (a) Explain the ways in which the attitudes and behaviour of managers in a company are liable to pose more threat to the success of its budgetary control system than are minor technical inadequacies that may be in the system.

(15 marks)

  (b) Explain briefly what the management accountant can do to minimize the disruptive effects of such attitudes and behaviour.

(5 marks)

11.31 What are the behavioural aspects which should be borne in mind by those who are designing and operating standard costing and budgetary control systems?

(20 marks)

11.32 In his study of 'The Impact of Budgets on People', published in 1953, C. Argyris reported *inter alia* the following comment by a financial controller on the practice of participation in the setting of budgets in his company:

'We bring in the supervisors of budget areas, we tell them that we want their frank opinion, but most of them just sit there and nod their heads. We know they're not coming out with exactly how they feel. I guess budgets scare them.'

You are required to suggest reasons why managers may be reluctant to participate fully in setting budgets, and to suggest also unwanted side-effects which may arise from the imposition of budgets by senior management.

(13 marks)

11.33 The typical budgetary control system in practice does not encourage *goal congruence*, contains *budgetary slack*, ignores the *aspiration levels* of participants and attempts to control operations by *feedback*, when *feed-forward* is likely to be more effective; in summary the typical budgetary control system is likely to have dysfunctional effects.

You are required to

  (a) explain briefly *each* of the terms in italics;

(6 marks)

  (b) describe how the major dysfunctional effects of budgeting could be avoided.

(11 marks)

(Total 17 marks)

Standard costing and variance analysis

12 In the previous chapter the major features of management accounting control systems were examined. The different types of controls used by companies were described so that the elements of management accounting control systems could be considered within the context of the overall control process. A broad approach to control was adopted and the detailed procedures of financial controls were not examined. In this chapter we shall focus on the detailed financial controls that are used by organizations.

We shall consider a financial control system that enables the deviations from budget to be analysed in detail, thus enabling costs to be controlled more effectively. This system of control is called standard costing. In particular, we shall examine how a standard costing system operates and how the variances are calculated. Standard costing systems are applied in standard cost centres which were described in the previous chapter. You will recall that the main features of standard cost centres are that output can be measured and the input required to produce each unit of output can be specified. Therefore standard costing is generally applied to manufacturing activities and non-manufacturing activities are not incorporated within a standard costing system. In addition, the sales variances that

LEARNING OBJECTIVES

After studying this chapter, you should be able to:

- explain how a standard costing system operates;
- explain how standard costs are set;
- explain the meaning of standard hours produced;
- define basic, ideal and currently attainable standards;
- identify and describe the purposes of a standard costing system;
- calculate labour, material, overhead and sales margin variances and reconcile actual profit with budgeted profit;
- identify the causes of labour, material, overhead and sales margin variances;
- construct a departmental performance report.

are described in this chapter can also be applied in revenue centres. In the next chapter we shall look at financial controls that are appropriate for measuring profit and investment centre performance.

Standard costs are predetermined costs; they are target costs that should be incurred under efficient operating conditions. They are not the same as budgeted costs. A budget relates to an entire activity or operation; a standard presents the same information on a per unit basis. A standard therefore provides cost expectations per unit of activity and a budget provides the cost expectation for the total activity. If the budget output for a product is for 10 000 units and the standard cost is £3 per unit, budgeted cost will be £30 000. We shall see that establishing standard costs for each unit produced enables a detailed analysis to be made of the difference between the budgeted cost and the actual cost so that costs can be controlled more effectively.

Operation of a standard costing system

Standard costing is most suited to an organization whose activities consist of a series of *common* or *repetitive* operations and the input required to produce each unit of output can be specified. It is therefore relevant in manufacturing companies, since the processes involved are often of a repetitive nature. Standard costing procedures can also be applied in service industries such as units within banks, where output can be measured in terms of the number of cheques or the number of loan applications processed, and there are also well-defined input–output relationships. Standard costing cannot, however, be applied to activities of a non-repetitive nature, since there is no basis for observing repetitive operations and consequently standards cannot be set.

A standard costing system can be applied to organizations that produce many different products, as long as production consists of a series of common operations. For example, if the output from a factory is the result of five common operations, it is possible to produce many different product variations from these operations. It is therefore possible that a large product range may result from a small number of common operations. Thus standard costs should be developed for repetitive operations and product standard costs are derived simply by combining the standard costs from the operations which are necessary to make the product. This process is illustrated in Exhibit 12.1.

It is assumed that the standard costs are £20, £30, £40 and £50 for each of the operations 1 to 4. The standard cost for *product* 100 is therefore £110, which consists of £20 for operation 1, plus £40 and £50 for operations 3 and 4. The standard costs for each of the other products are calculated in a similar manner. In addition, the total standard cost for the total output of each operation for the period has been calculated. For example, six items of operation number 1 have been completed, giving a total standard cost of £120 for this operation (six items at £20 each). Three items of operation 2 have been completed, giving a total standard cost of £90, and so on.

Variances allocated to responsibility centres

You can see from Exhibit 12.1 that different responsibility centres are responsible for each operation. For example, responsibility centre A is responsible for operation 1, responsibility centre B for operation 2, and so on. Consequently, there is no point in comparing the actual cost of *product* 100 with the standard cost of £110 for the purposes of control, since responsibility centres A, C and D are responsible for the variance. None of the responsibility centres is solely answerable for the variance. Cost control requires that responsibility centres be identified with the standard cost for the output achieved. Therefore if the actual costs for responsibility centre A are compared with the standard cost of £120 for the production of the six items (see first row of Exhibit 12.1), the manager of this responsibility centre will be answerable for the full amount of the variance. Only by comparing total actual costs with total standard costs *for each operation or responsibility centre* for a period can control be achieved effectively. A comparison of standard *product* costs (i.e. the columns in Exhibit 12.1) with actual costs that involves several different responsibility centres is clearly inappropriate.

Figure 12.1 provides an overview of the operation of a standard costing system. You will see that the standard costs for the actual output for a particular period are traced to the managers of responsibility centres who are responsible for the various operations. The actual costs for the same period are also charged to the responsibility centres. Standard and actual costs are compared and the variance is reported. For example, if the actual cost for the output of the six items produced in responsibility centre A during the period is £220 and the standard cost is £120 (Exhibit 12.1), a variance of £100 will be reported.

Detailed analysis of variances

Figure 12.1 provides an overview of a standard costing system. You can see from the box below the first arrow in Figure 12.1 that the operation of a standard costing system also enables a detailed analysis of the variances to be reported. For example, variances for each responsibility centre can be identified by each element of cost and analysed according to the price and quantity content. The accountant assists managers by pinpointing where the variances have arisen and the responsibility managers can undertake to carry out the appropriate investigations to identify the reasons for the variance. For example, the accountant might identify the reason for a direct materials variance as being excessive usage of a certain material in a particular process, but the responsibility centre manager must investigate this process and identify the reasons for the excessive usage. Such an investigation should result in appropriate remedial action being taken or, if it is found that the variance is due to a permanent change in the standard, the standard should be changed.

Actual product costs are not required

It is questionable whether the allocation of actual costs to products serves any useful purpose. Because standard costs represent *future* target costs, they are preferable to actual *past* costs for decision-making. Also, the external financial accounting regulations in most countries specify that if standard product costs provide a reasonable approximation of actual product costs, they are acceptable for inventory valuation calculations for external reporting.

There are therefore strong arguments for not producing actual *product* costs when a standard costing system exists, since this will lead to large clerical savings. However, it must be stressed that actual costs must be accumulated periodically for each operation or responsibility centre, so that comparisons can be made with standard costs. Nevertheless, there will be considerably fewer responsibility centres than products, and the accumulation of actual costs is therefore much less time-consuming.

Comparisons after the event

It may be argued that there is little point in comparing actual performance with standard performance, because such comparisons can only be made after the event. Nevertheless, if people know in advance that their performance is going to be judged, they are likely to act

EXHIBIT 12.1

*Standard costs
analysed by
operations and
products*

Responsibility centre	Operation no. and standard cost		Products							Total standard cost	Actual cost
	No.	(£)	100	101	102	103	104	105	106	(£)	
A	1	20	✓	✓		✓	✓	✓	✓	120	
B	2	30		✓		✓		✓		90	
C	3	40	✓		✓		✓			120	
D	4	50	✓	✓	✓				✓	200	
Standard product cost			£110	£100	£90	£50	£60	£50	£70	530	

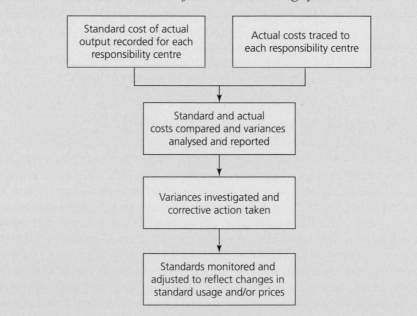

FIGURE 12.1   *An overview of a standard costing system*

differently from the way they would have done if they were aware that their performance
was not going to be measured. Furthermore, even though it is not possible for a manager to
change his or her performance after the event, an analysis of how well a person has
performed in the past may indicate – both to the person concerned and his or her superior –
ways of obtaining better performance in the future.

Establishing cost standards

Control over costs is best effected through action at the point where the costs are incurred. Hence the standards should be set for the quantities of material, labour and services to be consumed in performing an *operation*, rather than the complete *product* cost standards. Variances from these standards should be reported to show causes and responsibilities for deviations from standard. Product cost standards are derived by listing and adding the standard costs of operations required to produce a particular product. For example, if you refer to Exhibit 12.1 you will see that the standard cost of product 100 is £110 and is derived from the sum of the standard costs of operations 1, 3 and 4.

There are two approaches that can be used to set standard costs. First, past historical records can be used to estimate labour and material usage. Secondly, standards can be set based on **engineering studies**. With engineering studies a detailed study of each operation is undertaken based on careful specifications of materials, labour and equipment and on controlled observations of operations. If historical records are used to set standards, there is a danger that the latter will include past inefficiencies. With this approach, standards are set based on average past performance for the same or similar operations. Known excess usage of labour or materials should be eliminated or the standards may be tightened by an arbitrary percentage reduction in the quantity of resources required. The disadvantage of this method is that, unlike the engineering method, it does not focus attention on finding the best combination of resources, production methods and product quality. Nevertheless, standards derived from average historical usage do appear to be widely used in practice. (See Exhibit 12.3.)

Let us now consider how standards are established for each operation for direct labour, direct materials and overheads using the engineering studies approach. Note that the standard cost for each operation is derived from multiplying the quantity of input that should be used per unit of output (i.e. the quantity standard) by the amount that should be paid for each unit of input (i.e. the price standard).

Direct material standards

These are based on product specifications derived from an intensive study of the input *quantity* necessary for each operation. This study should establish the most suitable materials for each product, based on product design and quality policy, and also the optimal quantity that should be used after taking into account any wastage or loss that is considered inevitable in the production process. Material quantity standards are usually recorded on a **bill of materials**. This describes and states the required quantity of materials for each operation to complete the product. A separate bill of materials is maintained for each product. The standard material product cost is then found by multiplying the standard quantities by the appropriate standard prices.

The standard *prices* are obtained from the purchasing department. The standard material prices are based on the assumption that the purchasing department has carried out a suitable search of alternative suppliers and has selected suppliers who can provide the required quantity of sound quality materials at the most competitive price. Normally, price standards take into account the advantages to be obtained by determining the most economical order quantity and quantity discounts, best method of delivery and the most favourable credit terms. However, consideration should also be given to vendor reliability with respect to material quality and meeting scheduled delivery dates. Standard prices then provide a suitable base against which actual prices paid for materials can be evaluated.

Direct labour standards

To set labour standards, activities should be analysed by the different operations. Each operation is studied and an allowed time computed, usually after carrying out a time and motion study. The normal procedure for such a study is to analyse each operation to eliminate any unnecessary elements and to determine the most efficient production method. The most efficient methods of production, equipment and operating conditions are then standardized. This is followed by time measurements that are made to determine the number of standard hours required by an average worker to complete the job. Unavoidable delays such as machine breakdowns and routine maintenance are included in the standard time. Wage rate standards are normally either a matter of company policy or the result of negotiations between management and unions. The agreed wage rates are applied to the standard time allowed to determine the standard labour cost for each operation.

Overhead standards

The procedure for establishing standard manufacturing overhead rates for a standard costing system is the same as that which is used for establishing predetermined overhead rates as described in Chapter 5. Separate rates for fixed and variable overheads are essential for planning and control. Normally the standard overhead rate will be based on a rate per direct labour hour or machine hour of input.

Fixed overheads are largely independent of changes in activity, and remain constant over wide ranges of activity in the short term. It is therefore inappropriate for short-term cost control purposes to unitize fixed overheads to derive a fixed overhead rate per unit of activity. However, in order to meet the external financial reporting stock valuation requirements, fixed manufacturing overheads must be traced to products. It is therefore necessary to unitize fixed overheads for stock valuation purposes.

The main difference with the treatment of overheads under a standard costing system as opposed to a non-standard costing system is that the product overhead cost is based on the hourly overhead rates multiplied by the *standard hours* (that is, hours which should have been used) rather than the *actual hours* used.

At this stage it is appropriate if we summarize the approach that should be used to establish cost standards. Control over costs is best effected through action at the point where they are incurred. Hence standards should be set for labour, materials and variable overheads consumed in performing an *operation*. For stock valuation purposes it is necessary to establish *product cost* standards. Standard manufacturing product costs consist of the total of the standard costs of operations required to produce the product plus the product's standard fixed overhead cost. Note that standard costs are not established for non-manufacturing activities. A standard cost card should be maintained for each product and operation. It reveals the quantity of each unit of input that should be used to produce one unit of output. A typical product standard cost card is illustrated in Exhibit 12.2. In most organizations standard cost cards are now stored on a computer. Standards should be continuously reviewed, and, where significant changes in production methods or input prices occur, they should be changed in order to ensure that standards reflect current targets.

Standard hours produced

It is not possible to measure *output* in terms of units produced for a department making several different products or operations. For example, if a department produces 100 units of product X, 200 units of product Y and 300 units of product Z, it is not possible to add the production of these items together, since they are not homogeneous. This problem can be

EXHIBIT 12.2

An illustration of a standard cost card

Date standard set ....   Product: Sigma

Direct materials

Operation no.	Item code	Quantity (kg)	Standard price (£)	A	B	C	D	Totals (£)
					Department			
1	5.001	5	3		£15			
2	7.003	4	4			£16		
								31

Direct labour

Operation no.	Standard hours	Standard rate (£)	A	B	C	D	
1	7	9		£63			
2	8	9			£72		
							135

Factory overhead

Department	Standard hours	Standard rate (£)					
B	7	3		£21			
C	8	4			£32		
							53
Total manufacturing cost per unit (£)							219

overcome by ascertaining the amount of time, working under efficient conditions, it should take to make each product. This time calculation is called **standard hours produced**. In other words, **standard hours** are an *output* measure that can act as a common denominator for adding together the production of unlike items.

Let us assume that the following standard times are established for the production of one unit of each product:

Product X	5 standard hours
Product Y	2 standard hours
Product Z	3 standard hours

This means that it should take five hours to produce one unit of product X under efficient production conditions. Similar comments apply to products Y and Z. The production for the department will be calculated in standard hours as follows:

Product	Standard time per unit produced (hours)	Actual output (units)	Standard hours produced
X	5	100	500
Y	2	200	400
Z	3	300	900
			1800

Remember that standard hours produced is an output measure, and flexible budget allowances should be based on this. In the illustration we should expect the *output* of 1800 standard hours to take 1800 direct labour hours of *input* if the department works at the prescribed level of efficiency. The department will be inefficient if 1800 standard hours of output are produced using, say, 2000 direct labour hours of input. The flexible budget allowance should therefore be based on 1800 standard hours produced to ensure that no extra allowance is given for the 200 excess hours of input. Otherwise, a manager will obtain a higher budget allowance through being inefficient.

Types of cost standards

The determination of standard costs raises the problem of how demanding the standards should be. Should they represent ideal or faultless performance or should they represent easily attainable performance? Standards are normally classified into three broad categories:

1 basic cost standards;
2 ideal standards;
3 currently attainable standards.

Basic cost standards

Basic cost standards represent constant standards that are left unchanged over long periods. The main advantage of basic standards is that a base is provided for a comparison with actual costs through a period of years with the same standard, and efficiency trends can be established over time. When changes occur in methods of production, price levels or other relevant factors, basic standards are not very useful, since they do not represent *current* target costs. For this reason basic cost standards are seldom used.

Ideal standards

Ideal standards represent perfect performance. Ideal standard costs are the minimum costs that are possible under the most efficient operating conditions. Ideal standards are unlikely to be used in practice because they may have an adverse impact on employee motivation. Such standards constitute goals to be aimed for rather than performance that can currently be achieved.

Currently attainable standard costs

These standards represent those costs that should be incurred under efficient operating conditions. They are standards that are difficult, but not impossible, to achieve. **Attainable standards** are easier to achieve than ideal standards because allowances are made for normal spoilage, machine breakdowns and lost time. The fact that these standards represent a target that can be achieved under efficient conditions, but which is also viewed as being neither too easy to achieve nor impossible to achieve, provides the best norm to which actual costs should be compared. Attainable standards can vary in terms of the level of difficulty. For example, if tight attainable standards are set over a given time period, there might only be a 70% probability that the standard will be attained. On the other hand, looser

Since its introduction in the early 1900s standard costing has flourished and is now one of the most widely used management accounting techniques. Three independently conducted surveys of USA practice indicate highly consistent figures in terms of adopting standard costing systems. Cress and Pettijohn (1985) and Schwarzbach (1985) report an 85% adoption rate, while Cornick et al. (1988), found that 86% of the surveyed firms used a standard costing system. A Japanese survey by Scarborough et al. (1991) reported a 65% adoption rate. Surveys of UK companies by Drury et al. (1993) and New Zealand companies by Guilding et al. (1998) report adoption rates of 76% and 73% respectively.

In relation to the methods to set labour and material standards Drury et al. reported the following usage rates:

EXHIBIT 12.3

Surveys of company practice

	Extent of use (%)				
	Never	Rarely	Sometimes	Often	Always
Standards based on design/ engineering studies	18	11	19	31	21
Observations based on trial runs	18	16	36	25	5
Work study techniques	21	18	19	21	21
Average of historic usage	22	11	23	35	9

In the USA Lauderman and Schaeberle (1983) reported that 43% of the respondents used average historic usage, 67% used engineering studies, 11% used trial runs under controlled conditions and 15% used other methods. The results add up to more than 100% because some companies used more than one method.

Drury et al. (1993) also reported that the following types of standards were employed:

Maximum efficiency standards	5%
Achievable but difficult to attain standards	44%
Average past performance standards	46%
Other	5%

attainable standards might be set with a probability of 90% attainment. Attainable standards are equivalent to highly achievable standards described in Chapter 11.

Attainable standards that are likely to be achieved are preferable for planning and budgeting. It is preferable to prepare the master budget and cash budget using these standards. Clearly, it is inappropriate to use standards that may not be achieved for planning purposes. Hence attainable standards that are likely to be achieved lead to economies, since they can be used for both *planning* and *control*. However, easily attainable standards are unlikely to provide a challenging target that will motivate higher levels of efficiency.

For an indication of the types of cost standards that companies actually use you should refer to Exhibit 12.3.

Purposes of standard costing

Standard costing systems are widely used because they provide cost information for many different purposes such as the following.

- Providing a prediction of future costs that can be used for *decision-making purposes*. Standard costs can be derived from either traditional or activity-based costing systems. Because standard costs represent *future* target costs based on the elimination of avoidable inefficiencies they are preferable to estimates based on adjusted past costs which may incorporate inefficiencies. For example, in markets where competitive prices do not exist products may be priced on a bid basis. In these situations standard costs provide more appropriate information because efficient competitors will seek to eliminate avoidable costs. It is therefore unwise to assume that inefficiencies are recoverable within the bid price.

- Providing a *challenging target* which individuals are motivated to achieve. For example research evidence suggests that the existence of a defined quantitative goal or target is likely to motivate higher levels of performance than would be achieved if no such target was set.

- Assisting in *setting budgets* and evaluating managerial performance. Standard costs are particularly valuable for budgeting because a reliable and convenient source of data is provided for converting budgeted production into physical and monetary resource requirements. Budgetary preparation time is considerably reduced if standard costs are available because the standard costs of operations and products can be readily built up into total costs of any budgeted volume and product mix.

- Acting as a *control device* by highlighting those activities which do not conform to plan and thus alerting managers to those situations that may be 'out of control' and in need of corrective action. With a standard costing system variances are analysed in great detail such as by element of cost, and price and quantity elements. Useful feedback is therefore provided in pinpointing the areas where variances have arisen.

- Simplifying the task of tracing costs to products for *profit measurement and inventory valuation* purposes. Besides preparing annual financial accounting profit statements most organizations also prepare monthly internal profit statements. If actual costs are used a considerable amount of time is required in tracking costs so that monthly costs can be allocated between cost of sales and inventories. A data processing system is required which can track monthly costs in a resource efficient manner. Standard costing systems meet this requirement. You will see from Figure 12.2 that product costs are maintained at standard cost. Inventories and cost of goods sold are recorded at standard cost and a conversion to actual cost is made by writing off all variances arising during the period as a period cost. Note that the variances from standard cost are extracted by comparing actual with standard costs at the responsibility centre level, and not at the product level, so that actual costs are not assigned to individual products.

Variance analysis

It is possible to compute variances simply by committing to memory a series of variance formulae. If you adopt this approach, however, it will not help you to understand what a variance is intended to depict and what the relevant variables represent. In our discussion of each variance we shall therefore concentrate on the fundamental meaning of the variance, so that you can logically deduce the variance formulae as we go along.

All of the variances presented in this chapter are illustrated from the information contained in Example 12.1 on page 350. Note that the level of detail presented is highly simplified. A truly realistic situation would involve many products, operations and responsibility centres but would not give any further insights into the basic concepts or procedures.

Figure 12.3 shows the breakdown of the profit variance (the difference between budgeted and actual profit) into the component cost and revenue variances that can be

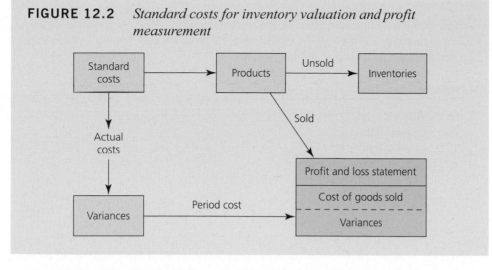

FIGURE 12.2   *Standard costs for inventory valuation and profit measurement*

calculated for a standard variable costing system. We shall now calculate the variances set out in Figure 12.3 using the data presented in Example 12.1.

Material variances

The costs of the materials which are used in a manufactured product are determined by two basic factors: the price paid for the materials, and the quantity of materials used in production. This gives rise to the possibility that the actual cost will differ from the standard cost because the *actual quantity* of materials used will be different from the *standard quantity* and/or that the *actual price* paid will be different from the *standard price*. We can therefore calculate a material usage and a material price variance.

Material price variances

The starting point for calculating this variance is simply to compare the standard price per unit of materials with the actual price per unit. You should now read Example 12.1. You will see that the standard price for material A is £10 per kg, but the actual price paid was £11 per kg. The price variance is £1 per kg. This is of little consequence if the excess purchase price has been paid only for a small number of units or purchases. But the consequences are important if the excess purchase price has been paid for a large number of units, since the effect of the variance will be greater.

The difference between the standard material price and the actual price per unit should therefore be multiplied by the quantity of materials purchased. For material A the price variance is £1 per unit; but since 19 000 kg were purchased, the excess price was paid out 19 000 times. Hence the total material price variance is £19 000 adverse. The formula for the material price variance now follows logically:

the **material price variance** is equal to the difference between the standard price (SP) and the actual price (AP) per unit of materials multiplied by the quantity of materials purchased (QP):

$$(SP - AP) \times QP$$

EXAMPLE 12.1

Alpha manufacturing company produces a single product, which is known as sigma. The product requires a single operation, and the standard cost for this operation is presented in the following standard cost card:

Standard cost card for product sigma	(£)
Direct materials:	
2 kg of A at £10 per kg	20.00
1 kg of B at £15 per kg	15.00
Direct labour (3 hours at £9 per hour)	27.00
Variable overhead (3 hours at £2 per direct labour hour)	6.00
Total standard variable cost	68.00
Standard contribution margin	20.00
Standard selling price	88.00

Alpha Ltd plan to produce 10 000 units of sigma in the month of April, and the budgeted costs based on the information contained in the standard cost card are as follows:

Budget based on the above standard costs and an output of 10 000 units	(£)	(£)	(£)
Sales (10 000 units of sigma at £88 per unit)			880 000
Direct materials:			
A: 20 000 kg at £10 per kg	200 000		
B: 10 000 kg at £15 per kg	150 000	350 000	
Direct labour (30 000 hours at £9 per hour)		270 000	
Variable overheads (30 000 hours at £2 per direct labour hour)		60 000	680 000
Budgeted contribution			200 000
Fixed overheads			120 000
Budgeted profit			80 000

Annual budgeted fixed overheads are £1 440 000 and are assumed to be incurred evenly throughout the year. The company uses a variable costing system for internal profit measurement purposes.

The actual results for April are:

	(£)	(£)
Sales (9000 units at £90)		810 000
Direct materials:		
A: 19 000 kg at £11 per kg	209 000	
B: 10 100 kg at £14 per kg	141 400	
Direct labour (28 500 hours at £9.60 per hour)	273 600	
Variable overheads	52 000	676 000
Contribution		134 000
Fixed overheads		116 000
Profit		18 000

Manufacturing overheads are charged to production on the basis of direct labour hours. Actual production and sales for the period were 9000 units.

FIGURE 12.3   *Variance analysis for a variable costing system*

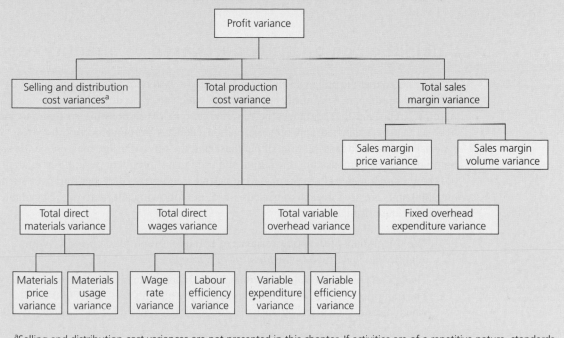

ᵃSelling and distribution cost variances are not presented in this chapter. If activities are of a repetitive nature, standards can be established and variances can be calculated in a similar manner to production cost variances. If standards cannot be established, costs should be controlled by comparing budgeted and actual costs.

Now refer to material B in Example 12.1. The standard price is £15, compared with an actual price of £14 giving a £1 saving per kg. As 10 100 kg were purchased, the total price variance will be £10 100 (10 100kg at £1). The variance for material B is favourable and that for material A is adverse. The normal procedure is to present the amount of the variances followed by symbols A or F to indicate either adverse or favourable variances.

Possible causes

It is incorrect to assume that the material price variance will always indicate the efficiency of the purchasing department. Actual prices may exceed standard prices because of a change in market conditions that causes a general price increase for the type of materials used. The price variance might therefore be beyond the control of the purchasing department. Alternatively, an adverse price variance may reflect a failure by the purchasing department to seek the most advantageous sources of supply. A favourable price variance might be due to the purchase of inferior quality materials, which may lead to inferior product quality or more wastage. For example, the price variance for material B is favourable, but we shall see in the next section that this is offset by excess usage. If the reason for this excess usage is the purchase of inferior quality materials then the material usage variance should be charged to the purchasing department.

It is also possible that another department may be responsible for all or part of the price variance. For example, a shortage of materials resulting from bad inventory control may necessitate an emergency purchase being made at short notice. The supplier may incur additional handling and freight charges on special rush orders, and may therefore charge a higher price for the materials. In this situation the price variance will be the responsibility of the stores department and not the purchasing department.

Calculation on quantity purchased or quantity used

We have noted that the price variance may be due to a variety of causes, some of which will be beyond a company's control, but others of which may be due to inefficiencies. It is therefore important that variances be reported as quickly as possible so that any inefficiencies can be identified and remedial action taken. A problem occurs, however, with material purchases in that the time of purchase and the time of usage may not be the same: materials may be purchased in one period and used in a subsequent period. For example, if 10 000 units of a material are purchased in period 1 at a price of £1 per unit over standard and 2000 units are used in each of periods 1 to 5, the following alternatives are available for calculating the price variance:

1   The full amount of the price variance of £10 000 is reported in *period 1* with quantity being defined as the *quantity purchased*.
2   The price variance is calculated with quantity being defined as the *quantity used*. The unit price variance of £1 is multiplied by the quantity used (i.e. 2000 units), which means that a price variance of £2000 will be reported for each of *periods 1 to 5.*

Method 1 is recommended, because the price variance can be reported in the period in which it is incurred, and reporting of the total variance is not delayed until months later when the materials are used. Also, adopting this approach enables corrective action to be taken earlier. For the sake of simplicity we shall assume in Example 12.1 that the actual purchases are identical with the actual usage.

Material usage variance

The starting point for calculating this quantity variance is simply to compare the standard quantity that should have been used with the actual quantity which has been used. Refer again to Example 12.1. You will see that the standard usage for the production of one unit of sigma is 2 kg for material A. As 9000 units of sigma are produced, 18 000 kg of material A should have been used; however, 19 000 kg are actually used, which means there has been an excess usage of 1000 kg.

The importance of this excess usage depends on the price of the materials. For example, if the price is £0.01 per kg then an excess usage of 1000 kg will not be very significant, but if the price is £10 per unit then an excess usage of 1000 kg will be very significant. It follows that to assess the importance of the excess usage, the variance should be expressed in monetary terms.

Calculation based on standard price or actual price

Should the standard material price per kg or the actual material price per kg be used to calculate the variance? The answer is the standard price. If the *actual* material price is used, the usage variance will be affected by the efficiency of the purchasing department, since any excess purchase price will be assigned to the excess usage. It is therefore necessary to remove the price effects from the usage variance calculation, and this is achieved by valuing the variance at the standard price. Hence the 1000 kg excess usage of material A is multiplied by the standard price of £10 per unit, which gives an adverse usage variance of £10 000. The formula for the variance is

the **material usage variance** is equal to the difference between the standard quantity (SQ) required for actual production and the actual quantity (AQ) used multiplied by the standard material price (SP):

$$(SQ - AQ) \times SP$$

For material B you will see from Example 12.1 that the standard quantity is 9000 kg (9000 units × 1 kg), but 10 100 kg have been used. The excess usage of 1100 kg is multiplied by the standard price of £15 per kg, which gives an adverse variance of £16 500. Note that the principles of flexible budgeting described in the previous chapter also apply here, with *standard quantity being based on actual production and not budgeted production.* This ensures that a manager is evaluated under the conditions in which he or she actually worked and not those envisaged at the time the budget was prepared.

Possible causes

The material usage variance is normally controllable by the manager of the appropriate production responsibility centre. Common causes of material usage variances include the careless handling of materials by production personnel, the purchase of inferior quality materials, pilferage, changes in quality control requirements, or changes in methods of production. Separate material usage variances should be calculated for each type of material used and allocated to each responsibility centre.

Total material variance

From Figure 12.3 you will see that this variance is the total variance before it is analysed into the price and usage elements. The formula for the variance is

the **total material variance** is the difference between the standard material cost (SC) for the actual production and the actual cost (AC):

$$SC - AC$$

For material A the standard material cost is £20 per unit (see Example 12.1), giving a total standard material cost of £180 000 (9000 units × £20). The actual cost is £209 000, and therefore the variance is £29 000 adverse. The price variance of £19 000 plus the usage variance of £10 000 agrees with the total material variance. Similarly, the total material variance for material B is £6400, consisting of a favourable price variance of £10 100 and an adverse usage variance of £16 500.

Note that if the price variance is calculated on the actual quantity *purchased* instead of the actual quantity *used*, the price variance plus the usage variance will agree with the total variance only when the quantity purchased is equal to the quantity which is used in the particular accounting period. Reconciling the price and usage variance with the total variance is merely a reconciliation exercise, and you should not be concerned if reconciliation of the sub-variances with the total variance is not possible.

Labour variances

The cost of labour is determined by the price paid for labour and the quantity of labour used. Thus a price and quantity variance will also arise for labour. Unlike materials, labour cannot be stored, because the purchase and usage of labour normally takes place at the same time. Hence the actual quantity of hours *purchased* will be equal to the actual quantity of hours *used* for each period. For this reason the price variance plus the quantity variance should agree with the total labour variance.

Wage rate variance

This variance is calculated by comparing the standard price per hour with the actual price paid per hour. In Example 12.1 the standard wage rate per hour is £9 and the actual wage rate is £9.60 per hour, giving a wage rate variance of £0.60 per hour. To determine the importance of the variance, it is necessary to ascertain how many times the excess payment of £0.60 per hour is paid. As 28 500 labour hours are used (see Example 12.1), we multiply 28 500 hours by £0.60. This gives an adverse wage rate variance of £17 100. The formula for the wage rate variance is

the **wage rate variance** is equal to the difference between the standard wage rate per hour (SR) and the actual wage rate (AR) multiplied by the actual number of hours worked (AH):

$$(SR - AR) \times AH$$

Note the similarity between this variance and the material price variance. Both variances multiply the difference between the standard price and the actual price paid for a unit of a resource by the actual quantity of resources used.

Possible causes

The wage rate variance may be due to a negotiated increase in wage rates not yet having been reflected in the standard wage rate. In a situation such as this the variance cannot be regarded as controllable. Unexpected overtime can also be a cause of this variance. Labour rate variances may also occur because a standard is used that represents a single average rate for a given operation performed by workers who are paid at several different rates. In this situation part of all of the variance may be due to the assignment of skilled labour to work that is normally performed by unskilled labour. The variance may then be regarded as the responsibility of the foreman, because he should have matched the appropriate grade of labour to the task at hand. However, the wage rate variance is probably the one that is least subject to control by management. In most cases the variance is due to wage rate standards not being kept in line with changes in actual wage rates, and for this reason it is not normally controllable by departmental managers.

Labour efficiency variance

The labour efficiency variance represents the quantity variance for direct labour. The quantity of labour that should be used for the actual output is expressed in terms of *standard hours produced*. In Example 12.1 the standard time for the production of one unit of sigma is 3 hours. Thus a production level of 9000 units results in an output of 27 000 standard hours. In other words, working at the prescribed level of efficiency, it should take 27 000 hours to produce 9000 units. However, 28 500 direct labour hours are actually required to produce this output, which means that 1500 excess direct labour hours are used. We multiply the excess direct labour hours by the *standard* wage rate to calculate the variance. This gives an adverse variance of £13 500. The formula for calculating the labour efficiency variance is

the **labour efficiency variance** is equal to the difference between the standard labour hours for actual production (SH) and the actual labour hours worked (AH) during the period multiplied by the standard wage rate per hour (SR):

$$(SH - AH) \times SR$$

This variance is similar to the material usage variance. Both variances multiply the difference between the standard quantity and actual quantity of resources consumed by the standard price.

Possible causes

The labour efficiency variance is normally controllable by the manager of the appropriate production responsibility centre and may be due to a variety of reasons. For example, the use of inferior quality materials, different grades of labour, failure to maintain machinery in proper condition, the introduction of new equipment or tools and changes in the production processes will all affect the efficiency of labour. An efficiency variance may not always be controllable by the production foreman; it may be due, for example, to poor production scheduling by the planning department, or to a change in quality control standards.

Total labour variance

From Figure 12.3 you will see that this variance represents the total variance before analysis into the price and quantity elements. The formula for the variance is

the **total labour variance** is the difference between the standard labour cost (SC) for the actual production and the actual labour cost (AC):

$$SC - AC$$

In Example 12.1 the actual production was 9000 units, and, with a standard labour cost of £27 per unit, the standard cost is £243 000. The actual cost is £273 600, which gives an adverse variance of £30 600. This consists of a wage rate variance of £17 100 and a labour efficiency variance of £13 500.

Variable overhead variances

A total variable overhead variance is calculated in the same way as the total direct labour and material variances. In Example 12.1 the output is 9000 units and the standard variable overhead cost is £6 *per unit* produced. The standard cost of production for variable overheads is thus £54 000. The actual variable overheads incurred are £52 000, giving a favourable variance of £2000. The formula for the variance is

Standard costing at Montclair Papers Division of Mohawk Forest Products

Montclair produces 1500 different products, including Forest Green Carnival. Its standard cost of $2900 per ton is derived from:

- Union wage rates for labour costs ('Pattern bargaining' virtually assured comparable labour costs among the major union firms, all of which were unionized).
- Standard yield rates for all manufacturing steps, based on latest performance measured against long-standing norms at the Montclair mill.
- Current market prices for all purchased components.
- Generally accepted industry procedures for building the 'normal' cost of scrap into the standard cost, after deducting the offset for the market value of the scrap generated.

The standards were updated annually for changes in purchase prices, process flows and yield targets. With more than 1500 products manufactured in the mill, more frequent updating was deemed unfeasible.

Manufacturing management accepted that the standard cost represented best practices of the mill and thus was an appropriate basis for monitoring monthly performance. Standard costs were also helpful to simplify calculating the month-end cost of goods sold and the ending inventory for financial statements. Updated only once a year, the standard cost was stable from month to month. Management viewed this stability as a positive feature in monitoring monthly performance against the annual plan.

Source: Shank, J.K. and Fisher, J. (1999) Target costing as a strategic tool, *Sloan Management Review*, Fall, **41**(1), pp. 73–82.

the **total variable overhead variance** is the difference between the standard variable overheads charged to production (SC) and the actual variable overheads incurred (AC):

$$SC - AC$$

Where variable overheads vary with direct labour or machine hours of *input* the total variable overhead variance will be due to one or both of the following:

1 A *price* variance arising from actual expenditure being different from budgeted expenditure.
2 A *quantity* variance arising from actual direct labour or machine hours of input being different from the hours of input, which *should* have been used.

These reasons give rise to the two sub-variances, which are shown in Figure 12.3: the variable overhead expenditure variance and the variable overhead efficiency variance.

Variable overhead expenditure variance

To compare the actual overhead expenditure with the budgeted expenditure, it is necessary to flex the budget. Because it is assumed in Example 12.1 that variable overheads will vary with direct labour hours of *input* the budget is flexed on this basis. Actual variable overhead expenditure is £52 000, resulting from 28 500 direct labour hours of input. For this level of activity variable overheads of £57 000, which consist of 28 500 input hours at £2 per hour, should have been spent. Spending was £5000 less than it should have been, and the result is a favourable variance.

If we compare the budgeted and the actual overhead costs for 28 500 direct labour hours of input, we shall ensure that any efficiency content is removed from the variance. This means that any difference must be due to actual variable overhead spending being different from the budgeted variable overhead spending. The formula for the variance is

the **variable overhead expenditure variance** is equal to the difference between the budgeted flexed variable overheads (BFVO) for the actual direct labour hours of input and the actual variable overhead costs incurred (AVO):

$$BFVO - AVO$$

Possible causes

Variable overhead represents the aggregation of a large number of individual items, such as indirect labour, indirect materials, electricity, maintenance and so on. The variable overhead variance can arise because the prices of individual items have changed. Alternatively, the variance can also be affected by how efficiently the individual variable overhead items are used. Waste or inefficiency, such as using more kilowatt-hours of power than should have been used will increase the cost of power and, thus, the total cost of variable overhead. The variable overhead expenditure on its own is therefore not very informative. Any meaningful analysis of this variance requires a comparison of the actual expenditure for each individual item of variable overhead expenditure against the budget. If you refer to the performance report presented in Exhibit 12.5 on page 362, you can see how the £5000 variable overhead expenditure variance can be analysed by individual items of expenditure. Control should be exercised by focusing on the individual line items of the expenditure variances and not the total variance.

Variable overhead efficiency variance

In Example 12.1 it is assumed that variable overheads vary with direct labour hours of input. The variable overhead efficiency variance arises because 28 500 direct labour hours of input were required to produce 9000 units. Working at the prescribed level of efficiency, it should take 27 000 hours to produce 9000 units of output. Therefore an extra 1500 direct labour hours of input were required. Because variable overheads are assumed to vary with direct labour hours of input, an additional £3000 (1500 hours at £2) variable overheads will be incurred. The formula for the variance is

the **variable overhead efficiency variance** is the difference between the standard hours of output (SH) and the actual hours of input (AH) for the period multiplied by the standard variable overhead rate (SR):

$$(SH - AH) \times SR$$

You should note that if it is assumed that variable overheads vary with direct labour hours of input, this variance is identical to the labour efficiency variance. Consequently, the reasons for the variance are the same as those described previously for the labour efficiency variance. If you refer again to Figure 12.3, you will see that the variable overhead expenditure variance (£5000 favourable) plus the variable efficiency variance (£3000 adverse) add up to the total variable overhead variance of £2000 favourable.

Similarities between materials, labour and overhead variances

So far, we have calculated price and quantity variances for direct material, direct labour and variable overheads. You will have noted the similarities between the computations of the three quantity and price variances. For example, we calculated the quantity variances (i.e. material usage, labour efficiency and variable overhead efficiency variances) by multiplying the difference between the standard quantity (SQ) of resources consumed for the actual production and the actual quantity (AQ) of resources consumed by the standard price (SP) per unit of the resource. Thus, the three quantity variances can be formulated as

$$(SQ - AQ) \times SP$$

Note that the standard quantity is derived from determining the quantity that should be used *for the actual production* for the period so that the principles of flexible budgeting are applied.

The price variances (i.e. material price, wage rate and variable overhead expenditure variances) were calculated by multiplying the difference between the standard price (SP) and the actual price (AP) per unit of a resource by the actual quantity (AQ) of resources acquired/used. The price variances can be formulated as

$$(SP - AP) \times AQ$$

This can be re-expressed as

$$(AQ \times SP) - (AQ \times AP)$$

Note that the first term in this formula (with AQ representing actual hours) is equivalent to the budgeted flexed variable overheads that we used to calculate the variable overhead expenditure variance. The last term represents the actual cost of the resources consumed.

We can therefore calculate all the price and quantity variances illustrated so far in this chapter by applying the formulae outlined above.

Fixed overhead expenditure or spending variance

The final variance shown in Figure 12.3 is the fixed overhead expenditure variance. With a variable costing system, fixed manufacturing overheads are not unitized and allocated to products. Instead, the total fixed overheads for the period are charged as an expense to the period in which they are incurred. Fixed overheads are assumed to remain unchanged in the short term in response to changes in the level of activity, but they may change in response to other factors. For example, price increases may cause expenditure on fixed overheads to increase. The fixed overhead expenditure variance therefore explains the difference between budgeted fixed overheads and the actual fixed overheads incurred. The formula for the **fixed overhead expenditure variance** is the difference between the budgeted fixed overheads (BFO) and the actual fixed overhead (AFO) spending:

$$BFO - AFO$$

In Example 12.1 budgeted fixed overhead expenditure is £120 000 and actual fixed overhead spending £116 000. Therefore the fixed overhead expenditure variance is £4000. Whenever the actual fixed overheads are less than the budgeted fixed overheads, the variance will be favourable. The total of the fixed overhead expenditure variance on its own is not particularly informative. Any meaningful analysis of this variance requires a comparison of the actual expenditure for each individual item of fixed overhead expenditure against the budget. The difference may be due to a variety of causes, such as changes in salaries paid to supervisors, or the appointment of additional supervisors. Only by comparing individual items of expenditure and ascertaining the reasons for the variances, can one determine whether the variance is controllable or uncontrollable. Generally, this variance is likely to be uncontrollable in the short term.

Sales variances

Sales variances can be used to analyse the performance of the sales function or revenue centres on broadly similar terms to those for manufacturing costs. The most significant feature of sales variance calculations is that they are calculated in terms of profit or contribution margins rather than sales values. Consider Example 12.2.

You will see that when the variances are calculated on the basis of sales *value*, it is necessary to compare the budgeted sales *value* of £110 000 with the actual sales of £120 000. This gives a favourable variance of £10 000. This calculation, however, ignores the impact of the sales effort on profit. The budgeted profit contribution is £40 000, which consists of 10 000 units at £4 per unit, but the actual impact of the sales effort in terms of profit margins indicates a profit contribution of £36 000, which consists of 12 000 units at £3 per unit, indicating an adverse variance of £4000. If we examine Example 12.2, we can see that the selling prices have been reduced, and that this has led not only to an increase in the total sales revenue but also to a reduction in total profits. The objective of the selling function is to influence total profits favourably. Thus a more meaningful performance measure will be obtained by comparing the results of the sales function in terms of profit or contribution margins rather than sales revenues.

Let us now calculate the sales variances for a standard variable costing system from the information contained in Example 12.1.

Total sales margin variance

Where a variable costing approach is adopted, the total sales *margin* variance seeks to identify the influence of the sales function on the difference between budget and actual profit contribution. In Example 12.1 the budgeted profit contribution is £200 000, which consists of budgeted sales of 10 000 units at a contribution of £20 per unit. This is compared with the contribution from the actual sales volume of 9000 units. Because the sales function

> **EXAMPLE 12.2**
>
> The budgeted sales for a company are £110 000 consisting of 10 000 units at £11 per unit. The standard cost per unit is £7. Actual sales are £120 000 (12 000 units at £10 per unit) and the actual cost per unit is £7.

is responsible for the sales volume and the unit selling price, but not the unit manufacturing costs, the standard cost of sales and not the actual cost of sales is deducted from the actual sales revenue. The calculation of *actual* contribution for ascertaining the total sales margin variance will therefore be as follows:

	(£)
Actual sales revenue (9000 units at £90)	810 000
Standard variable cost of sales for actual sales volume (9000 units at £68)	612 000
Actual profit contribution margin	198 000

To calculate the total sales margin variance, we compare the budgeted contribution of £200 000 with the actual contribution of £198 000. This gives an adverse variance of £2000 because the actual contribution is less that the budgeted profit contribution.

The formula for calculating the variance is as follows:

the **total sales margin variance** is the difference between the actual contribution (AC) and the budgeted contribution (BC) (both based on standard unit costs):

$$AC - BC$$

Using the standard cost to calculate both the budgeted and the actual contribution ensures that the production variances do not distort the calculation of the sales variances. The effect of using standard costs throughout the contribution margin calculations means that the sales variances arise because of changes in those variables controlled by the sales function (i.e. selling prices and sales quantity). Consequently, Figure 12.3 indicates that it is possible to analyse the total sales margin variance into two sub-variances – a sales margin price variance and a sales margin volume variance.

Sales margin price variance

In Example 12.1 the actual selling price is £90 but the budgeted selling price is £88. With a standard unit variable cost of £68, the change in selling price has led to an increase in the contribution margin from £20 per unit to £22 per unit. Because the actual sales volume is 9000 units, the increase in the selling price means that an increased contribution margin is obtained 9000 times, giving a favourable sales margin price variance of £18 000. The formula for calculating the variance is

the **sales margin price variance** is the difference between the actual contribution margin (AM) and the standard margin (SM) (both based on standard unit costs) multiplied by the actual sales volume (AV):

$$(AM - SM) \times AV$$

Sales margin volume variance

To ascertain the effect of changes in the sales volume on the difference between the budgeted and the actual contribution, we must compare the budgeted sales volume with the actual sales volume. You will see from Example 12.1 that the budgeted sales are 10 000 units but the actual sales are 9000 units, and to enable us to determine the impact of this reduction in sales volume on profit, we must multiply the 1000 units by the standard contribution margin of £20. This gives an adverse variance of £20 000.

The use of the standard margin (standard selling price less standard cost) ensures that the standard selling price is used in the calculation, and the volume variance will not be affected by any *changes* in the actual selling prices. The formula for calculating the variance is

the sales margin volume variance is the difference between the actual sales volume (AV) and the budgeted volume (BV) multiplied by the standard contribution margin (SM):

$$(AV - BV) \times SM$$

Difficulties in interpreting sales margin variances

The favourable sales margin price variance of £18 000 plus the adverse volume variance of £20 000 add up to the total adverse sales margin variance of £2000. It may be argued that it is not very meaningful to analyse the total sales margin variance into price and volume components, since changes in selling prices are likely to affect sales volume. Consequently, a favourable price variance will tend to be associated with an adverse volume variance, and vice versa. It may be unrealistic to sell more than the budgeted volume when selling prices have increased.

A further problem with sales variances is that the variances may arise from external factors and may not be controllable by management. For example, changes in selling prices may be the result of a response to changes in selling prices of competitors. Alternatively, a reduction in both selling prices and sales volume may be the result of an economic recession that was not foreseen when the budget was prepared. Manufacturing variances are not influenced as much by external factors, and for this reason management are likely to focus most of their attention on the control of the manufacturing variances. Nevertheless, sales margin variances provide useful information that enables the budgeted profit to be reconciled with the actual profit. However, for control and performance appraisal it is preferable to compare actual market share with target market share for each product. In addition, the trend in market shares should be monitored and selling prices should be compared with competitors' prices.

Reconciling budgeted profit and actual profit

Top management will be interested in the reason for the actual profit being different from the budgeted profit. By adding the favourable production and sales variances to the budgeted profit and deducting the adverse variances, the reconciliation of budgeted and actual profit shown in Exhibit 12.4 can be presented in respect of Example 12.1.

Example 12.1 assumes that Alpha Ltd produces a single product consisting of a single operation and that the activities are performed by one responsibility centre. In practice, most companies make many products, which require operations to be carried out in different responsibility centres. A reconciliation statement such as that presented in Exhibit 12.4 will therefore normally represent a summary of the variances for many responsibility

EXHIBIT 12.4

Reconciliation of budgeted and actual profits for a standard variable costing system

	(£)	(£)	(£)
Budgeted net profit			80 000
Sales variances:			
Sales margin price	18 000F		
Sales margin volume	20 000A	2 000A	
Direct cost variances:			
Material: Price	8 900A		
Usage	26 500A	35 400A	
Labour: Rate	17 100A		
Efficiency	13 500A	30 600A	
Manufacturing overhead variances:			
Fixed overhead expenditure	4 000F		
Variable overhead expenditure	5 000F		
Variable overhead efficiency	3 000A	6 000F	62 000A
Actual profit			18 000

centres. The reconciliation statement thus represents a broad picture to top management that explains the major reasons for any difference between the budgeted and actual profits.

EXHIBIT 12.5

A typical departmental performance report

DEPARTMENTAL PERFORMANCE REPORT

Department........................
Period............ April 20XX...........

Actual production   27 000 standard hours
Actual working hours   28 500 hours
Budgeted hours   30 000 hours

DIRECT MATERIALS

Type	Standard quantity	Actual quantity	Difference	Standard price	Usage variance	Reason
A	18 000 kg	19 000	1000	£10.00	£10 000A	
B	9 000 kg	10 100	1100	£15.00	£16 500A	

DIRECT LABOUR

Grade	Standard hours	Actual hours	Difference	Standard cost	Actual cost	Total variance	Analysis Efficiency	Rate	Reason
	27 000	28 500	1500	£243 000	£273 600	£30 600	£13 500A	£17 100A	

OVERHEADS

	Allowed cost	Actual cost	Expenditure variance	Reason	Variable overhead efficiency variance	
					(hours)	(£)
Controllable costs (variable):						
Indirect labour				Difference		
Power				between	1500	3000A
Maintenance				standard		
Indirect materials				hours and		
				actual		
				hours at		
				£2 per hour		
Total	£57 000	£52 000	£5000F		1500	3000A
Uncontrollable costs (fixed):						
Lighting and heating						
Depreciation						
Supervision						
	£120 000	116 000	4000F			

SUMMARY

	Variances (£)		Variances as a % of a standard cost	
	This month (£)	Cumulative (£)	This month (%)	Cumulative (%)
Direct materials usage	26 500A			
Direct labour:				
Efficiency	13 500A			
Wage rate	17 100A			
Controllable overheads:				
Expenditure	5 000F			
Variable overhead	3 000A			
Total	55 100A			

Comments:

Performance reports

The managers of responsibility centres will require a more detailed analysis of the variances to enable them to exercise control, and detailed performance reports should be prepared at monthly or weekly intervals to bring to their attention any significant variances. A typical performance report based on the information contained in Example 12.1 is presented in Exhibit 12.5. A departmental performance report should include only those items that the responsibility manager can control or influence. The material price variance is *not* presented, since it is not considered to be within the control of the manager of the responsibility centre. A comparison of current variances with those of previous periods and/or with those of the year to date is presented in the summary of the performance report. This information is often useful in establishing a framework within which current variances can be evaluated. In addition to weekly or monthly performance reports, the manager of a responsibility centre should receive daily reports on those variances that are controllable on a daily basis. This normally applies to material usage and labour efficiency. For these variances the weekly or monthly performance reports will provide a summary of the information that has previously been reported on a daily basis.

Summary

The following items relate to the learning objectives listed at the beginning of the chapter.

- **Explain how a standard costing system operates.**

  Standard costing is most suited to an organization whose activities consist of a series of repetitive operations and the input required to produce each unit of output can be specified. A standard costing system involves the following: (a) the standard costs for the actual output are recorded for each operation for each responsibility centre; (b) actual costs for each operation are traced to each responsibility centre; (c) the standard and actual costs are compared; (d) variances are investigated and corrective action is taken where appropriate; and (e) standards are monitored and adjusted to reflect changes in standard usage and/or prices.

- **Explain how standard costs are set.**

  Standards should be set for the quantities and prices of materials, labour and services to be consumed in performing each operation associated with a product. Product standard costs are derived by listing and adding the standard costs of operations required to produce a particular product. Two approaches are used for setting standard costs. First, past historical records can be used to estimate labour and material usage. Secondly, standards can be set based on engineering studies. With engineering studies a detailed study of each operation is undertaken under controlled conditions, based on high levels of efficiency, to ascertain the quantities of labour and materials required. Target prices are then applied based on efficient purchasing to ascertain the standard costs.

- **Explain the meaning of standard hours produced.**

  It is not possible to measure output in terms of units produced for a department making several different products or operations. This problem is overcome by ascertaining the amount of time, working under efficient operating conditions, it should take to make each product. This time calculation is called standard hours produced. Standard hours thus represents an output measure that acts as a common denominator for adding together the production of unlike items.

- **Define basic, ideal and currently attainable standards.**

  Basic cost standards represent constant standards that are left unchanged over long periods. Ideal standards represent perfect performance. They represent the minimum costs that are possible under the most efficient operating conditions. Currently attainable standards represent those costs that should be incurred under efficient operating conditions.

They are standards that are difficult, but not impossible, to achieve. Currently attainable standards are normally recommended for standard costing.

- **Identify and describe the purposes of a standard costing system.**

  Standard costing systems can be used for the following purposes: (a) providing a prediction of future costs that can be used for decision-making; (b) providing a challenging target which individuals are motivated to achieve; (c) providing a reliable and convenient source of data for budget preparation; (d) acting as a control device by highlighting those activities that do not conform to plan and thus alerting managers to those situations that may be 'out of control' and in need of corrective action; and (e) simplifying the task of tracing costs to products for profit measurement and inventory valuation purpose. Each purpose is described in more detail in Chapter 12.

- **Calculate labour, material, overhead and sales margin variances and reconcile actual profit with budgeted profit.**

  To reconcile actual profit with budget profit the favourable variances are added to the budgeted profit and adverse variances are deducted. The end result should be the actual profit. A summary of the formulae for the computation of the variances is presented in Exhibit 12.6. In each case the formula is presented so that so that a positive variance is favourable and a negative variance unfavourable.

- **Identify the causes of labour, material, overhead and sales margin variances.**

  Quantities cost variances arise because the actual quantity of resources consumed exceed actual usage. Examples include excess usage of materials and labour arising from the usage of inferior materials, careless handling of materials and failure to maintain machinery in proper condition. Price variances arise when the actual prices paid for resources exceed the standard prices. Examples include the failure of the purchasing function to seek the most efficient sources of supply or the use of a different grade of labour to that incorporated in the standard costs.

- **Construct a departmental performance report.**

  For an illustration of a departmental performance report you should refer to Exhibit 12.5.

Key terms and concepts

attainable standards (p. 346)

basic cost standards (p. 346)

bill of materials (p. 343)

budgeted costs (p. 340)

engineering studies (p. 343)

fixed overhead expenditure variance (p. 359)

ideal standards (p. 346)

labour efficiency variance (p. 355)

material price variance (p. 349)

material usage variance (p. 353)

sales margin price variance (p. 360)

sales margin volume variance (p. 361)

standard costs (p. 340)

standard hours (p. 345)

standard hours produced (p. 345)

total labour variance (p. 355)

total material variance (p. 353)

total sales margin variance (p. 360)

total variable overhead variance (p. 356)

variable overhead efficiency variance (p. 357)

variable overhead expenditure variance (p. 357)

wage rate variance (p. 354).

EXHIBIT 12.6

Summary of the formulae for the computation of the variances

The following variances are reported for both variable and absorption costing systems:

Materials and labour

1   Material price variance = (standard price per unit of material – actual price) × quantity of materials purchased

2   Material usage variance = (standard quantity of materials for actual production – actual quantity used) × standard price per unit

3   Total materials cost variance = (actual production × standard material cost per unit of production) – actual materials cost

4   Wage rate variance = (standard wage rate per hour – actual wage rate) × actual labour hours worked

5   Labour efficiency variance = (standard quantity of labour hours for actual production – actual labour hours) × standard wage rate

6   Total labour cost variance = (actual production × standard labour cost per unit of production) – actual labour cost

Fixed production overhead

7   Fixed overhead expenditure = budgeted fixed overheads – actual fixed overheads

Variable production overhead

8   Variable overhead expenditure variance = (budgeted variable overheads for actual input volume – actual variable overhead cost)

9   Variable overhead efficiency variance = (standard quantity of input hours for actual production – actual input hours) × variable overhead rate

10 Total variable overhead variance = (actual production × standard variable overhead rate per unit) – actual variable overhead cost

Sales margins

11 Sales margin price variance = (actual unit contribution margin – standard unit contribution margin) × actual sales volume

12 Sales margin volume variance = (actual sales volume – budgeted sales volume) × standard contribution margin

13 Total sales margin variance = total actual contribution – total budgeted contribution

Assessment material

Review questions

The review questions are short questions that enable you to assess your understanding of the main topics included in the chapter. The numbers in parentheses provide you with the page numbers to refer to if you cannot answer a specific question.

Review problems

The review problems are more complex and require you to relate and apply the chapter content to various business problems. The multiple-choice questions are the least demanding and normally take less than 10 minutes to complete. Further review problems for this chapter are available on the accompanying website, www.drury-online.com. The answers to these problems are available for lecturers on the lecturer's password-protected section of the website.

Case studies

The website also includes over 30 case study problems. A list of these cases is provided on pages 491–93. Several cases are relevant to the content of this chapter. Examples include Anjo Ltd, Boston Creamery and the Berkshire Toy Company.

Review questions

12.1   Describe the difference between budgeted and standard costs. (*p. 340*)

12.2   Explain how a standard costing system operates. (*pp. 340–42*)

12.3   Describe how standard costs are established using engineering studies. (*pp. 343–44*)

12.4   What are standard hours produced? What purpose do they serve? (*pp. 344–45*)

12.5   What are basic, ideal and currently attainable standards? Which type of standards are usually adopted? Why? (*pp. 346–47*)

12.6   Describe the different purposes of a standard costing system. (*p. 347*)

12.7   What are the possible causes of (a) material price and (b) material usage variances? (*pp. 351, 353*)

12.8   Explain why it is preferable for the material price variance to be computed at the point of purchase rather than the point of issue. (*p. 352*)

12.9   What are the possible causes of (a) wage rate and (b) labour efficiency variances? (*pp. 345–55*)

12.10   Explain how variable overhead efficiency and expenditure variances are computed. What are the possible causes of each of these variances? (*pp. 357–58*)

12.11   Why are sales variances based on contribution margins rather than sales revenues? (*p. 359*)

Review problems

12.12   During a period, 17 500 labour hours were worked at a standard cost of £6.50 per hour. The labour efficiency variance was £7800 favourable.

How many standard hours were produced?

A   1 200
B   16 300
C   17 500
D   18 700

12.13   T plc uses a standard costing system, which is material stock account being maintained at standard costs. The following details have been extracted from the standard cost card in respect of direct materials:

8 kg at £0.80/kg = £6.40 per unit
Budgeted production in April was 850 units.

The following details relate to actual materials purchased and issued to production during April, when actual production was 870 units:

| Materials purchased | 8200 kg costing £6888 |
| Materials issued to production | 7150 kg |

Which of the following correctly states the material price and usage variance to be reported?

	Price	Usage
A	£286 (A)	£152 (A)
B	£286 (A)	£280 (A)
C	£286 (A)	£294 (A)
D	£328 (A)	£152 (A)
E	£328 (A)	£280 (A)

12.14 PQ Limited operates a standard costing system for its only product. The standard cost card is as follows:

Direct material (4 kg at £2/kg)	£8.00
Direct labour (4 hours at £4/hour)	£16.00
Variable overhead (4 hours at £3/hour)	£12.00
Fixed overhead (4 hours at £5/hour)	£20.00

Fixed overheads are absorbed on the basis of labour hours. Fixed overhead costs are budgeted at £12 000 per annum, arising at a constant rate during the year.

Activity in period 3 is budgeted to be 10% of total activity for the year. Actual production during period 3 was 500 units, with actual fixed overhead costs incurred being £9800 and actual hours worked being 1970.

The fixed overhead expenditure variance for period 3 was:

A   £2200 (F)
B   £200 (F)
C   £50 (F)
D   £200 (A)
E   £2200 (A)

12.15 J Limited operates a standard cost accounting system. The following information has been extracted from its standard cost card and budgets:

Budgeted sales volume	5000 units
Budgeted selling price	£10.00 per unit
Standard variable cost	£5.60 per unit
Standard total cost	£7.50 per unit

If it used a standard marginal cost accounting system and its actual sales were 4500 units at a selling price of £12.00, its sales volume variance would be:

A   £1250 adverse
B   £2200 adverse
C   £2250 adverse
D   £3200 adverse
E   £5000 adverse

12.16 **Variance analysis and reconciliation of actual and budgeted profit**

BS Limited manufactures one standard product and operates a system of variance accounting using a fixed budget. As assistant management accountant, you are responsible for preparing the monthly operating statements. Data from the budget, the standard product cost and actual data for the month ended 31 October are given below.

Using the data given, you are required to prepare the operating statement for the month ended 31 October to show the budgeted profit; the variances for direct materials, direct wages, overhead and sales, each analysed into causes; and actual profit.

Budgeted and standard cost data:

Budgeted sales and production for the month: 10 000 units
   Standard cost for each unit of product:
   Direct material: X: 10 kg at £1 per kg
                    Y: 5 kg at £5 per kg
   Direct wages: 5 hours at £3 per hour
   Budgeted fixed overheads are £300 000

Budgeted sales price has been calculated to give a profit contribution of 50% of the selling price.

Actual data for month ended 31 October:

Production: 9500 units sold at a price of 10% higher than that budgeted
Direct materials consumed:
   X: 96 000 kg at £1.20 per kg
   Y: 48 000 kg at £4.70 per kg
Direct wages incurred 46 000 hours at £3.20 per hour
Fixed production overhead incurred £290 000

(30 marks)

12.17 Calculation of actual input data working back from variances

The following data relate to actual output, costs and variances for the four-weekly accounting period number 4 of a company that makes only one product. Opening and closing work in progress figures were the same.

	(£000)
Actual production of product XY	18 000 units
Actual costs incurred:	
Direct materials purchased and used (150 000 kg)	210
Direct wages for 32 000 hours	136
Variable production overhead	38

	(£000)
Variances:	
Direct materials price	15 F
Direct materials usage	9 A
Direct labour rate	8 A
Direct labour efficiency	16 F
Variable production overhead expenditure	6 A
Variable production overhead efficiency	4 F

Variable production overhead varies with labour hours worked.
A standard marginal costing system is operated.

You are required to:
(a) present a standard product cost sheet for one unit of product XY,

(16 marks)

(b) describe briefly *three* types of standard that can be used for a standard costing system, stating which is usually preferred in practice and why.

(9 marks)
(Total 25 marks)

12.18 Reconciliation of budgeted and actual contribution

JK plc operates a chain of fast-food restaurants. The company uses a standard marginal costing system to monitor the costs incurred in its outlets. The standard cost of one of its most popular meals is as follows:

		£ per meal
Ingredients	(1.08 units)	1.18
Labour	(1.5 minutes)	0.15
Variable conversion costs	(1.5 minutes)	0.06
The standard selling price of this meal is		1.99

In one of its outlets, which has budgeted sales and production activity level of 50 000 such meals, the number of such meals that were produced and sold during April 2003 was 49 700. The actual cost data was as follows:

		£
Ingredients	(55 000 units)	58 450
Labour	(1 200 hours)	6 800
Variable conversion costs	(1 200 hours)	3 250
The actual revenue from the sale of the meals was		96 480

Required:

(a) Calculate

  (i) the total budgeted contribution for April 2003;

  (ii) the total actual contribution for April 2003.

(3 marks)

(b) Present a statement that reconciles the budgeted and actual contribution for April 2003. Show all variances to the nearest £1 and in as much detail as possible.

(17 marks)
(Total 20 marks)

12.19 Calculation of labour variances and actual material inputs working backwards from variances

A company manufactures two components in one of its factories. Material A is one of several materials used in the manufacture of both components.

The standard direct labour hours per unit of production and budgeted production quantities for a 13-week period were:

	Standard direct labour hours	Budgeted production quantities
Component X	0.40 hours	36 000 units
Component Y	0.56 hours	22 000 units

The standard wage rate for all direct workers was £5.00 per hour. Throughout the 13-week period 53 direct workers were employed, working a standard 40-hour week.

The following actual information for the 13-week period is available:

Production:
    Component X, 35 000 units
    Component Y, 25 000 units
Direct wages paid, £138 500
Material A purchases, 47 000 kilos costing £85 110
Material A price variance, £430 F
Material A usage (component X), 33 426 kilos
Material A usage variance (component X), £320.32 A

Required:

(a) Calculate the direct labour variances for the period;

(5 marks)

(b) Calculate the standard purchase price for material A for the period and the standard usage of material A per unit of production of component X.

(8 marks)

(c) Describe the steps, and information, required to establish the material purchase quantity budget for material A for a period.

(7 marks)
(Total 20 marks)

Divisional financial performance measures

13 Large companies produce and sell a wide variety of products throughout the world. Because of the complexity of their operations, it is difficult for top management to directly control operations. It may therefore be appropriate to divide a company into separate self-contained segments or divisions and to allow divisional managers to operate with a great deal of independence. A divisional manager has responsibility for both the production and marketing activities of the division. The danger in creating autonomous divisions is that divisional managers might not pursue goals that are in the best interests of the company as a whole. The objective of this chapter is to consider financial performance measures that will motivate managers to pursue those goals that will best benefit the company as a whole. In other words, the objective is to develop performance measures that will achieve goal congruence.

In this chapter we shall focus on financial measures of divisional performance. However, financial measures cannot adequately measure all those factors that are critical to the success of a division. Emphasis should also be given to reporting key non-financial measures relating to such areas as competitiveness, product leadership, quality, delivery performance, innovation and flexibility to respond to changes in demand. In particular,

LEARNING OBJECTIVES

After studying this chapter, you should be able to:

- distinguish between functional and divisionalized organizational structures;
- explain why it is preferable to distinguish between managerial and economic performance;
- explain the factors that should be considered in designing financial performance measures for evaluating divisional managers;
- explain the meaning of return on investment, residual income and economic value added;
- compute economic value added;
- identify and explain the approaches that can be used to reduce the dysfunctional consequences of short-term financial measures.

performance measures should be developed that support the objectives and competitive strategies of the organization. Divisional financial performance measures should therefore be seen as one of a range of measures that should be used to measure and control divisional performance.

Functional and divisionalized organizational structures

A **functional organizational structure** is one in which all activities of a similar type within a company are placed under the control of the appropriate departmental head. A simplified organization chart for a functional organizational structure is illustrated in Figure 13.1(a). It is assumed that the company illustrated consists of five separate departments – production, marketing, financial administration, purchasing and research and development. In a typical functional organization none of the managers of the five departments is responsible for more than a part of the process of acquiring the raw materials, converting them into finished products, selling to customers, and administering the financial aspects of this process. For example, the production department is responsible for the manufacture of all products at a minimum cost, and of satisfactory quality, and to meet the delivery dates requested by the marketing department. The marketing department is responsible for the total sales revenue and any costs associated with selling and distributing the products, but not for the total profit. The purchasing department is responsible for purchasing supplies at a minimum cost and of satisfactory quality so that the production requirements can be met.

You will see from Figure 13.1 that the marketing function is a revenue centre and the remaining departments are cost centres. Revenues and costs (including the cost of investments) are combined together only at the chief executive, or corporate level, which is classified as an investment centre.

Let us now consider Figure 13.1(b), which shows a **divisionalized organizational structure**, which is split up into divisions in accordance with the products which are made. You will see from the diagram that each divisional manager is responsible for all of the operations relating to his or her particular product. To reflect this greater autonomy each division is either an investment centre or a profit centre. To simplify the presentation it is assumed that all of the divisions in Figure 13.1(b) are investment centres (we shall discuss the factors influencing the choice of investment or profit centres later in the chapter). Note that within each division there are multiple cost and revenue centres and also that a functional structure is applied within each division. Figure 13.1(b) shows a simplified illustration of a divisionalized organizational structure. In practice, however, only part of a company may be divisionalized. For example, activities such as research and development, industrial relations, and general administration may be structured centrally on a functional basis with a responsibility for providing services to all of the divisions.

The distinguishing feature between the functional structure (Figure 13.1(a)) and the divisionalized structure (Figure 13.1(b)) is that in the functional structure only the organization as a whole is an investment centre and below this level a functional structure applies throughout. In contrast, in a divisionalized structure the organization is divided into separate investment or profit centres and a functional structure applies below this level. In this chapter we shall focus on financial measures and controls at the profit or investment centre (i.e. divisional) level. Note that below this level the controls described in the two previous chapters should also be applied to cost centres and revenue centres that have been established within the divisionalised organizational structure.

Generally, a divisionalized organizational structure will lead to a decentralization of the decision-making process. For example, divisional managers will normally be free to set

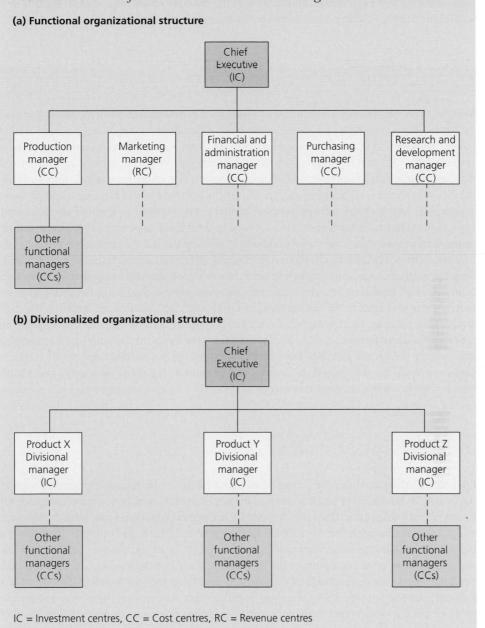

FIGURE 13.1   *A functional and divisionalized organizational structure*

(a) Functional organizational structure

(b) Divisionalized organizational structure

IC = Investment centres, CC = Cost centres, RC = Revenue centres

selling prices, choose which market to sell in, make product mix and output decisions, and select suppliers (this may include buying from other divisions within the company or from other companies). In a functional organizational structure pricing, product mix and output decisions will be made by central management. Consequently, the functional managers in a centralized organization will have far less independence than divisional managers. One way to express the difference between the two organizational structures is to say that the divisional managers have profit responsibility. They are responsible for generating revenues, controlling costs and earning a satisfactory return on the capital invested in their operations. The managers of the functional organizational structure do not have profit responsibility. For example, in Figure 13.1(a) the production manager has no control over sources of supply, selling prices, or product mix and output decisions.

Profit centres and investment centres

The creation of separate divisions may lead to the delegation of different degrees of authority; for example, in some organizations a divisional manager may, in addition to having authority to make decisions on sources of supply and choice of markets, also have responsibility for making capital investment decisions. Where this situation occurs, the division is known as an investment centre. Alternatively, where a manager cannot control the investment and is responsible only for the profits obtained from operating the fixed assets assigned to him or her by corporate headquarters, the segment is referred to as a profit centre. In contrast, the term cost centre is used to describe a responsibility centre in a functional organizational structure where a manager is responsible for costs but not profits.

Many firms attempt to simulate a divisionalized profit centre structure by creating separate manufacturing and marketing divisions in which the supplying division produces a product and transfers it to the marketing division, which then sells the product in the external market. Transfer prices are assigned to the products transferred between the divisions. This practice creates pseudo-divisionalized profit centres. Separate profits can be reported for each division, but the divisional managers have limited authority for sourcing and pricing decisions. To meet the true requirements of a divisionalized profit centre, a division should be able to sell the majority of its output to outside customers and should also be free to choose the sources of supply.

Advantages of divisionalization

Divisionalization can improve the decision-making process both from the point of view of the quality of the decision and the speed of the decision. The quality of the decisions should be improved because decisions can be made by the person who is familiar with the situation and who should therefore be able to make more informed judgements than central management who cannot be intimately acquainted with all the activities of the various segments of the business. Speedier decisions should also occur because information does not have to pass along the chain of command to and from top management. Decisions can be made on the spot by those who are familiar with the product lines and production processes and who can react to changes in local conditions in a speedy and efficient manner.

In addition, delegation of responsibility to divisional managers provides them with greater freedom, thus making their activities more challenging and providing the opportunity to achieve self-fulfilment. This process should mean that motivation and efficiency will be increased not just at the divisional manager level but throughout the whole division. A study by Dittman and Ferris (1978) of the attitudes of managers in companies in the USA found that those managers in charge of profit centres had greater job satisfaction than the managers of cost centres. They conclude that wherever possible, system designers ought to try to construct profit centres for organizational units.

Another important reason for adopting a divisionalized structure is that the distribution of decision-making responsibility to divisions frees top management from detailed involvement in day-to-day operations, and enables them to devote more effort to strategic planning and decision-making.

Disadvantages of divisionalization

If a company is divisionalized, there is a danger that divisions may compete with each other excessively and that divisional managers may be encouraged to take action which will increase their own profits at the expense of the profits of other divisions. This may adversely affect cooperation between the divisions and lead to a lack of harmony in achieving the overall organizational goals of the company. This in turn may lead to a reduction in total company profits.

A further argument against divisionalization is that top management loses some control by delegating decision-making to divisional managers. It is argued that a series of control reports is not as effective as detailed knowledge of a company's activities. However, with a good system of performance evaluation together with appropriate control information, top management should be able to effectively control operations.

Prerequisites for successful divisionalization

A divisionalized structure is most suited to companies engaged in several dissimilar activities. The reason is that it is difficult for top management to be intimately acquainted with all the diverse activities of the various segments of the business. On the other hand, when the major activities of a company are closely related, these activities should be carefully coordinated, and this coordination is more easily achieved in a centralized organizational structure. The results from a number of surveys suggest that divisionalization is more common in companies having diversified activities than when single or related activities are undertaken (Ezzamel and Hilton, 1980).

For successful divisionalization it is important that the activities of a division be as independent as possible of other activities. However, Solomons (1965) argues that even though substantial independence of divisions from each other is a necessary condition for divisionalization, if carried to the limit it would destroy the very idea that such divisions are an integral part of any single business. Divisions should be more than investments; they should contribute not only to the success of the company but to the success of each other.

According to Solomons, a further condition for the success of divisionalization is that the relations between divisions should be regulated so that no one division, by seeking its own profit, can reduce that of the company as a whole. He states that this is not the same as seeking profit at the expense of other divisions, but the amount that a division adds to its own profit must exceed the loss that it inflicts on another division. Unfortunately, conflicts between divisions do arise, and one of the important tasks of the accountant is to design an accounting control system that will discourage a division from improving its own profit at the expense of the company as a whole.

Distinguishing between the managerial and economic performance of the division

Before discussing the factors to be considered in determining how divisional profitability should be measured, we must decide whether the primary purpose is to measure the performance of the division or that of the divisional manager. The messages transmitted from these two measures may be quite different. For example, a manager may be assigned to an ailing division to improve performance, and might succeed in substantially improving the performance of the division. However, the division might still be unprofitable because of industry factors, such as overcapacity and a declining market. The future of the division might be uncertain, but the divisional manager may well be promoted as a result of the outstanding managerial performance. Conversely, a division might report significant profits but, because of management deficiencies, the performance may be unsatisfactory when the favourable economic environment is taken into account.

If the purpose is to evaluate the divisional manager then only those items directly controllable by the manager should be included in the profitability measure. Thus all allocations of indirect costs, such as central service and central administration costs, which cannot be influenced by divisional managers, ought not to be included in the profitability measure. Such costs can only be controlled where they are incurred; which means that central service managers should be held accountable for them.

Corporate headquarters, however, will also be interested in evaluating a division's economic performance for decision-making purposes, such as expansion, contraction and divestment decisions. In this situation a measure that includes only those amounts directly controllable by the divisional manager would overstate the economic performance of the division. This overstatement occurs because, if the divisions were independent companies, they would have to incur the costs of those services provided by head office. Therefore, to measure the economic performance of the division many items that the divisional manager cannot influence, such as interest expenses, taxes and the allocation of central administrative staff expenses, should be included in the profitability measure.

Alternative divisional profit measures

There are strong arguments for computing two measures of divisional profitability – one to evaluate managerial performance and the other to evaluate the economic performance of the division. In this chapter we shall focus on both these measures. The most common measures of divisional profitability are return on investment (that is, profit as a percentage of the investment in a division) residual income and economic value added. The reported divisional profit is a component of each of these measures. At this stage we shall restrict our attention purely to problems that are encountered with divisional profit measurement before turning our attention to the above three common measures of divisional profitability.

Exhibit 13.1 presents a divisional profit statement. You can see that there are four different profit measures that we can use to measure divisional performance. We shall focus initially on measuring *managerial* performance. The **variable short-run contribution margin** is inappropriate for performance evaluation, because it does not include fixed costs that are controllable by the divisional manager. For example, a manager may not be motivated to control non-variable labour costs or equipment rentals, since they fall below the variable short-run contribution line and are not included in the performance measure.

The **controllable contribution** is computed by deducting from total divisional revenues all those costs that are controllable by the division manager. This measure therefore includes controllable fixed costs such as non-variable labour, equipment rental and the cost of utilities. These costs are fixed in the short term, but in the longer term the divisional manager has the option of reducing them by altering the scale of operations or reducing the complexity and diversity of product lines and distribution channels. Where a division is a profit centre, depreciation is not a controllable cost, since the manager does not have authority to make capital investment decisions. Depreciation, however, should be deemed

EXHIBIT 13.1

Alternative divisional profit measures

Sales to outside customers	xxx
Transfers to other divisions	xxx
Total sales revenue	xxx
Less variable costs	xxx
1. Variable short-run contribution margin	xxx
Less controllable fixed costs	xxx
2. Controllable contribution	xxx
Less non-controllable avoidable costs	xxx
3. Divisional contribution	xxx
Less allocated corporate expenses	xxx
4. Divisional net profit before taxes	xxx

to be a controllable expense for an investment centre in respect of those assets that are controllable by the divisional manager.

Controllable contribution is the most appropriate measure of a divisional manager's performance, since it measures the ability of managers to use the resources under their control effectively. It should not be interpreted in isolation if it is used directly to evaluate the performance of a divisional manager. Instead, the controllable contribution reported by a division should be evaluated relative to a budgeted performance, so that market conditions can be taken into account.

In practice, it is extremely difficult to distinguish between controllable and non-controllable costs. However, three situations can be identified that will assist us in over-coming this problem. Where a division is completely free to shop around for a service and there is no rule requiring the division to obtain the service from within the company, the expense is clearly controllable. Alternatively, a division may not be free to choose an outside source of supply for the service in question, but it may be able to decide how much of this service is utilized. In this latter situation the quantity is controllable by the division but the price is not. An appropriate solution here is for the division to be charged with the actual quantity at the standard or budgeted cost for the service that has been obtained. Thus any difference between the budget and actual performance would relate solely to excess usage by the division recorded at the standard price. Finally, the division may not be free to decide on either the quantity of the service it utilizes or the price it will be charged. Industrial relations costs may fall into this category. Here the divisions have no choice but to accept an apportioned cost for the benefits they have received (such apportionments may be made for external reporting purposes). In situations like this, the costs charged to the division for the service can only be regarded as a non-controllable item of divisional overhead. Another general rule that can be applied for distinguishing between controllable and non-controllable costs is to follow the guideline suggested by Merchant (1998) – that is, hold managers accountable for those costs that you want them to pay attention to.

Controllable contribution provides an incomplete measure of the *economic* performance of a division, since it does not include those costs that are attributable to the division but which are not controllable by the divisional manager. For example, depreciation of divisional assets, and head office finance and legal staff who are assigned to providing services for specific divisions, would fall into this category. These expenses would be avoidable if a decision were taken to close the division. Those non-controllable expenses that are attributable to a division, and which would be avoidable if the division was closed, are deducted from controllable contribution to derive the **divisional contribution**. This is clearly a useful figure for evaluating the *economic* contribution of the division, since it represents the contribution that a division is making to corporate profits and overheads. It should not be used, however, to evaluate managerial performance, since it includes costs that are not controllable by divisional managers.

Many companies allocate all corporate general and administrative expenses to divisions to derive a **divisional net profit before taxes**. From a theoretical point of view, it is difficult to justify such allocations since they tend to be arbitrary and do not have any connection with the manner in which divisional activities influence the level of these corporate expenses. Divisional contribution would therefore seem to be the most appropriate measure of divisions' *economic* performance, since it is not distorted by arbitrary allocations. We have noted, however, that corporate headquarters may wish to compare a division's economic performance with that of comparable firms operating in the same industry. The divisional contribution would overstate the performance of the division, because if the division were independent, it would have to incur the costs of those services performed by head office. The apportioned head office costs are an approximation of the costs that the division would have to incur if it traded as a separate company. Consequently, companies may prefer to use divisional net profit when comparing the economic performance of a division with similar companies.

For the reasons mentioned above, divisional net profit is not a satisfactory measure for evaluating *managerial* performance. Despite the many theoretical arguments against divisional net profit, the empirical evidence indicates that this measure is used widely to evaluate both divisional *economic* and *managerial* performance (Reece and Cool, 1978; Fremgen and Liao, 1981; Ramadan, 1989; Skinner, 1990; Drury *et al.*, 1993). In the Fremgen and Liao survey respondents were asked why they allocated indirect costs. The most important managerial performance evaluation reason was to 'remind profit centre managers that indirect costs exist and that profit centre earnings must be adequate to cover a share of these costs'. The counter-argument to this is that if central management wishes to inform managers that divisions must be profitable enough to cover not only their own operations but corporate expenses as well, it is preferable to set a high budgeted controllable contribution target that takes account of these factors. Divisional managers can then concentrate on increasing controllable contribution by focusing on those costs and revenues that are under their control and not be concerned with costs that they cannot control.

A further reason for cost allocations cited in the surveys by Fremgen and Liao and Skinner was that by allocating central overhead costs to divisions, divisional managers are made aware of these costs, so they will exert pressure on central management to minimize the costs of central staff departments. There is also some evidence to suggest that companies hold managers accountable for divisional net profit because this is equivalent to the measure that financial markets focus on to evaluate the performance of the company as a whole (Joseph *et al.*, 1996). Top management therefore require their divisional managers to concentrate on the same measures as those used by financial markets.

A more recent UK study by El-Shishini and Drury (2001) asked the respondents to rank in order of importance the factors influencing organizations to allocate the cost of shared resources to divisions. In rank order the highest rankings were attributed to the following factors:

1 to show divisional managers the total costs of operating their divisions;
2 to make divisional managers aware that such costs exist and must be covered by divisional profits;
3 divisional managers would incur such costs if they were independent units;
4 divisional managers should bear the full business risk as if they were managers of non-divisionalized companies.

Return on investment

Instead of focusing purely on the absolute size of a division's profits, most organizations focus on the **return on investment (ROI)** of a division. Note that ROI is synonymous with accounting rate of return (ARR) described as an investment appraisal technique in Chapter 9. In Chapter 9 our focus was on future estimates (i.e. an *ex ante* measure) for making investment decisions. In this chapter we are focusing on an historic after-the-event (i.e. *ex post*) performance measure. ROI expresses divisional profit as a percentage of the assets employed in the division. Assets employed can be defined as total divisional assets, assets controllable by the divisional manager or net assets. We shall consider the alternative measures of assets employed later in the chapter.

ROI is the most widely used financial measure of divisional performance. Why? Consider a situation where division A earns a profit of £1 million and division B a profit of £2 million. Can we conclude that Division B is more profitable than Division A? The answer is no, since we should consider whether the divisions are returning a sufficiently high return on the capital invested in the division. Assume that £4 million capital is invested in division A and £20 million in division B. Division A's ROI is 25% (£1m/£4m) whereas the return for division B is 10% (£2m/£20m). Capital invested has alternative uses, and corporate management will wish to ascertain whether the returns being earned on the capital invested in a particular division exceeds the division's opportunity cost of capital (i.e. the returns available from the alternative use of the capital). If, in the above illustration, the return available on similar investments to that in division B is 15% then the economic viability of division B is questionable if profitability cannot be improved.

Another feature of the ROI is that it can be used as a common denominator for comparing the returns of dissimilar businesses, such as other divisions within the group or outside competitors. ROI has been widely used for many years in all types of organizations so that most managers understand what the measure reflects and consider it to be of considerable importance.

Despite the widespread use of ROI, a number of problems exist when this measure is used to evaluate the performance of divisional managers. For example, it is possible that divisional ROI can be increased by actions that will make the company as a whole worse off, and conversely, actions that decrease the divisional ROI may make the company as a whole better off. In other words, evaluating divisional managers on the basis of ROI may not encourage goal congruence. Consider the following example:

	Division X	Division Y
Investment project available	£10 million	£10 million
Controllable contribution	£2 million	£1.3 million
Return on the proposed project	20%	13%
ROI of divisions at present	25%	9%

It is assumed that neither project will result in any changes in non-controllable costs and that the overall cost of capital for the company is 15%. The manager of division X would be reluctant to invest the additional £10 million because the return on the proposed project is 20%, and this would reduce the existing overall ROI of 25%. On the other hand, the manager of division Y would wish to invest the £10 million because the return on the proposed project of 13% is in excess of the present return of 9%, and it would increase the division's overall ROI. Consequently, the managers of both divisions would make decisions that would not be in the best interests of the company. The company should accept only those projects where the return is in excess of the cost of capital of 15%, but the manager of division X would reject a potential return of 20% and the manager of division Y would accept a potential return of 13%. ROI can therefore lead to a lack of goal congruence.

Residual income

To overcome some of the dysfunctional consequences of ROI, the residual income approach can be used. For the purpose of evaluating the performance of *divisional managers*, residual income is defined as controllable contribution less a cost of capital charge on the investment controllable by the divisional manager. For evaluating the *economic performance* of the division residual income can be defined as divisional contribution (see Exhibit 13.1) less a cost of capital charge on the total investment in assets employed by the division. If residual income is used to measure the managerial performance of investment centres, there is a greater probability that managers will be encouraged, when acting in their own best interests, also to act in the best interests of the company. Returning to our previous illustration in respect of the investment decision for divisions X and Y, the residual income calculations are as follows:

	Division X (£)	Division Y (£)
Proposed investment	10 million	10 million
Controllable contribution	2 million	1.3 million
Cost of capital charge (15% of the investment cost)	1.5 million	1.5 million
Residual income	0.5 million	− 0.2 million

This calculation indicates that the residual income of division X will increase and that of division Y will decrease if both managers accept the project. Therefore the manager of division X would invest, whereas the manager of division Y would not. These actions are in the best interests of the company as a whole.

Residual income suffers from the disadvantages of being an absolute measure, which means that it is difficult to compare the performance of a division with that of other divisions or companies of a different size. For example, a large division is more likely to earn a larger residual income than a small division. To overcome this deficiency, targeted or budgeted levels of residual income should be set for each division that are consistent with asset size and the market conditions of the divisions.

In the case of profit centres, where divisional managers are not authorized to make capital investment decisions and where they cannot influence the investment in working capital, ROI is a satisfactory performance measure, because if the return on investment is maximized on a fixed quantity of capital, the absolute return itself will also be maximized. However, in the case of investment centres, or profit centres where managers can significantly influence the investment in working capital, ROI appears to be an unsatisfactory method of measuring managerial performance, and in these circumstances the residual income is preferable.

Surveys of methods used by companies to evaluate the performance of divisional managers indicate a strong preference for ROI over residual income. For example, the UK survey by Drury *et al.* (1993) reported that the following measures were used:

	(%)
A target ROI set by the group	55
Residual income	20
A target profit *before* charging interest on investment	61
A target cash flow figure	43

Why is ROI preferred to residual income? Skinner (1990) found evidence to suggest that firms prefer to use ROI because, being a ratio, it can be used for inter-division and inter-firm comparisons. ROI for a division can be compared with the return from other divisions within the group or with whole companies outside the group, whereas absolute monetary measures such as residual income are not appropriate in making such comparisons. A second possible reason for the preference for ROI is that 'outsiders' tend to use ROI as a measure of a company's overall performance. Corporate managers therefore want their divisional managers to focus on ROI so that their performance measure is congruent with outsiders' measure of the company's overall economic performance. A further reason, suggested by Kaplan and Atkinson (1998), is that managers find percentage measures of profitability such as ROI more convenient, since they enable a division's profitability to be compared with other financial measures (such as inflation rates, interest rates, and the ROI rates of other divisions and comparable companies outside the group).

Economic value added (EVA$^{(TM)}$)

During the 1990s residual income has been refined and renamed as economic value added (EVA$^{(TM)}$) by the Stern Stewart consulting organization and they have registered EVA$^{(TM)}$ as their trademark. An article in an issue of *Fortune* magazine (1993) described the apparent success that many companies had derived from using EVA$^{(TM)}$ to motivate and evaluate corporate and divisional managers. *The Economist* (1997) reported that more than 300 firms world-wide had adopted EVA$^{(TM)}$ including Coca-Cola, AT&T, ICL, Boots and the Burton Group. A UK study by El-Shishini and Drury (2001) reported that 23% of the responding organizations used EVA$^{(TM)}$ to evaluate divisional performance.

The EVA$^{(TM)}$ concept extends the traditional residual income measure by incorporating adjustments to the divisional financial performance measure for distortions introduced by generally accepted accounting principles (GAAP). EVA$^{(TM)}$ can be defined as:

$$EVA^{(TM)} = \text{Conventional divisional profit} \pm \text{accounting adjustments} - \text{cost of capital charge on divisional assets}$$

Our earlier discussion relating to which of the conventional alternative divisional profit measures listed in Exhibit 13.1 should be used also applies here. There are strong theoretical arguments for using controllable contribution as the divisional profit measure for *managerial* performance and divisional contribution for measuring *economic* performance. Many companies, however, use divisional net profit (after allocated costs) to evaluate both divisional managerial and economic performance.

Adjustments are made to the chosen conventional divisional profit measure in order to replace historic financial accounting data with a measure that attempts to approximate economic profit and asset values. Stern Stewart have stated that they have developed approximately 160 accounting adjustments that may need to be made to convert the conventional accounting profit into a sound measure of EVA$^{(TM)}$ but they have indicated that most organizations will only need to use about 10 of the adjustments. These adjustments result in the capitalization of many discretionary expenditures, such as research and development, marketing and advertising, by spreading these costs over the periods in which the benefits are received. Therefore adopting EVA$^{(TM)}$ should reduce some of the harmful side-effects arising from using financial measures that were discussed in Chapter 11. This is because managers will not bear the full costs of the discretionary expenditures in the period in which they are incurred if the expenses are capitalized. Instead, the cost will be spread across the periods when the benefits from the expenditure are estimated to be received. Also because it is a restatement of the residual income measure, compared with ROI, EVA$^{(TM)}$ is more likely to encourage goal congruence in terms of asset acquisition decisions. By making cost of capital visible managers are made aware that capital has a cost and they are thus encouraged to dispose of underutilized assets that do not generate sufficient income to cover their cost of capital.

There are a number of issues that apply to ROI, residual income or its replacement EVA$^{(TM)}$. They concern determining which assets should be included in a division's asset base, and the adjustments that should be made to financial accounting practices to derive managerial information that is closer to economic reality.

Determining which assets should be included in the investment base

We must determine which assets to include in a division's asset base to compute both ROI and EVA$^{(TM)}$. (Note that for the remainder of the chapter we shall use the term EVA$^{(TM)}$ to incorporate residual income.) If the purpose is to evaluate the performance of the divisional manager then only those assets that can be directly traced to the division and that are controllable by the divisional manager should be included in the asset base.

Any liabilities that are within the control of the division should be deducted from the asset base. For example, a division may finance its investment in stocks by the use of trade creditors; this liability for creditors should therefore be deducted. The term **controllable investment** is used to refer to the net asset base that is controllable by divisional managers. Our overall aim in analysing controllable and non-controllable investment is to produce performance measures that will encourage a manager to behave in the best interests of the organization and also to provide a good approximation of managerial performance. It is therefore appropriate to include in the investment base only those assets that a manager can influence, and any arbitrary apportionments should be excluded.

If the purpose is to evaluate the economic performance of the division, the profitability of the division will be overstated if controllable investment is used. This is because a division could not operate without the benefit of corporate assets such as buildings, cash and debtors managed at the corporate level. These assets would be included in the investment base if the divisions were separate independent companies. Therefore many divisionalized companies allocate corporate assets to divisions when comparing divisional profitability with comparable firms in the same industry.

The impact of depreciation

It is common to find fixed assets valued at either their original cost or their written down value for the purpose of calculating return on investment and EVA$^{(TM)}$, but both of these valuation methods are weak. Consider, for example, an investment in an asset of £1 million with a life of five years with annual cash flows of £350 000 and a cost of capital of 10%. This investment has a positive NPV of £326 850, and should be accepted. You can see from Exhibit 13.2 that the annual profit is £150 000 when straight line depreciation is used. If the asset is *valued at original cost*, there will be a return of 15% per annum for five years. This will understate the true return, because the economic valuation is unlikely to remain at £1 million each year for five years and then immediately fall to zero. If ROI is based on the *written-down value*, you can see from Exhibit 13.2 that the investment base will decline each year – and, with constant profits, the effect will be to show a steady increase in return on investment. This steady increase in return on investment will suggest

How the use of EVA analysis transformed Armstrong's financial performance

The financial mission of a company should be to invest and create cash flows in excess of the cost of capital. If an investment is announced that is expected to earn in excess of the cost of capital, then the value of the firm will immediately rise by the present value of that excess – as long as the market understands and believes the available projections. The question is: What is the best way to measure this?

Traditional measures of return, such as ROI, actually could unwittingly motivate and reward managers to shrink the value of the company. Therefore, the concept EVA was developed. In a nutshell, EVA is designed to measure the degree to which a company's after-tax operating profits exceed – or fall short of – the cost of capital invested in the business. It makes managers think more about the use of capital and the amount of capital in each business.

Armstrong World Industries Inc. is a multibillion-dollar manufacturer and supplier of floor coverings, insulation products, ceiling and wall systems, and installation products. In 1993 the decision was made to discontinue the ROI concept and use EVA for strategic planning, performance measurement, and compensation. EVA is computed from straightforward adjustments to convert book values on the income statement and balance sheet to an economic basis. Armstrong used about a dozen adjustments.

Armstrong considered EVA to be the best financial measure for accurately linking accounting measures to stock market value and performance, making it ideal for setting financial targets. Changes in behaviour have become focused on three basic actions: (1) improving profit without more capital; (2) investing in projects earning above the cost of capital; and (3) eliminating operations unable to earn above the cost of capital.

On a higher strategic level, EVA allowed Armstrong to step back to see where the company was losing value. In what the company called its 'sunken ship' chart it was clear that businesses earning above the cost of capital were providing huge amounts of EVA. However, the ship was being dragged down because actual EVA was only 50 per cent. The trouble was negative EVA businesses and corporate overhead. By benchmarking 'the best' companies, Armstrong found it needed to improve its organizational effectiveness and dramatically reduce worldwide overhead. By selling or combining negative EVA businesses and by growing and further reducing costs in its positive EVA businesses, the company provided the potential to more than double its EVA.

Source: Adapted from Institute of Management & Administration Report on Financial Analysis Planning and Reporting, September, 2002.

an improvement in managerial performance when the economic facts indicate that performance has remained unchanged over the five-year period.

Similar inconsistencies will also occur if the EVA$^{(TM)}$ method is used. If the asset is valued at the original cost, EVA$^{(TM)}$ of £50 000 will be reported each year (£150 000 profit – (10% cost of capital × 1 million)). On the other hand, if the cost of capital charge is based on the written-down value of the asset, the investment base will decline each year, and EVA$^{(TM)}$ will increase (see Exhibit 13.2).

Exhibit 13.2 serves to illustrate that if asset written-down values are used to determine the division's investment base, managers can improve their ROI or EVA$^{(TM)}$ by postponing new investments and operating with older assets with low written-down values. In contrast, divisional managers who invest in new equipment will have a lower ROI or EVA$^{(TM)}$. This

EXHIBIT 13.2

Profitability measures using straight-line depreciation

	1 (£)	2 (£)	3 (£)	4 (£)	5 (£)
Net cash flow	350 000	350 000	350 000	350 000	350 000
Depreciation	200 000	200 000	200 000	200 000	200 000
Profit	150 000	150 000	150 000	150 000	150 000
Cost of capital (10% of WDV)	100 000	80 000	60 000	40 000	20 000
EVA$^{(TM)}$	50 000	70 000	90 000	110 000	130 000
Opening WDV of the asset	1 000 000	800 000	600 000	400 000	200 000
ROI	15%	18.75%	25%	37.5%	75%

situation arises because financial accounting depreciation methods (including the reducing balance method) produce lower profitability measures in the earlier years of an asset's life.

To overcome the problems created by using financial accounting depreciation methods, alternative depreciation models have been recommended. For a discussion of these methods you should refer to Drury (2004, ch. 20). The theoretically correct solution to the problem is to value assets at their economic cost (i.e. the present value of future net cash inflows) but this presents serious practical difficulties. An appropriate solution to the practical problems is to value assets at their replacement cost (see Lee, 1996 for a discussion of this topic). Although this method is conceptually distinct from the present value method of valuation, it may provide answers which are reasonable approximations of what would be obtained using a present value approach. In addition, replacement cost is conceptually superior to the historical cost method of asset valuation. It follows that the depreciation charge on controllable investment based on replacement cost is preferable to a charge based on historical cost. The ROI and EVA$^{(TM)}$ for measuring managerial performance would then be calculated on controllable investment valued at replacement cost.

Addressing the dysfunctional consequences of short-term financial performance measures

The primary objective of profit-making organizations is to maximize shareholder value. Therefore performance measures should be based on the value created by each division. Unfortunately, direct measures of value creation are not possible because the shares for only the business as a whole are traded on the stockmarket. It is not possible to derive stock market values at the segmental or business unit level of an organization. Instead, most firms use accounting profit or ROI measures as a surrogate for changes in market values.

Unfortunately, using accounting measures such as ROI or EVA$^{(TM)}$ as performance measures can encourage managers to become short-term oriented. For example, it has been shown that in the short term managers can improve both of these measures, by rejecting profitable long-term investments. By not making the investments, they can reduce expenses in the current period and not suffer the lost revenues until future periods. Managers can also boost their performance measure in a particular period by destroying customer and employee goodwill. For example, they can force employees to work excessive overtime towards the end of a measurement period so that goods can be delivered and their sales revenues and profits reported for the period. If the products are of lower quality, customer satisfaction (and future sales) may diminish. In addition, the effects of increased work pressure may result in staff absenteeism, demotivation and increased labour turnover. These harmful effects are unlikely to have much impact on the financial performance measure in the short term and will only become apparent in future periods.

Consider also the situation where two divisional managers using exactly the same amount of investment produce exactly the same EVA$^{(TM)}$ or ROI. Does this mean that their performances are the same? The answer is no. Even though their performance measures would be identical this does not mean their performances are the same. One manager may have built up customer goodwill by offering excellent customer service, and also have paid great attention to training, education, research and development, etc., while another may not have given these items any consideration. Differences such as these would not show up initially in financial performance measures.

Return on investment and EVA$^{(TM)}$ are short-run concepts that deal only with the current reporting period, whereas managerial performance measures should focus on future results that can be expected because of present actions. Ideally, divisional performance should be evaluated on the basis of economic income by estimating future cash flows and discounting them to their present value. This calculation could be made for a division at the beginning and the end of a measurement period. The difference between the beginning and ending values represents the estimate of economic income.

The main problem with using estimates of economic income to evaluate performance is that it lacks precision and objectivity. A major difficulty with measuring economic income is that the individual that is most knowledgeable and in the best position to provide the cash flow estimates is usually the individual whose performance is being evaluated. Thus, managers will be tempted to bias their estimates.

Various approaches can be used to overcome the short-term orientation that can arise when accounting profit-related measures are used to evaluate divisional performance. One possibility is to improve the accounting measures. EVA$^{(TM)}$ represents such an approach. If you refer back to the formula for calculating EVA$^{(TM)}$ you will see that it is computed by making accounting adjustments to the conventional financial accounting divisional profit calculation. These adjustments, such as capitalizing research and development and advertising expenditure, represent an attempt to approximate economic income. Incorporating a cost of capital charge is also a further attempt to approximate economic income.

Another alternative for reducing the short-term orientation, and increasing congruence of accounting measures with economic income is to lengthen the measurement period. The longer the measurement period, the more congruent accounting measures of performance are with economic income. For example, profits over a three-year measurement period are a better indicator of economic income than profits over a six-monthly period. The disadvantage of lengthening the measurement period is that rewards are tied to the performance evaluation, and if they are provided a long time after actions are taken, there is a danger that they will lose much of their motivational effects.

Probably the most widely used approach to mitigate against the dysfunctional consequences that can arise from relying excessively on financial measures is to supplement them with non-financial measures that measure those factors that are critical to the long-term success and profits of the organization. These measures focus on areas such as competitiveness, product leadership, productivity, quality, delivery performance, innovation and flexibility in responding to changes in demand. If managers focus excessively on the short-term, the benefits from improved short-term financial performance may be counter-balanced by a deterioration in the non-financial measures. Such non-financial measures should provide a broad indication of the contribution of a divisional manager's current actions to the long-term success of the organization.

The incorporation of non-financial measures creates the need to link financial and non-financial measures of performance. In particular, there is a need for a balanced set of measures that provide both short-term performance measures and also leading indicators of future financial performance from current actions. The **balanced scorecard** emerged in the 1990s to meet these requirements. The balanced scorecard will be covered extensively in Chapter 16 but at this stage you should note that the financial performance evaluation measures discussed in this chapter ought to be seen as one of the elements within the balanced scorecard. Divisional performance evaluation should be based on a combination of financial and non-financial measures using the balanced scorecard approach.

Summary

The following items relate to the learning objectives listed at the beginning of the chapter.

- **Distinguish between functional and divisionalized organizational structures.**

  A functional structure is one in which all activities of a similar type within a company are placed under the control of a departmental head. The organization as a whole is an investment centre. With a divisionalized structure, the organization is split up into divisions that consist of either investment centres or profit centres. Thus, the distinguishing feature is that in a functional structure only the organization as a whole is an investment centre and below this level a functional structure applies throughout. In contrast, in a divisionalized structure the organization is divided into separate profit or investment centres, and a functional structure applies below this level.

- **Explain why it is preferable to distinguish between managerial and economic performance.**

  Divisional economic performance can be influenced by many factors beyond the control of divisional managers. For example, good or bad economic performance may arise mainly from a favourable or unfavourable economic climate faced by the division rather than the specific contribution of the divisional manager. To evaluate the performance of divisional managers an attempt ought to be made to distinguish between the economic and managerial performance.

- **Explain the factors that should be considered in designing financial performance measures for evaluating divisional managers.**

  To evaluate the performance of a divisional manager only those items directly controllable by the manager should be included in the divisional managerial performance financial measures. Thus, all allocations of indirect costs, such as those central service and administration costs that cannot be influenced by divisional managers, ought not to be included in the performance measure. Such costs can only be controlled where they are incurred, which means those central service managers should be held accountable for them.

- **Explain the meaning of return on investment (ROI), residual income and economic value added (EVA™).**

  ROI expresses divisional profit as a percentage of the assets employed in a division. Residual income is defined as divisional profit less a cost of capital charge on divisional investment (e.g. net assets or total assets). During the 1990s, residual income was refined and renamed as EVA™. It extends the traditional residual income measure by incorporating adjustments to the divisional financial performance measure for distortions introduced by using generally accepted accounting principles that are used for external financial reporting. Thus, EVA™ consists of a divisional profit measure plus or minus the accounting adjustments less a cost of capital charge. All three measures can be used either as measures of managerial or economic performance. For managerial performance controllable profit should be used whereas for economic performance divisional net profit can be used. To derive the ROI or cost of capital charge, controllable investment (e.g. controllable net assets) can be used for measuring managerial performance and total divisional investment can be used to measure economic performance.

- **Compute economic value added (EVA™).**

EVA™ is computed by starting with a conventional divisional profit measure and (a) adding or deducting adjustments for any distortions to divisional profit measures arising from using generally accepted accounting principles for external reporting, and (b) deducting a cost of capital charge on divisional assets. The measure can be used either as a measure of managerial or economic performance as described above. Typical accounting adjustments include the capitalization of discretionary expenditures, such as research and development expenditure.

- **Identify and explain the approaches that can be used to reduce the dysfunctional consequences of short-term financial measures.**

Methods suggested for reducing the dysfunctional consequences include (a) use of improved financial performance measures such as EVA™ that incorporate accounting adjustments that attempt to overcome the deficiencies of conventional accounting measures; (b) lengthen the performance measurement period; and (c) do not rely excessively on accounting measures and incorporate non-financial measures using the balanced scorecard approach described in Chapter 16.

 # Key terms and concepts

balanced scorecard (p. 388)
controllable contribution (p. 378)
controllable investment (p. 384)
cost centre (p. 376)
divisional contribution (p. 379)
divisional net profit before taxes (p. 380)
divisionalized organizational structure (p. 374)

economic value added (EVA™) (p. 383)
functional organizational structure (p. 374)
investment centre (p. 376)
profit centre (p. 376)
residual income (p. 382)
return on investment (ROI) (p. 381)
variable short-run contribution margin (p. 378)

Assessment material

Review questions

The review questions are short questions that enable you to assess your understanding of the main topics included in the chapter. The numbers in parentheses provide you with the page numbers to refer to if you cannot answer a specific question.

Review problems

The review problems are more complex and require you to relate and apply the chapter content to various business problems. The multiple-choice questions are the least demanding and normally take less than 10 minutes to complete. Fully worked solutions to the review problems are provided in a separate section at the end of the book. Further review problems for this chapter are available on the accompanying website, www.drury-online.com. The answers to these problems are available for lecturers on the lecturer's password-protected section of the website.

Case studies

The website also includes over 30 case study problems. A list of these cases is provided on pages 491–93. For an additional case study that is relevant to the content of this chapter see EVA Ault Foods Ltd (Drury, 2004; pp. 1151–63).

Review questions

13.1   Distinguish between a functional and divisionalized organizational structure. (*pp. 374–75*)

13.2   Distinguish between profit centres and investment centres. (*p. 376*)

13.3   What are the advantages and disadvantages of divisionalization? (*pp. 376–77*)

13.4   What are the prerequisites for successful divisionalization? (*pp. 377*)

13.5   Why might it be appropriate to distinguish between the managerial and economic performance of a division? (*pp. 377–78*)

13.6   Describe the four alternative profit measures that can be used to measure divisional performance. Which measures are preferable for (a) measuring divisional *managerial* performance and (b) measuring divisional *economic* performance? (*pp. 378–80*)

13.7   Why is it common practice not to distinguish between managerial and economic performance? (*pp. 380*)

13.8   Why is it common practice to allocate central costs to measure divisional managerial performance? (*p. 380*)

13.9   Distinguish between return on investment, residual income and economic value added. (*pp. 381–84*)

13.10   How does the use of return on investment as a performance measure lead to bad decisions? How do residual income and economic value added overcome this problem? (*pp. 381–83*)

13.11   Explain how economic value added is calculated. (*pp. 383–84*)

13.12   Explain the approaches that can be used to reduce the dysfunctional consequences of short-term financial measures. (*pp. 386–88*)

Review problems

13.13   Bollon uses residual income to appraise its divisions using a cost of capital of 10%. It gives the managers of these divisions considerable autonomy although it retains the cash control function at head office.

The following information was available for one of the divisions:

	Net profit after tax £'000	Profit before interest and tax £'000	Divisional net assets £'000	Cash/ (overdraft) £'000
Division 1	47	69	104	(21)

What is the residual income for this division based on controllable profit and controllable net assets?

A   £36 600
B   £56 500
C   £58 600
D   £60 700.

13.14   Division Q makes a single product. Information for the division for the year just
ended is:

Sales	30 000 units
Fixed costs	£487 000
Depreciation	£247 500
Residual income	£47 200
Net assets	£1 250 000

Head Office assesses divisional performance by the residual income achieved.
It uses a cost of capital of 12% a year.

Division Q's average contribution per unit was

A   £14.82
B   £22.81
C   £28.06
D   £31.06
E   £32.81

(*2 marks*)

13.15   **Conflict between NPV and performance measurement**

Linamix is the chemicals division of a large industrial corporation. George Elton,
the divisional general manager, is about to purchase new plant in order to
manufacture a new product. He can buy either the Aromatic or the Zoman plant,
each of which have the same capacity and expected four year life, but which differ
in their capital costs and expected net cash flows, as shown below:

	Aromatic	Zoman
Initial capital investment	£6 400 000	£5 200 000
Net cash flows (before tax)		
2001	£2 400 000	£2 600 000
2002	£2 400 000	£2 200 000
2003	£2 400 000	£1 500 000
2004	£2 400 000	£1 000 000
Net present value	£315 634	£189 615
(@ 16% p.a.)		

In the above calculations it has been assumed that the plant will be installed and
paid for by the end of December 2000, and that the net cash flows accrue at the
end of each calendar year. Neither plant is expected to have a residual value after
decommissioning costs.

Like all other divisional managers in the corporation, Elton is expected to
generate a before tax return on his divisional investment in excess of 16% p.a.,
which he is currently just managing to achieve. Anything less than a 16% return
would make him ineligible for a performance bonus and may reduce his pension
when he retires in early 2003. In calculating divisional returns, divisional assets
are valued at net book values at the beginning of the year. Depreciation is charged
on a straight line basis.

Requirements:

(a) Explain, with appropriate calculations, why neither return on investment nor residual income would motivate Elton to invest in the process showing the higher net present value. To what extent can the use of alternative accounting techniques assist in reconciling the conflict between using accounting-based performance measures and discounted cash flow investment appraisal techniques?

(12 marks)

(b) Managers tend to use post-tax cash flows to evaluate investment opportunities, but to evaluate divisional and managerial performance on the basis of pre-tax profits. Explain why this is so and discuss the potential problems that can arise, including suggestions as to how such problems can be overcome.

(8 marks)

(c) Discuss what steps can be taken to avoid dysfunctional behaviour which is motivated by accounting-based performance targets.

(5 marks)
(Total 25 marks)

13.16 **Computation and discussion of economic value added**

The managers of Toutplut Inc were surprised at a recent newspaper article which suggested that the company's performance in the last two years had been poor. The CEO commented that turnover had increased by nearly 17% and pre-tax profit by 25% between the last two financial years, and that the company compared well with others in the same industry.

	$ million	
	Profit and loss account extracts for the year	
	2000	*2001*
Turnover	326	380
Pre-tax accounting profit[1]	67	84
Taxation	23	29
Profit after tax	44	55
Dividends	15	18
Retained earnings	29	37

	Balance sheet extracts for the year ending	
	2000	*2001*
Fixed assets	120	156
Net current assets	130	160
	250	316
Financed by:		
Shareholders' funds	195	236
Medium- and long-term bank loans	55	80
	250	316

[1]After deduction of the economic depreciation of the company's fixed assets. This is also the depreciation used for tax purposes.

Other information:

(i) Toutplut had non-capitalized leases valued at $10 million in each year 1999–2001.

(ii) Balance Sheet capital employed at the end of 1999 was $223 million.

(iii) The company's pre-tax cost of debt was estimated to be 9% in 2000, and 10% in 2001.

(iv) The company's cost of equity was estimated to be 15% in 2000 and 17% in 2001.

(v) The target capital structure is 60% equity, 40% debt.

(vi) The effective tax rate was 35% in both 2000 and 2001.

(vii) Economic depreciation was $30 million in 2000 and $35 million in 2001.

(viii) Other non-cash expenses were $10 million per year in both 2000 and 2001.

(ix) Interest expense was $4 million in 2000 and $6 million in 2001.

Required:

(a) Estimate the Economic Valued Added (EVA) for Toutplut Inc for both 2000 and 2001. State clearly any assumptions that you make.

Comment upon the performance of the company.

(7 marks)

(b) Briefly discuss the advantages and disadvantages of EVA.

(6 marks)
(Total 13 marks)

13.17 A long-established, highly centralized company has grown to the extent that its chief executive, despite having a good supporting team, is finding difficulty in keeping up with the many decisions of importance in the company.

Consideration is therefore being given to reorganizing the company into profit centres. These would be product divisions, headed by a divisional managing director, who would be responsible for all the divisions' activities relating to its products.

You are required to explain, in outline:

(a) the types of decision areas that should be transferred to the new divisional managing directors if such a reorganization is to achieve its objectives;

(b) the types of decision areas that might reasonably be retained at company head office;

(c) the management accounting problems that might be expected to arise in introducing effective profit centre control.

(20 marks)

13.18 (a) Explain the meaning of each of the undernoted measures which may be used for divisional performance measurement and investment decision-making. Discuss the advantages and problems associated with the use of each.

(i) Return on capital employed.

(ii) Residual income.

(iii) Discounted future earnings.

(9 marks)

(b) Comment on the reasons why the measures listed in (a) above may give conflicting investment decision responses when applied to the same set of data. Use the following figures to illustrate the conflicting responses which may arise:

Additional investment of £60 000 for a 6 year life with nil residual value.

Average net profit per year: £9000 (after depreciation).

Cost of capital: 14%.

Existing capital employed: £300 000 with ROCE of 20%.

(8 marks)

(Solutions should ignore taxation implications.)

(Total 17 marks)

13.19 Residual Income and Return on Investment are commonly used measures of performance. However, they are frequently criticized for placing too great an emphasis on the achievement of short-term results, possibly damaging longer-term performance.

You are required to discuss

(a) the issues involved in the long-term:short-term conflict referred to in the above statement;

(11 marks)

(b) suggestions which have been made to reconcile this difference.

(11 marks)
(Total 22 marks)

Transfer pricing in divisionalized companies

14 In the previous chapter alternative financial measures for evaluating divisional performance were examined. However, all of the financial measure outcomes will be significantly affected when divisions transfer goods and services to each other. The established transfer price is a cost to the receiving division and revenue to the supplying division, which means that whatever transfer price is set, will affect the profitability of each division. In addition, this transfer price will also significantly influence each division's input and output decisions, and thus total company profits.

In this chapter we shall examine the various approaches that can be adopted to arrive at transfer prices between divisions. Although our focus will be on transfer pricing between divisions (i.e. profit or investment centres) transfer pricing can also apply between cost

LEARNING OBJECTIVES

After studying this chapter, you should be able to:

- describe the different purposes of a transfer pricing system;
- identify and describe the five different transfer pricing methods;
- explain why the correct transfer price is the external market price when there is a perfectly competitive market for the intermediate product;
- explain why cost-plus transfer prices will not result in the optimum output being achieved;
- explain the two methods of transfer pricing that have been advocated to resolve the conflicts between the decision-making and performance evaluation objectives;
- describe the additional factors that must be considered when setting transfer prices for multinational transactions;
- describe how optimum transfer prices can be determined when there is no external market or an imperfect external market for the intermediate product.

centres (typically support/service centres) or from cost centres to profit/investment centres. The same basic principles apply as those that apply between divisions, the only difference being that there is no need for a profit element to be included in the transfer price to reimburse the supplying cost centre.

Purposes of transfer pricing

A transfer pricing system can be used to meet the following purposes:

1 To provide information that motivates divisional managers to make good economic decisions. This will happen when actions that divisional managers take to improve the reported profit of their divisions also improves the profit of the company as a whole.

2 To provide information that is useful for evaluating the managerial and economic performance of the divisions.

3 To intentionally move profits between divisions or locations.

4 To ensure that divisional autonomy is not undermined.

Providing information for making good economic decisions

Goods transferred from the supplying division to the receiving division are known as **intermediate products**. The products sold by a receiving division to the outside world are known as **final products**. The objective of the receiving division is to subject the intermediate product to further processing before it is sold as a final product in the outside market. The transfer price of the intermediate product represents a cost to the receiving division and a revenue to the supplying division. Therefore transfer prices are used to determine how much of the intermediate product will be produced by the supplying division and how much will be acquired by the receiving division. In a centralized company the decision as to whether an intermediate product should be sold or processed further is determined by comparing the incremental cost of, and the revenues from, further processing. In a divisionalized organization structure, however, the manager of the receiving division will treat the price at which the intermediate product is transferred as an incremental cost, and this may lead to incorrect decisions being made.

For example, let us assume that the incremental cost of the intermediate product is £100, and the additional further processing costs of the receiving division are £60. The incremental cost of producing the final product will therefore be £160. Let us also assume that the supplying division has a temporary excess capacity which is being maintained in order to meet an expected resurgence in demand and that the market price of the final product is £200. To simplify the illustration, we assume there is no market for the intermediate product. The correct short-term decision would be to convert the intermediate product into the final product. In a centralized company this decision would be taken, but in a divisionalized organization structure where the transfer price for the intermediate product is £150 based on full cost plus a profit margin, the incremental cost of the receiving division will be £210 (£150 + £60). The divisional manager would therefore incorrectly decide not to purchase the intermediate product for further processing. This problem can be overcome if the transfer price is set at the incremental cost of the supplying division, which in this example is £100.

Evaluating divisional performance

When goods are transferred from one division to another, the revenue of the supplying division becomes a cost of the receiving division. Consequently, the prices at which goods are transferred can influence each division's reported profits, and there is a danger that an unsound transfer price will result in a misleading performance measure that may cause divisional managers to believe that the transfer price is affecting their performance rather unfairly. This may lead to disagreement and negative motivational consequences.

Conflict of objectives

Unfortunately, no single transfer price is likely to perfectly serve all of the four specified purposes. They often conflict and managers are forced to make trade-offs. In particular, the decision-making and the performance evaluation purposes may conflict with each other. For example, in some situations the transfer price that motivates the short-run optimal economic decision is marginal cost. If the supplier has excess capacity, this cost will probably equal variable cost. The supplying division will fail to cover any of its fixed costs when transfers are made at variable cost, and will therefore report a loss. Furthermore, if a transfer price equal to variable cost (£100 in the above example) is imposed on the manager of the supplying division, the concept of divisional autonomy and decentralization is undermined. On the other hand, a transfer price that may be satisfactory for evaluating divisional performance (£150 in the above example) may lead divisions to make suboptimal decisions when viewed from the overall company perspective.

Alternative transfer pricing methods

There are five primary types of transfer prices that companies can use to transfer goods and services.

1 **Market-based transfer prices:** These are usually based on the listed price of an identical or similar products or services, the actual price the supplying division sells the intermediate product to external customers (possibly less a discount that reflects the lower selling costs for inter-group transfers), or the price a competitor is offering.

2 **Marginal cost transfer prices:** Most accountants assume that marginal cost can be approximated by short-run variable cost which is interpreted as direct costs plus variable indirect costs.

3 **Full cost transfer prices:** The terms full cost or long-run cost are used to represent the sum of the cost of all of those resources that are committed to a product or service in the long-term. Some firms add an arbitrary mark-up to variable costs in order to cover fixed costs and thus approximate full costs. Such an approach is likely to result in an inaccurate estimate of full cost.

4 **Cost-plus a mark-up transfer prices:** With cost-based transfer prices the supplying divisions do not make any profits on the products or services transferred. Therefore they are not suitable for performance measurement. To overcome this problem a mark-up is added to enable the supplying divisions to earn a profit on inter-divisional transfers.

5 **Negotiated transfer prices:** In some cases transfer prices are negotiated between the managers of the supplying and receiving divisions. Information about the market

prices and marginal or full costs often provide an input into these negotiations, although there is no requirement that they must do so.

Exhibit 14.1 shows the results of surveys of the primary transfer pricing methods used in various countries. This exhibit shows that in the USA transfer prices are used by the vast majority of the firms surveyed. It is apparent from all of the surveys that a small minority (less than 10%) transfer at marginal or variable cost. A significant proportion of firms use each of the other methods with the largest proportions transferring goods or services at market prices or either full cost or full cost plus a mark-up. The following sections describe in detail each of the transfer pricing methods and the circumstances when they are appropriate.

Market-based transfer prices

In most circumstances, where a **perfectly competitive market** for an intermediate product exists it is optimal for both decision-making and performance evaluation purposes to set transfer prices at competitive market prices. A perfectly competitive market exists where the product is homogeneous and no individual buyer or seller can affect the market prices.

When transfers are recorded at market prices divisional performance is more likely to represent the real economic contribution of the division to total company profits. If the supplying division did not exist, the intermediate product would have to be purchased on the outside market at the current market price. Alternatively, if the receiving division did not exist, the intermediate product would have to be sold on the outside market at the current market price. Divisional profits are therefore likely to be similar to the profits that would be calculated if the divisions were separate organizations. Consequently, divisional profitability can be compared directly with the profitability of similar companies operating in the same type of business.

In a perfectly competitive market the supplying division should supply as much as the receiving division requires at the current market price, so long as the incremental cost is lower than the market price. If this supply is insufficient to meet the receiving division's demand, it must obtain additional supplies by purchasing from an outside supplier at the current market price. Alternatively, if the supplying division produces more of the intermediate product than the receiving division requires, the excess can be sold to the outside market at the current market price.

Where the selling costs for internal transfers of the intermediate product are identical with those that arise from sales in the outside market, it will not matter whether the supplying division's output is sold internally or externally. To illustrate this we shall consider two alternatives. First, assume initially that the output of the supplying division is sold *externally* and that the receiving division purchases its requirements *externally*. Now consider a second situation where the output of the intermediate product is transferred *internally* at the market price and is not sold on the outside market. You should now refer to Exhibit 14.2. The aim of this diagram is to show that divisional and total profits are not affected, whichever of these two alternatives is chosen.

Exhibit 14.2 illustrates a situation where the receiving division sells 1000 units of the final product in the external market. The incremental costs of the supplying division for the production of 1000 units of the intermediate product are £5000, with a market price for the output of £8000. The incremental costs of the receiving division for the additional processing of the 1000 units of the intermediate product are £4000. This output can be sold for £18 000. You will see that it does not matter whether the intermediate product is

EXHIBIT 14.1

*Surveys of
company practice*

The studies listed below relate to surveys of transfer pricing practices in various countries. It is apparent from these surveys that variable/marginal costs are not widely used, whereas full cost or full cost plus a mark-up are used extensively. Market price methods are also widely used.

Australian and Canadian Surveys

	Australia Joye and Blayney (1991)	Canada Tang (1992)
Market price-based	13%	34%
Cost-based:		
Variable Costs		6
Full costs		37
Other		3
Total	65	46
Negotiated	11	18
Other	11	2
	100	100

The Canadian survey asked the respondents to name the dominant objective of the transfer pricing system. Approximately 50% stated that it was performance evaluation and one third stated that it was for profit maximization of the consolidated firm.

UK Survey (Drury *et al.*, 1993)

	Extent of use		
	Never/rarely	Sometimes	Often/always
Unit variable cost	94%	4%	2%
Unit full cost	66	13	21
Unit variable cost-plus mark-up	83	6	11
Unit full cost-plus mark-up	55	18	27
Marginal/incremental cost	93	6	1
Market price/adjusted market price	53	14	33
Negotiated	41	29	30
Lump sum payment plus cost per unit transferred	95	4	1

USA Survey (Borkowski, 1990)

Number of Companies Participating 215
Percentage Using Transfer Prices 89.6%

Percentage using transfers on following bases		
Market price		
Full market price	20.2	
Adjusted market price	12.5	32.7
Negotiated		
To external price	13.6	
To manufacturing costs	3.0	
With no restrictions	6.0	22.6

Full cost		
Standard	14.3	
Actual	7.1	
Plus profit based on cost	14.9	
Plus fixed profit	2.4	
Other	2.4	41.1
Variable cost		
Standard	2.4	
Actual	0.6	
Plus contribution based on cost	0.6	
Plus fixed contribution	0.0	
Plus opportunity cost	0.0	3.6
Marginal (incremental) cost		0.0
Mathematical/programming models		0.0
Dual pricing		0.0
Total		100.00

transferred internally or sold externally – profits of each division and total company profits remain unchanged.

This of course assumes that the supplying division can sell all its output either internally or externally at the going market price. If this were not the case then it would be necessary to instruct the receiving division to purchase from the supplying division the quantity that it is prepared to supply at the market price. This is because the receiving division is indifferent to whether it purchases the intermediate product from the supplying division or from the external market.

If the supplying division cannot make a profit in the long run at the current outside market price then the company will be better off not to produce the product internally but to obtain its supply from the external market. Similarly, if the receiving division cannot make a long-run profit when transfers are made at the current market price, it should cease processing this product, and the supplying division should be allowed to sell all its output to the external market. Where there is a competitive market for the intermediate product, the market price can be used to allow the decisions of the supplying and receiving division to be made independently of each other.

The effect of selling expenses

In practice, it is likely that total company profits will be different when the intermediate product is acquired internally or externally. The supplying division will incur selling expenses when selling the intermediate product on the external market, but such expenses may not be incurred on inter-divisional transfers. If the transfer price is set at the current market price, the receiving division will be indifferent to whether the intermediate product is obtained internally or externally. However, if the receiving division purchases the intermediate product externally, the company will be worse off to the extent of the selling expenses incurred by the supplying division in disposing of its output on the external market. In practice, many companies modify the market price rule for pricing inter-divisional transfers and deduct a margin to take account of the savings in selling and collection expenses.

EXHIBIT 14.2

Profit impact using market-based transfer prices

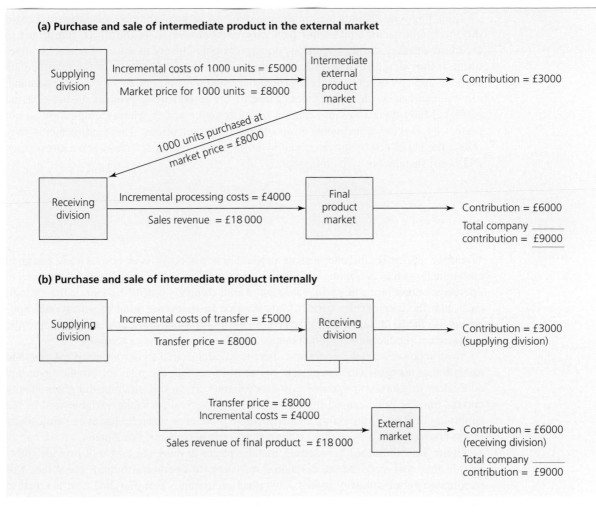

(a) Purchase and sale of intermediate product in the external market

(b) Purchase and sale of intermediate product internally

Other market imperfections

One of the major problems with using market prices is that the market is unlikely to be perfectly competitive. In addition, the transferred product may have special characteristics that differentiate it from other varieties of the same product. The market price for the intermediate product is appropriate only when quality, delivery, discounts and back-up services are identical. Furthermore, it may be possible to purchase the intermediate product in the external market from suppliers who are selling at a temporary distress price that is below total cost but above variable cost. If the supplying division has excess capacity, incorrect decisions may arise because of strict adherence to the market price rule.

For example, suppose that the supplying division has spare capacity and produces an intermediate product at an incremental cost of £1000; the transfer price for this product is set at the external market price of £1600. Now suppose that a supplier of the intermediate product is selling at a temporary distress price of £1500. Given this situation, the manager of the receiving division will prefer to purchase the intermediate product from the external supplier at £1500 than from the supplying division at a cost of £1600. Because the supplying division has spare capacity, the relevant cost of making the product internally is £1000, and the strict adherence to the market price rule can therefore motivate managers to take decisions that are not in the best interests of the company.

The complications indicated in the previous paragraphs arise because the market for the intermediate product is not perfectly competitive. It is therefore important to ascertain whether market conditions do approximate closely to those of perfect competition. If they do, the transfer price should be set at the market price of the intermediate product, and any excess of inter-divisional demand over supply, or supply over demand, can be resolved by the purchase and sale of the intermediate product on the external market. Many companies use market-based transfer prices where competition is not perfect by making adjustments from observed market prices. These adjustments may reflect the belief that the price quoted by an external supplier is a short-run distress price that is not sustainable in the long term.

Marginal cost transfer prices

When the market for the intermediate product is imperfect or even non-existent marginal cost transfer prices can motivate both the supplying and receiving division managers to operate at output levels that will maximize overall company profits. Economic theory indicates that the theoretically correct transfer price to encourage total organizational optimality is, in the absence of capacity constraints, the marginal cost of producing the intermediate product at the optimal output level for the company as a whole.

Most accountants have adopted a short-term perspective to derive marginal cost and assume that marginal cost is constant per unit throughout the relevant output range and equivalent to short-term variable cost (see Chapter 3). In this situation the theoretically correct transfer price can be interpreted as being equivalent to the variable cost of the supplying division of providing an intermediate product or service. However, using short-term variable cost is only optimal when a short-term perspective is adopted.

Figure 14.1 illustrates how setting transfer prices at marginal cost will provide information that will motivate the divisional managers to operate at output levels that will maximize overall company profits. This diagram assumes that marginal cost is equal to variable cost and constant throughout the entire production range. It therefore relates to a short-term time horizon. To keep things simple we shall assume that there is no market for the intermediate product. Note also that the net marginal revenue curve of the final product declines to reflect the fact that to sell more the price must be lowered. The term **net marginal revenue** refers to the marginal revenue of the final product less the marginal conversion costs (excluding the transfer price) incurred by the receiving division. The receiving division will purchase the intermediate product up to the point where net marginal revenue equals its marginal costs, as reflected by the transfer price. It will therefore be the optimal output from the overall company perspective (Q_2) only if the transfer price is set at the marginal cost of the intermediate product or service. If a higher price is set (as indicated by the green line) to cover full cost, or a mark-up is added to marginal cost, then the supplying division will restrict output to the sub-optimal level Q_1.

It is apparent from the surveys of company practice shown in Exhibit 14.1 that less than 10% of the companies transfer goods and services at marginal cost. The major reason for its low use is that when marginal cost is interpreted as being equivalent to variable cost it does not support the profit or investment responsibility structure because it provides poor

FIGURE 14.1   *A comparison of marginal cost and full cost or cost-plus
transfer pricing*

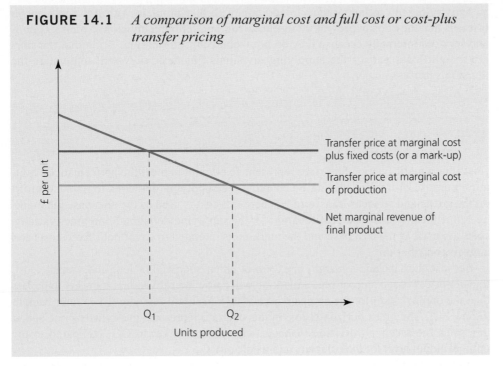

information for evaluating the performance of either the supplying or receiving divisions.
The supplying division will record losses on the capacity allocated to inter-divisional
transfers because it bears the full cost of production but only receives revenues that cover
variable cost. Conversely the profit of the receiving division will be overstated because it
will not bear any of the fixed capacity costs of the supplying division.

A further problem is that marginal costs may not be constant over the entire range of
output because step increases in fixed costs can occur. Measuring marginal cost is also
difficult in practice beyond a short-term period. The low usage of marginal cost transfer
prices suggests that managers reject the short-term interpretation of approximating
marginal costs with variable costs. Instead, they view product-related decisions as long-
range decisions that must reflect long-run pricing considerations and therefore the appropriate marginal cost to use is long-run marginal cost. We shall examine how long-run
marginal cost can be derived later in the chapter.

Full cost transfer prices

Exhibit 14.1 shows that full costs or full cost plus a mark-up are widely used in practice.
Their attraction is that, as indicated above, managers view product-related decisions as
long-run decisions and therefore require a measure of long-run marginal cost. Full costs
attempt to meet this requirement. In addition, they are preferable to short-run variable costs
for performance evaluation purposes since the supplying division can recover the full costs
of production, although no profit will be obtained on the goods or services transferred.

The major problem with full cost transfer prices is that they are often derived from
traditional costing systems which, as was pointed out in Chapter 6, can provide poor estimates of long-run marginal costs. Ideally, full cost transfer prices should be derived from

an activity-based costing system. In addition, a further problem with full cost transfer prices is that they do not provide an incentive for the supplying division to transfer goods and services internally because they do not include a profit margin. If internal transfers are a significant part of the supplying division's business, they will understate the division's profits.

Cost-plus a mark-up transfer prices

Cost-plus a mark-up transfer prices represent an attempt to meet the performance evaluation purpose of transfer pricing by enabling the supplying divisions to obtain a profit on the goods and services transferred. Where full cost is used as the cost base the mark-up is intended to provide a profit margin for the supplying division. Sometimes variable costs are used as the cost base and the mark-up is intended to cover both fixed costs and a profit contribution.

Because they include a margin in excess of either short-run or long-run variable cost, transfer prices based on cost-plus a mark-up will cause inter-divisional transfers to be less than the optimal level for the company as a whole. You will see why if you refer back to Figure 14.1. The green horizontal line in this diagram represents the transfer price and at this price the receiving division manager will restrict output to OQ_1 compared to the optimal output level for the company as a whole of OQ_2.

A further problem arises if we extend our analysis beyond two divisions to several divisions. If the first division in the process transfers goods to the second division at cost plus 20%, and the goods received from the second division are further processed and transferred at cost plus 20% to a third division, and so on, then the percentage margin becomes enormous by the time a mark-up is added by the final division in the process.

Negotiated transfer prices

The difficulties encountered in establishing a sound system of transfer pricing have led to suggestions that negotiated transfer prices should be used. Negotiated transfer prices are most appropriate in situations where some market imperfections exist for the intermediate product. When there are imperfections in the market, the respective divisional managers must have the freedom to buy and sell outside the company to enable them to engage in a bargaining process. It is claimed that if this is the case then the friction and bad feeling that may arise from a centrally controlled market transfer price will be eliminated without incurring a mis-allocation of resources.

There are strong arguments for believing that in certain situations, if divisions are allowed to bargain freely with each other, they will usually make decisions that will maximize total company profits – this is of course assuming that managers are competent and know how to use the accounting information. For negotiation to work effectively it is important that managers have equal bargaining power. If the receiving division has many sourcing possibilities for the intermediate product or service, but the supplying division has limited outlets, the bargaining power of the managers will be unequal. Unequal bargaining power can also occur if the transfers are a relatively small proportion of the business for one of the divisions and a relatively large proportion of the business of the other. The manager of the division where transfers are a small proportion of business has considerably more bargaining power because he, or she, will not suffer serious consequences if agreement is not reached on the proposed inter-divisional transfers.

It is important to note that negotiated transfer prices are inappropriate where there is a perfect market for the intermediate product, since in a perfect market situation transfer prices can be based on the competitive market price without the need for the managers to engage in a negotiating process. At the other extreme, where there is no market for the intermediate product, it is most unlikely that managers can engage in meaningful negotiation. Negotiated transfer prices are therefore best suited to situations where there is an imperfect external market for the intermediate product or service. Negotiated transfer prices do, however, suffer from the following limitations:

- because the agreed transfer price can depend on the negotiating skills and bargaining power of the managers involved, the final outcome may not be close to being optimal;
- they can lead to conflict between divisions and the resolution of such conflicts may require top management to mediate;
- measurement of divisional profitability can be dependent on the negotiating skills of managers, who may have unequal bargaining power;
- they are time-consuming for the managers involved, particularly where a large number of transactions are involved.

Even if negotiated prices do not result in an optimum output level, the motivational advantages of giving managers full independence over their input and output decisions may lead to increased profits that outweigh the loss of profits from negotiated non-optimal transfer prices.

Marginal cost plus opportunity cost

Setting transfer prices at the marginal (i.e. incremental) cost of the supplying division per unit transferred plus the opportunity cost per unit of the supplying division is often cited as a general rule that should lead to optimum decisions for the company as a whole. Opportunity cost is defined as the contribution forgone by the supplying division from transferring internally the intermediate product. Assuming that marginal cost is equivalent to variable cost, applying this rule will result in the transfer price being set at the variable cost per unit when there is no market for the intermediate product. Why? If the facilities are dedicated to the production of the intermediate product they will have no alternative use, so the opportunity cost will be zero.

Consider now a situation where there is a perfectly competitive external market for the intermediate product. Assume that the market price for the intermediate product is £20 per unit and the variable cost per unit of output is £5. If the supplying division has no spare capacity the contribution forgone from transferring the intermediate product is £15. Adding this to the variable cost per unit will result in the transfer price being set at the market price of £20 per unit. What is the transfer price if the supplying division has temporary spare capacity? In this situation there will be no forgone contribution and the transfer price will be set at the variable cost per unit of £5.

You should have noted that applying the above general rule leads to the same transfer price as was recommended earlier in this chapter. In other words, if there is a perfectly competitive external market for the intermediate product, the market price is the optimal transfer price. When there is no market for the intermediate product, transfers should be made at the marginal cost per unit of output of the intermediate product. Thus, the general rule is merely a restatement of the principles that have been established earlier. The major problem with applying this general rule is that it is difficult to apply in more complex situations such as when there is an imperfect market for the intermediate product.

An illustration of transfer pricing

The data used in Example 14.1 will now be used to illustrate the impact that transfer prices can have on divisional profitability and decision-making. You should now refer to Example 14.1.

At *the full cost plus a mark-up transfer price* of £35 the profit computations for each division will be as follows:

Oslo Division (Supplying division)

Output level (units) profit/(loss)	Transfer price revenues	Variable costs	Fixed costs	Total
1000	35 000	11 000	60 000	(36 000)
2000	70 000	22 000	60 000	(12 000)
3000	105 000	33 000	60 000	12 000
4000	140 000	44 000	60 000	36 000
5000	175 000	55 000	60 000	60 000
6000	210 000	66 000	60 000	84 000

Bergen Division (Receiving division)

Output level (units) profit/(loss)	Total revenues	Variable costs	Total cost of transfers	Fixed costs	Total
1000	100 000	7 000	35 000	90 000	(32 000)
2000	180 000	14 000	70 000	90 000	6 000
3000	240 000	21 000	105 000	90 000	24 000
4000	280 000	28 000	140 000	90 000	22 000
5000	300 000	35 000	175 000	90 000	0
6000	300 000	42 000	210 000	90 000	(42 000)

The supplying division maximizes profits at an output level of 6000 units whereas the receiving division maximizes profits at an output level of 3000 units. The receiving division will therefore purchase 3000 units from the supplying division. This is because the Bergen division will compare its net marginal revenue with the transfer price and expand output as long as the net marginal revenue of the additional output exceeds the transfer price. Remember that net marginal revenue was defined as the marginal revenue from the sale of the final product less the marginal conversion costs (excluding the transfer price). The calculations are as follows:

Units	Net marginal revenue (£)
1000	93 000 (100 000 – 7000)
2000	73 000 (80 000 – 7000)
3000	53 000 (60 000 – 7000)
4000	33 000 (40 000 – 7000)
5000	13 000 (20 000 – 7000)
6000	–7 000 (0 – 7000)

Faced with a transfer price of £35 000 per 1000 units the Bergen division will not expand output beyond 3000 units because the transfer price paid for each batch exceeds the net marginal revenue.

EXAMPLE 14.1

The Oslo division and the Bergen division are divisions within the Baltic Group. One of the products manufactured by the Oslo division is an intermediate product for which there is no external market. This intermediate product is transferred to the Bergen division where it is converted into a final product for sale on the external market. One unit of the intermediate product is used in the production of the final product. The expected units of the final product which the Bergen division estimates it can sell at various selling prices are as follows:

Net selling price (£)	Quantity sold Units
100	1000
90	2000
80	3000
70	4000
60	5000
50	6000

The costs of each division are as follows:

(£)	Oslo (£)	Bergen (£)
Variable cost per unit	11	7
Fixed costs attributable to the products	60 000	90 000

The transfer price of the intermediate product has been set at £35 based on a full cost plus a mark-up.

Let us now look at the profit at the different output levels for the company as a whole. Note that these calculations do not incorporate the transfer price since it represents inter-company trading with the revenue from the supplying division cancelling out the cost incurred by the receiving division.

Whole company profit computations

Output level (units)	Total revenues	Company variable costs	Company fixed costs	Company profit/(loss)
1000	100 000	18 000	150 000	(68 000)
2000	180 000	36 000	150 000	(6 000)
3000	240 000	54 000	150 000	36 000
4000	280 000	72 000	150 000	58 000
5000	300 000	90 000	150 000	60 000
6000	300 000	108 000	150 000	42 000

The profit maximizing output for the company as a whole is 5000 units. Therefore the current transfer pricing system does not motivate the divisional managers to operate at the optimum output level for the company as a whole.

To induce overall company optimality the *transfer price must be set at the marginal cost of the supplying division*, which over the time horizon and output levels under consideration, is the unit variable cost of £11 per unit. Therefore the transfer price for each batch of 1000 units would be £11 000. The receiving division will expand output as long as net marginal revenue exceeds the transfer price. Now look at the net marginal revenue that we calculated for the receiving division. You will see that the net marginal revenue from expanding output from 4000 to 5000 units is £13 000 and the transfer price that the receiving division must pay to acquire this batch of 1000 units is £11 000. Therefore expanding the output will increase the profits of the supplying division. Will the manager of the receiving division be motivated to expand output from 5000 to 6000 units? The answer is no because the net marginal revenue (–£7000) is less than the transfer price of purchasing the 1000 units.

Setting the transfer price at the unit marginal (variable) cost of the supplying division will motivate the divisional managers to operate at the optimum output level for the company as a whole provided that the supplying division manager is instructed to meet the demand of the receiving division at this transfer price. Although the variable cost transfer price encourages overall company optimality it is a poor measure of divisional performance. The supplying division manager will be credited with transfer price revenues of £11 000 per 1000 units. If you look back at the profit computations for the Oslo division you will see that the transfer price revenues will be identical to the variable cost column and therefore a loss equal to the fixed costs of £60 000 will be reported for all output levels. In the short-term the fixed costs are unavoidable and therefore the divisional manager is no worse off since these fixed costs will be still incurred but in the longer-term some, or all of them, may be avoidable and the manager would not wish to produce the intermediate product. The performance measure will overstate the performance of the receiving division because all of the contribution (sales less variable costs) from the sale of the final product will be credited to the manager of the receiving division.

Let us now consider a *full cost transfer price without the mark-up*. We need to estimate unit fixed costs at the planning stage for making decisions relating to output levels. You will also recall from Chapter 5 that it was pointed out that predetermined fixed overhead rates should be established. Let us assume that the 5000 units optimal output level for the company as a whole is used to determine the fixed overhead rate per unit. Therefore the fixed cost per unit for the intermediate product will be £12 per unit (£60 000 fixed costs/5000 units) giving a full cost of £23 (£11 variable cost plus £12 fixed cost). If the transfer price is set at £23 per unit (i.e. £23 000 per 1000 batch) the receiving division manager will expand output as long as net marginal revenues exceeds the transfer price. If you refer to the net marginal revenue schedule on page 408 you will see that the receiving division manager will choose to purchase 4000 units. The manager will choose not to expand output to the 5000 units optimal level for the company as a whole because the transfer cost of £23 000 exceeds the net marginal revenue of £13 000. Also at the selected output level of 4000 units the total transfer price revenues of the receiving division will be £92 000 (4000 units at £23) but you will see from the profit calculations for the Oslo division that the total costs are £104 000 (£44 000 + £60 000). Therefore the supplying division will report a loss because all of its fixed costs have not been recovered. Hence the transfer price is suitable for neither performance evaluation nor ensuring that optimal output decisions are made.

Would the managers be able to *negotiate a transfer price* that meets the decision-making and performance evaluation requirements? If the manager of the supplying division cannot avoid the fixed costs in the short-run he or she will have no bargaining power because there is no external market for the intermediate product and would accept any price as long as it is not below variable cost. Meaningful negotiation is not possible. If the fixed costs are avoidable the manager has some negotiating power since he or she can avoid £60 000 by not producing the intermediate product. The manager will try and negotiate a selling price in excess of full cost. If an output level of 5000 units is used to calculate the full cost the unit cost from our earlier calculations was £23 and the manager will try and negotiate a price in excess of £23. If you examine the net marginal revenue of the receiving division you will see that the manager of the receiving division will not expand output to 5000 units if the transfer price is set above £23 per unit. As indicated earlier negotiation is only likely to work when there is an external market for the intermediate market.

We can conclude from this illustration that to ensure overall company optimality the transfer price must be set at the marginal cost of the supplying division. Our analysis has focused on the short term, a period during which we have considered that fixed costs are irrelevant and unavoidable. In the longer term fixed costs are relevant and avoidable and thus represent a marginal cost that should be considered for decision-making. Thus for long-term decisions marginal cost should incorporate avoidable fixed costs but we have noted in earlier chapters that they should not be unitized since this is misleading because it gives the impression that they are variable with output. To incorporate avoidable fixed costs within long-run marginal cost they should be added as a lump-sum to short-run marginal (variable) costs. This is a feature of one of the proposals that we shall look at in the next section.

Proposals for resolving transfer pricing conflicts

Our discussion so far has indicated that in the absence of a perfect market for the intermediate product none of the transfer pricing methods can perfectly meet both the decision-making and performance evaluation requirements and also not undermine divisional autonomy. It has been suggested that if the external market for the intermediate product does not approximate closely those of perfect competition, then if long-run marginal cost can be accurately estimated, transfers at marginal cost should motivate decisions that are optimal from the overall company's perspective. However, transfers at short-run marginal cost are unsuitable for performance evaluation since they do not provide an incentive for the supplying division to transfer goods and services internally. This is because they do not contain a profit margin for the supplying division. Central headquarters intervention may be necessary to instruct the supplying division to meet the receiving division's demand at the marginal cost of the transfers. Thus, divisional autonomy will be undermined. Transferring at cost plus a mark-up creates the opposite conflict. Here the transfer price meets the performance evaluation requirement but will not induce managers to make optimal decisions.

To resolve the above conflicts the following transfer pricing methods have been suggested:

1 adopt a dual-rate transfer pricing system;
2 transfer at a marginal cost plus a fixed lump-sum fee.

Dual-rate transfer pricing system

Dual-rate transfer pricing uses two separate transfer prices to price each inter-divisional transaction. For example, the supplying division may receive the full cost plus a mark-up on each transaction and the receiving division may be charged at the marginal cost of the transfers. The former transfer price is intended to approximate the market price of the goods or services transferred. Exhibit 14.3, which relates to inter-divisional trading between two divisions in respect of 100 000 units on an intermediate product, is used to illustrate the application of a dual-rate transfer pricing system. You will see that if the transfer price is set

		(£)	(£)

EXHIBIT 14.3

Projected financial statement from inter-group trading

	(£)	(£)
Sale of final product: 100 000 units at £50		5 000 000
Marginal costs:		
Supplying division processing costs (100 000 units at £10)	1 000 000	
Receiving division conversion costs (100 000 units at £30)	3 000 000	4 000 000
Total contribution from inter-divisional trading		1 000 000

at the supplying division's marginal cost of £10 per unit for the intermediate product, the supplying division will be credited with a zero contribution from the transfers (£1 million transfers less £1 million marginal processing costs), and all of the total contribution of £1 million from inter-divisional trading will be assigned to the receiving division.

Dual-rate transfer pricing can be implemented by setting the transfer price to be charged to the receiving division at the marginal cost of the supplying division (£10 per unit). To keep things simple here, the transfer price that the supplying division receives is set at marginal cost plus 50%, giving a price of £15. It is assumed that the mark-up added will be sufficient to cover the supplying division's fixed costs and also provide a profit contribution. Therefore the receiving division manager will use the marginal cost of the supplying division which should ensure that decisions are made that are optimal from the company's perspective. The transfer price should also meet the performance evaluation requirements of the supplying division since each unit transferred generates a profit. Thus the supplying division manager is motivated to transfer the intermediate product internally. The reported outcomes for each division using the above dual-rate transfer prices, and the information shown in Exhibit 14.3 would be as follows:

Supplying division	(£)	*Receiving division*	(£)
Transfers to the supplying division at £15 (100 000 units at £10 plus 50%)	1 500 000	Sales of the final product at £50 (100 000 units)	5 000 000
Less: marginal processing costs	1 000 000	Less marginal costs:	
		Supplying division transfers (100 000 units at £10)	(1 000 000)
		Conversion costs (100 000 units at £30)	(3 000 000)
Profit contribution	500 000	Profit contribution	1 000 000

Note that the contribution for the company as a whole shown in Exhibit 14.3 is less than the sum of the divisional profits by £500 000, but this can be resolved by a simple accounting adjustment.

Dual-rate transfer prices are not widely used in practice for several reasons. First, the use of different transfer prices causes confusion, particularly when the transfers spread beyond two divisions. Secondly, they are considered to be artificial. Thirdly, they reduce divisional incentives to compete effectively. For example, the supplying division can easily generate internal sales to the receiving divisions when they are charged at marginal cost. This protects them from competition and gives them little incentive to improve their productivity. Finally, top-level managers do not like to double count internal profits because this can result in misleading information and create a false impression of divisional profits.

Marginal costs plus a fixed lump-sum fee

A solution that has been proposed where the market for the intermediate product is imperfect or non-existent, and where the supplying division has no capacity constraints, is to price all transfers at the short-run marginal cost and for the supplying division to also charge the receiving division a fixed fee for the privilege of obtaining these transfers at short-run marginal cost. This approach is sometimes described as a **two-part transfer pricing system**. With this system, the receiving division acquires additional units of the intermediate product at the marginal cost of production. Therefore when it equates its marginal costs with its marginal revenues to determine the optimum profit-maximizing output level, it will use the appropriate marginal costs of the supplying division. The supplying division can recover its fixed costs and earn a profit on the inter-divisional transfers through the fixed fee charged each period. The fixed fee is intended to compensate the supplying division for tying up some of its fixed capacity for providing products or services that are transferred internally. The fixed fee should cover a share of fixed costs of the supplying division and also provide a return on capital. For example, it can be based on the receiving division's budgeted use of the average capacity of the supplying division. Therefore if a particular receiving division plans to use 25% of a supplying division's average capacity, the division would be charged 25% of the fixed costs plus a further charge to reflect the required return on capital. The fixed fee plus the short-run marginal cost represents an estimate of long-run marginal cost.

The advantage of this approach is that transfers will be made at the marginal cost of the supplying division, and both divisions should also be able to report profits from inter-divisional trading. Furthermore, the receiving divisions are made aware, and charged for the full cost of obtaining intermediate products from other divisions, through the two components of the two-part transfer pricing system.

If you refer back to Example 14.1 you will see that this proposal would result in a transfer price at the short-run marginal (variable) cost of £11 per unit for the intermediate product plus a fixed fee lump-sum payment of £60 000 to cover the fixed costs of the capacity allocated to producing the intermediate product. In addition, a fixed sum to reflect the required return on the capital employed would be added to the £60 000. Adopting this approach the receiving division will use the short-run variable cost to equate with its net marginal revenue and choose to purchase the optimal output level for the company as a whole (5000 units). For longer-term decisions the receiving division will made aware that the revenues must be sufficient to cover the full cost of producing the intermediate product (£11 unit variable cost plus £60 000 fixed costs plus the opportunity cost of capital). When the lump-sum fixed fee is added to the short-run transfer price (£11 per unit) you will see that the supplying division will report a profit at all output levels.

International transfer pricing

So far we have concentrated on domestic transfer pricing. International transfer pricing is concerned with the prices that an organization uses to transfer products between divisions in different countries. The rise of multinational organizations introduces additional issues that must be considered when setting transfer prices.

When the supplying and the receiving divisions are located in different countries with different taxation rates, and the taxation rates in one country are much lower than those in

How a multinational pharmaceutical company solved its transfer pricing problems using ABC

Teva Pharmaceutical Industries Ltd reorganized its pharmaceutical operations into decentralized cost and profit centres. Teva's proposed a transfer pricing system based on marginal costs. But the proposed transfer pricing system generated a storm of controversy. First, some executives observed that the marketing divisions would report extremely high profits because they were being charged for the variable costs only. Second, the operations division would get 'credit' only for the variable expenses. There would be little pressure and motivation to control non-variable expenses. Third, if Teva's plants were less efficient than outside manufacturers of the pharmaceutical products, the marginal cost transfer price would give the marketing divisions no incentive to shift their source of supply. An alternative approach had to be found.

Teva's managers considered, but rejected, several traditional methods for establishing a new transfer pricing system. Market price was not feasible because no market existed for Teva's manufactured and packaged pharmaceutical products that had not been marketed to customers. A full cost calculation was rejected because the traditional methods for allocating overhead did not capture the actual cost structure in Teva's plants. Senior executives also believed strongly that negotiated transfer prices would lead to endless arguments among managers in the different divisions, which would consume excessive time on non-productive discussions.

Tava solved its transfer pricing problem by using ABC. Transfer prices are calculated in two different procedures. The first one assigns unit and batch-level costs, and the second assigns product-specific and plant-level costs. The marketing divisions are charged for unit-level costs (principally materials and labour) based on the actual quantities of each individual product they acquire. In addition, they are charged batch-level costs based on the actual number of production and packaging batches of each product they order. The product-specific and plant-level expenses are charged to marketing divisions annually in lump sums based on budgeted information.

What about unused capacity? To foster a sense of responsibility among marketing managers for the cost of supplying capacity resources, Teva charges the marketing division that experienced the decline in demand a lump-sum assignment for the cost of maintaining the unused production capacity in an existing line. When a marketing division initiates an increment in production capacity, it bears the costs of all the additional resources supplied. At that point, each marketing division would be charged based on its percentage of practical capacity used. The assignment of the plant-level costs receives much attention, particularly from the managers of the marketing divisions. They want to verify that these costs do indeed stay 'fixed' and don't creep upward each period. The marketing managers make sure that increases in plant-level costs occur only when they request a change in production capacity. The responsibility for the fixed cost increment is then clearly assignable to the requesting division.

Marketing managers now distinguish between products that cover all manufacturing costs versus those that cover only the unit and batch-level expenses but not their annual product-sustaining and plant-level expenses. Because of the assignment of unused capacity expenses to the responsible marketing division, the marketing managers incorporate information about available capacity when they make decisions about pricing, product mix and product introduction.

Source: Adapted from Kaplan R.S., Weiss, D. and Deseh, E. (1997) Transfer pricing with ABC, *Management Accounting (USA),* May, pp. 20–8.

the other, it would be in the company's interest if most of the profits were allocated to the division operating in the low taxation country. For example, consider an organization that manufactures products in Country A, which has a marginal tax rate of 25% and sells those products to Country B, which has a marginal tax rate of 40%. It is in the company's best interests to locate most of its profits in Country A, where the tax rate is lowest. Therefore it will wish to use the highest possible transfer price so that the receiving division operating in a Country B will have higher costs and report lower profits whereas the supplying division operating in Country A will be credited with higher revenues and thus report the higher profits. In many multinational organizations, the taxation issues outweigh other transfer pricing issues and the dominant consideration in the setting of transfer prices is the minimization of global taxes.

Taxation authorities in each country are aware that companies can use the transfer pricing system to manipulate the taxable profits that are declared in different countries and investigate the transfer pricing mechanisms of companies to ensure that they are not using the transfer pricing system to avoid paying local taxes. For example, in the UK the Income and Corporate Taxes Act 1988, Section 770 and the Finance Act 1998 (Chapter 36 – Schedules 16 and 17) deal with international transfer pricing issues. In an attempt to provide a world-wide consensus on the pricing of international intra-firm transactions the Organization for Economic Co-operation and Development issued a guideline statement in 1995 (OECD, Paris, 1995). This document is important because the taxation authorities in most countries have used it as the basis for regulating transfer pricing behaviour of international intra-firm transactions. The OECD guidelines are based on the requirement that transfer prices should be set using the arm's length price principle, which relates to the price that would have resulted if the prices actually used had been between two unrelated parties.

It would appear that multinational companies should use two transfer pricing systems – one for internal purposes based on our discussion in the earlier part of this chapter and another for taxation purposes. However, evidence of two transfer pricing systems is likely to attract the attention of the taxation authorities. It is easier for companies to claim that they are not manipulating profits to evade taxes if they use the same transfer pricing method for taxation and internal purposes. For this reason, and the greater simplicity, multinational companies tend to use the same transfer pricing method for both domestic and international transfers.

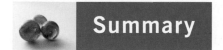

Summary

The following items relate to the learning objectives listed at the beginning of the chapter.

● **Describe the different purposes of a transfer pricing system.**

Transfer pricing can be used for the following purposes: (a) to provide information that motivates divisional managers to make good economic decisions; (b) to provide information that is useful for evaluating the managerial and economic performance of a division; (c) to intentionally move profits between divisions or locations; and (d) to ensure that divisional autonomy is not undermined.

● **Identify and describe the five different transfer pricing methods.**

The five main transfer pricing methods are (a) market-based transfer prices; (b) marginal cost transfer prices; (c) full cost transfer prices; (d) cost plus a mark-up transfer prices; and (e) negotiated transfer prices.

Governments around the world are scrabbling for scarce corporate taxes

In early January, the Inland Revenue Service (IRS) in the USA slapped GlaxoSmithKline, a big British drugs company, with a $5.2 billion bill, claiming that Glaxo Wellcome underpaid taxes on profits made in America from 1989 to 1996. Even though Glaxo had paid taxes on its profits in Britain, and although there is a 'double-taxation' agreement between Britain and America, which means that a company should not have to pay tax on the same profits in both countries, the IRS decided that much of this profit had, in fact, been made in America. GlaxoSmithKline is to fight the tax bill in court.

Whatever the outcome, the prospect of being taxed twice on the same profits has sent a shiver through the tax departments of multinationals everywhere. A tax partner at one big accounting firm says that 'transfer pricing' is the biggest worry for tax directors at the overwhelming majority of big companies. Transfer pricing is the method used by multinational firms to value goods and services bought and sold among subsidiaries, and is a big determinant of the profits and thus taxes paid in a given country. To cope with taxation issues arising from transfer pricing the big accounting firms are beefing up their transfer-pricing departments. In Britain alone, the combined numbers employed by the four biggest accounting firms in transfer pricing has tripled in recent years.

According to a United Nations agency an extraordinary 60 per cent of international trade is within multinationals, that is firms trading with themselves. Many have global brands, global research and development, and regional profit centres. The only reason for preparing national accounts is that tax authorities require it. But it is hard to say quite where global firms' profits are generated.

Navigating this mishmash of regulations is no easy task. Transfer prices are very tricky. Most countries set them at 'arm's length' – that is the price an independent party would pay for a given service or product. Although the principle is a nice one, the practice is complicated, particularly because companies are increasingly service-oriented and rely more on brands, intellectual property and other hard-to-price intangibles.

Transfer pricing is therefore open to manipulation. A report by America's Senate in 2001 claimed that multinationals evaded up to $45 billion in American taxes in 2000. Whatever the truth of this claim, some of the report's details were eye-catching: one firm sold toothbrushes between subsidiaries for $5655 each. Moreover, there is a mound of evidence, says James Hines, a tax expert at the University of Michigan, that shows that international companies tend to report higher taxable profits in countries where taxes are lower. Yet, as he says, this is not necessarily illegal or bad. Companies owe it to their shareholders to avoid paying unnecessary taxes. The trouble is that one person's abuse is another's smart planning. And the tension between those two views is likely to increase.

Source: The Economist, 31 January, 2004, pp. 71–2.

● **Explain why the correct transfer price is the external market price when there is a perfectly competitive market for the intermediate product.**

If there is a perfectly competitive market for the intermediate product transfers recorded at market prices are likely to represent the real economic contribution to total company profits. If the supplying division did not exist, the intermediate product would have to be purchased on the outside market at the current market price. Alternatively, if the receiving division did not exist, the intermediate product would have to be sold on the outside market at the current market price. Divisional profits are therefore likely to be similar to the profits that would be calculated if the divisions were separate organizations. For decision-making, if the receiving division does not acquire the intermediate product internally it would be able to acquire the product at the competitive external market price. Similarly, if the supplying division does transfer internally it will be able to sell the product at the external market price. Thus, the market price represents the opportunity cost of internal transfers.

● **Explain why cost-plus transfer prices will not result in the optimum output being achieved.**

If cost-plus transfer prices are used, the receiving division will determine its optimal output at the point where the marginal cost of its transfers is equal to its net marginal revenue (i.e. marginal revenue less marginal conversion costs, excluding the transfer price). However, the marginal cost of the transfers (i.e. the cost-plus transfer price) will be in excess of the marginal cost of producing the intermediate product for the company as a whole. Thus, marginal cost will be overstated and the receiving division manager will restrict output to the point where net marginal revenue equals the transfer price, rather than the marginal cost to the company of producing the intermediate product.

● **Explain the two methods of transfer pricing that have been advocated to resolve the conflicts between the decision-making and performance evaluation objectives.**

To overcome the decision-making and performance evaluation conflicts that can occur with cost-based transfer pricing two methods have been proposed – a dual-rate transfer pricing system and a two-part transfer pricing system. With a dual rate transfer pricing system the receiving division is charged with the marginal cost of the intermediate product and the supplying division is credited with the full cost per unit plus a profit margin. Therefore, the receiving division should choose the output level at which the marginal cost of the intermediate product is equal to the net marginal revenue of the final product. Also, the supplying division will earn a profit on inter-divisional transfers. Any inter-divisional profits are written off by an accounting adjustment. The two-part transfer pricing system involves transfers being made at the marginal cost per unit of output of the supplying division plus a lump-sum fixed fee charged by the supplying division to the receiving division for the use of the capacity allocated to the intermediate product. This transfer pricing system should also motivate the receiving division to choose the optimal output level and enable the supplying division to obtain a profit on inter-divisional trading.

● **Describe the additional factors that must be considered when setting transfer prices for multinational transactions.**

When divisions operate in different countries, taxation implications can be a dominant influence. The aim is to set transfer prices at levels which will ensure that most of the profits are allocated to divisions operating in low taxation countries. However, taxation authorities in the countries where the divisions are located and the OECD have introduced guidelines and legislation to ensure that companies do not use the transfer prices for taxation manipulation purposes.

● **Describe how optimum transfer prices can be determined when there is no external market or an imperfect external market for the intermediate product.**

The theoretically correct transfer price for both of the above situations, when there are no capacity constraints, is the marginal cost of producing the intermediate product at the optimum output level for the company as a whole. This chapter has illustrated how the optimum transfer price can be determined when there is no market for the intermediate product. For an illustration of how the optimum transfer price can be determined when there is an imperfect market for the intermediate product, you should refer to Drury (2004, Chapter 21).

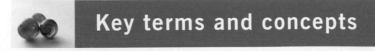

Key terms and concepts

cost-plus a mark-up transfer prices (p. 399)
dual-rate transfer pricing (p. 411)
final products (p. 398)
full cost transfer prices (p. 399)
intermediate products (p. 398)
marginal cost transfer prices (p. 399)

market-based transfer prices (p. 399)
negotiated transfer prices (p. 399)
net marginal revenue (p. 404)
perfectly competitive market (p. 400)
two-part transfer pricing system (p. 413)

Assessment material

Review questions

The review questions are short questions that enable you to assess your understanding of the main topics included in the chapter. The numbers in parentheses provide you with the page numbers to refer to if you cannot answer a specific question.

Review problems

The review problems are more complex and require you to relate and apply the chapter content to various business problems. The multiple-choice questions are the least demanding and normally take less than 10 minutes to complete. Fully worked solutions to the review problems are provided in a separate section at the end of the book. Further review problems for this chapter are available on the accompanying website, www.drury-online.com. The answers to these problems are available for lecturers on the lecturer's password-protected section of the website.

Case studies

The website also includes over 30 case study problems. A list of these cases is provided on page 491–93.

Review questions

14.1 Distinguish between intermediate products and final products. (*p. 398*)

14.2 Explain the four purposes for which transfer pricing can be used. (*pp. 398–99*)

14.3 Explain why a single transfer pricing method cannot serve all four purposes. (*p. 399*)

14.4 If an external, perfectly competitive market exists for an intermediate product what should be the transfer price? Why? (*pp. 400–402*)

14.5 Define the term 'net marginal revenue'. (*p. 404*)

14.6   If there is no external market for the intermediate product what is the optimal transfer price? Why? (*pp. 404–5*)

14.7   Why are full cost and cost-plus a mark-up transfer prices unlikely to result in the optimum output? (*pp. 405–6*)

14.8   Why are marginal cost transfer prices not widely used in practice? (*p. 405*)

14.9   Why are transfer prices based on full cost widely used in practice? (*pp. 405–6*)

14.10   Discuss the advantages and disadvantages of negotiated transfer prices. (*pp. 406–7*)

14.11   What are the circumstances that favour the use of negotiated transfer prices? (*pp. 406–7*)

14.12   Describe the two proposals that have been recommended for resolving transfer pricing conflicts. (*pp. 411–12*)

14.13   What are the special considerations that must be taken into account with international transfer pricing? (*pp. 413–15*)

14.14   When there is an imperfect market for the intermediate product what is the optimal transfer price? (*pp. 417–18*)

Review problems

14.15   X plc, a manufacturing company, has two divisions: Division A and Division B. Division A produces one type of product, ProdX, which it transfers to Division B and also sells externally. Division B has been approached by another company which has offered to supply 2500 units of ProdX for £35 each.

The following details for Division A are available:

	£
Sales revenue	
Sales to Division B @ £40 per unit	400 000
External sales @ £45 per unit	270 000
Less:	
Variable cost @ £22 per unit	352 000
Fixed costs	100 000
Profit	218 000

If Division B decides to buy from the other company, the impact of the decision on the profits of Division A and X plc, assuming external sales of ProdX cannot be increased, will be

	Division A	X plc
A	£12 500 decrease	£12 500 decrease
B	£15 625 decrease	£12 500 increase
C	£32 500 decrease	£32 500 increase
D	£45 000 decrease	£32 500 decrease
E	£45 000 decrease	£45 000 decrease

(*3 marks*)

14.16   Division A transfers 100 000 units of a component to Division B each year.

The market price of the component is £25.

Division A's variable cost is £15 per unit.

Division A's fixed costs are £500 000 each year.

What price would be credited to Division A for each component that it transfers to Division B under

(i)   dual pricing (based on marginal cost and market price)?

(ii) two-part tariff pricing (where the Divisions have agreed that the fixed fee will be £200 000)?

	Dual pricing	Two-part tariff pricing
A	£15	£15
B	£25	£15
C	£15	£17
D	£25	£17
E	£15	£20

(*2 marks*)

14.17   **Determining optimal transfer prices for three different scenarios**

Manuco Ltd has been offered supplies of special ingredient Z at a transfer price of £15 per kg by Helpco Ltd which is part of the same group of companies. Helpco Ltd processes and sells special ingredient Z to customers external to the group at £15 per kg. Helpco Ltd bases its transfer price on cost plus 25% profit mark-up. Total cost has been estimated as 75% variable and 25% fixed.

Required:

Discuss the transfer prices at which Helpco Ltd should offer to transfer special ingredient Z to Manuco Ltd in order that group profit maximizing decisions may be taken on financial grounds in each of the following situations:

(i)   Helpco Ltd has an external market for all of its production of special ingredient Z at a selling price of £15 per kg. Internal transfers to Manuco Ltd would enable £1.50 per kg of variable packing cost to be avoided.

(ii) Conditions are as per (i) but Helpco Ltd has production capacity for 3000 kg of special ingredient Z for which no external market is available.

(iii) Conditions are as per (ii) but Helpco Ltd has an alternative use for some of its spare production capacity. This alternative use is equivalent to 2000 kg of special ingredient Z and would earn a contribution of £6000.

(*13 marks*)

14.18   **Impact of cost-plus transfer price on decision-making and divisional profits**

Enormous Engineering (EE) plc is a large multidivisional engineering company having interests in a wide variety of product markets. The Industrial Products Division (IPD) sells component parts to consumer appliance manufacturers, both inside and outside the company. One such part, a motor unit, it sells solely to external customers, but buys the motor itself internally from the Electric Motor Division. The Electric Motor Division (EMD) makes the motor to IPD specifications and it does not expect to be able to sell it to any other customers.

In preparing the 2001 budgets IPD estimated the number of motor units it expects to be able to sell at various prices as follows:

Price (ex works) (£)	Quantity sold (units)
50	1000
40	2000
35	3000
30	4000
25	6000
20	8000

It then sought a quotation from EMD, who offered to supply the motors at £16 each based on the following estimate:

	(£)
Materials and bought-in parts	2
Direct labour costs	4
Factory overhead (150% of direct labour costs)	6
Total factory cost	12
Profit margin ($33\frac{1}{3}$% on factory cost)	4
Quoted price	£16

Factory overhead costs are fixed. All other costs are variable.

Although it considered the price quoted to be on the high side, IPD nevertheless believed that it could still sell the completed unit at a profit because it incurred costs of only £4 (material £1 and direct labour £3) on each unit made. It therefore placed an order for the coming year.

On reviewing the budget for 2001 the finance director of EE noted that the projected sales of the motor unit were considerably less than those for the previous year, which was disappointing as both divisions concerned were working well below their capacities. On making enquiries he was told by IPD that the price reduction required to sell more units would reduce rather than increase profit and that the main problem was the high price charged by EMD. EMD stated that they required the high price in order to meet their target profit margin for the year, and that any reduction would erode their pricing policy.

You are required to:

(a) develop tabulations for each division, and for the company as a whole, that indicate the anticipated effect of IPD selling the motor unit at each of the prices listed,

(*10 marks*)

(b) (i) show the selling price which IPD should select in order to maximize its own divisional profit on the motor unit,

(*2 marks*)

(ii) show the selling price which would be in the best interest of EE as a whole,

(*2 marks*)

(iii) explain why this latter price is not selected by IPD,

(*1 mark*)

(c) state:

    (i) what changes you would advise making to the transfer pricing system so that it will motivate divisional managers to make better decisions in future,

(5 marks)

    (ii) what transfer price will ensure overall optimality in this situation.

(5 marks)

(Total 25 marks)

14.19 **Calculating the effects of a transfer pricing system on divisional and company profits**

Division A of a large divisionalized organization manufactures a single standardized product. Some of the output is sold externally whilst the remainder is transferred to Division B where it is a subassembly in the manufacture of that division's product. The unit costs of Division A's product are as follows:

	(£)
Direct material	4
Direct labour	2
Direct expense	2
Variable manufacturing overheads	2
Fixed manufacturing overheads	4
Selling and packing expense – variable	1
	15

Annually 10 000 units of the product are sold externally at the standard price of £30.

In addition to the external sales, 5000 units are transferred annually to Division B at an internal transfer charge of £29 per unit. This transfer price is obtained by deducting variable selling and packing expense from the external price since this expense is not incurred for internal transfers.

Division B incorporates the transferred-in goods into a more advanced product. The unit costs of this product are as follows:

	(£)
Transferred-in item (from Division A)	29
Direct material and components	23
Direct labour	3
Variable overheads	12
Fixed overheads	12
Selling and packing expense – variable	1
	80

Division B's manager disagrees with the basis used to set the transfer price. He argues that the transfers should be made at variable cost plus an agreed (minimal) mark-up since he claims that his division is taking output that Division A would be unable to sell at the price of £30.

Partly because of this disagreement, a study of the relationship between selling price and demand has recently been made for each division by the company's sales director. The resulting report contains the following table:

Customer demand at various selling prices:

Division A			
Selling price	£20	£30	£40
Demand	15 000	10 000	5000
Division B			
Selling price	£80	£90	£100
Demand	7 200	5 000	2800

The manager of Division B claims that this study supports his case. He suggests that a transfer price of £12 would give Division A a reasonable contribution to its fixed overheads while allowing Division B to earn a reasonable profit. He also believes that it would lead to an increase of output and an improvement in the overall level of company profits.

You are required:

(a) to calculate the effect that the transfer pricing system has had on the company's profits, and

(*16 marks*)

(b) to establish the likely effect on profits of adopting the suggestion by the manager of Division B of a transfer price of £12.

(*6 marks*)
(*Total 22 marks*)

14.20 P plc is a multinational conglomerate company with manufacturing divisions, trading in numerous countries across various continents. Trade takes place between a number of the divisions in different countries, with partly-completed products being transferred between them. Where a transfer takes place between divisions trading in different countries, it is the policy of the Board of P plc to determine centrally the appropriate transfer price without reference to the divisional managers concerned. The Board of P plc justifies this policy to divisional managers on the grounds that its objective is to maximize the conglomerate's post-tax profits and that the global position can be monitored effectively only from the Head Office.

Requirements:

(a) Explain and critically appraise the possible reasoning behind P plc's policy of centrally determining transfer prices for goods traded between divisions operating in different countries.

(*10 marks*)

(b) Discuss the ethical implications of P plc's policy of imposing transfer prices on its overseas divisions in order to maximize post-tax profits.

(*10 marks*)
(*Total 20 marks*)

PART 4

Cost Management and Strategic Management Accounting

15	Cost management

16	Strategic management accounting

In Part Three the major features of traditional management accounting control systems and the mechanisms that can be used to control costs were described. The focus was on comparing actual results against a pre-set standard (typically the budget), identifying and analysing variances and taking remedial action to ensure that future outcomes conform with budgeted outcomes. Traditional cost control systems tend to be based on the preservation of the status quo and the ways of performing existing activities are not reviewed. The emphasis is on cost containment rather than cost reduction. In contrast, cost management focuses on cost reduction rather than cost containment. Chapter 15 examines the various approaches that fall within the area of cost management

During the late 1980s criticisms of traditional management accounting practices were widely publicized and new approaches were advocated which are more in tune with today's competitive and business environment. In particular, strategic management accounting has been identified as a way forward. However, there is still no comprehensive framework as to what constitutes strategic management accounting. Chapter 16 examines the elements of strategic management accounting and describes the different contributions that have been made to its development. In addition, recent developments that seek to incorporate performance measurement within the strategic management process are described.

Cost management

15 In Chapters 11–13 the major features of traditional management accounting control systems and the mechanisms that can be used to control costs were described. The focus was on comparing actual results against a pre-set standard (typically the budget), identifying and analysing variances and taking remedial action to ensure that future outcomes conform with budgeted outcomes. Traditional cost control systems tend to be based on the preservation of the status quo and the ways of performing existing activities are not reviewed. The emphasis is on cost containment rather than cost reduction.

Cost management focuses on cost reduction and continuous improvement and change rather than cost containment. Indeed, the term cost reduction could be used instead of cost management but the former is an emotive term. Therefore cost management is preferred.

LEARNING OBJECTIVES

After studying this chapter, you should be able to:

- distinguish between the features of a traditional management accounting control system and cost management;
- explain life-cycle costing and describe the typical pattern of cost commitment and cost incurrence during the three stages of a product's life cycle;
- describe the target costing approach to cost management;
- describe tear-down analysis, value engineering and functional analysis;
- distinguish between target costing and *kaizen* costing;
- describe activity-based cost management;
- distinguish between value added and non-value added activities;
- explain the purpose of a cost of quality report;
- describe how value chain analysis can be used to increase customer satisfaction and manage costs more effectively;
- explain the role of benchmarking within the cost management framework;
- outline the main features of a just-in-time philosophy.

Whereas traditional cost control systems are routinely applied on a continuous basis, cost management tends to be applied on an *ad hoc* basis when an opportunity for cost reduction is identified. Also many of the approaches that are incorporated within the area of cost management do not necessarily involve the use of accounting techniques. In contrast, cost control relies heavily on accounting techniques.

Cost management consists of those actions that are taken by managers to reduce costs, some of which are prioritized on the basis of information extracted from the accounting system. Other actions, however, are undertaken without the use of accounting information. They involve process improvements, where an opportunity has been identified to perform processes more effectively and efficiently, and which have obvious cost reduction outcomes. It is important that you are aware of all the approaches that can be used to reduce costs even if these methods do not rely on accounting information. You should also note that although cost management seeks to reduce costs, it should not be at the expense of customer satisfaction. Ideally, the aim is to take actions that will both reduce costs and enhance customer satisfaction.

Life-cycle costing

ADVANCED READING

Traditional management accounting control procedures have focused primarily on the manufacturing stage of a product's life cycle. Pre-manufacturing costs, such as research and development and design and post-manufacturing abandonment and disposal costs are treated as period costs. Therefore they are not incorporated in the product cost calculations, nor are they subject to the conventional management accounting control procedures.

Life-cycle costing estimates and accumulates costs over a product's entire life cycle in order to determine whether the profits earned during the manufacturing phase will cover the costs incurred during the pre- and post-manufacturing stages. Identifying the costs incurred during the different stages of a product's life cycle provides an insight into understanding and managing the total costs incurred throughout its life cycle. In particular, life-cycle costing helps management to understand the cost consequences of developing and making a product and to identify areas in which cost reduction efforts are likely to be most effective.

Figure 15.1 illustrates a typical pattern of cost commitment and cost incurrence during the three stages of a product's life cycle – the planning and design stage, the manufacturing stage and the service and abandonment stage. **Committed** or **locked-in costs** are those costs that have not been incurred but that will be incurred in the future on the basis of decisions that have already been made. It is difficult to significantly alter costs after they have been committed. For example, the product design specifications determine a product's material and labour inputs and the production process. At this stage costs become committed and broadly determine the future costs that will be incurred during the manufacturing stage.

You will see from Figure 15.1 that approximately 80% of a product's costs are *committed* during the planning and design stage. At this stage product designers determine the product's design and the production process. In contrast, the majority of costs are *incurred* at the manufacturing stage, but they have already become locked-in at the planning and design stage and are difficult to alter.

It is apparent from Figure 15.1 that cost management can be most effectively exercised during the planning and design stage and not at the manufacturing stage when the product design and processes have already been determined and costs have been committed. At this latter stage the focus is more on cost containment than cost management. An understanding of life-cycle costs and how they are committed and incurred at different stages throughout a product's life cycle led to the emergence of **target costing**, a technique that focuses on managing costs during a product's planning and design phase.

FIGURE 15.1   *Product life-cycle phases: relationship between costs committed and costs incurred*

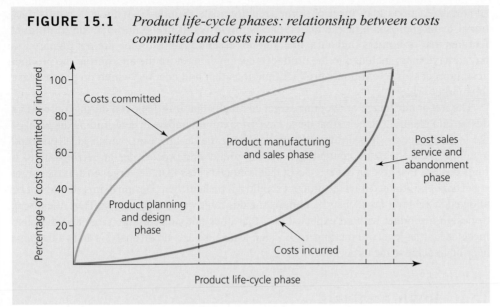

Target costing

In Chapter 7 we briefly looked at target costing as a mechanism for determining selling prices. We shall now consider how target costing can be used as a cost management tool. Target costing involves the following stages:

Stage 1:   Determine the target price which customers will be prepared to pay for the product.

Stage 2:   Deduct a target profit margin from the target price to determine the target cost.

Stage 3:   Estimate the actual cost of the product.

Stage 4:   If estimated actual cost exceeds the target cost investigate ways of driving down the actual cost to the target cost.

Target costing is a customer-oriented technique that is widely used by Japanese companies and which has recently been adopted by companies in Europe and the USA. The first stage requires market research to determine the customers' perceived value of the product based on its functions and its attributes (i.e. its functionality), its differentiation value relative to competing products and the price of competing products. The target profit margin depends on the planned return on investment for the organization as a whole and profit as a percentage of sales. This is then decomposed into a target profit for each product which is subsequently deducted from the target price to give the target cost. The target cost is compared with the predicted actual cost. If the predicted actual cost is above the target cost intensive efforts are made to close the gap so that the predicted cost equals the target cost.

A major feature of target costing is that a team approach is adopted to achieve the target cost. The team members include designers, engineers, purchasing, manufacturing, marketing and management accounting personnel. Their aim is to achieve the target cost specified for the product at the prescribed level of functionality and quality. The discipline of a team approach ensures that no particular group is able to impose their functional preferences. For example, design engineers pursuing their flair for design may design into products features that increase a product's costs but which customers do not value, or features that require the use of unique parts when alternative designs requiring standardized parts may meet customer requirements. Similarly, without a multi-functional team approach a marketing emphasis might result in the introduction of product features that customers find attractive, but not essential, and so they are not prepared to pay to have them included in the product's design. Therefore the aim during the product design process is to eliminate product functions that add cost but which do not increase the market price.

The major advantage of adopting target costing is that it is deployed during a product's design and planning stage so that it can have a maximum impact in determining the level of the locked-in costs. It is an iterative process with the design team, which ideally should result in the design team continuing with its product and process design attempts until it finds designs that give an expected cost that is equal or less than the target cost. If the target cost cannot be attained then the product should not be launched. Design teams should not be allowed to achieve target costs by eliminating desirable product functions. Thus, the aim is to design a product with an expected cost that does not exceed target cost and that also meets the target level of functionality. Design teams use tear-down analysis and value engineering to achieve the target cost.

Tear-down analysis

Tear-down analysis (also known as reverse engineering) involves examining a competitor's product in order to identify opportunities for product improvement and/or cost reduction. The competitor's product is dismantled to identify its functionality and design and to provide insights about the processes that are used and the cost to make the product. The aim is to benchmark provisional product designs with the designs of competitors and to incorporate any observed relative advantages of the competitor's approach to product design.

Value engineering

Value engineering (also known as value analysis) is a systematic interdisciplinary examination of factors affecting the cost of a product or service in order to devise means of achieving the specified purpose at the required standard of quality and reliability at the target cost. The aim of value engineering is to achieve the assigned target cost by (i) identifying improved product designs that reduce the product's cost without sacrificing functionality and/or (ii) eliminating unnecessary functions that increase the product's costs and for which customers are not prepared to pay extra.

Value engineering requires the use of functional analysis. This process involves decomposing the product into its many elements or attributes. For example, in the case of automobiles, functions might consist of style, comfort, operability, reliability, quality, attractiveness and many others (Kato, 1993). A price, or value, for each element is determined which reflects the amount the customer is prepared to pay. To obtain this information companies normally conduct surveys and interviews with customers. The total of the values for each function gives the estimated selling price from which the target profit is deducted to derive the target cost. The cost of each function of a product is compared with the benefits perceived by the customers. If the cost of the function exceeds the benefit to the customer, then the function should be either eliminated, modified to reduce its cost, or enhanced in terms of its perceived value so that its value exceeds the cost. Also by focusing on the product's functions, the design team will often consider components that perform the same function in other products, thus increasing the possibility of using standard components and reducing costs.

The need for accurate cost measurement systems

It is important that target costing is supported by an accurate cost system. In particular, cost drivers should be established that are the significant determinants of the costs of the activities so that cause-and-effect allocations are used. Arbitrary cost allocations should be avoided. If arbitrary cost allocations are used the allocation base will not be a significant determinant of cost. Let us assume that an arbitrary allocation base, say direct labour hours, is used to allocate support costs to products. To reduce the projected cost towards the target cost the target costing team will be motivated to focus on reducing direct labour hours. Why? Because this will result in a smaller proportion of the support costs being assigned to the product. However, the support costs incurred by the organization will not be reduced because there is no cause-and-effect relationship between direct labour hours and the resulting costs. Therefore the target costing exercise will merely result in a reduction in the costs that are allocated to the product but organizational costs will not be reduced. In contrast, if cause-and-effect allocation bases (i.e. cost drivers) are established, reductions in cost driver usage should be followed by a reduction in organizational support costs.

Therefore it is very important that cost systems use cost drivers that are the determinants of costs so that they will motivate designers to take actions that will reduce organizational costs. Decisions taken at the design stage lead to the committed usage of cost drivers which can be difficult to change in the future.

An illustration of target costing

Example 15.1 is used to illustrate the target costing process. You will have noted from reading the information presented in this example that the projected cost of the product is £700 compared with a target cost of £560. To achieve the target cost the company establishes a project team to undertake an intense target costing exercise. Example 15.1 indicates that the end result of the target costing exercise is a projected cost of £555 which is marginally below the target cost of £560. Let us now look at how the company has achieved the target cost and also how the costs shown in Example 15.1 have been derived.

In response to the need to reduce the projected cost the project team starts by purchasing video cameras from its main competitors and undertaking a tear-down analysis. This process involves dismantling the cameras to provide insights into potential design improvements for the new camera that will be launched. Value engineering is also undertaken with the project team working closely with the design engineers. Their objective is to identify new designs that will accomplish the same functions at a lower cost and also to eliminate any functions that are deemed to be unnecessary. This process results in a simplified design, a reduction in the number of parts and the replacement of some customized parts with standard parts. The outcome of the tear-down analysis and value engineering activities is a significant reduction in the projected direct materials, labour and rework costs, but the revised cost estimates still indicate that the projected cost exceeds the target cost.

Next the team engages in functional analysis. They identify the different elements, functions and attributes of the camera and potential customers are interviewed to ascertain the values that they place on each of the functions. This process indicates that several functions that have been included in the prototype are not valued by customers. The team therefore decide to eliminate these functions. The functional analysis results in further cost reductions being made, principally in the areas of materials and direct labour assembly costs, but the revised cost estimates still indicate that the target cost has not been attained.

The team now turn their attention to redesigning the production and support processes. They decide to redesign the ordering and receiving process by reducing the number of suppliers and working closely with a smaller number of suppliers. The suppliers are prepared to enter into contractual arrangements whereby they are periodically given a pre-determined production schedule and in return they will inspect the shipments and guarantee quality prior to delivery. In addition, the marketing, distribution and customer after-sales services relating to the product are subject to an intensive review, and process improvements are made that result in further reductions in costs that are attributable to the camera. The projected cost after undertaking all of the above activities is £555 compared with the target cost of £560 and at this point the target costing exercise is concluded.

Having described the target costing approach that the Digital Electronics Company has used let us now turn our attention to the derivation of the projected costs shown in Example 15.1. The projected cost for direct materials prior to the target costing exercise is £390 but value engineering and the functional analysis have resulted in a reduction in the number of parts that are required to manufacture the video camera. The elimination of most of the unique parts, and the use of standard parts that the company currently purchases in large volumes, also provides scope for further cost savings. The outcome of the redesign process is a direct material cost of £325.

The simplified product design enables the assembly time to be reduced thus resulting in the reduction of direct labour costs from £100 to £80. The direct machine costs relate to machinery that will be used exclusively for the production of the new product. The estimated cost of acquiring, maintaining and operating the machinery throughout the product's life cycle is £6 million. This is divided by the projected lifetime sales volume of the camera (300 000 units) giving a unit cost of £20. However, it has not been possible to reduce the unit cost because the machinery costs are committed, and fixed, and the target costing exercise has not resulted in a change in the predicted lifetime volume.

Prior to the target costing exercise 80 separate parts were included in the product specification. The estimated number of orders placed for each part throughout the product's life cycle is 150 and the predicted cost per order for the order and receiving activity is £200. Therefore the estimated lifetime costs are £2.4 million (80 parts × 150 orders × £200 per order) giving a unit cost of £8 (£2.4 million/300 000 units). The simplified design, and the parts standardization arising from the functional analysis and the value engineering activities, have enabled the number of parts to be reduced to 40. The redesign of the ordering and receiving process has also enabled the number of orders and the ordering cost to be reduced (the former from 150 to 100 and the latter from £200 to £150 per order). Thus the projected lifetime ordering and receiving costs after the target costing exercise are £600 000 (40 parts × 100 orders × £150 per order) giving a revised unit cost of £2 (£600 000/300 000 units).

Quality assurance involves inspecting and testing the cameras. Prior to the target costing exercise the projected cost was £60 (12 hours at £5 per hour) but the simplified design means that the camera will be easier to test resulting in revised cost of £50 (10 hours at £5 per hour). Rework costs of £15 represent the average rework costs per camera. Past experience with manufacturing similar products suggests that 10% of the output will require rework. Applying this rate to the estimated total lifetime volume of 300 000 cameras results in 30 000 cameras requiring rework at an estimated average cost of £150 per reworked camera. The total lifetime rework cost is therefore predicted to be £4.5 million (30 000 × £150) giving an average cost per unit of good output of £15 (£4.5 million/300 000). Because of the simplified product design the rework rate and the average rework cost will be reduced. The predicted rework rate is now 5% and the average rework cost will be reduced from £150 to £120. Thus, the revised estimate of the total lifetime cost is £1.8 million (15 000 reworked units at £120 per unit) and the projected unit cost is £6 (£1.8 million/300 000 units).

The predicted total lifetime engineering and design costs and other product-sustaining costs are predicted to be £3 million giving a unit cost of £10. The simplified design and reduced number of parts enables the lifetime cost to be reduced by 20%, to £2.4 million,

EXAMPLE 15.1

The Digital Electronics Company manufactures cameras and video equipment. It is in the process of introducing a new state-of-the art combined digital video and still camera. The company has undertaken market research to ascertain the customers' perceived value of the product based on its special features and a comparison with competitors' products. The results of the survey, and a comparison of the new camera with competitors' products and market prices, have been used to establish a target selling price and projected lifetime volume. In addition, cost estimates have been prepared based on the proposed product specification. The company has set a target profit margin of 30% on the proposed selling price and this has been deducted from the target selling price to determine the target cost. The following is a summary of the information that has been presented to management:

Projected lifetime sales volume	300 000 units
Target selling price	£800
Target profit margin (30% of selling price)	£240
Target cost (£800 – £240)	£560
Projected cost	£700

The excess of the projected cost over the target cost results in an intensive target costing exercise. After completing the target costing exercise the projected cost is £555 which is marginally below the target cost of £560. The analysis of the projected cost before and after the target costing exercise is as follows:

	Before (£)	Before (£)	After (£)	After (£)
Manufacturing cost				
Direct material (bought in parts)	390		325	
Direct labour	100		80	
Direct machining costs	20		20	
Ordering and receiving	8		2	
Quality assurance	60		50	
Rework	15		6	
Engineering and design	10	603	8	491
Non-manufacturing costs				
Marketing	40		25	
Distribution	30		20	
After-sales service and warranty costs	27	97	19	64
Total cost		700		555

and the unit cost to £8. The planned process improvements have also enabled the predicted marketing, distribution and after-sales service costs to be reduced. In addition, the simplified product design and the use of fewer parts has contributed to the reduction to the after-sales warranty costs. However, to keep our example brief the derivation of the non-manufacturing costs will not be presented, other than to note that the company uses an activity-based-costing system. All costs are assigned using cost drivers that are based on established cause-and-effect relationships.

Kaizen costing

In addition to target costing *kaizen* costing is widely used by Japanese organizations as a mechanism for reducing and managing costs. *Kaizen* is the Japanese term for making improvements to a process through small incremental amounts, rather than through large innovations. The major difference between target and *kaizen* costing is that target costing is applied during the design stage whereas *kaizen* costing is applied during the manufacturing stage of the product life cycle. With target costing the focus is on the product, and cost reductions are achieved primarily through product design. In contrast, *kaizen* costing focuses on the production processes and cost reductions are derived primarily through the increased efficiency of the production process. Therefore the potential cost reductions are smaller with *kaizen* costing because the products are already in the manufacturing stage of their life cycles and a significant proportion of the costs will have become locked-in.

Source: Image supplied by Toyota Manufacturing UK Ltd

The aim of *kaizen* costing is to reduce the cost of components and products by a pre-specified amount. Monden and Hamada (1991) describe the application of *kaizen* costing in a Japanese automobile plant. Each plant is assigned a target cost reduction ratio and this is applied to the previous year's actual costs to determine the target cost reduction. *Kaizen* costing relies heavily on employee empowerment. They are assumed to have superior knowledge about how to improve processes because they are closest to the manufacturing processes and customers and are likely to have greater insights into how costs can be reduced. Thus, a major feature of *kaizen* costing is that workers are given the responsibility to improve processes and reduce costs. Unlike target costing it is not accompanied by a set of techniques or procedures that are automatically applied to achieve the cost reductions.

Activity-based management

The early adopters of activity-based costing (ABC) used it to produce more accurate product (or service) costs but it soon became apparent to the users that it could be extended beyond purely product costing to a range of cost management applications. The terms **activity-based management (ABM)** or **activity-based cost management (ABCM)** are used to describe the cost management applications of ABC. To implement an ABM system only the first three of the four stages described in Chapter 6 for designing an activity-based product costing system are required. They are:

1 identifying the major activities that take place in an organization;

2 assigning costs to cost pools/cost centres for each activity;

3 determining the cost driver for each major activity.

ABM views the business as a set of linked activities that ultimately add value to the customer. It focuses on managing the business on the basis of the activities that make up the organization. ABM is based on the premise that activities consume costs. Therefore

Applying target costing to existing products at Montclair Papers Division

It is generally considered that target costing should normally be applied early in the product life cycle, but there is no conceptual reason why it cannot be applied to existing products. Montclair Papers Division of Mohawk Forest Products applied target costing to one of its existing products – Forest Green Carnival. The standard cost of this product was $2900 (see Real World Views 12.1) even though this resulted in a premium selling price with competitors selling at prices below the standard cost. Ajax Papers won over Montclair a bid of $1466 per ton, thereby setting the prevailing price in the market. The realization that an important competitor could operate under a dramatically different cost structure motivated managers to adopt a target costing approach and remove its standard cost blinders. Based on a target selling price of $1466, and deducting a target profit margin, a target cost of $1162 was derived. The target costing process focused on the four major cost components:

- Fibre cost (changing the mix of recycled paper and virgin pulp to reduce raw materials cost).
- Paper machine cost (getting on grade faster to improve yields).
- Dye costs.
- Conversion cost.

Fibre Cost. A project team began a series of manufacturing trials showing that the mill could increase the percentage of recycled paper in the raw-materials mix above the standard allowance of 22 per cent. Experience proved that recycled percentages ranging up to 75 per cent would not detrimentally affect the quality of the finished sheet if the scrap paper were handled carefully. Using 75 per cent scrap in the raw-material mix reduced the fibre cost by 60 per cent with no negative effect on paper quality.

Paper Machine Cost. Because the product had such poor yields, the mill scheduled a production run only about twice a year. A root-cause analysis of the long changeover time revealed that the biggest time loss was getting 'on shade' for a designer-created colour such as Forest Green. A project team tackled this problem by first observing that if the production run could start with a fibre mix closer to the desired shade, there was a dramatically reduced 'off shade' time. That implied starting with green fibre, rather than white. This had never been possible when 80 per cent of the fibre was virgin pulp that can only be purchased in one colour – white. But increasing the percentage of recycled fibre opened the possibility of buying green scrap paper instead of white. Since there was virtually no market demand for green 'broke' (scrap), the mill was able to buy unlimited quantities at low prices. Another project team experimented with Montclair's computerized colour-mixing system. They were able to develop proprietary software that allowed the colour-mixing crew to get 'on shade' in 40 minutes instead of 2 hours by starting with green broke. Reducing changeover time from 2 hours to 40 minutes raised the yield rate to 75 per cent when producing 2 hours of good paper.

Dye Costs. Starting the papermaking process with up to 75 per cent green fibre required much less dye to achieve the exact Forest Green shade. The newly developed proprietary software enabled getting on shade with an average dye cost that was an amazing $796 reduction in the cost per ton.

Conversion Costs. Another project team tackled this cost component by seriously considering the make-versus-buy option. Each converting department was challenged to develop competitive programmes or risk job loss to outsourcing. Over eighteen months, the $303 per ton conversion cost for Forest Green Carnival fell to $240 – a 20 per cent reduction.

By combining the improvements contributed by the four project teams, it was possible to envision lowering the manufacturing cost from $2900 to $1162.

Source: Shank, J.K. and Fisher, J. (1999) Target costing as a strategic tool, *Sloan Management Review,* Fall, **41**(1), pp. 73–82.

by managing activities costs will be managed in the long term. The goal of ABM is to enable customer needs to be satisfied while making fewer demands on organizational resources. Besides providing information on what activities are performed, ABM provides information on the cost of activities, why the activities are undertaken, and how well they are performed.

Traditional budget and control reports analyse costs by types of expense for each responsibility centre. In contrast, ABM analyses costs by activities and thus provides management with information on why costs are incurred and the output from the activity (in terms of cost drivers). Exhibit 15.1 illustrates the difference between the conventional analysis and the activity-based analysis in respect of customer order processing. The major differences are that the ABM approach reports by *activities* whereas the traditional analysis is by *departments*. Also ABM reporting is by sub-activities but traditional reporting is by expense categories. Another distinguishing feature of ABM reporting is that it often reports information on activities that cross departmental boundaries. For example, different production departments and the distribution department might undertake customer processing activities. They may resolve customer problems by expediting late deliveries. The finance department may assess customer credit worthiness and the remaining customer processing activities might be undertaken by the customer service department. Therefore the total cost of the customer processing activity could be considerably in excess of the costs that are assigned to the customer service department. However, to simplify the presentation it is assumed in Exhibit 15.1 that the departmental and activity costs are identical but if the cost of the customer order processing activity was found to be, say, three times the amount assigned to the customer service department, this would be important information because it may change the way in which the managers view the activity. For example, the managers may give more attention to reducing the costs of the customer processing activity.

It is apparent from an examination of Exhibit 15.1 that the ABM approach provides more meaningful information. It gives more visibility to the cost of undertaking the activities that make up the organization and may raise issues for management action that are not highlighted by the traditional analysis. For example, why is £90 000 spent on resolving customer problems? Attention-directing information such as this is important for managing the cost of the activities.

Johnson (1990) suggests that knowing costs by activities is a catalyst that eventually triggers the action necessary to become competitive. Consider a situation where salespersons, as a result of costing activities, are informed that it costs £50 to process a customer's order. They therefore become aware that it is questionable to pursue orders with

EXHIBIT 15.1

Customer order processing activity

	(£000s)
Traditional analysis	
Salaries	320
Stationery	40
Travel	140
Telephone	40
Depreciation of equipment	40
	580
ABM analysis	
Preparing quotations	120
Receiving customer orders	190
Assessing the creditworthiness of customers	100
Expediting	80
Resolving customer problems	90
	580

a low sales value. By eliminating many small orders, and concentrating on larger value orders, the demand for customer-processing activities should decrease, and future spending on this activity should be reduced.

Prior to the introduction of ABM most organizations have been unaware of the cost of undertaking the activities that make up the organization. Knowing the cost of activities enables those activities with the highest cost to be highlighted so that they can be prioritized for detailed studies to ascertain whether they can be eliminated or performed more efficiently. To identify and prioritize the potential for cost reduction many organizations have found it useful to classify activities as either value added or non-value added. Definitions of what constitutes value added and non-value added activities vary. A common definition is that a **value added activity** is an activity that customers perceive as adding usefulness to the product or service they purchase. For example, painting a car would be a value added activity in an organization that manufactures cars. Other definitions are an activity that is being performed as efficiently as possible or an activity that supports the primary objective of producing outputs.

In contrast, a **non-value added activity** is an activity where there is an opportunity for cost reduction without reducing the product's service potential to the customer. Examples of non-value added activities include inspecting, storing and moving raw materials. The cost of these activities can be reduced without reducing the value of the products to the customers. Non-value added activities are essentially those activities that customers should not be expected to pay for. Reporting the cost of non-value added activities draws management's attention to the vast amount of waste that has been tolerated by the organization. This should prioritize those activities with the greatest potential for cost reduction by eliminating or carrying them out more effectively, such as reducing material movements, improving production flows and taking actions to reduce stock levels. Taking action to reduce or eliminate non-value added activities is given top priority because by doing so the organization permanently reduces the cost it incurs without reducing the value of the product to the customer.

Our discussion so far has related to the application of ABM during the manufacturing or service phase of a product's life cycle. However, some organizations have used their activity-based costing systems to influence future costs at the design stage within the target costing process. For example, the Tektronix Portable Instruments Division assigned material support expenses using a single cost driver – number of part numbers. The company wanted to encourage design engineers to focus their attention on reducing the number of part numbers, parts and vendors in future generations of products. Product timeliness was seen as a critical success factor and this was facilitated by designs which simplified parts procurement and production processes. The cost system motivated engineers to design simpler products requiring less development time because they had fewer parts and part numbers. The cost system designers knew that most of the material support expenses were not incurred in direct proportion to the single cost driver chosen, but the simplified and imprecise cost system focused attention on factors deemed to be most critical to the division's future success.

A survey of activity-based costing applications by Innes and Mitchell (1995a) indicated that many organizations use cost driver rates as a measure of cost efficiency and performance for the activity concerned. The cost driver rate is computed by dividing the activity costs by the cost driver volume. For example, if the cost of processing 10 000 purchase orders is £100 000, the cost per purchasing order is £10. Assume now that improvements in procedures in the purchasing activity enable costs to be reduced to £80 000. If the same number of orders can be processed with fewer resources the cost of processing an order will be reduced to £8. Reporting and focusing on cost driver rates can thus be used to motivate managers to reduce the cost of performing activities.

There is a danger, however, that cost driver rates can encourage dysfunctional behaviour. An improvement in the cost driver rate can be achieved by splitting some purchase orders and increasing the orders processed to, say, 12 000. Assuming that the cost of the activity remains unchanged at £100 000 the cost per purchasing order will be reduced from £10 to £8.33 if all costs are fixed in the short term. The overall effect is that the workload will be increased and, in the long term, this could result in an increase in costs. Care should therefore be taken to avoid these dysfunctional consequences by using cost driver rates as feedback information to guide employees in improving the efficiency of performing activities. If the measures are interpreted in a recriminatory or threatening manner, there is a danger that they will lead to dysfunctional behaviour.

Business process re-engineering

Business process re-engineering involves examining business processes and making substantial changes to how the organization currently operates. It involves the redesign of how work is done through activities. A business process consists of a collection of activities that are linked together in a coordinated manner to achieve a specific objective. For example, material handling might be classed as a business process consisting of separate activities relating to scheduling production, storing materials, processing purchase orders, inspecting materials and paying suppliers.

The aim of business process re-engineering is to improve the key business processes in an organization by focusing on simplification, cost reduction, improved quality and enhanced customer satisfaction. Consider the materials handling process outlined in the above paragraph. The process might be re-engineered by sending the production schedule direct to nominated suppliers and entering into contractual agreements to deliver the materials in accordance with the production schedule and also guaranteeing their quality by inspecting them prior to delivery. The end result might be the elimination, or a permanent reduction, of the storing, purchasing and inspection activities. These activities are non-value added activities since they represent an opportunity for cost reduction without reducing the products' service potentials to customers.

REAL WORLD
VIEWS 15.2

Best practices in activity-based management

The American Productivity and Quality Center, the Consortium for Advanced Manufacturing International, and participating companies recently sponsored a research team to benchmark and study best practices in the implementation and use of ABM. Fifteen best practice companies were identified that have applied ABM in many different ways. Even though these applications were quite diverse, three broad categories were identified:

1 use for decision-making;

2 support for improvement initiatives; and

3 use for performance measurement.

Typically the best practice companies enter the ABM value cycle in one area, and migrate to other applications as their ABM systems evolve. First Tennessee Bank (FTB) illustrates how this migration can occur. Initially, FTB used ABM information to improve product and customer profitability. It found a classic case of cross-subsidization: profitable products and customers were supporting unprofitable products and customers, and pricing was often unrelated to services rendered. FTB used the activity cost information to adjust its mix of products and customers, and to move closer to a fee-for-service pricing structure.

After conducting profitability analysis, FTB began using ABM to support process improvement initiatives. Teams responsible for entire processes were formed, and through an activity analysis these process teams documented the high cost of inspection, paper movement and storage, and error correction in bank operations. One team identified the use of electronic transactions, which require less paper, fewer steps and fewer hand-offs among employees, as a cost savings opportunity. Processes were then redesigned to expand the bank's use of automated electronic transactions.

As a further migration, FTB began more recently to use ABM for benchmarking. The benchmarks apply to common activities, such as inspection, move, error and rework. The benchmarking process helps FTB identify improvement opportunities and prioritize action plans.

Source: Swenson, D. (2000) Best practices in activity-based management, in Reeve, J.M. (ed.), *Readings and Issues in Cost Management*, South Western Publishing Company (USA).

A distinguishing feature of business process re-engineering is that it involves radical and dramatic changes in processes by abandoning current practices and reinventing completely new methods of performing business processes. The focus is on major changes rather than marginal improvements. A further example of business process re-engineering is moving from a traditional functional plant layout to a just-in-time cellular product layout and adopting a just-in-time philosophy. Adopting a **just in time (JIT) system** and philosophy has important implications for cost management and performance reporting. It is therefore important that you understand the nature of such systems and how they differ from traditional systems, but rather than deviating at this point from our discussion of cost management the description of a JIT system will be deferred until the end of the chapter.

Cost of quality

To compete successfully in today's global competitive environment companies are becoming 'customer-driven' and making customer satisfaction an overriding priority. Customers are demanding ever-improving levels of service regarding cost, quality, reliability, delivery and the choice of innovative new products. Quality has become one of the key competitive variables and this has created the need for management accountants to become more involved in the provision of information relating to the quality of products and services and activities that produce them. In the UK quality related costs have been reported to range from 5 to 15% of total company sales revenue (Plunkett *et al.*, 1985). Eliminating inferior quality can therefore result in substantial savings and higher revenues.

Total quality management (TQM), a term used to describe a situation where *all* business functions are involved in a process of continuous quality improvement, has been adopted by many companies. TQM has broadened, from its early concentration on the statistical monitoring of manufacturing processes, to a customer-oriented process of continuous improvement that focuses on delivering products or services of consistent high quality in a timely fashion. In the 1980s most European and American companies considered quality to be an additional cost of manufacturing, but by the end of the decade they began to realize that quality saved money. The philosophy of emphasizing production volume over quality resulted in high levels of stocks at each production stage in order to protect against shortages caused by inferior quality at previous stages and excessive expenditure on inspection, rework, scrap and warranty repairs. Companies discovered that it was cheaper to produce the items correctly the first time rather than wasting resources by making substandard items that have to be detected, reworked, scrapped or returned by customers.

Management accounting systems can help organizations achieve their quality goals by providing a variety of reports and measures that motivate and evaluate managerial efforts to improve quality. These will include financial and non-financial measures. Many companies are currently not aware of how much they are spending on quality because the costs are incurred across many different departments and not accumulated as a separate cost object within the costing system. Managers need to know the costs of quality and how they are changing over time. A **cost of quality report** should be prepared to indicate the total cost to the organization of producing products or services that do not conform with quality requirements. Four categories of costs should be reported.

1. **Prevention costs** are the costs incurred in preventing the production of products that do not conform to specification. They include the costs of preventive maintenance, quality planning and training and the extra costs of acquiring higher quality raw materials.

2. **Appraisal costs** are the costs incurred to ensure that materials and products meet quality conformance standards. They include the costs of inspecting purchased parts, work in process and finished goods, quality audits and field tests.

3. **Internal failure costs** are the costs associated with materials and products that fail to meet quality standards. They include costs incurred before the product is despatched to the customer, such as the costs of scrap, repair, downtime and work stoppages caused by defects.

4. **External failure costs** are the costs incurred when products or services fail to conform to requirements or satisfy customer needs after they have been delivered. They include the costs of handling customer complaints, warranty replacement, repairs of returned products and the costs arising from a damaged company reputation. Costs within this category can have a dramatic impact on future sales.

	(£000s)	% of sales (£50 million)	
Prevention costs			
Quality training	1000		
Supplier reviews	300		
Quality engineering	400		
Preventive maintenance	500		
		2 200	4.4
Appraisal costs			
Inspection of materials received	500		
Inspection of WIP and completed units	1000		
Testing equipment	300		
Quality audits	800		
		2 600	5.2
Internal failure costs			
Scrap	800		
Rework	1000		
Downtime due to quality problems	600		
Retesting	400	2 800	5.6
External failure costs			
Returns	2000		
Recalls	1000		
Warranty repairs	800		
Handling customer complaints	500		
Foregone contribution from lost sales	3000		
		7 300	14.6
		14 900	29.8

EXHIBIT 15.2

Cost of quality report

Exhibit 15.2 presents a typical cost of quality report. Note that some of the items in the report will have to be estimated. For example, included in the external failure costs category is the forgone contribution from lost sales arising from poor quality. This cost is extremely difficult to estimate. Nevertheless, the lost contribution can be substantial and it is preferable to include an estimate rather than omit it from the report. By expressing each category of costs as a percentage of sales revenues comparisons can be made with previous periods, other organizations and divisions within the same group. Such comparisons can highlight problem areas. For example, comparisons of external failure costs with other companies can provide an indication of the current level of customer satisfaction.

The cost of quality report can be used as an attention-directing device to make the top management of a company aware of how much is being spent on quality-related costs. The report can also draw management's attention to the possibility of reducing total quality costs by a wiser allocation of costs among the four quality categories. For example, by spending more on the prevention costs, the amount of spending in the internal and external failure categories can be substantially reduced, and therefore total spending can be lowered. Also, by designing quality into the products and processes, appraisal costs can be reduced, since far less inspection is required.

Cost management and the value chain

Increasing attention is now being given to **value-chain analysis** as a means of increasing customer satisfaction and managing costs more effectively. The value chain is illustrated in Figure 15.2. It is the linked set of value-creating activities all the way from basic raw material sources for component suppliers through to the ultimate end-use product or service delivered to the customer. A value-chain analysis is used to analyse, coordinate and optimize linkages in the value chain. Coordinating the individual parts of the value chain together creates the conditions to improve customer satisfaction, particularly in terms of cost efficiency, quality and delivery. A firm which performs the value chain activities more efficiently, and at a lower cost, than its competitors will gain a competitive advantage. Therefore it is necessary to understand how value chain activities are performed and how they interact with each other. The activities are not just a collection of independent activities but a system of interdependent activities in which the performance of one activity affects the performance and cost of other activities.

The linkages in the value chain express the relationships between the performance of one activity and its effects on the performance of another activity. A linkage occurs when interdependence exists between activities and the higher the interdependence between activities the greater is the required coordination. Thus, it is appropriate to view the value chain from the customer's perspective, with each link being seen as the customer of the previous link. If each link in the value chain is designed to meet the needs of its customers, then end-customer satisfaction should ensue. Furthermore, by viewing each link in the value chain as a supplier–customer relationship, the opinions of the customers can be used to provide useful feedback information on assessing the quality of service provided by the supplier. Opportunities are thus identified for improving activities throughout the entire value chain.

Shank and Govindarajan (1992) also point out that focusing on the value chain results in the adoption of a broader strategic approach to cost management. They argue that traditional management accounting adopts an internal focus which, in terms of the value chain, starts too late and stops too soon. Starting cost analysis with purchases misses all the opportunities for exploiting linkages with the firm's suppliers and stopping cost analysis at the point of sale eliminates all opportunities for exploiting linkages with customers. Shank (1989) illustrates how an American automobile company failed to use the value chain approach to exploit links with suppliers and enhance profitability. The company had made significant internal savings from introducing JIT manufacturing techniques, but, at the same time, price increases from suppliers more than offset these internal cost savings. A value chain perspective revealed that 50% of the firm's costs related to purchases from parts suppliers. As the automobile company reduced its own need for buffer stocks, it placed major new strains on the manufacturing responsiveness of suppliers. The increase in the suppliers' manufacturing costs was greater than the decrease in the automobile company's internal costs. Shank states:

> For every dollar of manufacturing cost the assembly plants saved by moving towards JIT management concepts, the suppliers' plant spent much more than one dollar extra because of schedule instability arising from the introduction of JIT. Because of its narrow value added perspective, the auto company had ignored the impact of its changes on its suppliers' costs. Management had ignored the idea that JIT involves a partnership with suppliers (Shank, 1989, p. 51).

Similarly, by developing linkages with customers mutually beneficial relationships can be established. For example, Shank and Govindarajan (1992), drawing off research by Hergert and Morris (1989) point out that some container producers in the USA have

FIGURE 15.2 *The value chain*

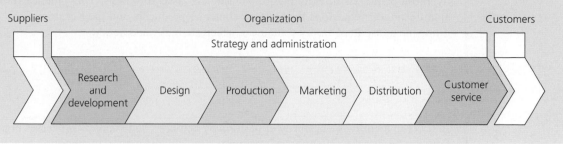

Value chain analysis in interfirm relationships

The following presents extracts from a case study on the use of an ABC cost model by a large UK retail firm (Sainsbury) and a group of suppliers for supporting their supply chain management practices. This cost model was based on the principles of value chain analysis and integrated cost information across the supply chain. It was used to improve supply chain operations by performing benchmark analyses, strategic what-if analyses and cost monitoring. The model was used to identify opportunities to reduce supply chain costs.

To be able to analyse the supply chain costs, cost and cost driver data were required from both Sainsbury and suppliers. Suppliers were free to choose whether or not they would participate in this initiative. When they decided to participate, they were required to deliver cost data and cost driver quantities to Sainsbury for feeding the supplier section of the model.

Benchmarking was used to compare suppliers' activity costs with the average of their network. In addition, cost comparisons were made between networks, regions and store types. By clustering suppliers into different networks the most important differences between their operations were eliminated, as suppliers within a network performed fairly comparable activities. The most important measure for the benchmark analysis was the cost per cost driver (i.e. the cost driver rate), as this measure could be compared directly with other suppliers. The benchmark analysis revealed the suppliers' relative performance against the network average. When a supplier deviated significantly from the average, the Logistics Operations department would initiate a discussion with the supplier to find out the cause(s) of the difference, by analysing the underlying activities, and to assess whether and how performance could be improved. In addition, as suppliers in different networks faced no competition, comparing the costs of their activities and analysing the differences in their operations could be used to transfer efficient supply chain practices across networks.

Strategic what-if analyses were performed to analyse the effects of changes in the supply chain on supply chain costs. When, for example, as a result of a benchmark analysis, Sainsbury and a supplier developed ideas or scenarios for improving supply chain processes, the model was used to calculate the expected changes in costs of each scenario.

Source: Adapted from Dekker, H.C. (2003) Value chain analysis in interfirm relationships: a field study, *Management Accounting Research*, **14**(1), pp. 1–23. With permission from Elsevier.

constructed manufacturing facilities near beer breweries and deliver the containers through overhead conveyers directly onto the customers' assembly lines. This practice results in significant cost reductions for both the container producers and their customers by expediting the transport of empty containers, which are bulky and heavy.

Benchmarking

In order to identify the best way of performing activities and business processes organizations are turning their attention to **benchmarking**, which involves comparing key activities with world-class best practices. Benchmarking attempts to identify an activity, such as customer order processing, that needs to be improved and finding a non-rival organization that is considered to represent world-class best practice for the activity and studying how it performs the activity. The objective is to find out how the activity can be improved and ensure that the improvements are implemented.

Benchmarking is cost beneficial since an organization can save time and money avoiding mistakes that other companies have made and/or the organization can avoid duplicating the efforts of other companies. The overall aim should be to find and implement best practice.

Environmental cost management

Environmental cost management is becoming increasingly important in many organizations. There are several reasons for this. First, environmental costs can be large for some industrial sectors. For example, Ranganathan and Ditz (1996) reported that Amoco's environmental costs at its Yorktown refinery were at least 22% of operating costs. Second, regulatory requirements involving huge fines for non-compliance have increased significantly over the past decade. Therefore, selecting the least costly method of compliance has become a major objective. Third, society is demanding that companies focus on becoming more environmentally friendly. Companies are finding that becoming a good social citizen and being environmentally responsible improves their image and enhances their ability to sell their products and services. These developments have created the need for companies to develop a system of measuring, reporting and monitoring environmental costs.

According to Epstein and Roy (1997) many companies cannot identify their total environmental costs and do not recognize that they can be controlled and reduced. In most cost accounting systems, environmental costs are hidden within general overheads and are either not allocated to cost objects, or they are allocated on an arbitrary basis within the allocation of general overheads. Thus, crucial relationships are not identified between environmental costs and the responsible products, processes and underlying activities. For example, Ranganathan and Ditz point out that the principal environmental issue facing Spectrum Glass, a major manufacturer of specialty sheet glass, is the use and release of cadmium. It discovered that only one product (Ruby red glass) was responsible for all of its cadmium emissions but the cost accounting system allocated a portion of this cost to all products. This process resulted in ruby red glass being undercosted and other products being overcosted.

Environmental costs should be accumulated by separate cost pools, analysed by appropriate categories and traced to the products or processes that caused the costs using ABC concepts. Knowledge of the amount and categories of environmental costs, and their causes, provides the information that managers need to not only manage environmental costs more effectively by process redesign but to also reduce the pollutants emitted to the environment.

Hansen and Mendoza (1999) point out that environmental costs are incurred because poor environmental quality exists and thus are similar in nature to quality costs discussed earlier in this chapter. They advocate that an environmental cost report should be periodically produced, based on the principles of a cost of quality report (see Exhibit 15.2) to indicate the total environmental costs to the organization associated with the creation, detection, remedy and prevention of environmental degradation. Adopting a similar classification as that used for quality costs, the following four categories of environmental costs can be reported:

1 **Environmental prevention costs** are the costs of activities undertaken to prevent the production of waste that could cause damage to the environment. Examples include the costs associated with the design and operation of processes to reduce contaminants, training employees, recycling products and obtaining certification relating to meeting the requirements of international and national standards.

2 **Environmental appraisal costs** are the costs incurred to ensure that a firm's activities, products and processes conform to regulatory laws and voluntary standards. Examples include inspection of products and processes to ensure regulatory compliance, auditing environmental activities and performing contamination tests.

3 **Environmental internal failure costs** are the costs incurred from performing activities that have been produced but not discharged into the environment. Such costs are incurred to eliminate or reduce waste to levels that comply with regulatory requirements. Examples include the costs of disposing of toxic materials and recycling scrap.

4 **Environmental external failure costs** are the costs incurred on activities performed after discharging waste into the environment. Examples include the costs of cleaning up contaminated soil, restoring land to its natural state and cleaning up oil spills and waste discharges. Clearly this category of costs has the greatest impact on a company in terms of adverse publicity.

The environmental cost report should be similar in format to the cost of quality report (see Exhibit 15.2) with each category of costs expressed as a percentage of sales revenues (or operating costs) so that comparisons can be made with previous periods, other organizations and divisions within the same group. The environmental cost report should be used as an attention-directing device to make top management aware of how much is being spent on environmental costs and the relative amount in each category. The report also draws management's attention to those areas that have the greatest potential for cost reduction.

Finally, you should note at this point that incorporating an environmental perspective within a balanced scorecard framework has been adopted by some companies to link their environmental strategy to concrete performance measures. The balanced scorecard framework requires that within the scorecard the environmental objectives are clearly specified and that these objectives should be translated into specific performance measures. In addition, within the scorecard, firms should describe the major initiatives for achieving each objective and also establish targets for each performance measure. For feedback reporting, actual performance measures should also be added. The balanced scorecard framework is described in the next chapter.

Just in time systems

Earlier in this chapter it was pointed out that reorganizing business processes and adopting a just in time (JIT) system was an illustration of business process engineering but so far a JIT system has not been explained. Given that implementing a JIT system is a mechanism for reducing non-value added costs and long-run costs it is important that you understand the nature of such a system and its cost management implications.

The success of Japanese firms in international markets generated interest among many Western companies as to how this success was achieved. The implementation of **just in time (JIT) production methods** was considered to be one of the major factors contributing to this success. The JIT approach aims to produce the required items, at the required quality and in the required quantities, at the precise time they are required. In particular, JIT seeks to achieve the following goals:

- elimination of non-value added activities;
- zero inventory;
- zero defects;
- batch sizes of one;
- zero breakdowns;
- a 100% on-time delivery service.

The above goals represent perfection, and are most unlikely to be achieved in practice. They do, however, offer targets, and create a climate for continuous improvement and excellence. Let us now examine the major features of a JIT manufacturing philosophy.

Elimination of non-value added activities

JIT manufacturing is best described as a philosophy of management dedicated to the elimination of waste. Waste is defined as anything that does not add value to a product. The lead or cycle time involved in manufacturing and selling a product consists of process time, inspection time, move time, queue time and storage time. Of these five steps, only process time actually adds value to the product. All the other activities add cost but no value to the product, and are thus deemed non-value added processes within the JIT philosophy. According to Berliner and Brimson (1988), process time is less than 10% of total manufacturing lead time in many organizations in the USA. Therefore 90% of the manufacturing lead time associated with a product adds costs, but no value, to the product. By adopting a JIT philosophy and focusing on reducing lead times, it is claimed that total costs can be significantly reduced. The ultimate goal of JIT is to convert raw materials to finished products with lead times equal to processing times, thus eliminating all non-value added activities.

Factory layout

The first stage in implementing JIT manufacturing techniques is to rearrange the production process away from a **batch production functional layout** towards a product layout using flow lines. With a functional plant layout products pass through a number of specialist departments that normally contain a group of similar machines. Products are processed in large batches so as to minimize the set-up times when machine settings are changed between processing batches of different products. Batches move via different and complex routes through the various departments, travelling over much of the factory floor before they are completed. Each process normally involves a considerable amount of waiting time. The consequences of this complex routing process are high work in progress stock levels and long manufacturing cycle times.

The JIT solution is to reorganize the production process by dividing the many different products that an organization makes into families of similar products or components. All of the products in a particular group will have similar production requirements and routings. Production is rearranged so that each product family is manufactured in a well-defined production cell based on flow line principles. In a **product flow line**, specialist departments containing *similar* machines no longer exist. Instead groups of *dissimilar* machines are organized into product or component family flow lines that function like an assembly line. For each product line the machines are placed close together in the order in which they are required by the group of products to be processed. Items in each product family can now move, one at a time, from process to process more easily, thereby reducing work in progress stocks and lead times.

JIT manufacturing aims to produce the right parts at the right time, only when they are needed, and only in the quantity needed. This philosophy has resulted in a **pull manufacturing system**, which means that parts move through the production system based on end-unit demand, focusing on maintaining a constant flow of components rather than batches of WIP. With the pull system, work on components does not commence until specifically requested by the next process. JIT techniques aim to keep the materials moving in a continuous flow with no stoppages and no storage.

The pull system is implemented by monitoring the consumption of parts at each operation stage and using various types of visible signalling systems (known as *Kanbans*) to authorize production and movement of the part to the using location. The producing cell cannot run the parts until authorized to do so. The signalling mechanism usually involves the use of *Kanban* containers. These containers hold materials or parts for movement from one work centre to another. The capacity of *Kanban* containers tends to vary from two to five units. They are just big enough to permit the production line to operate smoothly despite minor interruptions to individual work centres within the cell. To illustrate how the system works consider three machines forming part of a cell where the parts are first processed by machine A before being further processed on machine B and then machine C. The *Kanban*s are located between the machines. As long as the *Kanban* container is not full, the worker at machine A continues to produce parts, placing them in the *Kanban* container. When the container is full the worker stops producing and recommences when a part has been removed from the container by the worker operating machine B. A similar process applies between the operations of machines B and C. This process can result in idle time within certain locations within the cell, but the JIT philosophy considers that it is more beneficial to absorb short-run idle time rather than add to inventory during these periods. During idle time the workers perform preventive maintenance on the machines.

With a pull system problems arising in any part of the system will immediately halt the production line because work centres at the earlier stages will not receive the pull signal (because the *Kanban* container is full) if a problem arises at a later stage. Alternatively, work centres at a later stage will not have their pull signal answered (because of empty *Kanban* containers) when problems arise with work centres at the earlier stages of the production cycle. Thus attention is drawn immediately to production problems so that appropriate remedial action can be taken. This is deemed to be preferable to the approach adopted in a traditional manufacturing system where large stock levels provide a cushion for production to continue.

In contrast, the traditional manufacturing environment is based on a **push manufacturing system**. With this system, machines are grouped into work centres based on the similarity of their functional capabilities. Each manufactured part has a designated routing, and the preceding process supplies parts to the subsequent process without any consideration being given to whether the next process is ready to work on the parts or not. Hence the use of the term 'push-through system'.

Batch sizes of one

Set-up time is the amount of time required to adjust equipment and to retool for a different product. Long set-up times make the production of batches with a small number of units uneconomic. However, the production of large batches leads to substantial throughput delays and the creation of high inventory levels. Throughput delays arise because several lengthy production runs are required to process larger batches through the factory. A further problem with large batches is that they often have to wait for lengthy periods before they are processed by the next process or before they are sold. The JIT philosophy is to reduce set-up times. For example, by investing in advanced manufacturing technologies some machine settings can be adjusted automatically instead of manually.

If set-up times are approaching zero, this implies that there are no advantages in producing in batches. Therefore the optimal batch size can be one. With a batch size of one, the work can flow smoothly to the next stage without the need for storage and to schedule the next machine to accept this item. In many situations set-up times will not be approaching zero, but by significantly reducing set-up times, small batch sizes will be economical. Small batch sizes, combined with short throughput times, also enable a firm to adapt more readily to short-term fluctuations in market demand and respond faster to customer requests, since production is not dependent on long planning lead times.

JIT purchasing arrangements

The JIT philosophy also extends to adopting JIT purchasing techniques, whereby the delivery of materials immediately precedes their use. By arranging with suppliers for more frequent deliveries, stocks can be cut to a minimum. Considerable savings in material handling expenses can be obtained by requiring suppliers to inspect materials before their delivery and guaranteeing their quality. This improved service is obtained by giving more business to fewer suppliers and placing longer-term purchasing orders. Therefore the supplier has an assurance of long-term sales, and can plan to meet this demand.

Companies that have implemented JIT purchasing techniques claim to have substantially reduced their investment in raw materials and work in progress stocks. Other advantages include, savings in time from negotiating with fewer suppliers and a reduction in paperwork arising from issuing blanket long-term orders to a few suppliers rather than individual purchase orders to many suppliers.

JIT and management accounting

Management accountants in many organizations have been strongly criticized because of their failure to alter the management accounting system to reflect the move from a traditional manufacturing to a just in time manufacturing system. Conventional management accounting systems can encourage behaviour that is inconsistent with a just in time manufacturing philosophy. Management accounting must support just in time manufacturing by monitoring, identifying and communicating to decision-makers any delay, error and waste in the system. Modern management accounting systems are now placing greater emphasis on providing information on supplier reliability, set-up times, throughput cycle times, percentage of deliveries that are on time and defect rates. All of these measures are critical to supporting a just in time manufacturing philosophy and are discussed in more detail in the next chapter.

Because JIT manufacturing systems result in the establishment of production cells that are dedicated to the manufacturing of a single product or a family of similar products many of the support activities can be directly traced to the product dedicated cells. Thus, a high proportion of costs can be directly assigned to products. Therefore the benefits from implementing ABC product costing will be lower in JIT organizations.

Summary

The following items relate to the learning objectives listed at the beginning of the chapter.

- **Distinguish between the features of a traditional management accounting control system and cost management.**

A traditional management accounting control system tends to be based on the preservation of the status quo and the ways of performing existing activities are not reviewed. The emphasis is on cost containment rather than cost reduction. Cost management focuses on cost reduction rather than cost containment. Whereas traditional cost control systems are routinely applied on a continuous basis, cost management tends to be applied on an ad-hoc basis when an opportunity for cost reduction is identified. Also many of the approaches that are incorporated within the area of cost management do not involve the use of accounting techniques. In contrast, cost control relies heavily on accounting techniques.

- **Explain life-cycle costing and describe the typical pattern of cost commitment and cost incurrence during the three stages of a product's life cycle.**

Life-cycle costing estimates and accumulates costs over a product's entire life cycle in order to determine whether the profits earned during the manufacturing phase will cover the costs incurred during the pre- and post-manufacturing stages. Three stages of a product's life cycle can be identified – the planning and design stage, the manufacturing stage and the service and abandonment stage. Approximately 80% of a product's costs are committed during the planning and design stage. At this stage product designers determine the product's design and the production process. In contrast, the majority of costs are incurred at the manufacturing stage, but they have already become locked-in at the planning and design stage and are difficult to alter. Cost management can be most effectively exercised during the planning and design stage and not at the manufacturing stage when the product design and processes have already been determined and costs have been committed.

- **Describe the target costing approach to cost management.**

Target costing is a customer-oriented technique. The first stage requires market research to determine the target selling price for a product. Next a standard or desired profit margin is deducted to establish a target cost for the product. The target cost is compared with the predicted actual cost. If the predicted actual cost is above the target cost intensive efforts are made to close the gap. Value engineering and functional analysis are used to drive the predicted actual cost down to the target cost. The major advantage of adopting target costing is that it is deployed during a product's design and planning stage so that it can have a maximum impact in determining the level of the locked-in costs.

- **Describe tear-down analysis, value engineering and functional analysis.**

  Tear-down analysis involves examining a competitor's product in order to identify opportunities for product improvement and/or cost reduction. The aim of value engineering is to achieve the assigned target cost by (a) identifying improved product designs that reduce the product's cost without sacrificing functionality and/or (b) eliminating unnecessary functions that increase the product's costs and for which customers are not prepared to pay extra. Value engineering requires the use of functional analysis. This involves decomposing the product into its many elements or attributes. A value for each element is determined which reflects the amount the customer is prepared to pay. The cost of each function of a product is compared with the benefits perceived by the customers. If the cost of the function exceeds the benefit to the customer, then the function is either eliminated, modified to reduce its cost, or enhanced in terms of its perceived value so that its value exceeds the cost.

- **Distinguish between target costing and *kaizen* costing.**

  The major difference between target and *kaizen* costing is that target costing is applied during the design stage whereas *kaizen* costing is applied during the manufacturing stage of the product life cycle. With target costing, the focus is on the product and cost reductions are achieved primarily through product design. In contrast, *kaizen* costing focuses on the production processes and cost reductions are derived primarily through the increased efficiency of the production process. The aim of *kaizen* costing is to reduce the cost of components and products by a pre-specified amount. A major feature is that workers are given the responsibility to improve processes and reduce costs.

- **Describe activity-based cost management.**

  Activity-based management (ABM) focuses on managing the business on the basis of the activities that make up the organization. It is based on the premise that activities consume costs. Therefore, by managing activities, costs will be managed in the long term. The goal of ABM is to enable customer needs to be satisfied while making fewer demands on organization resources. Prior to the introduction of ABM most organizations have been unaware of the cost of undertaking the activities that make up the organization. Knowing the cost of activities enables those activities with the highest cost to be highlighted so that they can be prioritized for detailed studies to ascertain whether they can be eliminated or performed more efficiently.

- **Distinguish between value added and non-value added activities.**

  To identify and prioritize the potential for cost reduction using ABM, many organizations have found it useful to classify activities as either value added or non-value added. A value added activity is an activity that customers perceive as adding usefulness to the product or service they purchase whereas a non-value added activity is an activity where there is an opportunity for cost reduction without reducing the product's service potential to the customer. Taking action to reduce or eliminate non-value added activities is given top priority because by doing so the organization permanently reduces the cost it incurs without reducing the value of the product to the customer.

- **Explain the purpose of a cost of quality report.**

  A cost of quality report indicates the total cost to the organization of producing products or services that do not conform with quality requirements. Quality costs are analysed by four categories for reporting purposes (prevention, appraisal, and internal and external failure costs). The report draws management's attention to the possibility of reducing total quality costs by a wiser allocation of costs among the four quality categories.

● **Describe how value chain analysis can be used to increase customer satisfaction and manage costs more effectively.**

Increasing attention is now being given to value chain analysis as a means of increasing customer satisfaction and managing costs more effectively. The value chain is the linked set of value-creating activities all the way from basic raw material sources from component suppliers through to the ultimate end-use product or service delivered to the customer. Understanding how value chain activities are performed and how they interact with each other creates the conditions to improve customer satisfaction, particularly in terms of cost efficiency, quality and delivery.

● **Explain the role of benchmarking within the cost management framework.**

Benchmarking involves comparing key activities with world-class best practices by identifying an activity that needs to be improved, finding a non-rival organization that is considered to represent world-class best practice for the activity, and studying how it performs the activity. The objective is to establish how the activity can be improved and ensure that the improvements are implemented. The outcome should be reduced costs for the activity or process or performing the activity more effectively, thus increasing customer satisfaction.

● **Outline the main features of a just-in-time philosophy.**

In recent years many companies have sought to eliminate and/or reduce the costs of non-value added activities by introducing just in time (JIT) systems. The aims of a JIT system are to produce the required items, at the required quality and in the required quantities, at the precise time they are required. In particular, JIT aims to eliminate waste by minimizing inventories and reducing cycle or throughput times (i.e. the time elapsed from when customers place an order until the time when they receive the desired product or service). Adopting a JIT manufacturing system involves moving from a batch production functional layout to a cellular flow line manufacturing system. The JIT philosophy also extends to adopting JIT purchasing techniques, whereby the delivery of materials immediately precedes their use. By arranging with suppliers for more frequent deliveries, stocks can be cut to a minimum.

 Key terms and concepts

activity-based cost management (p. 436)
activity-based management (p. 436)
appraisal costs (p. 442)
batch production functional layout (p. 448)
benchmarking (p. 446)
business process re-engineering (p. 440)
committed costs (p. 430)
cost of quality report (p. 442)
environmental appraisal costs (p. 447)
environmental external failure costs (p. 447)
environmental internal failure costs (p. 447)
environmental prevention costs (p. 447)
external failure costs (p. 442)
functional analysis (p. 432)
internal failure costs (p. 442)
just in time (JIT) system (p. 441)
kaizen costing (p. 436)

Kanbans (p. 449)
life-cycle costing (p. 430)
locked-in costs (p. 430)
non-value added activity (p. 439)
prevention costs (p. 442)
product flow line (p. 449)
pull manufacturing system (p. 449)
push manufacturing system (p. 449)
reverse engineering (p. 432)
target costing (p. 430)
tear-down analysis (p. 432)
total quality management (p. 442)
value added activity (p. 439)
value analysis (p. 432)
value-chain analysis (p. 444)
value engineering (p. 432)

Assessment material

Review questions

The review questions are short questions that enable you to assess your understanding of the main topics included in the chapter. The numbers in parentheses provide you with the page numbers to refer to if you cannot answer a specific question.

Review problems

The review problems are more complex and require you to relate and apply the chapter content to various business problems. Fully worked solutions to the review problems are provided in a separate section at the end of the book. Further review problems for this chapter are available on the accompanying website, www.drury-online.com. The answers to these problems are available for lecturers on the lecturer's password-protected section of the website.

Case studies

The website also includes over 30 case study problems. A list of these cases is provided on pages 491–93.

Review questions

15.1 How does cost management differ from traditional management accounting control systems? (*pp. 429–30*)

15.2 What are committed (locked-in) costs? (*p. 430*)

15.3 Explain the essential features of life-cycle costing. (*p. 430*)

15.4 Describe the stages involved with target costing. Describe how costs are reduced so that the target cost can be achieved. (*pp. 431–32*)

15.5 What is *kaizen* costing? (*p. 436*)

15.6 What are the distinguishing features of activity-based management? (*pp. 436–40*)

15.7 Distinguish between value added and non-value added activities. (*p. 439*)

15.8 What is business process re-engineering? (*pp. 440–41*)

15.9 Identify and discuss the four kinds of quality costs that are included in a cost of quality report. Give examples of costs that fall within each category. (*p. 442*)

15.10 Discuss the value of a cost of quality report. (*pp. 442–43*)

15.11 Explain what is meant by value-chain analysis. Illustrate how value-chain analysis can be applied. (*pp. 443–5*)

15.12 Explain how benchmarking can be used to manage costs and improve activity performance. What are the major features of a just in time manufacturing philosophy? (*pp. 446–47, pp. 448–51*)

15.13 Distinguish between a pull and push manufacturing system. (*pp. 449–50*)

15.14 What are the essential features of just in time purchasing arrangements? (*p. 450*)

Review problems

15.15 **Cost of quality reporting**

Burdoy plc has a dedicated set of production facilities for component X. A just in time system is in place such that no stock of materials; work in progress or finished goods are held.

At the beginning of period 1, the planned information relating to the production of component X through the dedicated facilities is as follows:

(i) Each unit of component X has input materials: 3 units of material A at £18 per unit and 2 units of material B at £9 per unit.

(ii) Variable cost per unit of component X (excluding materials) is £15 per unit worked on.

(iii) Fixed costs of the dedicated facilities for the period: £162 000.

(iv) It is anticipated that 10% of the units of X worked on in the process will be defective and will be scrapped.

It is estimated that customers will require replacement (free of charge) of faulty units of component X at the rate of 2% of the quantity invoiced to them in fulfilment of orders.

Burdoy plc is pursuing a total quality management philosophy. Consequently all losses will be treated as abnormal in recognition of a zero defect policy and will be valued at variable cost of production.

Actual statistics for each periods 1 to 3 for component X are shown in Appendix 3.1. No changes have occurred from the planned price levels for materials, variable overhead or fixed overhead costs.

Required:

(a) Prepare an analysis of the relevant figures provided in Appendix 3.1 to show that the period 1 actual results were achieved at the planned level in respect of (i) quantities and losses and (ii) unit cost levels for materials and variable costs.

(*5 marks*)

(b) Use your analysis from (a) in order to calculate the value of the planned level of each of internal and external failure costs for period 1.

(3 marks)

(c) Actual free replacements of component X to customers were 170 units and 40 units in periods 2 and 3 respectively. Other data relating to periods 2 and 3 is shown in Appendix 3.1.

Burdoy plc authorized additional expenditure during periods 2 and 3 as follows: Period 2: Equipment accuracy checks of £10 000 and staff training of £5000. Period 3: Equipment accuracy checks of £10 000 plus £5000 of inspection costs; also staff training costs of £5000 plus £3000 on extra planned maintenance of equipment.

Required:

(i) Prepare an analysis for EACH of periods 2 and 3 which reconciles the number of components invoiced to customers with those worked on in the production process. The analysis should show the changes from the planned quantity of process losses and changes from the planned quantity of replacement of faulty components in customer hands;
(All relevant working notes should be shown)

(8 marks)

(ii) Prepare a cost analysis for EACH of periods 2 and 3 which shows actual internal failure costs, external failure costs, appraisal costs and prevention costs;

(6 marks)

(iii) Prepare a report which explains the meaning and interrelationship of the figures in Appendix 3.1 and in the analysis in (a), (b) and (c) (i)/(ii). The report should also give examples of each cost type and comment on their use in the monitoring and progressing of the TQM policy being pursued by Burdoy plc.

(13 marks)
(Total 35 marks)

Appendix 3.1
Actual statistics for component X

	Period 1	Period 2	Period 3
Invoiced to customers (units)	5 400	5 500	5 450
Worked on in the process (units)	6 120	6 200	5 780
Total costs:			
Materials A and B (£)	440 640	446 400	416 160
Variable cost of production (£)			
(excluding material cost)	91 800	93 000	86 700
Fixed cost (£)	162 000	177 000	185 000

15.16 **Traditional and activity-based budget statements and life-cycle costing**

The budget for the Production, Planning and Development Department of Obba plc, is currently prepared as part of a traditional budgetary planning and control system. The analysis of costs by expense type for the period ended 30 November 2000 where this system is in use is as follows:

Expense type	Budget %	Actual %
Salaries	60	63
Supplies	6	5
Travel cost	12	12
Technology cost	10	7
Occupancy cost	12	13

The total budget and actual costs for the department for the period ended 30 November 2000 are £1 000 000 and £1 060 000 respectively.

The company now feels that an activity-based budgeting approach should be used. A number of activities have been identified for the Production, Planning and Development Department. An investigation has indicated that total budget and actual costs should be attributed to the activities on the following basis:

	Budget %	Actual %
Activities		
1. Routing/scheduling – new products	20	16
2. Routing/scheduling – existing products	40	34
3. Remedial re-routing/scheduling	5	12
4. Special studies – specific orders	10	8
5. Training	10	15
6. Management and administration	15	15

Required:

(a) (i) Prepare *two* budget control statements for the Production Planning and Development Department for the period ended 30 November 2000 which compare budget with actual cost and show variances using
1. a traditional expense-based analysis and
2. an activity-based analysis.

(*6 marks*)

(ii) Identify and comment on *four* advantages claimed for the use of activity-based budgeting over traditional budgeting using the Production Planning and Development example to illustrate your answer.

(*12 marks*)

(iii) Comment on the use of the information provided in the activity-based statement which you prepared in (i) in activity-based performance measurement and suggest additional information which would assist in such performance measurement.

(*8 marks*)

(b) Other activities have been identified and the budget quantified for the three months ended 31 March 2001 as follows:

Activities	Cost driver unit basis	Units of cost driver	Cost (£000)
Product design	design hours	8 000	2000 (see note 1)
Purchasing	purchase orders	4 000	200
Production	machine hours	12 000	1500 (see note 2)
Packing	volume (cu.m.)	20 000	400
Distribution	weight (kg)	120 000	600

Note 1: this includes all design costs for new products released this period.

Note 2: this includes a depreciation provision of £300 000 of which £8000 applies to 3 months' depreciation on a straight line basis for a new product (NPD). The remainder applies to other products.

New product NPD is included in the above budget. The following additional information applies to NPD:

(i) Estimated total output over the product life cycle: 5000 units (4 years life cycle).

(ii) Product design requirement: 400 design hours

(iii) Output in quarter ended 31 March 2001: 250 units

(iv) Equivalent batch size per purchase order: 50 units

(v) Other product unit data: production time 0.75 machine hours: volume 0.4 cu. metres; weight 3 kg.

Required:

Prepare a unit overhead cost for product NPD using an activity-based approach which includes an appropriate share of life cycle costs using the information provided in (b) above.

(9 marks)

(Total 35 marks)

15.17 The implementation of budgeting in a world-class manufacturing environment may be affected by the impact of (i) a total quality ethos (ii) a just in time philosophy and (iii) an activity-based focus.

Briefly describe the principles incorporated in EACH of (i) to (iii) and discuss ways in which each may result in changes in the way in which budgets are prepared as compared to a traditional incremental budgeting system.

(15 marks)

15.18 New techniques are often described as contributing to cost reduction, but when cost reduction is necessary it is not obvious that such new approaches are used in preference to more established approaches. Three examples are:

new technique	compared with	*established approach*
(a) benchmarking		inter-firm comparison
(b) activity-based budgeting		zero base budgeting
(c) target costing		continuous cost improvement

You are required, for two of the three newer techniques mentioned above:

- to explain its objectives
- to explain its workings
- to differentiate it from the related approach identified
- to explain how it would contribute to a cost reduction programme.

(*20 marks*)

15.19 'ABC is still at a relatively early stage of its development and its implications for process control may in the final analysis be more important than its product costing implications. It is a good time for every organization to consider whether or not ABC is appropriate to its particular circumstances.'

J. Innes & F. Mitchell, *Activity Based Costing, A Review with Case Studies*, CIMA, 1990.

You are required:

(a) to contrast the feature of organizations which would benefit from ABC with those which would not;

(*8 marks*)

(b) to explain in what ways ABC may be used to manage costs, and the limitations of these approaches;

(*11 marks*)

(c) to explain and to discuss the use of target costing to control product costs.

(*6 marks*)
(*Total 25 marks*)

Strategic management accounting

16 During the late 1980s criticisms of traditional management accounting practices were widely publicized and new approaches were advocated which are more in tune with today's competitive and business environment. In particular, strategic management accounting has been identified as a way forward. However, there is still no comprehensive framework as to what constitutes strategic management accounting. In this chapter we shall examine the elements of strategic management accounting and describe the different contributions that have been made to its development.

One of the elements of strategic management accounting involves the provision of information for the formulation of an organization's strategy and managing strategy implementation. To encourage behaviour that is consistent with an organization's strategy, attention is now being given to developing an integrated framework of performance measurement that can be used to clarify, communicate and manage strategy. In the latter part of this chapter recent developments that seek to incorporate performance measurement within the strategic management process are described.

LEARNING OBJECTIVES:

After studying this chapter, you should be able to:

- describe the different elements of strategic management accounting;
- describe the balanced scorecard;
- explain each of the four perspectives of the balanced scorecard;
- provide illustrations of performance measures for each of the four perspectives;
- describe the distinguishing characteristics of service organizations that influence performance measurement.

What is strategic management accounting?

For many years strategic management accounting has been advocated as a potential area of development that would enhance the future contribution of management accounting. In the late 1980s the UK Chartered Institute of Management Accountants commissioned an investigation to review the current state of development of management accounting. The findings were published in a report entitled *Management Accounting: Evolution not Revolution*, authored by Bromwich and Bhimani (1989). In the report, and a follow-up report (*Management Accounting: Pathways to Progress*, 1994) Bromwich and Bhimani drew attention to strategic management accounting as an area for future development. Despite the publicity that strategic management accounting has received there is still no comprehensive conceptual framework of what strategic management accounting is (Tomkins and Carr, 1996). For example, Coad (1996) states:

> *Strategic management accounting is an emerging field whose boundaries are loose and, as yet, there is no unified view of what it is or how it might develop. The existing literature in the field is both disparate and disjointed (Coad, 1996, p. 392).*

Innes (1998) defines strategic management accounting as the provision of information to support the strategic decisions in organizations. Strategic decisions usually involve the longer-term, have a significant effect on the organization and, although they may have an internal element, they also have an external element. Adopting this definition suggests that the provision of information that supports an organization's major long-term decisions, such as the use of activity-based costing information for providing information relating to product mix, introduction and abandonment decisions falls within the domain of strategic management accounting. This view is supported by Cooper and Kaplan (1988) who state that strategic accounting techniques are designed to support the overall competitive strategy of the organization, principally by the power of using information technology to develop more refined product and service costs. Various writers have suggested that other management accounting techniques that fall within the domain of strategic management accounting are target costing, life-cycle costing and activity-based management (see Chapter 15 for a discussion of these techniques).

Other writers, however, have adopted definitions that emphasize that strategic management accounting is externally focused. Simmonds (1981, 1982), who first coined the term strategic management accounting, views it as the provision and analysis of management accounting data about a business and its competitors which is of use in the development and monitoring of the strategy of that business. He views profits as emerging not from internal efficiencies but from the firm's competitive position in its markets. More recently, Bromwich (1990), a principal advocate of strategic management accounting, has provided the following definition:

> *The provision and analysis of financial information on the firm's product markets and competitors' costs and cost structures and the monitoring of the enterprise's strategies and those of its competitors in these markets over a number of periods (Bromwich, 1990, p. 28).*

The Chartered Institute of Management Accountants (CIMA) in the UK defines strategic management accounting as:

> *A form of management accounting in which emphasis is placed on information which relates to factors external to the firm, as well as non-financial information and internally generated information (CIMA Official Terminology, 2000, p. 50).*

Because of its external focus, and the fact that it is a market driven approach to product pricing and cost management, Roslender (1995) has identified target costing as falling within the domain of strategic management accounting.

The lack of consensus on what constitutes strategic management accounting resulted in Lord (1996) reviewing the literature. Several strands were identified that had been used to characterize strategic management accounting. They included:

1 The extension of traditional management accounting's internal focus to include external information about competitors.

2 The relationship between the strategic position chosen by a firm and the expected emphasis on management accounting (i.e. accounting in relation to strategic positioning).

3 Gaining competitive advantage by analysing ways to decrease costs and/or enhance the differentiation of a firm's products, through exploiting linkages in the value chain and optimizing cost drivers.

Let us now examine each of the above characteristics in more detail.

External information about competitors

Much of the early work relating to strategic management accounting can be attributed to the writings of Simmonds (1981, 1982, 1986). He argued that management accounting should be more outward looking and should help the firm evaluate its competitive position relative to the rest of the industry by collecting data on costs and prices, sales volumes and market shares, and cash flows and resources availability for its main competitors. To protect an organization's strategic position and determine strategies to improve its future competitiveness managers require information that indicates by whom, by how much and why they are gaining or being beaten. This information provides advance warning of the need for a change in competitive strategy. Competitive information is available from public sources such as company annual reports, press, official institutions and informal sources (e.g. sales personnel, analysing competitors' products, industry specialists, consultants, etc.).

Simmonds also stressed the importance of the learning curve as a means of obtaining strategic advantage by forecasting cost reductions and consequently selling price reductions of competitors. He also drew attention to the importance of early experience with a new product as a means of conferring an unbeatable lead over competitors. The leading competitor should be able to reduce its selling price for the product (through the learning curve effect) which should further increase its volume and market share and eventually force some lagging competitors out of the industry.

An organization may also seek to gain strategic advantage by its pricing policy. Here the management accounting function can assist by attempting to assess each major competitor's cost structure and relate this to their prices. In particular, Simmonds suggests that it may be possible to assess the cost–volume–profit relationship of competitors in order to predict their pricing responses. He states:

Clearly, competitor reactions can substantially influence the outcome of a price move. Moreover, likely reactions may not be self-evident when each competitor faces a different cost–volume–profit situation. Competitors may not follow a price lead nor even march in perfect step as they each act to defend or build their own positions. For an adequate assessment of the likelihood of competitor price reactions, then, some calculation is needed of the impact of possible price moves on the performance of individual competitors. Such an assessment in turn requires an accounting approach that can depict both competitor cost–volume–profit situations and their financial resources (Simmonds, 1982, p. 207).

Besides dealing with costs and prices Simmonds focused on volume and market share. By monitoring movements in market share for its major products, an organization can see whether it is gaining or losing position, and an examination of relative market shares will indicate the strength of different competitors. Including market-share details in management accounting reports helps to make management accounting more strategically relevant. Competitor information may be obtained through public, formal sources, such as published reports and the business press, or through informal channels, such as the firm's salesforce, its customers and its suppliers.

Simmonds (1981) also suggested some changes and additions to traditional management accounting reporting systems in order to include the above information. Market share statements could be incorporated into management accounts. In addition, budgets could be routinely presented in a strategic format with columns for Ourselves, Competitor A, Competitor B, etc. According to Ward (1992) very few firms regularly report competitor information.

Accounting in relation to strategic positioning

Various classifications of strategic positions that firms may choose have been identified in the strategic management literature. Porter (1985) suggests that a firm has a choice of three generic strategies in order to achieve sustainable competitive advantage. They are:

- *cost leadership*, whereby an enterprise aims to be the lowest-cost producer within the industry thus enabling it to compete on the basis of lower selling prices rather than providing unique products or services. The source of this competitive advantage may arise from factors such as economies of scale, access to favourable raw materials prices and superior technology (Langfield-Smith, 1997).

- *differentiation*, whereby the enterprise seeks to offer products or services that are considered by its customers to be superior and unique relative to its competitors. Examples include the quality or dependability of the product, after-sales service, the wide availability of the product and product flexibility (Langfield-Smith, 1997).

- *focus*, which involves seeking advantage by focusing on a narrow segment of the market that has special needs that are poorly served by other competitors in the industry. Competitive advantage is based on either cost leadership or product differentiation.

Miles and Snow (1978) distinguish between *defenders* and *prospectors*. Defenders operate in relatively stable areas, have limited product lines and employ a mass production routine technology. They compete through making operations efficient through cost, quality and service leadership, and engage in little product/market development. Prospectors compete through new product innovations and market development and are constantly looking for new market opportunities. Hence, they face a more uncertain task environment.

The accounting literature suggests that firms will place more emphasis on particular accounting techniques, depending on which strategic position they adopt. For example, Porter (1980) suggested that tight cost controls are more appropriate when a cost leadership strategy is followed. Simons (1987) found that business units that follow a defender strategy tend to place a greater emphasis on the use of financial measures (e.g., short-term budget targets) for compensating financial managers. Prospector firms placed a greater emphasis on forecast data and reduced importance on cost control. Ittner *et al.* (1997) also found that the use of non-financial measures for determining executive's bonuses increases with the extent to which firms follow an innovation-oriented prospector strategy. Shank

(1989) stresses the need for management accounting to support a firm's competitive strategies, and illustrates how two different competitive strategies – cost leadership and product differentiation – demand different cost analysis perspectives. For example, carefully engineered product cost standards are likely to be a very important management control tool for a firm that pursues a cost leadership strategy in a mature commodity business. In contrast, carefully engineered manufacturing cost standards are likely to be less important for a firm following a product differentiation strategy in a market-driven, rapidly changing and fast-growing business. A firm pursuing a product differentiation strategy is likely to require more information than a cost leader about new product innovations, design cycle times, research and development expenditures and marketing cost analysis. Exhibit 16.1 illustrates some potential differences in cost management emphasis, depending on the primary strategic thrust of the firm.

Gaining competitive advantage

Porter (1985) advocated using **value-chain analysis** (see Chapter 15) to gain competitive advantage. The aim of value chain analysis is to find linkages between value-creating activities which result in lower cost and/or enhanced differentiation. These linkages can be within the firm or between the firm and its suppliers, and customers. The value chain comprises five primary activities and a number of support activities. The primary activities are defined sequentially as inbound logistics, operations, outbound logistics, marketing and sales and services. The secondary activities exist to support the primary activities and include the firm's infrastructure, human resource management, technology and procurement. Costs and assets are assigned to each activity in the value chain. The cost behaviour pattern of each activity depends on a number of causal factors which Porter calls cost drivers. These cost drivers operate in an interactive way and it is management's success in coping with them which determines the cost structure.

Strategic cost analysis also involves identifying the value chain and the operation of cost drivers of competitors in order to understand relative competitiveness. Porter advocates that organizations should use this information to identify opportunities for cost reduction, either by improving control of the cost drivers or reconfiguring the value chain. The latter involves deciding on those areas of the value chain where the firm has a comparative advantage and those which it should source to suppliers. It is essential that the cost reduction performance of both the organization and its principal competitors is continually monitored if competitive advantage is to be sustained.

You may be able to remember the illustration in the previous chapter relating to how an American automobile company failed to use the value chain approach to exploit links with suppliers and enhance profitability.[1] The company had made significant internal savings from introducing JIT manufacturing techniques, but, at the same time, price increases from suppliers more than offset these internal cost savings. A value chain perspective revealed that 50% of the firm's costs related to purchases from parts suppliers. As the automobile company reduced its own need for buffer stocks, it placed major new strains on the manufacturing responsiveness of suppliers. The increase in the suppliers' manufacturing costs was greater than the decrease in the automobile company's internal costs. Shank (1989) states:

> For every dollar of manufacturing cost the assembly plants saved by moving towards JIT management concepts, the suppliers' plant spent much more than one dollar extra because of schedule instability arising from the introduction of JIT. Because of its narrow value added perspective, the auto company had ignored the impact of its changes on its suppliers' costs. Management had ignored the idea that JIT involves a partnership with suppliers (Shank, 1989, p. 51).

EXHIBIT 16.1

Relationship between strategies and cost management emphasis

	Product differentiation	Cost leadership
Role of standard costs in assessing performance	Not very important	Very important
Importance of such concepts as flexible budgeting for manufacturing cost control	Moderate to low	High to very high
Perceived importance of meeting budgets	Moderate to low	High to very high
Importance of marketing cost analysis	Critical to success	Often not done at all on a formal basis
Importance of product cost as an input to pricing decisions	Low	High
Importance of competitor cost analysis	Low	High

Source: Shank (1989)

Surveys of strategic management accounting practices

Little research has been undertaken on the extent to which companies use strategic management accounting practices. A notable exception is a survey undertaken by Guilding *et al.* (2000). The survey consisted of a sample of 312 large companies comprising 63 from the UK, 127 from the USA and 124 from New Zealand.

Guilding *et al.* acknowledge the difficulty in identifying what are generally accepted as constituting strategic management accounting practices. Based on a review of the literature they identified 12 strategic management accounting practices. The criteria that they used for identifying the practices were that they must exhibit one or more of the following characteristics: environmental or marketing orientation; focus on competitors; and long-term, forward-looking orientation. The average usage of the identified practices and their perceived merits are reported in Exhibit 16.2. Three of the 12 listed practices, namely quality costing (involving the use of cost of quality reports), life-cycle costing and target costing, were described in the previous chapter. Although some of the remaining eight practices have been described in this chapter they can be subject to different interpretations and definitions. The following represent the definitions of these eight terms given to the respondents participating in the survey:

- *Competitive position monitoring* The analysis of competitor positions within the industry by assessing and monitoring trends in competitor sales, market share, volume, unit costs and return on sales. This information can provide a basis for the assessment of a competitor's market strategy.

- *Strategic pricing* The analysis of strategic factors in the pricing decision process. These factors may include: competitor price reaction; price elasticity; market growth; economies of scale and experience.

- *Competitor performance appraisal based on published financial statements* The numerical analysis of a competitor's published statements as part of an assessment of the competitor's key sources of competitive advantage.

EXHIBIT 16.2

Usage and perceived merit of strategic management accounting practices

Strategic management accounting practice	Average usage score[a]	Ranking	Average perceived merit score[b]	Ranking
Competitive position monitoring	4.99	1	5.73	1
Strategic pricing	4.54	2	5.45	2
Competitor performance appraisal based on published financial statements	4.42	3	5.31	3
Competitor cost assessment	4.07	4	5.27	4
Strategic costing	3.49	5	4.91	5
Quality costing	3.22	6	4.29	6
Target costing	3.12	7	3.94	8
Value-chain costing	3.04	8	4.27	7
Brand value monitoring	2.73	9	3.38	11
Life-cycle costing	2.60	10	3.58	9
Attribute costing	2.33	11	3.49	10
Brand value budgeting	2.32	12	3.33	12

Notes

[a]All items scored on a Likert scale where 1 denotes used 'not at all' and 7 denotes used 'to a great extent'.

[b]All items scored on a Likert scale where 1 denotes 'not at all helpful' and 7 denotes 'helpful to a great extent'.

- *Competitor cost assessment* The provision of regularly updated estimates of a competitor's costs based on, for example, appraisal of facilities, technology, economies of scale. Sources include direct observation, mutual suppliers, mutual customers and ex-employees.

- *Strategic costing* The use of cost data based on strategic and marketing information to develop and identify superior strategies that will sustain a competitive advantage.

- *Value-chain costing* An activity-based costing approach where costs are allocated to activities required to design, procure, produce, market, distribute and service a product or service.

- *Brand value monitoring* The financial valuation of a brand through the assessment of brand strength factors such as: leadership; stability; market; internationality; trend; support; and protection combined with historical brand profits.

- *Brand value budgeting* The use of brand value as a basis for managerial decisions on the allocation of resources to support/enhance a brand position, thus placing attention on management dialogue on brand issues.

It is apparent from Exhibit 16.2 that the three competitor accounting practices and strategic pricing are the most popular strategic management accounting practices. They all have average scores above the mid-point on the seven-point scale for the 'not at all/to a large extent' used measure. You will also see from Exhibit 16.2 that the usage rates for the remaining eight strategic management accounting practices are below the mid-point of the '1–7' measurement scale used, thus suggesting that these practices are not widely used by the responding organizations.

In terms of the perceived merit of the 12 practices, the rankings shown in Exhibit 16.2 are similar to those reported for the extent of usage. Guilding *et al.* conclude that while usage rates for most of the practices appraised scored relatively lowly, two factors suggest that it would be inappropriate to dismiss their potential. First, for all of the strategic management accounting practices appraised, the perceived merit scores are significantly greater than the usage rate scores. Secondly, for the eight strategic management accounting practices where relatively low usage rates were observed, three (strategic costing, quality costing and value-chain costing) scored above the mid-point with respect to perceived merit. These observations suggest that there is a gap between what is needed and what is reported by an accounting system.

Guilding *et al.* also examined the familiarity of practising accountants with the term 'strategic management accounting'. The responses suggest that there was negligible use of the term in organizations and practising accountants have a limited appreciation of what the term means. This reinforces Tomkins and Carr's (1996) claim, made in an academic context, that strategic management accounting is ill-defined.

The balanced scorecard

More recent contributions to strategic management accounting have emphasized the role of management accounting in formulating and supporting the overall competitive strategy of an organization. To encourage behaviour that is consistent with an organization's strategy, attention is now being given to developing an integrated framework of performance measurement that can be used to clarify, communicate and manage strategy implementation. In the remainder of the chapter our focus will be on integrated approaches to performance measurement that are linked to an organization's strategy. These approaches differ from the financial performance measures that have been described in Chapters 11–13. These measures tend to be used primarily as a financial control mechanism whereas the approaches that are described in the remainder of this chapter attempt to integrate both financial and non-financial measures and incorporate performance measurement within the strategic management process.

Prior to the 1980s management accounting control systems tended to focus mainly on financial measures of performance. The inclusion of only those items that could be expressed in monetary terms motivated managers to focus excessively on cost reduction and ignore other important variables which were necessary to compete in the global competitive environment that emerged during the 1980s. Product quality, delivery, reliability, after-sales service and customer satisfaction became key competitive variables but none of these were given much importance by the traditional management accounting performance measurement system.

During the 1980s much greater emphasis was given to incorporating into the management reporting system those non-financial performance measures that provided feedback on the key variables that are required to compete successfully in a global economic environment. However, a proliferation of performance measures emerged. This resulted in confusion when some of the measures conflicted with each other and it was possible to enhance one measure at the expense of another. It was also not clear to managers how the non-financial measures they were evaluated on contributed to the whole picture of achieving success in financial terms. According to Kaplan and Norton (2001a) previous systems that incorporated non-financial measurements used ad hoc collections of such measures, more like checklists of measures for managers to keep track of and improve than a comprehensive system of linked measurements.

The need to integrate financial and non-financial measures of performance and identify key performance measures that link measurements to strategy led to the emergence of the **balanced scorecard** – an integrated set of performance measures derived from the company's strategy that gives *top* management a fast but comprehensive view of the organizational unit (i.e. a division/strategic business unit). The balanced scorecard was devised by Kaplan and Norton (1992) and refined in later publications (Kaplan and Norton, 1993, 1996a, 1996b, 2001a, 2001b). Therefore the following discussion is a summary of Kaplan and Norton's writings on this topic. They use the diagram reproduced in Figure 16.1 to illustrate how the balanced scorecard links performance measures.

Figure 16.1 emphasizes that the balanced scorecard philosophy assumes that an organization's vision and strategy is best achieved when the organization is viewed from the following four perspectives:

1 **customer perspective** (How do customers see us?)

2 **internal business process perspective** (What must we excel at?)

3 **learning and growth perspective** (Can we continue to improve and create value?)

4 **financial perspective** (How do we look to shareholders?)

The balanced scorecard is a strategic management technique for communicating and evaluating the achievement of the mission and strategy of the organization. You will see by referring to Figure 16.1 that to implement the balanced scorecard the major objectives for each of the four perspectives should be articulated. Figure 16.1 also shows that these objectives should then be translated into specific performance measures. There may be one or more objectives for each perspective and one or more performance measure linked to each objective. Figure 16.1 also shows that Kaplan and Norton recommend that in the scorecard firms should identify and describe the major initiatives for achieving each objective and also establish targets for each performance measure. For feedback reporting actual performance measures can also be added. The aim of the scorecard is to provide a comprehensive framework for translating a company's strategic objectives into a coherent set of performance measures. In order to minimize information overload and avoid a proliferation of performance measures the number of measures in each of the boxes used for each of the four perspectives in Figure 16.1 is limited. Only the critical measures are incorporated in the scorecard. Typically each box perspective ought to comprise four to seven separate measures.

A critical assumption of the balanced scorecard is that each performance measure is part of a cause-and-effect relationship involving a linkage from strategy formulation to financial outcomes. Measures of organizational learning and growth are assumed to be the drivers of the internal business processes. The measures of these processes are in turn assumed to be the drivers of measures of customer perspective, while these measures are the driver of the financial perspective. The assumption that there is a cause-and-effect relationship is necessary because it allows the measurements relating to the non-financial perspectives to be used to predict future financial performance. In this context, Kaplan and Norton (1996b) indicate that the chain of cause-and-effect relationships encompasses all four perspectives of the balanced scorecard such that economic value added (see Chapter 13) may be an outcome measure for the financial perspective. The driver of this measure could be an expansion of sales from existing customers. This expansion may be achieved by enhancing customers' loyalty by meeting their preference from on-time delivery. Thus the improved on-time delivery is expected to lead to higher customer loyalty which in turn leads to higher financial performance. The on-time delivery is part of the internal process

REAL WORLD VIEWS 16.1

How Southwest Airlines developed its balanced scorecard analysis

Southwest Airlines set 'operating efficiency' as its strategic theme. The four perspectives embodied in the balanced scorecard were linked together by a series of relatively simple questions and answers:

Financial: What will drive operating efficiency? *Answer:* More customers on fewer planes.

Customer: How will we get more customers on fewer planes? *Answer:* Attract targeted segments of customers who value price and on-time arrivals.

Internal: What must our internal focus be? *Answer:* Fast aircraft turnaround time.

Learning: How will our people accomplish fast turnaround? *Answer:* Educate and compensate the ground crew regarding how they contribute to the firm's success. Also, use the employee stockholder programme.

The chart below shows how Southwest used this framework to lay out its balanced scorecard model. The first column of the chart contains the 'strategy map', that illustrates the cause-and-effect relationships between strategic objectives. The Objectives column shows what each strategy must achieve and what is critical to its success. The Measurement column shows how success in achieving each strategy will be measured and tracked. The Target column spells out the level of performance or rate of improvement that is needed. The Initiative column contains key action programmes required to achieve objectives. Note that all of the measures, targets and initiatives are all aligned to each objective.

The company extended the effort to the department level, and the degree of development varied between departments. The goal was to identify key performance measures in each segment for the operating personnel. Some of the non-financial metrics that have emerged on a departmental level include: load factor (percentage of seats occupied); utilization factors on aircraft and personnel; on-time performance; available seat miles; denied-boarding rate; lost-bag reports per 10 000 passengers; flight cancellation rate; employee head count; and customer complaints per 10 000 passengers filed with the Department of Transportation.

Southwest Airlines' Balanced Scorecard Framework

Strategic Theme: Operating Efficiency	Objectives	Measurement	Target	Initiative
Financial — Profitability; Fewer planes; More customers	Profitability / More customers / Fewer planes	Market value / Seat revenue / Plane lease cost	30% CAGR / 20% CAGR / 5% CAGR	
Customer — Flight is on time; Lowest prices	Flight is on time / Lowest prices	FAA on time arrival rating / Customer ranking (market survey)	#1 / #1	Quality management / Customer loyalty program
Internal — Fast ground turnaround	Fast ground turnaround	On ground time / On time departure	30 minutes / 90%	Cycle time optimization
Learning — Ground crew alignment	Ground crew alignment	% Ground crew trained / % Ground crew stockholders	Yr. 1 70% / Yr. 3 90% / Yr. 5 100%	ESOP Ground crew training

(Source: Balanced Scorecard Collaborative)

Source: Adapted from Institute of Management & Administration Report on Financial Analysis Planning and Reporting, July 2002.

FIGURE 16.1   *The balanced scorecard*

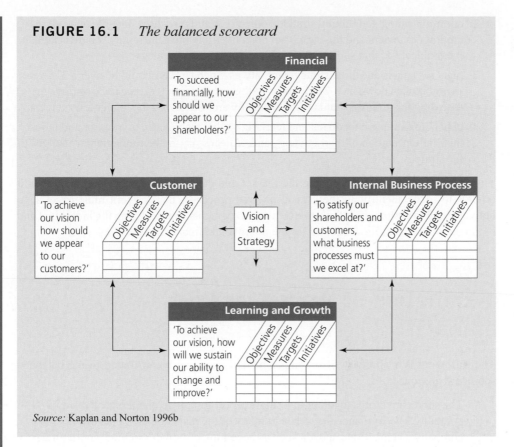

Source: Kaplan and Norton 1996b

perspective and to achieve it the business needs to achieve a short cycle time in operating processes and the short cycle time can be achieved by training the employees, this goal being part of the learning and growth perspective.

The balanced scorecard thus consists of two types of performance measures. The first consists of **lagging measures**. These are the financial (outcome) measures within the financial perspective that are the results of past actions. Mostly these measures do not incorporate the effect of decisions when they are made. Instead, they show the financial impact of the decisions as their impact materializes and this can be long after the decisions were made. The second are **leading measures** that are the drivers of future financial performance. These are the non-financial measures relating to the customer, internal business process and learning and growth perspectives.

The balanced scorecard as a strategic management system

Kaplan and Norton (1996b) describe how innovative companies are using the measurement focus of the scorecard to accomplish the following critical management processes:

1   clarifying and translating vision and strategy into specific strategic objectives and identifying the critical drivers of the strategic objectives;

2 communicating and linking strategic objectives and measures. Ideally, once all the employees understand the high level objectives and measures, they should establish local objectives that support the business unit's global strategy;

3 plan, set targets and align strategic initiatives. Such targets should be over a 3–5 year period broken down on a yearly basis so that progression targets can be set for assessing the progress that is being made towards achieving the longer-term targets;

4 enhancing strategic feedback and learning so that managers can monitor and adjust the implementation of their strategy, and, if necessary, make fundamental changes to the strategy itself.

They approach strategy as choosing the market and customer segments the business unit intends to serve, identifying the critical internal processes that the unit must excel at to deliver value to customers in the targeted market segments, and selecting the individual and organizational capabilities required for the internal and financial objectives.

Benefits and limitation of the balanced scorecard approach

The following is a summary of the major benefits that can be attributed to the balanced scorecard approach:

1 The scorecard brings together in a single report four different perspectives on a company's performance that relate to many of the disparate elements of the company's competitive agenda such as becoming customer oriented, shortening response time, improving quality, emphasizing teamwork, reducing new product launch times and managing for the long term. Many organizations collect some performance measures relating to each of the four perspectives but they are typically presented in several different large reports that often prove to be unhelpful because they suffer from information overload.

2 The approach provides a comprehensive framework for translating a company's strategic goals into a coherent set of performance measures by developing the major goals for the four perspectives and then translating these goals into specific performance measures.

3 The scorecard helps managers to consider all the important operational measures together. It enables managers see whether improvements in one area may have been at the expense of another.

4 The approach improves communications within the organization and promotes the active formulation and implementation of organizational strategy by making it highly visible through the linkage performance measures to business unit strategy.

The balanced scorecard has also been subject to frequent criticisms. Most of them question the assumption of the cause-and-effect relationship on the grounds that they are too ambiguous and lack a theoretical underpinning or empirical support. The empirical studies that have been undertaken have failed to provide evidence on the underlying linkages between non-financial data and future financial performance (American Accounting Association Financial Accounting Standards Committee, 2002). Other criticisms relate to the omission of important perspectives, the most notable being the environmental/impact on society perspective (see Chapter 15) and an employee perspective. It should be noted, however, that Kaplan and Norton presented the four perspectives as a suggested framework rather than a constraining straitjacket. There is nothing to prevent companies adding additional perspectives to meet their own requirements but they must avoid the temptation of creating too many perspectives and performance measures since one of the major benefits of the balanced scorecard is its conciseness and clarity of presentation.

Establishing objectives and performance measures

Having explained the general principles of the balanced scorecard we shall now consider the process of establishing objectives and performance measures in each of the four scorecard perspectives (financial, customer, internal business process, and learning and growth). Throughout this section the generic measures that have been presented by Kaplan and Norton are described. In practice, companies should customize these measures to fit their own specific strategies. Exhibit 16.3 provides an illustration of potential performance measures for organizations operating in different business sectors. You will also find it is appropriate at this point to refer to Exhibit 16.4 which summarizes surveys of practice relating to the usage of the balanced scorecard.

The financial perspective

In Chapters 11–13 financial performance measures have been extensively discussed. At the strategic business unit level operating profit, return on investment, residual income and economic value added were discussed and such measures should be used for measuring the financial objective of the business unit. Other financial objectives include revenue growth, cost reduction and asset utilization. Typical financial objectives are to increase return on investment by 20% and/or to increase sales and operating income by 100% over the next five years. Because the financial measures have already been described in earlier chapters we shall concentrate mainly on the remaining three scorecard perspectives.

The customer perspective

In the customer perspective of the balanced scorecard managers should identify the customer and market segments in which the businesses unit will compete. Target segments may include both existing and potential customers. Managers should then develop performance measures that track the business unit's ability to create satisfied and loyal customers in the targeted segments. The customer perspective typically includes several core or generic objectives and measures that relate to customer loyalty and the outcomes of the strategy in the targeted segments. They include core objectives relating to increasing market share, customer retention, new customer acquisition, customer satisfaction and customer profitability. Possible performance measures for these objectives are discussed below.

Market share

Market share represents the proportion of sales in a particular market that a business obtains. It can be measured in terms of sales revenues, unit sales volume or number of customers.

EXHIBIT 16.3

Potential scorecard measures in different business sectors

	Generic	Health care	Airlines	Banking
Financial Strength (Looking Back)	Market share Revenue growth Operating profits Return on equity Stock market performance Growth in margin	Patient census Unit profitability Funds raised for capital improvements Cost per care Percentage of revenue – new programmes	Revenue/cost per available passenger mile Mix of freight Mix of full fare to discounted Average age of fleet Available seat miles and related yields	Outstanding loan balances Deposit balances Non-interest income
Customer Service and Satisfaction (Looking from the outside in)	Customer satisfaction Customer retention Quality customer service Sales from new products/services	Patient satisfaction survey Patient retention Patient referral rate Admittance or discharge timeliness Medical plan awareness	Lost bag reports per 10 000 passengers Denied boarding rate Flight cancellation rate Customer complaints filed with the DOT	Customer retention Number of new customers Number of products per customer Face time spent between loan officers and customers
Internal Operating Efficiency (Looking from the inside out)	Delivery time Cost Process quality Error rates on shipments Supplier satisfaction	Weekly patient complaints Patient loads Breakthroughs in treatments and medicines Infection rates Readmission rate Length of stay	Load factors (percentage of seats occupied) Utilization factors on aircraft and personnel On-time performance	Sales calls to potential customers Thank you calls or cards to new and existing customers Cross-selling statistics
Learning and Growth (Looking ahead)	Employee skill level Training availability Employee satisfaction Job retention Amount of overtime worked Amount of vacation time taken	Training hours per caregiver Number of peer reviewed papers published Number of grants awarded (NIH) Referring MDs Employee turnover rate	Employee absenteeism Worker safety statistics Performance appraisals completed Training programme hours per employee	Test results from training knowledge of product offerings, sales and service Employee satisfaction survey

Source: Leauby and Wentzel, 2002

EXHIBIT 16.4

Surveys of practice relating to balanced scorecard usage

Surveys indicate that even though the balanced scorecard did not emerge until the early 1990s it is now widely used in many countries throughout the world. A US survey by Silk (1998) estimates that 60% of Fortune 1000 firms have experimented with the balanced scorecard. In the UK a survey of large divisionalized companies (annual sales turnover in excess of £100 million) by El Shishini and Drury (2001) indicated that 43% used the balanced scorecard at the divisional level. Other studies in mainland Europe indicate significant usage. Pere (1999) reported a 31% usage rate of companies in Finland with a further 30% in the process of implementing it. In Sweden Kald and Nilsson (2000) reported that 27% of major Swedish companies have implemented the approach. Other studies by Oliveras and Amat (2002) and Speckbacher *et al.* (2003) respectively report widespread usage in Spain and German-speaking countries (Germany, Austria and Switzerland). Major companies adopting the balanced scorecard include KPMG Peat Marwick, Allstate Insurance and AT&T (Chow *et al.*, 1997).

In terms of the perspectives used Malmi (2001) conducted a study involving semi-structured interviews in 17 companies in Finland. He found that 15 companies used the 4 perspectives identified by Kaplan and Norton and 2 companies added a fifth – an employee's perspective. A study by Olve *et al.* (2000) found that 15–20 performance measures are customarily used. There is also evidence to indicate that the balanced scorecard approach is linked to incentive compensation schemes. Epstein and Manzoni (1998) reported that 60% of the 100 large US organizations surveyed linked the balanced scorecard approach to incentive pay for their senior executives.

It is a measure of market penetration. Estimates of total market size can sometimes be derived from public sources such as trade associations and industry groupings. The major contribution of this measure is that it indicates whether the strategy adopted is achieving the expected results in the targeted market segment.

Customer retention and loyalty

One method of maintaining or increasing market share in targeted customer segments is to ensure that existing customers are retained in those segments. Customer retention can be measured in terms of the average duration of a customer relationship. In addition surveying defecting customers to ascertain where they have taken their business and why they have left can provide valuable feedback on the effectiveness of the firm's strategy. Customer loyalty can be measured by the number of new customers referred by existing customers since this would suggest that a customer must be highly satisfied before recommending a company's products or services to others.

Customer acquisition

Customer acquisition can be measured by either the number of new customers or the total sales to new customers in the desired market segment. Other measures include the number of new customers expressed as a percentage of prospective inquiries or the ratio of new customers per sales call.

Customer satisfaction

Measuring customer satisfaction typically involves the use of questionnaire surveys and customer response cards. Customer satisfaction can also be measured by examining letters of complaint, feedback from sales representatives and the use of 'mystery shoppers'. The latter normally involves external agencies sampling the service as customers and formally reporting back on their findings. The major limitation of customer satisfaction measures is that they measure attitudes and not actual buying behaviour.

Customer profitability

A company can be very successful in terms of market share, customer retention and acquisition, and customer satisfaction but this may be achieved at the expense of customer profitability. A company does not want just satisfied customers, it also wants profitable customers. The four measures described above relate to the means required to achieve customer profitability but they do not measure the outcome. Customer profitability measures meet this requirement. Profitability should be analysed by different customer segments and unprofitable segments identified. Newly acquired customers may initially be unprofitable and life-cycle profitability analysis should be used for determining whether the focus should be on retention or on abandoning them. For unprofitable existing customers, actions should be taken to try and make them profitable. Such actions might include trying to alter their buying behaviour so that they consume less resources, or price increases. If neither of these strategies is successful they should not be retained.

The internal business perspective

The internal business process measures should focus on the internal processes that are required to achieve the organization's customer and financial objectives. Kaplan and Norton (1996b) identify three principal internal business processes. They are:

1 innovation processes;
2 operation processes;
3 post-service sales processes.

Innovation processes

Objectives for the innovation process include increasing the number of new products, decreasing the time to develop new products and identifying new markets and customers. In the innovation process, managers research the needs of customers and then create the products or services that will meet those needs. In particular, companies identify new markets, new customers, and the emerging and latent needs of existing customers. They then design and develop new products and services that enable them to reach these new markets and customers.

Historically, because of difficult measurement problems and the over-emphasis on easily quantifiable financial measures little attention has been given to developing performance measures for product design and development processes. Companies are becoming increasingly aware that success in developing a continuous stream of innovative products and services can provide a competitive advantage. Research and development has therefore become a more important element in the value chain of most businesses and increasing attention is now being given to specifying objectives and measures for this business process.

Kaplan and Norton (1996b) highlight some of the innovation measures they have observed in organizations using balanced scorecards. They include:

1 percentage of sales from new products;
2 new product introduction versus competitors'; also new product introduction versus plan;
3 time to develop next generation of the products;
4 number of key items in which the company is first or second to the market;
5 break-even time, being the time from the beginning of product development work until the product has been introduced and has generated enough profit to pay back the investment originally made in its development.

Operations process

The operations process starts with the receipt of a customer order and finishes with the delivery of the product or service to the customer. Objectives for the operations process include decreasing process time, increasing process efficiency, increasing process quality and decreasing process cost. Historically, the operations process has been the major focus of most of an organization's performance measurement system. The performance and control measures have traditionally relied on financial measures such as standard costs, budgets and variance analysis. The over-emphasis on financial measures, particularly price and efficiency variances, sometimes motivated dysfunctional actions. For example, the pursuit of efficiency encouraged the maximum utilization of labour and machines resulting in excessive inventories that were not related to current customer orders.

The emergence of the global competitive environment and the need to make customer satisfaction an overriding priority has resulted in many companies supplementing their financial measures with measures of quality, reliability, delivery and those characteristics of product and service offerings that create value for customers. Companies that can identify the differentiating characteristics of their products and services should incorporate measures of these characteristics in the operation processes component of the balanced scorecard. These developments have created the need to focus on measures relating to achieving excellence in terms of time, quality and cost.

Cycle time measures

Many customers place a high value on short and reliable lead times, measured from the time elapsed from when they place an order until the time when they receive the desired product or service. Traditionally companies met this requirement by holding large inventories of many different products but, as indicated in the previous chapter, this approach is not consistent with being a low-cost supplier. Because of this many companies are adopting just in time (JIT) production systems with the aim of achieving both the low-cost and short lead time objectives. Reducing cycle or throughput times is therefore of critical importance for JIT companies.

Delivery performance can focus on **cycle time measures** and supplier delivery performance. Cycle times can be measured in various ways. Total cycle time measures the length of time required from the placing of an order by a customer to the delivery of the product or service to the customer. Manufacturing cycle time measures the time it takes from starting and finishing the production process. Cycle times should be measured and monitored and trends observed.

The total manufacturing cycle time consists of the sum of processing time, inspection time, wait time and move time. Only processing time adds value, and the remaining activities are non-value added activities. The aim is to reduce the time spent on non-value added activities and thus minimize manufacturing cycle time. A measure of cycle time that has been adopted is **manufacturing cycle efficiency (MCE)**:

$$MCE = \frac{processing\ time}{processing\ time + inspection\ time + wait\ time + move\ time}$$

The MCE measure is particularly important for JIT manufacturing companies. With a computerized manufacturing process, it may be possible to report the time taken on each of the above non-value added activities. This will pinpoint those activities that are causing excessive manufacturing cycle times. At the operational level, cycle times should be measured for each product or product line, and trends reported. The emphasis should be on continuous improvements and a shortening of the cycle times.

Although JIT production processes and MCE measures were initially developed for manufacturing operations, they are also applicable to service companies. For example, many customers are forced to queue to receive a service. Companies that can eliminate waiting time for a service will find it easier to attract customers. The time taken to process mortgage and loan applications by financial institutions can take a considerable time period involving a considerable amount of non-value added waiting time. Thus, reducing the time to process the applications enhances customer satisfaction and creates the potential for increasing sales revenues.

Quality measures

Besides time, **quality measures** should also be included in the measures relating to operating processes. Most organizations now have established quality programmes and use all, or some of the following process quality measurements:

- process parts-per-million (PPM) defect rates
- yields (ratio of good items produced to good items entering the process)
- first-pass yields
- waste
- scrap
- rework
- returns
- percentages of processes under statistical process control.

In many companies suppliers also have a significant influence on the ability of a company to achieve its time, quality and cost objectives. Performance measures relating to suppliers' performance include the frequency of defects, the number of late deliveries and price trends.

Cost measurement

Kaplan and Norton (1996b) recommend that activity-based costing should be used to produce **cost measures** of the important internal business processes. These costs, together with measurements relating time and quality should be monitored over time and/or benchmarked with a view to continuous improvement or process re-engineering.

The above measures represent generic measures but aspects of quality, time and cost measurement are likely to be included as critical performance measures in any organization's internal business perspective within its balanced scorecard.

Post-sales service processes

This final category relating to the internal business process perspective includes warranty and repair activities, treatment of defects and returns and the process and administration of customer payments. Increasing quality, increasing efficiency and decreasing process time are also objectives that apply to the post-sales service. In addition, excellent community relations is an important strategic objective for ensuring continuing community support to operate manufacturing facilities in companies where environmental factors are involved. For such companies appropriate environmental measures, such as those relating to the safe disposal of waste and by-products, should be established.

Kaplan and Norton suggest that companies attempting to meet their target customers' expectations for superior post-sales service can measure their performance by applying some of the time, quality and cost measurements that have been suggested for the operating processes. For example, cycle time from customer request to the ultimate resolution of the problem can measure the speed of response to failures. Activity-cost measurement can be used to measure the cost of the resources used for the post-sale service processes. Also first-pass yields can measure what percentage of customer requests are handled with a single service call, rather than requiring multiple calls to resolve the problem.

The learning and growth perspective

To ensure that an organization will continue to have satisfied and loyal customers in the future and continue to make excellent use of its resources, the organization and its employees must keep learning and developing. Hence there is a need for an additional perspective that focuses on a group of indicators that capture the company's performance with respect to learning, growth and innovation. Thus, the fourth and final perspective on the balanced scorecard identifies the infrastructure that the business must build to create long-term growth and improvement. This perspective stresses the importance of investing for the future in areas other than investing in assets and new product research and development (which is included in the innovation process of the internal business perspective). Organizations must also invest in their infrastructure (people, systems and organizational procedures) to provide the capabilities that enable the accomplishment of the other three perspectives' objectives. Kaplan and Norton have identified the following three principal categories, or enablers, for the learning and growth objectives:

1 employee capabilities;
2 information system capabilities;
3 motivation, empowerment and alignment.

Employee capabilities

Kaplan and Norton (1996b) observed that most companies use three common core measurement outcomes – employee satisfaction, employee retention and employee productivity. Within this core, the employee satisfaction objective is generally considered to be the driver of the other two measures. Satisfied employees are normally a pre-condition for increasing customer satisfaction. Many companies periodically measure employee satisfaction using surveys. For example, questions may relate to involvement in decisions and active encouragement to be creative and to use one's initiative. An aggregate index is constructed which can be analysed on a departmental or divisional basis.

Employee retention can be measured by the annual percentage of key staff that leave and many different methods can be used to measure employee productivity. A generic measure of employee productivity that can be applied throughout the organization and compared with different divisions is the sales revenue per employee.

Information system capabilities

For employees to be effective in today's competitive environment they need excellent information on customers, internal processes and the financial consequences of their decisions. Measures of strategic information availability suggested by Kaplan and Norton (1996b) include percentage of processes with real time quality, cycle time and cost feedback available and the percentage of customer-facing employees having on-line information about customers. These measures seek to provide an indication of the availability of internal process information to front-line employees.

Motivation, empowerment and alignment

The number of suggested improvements per employee is proposed as a measure relating to having motivated and empowered employees. The performance drivers for individual and organizational alignment focus on whether departments and individuals have their goals aligned with the company objectives articulated in the balanced scorecard. A suggested outcome measure is the percentage of employees with personal goals aligned to the balanced scorecard and the percentage of employees who achieve personal goals.

Performance measurement in service organizations

Although Kaplan and Norton (1996b) illustrate how the balanced scorecard can be applied in both the manufacturing and service sectors, much of the performance measurement literature concentrates on the manufacturing sector. To remedy this deficiency this section focuses on performance measurement in the service sector. Based on their research into the management accounting practices of a range of companies in several different service industries Fitzgerald *et al.* (1989) identified four unique characteristics distinguishing service companies from manufacturing organizations. First, most services are intangible. Fitzgerald *et al.* state:

> *In travelling on a particular airline the customer will be influenced by the comfort of the seat, the meals served, the attitudes and confidence of the cabin staff, the boarding process and so on. This makes managing and controlling the operation complex because it is difficult to establish exactly what an individual customer is buying; is it the journey or the treatment? (Fitzgerald* et al., *1989, p. 2)*

Secondly, service outputs vary from day to day, since services tend to be provided by individuals whose performance is subject to variability that significantly affects the service quality the customer receives. Thirdly, the production and consumption of many services are inseparable such as in taking a rail journey. Fourthly, services are perishable and cannot be stored. Fitzgerald *et al.* illustrate this characteristic with a hotel, which contains a fixed number of rooms. If a room is unoccupied, the sales opportunity is lost for ever and the resource is wasted.

With regard to the control of the intangible aspects, the authors found that companies used the following methods to measure performance:

1 *Measures of satisfaction after the service.* The most common method was the monitoring and analysis of letters of complaint, but some companies interviewed samples of customers or used questionnaires to ascertain the customers' perception of service quality.

2 *Measures during the service.* An approach used by some companies was for management to make unannounced visits, with the aim of observing the quality of service offered. Another mechanism was the use of mystery shoppers, where staff employed by external agencies were sent out to sample the service as customers and formally report back on their findings.

3 *Tangibles as surrogates for intangibles.* The researchers observed that some firms used internal measures of tangible aspects of the service as indicators of how the customers might perceive the service. Some companies measured waiting times and the conditions of the waiting environment as surrogates of customers' satisfaction with the service.

Fitzgerald *et al.* also draw attention to the importance of relating the performance measures to the corporate and marketing strategies of the organizations. For example, if the delivery of high quality service is seen to be a key strategic variable then quality measures should be the dominant performance measures. On the other hand, if a low cost of the service relative to competitors is seen as the key strategic variable then strict adherence to budgets will be a key feature of the control system. There is also a greater danger in service organizations of focusing excessively on financial performance measures, which can be easily quantified, thus placing an undue emphasis on maximizing short-term performance, even if this conflicts with maximizing long-term performance. Consequently, it is more important in service organizations that a range of non-financial performance indicators be developed providing better predictors for the attainment of long-term profitability goals.

Dimensions of performance measurement

Fitzgerald *et al.* (1991) advocate the measurement of service business performance across six dimensions. They propose that managers of every service organization need to develop their own set of performance measures across the six dimensions to monitor the continued relevance of their competitive strategy. Exhibit 16.5 shows the six dimensions with examples of types of performance measures for each dimension. You should note that the dimensions fall into two conceptually different categories. Competitiveness and financial performance reflect the success of the chosen strategy (i.e. ends or results). The remaining four dimensions (quality, flexibility, resource utilization and innovation) are the drivers or determinants that determine competitive success. Fitzgerald *et al.* conclude that the design of a balanced range of performance measures should be dependent upon the company's service type, competitive environment and chosen strategy.

EXHIBIT 16.5

Performance measures for service organizations

	Dimensions of performance	Types of measures
Results	Competitiveness	Relative market share and position
		Sales growth
		Measures of the customer base
	Financial performance	Profitability
		Liquidity
		Capital structure
		Market ratios
Determinants	Quality of service	Reliability
		Responsiveness
		Aesthetics/appearance
		Cleanliness/tidiness
		Comfort
		Friendliness
		Communication
		Courtesy
		Competence
		Access
		Availability
		Security
	Flexibility	Volume flexibility
		Delivery speed flexibility
		Specification flexibility
	Resource utilization	Productivity
		Efficiency
	Innovation	Performance of the innovation process
		Performance of individual innovations

Source: Fitzgerald *et al.*, 1991

Moon and Fitzgerald (1996) point out the similarities between the Fitzgerald *et al.* framework and the balanced scorecard. Both frameworks emphasize the need to link performance measures to corporate strategy, include external (customer type) as well as internal measures, include non-financial as well as financial measures and make explicit the trade-offs between the various measures of performance. In addition, both frameworks distinguish between 'results' of actions taken and the 'drivers' or 'determinants' of future performance. The balanced scorecard complements financial measures with operational measures on customer satisfaction, internal processes, and the organization's innovation and improvement activities that are the drivers of future financial performance (Kaplan and Norton, 1992). The Fitzgerald *et al.* framework specifies that measures of financial performance and competitiveness are the 'results' of actions previously taken and reflect the success of the chosen strategy. The remaining four dimensions (quality, flexibility, resource utilization and innovation) are the factors or drivers that determine competitive success, either now or in the future. The objective of both approaches is to ensure that a balanced set of performance measures is used so that no dimension is overly stressed to the detriment of another.

Summary

The following items relate to the learning objectives listed at the beginning of the chapter.

- **Describe the different elements of strategic management accounting.**

  Despite the publicity that strategic management accounting has received there is still no comprehensive conceptual framework of what strategic management accounting is. Because of the lack of consensus on what constitutes strategic management accounting the elements that have been identified in the literature to characterize strategic management accounting have been described. Three elements can be identified: (a) the extension of traditional management accounting's internal focus to include external information about competitors; (b) the relationship between the strategic position chosen by a firm and the expected emphasis on management accounting; and (c) gaining competitive advantage by analysing ways to decrease costs and/or enhance the differentiation of a firm's products, through exploiting linkages in the value chain and optimizing cost drivers. Some authors have adopted a broader view of strategic management accounting that encompasses activity-based costing, target costing and the cost management approaches described in the previous chapter.

- **Describe the balanced scorecard.**

  Recent developments in performance evaluation have sought to integrate financial and non-financial measures and assist in clarifying, communicating and managing strategy. The balanced scorecard attempts to meet these requirements. It requires that managers view the business from the following four different perspectives: (a) customer perspective (how do customers see us?); (b) internal business process perspective (what must we excel at?); (c) learning and growth perspective (can we continue to improve and create value?), and (d) financial perspective (how do we look to shareholders?). Organizations should articulate the major goals for each of the four perspectives and then translate these goals into specific performance measures. Each organization must decide what are its critical performance measures. The choice will vary over time and should be linked to the strategy that the organization is following.

- **Explain each of the four perspectives of the balanced scorecard.**

  The financial perspective provides performance measures relating to the financial outcomes of past actions. Thus, it provides feedback on the success of pursuing the objectives identified for the other three perspectives. In the customer perspective managers identify the customer and market segments in which the businesses unit will compete. Performance measures should be developed within this perspective that track a business unit's ability to create satisfied and loyal customers in the targeted segments. They include market share, customer retention, new customer acquisition, customer satisfaction and customer profitability. In the internal business perspective, managers identify the critical internal processes for which the organization must excel in implementing its strategy. The internal business process measures should focus on the internal processes that will have the greatest impact on customer satisfaction and achieving the organization's financial objectives. The principal internal business processes include the innovation processes, operation processes and post-service sales processes. The final perspective on the balanced scorecard identifies the infrastructure that the business must build to create long-term growth and improvement. The following three categories have been identified as falling within this perspective: employee capabilities, information system capabilities and motivation, empowerment and alignment.

- **Provide illustrations of performance measures for each of the four perspectives.**

  Within the financial perspective examples include economic value added and residual income. Market share and customer satisfaction are generic measures within the customer perspective. Typical internal business perspective measures include percentage of sales from new products (innovation processes), cycle time measures such as manufacturing cycle efficiency (operation processes) and percentage returns from customers (post-service sales processes). Measures of employee satisfaction represent generic measures within the learning and growth satisfaction.

- **Describe the distinguishing characteristics of service organizations that influence performance measurement.**

  Four unique characteristics distinguishing service companies from manufacturing organizations can be identified. They are (a) most services are intangible; (b) service outputs vary from day to day, since services tend to be provided by individuals whose performance is subject to variability that significantly affects the service quality the customer receives; (c) the production and consumption of many services are inseparable such as in taking a rail journey; and (d) services are perishable and cannot be stored. For example, a hotel contains a fixed number of rooms. If a room is unoccupied, the sales opportunity is lost forever and the resource is wasted.

Note

1 This illustration has been derived from Shank (1989).

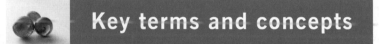

Key terms and concepts

balanced scorecard (p. 469)
brand value budgeting (p. 467)
brand value monitoring (p. 467)
competitive position monitoring (p. 466)
competitor cost assessment (p. 467)
competitor performance appraisal (p. 466)
cost measures (p. 478)
customer perspective (p. 469)
cycle time measures (p. 477)
financial perspective (p. 469)
internal business process perspective (p. 469)
lagging measures (p. 471)

leading measures (p. 471)
learning and growth perspective (p. 469)
learning curve (p. 463)
manufacturing cycle efficiency (MCE) (p. 478)
quality measures (p. 478)
strategic costing (p. 467)
strategic management accounting (p. 462)
strategic pricing (p. 466)
target costing (p. 462)
value-chain analysis (p. 465)
value-chain costing (p. 467)

Assessment material

Review questions

The review questions are short questions that enable you to assess your understanding of the main topics included in the chapter. The numbers in parentheses provide you with the page numbers to refer to if you cannot answer a specific question.

Review problems

The review problems are more complex and require you to relate and apply the chapter content to various business problems. Fully worked solutions to the review problems are provided in a separate section at the end of the book. Further review problems for this chapter are available on the accompanying website, www.drury-online.com. The answers to these problems are available for lecturers on the lecturer's password-protected section of the website.

Case studies

The website also includes over 30 case study problems. A list of these cases is provided on pages 491–93. Several cases are relevant to the content of this chapter. Brunswick Plastics, Kinkead Equipment Ltd and Majestic Lodge cases include elements of strategic management accounting.

Review questions

16.1   Provide a definition of strategic management accounting. (*p. 462*)

16.2   Describe the three major strands of strategic management accounting that can be identified from the literature. (*pp. 463–65*)

16.3   How do different competitive strategies influence the emphasis that is given to particular management accounting techniques? (*pp. 464–65*)

16.4   What is the purpose of a balanced scorecard? (*pp. 467–69*)

16.5   Describe the four perspectives of the balanced scorecard. (*pp. 469–71*)

16.6   Explain the differences between lag measures and lead measures. (*p. 471*)

16.7   Explain what is meant by cause-and-effect relationships within the balanced scorecard. (*pp. 469–70*)

16.8   Discuss the benefits and limitations of the balanced scorecard. (*pp. 472–73*)

16.9   Identify and describe the core objectives of the customer perspective. (*pp. 473–76*)

16.10   Describe the three principal internal business processes that can be included within the internal business perspective. (*pp. 476–79*)

16.11   What is manufacturing cycle efficiency? (*p. 478*)

16.12   Describe three principal categories within the learning and growth perspective. (*pp. 479–80*)

16.13   Provide examples of performance measures within each of the four perspectives of the balanced scorecard. (*pp. 473–80*)

16.14   Describe the four unique characteristics distinguishing service companies from manufacturing organizations. (*pp. 480–81*)

Review problems

16.15   **Financial and non-financial performance measures**

BS Ltd provides consultancy services to small and medium sized businesses. Three types of consultants are employed offering administrative, data processing and marketing advice respectively. The consultants work partly on the client's premises and partly in BS Ltd premises, where chargeable development work in relation to each client contract will be undertaken. Consultants spend some time negotiating with potential clients, attempting to secure contracts from them. BS Ltd has recently implemented a policy change which allows for a number of follow-up (remedial) hours at the client's premises after completion of the contract in order to eliminate any problems which have arisen in the initial stages of operation of the system. Contract negotiation and remedial work hours are not charged directly to each client. BS Ltd carries out consultancy for new systems and also to offer advice on existing systems which a client may have introduced before BS Ltd became involved. BS Ltd has a policy of retaining its consultancy staff at a level of 60 consultants on an ongoing basis.

Additional information for the year ended 30 April is as follows:

(i)   BS Ltd invoices clients £75 per chargeable consultant hour.

(ii)   Consultant salaries are budgeted at an average per consultant of £30 000 per annum. Actual salaries include a bonus for hours in excess of budget paid for at the budgeted average rate per hour.

(iii) Sundry operating costs (other than consultant salaries) were budgeted at £3 500 000. Actual was £4 100 000.

(iv)   BS Ltd capital employed (start year) was £6 500 000.

(v)   Table 1 shows an analysis of sundry budgeted and actual quantitative data.

Required:

(a) (i) Prepare an analysis of actual consultancy hours for the year ended 30 April which shows the increase or decrease from the standard/allowed non-chargeable hours. This increase or decrease should be analysed to show the extent to which it may be shown to be attributable to a change from standard in:

1. standard chargeable hours; 2. remedial advice hours; 3. contract negotiation hours; 4. other non-chargeable hours.

(13 marks)

(ii) Calculate the total value of each of 1 to 4 in (a) above in terms of chargeable client income per hour.

(4 marks)

(b) BS Ltd measure business performance in a number of ways. For each of the undernoted measures, comment on the performance of BS Ltd using quantitative data from the question and your answer to (a) to assist in illustrating your answer:

(i) Financial performance

(ii) Competitive performance

(iii) Quality of service

(iv) Flexibility

(v) Resource utilization

(vi) Innovation.

(18 marks)

(Total 35 marks)

Table 1: BS Ltd Sundry statistics for year ended 30 April

	Budget	Actual
Number of consultants:		
Administration	30	23
Data processing	12	20
Marketing	18	17
Consultants hours analysis:		
contract negotiation hours	4 800	9 240
remedial advice hours	2 400	7 920
other non-chargeable hours	12 000	22 440
general development work hours (chargeable)	12 000	6 600
customer premises contract hours	88 800	85 800
Gross hours	120 000	132 000
Chargeable hours analysis:		
new systems	70%	60%
existing systems advice	30%	40%
Number of clients enquiries received:		
new systems	450	600
existing systems advice	400	360
Number of client contracts worked on:		
new systems	180	210
existing systems advice	300	288
Number of client complaints	5	20
Contracts requiring remedial advice	48	75

16.16 **Financial and non-financial performance measurement in a service organization**

The owners of *The Eatwell Restaurant* have diversified business interests and operate in a wide range of commercial areas. Since buying the restaurant in 1997 they have carefully recorded the data below.

Recorded Data for The Eatwell Restaurant (1998–2001)

	1998	1999	2000	2001
Total meals served	3 750	5 100	6 200	6 700
Regular customers attending weekly	5	11	15	26
Number of items on offer per day	4	4	7	9
Reported cases of food poisoning	4	5	7	7
Special theme evenings introduced	0	3	9	13
Annual operating hours with no customers	380	307	187	126
Proposals submitted to cater for special events	10	17	29	38
Contracts won to cater for special events	2	5	15	25
Complimentary letters from satisfied customers	0	4	3	6
Average number of customers at peak times	18	23	37	39
Average service delay at peak time (mins)	32	47	15	35
Maximum seating capacity	25	25	40	40
Weekly opening hours	36	36	40	36
Written complaints received	8	12	14	14
Idle time	570	540	465	187
New meals introduced during the year	16	8	27	11

Financial Data	£	£	£	£
Average customer spend on wine	3	4	4	7
Total Turnover	83 000	124 500	137 000	185 000
Turnover from special events	2 000	13 000	25 000	55 000
Profit	11 600	21 400	43 700	57 200
Value of food wasted in preparation	1 700	1 900	3 600	1 450
Total turnover of all restaurants in locality	895 000	1 234 000	980 000	1 056 000

Required:

(a) Assess the overall performance of the business and submit your comments to the owners. They wish to compare the performance of the restaurant with their other business interests and require your comments to be grouped into the key areas of performance such as those described by Fitzgerald and Moon.

(*14 marks*)

(b) Identify any additional information that you would consider of assistance in assessing the performance of *The Eatwell Restaurant* in comparison with another restaurant. Give reasons for your selection and explain how they would relate to the key performance area categories used in (a).

(6 marks)
(Total 20 marks)

16.17 CM Limited was formed ten years ago to provide business equipment solutions to local businesses. It has separate divisions for research, marketing, product design, technology and communication services, and now manufactures and supplies a wide range of business equipment (copiers, scanners, printers, fax machines and similar items).

To date it has evaluated its performance using monthly financial reports that analyse profitability by type of equipment.

The Managing Director of CM Limited has recently returned from a course on which it had been suggested that the 'Balanced Scorecard' could be a useful way of measuring performance.

Required:

(a) Explain the 'Balanced Scorecard' and how it could be used by CM Limited to measure its performance.

(13 marks)

While on the course, the Managing Director of CM Limited overheard someone mention how the performance of their company had improved after they introduced 'Benchmarking'.

Required:

(b) Explain 'Benchmarking' and how it could be used to improve the performance of CM Limited.

(12 marks)
(Total 25 marks)

16.18 The introduction of improved quality into products has been a strategy applied by many organizations to obtain competitive advantage. Some organizations believe it is necessary to improve levels of product quality if competitive advantage is to be preserved or strengthened.

Requirement:

Discuss how a management accountant can assist an organization to achieve competitive advantage by measuring the increase in added value from improvement in its product quality.

(20 marks)

16.19 **Performance measurement in non-profit organizations**

(a) The absence of the profit measure in Not-for-Profit (NFP) organizations causes problems for the measurement of their efficiency and effectiveness.

You are required to explain:

(i) why the absence of the profit measure should be a cause of the problems referred to

(9 marks)

(ii) how these problems extend to activities within business entities which have a profit motive. Support your answer with examples.

(4 marks)

(b) A public health clinic is the subject of a scheme to measure its efficiency and effectiveness. Amongst a number of factors, the 'quality of care provided' has been included as an aspect of the clinic's service to be measured. Three features of 'quality of care provided' have been listed:

Clinic's adherence to appointment times
Patients' ability to contact the clinic and make appointments without difficulty
The provision of a comprehensive patient health monitoring programme.

You are required to:

(i) suggest a set of quantitative measures which can be used to identify the effective level of achievement of each of the features listed;

(9 marks)

(ii) indicate how these measures could be combined into a single 'quality of care' measure.

(3 marks)
(Total 25 marks)

CASE STUDIES

Case studies available from the website

The dedicated website for this book includes over 30 case studies. Both students and lecturers can download these case studies from the open access website. The authors of the cases have provided teaching notes for each case and these can be downloaded only by lecturers from the password-protected lecturer's section of the website.

The cases generally cover the content of several chapters and contain questions to which there is no ideal answer. They are intended to encourage independent thought and initiative and to relate and apply the content of this book to more uncertain situations. They are also intended to develop critical thinking and analytical skills. Details relating to the cases that are available from the website are listed on the following pages.

Airport Complex Peter Nordgaard and Carsten Rhode, Copenhagen Business School
A general case providing material for discussion of several aspects involved in the management control of a service company, which is mainly characterized by mass services.

Anjo Ltd Lin Fitzgerald, Loughborough University Business School
Variance analysis that provides the opportunity to be used as a role playing exercise.

Berkshire Threaded Fasteners Company John Shank, The Amos Tuck School of Business Administration Dartmouth College
Cost analysis for dropping a product, for pricing, for product mix and product improvement.

Berkshire Toy Company D. Crawford and E.G. Henry, State University of New York (SUNY) at Oswego
Variance analysis, performance evaluation, responsibility accounting and the balanced scorecard.

Blessed Farm Partnership Rona O'Brien, Sheffield Hallam University
Strategic decision-making, evaluation of alternatives, ethics, sources of information.

Boston Creamery John Shank, The Amos Tuck School of Business Administration Dartmouth College
Management control systems, profit planning, profit variance analysis and flexible budgets.

Brunswick Plastics Anthony Atkinson, University of Waterloo and adapted by John Shank, The Amos Tuck School of Business Administration Dartmouth College
Relevant cost analysis for a new product, short-run versus strategic considerations, pricing considerations.

Company A Mike Tayles, Universtiy of Hull Business School and Paul Walley, Warwick Business School
Evaluation of a product costing system and suggested performance measures to support key success factors.

Company B Mike Tayles, Universtiy of Hull Business School and Paul Walley, Warwick Business School
The impact of a change in manufacturing strategy and method upon product costing and performance measurement systems.

Danfoss Drives Dan Otzen, Copenhagen Business School
The linkage between operational management and management accounting/control of a company including a discussion of the operational implications of JIT for management accounting.

Dumbellow Ltd Stan Brignall, Aston Business School
Marginal costing versus absorption costing, relevant costs and cost–volume–profit analysis.

Electronic Boards plc John Innes, University of Dundee and Falconer Mitchell, University of Edinburgh
A general case that may be used at an introductory stage to illustrate the basics of management accounting and the role it can play within a firm.

Endeavour Twoplise Ltd Jayne Ducker, Antony Head, Brenda McDonnell, Sheffield Hallam University and Susan Richardson, University of Bradford Management Centre
Functional budget and master budget construction, budgetary control and decision-making.

Fleet Ltd Lin Fitzgerald, Loughborough University Business School
Outsourcing decision involving relevant costs and qualitative factors.

Global Ltd Susan Richardson, University of Bradford Management Centre
Cash budgeting, links between cash and profit, pricing/bidding, information system design and behavioural aspects of management control.

Gustavsson, AB Colin Drury, Huddersfield University Business School
Alternative choice of cost centres and their implication for overhead assignments for various decisions.

Hardhat Ltd Stan Brignall, Aston Business School
Cost–volume–profit analysis.

High Street Reproduction Furniture Ltd Jayne Ducker, Antony Head, Rona O'Brien, Sheffield Hallam University and Sue Richardson, University of Bradford Management Centre
Relevant costs, strategic decision-making and limiting factors.

Integrated Technology Services (UK) Ltd Mike Johnson, University of Dundee
An examination of the planning and control framework of an information services business which provides outsourced computing support services to large industrial and government organizations.

Kinkead Equipment Ltd John Shank, The Amos Tuck School of Business Administration Dartmouth College
Profit variance analysis that emphasizes how variance analysis should be redirected to consider strategic issues.

Lynch Printers Peter Clarke, University College Dublin
Cost-plus pricing within the context of correctly forecasting activity for a forthcoming period in order to determine the overhead rates. The case illustrates that a company can make a loss even when an anticipated profit margin is added to all jobs.

Majestic Lodge John Shank, The Amos Tuck School of Business Administration Dartmouth College
Relevant costs and cost–volume–profit analysis.

Merrion Products Ltd Peter Clarke, University College Dublin
Cost–volume–profit analysis, relevant costs and limiting factors.

Moult Hall Jayne Ducker, Antony Head, Brenda McDonnell, Sheffield Hallam University
and Susan Richardson, University of Bradford Management Centre
*Organizational objectives, strategic decision-making, evaluation of alternatives,
relevant costs, debating the profit ethos, break-even analysis.*

Oak City R.W. Ingram, W.C. Parsons, University of Alabama and W.A. Robbins,
Attorney, Pearson and Sutton
*Cost allocation in a government setting to determine the amount of costs that should
be charged to business for municipal services. The case also includes ethical
considerations.*

Quality Shopping Rona O'Brien, Sheffield Hallam University
*Departmental budget construction, credit checking, environmental issues, behavioural
issues and management control systems.*

Rawhide Development Company Bill Doolin, University of Waikato and Deryl
Northcott, University of Manchester
*Capital investment appraisal involving relevant cash flows, uncertainty, application of
spreadsheet tools and social considerations.*

Reichard Maschinen, GmbH Professor John Shank, The Amos Tuck School of Business
Administration Dartmouth College
Relevant costs and pricing decisions

Rogatec Ltd Jayne Ducker, Antony Head, Brenda McDonnell, Sheffield Hallam
University and Susan Richardson, University of Bradford Management Centre
Standard costing and variance analysis, budgets, ethics, sources of information.

Traditions Ltd. Jayne Ducker, Antony Head, Brenda McDonnell, Sheffield Hallam
University and Susan Richardson, University of Bradford Management Centre
Relevant cost analysis relating to a discontinuation decision and budgeting.

BIBLIOGRAPHY

Accounting Standards Committee (1988), Accounting for Stocks and Work-in-Progress (SSAP9).

Ackoff, R.L. (1981) *Creating the Corporate Future*, Wiley.

American Accounting Association (1966) *A Statement of Basic Accounting Theory*, American Accounting Association.

American Accounting Association Financial Accounting Standards Committee (2002), Recommendations on disclosure of non-financial performance measures, *Accounting Horizons*, Vol 16, No. 4, 353–362.

Ansari, S. (1979) Towards an open system approach to budgeting, *Accounting, Organisations and Society*, **4**(3), 149–61.

Argyris, C. (1953) Human problems with budgets, *Harvard Business Review*, January–February, 97–110.

Armitage, H.M. and Nicholson, R. (1993) Activity based costing: a survey of Canadian practice, Issue Paper No. 3, Society of Management Accountants of Canada.

Arnold, G.C. and Hatzopoulos, P.D. (2000) The theory–practice gap in capital budgeting: evidence from the United Kingdom, *Journal of Business Finance and Accounting*, **27**(5) and (6), June/July, 603–26.

Ask, U. and Ax, C. (1992) Trends in the Development of Product Costing Practices and Techniques – A Survey of Swedish Manufacturing Industry, Paper presented at the 15th Annual Congress of the European Accounting Association, Madrid.

Ask, U., Ax, C. and Jonsson, S. (1996) Cost management in Sweden: from modern to post-modern, in Bhimani, A. (ed.) *Management Accounting: European Perspectives*, Oxford, Oxford University Press, 199–217.

Ballas, A. and Venieris, G. (1996) A survey of management accounting practices in Greek firms, in Bhimani, A. (ed.) *Management Accounting: European Perspectives*, Oxford, Oxford University Press, 123–39.

Banerjee, J. and Kane, W. (1996) Report on CIMA/JBA survey, *Management Accounting*, October, **30**, 37.

Barbato, M.B., Collini, P. and Quagli, (1996) Management accounting in Italy, in Bhimani, A. (ed.) *Management Accounting: European Perspectives*, Oxford, Oxford University Press, 140–163.

Barrett, M.E. and Fraser, L.B. (1977) Conflicting roles in budget operations, *Harvard Business Review*, July–August, 137–46.

Baxter, W.T. and Oxenfeldt, A.R. (1961) Costing and pricing: the cost accountant versus the economist, *Business Horizons*, Winter, 77–90; also in *Studies in Cost Analysis*, 2nd edn (ed. D. Solomons) Sweet and Maxwell (1968), 293–312.

Berliner, C. and Brimson, J.A. (1988) *Cost Management for Today's Advanced Manufacturing*, Harvard Business School Press.

Bjornenak T. (1997a) Diffusion and accounting: the case of ABC in Norway, *Management Accounting Research*, **8**(1), 317.

Bjornenak T. (1997b) Conventional wisdom and accounting practices, *Management Accounting Research*, **8**(4), 367–82.

Blayney, P. and Yokoyama, I. (1991) Comparative analysis of Japanese and Australian cost accounting and management practices, Working paper, University of Sydney, Australia.

Boons, A., Roozen, R.A. and Weerd, R.J. de (1994) Kosteninformatie in de Nederlandse Industrie, in *Relevantie methoden en ontwikkelingen* (Rotterdam: Coopers and Lybrand).

Borkowski, S.C. (1990) Environmental and organizational factors affecting transfer pricing: a survey, *Journal of Management Accounting Research*, **2**, 78–99.

Brealey, R.A. and Myers, S.C. (2003) *Principles of Corporate Finance*, McGraw-Hill, New York.

Bromwich, M. (1990) The case for strategic management accounting: the role of accounting information for strategy in competitive markets, *Accounting, Organisations and Society*, **1**, 27–46.

Bromwich, M. and Bhimani, A. (1989) *Management Accounting: Evolution not Revolution*, Chartered Institute of Management Accountants.

Bromwich, M. and Bhimani, A. (1994) *Management Accounting: Pathways to Progress*, Chartered Institute of Management Accountants.

Brownell, P. (1981) Participation in budgeting, locus of control and organisational effectiveness, *The Accounting Review*, October, 944–58.

Bruggeman, W., Slagmulder, R. and Waeytens, D. (1996) Management accounting changes; the Belgian experience, in Bhimani, A. (ed.) *Management Accounting: European Perspectives*, Oxford, Oxford University Press, 1–30.

Chartered Institute of Management Accountants (2000) *Management Accounting: Official Terminology*, CIMA.

Chenhall, R.H. and Langfield-Smith, K. (1998) Adoption and benefits of management accounting practices: an Australian perspective, *Management Accounting Research*, **9**(1), 120.

Chow, C., Haddad, K. and Williamson, J. (1997) Applying the Balanced Scorecard to Small Companies, *Management Accounting*, August, 21–7.

Chow, C.W. (1983) The effect of job standards, tightness and compensation schemes on performance: an exploration of linkages, *The Accounting Review,* October, 667–85.

Clarke, P.J. (1992) Management Accounting Practices and Techniques in Irish Manufacturing Firms, The 15th Annual Congress of the European Accounting Association, Madrid, Spain.

Clarke, P. (1995), Management accounting practices and techniques in Irish manufacturing companies, Working paper, Trinity College, Dublin.

Coad, A. (1996) Smart work and hard work: explicating a learning orientation in strategic management accounting, *Management Accounting Research*, **7**(4), 387–408.

Cooper, R. (1990a) Cost classifications in unit-based and activity-based manufacturing cost systems, *Journal of Cost Management*, Fall, 4–14.

Cooper, R. (1990b) Explicating the logic of ABC, *Management Accounting*, November, 5860.

Cooper, R. (1997) Activity-Based Costing: Theory and Practice, in Brinker, B.J. (ed.), *Handbook of Cost Management*, Warren, Gorham and Lamont, B1–B33.

Cooper, R. and Kaplan, R.S. (1987) How cost accounting systematically distorts product costs, in *Accounting and Management: Field Study Perspectives* (eds W.J. Bruns and R.S. Kaplan), Harvard Business School Press, Ch. 8.

Cooper, R. and Kaplan, R.S. (1988) Measure costs right: make the right decisions, *Harvard Business Review*, September/October, 96–103.

Cooper, R. and Kaplan, R.S. (1991) *The Design of Cost Management Systems: Text, Cases and Readings*, Prentice-Hall.

Cooper, R. and Kaplan, R.S. (1992) Activity based systems: measuring the costs of resource usage, *Accounting Horizons*, September, 1–13.

Cornick, M., Cooper, W. and Wilson, S. (1988) How do companies analyse overhead?, *Management Accounting*, June, 41–3.

Cress, W. and Pettijohn, J. (1985) A survey of budget-related planning and control policies and procedures, *Journal of Accounting Education*, **3**, Fall, 61–78.

Cyert, R.M. and March, J.G. (1969) *A Behavioural Theory of the Firm*, Prentice-Hall.

Dardenne, P. (1998) Capital budgeting practices – Procedures and techniques by large companies in Belgium, paper presented at the 21st Annual Congress of the European Accounting Association, Antwerp, Belgium.

Dekker, H.C. (2003) Value chain analysis in interfirm relationships: a field study, *Management Accounting Research*, **14**(1), 1–23.

Dekker, H. and Smidt, P. (2003) A survey of the adoption and use of target costing in Dutch firms, *International Journal of Production Economics*, **84**(3), 293–306.

Dittman, D.A. and Ferris, KR. (1978) Profit centre: a satisfaction generating concept, *Accounting and Business Research*, **8**(32), Autumn, 242–5.

Drucker, P.F. (1964) Controls, control and management, in *Management Controls: New Directions in Basic Research* (eds C.P. Bonini, R. Jaedicke and H. Wagner), McGraw-Hill.

Drury, C. (2004) *Management and Cost Accounting*, 6th edn, Thomson Learning, London.

Drury C. and Tayles M. (1994) Product costing in UK manufacturing organisations, *The European Accounting Review*, **3**(3), 443–69.

Drury C. and Tayles M. (2000), *Cost system design and profitability analysis in UK companies*, Chartered Institute of Management Accountants.

Drury, C., Braund, S., Osborne, P. and Tayles, M. (1993) A survey of management accounting practices in UK manufacturing companies, ACCA Research Paper, Chartered Association of Certified Accountants.

El-Shishini, H. and Drury, C. (2001) Divisional performance measurement in UK companies, Paper presented to the Annual Congress of the European Accounting Association, Athens.

Emmanuel, C., Otley, D. and Merchant, K. (1990) *Accounting for Management Control*, International Thomson Business Press, London.

Emore, J.R. and Ness, J.A. (1991) The slow pace of meaningful changes in cost systems, *Journal of Cost Management for the Manufacturing Industry*, Winter, 36–45.

Epstein, M. and Manzoni, J.F. (1998) Implementing corporate strategy: From tableaux de bord to balanced scorecards, *European Management Journal*, **16**(2), 190–203.

Epstein, M. and Roy, M.J. (1997) Environmental management to improve corporate profitability, *Journal of Cost Management*, November–December, 26–34.

Evans, H. and Ashworth, G. (1996) Survey conclusions: wakeup to the competition, *Management Accounting* (UK), May, 16–18.

Ezzamel, M. and Hart, H. (1987) *Advanced Management Accounting: An Organisational Emphasis*. Cassell, London.

Ezzamel, M.A. and Hilton, K. (1980) Divisionalization in British industry: a preliminary study, *Accounting and Business Research*, Summer, 197 214.

Fitzgerald, L., Johnston, R., Silvestro, R. and Steele, A. (1989) Management control in service industries, *Management Accounting*, April, 44–6.

Fitzgerald, L., Johnston, R., Brignall, T.J., Silvestro, R. and Voss, C. (1991) *Performance Measurement in Service Businesses*, Chartered Institute of Management Accountants.

Fitzgerald, L. and Moon, P. (1996) *Performance Management in Service Industries*, Chartered Institute of Management Accountants.

Fremgen, J.M. and Liao, S.S. (1981) The Allocation of Corporate Indirect Costs, National Association of Accountants, New York.

Friedman, A.L. and Lyne, S.R. (1995) *Activity-based Techniques: The Real Life Consequences*, Chartered Institute of Management Accountants.

Friedman, A.L. and Lyne, S.R. (1997) Activity-based techniques and the death of the beancounter, *The European Accounting Review*, **6**(1), 19–44.

Friedman, A.L. and Lyne, S.R. (1999) *Success and Failure of Activity-based Techniques: A long-term perspective*, Chartered Institute of Management Accountants.

Gardiner, S.C. (1993) Measures of product attractiveness and the theory of constraints. *International Journal of Retail and Distribution*, **21**(7), 37–40.

Granlund, M. and Lukka, K. (1998) It's a small world of management accounting practices, *Journal of Management Accounting Research*, **10**, 151–79.

Green, F.B. and Amenkhienan, F.E. (1992) Accounting innovations: A cross sectional survey of manufacturing firms, *Journal of Cost Management for the Manufacturing Industry*, Spring 58–64.

Guilding, C., Craven, K.S. and Tayles, M. (2000) An international comparison of strategic management accounting practices, *Management Accounting Research*, **11**(1), 113–35.

Guilding, C., Lamminmaki, D. and Drury, C. (1998) Budgeting and standard costing practices in New Zealand and the United Kingdom, *The International Journal of Accounting*, **33**(5), 41–60.

Hansen, D.R. and Mendoza, R. (1999) Costos de impacto ambiental: Su medicion, asignacion, y control. *INCA Revista*, vol x, No. 2, 1999.

Hergert, M. and Morris, D. (1989) Accounting data for value chain analysis, *Strategic Management Journal*, **10**, 175–88.

Holzer, H.P. and Norreklit, H. (1991) Some thoughts on the cost accounting developments in the United States, *Management Accounting Research*, March, 3–13.

Hopwood, A.G. (1976) *Accountancy and Human Behaviour*, Prentice-Hall.

Hopwood, A.G. (1978) Towards an organisational perspective for the study of accounting and information systems, *Accounting, Organisations and Society*, **3**(1), 3–14.

Hornyak, S. (2000) Budgeting made easy, in Reeve, J.M. (ed.), *Readings and Issues in Cost Management*, South Western College Publishing, 341–6.

Imoisili, O.A. (1989) The role of budget data in the evaluation of managerial performance, *Accounting, Organizations and Society*, **14**(4), 325–35.

Innes, J. and Mitchell, F. (1991) ABC: A survey of CIMA members, *Management Accounting*, October, 28–30.

Innes, J. and Mitchell, F. (1995a) A survey of activity-based costing in the UK's largest companies, *Management Accounting Research*, June, 137–54.

Innes, J. and Mitchell, F. (1995b) Activity-based costing, in *Issues in Management Accounting* (eds D. Ashton, T. Hopper and R.W. Scapens), Prentice-Hall, 115–36.

Innes, J. and Mitchell, F. (1997) The application of activity-based costing in the United Kingdom's largest financial institutions, *The Service Industries Journal*, **17**(1), 190–203.

Innes, J. (1998) Strategic management accounting, in Innes, J. (ed.) *Handbook of Management Accounting*, Gee, London.

Innes, J., Mitchell, F. and Sinclair, D. (2000) Activity-based costing in the UK's largest companies: a comparison of 1994 and 1999 survey results, *Management Accounting Research*, **11**(3), 349–62.

Israelsen, P., Anderson, M., Rohde, C. and Sorensen, P.E. (1996) Management accounting in Denmark: theory and practice, in Bhimani, A. (ed.) *Management Accounting: European Perspectives*, Oxford, Oxford University Press, 3153.

Ittner, C.D., Larcker, D.F. and Rajan, M.V. (1997) The choice of performance measures in annual bonus contracts, *The Accounting Review*, **72**(2), 231–55.

Johnson, H.T. (1990) Professors, customers and value: bringing a global perspective to management accounting education, in *Performance Excellence in Manufacturing and Services Organizations* (ed. P. Turney), American Accounting Association.

Johnson, H.T. and Kaplan, R.S. (1987) *Relevance Lost: The Rise and Fall of Management Accounting*, Harvard Business School Press.

Johnson, G. and Scholes, K. (1999) *Exploring Corporate Strategy*, Prentice-Hall.

Johnson, G. and Scholes, K. (2002) *Exploring Corporate Strategy*, Prentice-Hall.

Joseph, N., Turley, S., Burns, J., Lewis, L., Scapens, R.W. and Southworth, A. (1996) External financial reporting and management information: A survey of UK management accountants, *Management Accounting Research* **7**(1), 73–94.

Joshi, P.L. (1998) An explanatory study of activity-based costing practices and benefits in large size manufacturing companies in India, *Accounting and Business Review*, **5**(1), 65–93.

Joye, M.P. and Blayney, P.J. (1990) Cost and management accounting practice in Australian manufacturing companies: survey results, Monograph No. 7, University of Sydney.

Joye, M.P. and Blayney, P.J. (1991) Strategic management accounting survey, Monograph No. 8, University of Sydney.

Kald, M. and Nilsson, F. (2000) Performance measurement at Nordic companies, *European Management Journal*, **1**, 113–27.

Kaplan, R.S. (1990) Contribution margin analysis: no longer relevant/strategic cost management: the new paradigm, *Journal of Management Accounting Research* (USA), Fall, 2–15.

Kaplan, R.S. (1994) Management accounting (1984–1994): development of new practice and theory, *Management Accounting Research*, September and December, 247–60.

Kaplan, R.S. and Atkinson, A.A. (1998) *Advanced Management Accounting*, Prentice-Hall, Ch. 3

Kaplan, R.S. and Cooper, R. (1998) *Cost and Effect: Using Integrated Systems to Drive Profitability and Performance*, Harvard Business School Press.

Kaplan, R.S. and Norton, D.P. (1992) The balanced scorecard: measures that drive performance, *Harvard Business Review*, Jan–Feb, 71–9.

Kaplan, R.S. and Norton, D.P. (1993) Putting the balanced scorecard to work, *Harvard Business Review*, September–October, 134–47.

Kaplan, R.S. and Norton, D.P. (1996a) Using the balanced scorecard as a strategic management system, *Harvard Business Review*, Jan–Feb, 75–85.

Kaplan, R.S. and Norton, D.P. (1996b) *The Balanced Scorecard: Translating strategy into action*, Harvard Business School Press.

Kaplan, R.S. and Norton, D.P. (2001a) *The Strategy-focused Organization*, Harvard Business School Press.

Kaplan, R.S. and Norton, D.P. (2001b) Balance without profit, *Financial Management*, January, 23–6.

Kaplan R.S., Weiss, D. and Deseh, E. (1997) Transfer pricing with ABC, *Management Accounting (USA)*, 20–8.

Kato, Y. (1993) Target costing support systems: lessons from leading Japanese companies, *Management Accounting Research*, March, 33–48.

Langfield-Smith, K. (1997) Management control systems and strategy: a critical review, *Accounting, Organizations and Society*, **22**, 207–32.

Lauderman, M. and Schaeberle, F.W. (1983) The cost accounting practices of firms using standard costs, *Cost and Management* (Canada), July/August, 21–5.

Leauby, B.A. and Wentzel, K. (2002) Know the score: The balanced scorecard approach to strategically assist clients, *Pennsylvania CPA Journal*, Spring, 29–32.

Lee, T.A. (1996) *Income and Value Measurement*, Thomson Business Press, London.

Lord, B.R. (1996), Strategic management accounting: the emperor's new clothes? *Management Accounting Research*, **7**(3), 347–66.

Lukka, K. and Granlund, M. (1996) Cost accounting in Finland: Current practice and trends of development, *The European Accounting Review*, **5**(1), 1–28.

Macintosh, N.B. (1985) *The Social Software of Accounting and Information Systems*, Wiley.

Malmi, T. (2001) Balanced scorecards in Finnish companies: a research note. *Management Accounting Research*, **12**(2), 207–20.

McGowan, A.S. and Klammer, T.P. (1997) Satisfaction with activity-based cost management, *Journal of Management Accounting Research*, **9**, 217–38.

Merchant, K.A. (1989) *Rewarding Results: Motivating Profit Center Managers*, Harvard Business School Press.

Merchant, K.A. (1990) How challenging should profit budget targets be? *Management Accounting*, November, 46–8.

Merchant, K.A. (1998) *Modern Management Control Systems: Text and Cases*, Prentice-Hall, New Jersey.

Miles, R.E. and Snow, C.C. (1978) *Organizational Strategies, Structure and Process*, McGraw-Hill, New York.

Monden, Y. and Hamada, K. (1991) Target costing and *Kaizen* costing in Japanese automobile companies, *Journal of Management Accounting Research*, Autumn, 16–34.

Moon, P. and Fitzgerald, L. (1996) *Performance Measurement in Service Industries: Making it Work*, Chartered Institute of Management Accountants, London.

Moore, P.G. and Thomas, H. (1991) *The Anatomy of Decisions*, Penguin, Harmondsworth.

Nicholls, B. (1992) ABC in the UK – a status report, *Management Accounting*, May, 22–3.

Oliveras, E. and Amat, O. (2002) The balanced scorecard assumptions and the drivers of business growth, Paper presented at the 25th Annual Congress of the European Accounting Association, Copenhagen, Denmark.

Olve, N., Roy, J. and Wetter, M. (2000) *Performance Drivers: A Practical Guide to Using the Balanced Scorecard*, John Wiley & Sons.

Otley, D.T. (1978) Budget use and managerial performance, *Journal of Accounting Research*, **16**(1), Spring, 122–49.

Otley, D.T. (1987) *Accounting Control and Organizational Behaviour*, Heinemann, London.

Ouchi, W.G. (1979) A conceptual framework for the design of organizational control mechanisms, *Management Science*, 833–48.

Pendlebury, M. (1996) Management accounting in local government, in *Handbook of Management Accounting Practice* (ed. C. Drury), Butterworth-Heinemann, London.

Pere, T. (1999) How the execution of strategy is followed in large organisations located in Finland, Masters Thesis (Helsinki School of Economics and Business Administration).

Phyrr, P.A. (1976) Zero-based budgeting – where to use it and how to begin, *S.A.M. Advanced Management Journal*, Summer, 5.

Pike, R.H. (1996) A longitudinal study of capital budgeting practices, *Journal of Business Finance and Accounting*, 23(1), 79–92.

Pike, R. and Neale, B. (2003) *Corporate Finance and Investment*, Prentice-Hall Europe.

Plunkett, J.J., Dale, B.G. and Tyrrell, R.W. (1985) *Quality Costs*, Department of Trade and Industry, London.

Porter, M. (1980) *Competitive strategy techniques analysing industries and competitors*, New York, Free Press.

Porter, M. (1985) *Competitive Advantage*, New York, Free Press.

Ramadan, S.S. (1989) The rationale for cost allocation: A study of UK companies, *Accounting and Business Research*, Winter, 31–7.

Ranganathan, J. and Ditz, D. (1996) Environmental accounting: a tool for better management, *Management Accounting*, February, 38–40.

Reece, J.S. and Cool, W.R. (1978) Measuring investment centre performance, *Harvard Business Review*, May/June 29–49.

Roslender, R. (1992) *Sociological Perspectives on Modern Accountancy*, Routledge, London.

Roslender, R. (1995) Accounting for strategic positioning: Responding to the crisis in management accounting, *British Journal of Management*, 6, 45–57.

Roslender, R. (1996) Relevance lost and found: Critical perspectives on the promise of management accounting, *Critical Perspectives on Accounting*, 7(5), 533–61.

Saez-Torrecilla, A., Fernandez-Fernandez, A., Texeira-Quiros, J. and Vequera-Mosquero, M. (1996) Management accounting in Spain: trends in thought and practice, in Bhimari, A. (ed.) *Management Accounting: European Perspective 3*, Oxford, Oxford University Press, 180–90.

Scapens, R., Jazayeri, M. and Scapens, J. (1998) SAP: Integrated information systems and the implications for management accountants, *Management Accounting (UK)*, September, 46–8.

Scapens, R.W. (1991) *Management Accounting: A Review of Recent Developments*, Macmillan.

Scarborough, P.A., Nanni, A. and Sakuri, M. (1991) Japanese management accounting practices and the effects of assembly and process automation. *Management Accounting Research*, 2, 27–46.

Scherrer, G. (1996) Management accounting: a German perspective, in Bhimani, A. (ed.), *Management Accounting: European Perspectives*, Oxford, Oxford University Press, 100–22.

Schwarzbach, H.R. (1985) The impact of automation on accounting for direct costs, *Management Accounting* (USA), 67(6), 45–50.

Shank, J.K. (1989) Strategic cost management: new wine or just new bottles?, *Journal of Management Accounting Research* (USA), Fall, 47–65.

Shank, J. and Govindarajan, V. (1992) Strategic cost management: the value chain perspective, *Journal of Management Accounting Research*, 4, 179–97.

Shields, M.D. (1995) An empirical analysis of firms' implementation experiences with activity-based costing, *Journal of Management Accounting Research*, 7, Fall, 148–66.

Shim, E. and Stagliano, A. (1997) A survey of US manufacturers on implementation of ABC, *Journal of Cost Management*, March/April, 39–41.

Silk, S. (1998) Automating the balanced scorecard, *Management Accounting*, May, 38–44.

Simmonds, K. (1981) Strategic management accounting, *Management Accounting*, 59(4), 26–9.

Simmonds, K. (1982) Strategic management accounting for pricing: a case example, *Accounting and Business Research*, 12(47), 206–14.

Simmonds, K. (1986) The accounting assessment of competitive position, *European Journal of Marketing, Organisations and Society*, 12(4), 357–74.

Simon, H.A. (1959) Theories of decision making in economics and behavioural science, *The American Economic Review*, June, 233–83.

Simons, R. (1987) Accounting control systems and business strategy, *Accounting, Organizations and Society*, 12(4), 357–74.

Simons, R. (1999) *Performance Measurement and Control Systems for Implementing Strategy*, Prentice-Hall, New Jersey.

Sizer, J. (1989) *An Insight into Management Accounting*, Penguin, Harmondsworth, Chs 11, 12.

Skinner, R.C. (1990) The role of profitability in divisional decision making and performance, *Accounting and Business Research*, Spring, 135–41.

Solomons, D. (1965) *Divisional Performance: Measurement and Control*, R.D. Irwin.

Speckbacher, G., Bischof, J. and Pfeiffer, T. (2003) A Descriptive Analysis on the Implementation of Balanced Scorecards in German-Speaking Countries, *Management Accounting Research*, 14(4), 361–88.

Stewart, G.B. (1991) *The Quest for Value: A Guide for Senior Managers*, Harper Collins, New York.

Stewart, G.B. (1994) EVA(TM): Fact and Fantasy, *Journal of Applied Corporate Finance*, Summer, 71–84.

Stewart, G.B. (1995) EVA(TM) works But not if you make common mistakes, *Fortune*, 1 May, 81–2.

Tang, R. (1992) Canadian transfer pricing in the 1990s, *Management Accounting* (USA), February.

Tani, T., Okano, H., Shimizu, N., Iwabuchi, Y, Fukuda, J. and Cooray, S. (1994) Target cost management in Japanese companies: current state of the art, *Management Accounting Research*, 5(1), 67–82.

Thompson, J.L. (2001) *Strategic Management*, Chapman and Hall, London.

Tomkins, C. (1973) *Financial Planning in Divisionalised Companies*, Haymarket, Chs 4 and 8.

Tomkins, C. and Carr, C. (1996) Editorial in Special Issue of Management Accounting Research: Strategic Management Accounting, *Management Accounting Research*, 7(2), 165–7.

Trahan, E.A. and Gitman, L.J. (1995) Bridging the theory–practice gap in corporate finance: A survey of chief finance officers, *The Quarterly Review of Economics and Finance*, 35(1), Spring, 73–87.

Turney, P. (1993) *Common Cents: The ABC Performance Breakthrough*, Cost Technology, Hillsboro, Oregon, USA.

Umapathy, S. (1987) *Current Budgeting Practices in U.S. Industry: The State of the Art*, New York, Quorum.

Virtanen, K., Malmi, T., Vaivio, J. and Kasanen, E. (1996) Drivers of management accounting in Finland, in Bhimani, A. (ed.) *Management Accounting: European Perspectives*, Oxford, Oxford University Press, 218–41.

Vroom, V.H. (1960) *Some Personality Determinants of the Effects of Participation*, Prentice-Hall.

Ward, K. (1992) Accounting for marketing strategies, in *Management Accounting Handbook* (ed. C. Drury), Butterworth-Heinemann, Ch. 7.

Watson, D.H. and Baumler, J.V. (1975) Transfer pricing: a behavioural context, *Accounting Review*, 50(3), July, 466–74.

Yoshikawa, T., Innes, J., Mitchell, F. and Tanaka, M. (1993) *Contemporary Cost Management*, Chapman and Hall.

APPENDICES

Appendix A: Present value of £1

Years hence	1%	2%	4%	6%	8%	10%	12%	14%	15%	16%
1	0.990	0.980	0.962	0.943	0.926	0.909	0.893	0.877	0.870	0.862
2	0.980	0.961	0.925	0.890	0.857	0.826	0.797	0.769	0.756	0.743
3	0.971	0.942	0.889	0.840	0.794	0.751	0.712	0.675	0.658	0.641
4	0.961	0.924	0.855	0.792	0.735	0.683	0.636	0.592	0.572	0.552
5	0.951	0.906	0.822	0.747	0.681	0.621	0.567	0.519	0.497	0.476
6	0.942	0.888	0.790	0.705	0.630	0.564	0.507	0.456	0.432	0.410
7	0.933	0.871	0.760	0.665	0.583	0.513	0.452	0.400	0.376	0.354
8	0.923	0.853	0.731	0.627	0.540	0.467	0.404	0.351	0.327	0.305
9	0.914	0.837	0.703	0.592	0.500	0.424	0.361	0.308	0.284	0.263
10	0.905	0.820	0.676	0.558	0.463	0.386	0.322	0.270	0.247	0.227
11	0.896	0.804	0.650	0.527	0.429	0.350	0.287	0.237	0.215	0.195
12	0.887	0.788	0.625	0.497	0.397	0.319	0.257	0.208	0.187	0.168
13	0.879	0.773	0.601	0.469	0.368	0.290	0.229	0.182	0.163	0.145
14	0.870	0.758	0.577	0.442	0.340	0.263	0.205	0.160	0.141	0.125
15	0.861	0.743	0.555	0.417	0.315	0.239	0.183	0.140	0.123	0.108
16	0.853	0.728	0.534	0.394	0.292	0.218	0.163	0.123	0.107	0.093
17	0.844	0.714	0.513	0.371	0.270	0.198	0.146	0.108	0.093	0.080
18	0.836	0.700	0.494	0.350	0.250	0.180	0.130	0.095	0.081	0.069
19	0.828	0.686	0.475	0.331	0.232	0.164	0.116	0.083	0.070	0.060
20	0.820	0.673	0.456	0.312	0.215	0.149	0.104	0.073	0.061	0.051

18%	20%	22%	24%	25%	26%	28%	30%	35%	Years hence
0.847	0.833	0.820	0.806	0.800	0.794	0.781	0.769	0.741	1
0.718	0.694	0.672	0.650	0.640	0.630	0.610	0.592	0.549	2
0.609	0.579	0.551	0.524	0.512	0.500	0.477	0.455	0.406	3
0.516	0.482	0.451	0.423	0.410	0.397	0.373	0.350	0.301	4
0.437	0.402	0.370	0.341	0.328	0.315	0.291	0.269	0.223	5
0.370	0.335	0.303	0.275	0.262	0.250	0.227	0.207	0.165	6
0.933	0.279	0.249	0.222	0.210	0.198	0.178	0.159	0.122	7
0.266	0.233	0.204	0.179	0.168	0.157	0.139	0.123	0.091	8
0.225	0.194	0.167	0.144	0.134	0.125	0.108	0.094	0.067	9
0.191	0.162	0.137	0.116	0.107	0.099	0.085	0.073	0.050	10
0.162	0.135	0.112	0.094	0.086	0.079	0.066	0.056	0.037	11
0.137	0.112	0.092	0.076	0.069	0.062	0.052	0.043	0.027	12
0.116	0.093	0.075	0.061	0.055	0.050	0.040	0.033	0.020	13
0.099	0.078	0.062	0.049	0.044	0.039	0.032	0.025	0.015	14
0.084	0.065	0.051	0.040	0.035	0.031	0.025	0.020	0.011	15
0.071	0.054	0.042	0.032	0.028	0.025	0.019	0.015	0.008	16
0.060	0.045	0.034	0.026	0.023	0.020	0.015	0.012	0.006	17
0.051	0.038	0.028	0.021	0.018	0.016	0.012	0.009	0.005	18
0.043	0.031	0.023	0.017	0.014	0.012	0.009	0.007	0.003	19
0.037	0.026	0.019	0.014	0.012	0.010	0.007	0.005	0.002	20

Appendix B: Present value of £1 received annually for n years

Years hence	1%	2%	4%	6%	8%	10%	12%	14%	15%	16%	18%
1	0.990	0.980	0.962	0.943	0.926	0.909	0.893	0.877	0.870	0.862	0.847
2	1.970	1.942	1.886	1.833	1.783	1.736	1.690	1.647	1.626	1.605	1.566
3	2.941	2.884	2.775	2.673	2.577	2.487	2.402	2.322	2.283	2.246	2.174
4	3.902	3.808	3.630	3.465	3.312	3.170	3.037	2.914	2.855	2.798	2.690
5	4.853	4.713	4.452	4.212	3.993	3.791	3.605	3.433	3.352	3.274	3.127
6	5.795	5.601	5.242	4.917	4.623	4.355	4.111	3.889	3.784	3.685	3.498
7	6.728	6.472	6.002	5.582	5.206	4.868	4.564	4.288	4.160	4.039	3.812
8	7.652	7.325	6.733	6.210	5.747	5.335	4.968	4.639	4.487	4.344	4.078
9	8.556	8.162	7.435	6.802	6.247	5.759	5.328	4.946	4.772	4.607	4.303
10	9.471	8.983	8.111	7.360	6.710	6.145	5.650	5.216	5.019	4.833	4.494
11	10.368	9.787	8.760	7.887	7.139	6.495	5.937	5.453	5.234	5.029	4.656
12	11.255	10.575	9.385	8.384	7.536	6.814	6.194	5.660	5.421	5.197	4.793
13	12.134	11.343	9.986	8.853	7.904	7.103	6.424	5.842	5.583	5.342	4.910
14	13.004	12.106	10.563	9.295	8.244	7.367	6.628	6.002	5.724	5.468	5.008
15	13.865	12.849	11.118	9.712	8.559	7.606	6.811	6.142	5.847	5.575	5.092
16	14.718	13.578	11.652	10.106	8.851	7.824	6.974	6.265	5.954	5.669	5.162
17	15.562	14.292	12.166	10.477	9.122	8.022	7.120	6.373	6.047	5.749	5.222
18	16.398	14.992	12.659	10.828	9.372	8.201	7.250	6.467	6.128	5.818	5.273
19	17.226	15.678	13.134	11.158	9.604	8.365	7.366	6.550	6.198	5.877	5.316
20	18.046	16.351	13.590	11.470	9.818	8.514	7.469	6.623	6.259	5.929	5.353

20%	22%	24%	25%	26%	28%	30%	35%	36%	37%	Years hence
0.833	0.820	0.806	0.800	0.794	0.781	0.769	0.741	0.735	0.730	1
1.528	1.492	1.457	1.440	1.424	1.392	1.361	1.289	1.276	1.263	2
2.106	2.042	1.981	1.952	1.923	1.868	1.816	1.696	1.673	1.652	3
2.589	2.494	2.404	2.362	2.320	2.241	2.166	1.997	1.966	1.935	4
2.991	2.864	2.745	2.689	2.635	2.532	2.436	2.220	2.181	2.143	5
3.326	3.167	3.020	2.951	2.885	2.759	2.643	2.385	2.339	2.294	6
3.605	3.416	3.242	3.161	3.083	2.937	2.802	2.508	2.455	2.404	7
3.837	3.619	3.421	3.329	3.241	3.076	2.925	2.598	2.540	2.485	8
4.031	3.786	3.566	3.463	3.366	3.184	3.019	2.665	2.603	2.544	9
4.192	3.923	3.682	3.571	3.465	3.269	3.092	2.715	2.649	2.587	10
4.327	4.035	3.776	3.656	3.544	3.335	3.147	2.752	2.683	2.618	11
4.439	4.127	3.851	3.725	3.606	3.387	3.190	2.779	2.708	2.641	12
4.533	4.203	3.912	3.780	3.656	3.427	3.223	2.799	2.727	2.658	13
4.611	4.265	3.962	3.824	3.695	3.459	3.249	2.814	2.740	2.670	14
4.675	4.315	4.001	3.859	3.726	3.483	3.268	2.825	2.750	2.679	15
4.730	4.357	4.033	3.887	3.751	3.503	3.283	2.834	2.757	2.685	16
4.775	4.391	4.059	3.910	3.771	3.518	3.295	2.840	2.763	2.690	17
4.812	4.419	4.080	3.928	3.786	3.529	3.304	2.844	2.767	2.693	18
4.844	4.442	4.097	3.942	3.799	3.539	3.311	2.848	2.770	2.696	19
4.870	4.460	4.110	3.954	3.808	3.546	3.316	2.850	2.772	2.698	20

ANSWERS TO REVIEW PROBLEMS

Chapter 2

2.15 (a) SV (or variable if direct labour can be matched exactly to output)
  (b) F
  (c) F
  (d) V
  (e) F (Advertising is a discretionary cost. See Chapter 10, Zero-based budgeting for an explanation of this cost.)
  (f) SV
  (g) F
  (h) SF
  (i) V

2.16 Controllable c, d, f
  Non-controllable a, b, e, g, h

2.17 Answer = B

2.18 Answer = B

2.19 Answer = B

2.20 (a) (i) Schedule of annual mileage costs

	5000 miles (£)	10 000 miles (£)	15 000 miles (£)	30 000 miles (£)
Variable costs:				
Spares	100	200	300	600
Petrol	380	760	1140	2280
Total variable cost	480	960	1440	2880
Variable cost per mile	0.096	0.096	0.096	0.096
Fixed costs				
Depreciation[a]	2000	2000	2000	2000
Maintenance	120	120	120	120
Vehicle licence	80	80	80	80
Insurance	150	150	150	150
Tyres[b]	—	—	75	150
	2350	2350	2425	2500
Fixed cost per mile	0.47	0.235	0.162	0.083
Total cost	2830	3310	3865	5380
Total cost per mile	0.566	0.331	0.258	0.179

Notes

[a] Annual depreciation $= \dfrac{£5500 \text{ (cost)} - £1500 \text{ (trade-in price)}}{2 \text{ years}} = £2000$

[b] At 15 000 miles per annum tyres will be replaced once during the two-year period at a cost of £150. The average cost per year is £75. At 30 000 miles per annum tyres will be replaced once each year.

Comments

Tyres are a semi-fixed cost. In the above calculations they have been regarded as a step fixed cost. An alternative approach would be to regard the semi-fixed cost as a variable cost by dividing £150 tyre replacement by 25 000 miles. This results in a variable cost per mile of £0.006.

Depreciation and maintenance cost have been classified as fixed costs. They are likely to be semi-variable costs, but in the absence of any additional information they have been classified as fixed costs.

  (ii) See Figure 2.20.
  (iii) The respective costs can be obtained from the vertical dashed lines in the graph (Figure 2.20).
  (b) The *cost per mile* declines as activity increases. This is because the majority of costs are fixed and do not increase when mileage increases. However, *total cost* will increase with increases in mileage.

FIGURE 2.20 *The step increase in fixed cost is assumed to occur at an annual mileage of 12 500 and 25 000 miles, because tyres are assumed to be replaced at this mileage*

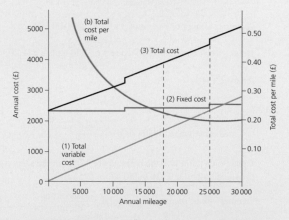

2.21 (a) (i) For an explanation of sunk and opportunity costs see Chapter 2. The down payment of £5000 represents a sunk cost. The lost profit from subletting the shop of £1600 p.a. ((£550 × 12) – £5000) is an example of an opportunity cost. Note that only the £5000 additional rental is included in the opportunity cost calculation. (The £5000 sunk cost is excluded from the calculation.)

(ii) The relevant information for running the shop is:

	(£)
Net sales	100 000
Costs (£87 000 – £5000 sunk cost)	82 000
	18 000
Less opportunity cost from subletting	1 600
Profit	16 400

The above indicates that £16 400 additional profits will be obtained from using the shop for the sale of clothing. It is assumed that Mrs Johnson will not suffer any other loss of income if she devotes half her time to running the shop.

(b) The CIMA terminology defines a notional cost as 'A hypothetical cost taken into account in a particular situation to represent a benefit enjoyed by an entity in respect of which no actual expense is incurred.' Examples of notional cost include:

(i) Interest on capital to represent the notional cost of using an asset rather than investing the capital elsewhere.

(ii) Including rent as a cost for premises owned by the company so as to represent the lost rent income resulting from using the premises for business purposes.

Chapter 3

3.11

	Product X	Product Y	Total
Budgeted sales volume (units)	80 000	20 000	
Budgeted contribution per unit	£4	£5	
Budgeted total contribution	£320 000	£100 000	£420 000
Budgeted sales revenue	£960 000	£160 000	£1 120 000

Average contribution per unit = £420 000/100 000 units = £4.20

$$\text{Break-even point} = \frac{\text{Fixed costs (£273 000)}}{\text{Average contribution per unit (£4.20)}} = 65\ 000 \text{ units}$$

Average selling price per unit = £1 120 000/100 000 units
= £11.20

Break-even point in sales revenue = 65 000 units × £11.20
= £728 000

Answer = D

3.12

Average contribution to sales ratio = $\frac{(40\% \times 1) + (50\% \times 3)}{4} = 47.5\%$

Break-even point is at the point where 47.5% of the sales equal the fixed costs (i.e. £120 000/0.475 = £252 632).

In other words, the break-even point = $\frac{\text{Fixed costs}}{\text{PV ratio}}$

Answer = C

3.13

	Total cost (1000 units) (£)	Total cost (2000 units) (£)
Production overhead	3500 (£3.50 × 1000)	5000 (£2.50 × 2000)
Selling overhead	1000 (£1 × 1000)	1000 (£0.5 × 2000)

Variable cost per unit = $\frac{\text{Change in cost}}{\text{Change in activity}}$

Production overhead = £1500/1000 units = £1.50

Selling overhead = Fixed cost since total costs remain unchanged.

The unit costs of direct materials are constant at both activity levels and are therefore variable.

Production overheads fixed cost element = Total cost (£3500) – Variable cost (1000 × £1.50) = £2000

Total fixed cost = £2000 + £1000 = £3000

Unit variable cost £4 + £3 + £1.50 = £8.50

Answer = E

3.14

Contribution/sales (%) = (0.33 × 40% Aye) + (0.33 × 50% Bee) + (0.33 × ? Cee) = 48%

Cee = 54% (Balancing figure)

The total contribution/sales ratio for the revised sales mix is:

(0.40 × 40% Aye) + (0.25 × 50% Bee) + (0.35 × 54% Cee)
= 47.4%

Answer = C

3.15

Sales	100	110 (100 + 10%)
Variable cost	60	60
Contribution	40	50

Increase = 25%

Answer = D

3.16

Contribution per unit = 40% × £20 = £8

$$\text{Break-even point} = \frac{\text{Fixed costs (£60 000)}}{\text{Contribution per units (£8)}} = 7500 \text{ units}$$

Answer = E

3.17

Break-even point in sales value	= Fixed costs (£76 800)/Profit–volume ratio (i.e. contribution/sales ratio)
	= £76 800/(0.40)
	= £192 000
Actual sales	= £224 000
Margin of safety	= £32 000 (in sales revenues)
Margin of safety in units	= £2000 (£32 000/£16)

Answer = A

3.18

(i)
p	=	total sales revenue
q	=	total cost (fixed cost + variable cost)
r	=	total variable cost
s	=	fixed costs at the specific level of activity
t	=	total loss at the specific level of activity
u	=	total profit at that level of activity
v	=	total contribution at the specific level of activity
w	=	total contribution at a lower level of activity
x	=	level of activity of output sales
y	=	monetary value of cost and revenue function for level of activity

(ii) At event m the selling price per *unit* decreases, but it remains constant. Note that p is a straight line, but with a lower gradient above m compared with below m.

At event n there is an increase in fixed costs equal to the dotted line. This is probably due to an increase in capital expenditure in order to expand output beyond this point. Also note that at this point the variable cost per unit declines as reflected by the gradient of the variable cost line. This might be due to more efficient production methods associated with increased investment in capital equipment.

(iii) Break-even analysis is of limited use in a multi-product company, but the analysis can be a useful aid to the management of a small single product company. The following are some of the main benefits:

(a) Break-even analysis forces management to consider the functional relationship between costs, revenue and activity, and gives an insight into how costs and revenue change with changes in the level of activity.

(b) Break-even analysis forces management to consider the fixed costs at various levels of activity and the selling price that will be required to achieve various levels of output.

You should refer to Chapter 3 for a discussion of more specific issues of break-even analysis. Break-even analysis can be a useful tool, but it is subject to a number of assumptions that restrict its usefulness (see, especially, 'Cost–volume–profit analysis assumptions').

3.19 *Preliminary calculations:*

	Sales (units)	Profit/(loss)
November	30 000	£40 000
December	35 000	£60 000
Increase	5 000	£20 000

An increase in sales of 5000 units increases contribution (profits) by £20 000. Therefore contribution is £4 per unit. Selling price is £10 per unit (given) and variable cost per unit will be £6.
At £30 000 unit sales:

Contribution   minus Fixed costs = Profit
£120 000   minus   ?   = £40 000
∴ Fixed costs = £80 000

The above information can now be plotted on a graph. A break-even chart or a profit–volume graph could be constructed. A profit–volume graph avoids the need to calculate the profits since the information can be read directly from the graph. (See Figure 3.20a for a break-even chart and Figure 3.20b for a profit–volume graph.)

(a) (i) Fixed costs = £80 000.
(ii) Variable cost per unit = £6.
(iii) Profit–volume =
$$\frac{\text{Contribution per unit (£4)}}{\text{Selling price per unit (£10)}} \times 100 = 40\%$$
(iv) Break-even point = 20 000 units.
(v) The margin of safety represents the difference between actual or expected sales volume and the break-even point. Therefore the margin of safety will be different for each month's sales. For example, the margin of safety in November is 10 000 units (30 000 units – 20 000 units). The margin of safety can be read from Figure 3.20b for various sales levels.

(b) and (c) See the sections on 'The accountants' cost–volume–profit model' and 'Cost–volume–profit analysis assumptions' in Chapter 3 for the answers.

FIGURE 3.20a   *Break-even chart*

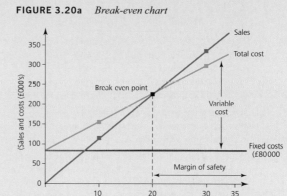

FIGURE 3.20b   *Profit–volume graph*

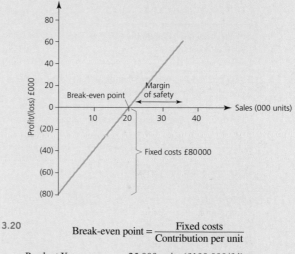

3.20

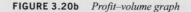

$$\text{Break-even point} = \frac{\text{Fixed costs}}{\text{Contribution per unit}}$$

Product X	25 000 units (£100 000/£4)
Product Y	25 000 units (£200 000/£8)
Company as a whole	57 692 units (£300 000/£5.20[a])

Note:
[a]Average contribution per unit
$$= \frac{(70\,000 \times £4) + (30\,000 \times £8)}{100\,000 \text{ units}}$$
$$= £5.20$$

The sum of the product break-even points is less than the break-even point for the company as a whole. It is incorrect to add the product break-even points because the sales mix will be different from the planned sales mix. The sum of the product break-even points assumes a sales mix of 50% to X and 50% to Y. The break-even point for the company as a whole assumes a planned sales mix of 70% to X and 30% to Y. CVP analysis will yield correct results only if the planned sales mix is equal to the actual sales mix.

3.21

Workings:	(000)
Sales	1000
Variable costs	600
Contribution	400
Fixed costs	500
Profit/(loss)	(100)

Unit selling price = £20 (£1m/50 000)
Unit variable cost = £12 (£600 000/50 000)
Unit contribution = £8

(a) Sales commission will be £2 per unit, thus reducing the contribution per unit to £6. The break-even point will be 83 333 units (£500 000/£6) or £1 666 666 sales value. This requires an increase of 67% on previous sales and the company must assess whether or not sales can be increased by such a high percentage.

(b) A 10% decrease in selling price will decrease the selling price by £2 per unit and the revised unit contribution will be £6:

	(£)
Revised total contribution (65 000 × £6)	390 000
Less fixed costs	500 000
Profit/(loss)	(110 000)

The estimated loss is worse than last year and the proposal is therefore not recommended.

(c) Wages will increase by 25% – that is, from £200 000 to £250 000 – causing output to increase by 20%.

		(£)
Sales		1 200 000
Direct materials and variable overheads	480 000	
Direct wages	250 000	730 000
Contribution		470 000
Less fixed costs		550 000
Profit/(loss)		(80 000)

This represents an improvement of £20 000 on last year's loss of £100 000.

(d) Revised selling price = £24

Let X = Revised sales volume
∴ sales revenue less (variable costs + fixed costs) = Profit
24X less (12X + 800 000) = 0.1 (24X)
∴ 9.6X = 800 000
∴ X = 83 333 units

Clearly this proposal is preferable since it is the only proposal to yield a profit. However, the probability of increasing sales volume by approximately 67% plus the risk involved from increasing fixed costs by £300 000 must be considered.

3.22 (a)

$$BEP = \frac{400\ 000\ (\text{fixed costs}) \times £1\ 000\ 000\ (\text{sales})}{£420\ 000\ (\text{contribution})}$$

= 952 380

(b) (i)

	(£)	(£)
Revised selling price		9.00
Less variable costs:		
Direct materials	1.00	
Direct labour	3.50	
Variable overhead	0.60	
Delivery expenses	0.50	
Sales commission	0.18	
(2% of selling price)		5.78
Contribution per unit		3.22
Number of units sold		140 000
Total contribution (140 000 × 3.22)		450 800
Fixed costs		400 000
Profit from proposal (i)		50 800

(ii)

Desired contribution	= 480 000
Contribution per unit for present proposal	= 3.22
Required units to earn large profit	= 149 068

(c) (i) The variable cost of selling to the mail order firm is:

	(£)
Direct material	1.00
Direct labour	3.50
Variable overhead	0.60
Delivery expenses	nil
Sales commission	nil
Additional package cost	0.50
	5.60

To break even, a contribution of £1.20 is required (60 000 fixed cost/50 000 units sold). Therefore selling price to break even is £6.80 (£5.60 + £1.20).

(ii) To earn £50 800 profit, a contribution of £110 800 (£60 000 + £50 800) is required.
That is, a contribution of £2.22 per unit is required. Therefore required selling price is £7.82 (£5.60 + £2.22).

(iii) To earn the target profit of £80 000, a contribution of £140 000 is required. That is, £2.80 per unit. Therefore required selling price = £8.40 (£5.60 + £2.80).

(d) Contribution per unit is £3.22 per (B)

Unit sold	160 000
Total contribution	£515 200
Fixed costs	£430 000
Profit	£85 200

Chapter 4

4.13

	X	Y	Z
Contribution per unit	£41	£54	£50
Kg used (Limiting factor)	2 (£10/5)	1	3
Contribution per kg	£20.5	£54	£16.67
Ranking	2	1	3

Answer = B

4.14
The material is in regular use and if used will have to be replaced at a cost of £1950 (600 × £3.25). The cash flow consequences are £1950.
Answer = D

4.15
The shadow price is the opportunity cost or contribution per unit of a scarce resource.

	Quone	Qutwo
Contribution per unit	£8	£8.50
Kg per unit	3 (£6/£2)	2.50 (£5/£2)
Contribution per kg	£2.67	£3.40

Scarce materials will be used to make Qutwos and will yield a contribution of £3.40 per kg. Therefore the opportunity cost is £3.40 per kg.
Answer = D

4.16
Assuming that fixed costs will remain unchanged whether or not the company makes or buys the components the relevant cost of manufacture will be the variable cost. Under these circumstances the company should only purchase components if the purchase price is less than the variable cost. Therefore the company should only purchase component T.
Answer = D

4.17
Incremental cost of new employees = £40 000 × 4 = £160 000
Supervision is not an incremental cost.
Incremental costs of retraining
= £15 000 + £100 000 replacement cost = £115 000
Retraining is the cheaper alternative and therefore the relevant cost of the contract is £115 000.
Answer = B

4.18
The material is readily available and the use of the materials will necessitate their replacement. The relevant cost is therefore the replacement cost of £4050 (1250 kg at £3.24).
Answer = B

4.19
Specific (avoidable) fixed overheads per division = £262.5 × 60% = £157.5/3 = £52.5
The specific fixed costs are deducted from the divisional contributions to derive the following contributions (£000's) to general fixed costs:
Division A = £17.5
Division B = £157.5
Division C = −£22.5
Only divisions A and B should remain open since they both provide positive contributions to general fixed costs.
Answer = B

4.20 (a)

	North East (£)	South coast (£)
Material X from stock (i)	19 440	
Material Y from stock (ii)		49 600
Firm orders of material X (iii)	27 360	
Material X not yet ordered (iv)	60 000	
Material Z not yet ordered (v)		71 200
Labour (vi)	86 000	110 000
Site management (vii)	—	
Staff accommodation and travel for site management (viii)	6 800	5 600
Plant rental received (ix)	(6000)	—
Penalty clause (x)		28 000
	193 600	264 400
Contract price	288 000	352 000
Net benefit	94 400	87 600

(b) (i) If material X is not used on the North East contract the most beneficial use is to use it as a substitute material thus avoiding future purchases of £19 440 (0.9 × 21 600). Therefore by using the stock quantity of material X the company will have to spend £19 440 on the other materials.

(ii) Material Y is in common use and the company should not dispose of it. Using the materials on the South coast contract will mean that they will have to be replaced at a cost of £49 600 (£24 800 × 2). Therefore the future cash flow impact of taking on the contract is £49 600.

(iii) It is assumed that with firm orders for materials it is not possible to cancel the purchase. Therefore the cost will occur whatever future alternative is selected. The materials will be used as a substitute material if they are not used on the contract and therefore, based on the same reasoning as note (i) above, the relevant cost is the purchase price of the substitute material (0.9 × £30 400).

(iv) The material has not been ordered and the cost will only be incurred if the contract is undertaken. Therefore additional cash flows of £60 000 will be incurred if the company takes on the North East contract.

(v) The same principles apply here as were explained in note (iv) and additional cash flows of £71 200 will be incurred only if the company takes on the South coast contract.

(vi) It is assumed that labour is an incremental cost and therefore relevant.

(vii) The site management function is performed by staff at central headquarters. It is assumed that the total company costs in respect of site management will remain unchanged in the short term whatever contracts are taken on. Site management costs are therefore irrelevant.

(viii) The costs would be undertaken only if the contracts are undertaken. Therefore they are relevant costs.

(ix) If the North East contract is undertaken the company will be able to hire out surplus plant and obtain a £6000 cash inflow.

(x) If the South coast contract is undertaken the company will have to withdraw from the North East contract and incur a penalty cost of £28 000.

(xi) The headquarter costs will continue whichever alternative is selected and they are not relevant costs.

(xii) It is assumed that there will be no differential cash flows relating to notional interest. However, if the interest costs associated with the contract differ then they would be relevant and should be included in the analysis.

(xiii) Depreciation is a sunk cost and irrelevant for decision-making.

4.21 (a) (i)

Product	A	B	C
	(£)	(£)	(£)
Selling price	15	12	11
Less variable costs:			
Materials	(5)	(4)	(3)
Labour	(3)	(2)	(1.5)
Variable overhead (1)	(3.50)	(2)	(1.5)
Contribution	3.50	4	5

Note:

(1) Fixed overheads are apportioned to products on the basis of sales volume and the remaining overheads are variable with output.

(ii)

Product	B	C
	(£)	(£)
Selling price	12	9.50
Less variable costs:		
Materials	(4)	(3)
Labour	(2)	(1.80)
Variable overhead	(2)	(1.50)
Contribution	4	3.20

(b) (i)

Product	A	B	C	Total
Total contribution	350 000	480 000	400 000	1 230 000
Less fixed costs:				
Labour				(220 000)
Fixed administration				(900 000)
Profit				110 000

(ii)

Product	B	C	Total
Total contribution[a]	480 000	576 000	1 056 000
Less fixed costs:			
Labour[b]			(160 000)
Fixed administration[c]			(850 000)
Profit			46 000

Notes:
[a] B = 120 000 units × £4 contribution,
  C = 18 000 units × £3.20 contribution.
[b] (25% × £320 000 for B) plus (25% × £160 000 × 2 for C).
[c] Fixed administration costs will decline by 1/6 of the amount apportioned to Product A (100/300 × £900 000). Therefore fixed overheads will decline from £900 000 to £850 000.

(c) Product A should not be eliminated even though a loss is reported for this product. If Product A is eliminated the majority of fixed costs allocated to it will still continue and will be borne by the remaining products. Product A generates a contribution of £350 000 towards fixed costs but the capacity released can be used to obtain an additional contribution from Product C of £176 000 (£576 000 – £400 000). This will result in a net loss in contribution of £174 000. However, fixed cost savings of £110 000 (£50 000 administration apportioned to Product A plus £100 000 labour for A less an extra £40 000 labour for Product C) can be obtained if Product A is abandoned. Therefore there will be a net loss in contribution of £64 000 (£174 000 – £110 000) and profits will decline from £110 000 to £64 000.

4.22 The following information represents a comparison of alternatives 1 and 2 with the sale of material XY.

Alternative 1: Conversion versus immediate sale	(£)	(£)	(£)
1. Sales revenue (900 units at £400 per unit			360 000
Less Relevant costs:			
2. Material XY opportunity cost		21 000	
3. Material A (600 units at £90)		54 000	
4. Material B (1000 units at £45)		45 000	
5. Direct labour:			
Unskilled (5000 hrs at £6)	30 000		
Semi-skilled	nil		
Highly skilled (5000 hrs at £17)	85 000	115 000	
6. Variable overheads (15 000 hrs at £1)		15 000	
7. Selling and delivery expenses		27 000	
Advertising		18 000	
8. Fixed overheads		—	295 000
Excess of relevant revenues			65 000

Alternative 2: Adaptation versus immediate sale			
9. Saving on purchase of sub-assembly:			
Normal spending (1200 units at £900)		1 080 000	
Revised spending (900 units at £950)		855 000	225 000
Less relevant costs:			
2. Material XY opportunity cost		21 000	
10. Material C (1000 units at £55)		55 000	
5. Direct labour:			
Unskilled (4000 hrs at £6)	24 000		
Semi-skilled	nil		
Skilled (4000 hrs at £16)	64 000	88 000	
6. Variable overheads (9000 hrs at £1)		9 000	
8. Fixed overheads		nil	173 000
Net relevant savings			52 000

Notes

1. There will be additional sales revenue of £360 000 if alternative 1 is chosen.

2. Acceptance of either alternative 1 or 2 will mean a loss of revenue of £21 000 from the sale of the obsolete material XY. This is an opportunity cost, which must be covered whichever alternative is chosen. The original purchase cost of £75 000 for material XY is a sunk cost and is irrelevant.

3. Acceptance of alternative 1 will mean that material A must be replaced at an additional cost of £54 000.

4. Acceptance of alternative 1 will mean that material B will be diverted from the production of product Z. The excess of relevant revenues over relevant cost for product Z is £180 and each unit of product Z uses four units of material. The lost contribution (excluding the cost of material B which is incurred for both alternatives) will therefore be £45 for each unit of material B that is used in converting the raw materials into a specialized product.

5. Unskilled labour can be matched exactly to the company's production requirements. The acceptance of either alternative 1 or 2 will cause the company to incur additional unskilled labour costs of £6 for each hour of unskilled labour that is used. It is assumed that the semi-skilled labour would be retained and that there would be sufficient excess supply for either alternative at no extra cost to the company. In these circumstances semi-skilled labour will not have a relevant cost. Skilled labour is in short supply and can only be obtained by reducing production of product L, resulting in a lost contribution of £24 or £6 per hour of skilled labour. We have already established that the relevant cost for labour that is in short supply is the hourly labour cost plus the lost contribution per hour, so the relevant labour cost here will be £16 per hour.

6. It is assumed that for each direct labour hour of input variable overheads will increase by £1. As each alternative uses additional direct labour hours, variable overheads will increase, giving a relevant cost of £1 per direct labour hour.

7. As advertising selling and distribution expenses will be different if alternative 1 is chosen, these costs are clearly relevant to the decision.
8. The company's fixed overheads will remain the same whichever alternative is chosen, and so fixed overheads are not a relevant cost for either alternative.
9. The cost of purchasing the sub-assembly will be reduced by £225 000 if the second alternative is chosen, and so these savings are relevant to the decision.
10. The company will incur additional variable costs of £55 for each unit of material C that is manufactured, so the fixed overheads for material C are not a relevant cost.

When considering a problem such as this one, there are many different ways in which the information may be presented. The way in which we have dealt with the problem here is to compare each of the two stated alternatives with the other possibility of selling off material XY for its scrap value of £21 000. The above answer sets out the relevant information, and shows that of the three possibilities alternative 1 is to be preferred.

An alternative presentation of this information, which you may prefer, is as follows:

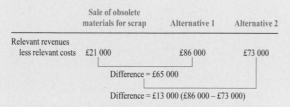

	Sale of obsolete materials for scrap	Alternative 1	Alternative 2
Relevant revenues less relevant costs	£21 000	£86 000	£73 000

Difference = £65 000

Difference = £13 000 (£86 000 – £73 000)

We show here *the sale of the obsolete materials as a separate alternative*, and so the opportunity cost of material XY, amounting to £21 000 (see item 2 in the answer) is not included in either alternative 1 or 2, since it is brought into the analysis under the heading 'Sale of obsolete materials for scrap' in the above alternative presentation. Consequently, in both alternatives 1 and 2 the relevant revenues less relevant costs figure is increased by £21 000. The differences between alternative 1 and 2 and the sale of the obsolete materials are still, however, £65 000 and £52 000 respectively, which gives an identical result to that obtained in the above solution.

4.23 (a) *Preliminary calculations*

Variable costs are quoted per acre, but selling prices are quoted per tonne. Therefore, it is necessary to calculate the planned sales revenue per acre. The calculation of the selling price and contribution per acre is as follows:

	Potatoes	Turnips	Parsnips	Carrots
(a) Yield per acre in tonnes	10	8	9	12
(b) Selling price per tonne	£100	£125	£150	£135
(c) Sales revenue per acre, (a) × (b)	£1000	£1000	£1350	£1620
(d) Variable cost per acre	£470	£510	£595	£660
(e) Contribution per acre	£530	£490	£755	£960
(a) (i)				

(i) Profit statement for current year

	Potatoes	Turnips	Parsnips	Carrots	Total
(a) Acres	25	20	30	25	
(b) Contribution per acre	£530	£490	£755	£960	
(c) Total contribution (a × b)	£13 250	£9800	£22 650	£24 000	£69 700
				Less fixed costs	£54 000
				Profit	£15 700

(ii) Profit statement for recommended mix

	Area A (45 acres)		Area B (55 acres)		
	Potatoes	Turnips	Parsnips	Carrots	Total
(a) Contribution per acre	£530	£490	£755	£960	
(b) Ranking	1	2	2	1	
(c) Minimum sales requirements in acres[a]		5	4		
(d) Acres allocated[b]	40			51	
(e) Recommended mix (acres)	40	5	4	51	
(f) Total contribution, (a) × (e)	£21 200	£2450	£3020	£48 960	£75 630
				Less fixed costs	£54 000
				Profit	£21 630

Notes

[a]The minimum sales requirement for turnips is 40 tonnes, and this will require the allocation of 5 acres (40 tonnes/8 tonnes yield per acre). The minimum sales requirement for parsnips is 36 tonnes, requiring the allocation of 4 acres (36 tonnes/9 tonnes yield per acre).
[b]Allocation of available acres to products on basis of a ranking that assumes that acres are the key factor.

(b) (i) Production should be concentrated on carrots, which have the highest contribution per acre (£960).

	(£)

(ii) Contribution from 100 acres of carrots

	(£)
(100 × £960)	96 000
Fixed overhead	54 000
Profit from carrots	42 000

(iii) Break-even point in acres for carrots $= \dfrac{\text{fixed costs (£54 000)}}{\text{contribution per acre (£960)}}$

= 56.25 acres

Contribution in sales value for carrots
= £91 125 (56.25 acres at £1620 sales revenue per acre).

Chapter 5

5.12 Overhead absorbed (£714 000) = Actual hours (119 000) × Pre-determined overhead rate.
Pre-determined overhead rate = £714 000/119 000 = £6.
Budgeted overheads (£720 000) = Budgeted machine hours × Budgeted overhead rate (£6).
Budgeted machine hours = £720 000/£6 = 120 000 hours.
Answer = C

5.13 Budgeted overhead rate = £258 750/11 250 hours = £23 per machine hour
Overheads absorbed = £23 × 10 980 Actual hours = £252 540
Overheads incurred = £254 692
Overheads absorbed = £252 540
Under-absorbed overheads = £2152
Answer = A

5.14 (i) Budgeted overhead rates and not actual overhead rates should be used as indicated in Chapter 3.
Overhead rate = £148 750/8500 hours = £17.50 per hour.
Answer = A
(ii)

	(£)
Actual overheads incurred	146 200
Overheads absorbed (7928 × £17.50)	138 740
Under-absorbed overheads	7 460

Answer = D

5.15 (i) It is assumed that labour cost is to be used as the allocation base.

Total labour cost = £14 500 + £3500 + £24 600 = £42 600

Overhead recovery rate = £126 000/£42 600 = £2.9578 per £1 of labour

Overhead charged to Job CC20 = £24 600 × £2.9578 = £72 761

Answer = C

(ii)

	(£)
Opening WIP	42 790
Direct labour	3 500
Overhead (£3500 × £2.9578)	10 352
	56 642
Selling price (£56 642/0.667)	84 921
or £56 642 divided by 2/3 =	£84 963

Answer = C

(iii) Closing WIP = Total cost of AA10 and CC20

	Total (£)	AA10 (£)	CC20 (£)
Opening WIP		26 800	0
Materials in period		17 275	18 500
Labour in period		14 500	24 600
Overheads in period:			
2.9577465 × £14 500		42 887	
2.9577465 × £24 600			72 761
	217 323	101 462	115 861

Answer = D

5.16 Answer = D

5.17 Because production is highly automated it is assumed that overheads will be most closely associated with machine hours. The predetermined overhead rate will therefore be £18 derived from dividing budgeted overheads (£180 000) by the budgeted machine hours (10 000). Therefore the answer is B.

5.18 (a)

	Total (£)	A (£)	Departments B (£)	C (£)	X (£)	Y (£)
Rent and rates[a]	12 800	6 000	3 600	1 200	1200	800
Machine insurance[b]	6 000	3 000	1 250	1 000	500	250
Telephone charges[c]	3 200	1 500	900	300	300	200
Depreciation[b]	18 000	9 000	3 750	3 000	1500	750
Supervisors' salaries[d]	24 000	12 800	7 200	4 000		
Heat and light[a]	6 400	3 000	1 800	600	600	400
	70 400					
Allocated		2 800	1 700	1 200	800	600
	38 100	20 200	11 300	4900	3000	
Reapportionment of X		2 450 (50%)	1 225 (25%)	1 225 (25%)	(4900)	
Reapportionment of Y		600 (20%)	900 (30%)	1 500 (50%)		(3000)
		£41 150	£22 325	£14 025		
Budgeted D.L. hours[e]		3 200	1 800	1 000		
Absorption rates		£12.86	£12.40	£14.02		

Notes

[a]Apportioned on the basis of floor area.

[b]Apportioned on the basis of machine value.

[c]Should be apportioned on the basis of the number of telephone points or estimated usage. This information is not given and an alternative arbitrary method of apportionment should be chosen. In the above analysis telephone charges have been apportioned on the basis of floor area.

[d]Apportioned on the basis of direct labour hours.

[e]Machine hours are not given but direct labour hours are. It is assumed that the examiner requires absorption to be on the basis of direct labour hours.

(b)

	Job 123 (£)	Job 124 (£)
Direct material	154.00	108.00
Direct labour:		
Department A	76.00	60.80
Department B	42.00	35.00
Department C	34.00	47.60
Total direct cost	306.00	251.40
Overhead:		
Department A	257.20	205.76
Department B	148.80	124.00
Department C	140.20	196.28
Total cost	852.20	777.44
Profit	284.07	259.15

(c) Listed selling price   1136.27   1036.59

Note

Let SP represent selling price.

Cost + 0.25SP = SP

Job 123: £852.20 + 0.25SP = 1SP

$\quad\quad\quad\quad\quad$ 0.75SP = £852.20

$\quad\quad\quad\quad\quad$ Hence SP = £1136.27

For Job 124: $\quad$ 0.75SP = £777.44

$\quad\quad\quad\quad\quad$ Hence SP = £1036.59

5.19 (a) (i) Calculation of budgeted overhead absorption rates:

Apportionment of overheads to production departments

	Machine shop (£)	Fitting section (£)	Canteen (£)	Machine maintenance section (£)	Total (£)
Allocated overheads	27 660	19 470	16 600	26 650	90 380
Rent, rates, heat and light[a]	9 000	3 500	2 500	2 000	17 000
Depreciation and insurance of equipment[a]	12 500	6 250	2 500	3 750	25 000
	49 160	29 220	21 600	32 400	132 380
Service department apportionment					
Canteen[b]	10 800	8 400	(21 600)	2 400	—
Machine maintenance section	24 360	10 440	—	(34 800)	—
	84 320	48 060	—	—	132 380

Calculation of absorption bases

	Machine shop			Fitting section	
Product	Budgeted production	Machine hours per product	Total machine hours	Direct labour cost per product (£)	Total direct wages (£)
X	4200 units	6	25 200	12	50 400
Y	6900 units	3	20 700	3	20 700
Z	1700 units	4	6 800	21	35 700
			52 700		106 800

Budgeted overhead absorption rates

Machine shop	Fitting section
$\dfrac{\text{budgeted overheads}}{\text{budgeted machine hours}} = \dfrac{£84\,320}{£52\,700}$	$\dfrac{\text{budgeted overheads}}{\text{budgeted direct wages}} = \dfrac{48\,060}{106\,800}$
= £1.60 per machine hour	= 45% of direct wages

Notes

[a]Rents, rates, heat and light are apportioned on the basis of floor area. Depreciation and insurance of equipment are apportioned on the basis of book value.

[b]Canteen costs are reapportioned according to the number of employees. Machine maintenance section costs are reapportioned according to the percentages given in the question.

(ii) The budgeted manufacturing overhead cost for producing one unit of product X is as follows:

	(£)
Machine shop: 6 hours at £1.60 per hour	9.60
Fittings section: 45% of £12	5.40
	15.00

(b) The answer should discuss the limitations of blanket overhead rates and actual overhead rates. See 'Blanket overhead rates' and 'Budgeted overhead rates' in Chapter 5 for the answer to this question.

5.20 (a) The calculation of the overhead absorption rates are as follows:
Forming department machine hour rate = £6.15 per machine hour (£602 700/98 000 hours)
Finishing department labour hour rate = £2.25 per labour hour (£346 500/154 000 hours)
The forming department is mechanized, and it is likely that a significant proportion of overheads will be incurred as a consequence of employing and running the machines. Therefore a machine hour rate has been used. In the finishing department several grades of labour are used. Consequently the direct wages percentage method is inappropriate, and the direct labour hour method should be used.

(b) The decision should be based on a comparison of the incremental costs with the purchase price of an outside supplier if spare capacity exists. If no spare capacity exists then the lost contribution on displaced work must be considered. The calculation of incremental costs requires that the variable element of the total overhead absorption rate must be calculated. The calculation is:
Forming department variable machine hour rate = £2.05 (£200 900/98 000 hours)
Finishing department variable direct labour hour rate = £0.75 (£115 500/154 000 hours)
The calculation of the variable costs per unit of each component is:

	A (£)	B (£)	C (£)
Prime cost	24.00	31.00	29.00
Variable overheads: Forming	8.20	6.15	4.10
Finishing	2.25	7.50	1.50
Variable unit manufacturing cost	34.45	44.65	34.60
Purchase price	£30	£65	£60

On the basis of the above information, component A should be purchased and components B and C manufactured. This decision is based on the following assumptions:
(i) Variable overheads vary in proportion to machine hours (forming department) and direct labour hours (finishing department).
(ii) Fixed overheads remain unaffected by any changes in activity.
(iii) Spare capacity exists.
For a discussion of make-or-buy decisions see Chapter 4.

(c) Production overhead absorption rates are calculated in order to ascertain costs per unit of output for stock valuation and profit measurement purposes. Such costs are inappropriate for decision-making and cost control. For an explanation of this see the section in Chapter 5 titled 'Different costs for different purposes'.

Chapter 6

6.19

	W (£000)	X (£000)	Y (£000)
Gross margin	1100	1750	1200
Less customer related costs:			
Sales visits at £500 per visit	55	50	85
Order processing at £100 per order placed	100	100	150
Despatch costs at £100 per order placed	100	100	150
Billing and collections at £175 per invoice raised	157	210	262
Profit/(loss)	688	1290	553
Ranking	2	1	3

Answer = C

6.20 Budgeted number of batches per product:

D = 1000 (100 000/100)
R = 2000 (100 000/50)
P = 2000 (50 000/25)
    5000

Budgeted machine set-ups:

D = 3 000 (1000 × 3)
R = 8 000 (2000 × 4)
P = 12 000 (2000 × 6)
    23 000

Budgeted cost per set-up = £150 000/23 000 = £6.52
Budgeted set-up cost per unit of R = (£6.52 × 4)/50 = £0.52
Answer = A

6.21 The answer to the question should describe the two-stage overhead allocation process and indicate that most cost systems use direct labour hours in the second stage. In today's production environment direct labour costs have fallen to about 10% of total costs for many firms and it is argued that direct labour is no longer a suitable base for assigning overheads to products. Using direct labour encourages managers to focus on reducing direct labour costs when they represent only a small percentage of total costs.
Approaches which are being adopted include:
(i) Changing from a direct labour overhead-recovery rate to recovery methods based on machine time. The justification for this is that overheads are caused by machine time rather than direct labour hours and cost.
(ii) Implementing activity-based costing systems that use many different cost drivers in the second stage of the two-stage overhead allocation procedure.
The answer should then go on to describe the benefits of ABC outlined in Chapter 6. Attention should also be drawn to the widespread use of direct labour hours by Japanese companies. According to Hiromoto[1] Japanese companies allocate overhead costs using the direct labour cost/hours to focus design engineers' attention on identifying opportunities to reduce the products' labour content. They use direct labour to encourage designers to make greater use of technology because this frequently improves long-term competitiveness by increasing quality, speed and flexibility of manufacturing.

Notes
[1] Hiromoto, T. (1988) 'Another hidden edge – Japanese management accounting', *Harvard Business Review*, July/August, pp. 22–6.

6.22 (a) Large-scale service organizations have a number of features that have been identified as being necessary to derive significant benefits from the introduction of ABC:

(i) They operate in a highly competitive environment;

(ii) They incur a large proportion of indirect costs that cannot be directly assigned to specific cost objects;

(iii) Products and customers differ significantly in terms of consuming overhead resources;

(iv) They market many different products and services.

Furthermore, many of the constraints imposed on manufacturing organizations, such as also having to meet financial accounting stock valuation requirements, or a reluctance to change or scrap existing systems, do not apply. Many service organizations have only recently implemented cost systems for the first time. This has occurred at the same time as when the weaknesses of existing systems and the benefits of ABC systems were being widely publicized. These conditions have provided a strong incentive for introducing ABC systems.

(b) The following may create problems for the application of ABC:

(i) Facility sustaining costs (such as property rents etc.) represent a significant proportion of total costs and may only be avoidable if the organization ceases business. It may be impossible to establish appropriate cost drivers;

(ii) It is often difficult to define products where they are of an intangible nature. Cost objects can therefore be difficult to specify;

(iii) Many service organizations have not previously had a costing system and much of the information required to set up an ABC system will be nonexistent. Therefore introducing ABC is likely to be expensive.

(c) The uses for ABC information for service industries are similar to those for manufacturing organizations:

(i) It leads to more accurate product costs as a basis for pricing decisions when cost-plus pricing methods are used;

(ii) It results in more accurate product and customer profitability analysis statements that provide a more appropriate basis for decision-making;

(iii) ABC attaches costs to activities and identifies the cost drivers that cause the costs. Thus ABC provides a better understanding of what causes costs and highlights ways of performing activities more effectively by reducing cost driver transactions. Costs can therefore be managed more effectively in the long term. Activities can also be analysed into value added and non-value added activities and by highlighting the costs of non-value added activities attention is drawn to areas where there is a potential for cost reduction without reducing the products' service potentials to customers.

(d) The following aspects would be of most interest to a regulator:

(i) The costing method used (e.g. marginal, traditional full cost or ABC). This is of particular importance to verify whether or not reasonable prices are being set and that the organization is not taking advantage of its monopolistic situation. Costing information is also necessary to ascertain whether joint costs are fairly allocated so that cross-subsidization from one service to another does not apply;

(ii) Consistency in costing methods from period to period so that changes in costing methods are not used to distort pricing and profitability analysis;

(iii) In many situations a regulator may be interested in the ROI of the different services in order to ensure that excessive returns are not being obtained. A regulator will therefore be interested in the methods and depreciation policy used to value assets and how the costs of assets that are common to several services (e.g. corporate headquarters) are allocated. The methods used will influence the ROI of the different services.

6.23 (a) (i) Direct labour overhead rate

$$= \frac{\text{total overheads (£1 848 000)}}{\text{total direct labour hours (88 000)}}$$

$$= £21 \text{ per direct labour hour}$$

Product costs

Product	X (£)	Y (£)	Z (£)
Direct labour	8	12	6
Direct materials	25	20	11
Overhead[a]	28	42	21
Total cost	61	74	38

Note
[a]X = 1⅓ hours × £21
Y = 2 hours × £21
Z = 1 hour × £21

(ii) Materials handling
Overhead rate

$$= \frac{\text{receiving department overheads (£435 000)}}{\text{direct material cost (£1 238 000)}} \times 100$$

$$= 35.14\% \text{ of direct material cost}$$

Machine hour overhead rate

$$= \frac{\text{other overheads (£1 413 000)}}{76 000 \text{ machine hours}}$$

$$= £18.59 \text{ per machine hour}$$

Product costs

Product	X (£)	Y (£)	Z (£)
Direct labour	8.00	12.00	6.00
Direct materials	25.00	20.00	11.00
Materials handling overhead	8.78 (£25 × 35.14%)	7.03 (£20 × 35.14%)	3.87 (£11 × 35.14%)
Other overheads[a] (machine hour basis)	24.79	18.59	37.18
Total cost	66.57	57.62	58.05

Note
[a]X = 1⅓ × £18.59
Y = 1 × £18.59
Z = 2 × £18.59

(b) The cost per transaction or activity for each of the cost centres is as follows:

Set-up cost
Cost per set-up

$$= \frac{\text{set-up cost (£30 000)}}{\text{number of production runs (30)}} = £1000$$

Receiving

Cost per receiving order

$$= \frac{\text{receiving cost (£435 000)}}{\text{number of orders (270)}} = £1611$$

Packing

Cost per packing order

$$= \frac{\text{packing cost (£250 000)}}{\text{number of orders (32)}} = £7812$$

Engineering

Cost per production order

$$= \frac{\text{engineering cost (£373 000)}}{\text{number of production orders (50)}} = £7460$$

The total set-up cost for the period was £30 000 and the cost per transaction or activity for the period is £1000 per set-up. Product X required three production runs, and thus £3000 of the set-up cost is traced to the production of product X for the period. Thus the cost per set-up per unit produced for product X is £0.10 (£3000/30 000 units).

Similarly, product Z required 20 set-ups, and so £20 000 is traced to product Z. Hence the cost per set-up for product Z is £2.50 (£20 000/8000 units).

The share of a support department's cost that is traced to each unit of output for each product is therefore calculated as follows:

cost per transaction

$$\times \frac{\text{number of transactions per product}}{\text{number of units produced}}$$

The unit standard costs for products X, Y and Z using an activity-based costing system are

	X	Y	Z
Direct labour	£8.00	£12.00	£6.00
Direct materials	25.00	20.00	11.00
Machine overhead[a]	13.33	10.00	20.00
Set-up costs	0.10	0.35	2.50
Receiving[b]	0.81	2.82	44.30
Packing[c]	2.34	1.17	19.53
Engineering[d]	3.73	3.73	23.31
Total manufacturing cost	53.31	50.07	126.64

Notes

[a]Machine hours × machine overhead rate (£760 000/ 76 000 hrs)

[b]X = (£1611 × 15)/30 000
Y = (£1611× 35)/20 000
Z = (£1611 × 220)/8000

[c]X = (£7812 × 9)/30 000
Y = (£7812 × 3)/20 000
Z = (£7812 × 20)/8000

[d]X = (£7460 × 15)/30 000
Y = (£7460 × 10)/20 000
Z = (£7460 × 25)/8000

(c) The traditional product costing system assumes that products consume resources in relation to volume measures such as direct labour, direct materials or machine hours. The activity-based system recognizes that some overheads are unrelated to production volume, and uses cost drivers that are independent of production volume. For example, the activity-based system assigns the following percentage of costs to product Z, the low volume product:

Set-up-related costs   66.67%
(20 out of 30 set-ups)
Delivery-related costs   62.5%
(20 out of 32 deliveries)
Receiving costs   81.5%
(220 out of 270 receiving orders)
Engineering-related costs   50%
(25 out of 50 production orders)

In contrast, the current costing system assigns the cost of the above activities according to production volume, measured in machine hours. The total machine hours are

Product X 40 000 (30 000 × 1⅓)
Product Y 20 000 (20 000 × 1)
Product Z 16 000 (8 000 × 2)
76 000

Therefore 21% (16 000/76 000) of the non-volume-related costs are assigned to product Z if machine hours are used as the allocation base. Hence the traditional system undercosts the low-volume product, and, on applying the above approach, it can be shown that the high-volume product (product X) is overcosted. For example, 53% of the costs (40 000/76 000) are traced to product X with the current system, whereas the activity-based system assigns a much lower proportion of non-volume-related costs to this product.

6.24   (a) (i)   *Conventional Absorption Costing Profit Statement:*

	XYI	YZT	ABW
(1) Sales volume (000 units)	50	40	30
	£	£	£
(2) Selling price per unit	45	95	73
(3) Prime cost per unit	32	84	65
(4) Contribution per unit	13	11	8
(5) Total contribution in £000s (1 × 4)	650	440	240
(6) Machine department overheads[a]	120	240	144
(7) Assembly department overheads[b]	288.75	99	49.5
Profit (£000s)	241.25	101	46.5

Total profit = £388 750

Notes:
[a]XYI = 50 000 × 2 hrs × £1.20, YZT = 40 000 × 5 hrs × £1.20
[b]XYI = 50 000 × 7 hrs × £0.825, YZT = 40 000 × 3 hrs × £0.825

(ii) *Cost pools:*

	Machining services	Assembly services	Set-ups	Order processing	Purchasing
£000	357	318	26	156	84
Cost drivers	420 000 machine hours	530 000 direct labour hours	520 set-ups	32 000 customer orders	11 200 suppliers' orders
Cost driver rates	£0.85 per machine hour	£0.60 per direct labour hour	£50 per set-up	£4.875 per customer order	£7.50 per suppliers' order

ABC Profit Statement:

	XYI (£000)	YZT (£000)	ABW (£000)
Total contribution	650	440	240
Less overheads:			
Machine department at £0.85 per hour	85	170	102
Assembly at £0.60 per hour	210	72	36
Set-up costs at £50 per set-up	6	10	10
Order processing at £4.875 per order	39	39	78
Purchasing at £7.50 per order	22.5	30	31.5
Profit (Loss)	287.5	119	(17.5)

Total profit = £389 000

(b) See the sections on 'Comparison of traditional and ABC costing systems' and 'Volume-based and non-volume-based cost drivers' in Chapter 6 for the answer to this question.

Material ordering cost per unit of output:

Product A (1 × £192)/500	= £0.38
B (4 × £192)/5000	= £0.15
C (1 × £192)/600	= £0.32
D (4 × £192)/7000	= £0.11

Material handling related costs

Cost per material handling = £7580/27 = £280.74

Material handling cost per unit of output:

Product A (2 × £280.74)/500	= £1.12
B (10 × £280.74)/5000	= £0.56
C (3 × £280.74)/600	= £1.40
D (12 × £280.74)/7000	= £0.48

Spare parts

Cost per part = £8600/12 = £716.67

Administration of spare parts cost per unit of output:

Product A (2 × £716.67)/500	= £2.87
B (5 × £716.67)/5000	= £0.72
C (1 × £716.67)/600	= £1.19
D (4 × £716.67)/7000	= £0.41

Overhead cost per unit of output

Product	A (£)	B (£)	C (£)	D (£)
ABC overhead cost:				
Machine overheads	0.75	0.75	3.00	4.50
Set-ups	0.51	0.31	0.85	0.29
Material ordering	0.38	0.15	0.32	0.11
Material handling	1.12	0.56	1.40	0.48
Spare parts	2.87	0.72	1.19	0.41
	5.63	2.49	6.76	5.79
Present system	1.20	1.20	4.80	7.20
Difference	+4.43	+1.29	+1.96	−1.41

The present system is based on the assumption that all overhead expenditure is volume-related, measured in terms of machine hours. However, the overheads for the five support activities listed in the question are unlikely to be related to machine hours. Instead, they are related to the factors that influence the spending on support activities (i.e. the cost drivers). The ABC system traces cost to products based on the quantity (cost drivers) of activities consumed. Product D is the high volume product, and thus the present volume-based system traces a large share of overheads to this product. In contrast, the ABC system recognizes that product D consumes overheads according to activity consumption and traces a lower amount of overhead to this product. The overall effect is that, with the present system, product D is overcosted and the remaining products are undercosted. For a more detailed explanation of the difference in resource consumption between products for an ABC and traditional cost system see 'A comparison of traditional and ABC systems' and 'Volume-based and non-volume-based cost drivers' in Chapter 6 for the answer to this question.

Chapter 7

7.17

Units	Total variable costs (£)	Selling price per unit (£)	Total sales revenue (£)	Total contribution (£)
10	40 000	6 500	65 000	25 000
11	44 400	6 350	69 850	25 450
12	49 200	6 200	74 400	25 200
13	54 400	6 050	78 650	24 250

It is apparent from the cost and revenue functions that contribution declines beyond an output of 11 units so there is no need to compute the contribution for 14 and 20 units. The most profitable output is 11 units.

Answer = B

7.18 (a) Variable cost plus 20% = £30 × 1.20 = £36
Total cost plus 20% = £37 × 1.20 = £44.40

Advantages of variable costs include that it avoids arbitrary allocations, identifies short-term relevant costs, simplicity and mark-up can be increased to provide a contribution to fixed costs and profit. The disadvantages are that it represents only a partial cost, it is short-term oriented and ignores price/demand relationships.

Advantages of total cost include that it attempts to include all costs, reduces the possibility that fixed costs will not be covered and simplicity. The disadvantages are that total cost is likely to involve some arbitrary apportionments and the price/demand relationship is ignored.

(b) See 'Pricing policies' in Chapter 7 for the answer to this question. The answer should point out that price skimming is likely to lead to a higher initial price whereas a pricing penetration policy is likely to lead to a lower initial price.

7.19 (a) *Computation of full costs and budgeted cost-plus selling price*

	EXE (£m)	WYE (£m)	Stores (£m)	Maintenance (£m)	Admin (£m)
Material	1.800	0.700	0.100		
Other variable	0.800	0.500	0.100	0.200	0.200
Gen factory	1.440	1.080	0.540	0.180	0.360
					0.560
Admin reallocation	0.224	0.168	0.112	0.056	(0.560)
				0.536	
Maintenance reallocation	0.268	0.134	0.134	(0.536)	
			0.986		
Stores	0.592	0.394	(0.986)		
	5.124	2.976			
Volume	150 000	70 000			
	(£)	(£)			
Full cost	34.16	42.51			
Mark up (25%)	8.54	10.63			
Price	42.70	53.14			

(b) (i) The incremental costs for the order consist of the variable costs. The calculation of the unit variable cost is as follows:

	EXE (£m)	WYE (£m)	Stores (£m)	Maintenance (£m)	Admin (£m)
Material	1.800	0.700	0.100	0.100	
Other variable	0.800	0.500	0.100	0.200	0.200
Admin	0.080	0.060	0.040	0.020	(0.200)
				0.320	
Maintenance	0.160	0.080	0.080	(0.320)	
			0.320		
Stores	0.192	0.128	(0.320)		
	3.032	1.468			
Volume	150 000	70 000			
	(£)	(£)			
Variable cost	20.21	20.97			

The proposed selling price exceeds the incremental cost and provides a contribution towards fixed costs and profits of £14.03 (£35 – £20.97) per unit thus giving a total contribution of £42 090. Given that the company has spare capacity no lost business will be involved and it appears that the order is a one-off short-term special order. Therefore the order is acceptable provided it does not have an impact on the selling price in the existing market or utilize capacity that has alternative uses. Given that the markets are segregated the former would appear to be an unlikely event. However, if the order were to generate further regular business the longer-term cost considerations described in Chapter 7 should be taken into account in determining an acceptable long-run price.

(ii) The proposed selling price is £46.76 (full cost of £42.51 plus 10%). This will generate a contribution of £25.79 (£46.76 – £20.97) per unit. Un-utilized capacity is 30 000 units but the order is for 50 000 units. Therefore the order can only be met by reducing existing business by 20 000 units. The financial evaluation is as follows:

Increase in contribution from existing business	
(50 000 units at a contribution of £25.79)	£1 289 500
Lost contribution from existing business	
(20 000 units at a contribution of (£53.14 – £20.97))	643 400
Net increase in contribution	646 100

Before accepting the order the longer term implications should be considered. The inability to meet the full demand from existing customers may result in a significant reduction in customer goodwill and the lost contribution from future sales to these customers may exceed the short-term gain of £646 100. Also the above analysis has not considered the alternative use of the un-utilized capacity of 30 000 units. If the cost savings from reducing the capacity exceed £646 100 for the period under consideration the order will not be worthwhile. The order will also result in the company operating at full capacity and it is possible that the cost structure may change if the company is operating outside its normal production range.

If the company does not rely on customer repeat orders and customer goodwill it is unlikely to be affected and the order would appear to be profitable. It is important, however, that long-term considerations are taken into account when evaluating the order. In particular, consideration should be given to the negotiation of a longer-term contract on both price and volume.

7.20 (a) For the answer to this question you should refer to Chapter 7. In particular the answer should discuss the role of cost information in the following situations:

1 a price setting firm facing short-run pricing decisions;
2 a price setting firm facing long-run decisions;
3 a price taker firm facing short-run product-mix decisions;
4 a price taker firm facing long-run decisions.

(b) *Calculation of variable overhead absorption rates*

	Moulding (£000)	Finishing (£000)	General Factory (£000)
Allocated overheads	1600	500	1050
Reallocation of general factory based on machine hours	600	450	(1050)
	2200	950	
Machine hours	800	600	
Variable overhead rate per hour	£2.75	£1.583	

Calculation of fixed overhead absorption rates

	Moulding (£000)	Finishing (£000)	General Factory (£000)
Allocated overheads	2500	850	1750
Reallocation of General Factory based on machine hours	1050	700	(1750)
	3550	1550	
Machine hours	800	600	
Variable overhead rate per hour	£4.4375	£2.583	

Calculation of full manufacturing cost

		(£)
Direct material		9.00
Direct labour	10.00 (2 × £5)	
	16.50 (3 × £5.50)	26.50
Variable overheads	11.00 (4 × £2.75)	
	4.75 (3 × £1.583)	15.75
Variable manufacturing cost		51.25
Fixed overheads	17.75 (4 × £4.4375)	
	7.75 (3 × £2.583)	25.50
Full manufacturing cost		76.75

Prices based on full manufacturing cost
25% mark up = £95.94
30% mark up = £99.78
35% mark up = £103.61

Minimum prices based on short-term variable cost and incremental cost are as follows:

Variable cost = £51.25
Incremental cost = £59.60 (£51.25 plus specific fixed costs of £8.35)

The specific fixed cost per unit is calculated by dividing the fixed costs of £167 000 by the estimated sales volume (10% × 200 000).

(c) The cost information is more likely to provide a general guide to the pricing decision but the final pricing decision will be influenced by the prices of competitors' products (£90 – £100). The full cost prices indicate prices within a range of £96 – £104. The variable/incremental price indicates a minimum short-run price that may be appropriate if the company wishes to pursue a price skimming policy. Given that the product is an improvement on competitors, a price in the region of £100 would seem to be appropriate but the final decision should be based on marketing considerations drawing off the knowledge of the marketing staff. The role of the cost information has been to indicate that a price within this range should provide a reasonable margin and contribution to general fixed costs.

Chapter 8

8.11 The calculation of accurate expected values are dependent on the accuracy of the probability distribution. It also takes no account of risk.
Therefore the answer is D.

8.12 Expected income with advertising = (£200 000 × 0.95) + (£70 000 × 0.05) = £193 500
Expected income without advertising = (£200 000 × 0.7) + (£70 000 × 0.3) = £161 000
The maximum amount the company should pay for advertising is the increase in expected value of £32 500.
Therefore the answer is A.

8.13 (a)

Expected cash flows	Ranking
L = (£500 × 0.2) + (£470 × 0.5) + (£550 × 0.3) = £500	2
M = (£400 × 0.2) + (£550 × 0.5) + (£570 × 0.3) = £526	1
N = (£450 × 0.2) + (£400 × 0.5) + (£475 × 0.3) = £432.5	4
O = (£360 × 0.2) + (£400 × 0.5) + (£420 × 0.3) = £398	5
P = (£600 × 0.2) + (£500 × 0.5) + (£425 × 0.3) = £497.5	3

Answer = B

(b) Without additional information machine M (see part a) will be purchased. If perfect information is obtained the choice will be matched with the level of demand. Therefore if the market condition is predicted to be poor P will be chosen and if the market condition is predicted to be good or excellent M will be chosen. The expected values of these outcomes is:

(£600 × 0.2 for P) + (£550 × 0.5 for M) + (£570 × 0.3 for M) = £566
This represents an increase in £40 000 expected value (£566 – £526)
Answer = D

8.14 (a) (i) See the decision tree shown in Figure Q8.14.
(ii) 1. The assumption underlying the maximin technique is that the worst outcome will occur. The decision-maker should select the outcome with the largest possible payoff assuming the worst possible outcome occurs. From the decision tree we can see that the payoffs for the worst possible outcomes are as follows:

	Payoff (£000)
Hire of machine 200	55
Hire of machine 300	45
Hire of machine 600	38.5
Do not franchise	90

The decision is not to franchise using the maximum criterion.

2. The expected values for each alternative (see Figure Q8.14) are as follows:

	(£000)
Hire of machine 200	87.0
Hire of machine 300	101.0
Hire of machine 600	99.0
Do not franchise	90.0

The company will maximize the expected value of the contributions if it hires the 300 batch machine.

FIGURE Q8.14

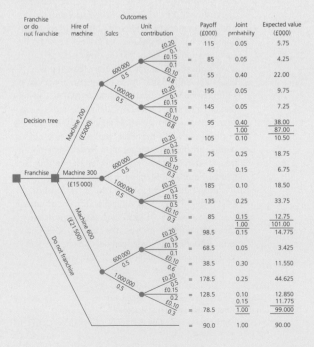

3. The probability of a contribution of less than £100 000 for each alternative can be found by adding the joint probabilities from payoffs of less than £100 000. The probabilities are as follows:

Hire of machine 200 = 0.85
Hire of machine 300 = 0.55
Hire of machine 600 = 0.65
Do not franchise = 1.00

The company should hire the 300 machine adopting this decision criterion.

(b) The approaches in part (a) enable uncertainty to be incorporated into the analysis and for decisions to be based on range of outcomes rather than a single outcome. This approach should produce better decisions in the long run. The main problem with this approach is that only a few selected outcomes with related probabilities are chosen as being representative of the entire distribution of possible outcomes. The approach also gives the impression of accuracy, which is not justified. Comments on the specific methods used in (a) are as follows:

Maximin: Enables an approach to be adopted which minimizes risk. The main disadvantage is that such a risk-averse approach will not result in decisions that will maximize long-run profits.

Expected value: For the advantages of this approach see 'Expected value' in Chapter 8. The weaknesses of expected value are as follows:

(i) It ignores risk. Decisions should not be made on expected value alone. It should be used in conjunction with measures of dispersion.

(ii) It is a long-run average payoff. Therefore it is best suited to repetitive decisions.

(iii) Because it is an average, it is unlikely that the expected value will occur.

Probability of earning an annual contribution of less than £100 000: This method enables decision-makers to specify their attitude towards risk and return and choose the alternative that meets the decision-makers risk–return preference. It is unlikely that this approach will be profit-maximizing or result in expected value being maximized.

8.15 (a) For each selling price there are three possible outcomes for sales demand, unit variable cost and fixed costs. Consequently, there are 27 possible outcomes. In order to present probability distributions for the two possible selling prices, it would be necessary to compute profits for 54 outcomes. Clearly, there would be insufficient time to perform these calculations within the examination time that can be allocated to this question. It is therefore assumed that the examiner requires the calculations to be based on an expected value approach.

The expected value calculations are as follows:

(i) *Variable cost*

	(£)
(£10 + 10%) × 10/20 =	5.50
£10 × 6/20 =	3.00
(£10 − 5%) × 4/20 =	1.90
	10.40

(ii) *Fixed costs*

	(£)
£82 000 × 0.3 =	24 600
£85 000 × 0.5 =	42 500
£90 000 × 0.2 =	18 000
	85 100

(iii) *£17 selling price*

	(units)
21 000 units × 0.2 =	4 200
19 000 units × 0.5 =	9 500
16 500 units × 0.3 =	4 950
	18 650

(iv) *£18 selling price*

	(units)
19 000 units × 0.2 =	3 800
17 500 units × 0.5 =	8 750
15 500 units × 0.3 =	4 650
	17 200

Expected contribution

£17 selling price = (£17 − £10.40) × 18 650 = £123 090
£18 selling price = (£18 − £10.40) × 17 200 = £130 720

The existing selling price is £16, and if demand continues at 20 000 units per annum then the total contribution will be £112 000 [(£16 − £10.40) × 20 000 units].

Using the expected value approach, a selling price of £18 is recommended.

(b) Expected profit − £130 720 − £85 100 fixed costs = £45 620
Break-even point = fixed costs (£85 100)/contribution per unit (£7.60) = 11 197 units
Margin of safety = expected demand (17 200 units) − 11 197 units = 6003 units
% margin of safety = 6003/17 200 = 34.9% of sales
Note that the most pessimistic estimate is above the break-even point.

(c) An expected value approach has been used. The answer should draw attention to the limitations of basing the decision solely on expected values. In particular, it should be stressed that risk is ignored and the range of possible outcomes is not considered. The decision ought to be based on a comparison of the probability distributions for the proposed selling prices. For a more detailed answer see 'Probability distributions and expected value' and 'Measuring the amount of uncertainty' in Chapter 8.

(d) Computer assistance would enable a more complex analysis to be undertaken. In particular, different scenarios could be considered, based on different combinations of assumptions regarding variable cost, fixed cost, selling prices and demand.

8.16 (a)

Alternative types of machine hire	Possible outcomes (level of orders)	Probability of outcomes	Payoff (£000)
High	High	0.25	2200 [(0.3 × £15 000) – £2300]
	Medium	0.45	250 [(0.3 × £8500) – £2300]
	Low	0.30	–1100 [(0.3 × £4000) – £2300]
Medium	High	0.25	1700 (0.3 × £15 000) – £1500 – £1300
	Medium	0.45	1050 [(0.3 × £8500) – £1500]
	Low	0.30	–300 [(0.3 × £4000) – £1500]
Low	High	0.25	1350 (0.3 × £15 000) – £1000 – £2150
	Medium	0.45	700 (0.3 × £8500) – £1000 – £850
	Low	0.30	200 [(0.3 × £4000) – £1000]

(b) Expected values:

$$\text{High hire level} = (0.25 \times £2200) + (0.45 \times £250) - (0.3 \times £1100)$$
$$= £332\ 500$$
$$\text{Medium hire level} = (0.25 \times £1700) + (0.45 \times £1050) - (0.3 \times £300)$$
$$= £807\ 500$$
$$\text{Low hire level} = (0.25 \times £1350) + (0.45 \times £700) + (0.3 \times £200)$$
$$= £712\ 500$$

Using the expected value decision rule, the medium hire contract should be entered into.

(c) Managers may be risk-averse, risk-neutral or risk-seeking. A risk-averse manager might adopt a maximin approach and focus on the worst possible outcome for each alternative and then select the alternative with the largest payoff. This approach would lead to the selection of the low initial hire level. A risk-seeking manager might adopt a maximax approach and focus on the best possible outcomes. This approach would lead to choosing the high initial hire contract, since this has the largest payoff when only the most optimistic outcomes are considered.

(d) With perfect information, the company would select the advance plant and machinery hire alternative that would maximize the payoff. The probabilities of the consultants predicting high, medium and low demand are respectively 0.25, 0.45 and 0.30. The expected value calculation with the consultant's information would be:

	Advance hire level	Payoff (£000)	Probability	Expected value (£000)
High market	high	2200	0.25	550
Medium market	medium	1050	0.45	472.5
Low market	low	200	0.30	60
				1082.5
				(£)

Expected value with consultant's information	1 082 500
Expected value without consultant's information	807 500
Maximum amount payable to consultant	275 000

Chapter 9

9.15 Using the interpolation method the IRR is:
$$15\% + \frac{£3664}{(£3664 + £21\ 451)} \times (20\% - 15\%) = 15.7\%$$
Answer = A

9.16 Because the same amount is paid each period the cumulative (annuity) discount tables in Appendix B can be used. For 12 periods at 3% the annuity factor is 9.954. The present value 3 months from now will be £2986 (300 × 9.954). Assuming that the first payment is made at the beginning of month 3 this is the equivalent to the end of month 2 for discounting purposes. Therefore it is necessary to discount the present value back two months (periods) to today (time zero). Using the discount factor from Appendix A for 3% and 2 periods the present value at time zero is £2816 (£2986 × 0.9426). Therefore the answer is A.

9.17 (a) (i) Average capital invested
$$= \frac{£50\ 000 + £10\ 000}{2} = £30\ 000$$

For an explanation of why the project's scrap value is added to the initial cost to calculate the average capital employed, you should refer to note 1 at the end of Chapter 9.

Note that the mid-point of the project's life is two years and the written down value at the end of year 2 is £30 000.

Average annual profit (Project A)
$$= \frac{£25\ 000 + £20\ 000 + £15\ 000 + £10\ 000}{4}$$
$$= £17\ 500$$

Average annual profit (Project B)
$$= \frac{£10\ 000 + £10\ 000 + £14\ 000 + £26\ 000}{4}$$
$$= £15\ 000$$

Average annual return:
$$\begin{array}{ll} A & \left(\frac{£17\ 500}{£30\ 000} \times 100\right) \\ 58.33\% & \end{array}$$
$$\begin{array}{ll} B & \left(\frac{£15\ 000}{£30\ 000} \times 100\right) \\ 50\% & \end{array}$$

(ii) Payback period:
$$\begin{array}{ll} \text{Project A} & \left(1 + \frac{£15\ 000}{£30\ 000}\right) \\ 1.5\ \text{years} & \end{array}$$
$$\begin{array}{ll} \text{Project B} & \left(2 + \frac{£10\ 000}{£24\ 000}\right) \\ 2.4\ \text{years} & \end{array}$$

(iii)

Year	Project A Cash inflows (W1) (£)	Project B Cash inflows (W1) (£)	Discount factor	Project A PV (£)	Project B PV (£)
1	35 000	20 000	0.909	31 815	18 180
2	30 000	20 000	0.826	24 780	16 520
3	25 000	24 000	0.751	18 775	18 024
4	20 000	36 000	0.683	13 660	24 588
4	10 000	10 000	0.683	6 830	6 830
				95 860	84 142
		Investment cost		(50 000)	(50 000)
		NPV		45 860	34 142

Workings:
(W1) Cash flows = Profit + depreciation.
Note that the estimated resale value is included as a year 4 cash inflow.

(b) See Chapter 9 for the answer to this section of the problem.

(c) Project A is recommended because it has the highest NPV and also the shortest payback period.

9.18 (a) The IRR is where:

annual cash inflows × discount factor = investment cost
i.e.   £4000 × discount factor = £14 000
Therefore   discount factor = $\dfrac{£14\,000}{£4\,000}$
                                   = 3.5

We now work along the five-row table of the cumulative discount tables to find the discount rate with a discount factor closest to 3.5. This is 13%. Therefore the IRR is 13%.

(b) The annual saving necessary to achieve a 12% internal rate of return is where:

annual savings × 12% discount factor = investment cost
i.e. annual savings × 3.605   = £14 000
Therefore annual savings   = $\dfrac{£14\,000}{3.605}$
                                     = £3 883

(c) NPV is calculated as follows:

	(£)
£4000 received annually from years 1–5:	
£4000 × 3.791 discount factor	15 164
Less investment cost	14 000
NPV	1 164

9.19 (a)

$$\text{Project A} = 3 \text{ years} + \frac{350 - 314}{112} = 3.32 \text{ years}$$

Project B = 3.0 years

Project C = 2.00 years

(b) Accounting rate of return = average profit/average investment

$$\text{Project A} = 79/175 = 45\%$$
$$\text{Project B} = 84/175 = 48\%$$
$$\text{Project C} = 70/175 = 40\%$$

Note that average profit = (sum of cash flows – investment cost)/project's life.

(c) The report should include:
(i) NPVs of each project (project A = £83 200 (W1), project B = £64 000 (W2), project C = £79 000 (W3). A simple description of NPV should also be provided. For example, the NPV is the amount over and above the cost of the project which could be borrowed, secure in the knowledge that the cash flows from the project will repay the loan.
(ii) The following rankings are based on the different evaluation procedures:

Project	IRR	Payback	ARR	NPV
A	2	3	2	1
B	3	2	1	3
C	1	1	3	2

(iii) A discussion of each of the above evaluation procedures.
(iv) IRR is subject to the following criticisms:
1. Multiple rates of return can occur when a project has unconventional cash flows.
2. It is assumed that the cash flows received from a project are re-invested at the IRR and not the cost of capital.
3. Inability to rank mutually exclusive projects.
4. It cannot deal with different sized projects. For example, it is better to earn a return of 35% on £100 000 than 40% on £10 000.
Note that the above points are explained in detail in Chapter 9.
(v) Payback ignores cash flows outside the payback period, and it also ignores the timing of cash flows within the payback period. For example, the large cash flows for project A are ignored after the payback period. This method may be appropriate for companies experiencing liquidity problems who wish to recover their initial investment quickly.
(vi) Accounting rate of return ignores the timing of cash flows, but it is considered an important measure by those who believe reported profits have a significant impact on share prices.
(vii) NPV is generally believed to be the theoretically correct evaluation procedure. A positive NPV from an investment is supposed to indicate the increase in the market value of the shareholders' funds, but this claim depends upon the belief that the share price is the discounted present value of the future dividend stream. If the market uses some other method of valuing shares then a positive NPV may not represent the increase in market value of shareholders' funds. Note that the cash flows have been discounted at the company's cost of capital. It is only suitable to use the company's cost of capital as the discount rate if projects A, B and C are equivalent to the average risk of all the company's existing projects. If they are not of average risk then project risk-adjusted discount rates should be used.
(viii) The projects have unequal lives. It is assumed that the equipment will not be replaced.
(ix) It is recommended that NPV method is used and project A should be selected.

(d) Stadler prefers project C because it produces the highest accounting profit in year 3. Stadler is assuming that share prices are influenced by short-run reported profits. This is in contrast with theory, which assumes that the share price is the discounted present value of the future dividend stream. Stadler is also assuming that the market only has access to reported historical profits and is not aware of the future benefits arising from the projects. The stock market also obtains company information on future prospects from sources other than reported profits. For example, press releases, chairman's report and signals of future prosperity via increased dividend payments.

Workings

(W1) Project A = (100 × 0.8333) + (110 × 0.6944) +
(104 × 0.5787) + (112 × 0.4823) +
(138 × 0.4019) + (160 × 0.3349) +
(180 × 0.2791) − £350

(W2) Project B = (40 × 0.8333) + (100 × 0.6944) +
(210 × 0.5787) + (260 × 0.4823) +
(160 × 0.4019) − £350

(W3) Project C = (200 × 0.8333) + (150 × 0.6944) +
(240 × 0.5787) + (40 × 0.4823) − £350

9.20 The report should include the information contained in items (a) to (c) below:

(a) Depreciation is not a cash flow. The operating net cash inflows (before tax) therefore consist of sales less materials and labour costs. The NPV calculation is as follows:

Year	0 (£)	1 (£)	2 (£)	3 (£)	4 (£)
Net cash inflows before tax		80 000	75 000	69 750	
Tax[a]			(14 025)	(15 469)	4826
Investment outlay	(150 000)				
Net cash flow	(150 000)	80 000	60 975	54 281	4826
Discount factor (18%)	1.000	0.847	0.718	0.609	0.516
Present value	(150 000)	67 760	43 780	33 057	2490
NPV = −£2913					

Note:

The tax computation is as follows:

Year	1 (£)	2 (£)	3 (£)
Net cash inflows before tax	80 000	75 000	69 750
Writing down allowances	37 500	28 125	84 375
Taxable profit	42 500	46 875	(14 625)
Tax at 33%	14 025	15 469	(4 826)
Writing down allowances:			
Opening WDV	150 000	112 500	84 375
Writing down allowances (25%)	37 500	28 125	
Closing WDV	112 500	84 375	Nil
Balancing allowance			84 375

(b) Because corporation taxes are payable on taxable profits and not accounting profits depreciation has been replaced by the Inland Revenue's allowable depreciation (known as written-down allowances). The net cost of the asset is £150 000 and written-down allowances received amounted to £65 625 (£37 500 + £28 125). Therefore a balancing allowance is available at the end of the asset's life of £84 375 (£150 000 − £65 625). The Inland Revenue allows the net cost of the asset to be claimed over its life with a balancing adjustment in the final year.

Because taxation is normally payable 9 months after the company's accounting year end the taxation cash flows are shown to be delayed by one year. This is a simplification of the actual situation but is normally sufficiently accurate for appraising investments.

(c) Other factors to be considered include:
   (i) The probability of obtaining a subsequent contract. There would be no need to purchase a further machine and the project would therefore yield a positive NPV.
   (ii) The negative NPV is very small and if the company has other profitable activities it may be worthwhile accepting in order to have the chance of obtaining a second contract and establishing long-term relationships with a large multinational customer.
   (iii) Capacity that is available. If other profitable opportunities have to be forgone to undertake the contract because of shortage of capacity then the opportunity cost should be included in the financial analysis.

Chapter 10

10.17 Answer = A

10.18

	(£)	(£)
Cash sales		22 000
Credit sales		
April (70% × 0.6 × 0.98 × £70 000)	28 812	
March (27% × 0.6 × £60 000)	9 720	38 532
		60 532

Answer = C

10.19 Total variable costs for year ended March 2002 = £647 080
(£924 400 × 70%)
Analysed by:

	Passengers	Parcels
Variable costs	£388 248 (60%)	258 832 (40%)
Activity for year ending March 2002	1024	24 250 kg
£ per passenger	£379.148	
£ per kg		£10.674
Revised costs based on 3% increase	£390.52	£10.994
Activity for period ending September 2002	209	7200 kg
Budgeted cost (Activity × Revised cost)	£81 619	£79 157

The answer is A for part (a) and C for part (b)

10.20 (a) Production budget

Product	A	B
Sales	2000	1500
Opening stock	(100)	(200)
Closing stock		
(10% × sales level)	200	150
	2100	1450

(b) Materials usage budget

Material type	X kg	Y litres
Usage		
$(2100 \times 2) + (1450 \times 3)$	8550	
$(2100 \times 1) + (1450 \times 4)$		7900

(c) Materials purchases budget

	X kg	Y litres
Usage	8550	7900
Opening stock	(300)	(1000)
Closing stock[a]	850	800
	9100	7700
	× £10	× £7
	£91 000	£53 900

(d) Labour budget

	Skilled hours	Semi skilled hours
$(2100 \times 4) + (1450 \times 2)$	11 300	
$(2100 \times 2) + (1450 \times 5)$		11 450
	× £12	× £8
	£135 600	£91 600

Note:
[a]Material Closing Stock
Material X $(2000 \times 2 + 1500 \times 3) \times 10\% = 850$
Material Y $(2000 \times 1 + 1500 \times 4) \times 10\% = 850$

10.21

Task 1

Alderley Ltd Budget Statements 13 weeks to 4 April

(a) Production Budget

	Elgar units	Holst units
Budgeted sales volume	845	1235
Add closing stock[a]	78	1266
Less Opening stock	(163)	(361)
Units of production	760	1140

(b) Material Purchases Budget

	Elgar kg	Holst kg	Total kg
Material consumed	5320 (760×7)	9120 (1140×8)	14 440
Add raw material closing stock[b]			2 888
Less raw material opening stock			(2 328)
Purchases (kg)			15 000

(c) Purchases (£) $(1500 \times £12)$ £180 000

(d) Production Labour Budget

	Elgar hours	Holst hours	Total hours
Standard hours produced[c]	6080	5700	11 780
Productivity adjustment $(5/95 \times 11\ 780)$			620
Total hours employed			12 400
Normal hours employed[d]			11 544
Overtime hours			856

(e) Labour cost

	£
Normal hours $(11\ 544 \times £8)$	92 352
Overtime $(856 \times £8 \times 125\%)$	8 560
Total	100 912

Notes:
[a]Number of days per period = 13 weeks × 5 days = 65
  Stock: Elgar = $(6/65) \times 845 = 78$, Holst = $(14/65) \times 1235 = 266$
[b]$(13/65) \times (5320 + 9120) = 2888$
[c]Elgar 760 × 8 hours = 6080, Holst 1140 × 5 hours = 5700
[d]24 employees × 37 hours × 13 weeks = 11 544

Task 2

(a) Four ways of forecasting future sales volume are:
   (i) Where the number of customers is small it is possible to interview them to ascertain what their likely demand will be over the forecasting period.
   (ii) Produce estimates based on the opinion of executives and sales personnel. For example, sales personnel may be asked to estimate the sales of each product to their customers, or regional sales managers may estimate the total sales for each of their regions.
   (iii) Market research may be necessary where it is intended to develop new products or new markets. This may involve interviews with existing and potential customers in order to estimate potential demand.
   (iv) Estimates involving statistical techniques that incorporate general business and market conditions and past growth in sales.

(b) Interviewing customers and basing estimates on the opinions of sales personnel are likely to be more appropriate for existing products and customers involving repeat sales. Market research is appropriate for new products or markets and where the market is large and anticipated revenues are likely to be sufficient to justify the cost of undertaking the research.

Statistical estimates derived from past data are likely to be appropriate where conditions are likely to be stable and past demand patterns are likely to be repeated through time. This method is most suited to existing products or markets where sufficient data is available to establish a trend in demand.

(c) The major limitation of interviewing customers is that they may not be prepared to divulge the information if their future plans are commercially sensitive. There is also no guarantee that the orders will be placed with Alderley Ltd. They may place their orders with competitors.

Where estimates are derived from sales personnel there is a danger that they might produce over-optimistic estimates in order to obtain a favourable performance rating at the budget setting stage. Alternatively, if their future performance is judged by their ability to achieve the budgeted sales they may be motivated to under-estimate sales demand.

Market research is expensive and may produce unreliable estimates if inexperienced researchers are used. Also small samples are often used which may not be indicative of the population and this can result in inaccurate estimates.

Statistical estimates will produce poor demand estimates where insufficient past data is available, demand is unstable over time and the future environment is likely to be significantly different from the past. Statistical estimates are likely to be inappropriate for new products and new markets where past data is unavailable.

10.22 (a) (i) *Cash budget for weeks 1–6*

	Week 1 (£)	Week 2 (£)	Week 3 (£)	Week 4 (£)	Week 5 (£)	Week 6 (£)
Receipts from debtors^a	24 000	24 000	28 200	25 800	19 800	5 400
Payments:						
To material suppliers^b	8 000	12 500	6 000	nil	nil	nil
To direct workers^c	3 200	4 200	2 800	nil	nil	nil
For variable overheads^d	4 800	3 200	nil	nil	nil	nil
For fixed overhead^e	8 300	8 300	6 800	6 800	6 800	6 800
Total payments	24 300	28 200	15 600	6 800	6 800	6 800
Net movement	(300)	(4 200)	12 600	19 000	13 000	(1 400)
Opening balance (week 1 given)	1 000	700	(3 500)	9 100	28 100	41 100
Closing balance	700	(3 500)	9 100	28 100	41 100	39 700

Notes
^{a}Debtors:

	Week 1	Week 2	Week 3	Week 4	Week 5	Week 6
Units sold*	400	500	400	300	—	—
Sales (£)	24 000	30 000	24 000	18 000	—	—
Cash received (70%)		16 800	21 000	16 800	12 600	
(30%)			7 200	9 000	7 200	5 400
Given	24 000	7 200				
Total receipts (£)	24 000	24 000	28 200	25 800	19 800	5 400

*Sales in week 4 = opening stock (600 units) + production in weeks 1 and 2 (1000 units) less sales in weeks 1–3 (1300 units) = 300 units.

^{b}Creditors:

	Week 1 (£)	Week 2 (£)	Week 3 (£)	Week 4	Week 5	Week 6
Materials consumed at £15	9 000	6 000	—	—	—	—
Increase in stocks	3 500	—				
Materials purchased	12 500	6 000				
Payment to suppliers	8 000 (given)	12 500	6000	nil	nil	nil

^{c}Wages:

	Week 1 (£)	Week 2 (£)	Week 3 (£)	Week 4	Week 5	Week 6
Wages consumed at £7	4200	2800	nil	nil	nil	nil
Wages paid	3200 (given)	4200	2800	—	—	—

^{d}Variable overhead payment = budgeted production × budgeted cost per unit.
^{e}Fixed overhead payments for weeks 1–2 = fixed overhead per week (£9000).
less weekly depreciation (£700).
Fixed overhead payments for weeks 3–6 = £8300 normal payment less £1500 per week.

(ii) *Comments*
1. Finance will be required to meet the cash deficit in week 2, but a lowering of the budgeted material stocks at the end of week 1 would reduce the amount of cash to be borrowed at the end of week 2.
2. The surplus cash after the end of week 2 should be invested on a short-term basis.
3. After week 6, there will be no cash receipts, but cash outflows will be £6800 per week. The closing balance of £39 700 at the end of week 6 will be sufficient to finance outflows for a further 5 or 6 weeks (£39 700/£6800 per week).

(b) The answer should include a discussion of the matching concept, emphasizing that revenues and expenses may not be attributed to the period when the associated cash inflows and outflows occur. Also, some items of expense do not affect cash outflow (e.g. depreciation).

10.23 (a) See 'Zero-base budgeting' in Chapter 10 for the answer to this question. In particular the answer should stress that the first stage should be to explicitly state the objectives that each part of the organization is trying to achieve. The activities for achieving these objectives should be described in a decision package. A decision package should consist of a base package, which would normally represent a minimum level of activity, plus incremental packages for higher levels of activity and costs. The packages are then evaluated and ranked in order of their decreasing benefits. A cut-off point is determined by the budgeted spending level, and packages are allocated according to their ranking until the budgeted spending level is reached.

(b) For the answer to this question see 'Zero-base budgeting' in Chapter 10.

(c) The problems that might be faced in introducing a zero-base budgeting scheme are:
(i) Implementation of zero-base budgeting might be resisted by staff. Traditional incremental budgeting tends to protect the empire that a manager has built. Zero-base budgeting challenges this empire, and so there is a strong possibility that managers might resist the introduction of such a system.
(ii) There is a need to combat a feeling that current operations are efficient.
(iii) The introduction of zero-base budgeting is time-consuming, and management may lack the necessary expertise.
(iv) Lack of top-management support.

(d) Beneficial results are likely to be obtained from a company with the following features:
(i) A large proportion of the expenditure is of a discretionary nature.
(ii) Management and employees of the company are unlikely to be resistant to change.
(iii) Suitable output measures can be developed.
(iv) A senior manager is employed who has some experience from another organization of implementing zero-base budgeting.

10.24 (a) Incremental budgeting uses the previous year's budget as the starting point for the preparation of next year's budget. It is assumed that the basic structure of the budget will remain unchanged and that adjustments will be made to allow for changes in volume, efficiency and price levels. The budget is therefore concerned with increments to operations that will occur during the period and the focus is on existing use of resources rather than considering alternative strategies for the future budget period. Incremental budgeting suffers from the following weaknesses:
(i) it perpetuates past inefficiencies;
(ii) there is insufficient focus on improving efficiency and effectiveness;
(iii) the resource allocation tends to be based on existing strategies rather than considering future strategies;
(iv) it tends to focus excessively on the short term and often leads to arbitrary cuts being made in order to achieve short-term financial targets.

(b) See 'Activity-based budgeting' in Chapter 10 for the answer to this question. In particular, the answer should stress that:

(i)   the focus is on managing activities;

(ii) the focus is on the resources that are required for undertaking activities and identifying those activity resources that are un-utilized or which are insufficient to meet the requirements specified in the budget;

(iii) attention is given to eliminating non-value-added activities;

(iv) the focus is on the control of the causes of costs (i.e. the cost drivers).

For a more detailed discussion of some of the above points you should also refer to 'Activity-based management' in Chapter 15.

10.25 (a) *Cumbersome process*

The answer to the first comment in the question should include a very brief summary of 'Stages in the budgeting process' in Chapter 10. The process involves detailed negotiations between the budget holders and their superiors and the accountancy staff. Because the process is very time consuming it must be started well before the start of the budget year. Subsequent changes in the environment, and the fact that the outcomes reflected in the master budget may not meet financial targets, may necessitate budget revisions and a repeat of the negotiation process. The renegotiating stage may well be omitted because of time constraints. Instead, across the board cost reductions may be imposed to meet the budget targets.

Concentration on short-term financial control

Short-term financial targets are normally set for the budget year and the budget is used as the mechanism for achieving the targets. Budget adjustments are made to ensure that the targets are achieved often with little consideration being given to the impact such adjustments will have on the longer-term plans.

Undesirable motivation effects on managers

Managers are often rewarded or punished based on their budget performance in terms of achieving or exceeding the budget. There is a danger that the budget will be viewed as a punitive device rather than as an aid to managers in managing their areas of responsibility. This can result in dysfunctional consequences such as attempting to build slack into the budgeting system by overstating costs and understating revenues. Alternatively, cuts may be made in discretionary expenses which could have adverse long-term consequences. The overriding aim becomes to achieve the budget, even if this is done in a manner that is not in the organization's best interests.

Emphasizing formal organizational structure

Budgets are normally structured around functional responsibility centres, such as departments and business units. A functional structure is likely to encourage bureaucracy and slow responses to environmental and competitive changes. There is a danger that there will be a lack of goal congruence and that managers may focus on their own departments to the detriment of the organization. Also if budgets are extended to the lower levels of the organization employees will focus excessively on meeting the budget and this may constrain their activities in terms of the flexibility that is required when dealing with customers.

(b) *Cumbersome process*

Managers could be given greater flexibility on how they will meet their targets. For example, top management might agree specific targets with the managers and the managers given authority to achieve the targets in their own way. Detailed budgets are not required and the emphasis is placed on managers achieving their overall targets.

Another alternative is to reduce the budget planning period by implementing a system of continuous or rolling budgets.

Concentration on short-term financial control

This might be overcome by placing more stress on a manager's long-term performance and adopting a profit-conscious style of budget evaluation (see 'Side effects from using accounting information for performance evaluation' in Chapter 11) and also placing more emphasis on participative budgeting (see 'Participation in the budget process' in Chapter 11). Attention should also be given to widening the performance measurement system and focusing on key result areas that deal with both short-term and long-term considerations. In particular a balanced scorecard approach (see Chapter 16) might be adopted.

Undesirable motivation effects on managers

The same points as those made above (i.e. profit-conscious style of evaluation, participative budgeting and a broader range of performance measures) also apply here. In addition, the rewards and punishment system must be changed so that it is linked to a range of performance criteria rather than being dominated by short-term financial budget performance. Consideration could also be given to changing the reward system from focusing on responsibility centre performance to rewards being based on overall company performance.

Emphasizing formal organizational structure

Here the answer could discuss activity-based budgeting with the emphasis being on activity centres and business processes, rather than functional responsibility centres that normally consist of departments. For a discussion of these issues you should refer to 'Activity-based budgeting' in Chapter 10 and 'Activity-based cost management' in Chapter 15. Consideration should also given to converting cost centres to profit centres and establishing a system of internal transfer prices. This would encourage managers to focus more widely on profits rather than just costs. Finally, budgets should not be extended to lower levels of the organization and more emphasis should be given to empowering employees to manage their own activities (see 'Employee empowerment' in Chapter 1).

Chapter 11

11.22 *Task 1*

Reclamation Division Performance Report – 4 weeks to
31 May:

Original budget   250 tonnes

Actual output   200 tonnes

	Budget based on 200 tonnes	Actual	Variance	Comments
Controllable expenses:				
Wages and social security costs*ᵃ*	43 936	46 133	2197A	
Fuel*ᵇ*	15 000	15 500	500A	
Consumables*ᶜ*	2 000	2 100	100A	
Power*ᵈ*	1 500	1 590	90A	
Directly attributable overheads*ᵉ*	20 000	21 000	1000A	
	82 436	86 323	3887A	
Non-controllable expenses:				
Plant maintenance*ᵉ*	5 950	6 900	950A	
Central services*ᵉ*	6 850	7 300	450A	
	12 800	14 200	1400A	
Total	95 236	100 523	5287A	

Notes:
*ᵃ*6 employees × 4 teams × 42 hours per week × £7.50 per hour × 4 weeks = £30 240.
*ᵇ*200 tonnes × £75
*ᶜ*200 tonnes × £10
ᵈ£500 + (£5 × 200) = £1500
*ᵉ*It is assumed that directly attributable expenses, plant maintenance and central services are non-variable expenses.

Task 2

(a) (i) Past knowledge can provide useful information on future outcomes but ideally budgets ought to be based on the most up-to-date information. Budgeting should be related to the current environment and the use of past information that is two years old can only be justified where the operating conditions and environment are expected to remain unchanged.

(ii) For motivation and planning purposes budgets should represent targets based on what we are proposing to do. For control purposes budgets should be flexed based on what was actually done so that actual costs for actual output can be compared with budgeted costs for the actual output. This ensures that valid comparisons will be made.

(iii) For variable expenses the original budget should be reduced in proportion to reduced output in order to reflect cost behaviour. Fixed costs are not adjusted since they are unaffected in the short-term by output changes. Flexible budgeting ensures that like is being compared with like so that reduced output does not increase the probability that favourable cost variances will be reported. However, if less was produced because of actual sales being less than budget this will result in an adverse sales variance and possibly an adverse profit variance.

(iv) Plant maintenance costs are apportioned on the basis of capital values and therefore newer equipment (with higher written-down values) will be charged with a higher maintenance cost. Such an approach does not provide a meaningful estimate of maintenance resources consumed by departments since older equipment is likely to be more expensive to maintain. The method of recharging should be reviewed and ideally based on estimated usage according to maintenance records. The charging of the overspending by the maintenance department to user departments is questionable since this masks inefficiencies. Ideally, maintenance department costs should be recharged based on actual usage at budgeted cost and the maintenance department made accountable for the adverse spending (price) variance.

(v) The comments do not explain the causes of the variances and are presented in a negative tone. No comments are made, nor is any praise given, for the favourable variances.

(vi) Not all variances should be investigated. The decision to investigate should depend on both their absolute and relative size and the likely benefits arising from an investigation.

(vii) Central service costs are not controllable by divisional managers. However, even though the divisional manager cannot control these costs there is an argument for including them as non-controllable costs in the performance report. The justification for this is that divisional managers are made aware of central service costs and may put pressure on central service staff to control such costs more effectively. It should be made clear to divisional managers that they are not accountable for any non-controllable expenses that are included in their performance reports.

11.23 (a) (i) Activity varies from month to month, but quarterly budgets are set by dividing total annual expenditure by 4.

(ii) The budget ought to be analysed by shorter intervals (e.g. monthly) and costs estimated in relation to monthly activity.

(iii) For control purposes monthly comparisons and cumulative monthly comparisons of planned and actual expenditure to date should be made.

(iv) The budget holder does not participate in the setting of budgets.

(v) An incremental budget approach is adopted. A zero-based approach would be more appropriate.

(vi) The budget should distinguish between controllable and uncontrollable expenditure.

(b) The information that should flow from a comparison of the actual and budgeted expenditure would consist of the variances for the month and year to date analysed into the following categories:

(i) controllable and uncontrollable items;

(ii) price and quantity variances with price variance analysed by inflationary and non-inflationary effects.

(c) (i) Flexible budgets should be prepared on a monthly basis. Possible measures of activity are number of patient days or expected laundry weight.

(ii) The laundry manager should participate in the budgetary process.

(iii) Costs should be classified into controllable and non-controllable items.

(iv) Variances should be reported and analysed by price and quantity on a monthly and cumulative basis.

(v) Comments should be added explaining possible reasons for the variances.

11.24

Task 1:

Performance Statement – Month to 31 October

| Number of guest days = Original budget | | 9 600 |
| Flexed budget | | 11 160 |

	Flexed budget (£)	Actual (£)	Variance (£)
Controllable expenses			
Food (1)	23 436	20 500	2936F
Cleaning materials (2)	2 232	2 232	0
Heat, light and power (3)	2 790	2 050	740F
Catering staff wages (4)	8 370	8 400	30A
	36 828	33 182	3646F
Non-controllable expenses			
Rent, rates, insurance and depreciation (5)	1 860	1 860	0

Notes:
(1) £20 160/9600 × 11 160.
(2) £1920/9600 × 11 160.
(3) £2400/9600 × 11 160.
(4) £11 160/40 × £30.
(5) Original fixed budget based on 30 days but October is a 31-day month (£1800/30 × 31).

Task 2:

(a) See the sections on the multiple functions of budgets (motivation) in Chapter 10, and 'Setting financial performance targets' in Chapter 11 for the answers to this question.

(b) Motivating managers ought to result in improved performance. However, besides motivation, improved performance is also dependent on managerial ability, training, education and the existence of a favourable environment. Therefore motivating managers is not guaranteed to lead to improved performance.

(c) The use of a fixed budget is unlikely to encourage managers to become more efficient where budgeted expenses are variable with activity. In the original performance report actual expenditure for 11.160 guest days is compared with budgeted expenditure for 9600 days. It is misleading to compare actual costs at one level of activity with budgeted costs at another level of activity. Where the actual level of activity is above the budgeted level adverse variances are likely to be reported for variable cost items. Managers will therefore be motivated to reduce activity so that favourable variances will be reported. Therefore it is not surprising that Susan Green has expressed concern that the performance statement does not reflect a valid reflection of her performance. In contrast, most of Brian Hilton's expenses are fixed and costs will not increase when volume increases. A failure to flex the budget will therefore not distort his performance.

To motivate, challenging budgets should be set and small adverse variances should normally be regarded as a healthy sign and not something to be avoided. If budgets are always achieved with no adverse variances this may indicate that undemanding budgets may have been set which are unlikely to motivate best possible performance. This situation could apply to Brian Hilton who always appears to report favourable variances.

11.25 (a) Recommendations are as follows:

(i) For cost control and managerial performance evaluation, expenses should be separated into their controllable and non-controllable categories. Two separate profit calculations should be presented: controllable profit, which is appropriate for measuring managerial performance, and a 'bottom line' net profit, which measures the economic performance of each store rather than the manager.

(ii) The report should be based on an ex-post basis. In other words, if the environment is different from that when the original budget was set, actual performance should be compared with a budget that reflects any changed conditions. For example, the budget should be adjusted to reflect the effect of the roadworks.

(iii) Actual expenses should be compared with flexed budgets and not the original budget.

(iv) Each store consists of three departments. The report should therefore analyse gross profits by departments. Selling prices and the cost of goods sold are beyond the control of the stores' managers, but each departmental manager can influence sales volume. An analysis of gross profits by departments and a comparison with previous periods should provide useful feedback on sales performance and help in deciding how much space should be allocated to each activity.

(v) Stock losses should be minimized. Such losses are controllable by departmental managers. The cost of stock losses should therefore be monitored and separately reported.

(vi) The budget should include cumulative figures to give an indication of trends, performance to date and the potential annual bonus.

(vii) Any imputed interest charges should be based on economic values of assets and not historic costs.

(b) The report should include a discussion of the following:

(i) *Review of delegation policies:* Head office purchases the goods for sale, fixes selling prices, appoints permanent staff and sets pay levels. Stores managers are responsible for stores' running expenses, employment of temporary staff and control of stocks.

Purchasing is centralized, thus enabling the benefits of specialized buying and bulk purchasing to be obtained. Purchasing policies are coordinated with expected sales by consultation between head office buyers and stores and departmental managers. It is wise to make stores managers responsible for controlling stocks because they are in the best position to assess current and future demand.

Managers are responsible for sales volume but they cannot fix selling prices. There are strong arguments for allowing stores to set selling prices, and offer special discounts on certain goods. Central management may wish to retain some overall control by requiring proposed price changes beyond certain limits referred to them for approval. There are also strong arguments for allowing the stores' managers to appoint permanent staff. The stores' managers are likely to be in a better position to be able to assess the abilities necessary to be a successful member of their own team.

(ii) *Strengths of the management control system:*
1. Sales targets are set after consultation between head office and the departmental managers.
2. The budgets are prepared well in advance of the start of the budget year, thus giving adequate time for consultation.
3. Performance reports are available one week after the end of the period.
4. Budgets are adjusted for seasonal factors.
5. Significant variations in performance are investigated and appropriate action is taken.

(iii) *Weaknesses of the management control system:*
1. There is no consultation in the setting of expense budgets.
2. Actual costs are compared with a fixed budget and not a flexible budget.
3. Costs are not separated into controllable and non-controllable categories.
4. Budgets are set on an incremental basis with budgets set by taking last year's base and adjusting for inflation.
5. Budgets are not revised for control purposes. Targets set for the original budget before the start of the year may be inappropriate for comparison with actual expenses incurred towards the end of the budget year.
6. Using a budget that does not include ex-post results and that is not linked to controllable profit is likely to be demotivating, and results in managers having little confidence in the budget system.

(iv) *Recommendations:*
1. Compare actual costs with a flexed budget.
2. The performance report should separate costs into controllable and uncontrollable categories, and controllable profit should be highlighted. Any bonus payments should be related to controllable profit and not 'bottom-line' profits.
3. Introduce monthly or quarterly rolling budgets.
4. Ensure that the store's managers participate in setting the budget and accept the target against which they will be judged.
5. Set targets using a zero-base approach.
6. Consider extending the bonus scheme to departmental managers.

11.26 (a) The cybernetic system referred to in the question is illustrated in Fig. 11.1 in Chapter 11. The main limitations are:
(i) The human dimension is ignored. Individual behaviour varies and they do not react to deviations from objectives in a single prescribed manner as predicted by the model.
(ii) The time dimension is not incorporated into the model. If feedback response and action is too rapid then this may be counterproductive, whereas inefficiencies will be allowed to continue if feedback is too slow.
(iii) The model is based on feedback controls whereas it is more appropriate for organizations to focus on feedforward controls.

(iv) The model assumes that control operates only on the inputs to the system, whereas control may entail changing the goals, expected outputs or the measurement system.

(b) (i) The main prerequisites are:
1. A single clearly specified objective (or multiple objectives if they are all consistent).
2. A clear input–output relation so that the impact that changing the inputs has on outputs can be predicted.
3. Outputs can be easily and accurately measured.
4. Clearly specified control responses where actual outcomes differ from predicted outcomes.
If the above conditions exist then it is likely that the system will work in a similar manner to that predicted by the mechanical control system.

(ii) The answer should draw attention to the fact that there is no single unifying objective such as profit. Instead, they are likely to have several objectives some of which may conflict. Consequently, it is difficult to specify clear aims for the system. Furthermore, management perceptives of what are the major objectives may differ. This is likely to result in conflict and raise political issues.

Because of the multiple objectives and the absence of an over-riding profit motive it is difficult to measure the outputs. Hence, there is a greater emphasis on subjective rather than objective measurement. Control is therefore difficult to implement because it is difficult to predict the impact that changes in inputs will have on outputs. As a result, there tends to be an overemphasis on measuring inputs rather than outputs.

11.27 (i) Budgets are used for a variety of purposes, one of which is to evaluate the performance of budgetees. When budgets form the basis for future performance evaluation, there is a possibility that budgetees will introduce bias into the process for personal gain and self-protection. Factors that are likely to cause managers to submit budget estimates that do not represent their best estimates include:
1. *The reward system:* If managers believe that rewards depend upon budget attainment then they might be encouraged to underestimate sales budgets and overestimate cost budgets.
2. *Past performance:* If recent performance has been poor, managers may submit favourable plans so as to obtain approval from their supervisors. Such an approach represents a trade-off advantage of short-run security and approval against the risk of not being able to meet the more optimistic plans.
3. *Incremental budgeting:* Incremental budgeting involves adding increments to past budgets to reflect expected future changes. Consequently, the current budget will include bias that has been built into previous budgets.
4. *External influences:* If managers believe that their performance is subject to random external influences then, from a self-protection point of view, they might submit budgets that can easily be attained.
5. *Style of performance evaluation:* A budget-constrained style of evaluation might encourage the budgetee to meet the budget at all costs. Consequently, budgetees will be motivated to bias their budget estimates.

(ii) The following procedures should be introduced to minimize the likelihood of biased estimates:
1. Encourage managers to adopt a profit-conscious style of evaluation.
2. Adopt a system of zero-base budgeting.
3. Key figures in the budget process (e.g. sales estimates) should be checked by using information from different sources.
4. Planning and operating variances (see 'Ex-post budget adjustments' in Chapter 11 for a discussion of planning and operating variances) should be segregated. Managers might be motivated to submit more genuine estimates if they are aware that an ex-post budget will be used as a basis for performance appraisal.
5. Participation by the budgetees in the budget process should be encouraged so as to secure a greater commitment to the budget process and improve communication between budgetees, their superior and the budget accountants.

11.28 (a) See Chapter 11 for the answer to this question. In particular, your answer should stress:
   (i) The need for a system of responsibility accounting based on a clear definition of a manager's authority and responsibility.
   (ii) The production of performance reports at frequent intervals comparing actual and budget costs for individual expense items. Variances should be analysed according to whether they are controllable or non-controllable by the manager.
   (iii) The managers should participate in the setting of budgets and standards.
   (iv) The system should ensure that variances are investigated, causes found and remedial action is taken.
   (v) An effective cost control system must not be used as a punitive device, but should be seen as a system that helps managers to control their costs more effectively.
   (b) Possible problems include:
   (i) Difficulties in setting standards for non-repetitive work.
   (ii) Non-acceptance by budgetees if they view the system as a punitive device to judge their performance.
   (iii) Isolating variances where interdependencies exist.

11.29 (a) See 'Planning', 'Motivation' and 'Performance evaluation' in the section on the multiple functions of budgets in Chapter 10 for the answer to this question. The answer should emphasize that the role of motivation is to encourage goal congruence between the company and the employees.
   (b) See 'Conflicting roles of budgets' in Chapter 10 for an explanation of how the planning and motivation roles can conflict. Prior to the commencement of the budget period, management should prepare budgets that represent targets to be achieved based upon anticipated environmental variables. It is possible that at the end of the budget period the *actual* environmental variables will be different from those envisaged when the budget was prepared. Therefore actual performance will be determined by the actual environment variables, but the plans reflected in the budget may be based on different environmental variables. It is inappropriate to compare actual performance based on one set of environmental variables with budgeted performance based on another set of environmental variables. Consequently, a budget that is used for planning purposes will be in conflict with one that is used for performance evaluation.

The conflict between motivation and evaluation is described by Barrett and Fraser (1977) (see Bibliography in main text) as follows:

In many situations the budget that is most effective in the evaluation role might be called an ex-post facto budget. It is one that considers the impact of uncontrollable or unforeseeable events, and it is constructed or adjusted after the fact.

The potential role conflict between the motivation and evaluation roles involves the impact on motivation of using an ex-post facto standard in the evaluation process. Managers are unlikely to be totally committed to achieving the budget's objectives if they know that the performance standards by which they are to be judged may change.

In other words, for evaluation purposes the budget might be adjusted to reflect changes in environmental variables. If a manager expects that the budget will be changed for evaluation purposes, there is a danger that he or she will not be as highly motivated to achieve the original budget.

(c) (i) The planning and motivation conflict might be resolved by setting two budgets. A budget based on most likely outcomes could be set for planning purposes and a separate, more demanding budget could be used for motivation purposes.
   (ii) The planning and evaluation role conflict can be resolved by comparing actual performance with an ex-post budget. See 'Ex-post budget adjustments' in Chapter 11 for an indication of how this conflict can be resolved.
   (iii) Barrett and Fraser (1977) suggest the following approach for resolving the motivation and evaluation conflict:

The conflict between the motivation and evaluation roles can also be reduced by using 'adjustable budgets'. These are operational budgets whose objectives can be modified under predetermined sets of circumstances. Thus revision is possible during the operating period and the performance standard can be changed.

In one company that uses such a budgeting system, managers commit themselves to a budget with the understanding that, if there are substantial changes in any of five key economic or environmental variables, top management will revise the budget and new performance criteria will be set. This company automatically makes budget revisions whenever there are significant changes in any of these five variables. Naturally, the threshold that triggers a new budget will depend on the relative importance of each variable. With this system, managers know they are expected to meet their budgets. The budget retains its motivating characteristics because it represents objectives that are possible to achieve. Uncontrollable events are not allowed to affect budgeted objectives in such a way that they stand little chance of being met. Yet revisions that are made do not have to adversely affect commitment, since revisions are agreed to in advance and procedures for making them are structured into the overall budgeting system.

A more detailed answer to this question can be found in Barrett and Fraser (1977).

11.30 (a) The answer should include a discussion of the following points:

(i) Constant pressure from top management for greater production may result in the creation of anti-management work groups and reduced efficiency, so that budgetees can protect themselves against what they consider to be increasingly stringent targets.

(ii) Non-acceptance of budgets if the budgetees have not been allowed to participate in setting the budgets.

(iii) Negative attitudes if the budget is considered to be a punitive control device instead of a system to help managers do a better job. The negative attitudes might take the form of reducing cooperation between departments and also with the accounting department. Steps might be taken to ensure that costs do not fall below budget, so that the budget will not be reduced next year. There is a danger that data will be falsified, and more effort will be directed to finding excuses for failing to achieve the budget than trying to control or reduce costs.

(iv) Managers might try and achieve the budget at all costs even if this results in actions that are not in the best interests of the organization, e.g. delaying maintenance costs.

(v) Organizational atmosphere may become one of competition and conflict rather than one of cooperation and conciliation.

(vi) Suspicion and mistrust of top management, resulting in the whole budgeting process being undermined.

(vii) Belief that the system of evaluation is unjust and widespread worry and tension by the budgetees. Tension might be relieved by falsifying information, blaming others or absenteeism.

(b) For the answer to this question see 'Dealing with the distorting effects of uncontrollable factors before (and after) the measurement period' in Chapter 11.

11.31 The answer should include a discussion of the following:
(i) The impact of targets on performance.
(ii) The use of accounting control techniques for performance evaluation.
(iii) Participation in the budgeting and standard setting process.
(iv) Bias in the budget process.
(v) Management use of budgets and the role of the accountant in the education process.
See Chapter 11 for a discussion of each of the above items.

11.32 Managers may be reluctant to participate in setting budgets for the following reasons:

(i) Managers may consider that they do not engage in true participation if they cannot influence the budget. They may consider the process to be one of the senior managers securing formal acceptance of previously determined target levels.

(ii) Personality of budgetees may result in authoritarian managers having authoritarian expectations of their superiors. Consequently, authoritarian budgetees may be reluctant to participate in the budget process.

(iii) The degree to which individuals have control over their own destiny appears to influence the desire for participation. Managers may believe that they cannot significantly influence results and thus consider participation to be inappropriate.

(iv) Bad management/superior relationships.

(v) Lack of understanding of the budget process or a belief by the budgetees that they will be engaging in a process that will be used in a recriminatory manner by their superiors.

The unwanted side-effects that might arise from the imposition of budgets by senior management include the following:

(i) Non-acceptance of budgets.

(ii) The budgetees might consider the method of performance evaluation to be unjust.

(iii) Creation of anti-management cohesive work groups.

(iv) Reduced efficiency by work groups so as to protect themselves against what they consider to be increasingly stringent targets.

(v) The budget system will be undermined. The real problem is the way management use the system rather than inadequacies of the budget system itself.

(vi) An increase in suspicion and mistrust, so undermining the whole budgeting process.

(vii) Encouraging budgetees to falsify and manipulate information presented to management.

(viii) Organizational atmosphere may become one of competition and conflict rather than one of cooperation and conciliation.

(ix) Managers might try to achieve the budget at all costs even if this results in actions that are not in the best interests of the organization.

11.33 (a) For a discussion of feedback and feed-forward controls see Chapter 11. The remaining terms are also discussed in Chapter 11.

(b) For the answer to this question see 'Dealing with the distorting effects of uncontrollable factors before (and after) the measurement period', 'Participation in the budget and target setting process' and 'Side effects from using accounting information for performance evaluation' in Chapter 11.

Chapter 12

12.12 A favourable labour efficiency variance indicates that actual hours used were less than the standard hours produced. The favourable variance was £7800. Therefore the standard hours produced were 18 700 (17 500 + £7800/£6.50).
Answer = D

12.13 Materials price variance = (Standard price – Actual price) × Actual quantity

= (Actual quantity × Standard price) – Actual cost

= (8200 × £0.80) – £6888

= £328 Adverse

Material usage variance = (Standard quantity – Actual quantity) × Standard price

= (870 × 8 kg = 6960 – 7150) × £0.80

= £152 Adverse

Answer = D

12.14 Fixed overhead variance = Budgeted cost (not flexed) – Actual cost

= £10 000 per month – £9800

= £200 Favourable

Answer = B

12.15 Sales volume variance = (Actual sales volume – Budgeted sales volume) × Standard contribution margin

= (4500 – 5000) £4.40

= £2200 Adverse

Answer = B

12.16 1. *Preliminary calculations*

The standard product cost and selling price are calculated as follows:

	(£)
Direct materials	
X (10 kg at £1)	10
Y (5 kg at £5)	25
Direct wages (5 hours × £3)	15
Standard variable cost	50
Profit (Contribution margin)	50
Selling price	100

The actual profit for the period is calculated as follows:

	(£)	(£)
Sales (9500 at £110)		1 045 000
Direct materials: X	115 200	
Y	225 600	
Direct wages (46 000 × £3.20)	147 200	
Fixed overhead	290 000	778 000
Actual profit		267 000

It is assumed that the term 'using a fixed budget' refers to the requirement to reconcile the budget with the original fixed budget.

	(£)	(£)
Material price variance:		
(standard price – actual price)		
× actual quantity		
X: (£1 – £1.20) × 96 000	19 200 A	
Y: (£5 – £4.70) × 48 000	14 440 F	4800 A
Material usage variance:		
(standard quantity – actual quantity)		
× standard price		
X: (9500 × 10 = 95 000 – 96 000) × £1	1 000 A	
Y: (9500 × 5 = 47 500 – 48 000) × £5	2 500 A	3500 A

The actual materials used are in standard proportions. Therefore there is no mix variance.

	(£)	(£)
Wage rate variance:		
(standard rate – actual rate) × actual hours		
(£3 – £3.20) × 46 000	9 200 A	
Labour efficiency variance:		
(standard hours – actual hours) × standard rate		
(9500 × 5 = 47 500 – 46 000) × £3	4 500 F	4 700 A
Fixed overhead expenditure:		
budgeted fixed overheads – actual fixed overheads		
(10 000 × £30 = £300 000 – £290 000)		10 000 F
Sales margin price variance:		
(actual margin – standard margin) × actual		
sales volume (£60 – £50) × 9500		95 000 F
Sales margin volume variance:		
(actual sales volume – budgeted sales volume)		
× Standard margin		
(9500 – 10 000) × £50	25 000 A	70 000 F
Total variance		67 000 F

	(£)
Budgeted profit contribution	
(10 000 units at £50)	500 000
Less budgeted fixed overheads	300 000
Budgeted profit	200 000
Add favourable variances (see above)	67 000
Actual profit	267 000

12.17 (a) *Standard product cost for one unit of product XY*

	(£)
Direct materials (8 kg (W2) at £1.50 (W1) per kg)	12.00
Direct wages (2 hours (W4) at £4 (W3) per hour)	8.00
Variable overhead (2 hours (W4) at £1 (W5) per hour)	2.00
	22.00

Workings

(W1) Actual quantity of materials purchased at standard price is £225 000 (actual cost plus favourable material price variance).
Therefore standard price = £1.50 (£225 000/150 000 kg).

(W2) Material usage variance = 6000 kg (£9000/£1.50 standard price).
Therefore standard quantity for actual production = 144 000 kg (150 000 – 6000 kg).
Therefore standard quantity per unit = 8 kg (144 000 kg/18 000 units).

(W3) Actual hours worked at standard rate = £128 000 (£136 000 – £8000).
Therefore standard rate per hour = £4 (£128 000/32 000 hours).

(W4) Labour efficiency variance = 4000 hours (£16 000/£4).
Therefore standard hours for actual production = 36 000 hours (32 000 + 4000).
Therefore standard hours per unit = 2 hours (36 000 hours/18 000 units).

(W5) Actual hours worked at the standard variable overhead rate is £32 000 (£38 000 actual variable overheads less £6000 favourable expenditure variance).
Therefore, standard variable overhead rate = £1 (£32 000/32 000 hours).

(b) See 'Types of cost standards' in Chapter 12 for the answer to this question.

12.18 (a) Budgeted contribution = Standard unit contribution
(£1.99 – £1.39 = £0.60) × 50 000 = £30 000
Actual contribution = £96 480 – (£58 450 + £6800 + £3250) = £27 980

(b) Sales margin price = (Actual price – Standard price) × Actual sales volume
= Actual sales (£96 480) – Actual sales volume (49 700) × Standard price (£1.99)
= £2423A (note that the same answer would be obtained using contribution margins in the above formula)

Sales margin volume = (Actual volume – Budgeted volume) × Standard unit contribution
= (49 700 – 50 000) × £0.60 = £180A

Ingredients price $= (SP - AP)AQ = (AQ \times SP) - (AQ \times AP)$
$= (55\,000 \times £1.18/1.08 = £60\,093) - £58\,450 = £1643F$

Ingredients usage $= (SQ - AQ)SP = (49\,700 \times 1.08 =$
$53\,676 - 55\,000)\,£1.18/1.08 = £1447A$

Wage rate $= (SP - AP)AH = (AH \times SP) - (AH \times AP)$
$= (1200 \times £6^1 = £7200) - £6800 = £400F$

Labour efficiency $= (SH - AH)SP = (49\,700 \times 1.5$
minutes $= 1242.5$ hours
$- 1200$ hours$) \times £6 = £255F$

Variable conversion price $= (SP - AP)AH = (AH \times SP) -$
$(AH \times AP)$
$= (1200 \times £2.40^2 = £2880 - £3250 = £370A$

Variable conversion efficiency $= (SH - AH)SP = (49\,700$
$\times 1.5$ minutes $= 1242.5$ hours $- 1200$ hours$) \times £2.40 =$
$£102F$

Notes
[1]Actual price paid for labour $= £0.15/1.5$ minutes $= £0.10$
per minute $= £6$ per hour
[2]Actual variable overhead price $= £0.06/1.5$ minutes $=$
$£0.04$ per minute $= £2.40$ per hour

Reconciliation statement

	(£)	
Budgeted contribution	30 000	
Sales volume contribution variance	180	(A)
Standard contribution on actual sales	29 820	
Sales price variance	2 423	(A)
	27 397	

Cost variances		A	F	
Ingredients:	Price		1643	
	Usage	1447		
Labour	Rate		400	
	Efficiency		255	
Conversion cost	Expenditure	370		
	Efficiency		102	583 (F)
Total		1817	2400	27 980
Actual contribution				

12.19 (a) Wage rate variance $= (SP - AP)AH = (SP \times AH) -$
$(AP \times AH)$
$= (£5 \times 53$ workers $\times 13$ weeks $\times 40$ hrs$) - £138\,500$
$= £700A$

Labour efficiency $= (SH - AH)SP$

SH (Standard hours) $= (35\,000 \times 0.4$ hrs$) + (25\,000 \times$
0.56 hrs$)$
$= 28\,000$

AH (Actual hours) $= 53$ workers $\times 13$ weeks $\times 40$ hrs $=$
$27\,560$

Variance $= (28\,000 - 27\,560) \times £5 = £2200A$

(b) Material price variance $= (SP - AP)AQ$
$= (AQ \times SP) - (AQ \times AP)$
$£430F$ (given) $= 47\,000\,SP - £85\,110$
SP (Standard price) $= \dfrac{£430 + 85\,110}{47\,000}$
$= £1.82$

Material usage variance $= (SQ - AQ)SP$
$= (SQ \times SP) - (AQ \times SP)$

$£320.32A$ (given)	$= £1.82\,SQ - (33\,426 \times £1.82)$
$- £320.32A$	$= £1.82\,SQ - £60\,835.32$
$£1.82\,SQ$	$= £60\,515$
SQ	$= £60\,515/£1.82 = 33\,250$
Note that SQ	$=$ Actual production (35 000 units) $\times$ Standard usage

Therefore $35\,000 \times$ Standard usage $= 33\,250$

Standard usage	$= 33\,250/35\,000$
	$= 0.95$ kg per unit of component X

(c) For the answer to this question you should refer to the detailed illustration of the budget process shown in Chapter 10. In particular, the answer should indicate that if sales are the limiting factor the production budget should be linked to the sales budget. Once the production budget has been established for the two components, the production quantity of each component multiplied by the standard usage of material A per unit of component output determines the required quantity of material to meet the production requirements. The budgeted purchase quantity of material A consists of the quantity to meet the production usage requirements plus or minus an adjustment to take account of any planned change in the level of raw material stock.

Chapter 13

13.13 Divisional managers do not control the cash function. Therefore controllable net assets should exclude the cash overdraft so controllable net assets are £125 000 (£101 000 + £24 000).

Controllable residual income	= £69 000 (Profit before interest and tax)
Less cost of capital	= 12 500 (10% × 125 000)
Residual income	= 56 500
Answer = B	

13.14 Working backwards to derive the divisional contribution:

	£
Cost of capital charge	150 000 (£1.25m × 12%)
Residual income	47 200
Profit	197 200
Depreciation	247 500
Fixed costs	487 000
Total contribution	931 700

Contribution per unit = £31.06 (£931 700/30 000 units)
Answer = D

13.15 (a) The annual ROI and residual income calculations for each plant are as follows:

	2001	2002	2003	2004	Total
Aromatic					
(1) Net cash flow (£m)	2.4	2.4	2.4	2.4	9.6
(2) Depreciation	1.6	1.6	1.6	1.6	
(3) Profit	0.8	0.8	0.8	0.8	3.2
(4) Cost of capital (16% of 6)	(1.02)	(0.77)	(0.51)	(0.26)	
(5) Residual income	(0.22)	0.03	0.29	0.54	
(6) Opening WDV of asset	6.4	4.8	3.2	1.6	
(7) ROI (Row 3/Row 6)	12.5%	16.67%	25%	50%	
Zoman					
(1) Net cash flow	2.6	2.2	1.5	1.0	7.3
(2) Depreciation	1.3	1.3	1.3	1.3	
(3) Profit	1.3	0.9	0.2	(0.3)	2.1
(4) Cost of capital (16%)	(0.83)	(0.62)	(0.42)	(0.21)	
(5) Residual income	0.47	0.28	(0.22)	(0.51)	
(6) Opening WDV of asset	5.2	3.9	2.6	1.3	
(7) ROI	25%	23%	7.7%	(23%)	

The answer should indicate:

(i) Over the whole life of the project both ROI and residual income (RI) favour the Aromatic plant. The average ROI and RI figures are 25% and £0.16m (£0.64m/4) for the Aromatic plant and 20% and £0.005m (£0.02m/4) for the Zoman plant. The ROI calculations are based on expressing the average profits as a percentage of the average investment (defined as one half of the initial capital investment).

(ii) An explanation that Mr Elton will favour the Zoman plant because it yields a higher ROI and RI over the first two years. Mr Elton will probably focus on a two-year time horizon because of his personal circumstances, since choosing the Aromatic plant is likely to result in him losing his bonus. Therefore he will choose the plant with the lower NPV and there will be a lack of goal congruence.

(iii) Suggestions as to how alternative accounting techniques can assist in reconciling the conflict between accounting performance measures and DCF techniques:

1. Avoiding short-term evaluations and evaluating performance at the end of the project's life. Thus bonuses would be awarded with hindsight;

2. Use alternative asset valuations other than historic cost (e.g. replacement cost);

3. Choose alternative depreciation methods that are most consistent with NPV calculations (e.g. annuity depreciation);

4. Incorporate a range of variables (both financial and non-financial when evaluating managerial performance) that give a better indication of future results that can be expected from current actions.

(b) Managers may use pre-tax profits to evaluate divisional performance because it is assumed that taxation is non-controllable. Taxation payable is based on total group profits and present and past capital expenditure rather than individual divisional profitability. After tax cash flows are used to appraise capital investments because the focus is on decision-making and accepting those projects that earn a return in excess of the investors' opportunity cost of capital. To do this IRRs and NPVs should be based on after-tax cash flows.

The following potential problems can arise:

(i) Managers may ignore the taxation impact at the decision-making stage because it is not considered when evaluating their performance;

(ii) Confusion and demotivation can occur when different criteria are used for decision-making and performance evaluation.

Possible solutions include evaluating divisional profitability after taxes or evaluating performance based on a comparison of budgeted and actual cash flows. Adopting the latter approach is an attempt to ensure that the same criteria is used for decision-making and performance evaluation.

(c) Steps that can be taken to avoid dysfunctional behaviour include:

(i) Not placing too much emphasis on short-term performance measures and placing greater emphasis on the long term by adopting a profit-conscious style of evaluation.

(ii) Focusing on controllable residual income or economic value added combined with asset valuations derived from depreciation models that are consistent with NPV calculations. Alternatively, performance evaluation might be based on a comparison of budgeted and actual cash flows. The budgeted cash flows should be based on cash flows that are used to appraise capital investments.

(iii) Supplementing financial performance measures with non-financial measures when evaluating performance (see 'Addressing the dysfunctional consequences of short-term financial measures' in Chapter 13).

13.16 (a) To compute EVA, adjustments must be made to the conventional after tax profit measures of $44m and $55m shown in the question. Normally an adjustment is made to convert conventional financial accounting depreciation to an estimate of economic depreciation, but the question indicates that profits have already been computed using economic depreciation. Non-cash expenses are added back since the adjusted profit attempts to approximate cash flow after taking into account economic depreciation. Net interest is also added back because the returns required by the providers of funds will be reflected in the cost of capital deduction. Note that net interest is added back because interest will have been allowed as an expense in determining the taxation payment.

The capital employed used to calculate EVA should be based on adjustments that seek to approximate book economic value at the start of each period. Because insufficient information is given, the book value of shareholders funds plus medium- and long-term loans at the end of 2000 is used as the starting point to determine economic capital employed at the beginning of 2001.

	2000 ($m)	20001 ($m)
Adjusted profit	56.6 (44 + 10 + (4 × 0.65))	68.9 (55 + 10 + (6 × 0.65))
Capital employed	233 (223 + 10)	260 (250 + 10)

The weighted average cost of capital should be based on the target capital structure. The calculation is as follows:

$2000 = (15\% \times 0.6) + (9\% \times 0.65 \times 0.4) = 11.34\%$
$2001 = (17\% \times 0.6) + (10\% \times 0.65 \times 0.4) = 12.8\%$
EVA $2000 = 56.6 - (233 \times 0.1134) = \$30.18m$
EVA $2001 = 68.9 - (260 \times 0.128) = \$35.62$

The EVA measures indicate that the company has added significant value in both years and achieved a satisfactory level of performance.

(b) Advantages of EVA include:
1 because some discretionary expenses are capitalized the harmful side-effects of financial measures described in Chapters 11 and 13 are reduced;
2 EVA is consistent with maximizing shareholders funds;
3 EVA is easily understood by managers;
4 EVA can also be linked to managerial bonus schemes and motivate managers to take decisions that increase shareholder value.

Disadvantages of EVA include:
1 the EVA computation can be complicated when many adjustments are required;
2 EVA is difficult to use for inter-firm and inter-divisional comparisons because it is not a ratio measure;
3 if economic depreciation is not used, the short-term measure can conflict with the long-term measure;
4 economic depreciation is difficult to estimate and conflicts with generally accepted accounting principles which may hinder its acceptance by financial managers.

13.17 (a) Examples of the types of decisions that should be transferred to the new divisional managers include:
(i)   Product decisions such as product mix, promotion and pricing.
(ii) Employment decisions, except perhaps for the appointment of senior managers.
(iii) Short-term operating decisions of all kinds. Examples include production scheduling, subcontracting and direction of marketing effort.
(iv) Capital expenditure and disinvestment decisions (with some constraints).
(v)   Short-term financing decisions (with some constraints).

(b) The following decisions might be retained at company head office:
(i)   Strategic investment decisions that are critical to the survival of the company as a whole.
(ii) Certain financing decisions that require that an overall view be taken. For example, borrowing commitments and the level of financial gearing should be determined for the group as a whole.
(iii) Appointment of top management.
(iv) Sourcing decisions such as bulk buying of raw materials if corporate interests are best served by centralized buying.
(v)   Capital expenditure decisions above certain limits.
(vi) Common services that are required by all profit centres. Corporate interests might best be served by operating centralized service departments such as an industrial relations department. Possible benefits include reduced costs and the extra benefits of specialization.

(vii) Arbitration decisions on transfer pricing disputes.
(viii) Decisions on items which benefit the company rather than an individual division, e.g. taxation and computer applications.

(c) The answer to this question should focus on the importance of designing performance reports which encourage goal congruence. For a discussion of this topic see Chapter 13.

13.18 (a) For the answer to this question see 'Return on investment' and 'Residual income' in Chapter 13. Note that discounted future earnings are the equivalent to discounted future profits.

(b) The existing ROCE is 20% and the estimated ROCE on the additional investment is 15% (£9000/£60 000). The divisional manager will therefore reject the additional investment, since adding this to the existing investments will result in a decline in the existing ROCE of 20%.

The residual income on the additional investment is £600 (£9000 average profit for the year less an imputed interest charge of 14% × £6000 = £8400). The manager will accept the additional investment, since it results in an increase in residual income.

If the discounted future earnings method is used, the investment would be accepted, since it will yield a positive figure for the year (that is, £9000 × 3.889 discount factor).

Note that the annual future cash flows are £19 000 (£9000 net profit plus £10 000 depreciation provision). The project has a 6-year life. The annual cash inflow must be in excess of £15 428 (£60 000/3.889 annuity factor – 6 years at 14%) if the investment is to yield a positive NPV. If annual cash flows are £19 000 each year for the next 6 years, the project should be accepted.

The residual income and discounted future earnings methods of evaluation will induce the manager to accept the investment. These methods are consistent with the correct economic evaluation using the NPV method. If ROCE is used to evaluate performance, the manager will incorrectly reject the investment. This is because the manager will only accept projects that yield a return in excess of the current ROCE of 20%.

Note that the above analysis assumes that the cash flows/profits are constant from year to year.

13.19 (a) For cost control and performance measurement purposes it is necessary to measure performance at frequent intervals. Managers tend to be evaluated on short-term (monthly, quarterly or even yearly) performance measures such as residual income (RI) or return on investment (ROI). Such short-term performance measures focus only on the performance for the particular control period. If a great deal of stress is placed on managers meeting short-term performance measure targets, there is a danger that they will take action that will improve short-term performance but that will not maximize long-term profits. For example, by skimping on expenditure on advertising, customer services, maintenance, and training and staff development costs, it is possible to improve short-term performance. However, such actions may not maximize long-term profits.

Ideally, performance measures ought to be based on future results that can be expected from a manager's actions during a period. This would involve a comparison of the present value of future cash flows at the start and end of the period, and a manager's performance would be based on the increase in present value during the period. Such a system is not feasible, given the difficulty in predicting and measuring outcomes from current actions.

ROI and RI represent single summary measures of performance. It is virtually impossible to capture in summary financial measures all the variables that measure the success of a manager. It is therefore important that accountants broaden their reporting systems to include additional non-financial measures of performance that give clues to future outcomes from present actions.

It is probably impossible to design performance measures which will ensure that maximizing the short-run performance measure will also maximize long-term performance. Some steps, however, can be taken to improve the short-term performance measures so that they minimize the potential conflict. For example, during times of rising prices, short-term performance measures can be distorted if no attempt is made to adjust for the changing price levels. ROI has a number of deficiencies. In particular, it encourages managers to accept only those investments that are in excess of the current ROI, and this can lead to the rejection of profitable projects. Such actions can be reduced by replacing ROI with RI as the performance measure. However, merely changing from ROI to RI will not eliminate the short-run versus long-run conflicts.

(b) One suggestion that has been made to overcome the conflict between short-term and long-term measures is for accountants to broaden their reporting systems and include non-financial performance measures in the performance reports. For example, obtaining feedback from customers regarding the quality of service encourages managers not to skimp on reducing the quality of service in order to save costs in the short term. For a discussion of the potential contribution from including non-financial measures in the reporting system see 'Addressing the dysfunctional consequences of short-term financial performance measures' in Chapter 13.

Other suggestions have focused on refining the financial measures so that they will reduce the potential for conflict between actions that improve short-term performance at the expense of long-term performance. For a description of these suggestions see 'The impact of depreciation' in Chapter 13.

Chapter 14

14.15 The loss of contribution (profits) in Division A from lost internal sales of 2500 units at £18 (£40 – £22) is £45 000.

The impact on the whole company is that the external purchase cost is £87 500 (2500 × £35) compared with the incremental cost of manufacture of £55 000 (2500 × £22). Therefore the company will be worse off by £32 500. Answer = D

14.16 The dual market price in respect of Division A will be the market price of £25. The two-part tariff transfer price per unit is the marginal cost of £15.
Answer = B

14.17 (i) The proposed transfer price of £15 is based on cost plus 25% implying that the total cost is £12. This comprises of £9 variable cost (75%) and £3 fixed cost. The general transfer pricing guideline described in Chapter 14 can be applied to this question. That is the transfer price that should be set at marginal cost plus opportunity. It is assumed in the first situation that transferring internally will result in Helpco having a lost contribution of £9 (£15 external market price less £9 variable cost for the external market). The marginal cost of the transfer is £7.50 (£9 external variable cost less £1.50 packaging costs not required for internal sales). Adding the opportunity cost of £6 gives a transfer price of £13.50 per kg. This is equivalent to applying the market price rule where the transfer price is set at the external market price (£15) less selling costs avoided (£1.50) by transferring internally.

(ii) For the 3000 kg where no external market is available the opportunity cost will not apply and transfers should be at the variable cost of £7.50. The remaining output should be transferred at £13.50 as described above.

(iii) The lost contribution for the 2000 kg is £3 per kg (£6000/2000 kg) giving a transfer price of £10.50 (£7.50 variable cost plus £3 opportunity cost). The remaining 1000 kg for which there is no external market should be transferred at £7.50 variable cost and the balance for which there is an external market transferred at £13.50.

14.18 (a) The effects on each division and the company as a whole of selling the motor unit at each possible selling price are presented in the following schedules:

(i) *EM division*

Output level (units)	Total revenues (£)	Variable costs (£)	Total contribution (£)
1000	16 000	6 000	10 000
2000	32 000	12 000	20 000
3000	48 000	18 000	30 000
4000	64 000	24 000	40 000
6000	96 000	36 000	60 000
8000	128 000	48 000	**80 000**

(ii) *IP division*

Output level (units)	Total revenues (£)	Variable costs (£)	Total cost of transfers (£)	Total contribution (£)
1000	50 000	4 000	16 000	30 000
2000	80 000	8 000	32 000	40 000
3000	105 000	12 000	48 000	**45 000**
4000	120 000	16 000	64 000	40 000
6000	150 000	24 000	96 000	30 000
8000	160 000	32 000	128 000	nil

(iii) *Enormous Engineering plc*

Output level (units)	Total revenues (£)	Variable costs (EMD) (£)	Variable costs (IPD) (£)	Total contribution (£)
1000	50 000	6 000	4 000	40 000
2000	80 000	12 000	8 000	60 000
3000	105 000	18 000	12 000	75 000
4000	120 000	24 000	16 000	80 000
6000	150 000	36 000	24 000	**90 000**
8000	160 000	48 000	32 000	80 000

The above schedules indicate that EM division maximizes profits at an output of 8000 units, whereas IP division maximizes profits at an output level of 3000 units. Profits are maximized for the company as a whole at an output level of 6000 units.

(b) (i) Based on the tabulation in (a), IPD should select a selling price of £35 per unit. This selling price produces a maximum divisional contribution of £45 000.

(ii) The company as a whole should select a selling price of £25 per unit. This selling price produces a maximum company contribution of £90 000.

(iii) If IPD selected a selling price of £25 per unit instead of £35 per unit, its overall marginal revenue would increase by £45 000 but its marginal cost would increase by £60 000. Consequently it is not in IPD's interest to lower the price from £35 to £25 when the transfer price of the intermediate product is set at £16.

(c) (i) Presumably profit centres have been established so as to provide a profit incentive for each division and to enable divisional managers to exercise a high degree of divisional autonomy. The maintenance of divisional autonomy and the profitability incentive can lead to sub-optimal decisions. The costs of sub-optimization may be acceptable to a certain extent in order to preserve the motivational advantages which arise with divisional autonomy.

Within the EE group, EMD has decision-making autonomy with respect to the setting of transfer prices. EMD sets transfer prices on a full cost-plus basis in order to earn a target profit. The resulting transfer price causes IPD to restrict output to 3000 units, which is less than the group optimum. The cost of this sub-optimal decision is £15 000 (£90 000 – £75 000). A solution to the problem is to set the transfer price at the variable cost per unit of the supplying division. This transfer price will result in IPD selecting the optimum output level, but will destroy the profit incentive for the EM division. Note that fixed costs will not be covered and there is no external market for the intermediate product.

Possible solutions to achieving the motivational and optimality objectives include:
1. operating a dual transfer pricing system;
2. lump sum payments.
See 'Proposals for resolving transfer pricing conflicts' in Chapter 14 for an explanation of the above items.

(ii) Where there is no market for the intermediate product and the supplying division has no capacity constraints, the correct transfer price is the marginal cost of the supplying division for that output at which marginal cost equals the receiving division's net marginal revenue from converting the intermediate product. When unit variable cost is constant and fixed costs remain unchanged, this rule will result in a transfer price which is equal to the supplying division's unit variable cost. Therefore the transfer price will be set at £6 per unit when the variable cost transfer pricing rule is applied. IPD will then be faced with the following marginal cost and net marginal revenue schedule:

Output level (units)	Marginal cost of transfers (£)	Net marginal revenue of IPD (£)
1000		
2000	6 000	26 000
3000	6 000	21 000
4000	6 000	11 000
6000	12 000	22 000
8000	12 000	2 000

IPD will select an output level of 6000 units and will not go beyond this because NMR < marginal cost. This is the optimal output for the group, but the profits from the sale of the motor unit will accrue entirely to the IP division, and the EM division will make a loss equal to the fixed costs.

14.19 (a) The variable costs per unit of output for sales *outside* the company are £11 for the intermediate product and £49 [£10(A) + £39(B)] for the final product. Note that selling and packing expenses are not incurred by the supplying division for the transfer of the intermediate product. It is assumed that the company has sufficient capacity to meet demand at the various selling prices.

Optimal output of intermediate product for sale on external market

Selling price (£)	20	30	40
Unit contribution (£)	9	19	29
Demand (units)	15 000	10 000	5 000
Total contribution (£)	135 000	190 000	145 000

Optimal output is 10 000 units at a selling price of £30.

Optimal output for final product

Selling price (£)	80	90	100
Unit contribution (£)	31	41	51
Demand (units)	7 200	5 000	2 800
Total contribution (£)	223 200	205 000	142 800

Optimal output is 7200 units at a selling price of £80.

Optimal output of Division B based on a transfer price of £29
Division B will regard the transfer price as a variable cost. Therefore total variable cost per unit will be £68 (£29 + £39), and Division B will calculate the following contributions:

Selling price (£)	80	90	100
Unit contribution (£)	12	22	32
Demand (units)	7 200	5 000	2 800
Total contribution (£)	86 400	110 000	89 600

The manager of Division B will choose an output level of 5000 units at a selling price of £90. This is sub-optimal for the company as a whole. Profits for the *company as a whole* from the sale of the final product are reduced from £223 200 (7200 units) to £205 000 (5000 units). The £205 000 profits would be allocated as follows:

Division A £95 000 [5000 units at (£29 – £10)]
Division B £110 000

(b) At a transfer price of £12, the variable cost per unit produced in Division B will be £51 (£12 + £39). Division B will calculate the following contributions:

Selling price (£)	80	90	100
Unit contribution (£)	29	39	49
Demand (units)	7 200	5 000	2 800
Total contribution (£)	208 800	195 000	137 200

The manager of Division B will choose an output level of 7200 units and a selling price of £80. This is the optimum output level for the company as a whole. Division A would obtain a contribution of £14 400 [7200 × (£12 – £10)] from internal transfers of the intermediate product, whereas Division B would obtain a contribution of £208 800 from converting the intermediate product and selling as a final product. Total contribution for the company as a whole would be £223 200. Note that Division A would also earn a contribution of £190 000 from the sale of the intermediate product to the external market.

14.20 (a) See 'International transfer pricing' in Chapter 14 for the answer to this question. Besides the ethical issues and legal considerations other criticisms relate to the distortions in the divisional profit reporting system. Also divisional autonomy will be undermined if the transfer prices are imposed on the divisional managers.

(b) The ethical limitations relate to multinational companies using the transfer pricing system to reduce the amount paid in custom duties, taxation and the manipulation of dividends remitted. Furthermore, using the transfer prices for these purposes is likely to be illegal, although there is still likely to be some scope for manipulation that is within the law. It is important that multinational companies are seen to be acting in a socially responsible manner. Any bad publicity relating to using the transfer pricing system purely to avoid taxes and custom duties will be very harmful to the image of the organization. Nevertheless tax management and the ability to minimize corporate taxes is an important task for management if it is to maximize shareholder value. Thus it is important that management distinguish between tax avoidance and tax evasion. Adopting illegal practices is not acceptable and management must ensure that their transfer pricing policies do not contravene the regulations and laws of the host counties in which they operate.

Chapter 15

15.15 (a) (i)

	Units
Components worked on in the process	6120
Less: planned defective units	612
replacements to customers (2% × 5400)	108
Components invoiced to customers	5400

Therefore actual results agree with planned results.

(ii) Planned component cost = (3 × £18 for material A) + (2 × £9 for material B) + £15 variable cost = £87
Comparing with the data in the appendix:
Materials = £440 640/6120 = £72
Variable overhead = £91 800/6120 = £15
This indicates that prices were at the planned levels.

(b) Internal failure costs = £53 244 (612 units × £87)
External failure costs = £9396 (108 units × £87)

(c) (i)

	Period 2 (units)	Period 3 (units)
Components invoiced to customers	5500	5450
Planned replacement (2%)	110	109
Unplanned replacements	60 (170 – 110)	–69 (40 – 109)
Components delivered to customers	5670	5490
Planned process defects (10% of worked on in the process)	620	578
Unplanned defects (difference to agree with final row)	–90	–288
Components worked on in the process	6200	5780

(ii)

	Period 2 (£)	Period 3 (£)
Internal failure costs £87	46 110 (620 – 90) × £87	25 230 (578 – 288) × £87
External failure costs	14 790 (110 + 60) × £87	3 480 (109 – 69) × £87
Appraisal costs	10 000	15 000
Prevention costs	5 000	8 000

(iii) The following points should be included in the report:
1. Insufficient detail is provided in the statistics shown in the appendix thus resulting in the need to for an improvement in reporting.
2. The information presented in (c) (i) indicates that free replacements to customers were 60 greater than planned in period 2 but approximately 70 less than planned in period 3. In contrast, the in process defects were 90 less than planned (approximately 15%) in period 2 and 288 less than plan (approximately 50%) in period 3.
3. Internal failures costs show a downward trend from periods 1–3 with a substantial decline in period 3. External failure costs increased in period 2 but declined significantly in period 3.
4. The cost savings arising in periods 2 and 3 are as follows:

	Period 2 (£)	Period 3 (£)
Increase/decrease from previous period:		
Internal failure costs	–7134 (£53 244 – £46 110)	–20 880 (£46 110 – £25 230)
External failure costs	+5394 (£9396 – £14 790)	–11 310 (£14 790 – £3480)
Total decrease	–1740	–32 190

The above savings should be compared against the investment of £10 000 appraisal costs and £5000 prevention costs for period 2 and £15 000 and £8000 respectively in period 3. It can be seen that the costs exceed the savings in period 2 but the savings exceeded the costs in period 3. There has also been an increase in the external failure costs from period 1 to period 2. Investigations should be made relating to the likely time lag from incurring prevention/appraisal costs and their subsequent benefits.

5. The impact on customer goodwill from the reduction in replacements should also be examined.

15.16 (a) (i) *Performance report for period ending 30 November (Traditional analysis)*

Expenses

	Budget (£)	Actual (£)	Variance (£)
Salaries	600 000	667 800	67 800A
Supplies	60 000	53 000	7 000F
Travel cost	120 000	127 200	7 200A
Technology cost	100 000	74 200	25 800F
Occupancy cost	120 000	137 800	17 800A
Total	1 000 000	1 060 000	60 000A

Performance report for period ending 30 November (Activity-based analysis)

Activities

	(£)	(£)	(£)
Routing/scheduling – new products	200 000	169 600	30 400F
Routing/scheduling – existing products	400 000	360 400	39 600F
Remedial re-routing/scheduling	50 000	127 200	77 200A
Special studies – specific orders	100 000	84 800	15 200F
Training	100 000	159 000	59 000A
Management and administration	150 000	159 000	9 000A
Total	1 000 000	1 060 000	60 000A

(ii) See 'Activity-based budgeting' in Chapter 10 for the answer to this question. In particular, the answer should stress:

(i) The enhanced visibility of activity-based budgeting (ABB) by focusing on outcomes (activities) rather than a listing by expense categories.

(ii) The cost of activities are highlighted thus identifying high cost non-value added activities that need to be investigated.

(iii) ABB identifies resource requirements to meet the demand for activities whereas traditional budgeting adopts an incremental approach.

(iv) Excess resources are identified that can be eliminated or redeployed.

(v) ABB enables more realistic budgets to be set.

(vi) ABB avoids arbitrary cuts in specific budget areas in order to meet overall financial targets.

(vii) It is claimed that ABB leads to increased management commitment to the budget process because it enables management to focus on the objectives of each activity and compare the outcomes with the costs that are allocated to the activity.

(iii) The ABB statement shows a comparison of actual with budget by activities. All of the primary value-adding activities (i.e. the first, second and fourth activities in the budget statement) have favourable

variances. Remedial rerouting is a non-value added activity and has the highest adverse variance. Given the high cost, top priority should be given to investigating the activity with a view to eliminating it, or to substantially reducing the cost by adopting alternative working practices. Training and management and administration are secondary activities which support the primary activities. Actual training expenditure exceeds budget by 50% and the reason for the over-spending should be investigated.

For each activity it would be helpful if the costs were analysed by expense items (such as salaries, supplies, etc.) to pinpoint the cost build up of the activities and to provide clues indicating why an overspending on some activities has occurred.

Cost driver usage details should also be presented in a manner similar to that illustrated in Exhibit 10.1 in Chapter 10. Many organizations that have adopted ABC have found it useful to report budgeted and actual cost driver rates. The trend in cost driver rates is monitored and compared with similar activities undertaken within other divisions where a divisionalized structure applies. As indicated in Chapter 15, care must be taken when interpreting cost driver rates.

For additional points to be included in the answer see 'Activity-based management' in Chapter 15.

(b) The cost driver rates are as follows:
Product design = £250 per design hour (£2m/8000 hours)
Purchasing = £50 per purchase order (£200 000/4000 orders)
Production (excluding depreciation) = £100 per machine hour ((£1 500 000 – £300 000)/12 000 hours)
Packing = £20 per cubic metre (£400 000/20 000)
Distribution = £5 per kg (£600 000/120 000)
The activity-based overhead cost per unit is as follows:

		(£)
Product design	(400 design hours at £250 per hour = £100 000 divided by life-cycle output of 5000 units)	20.00
Purchasing	(5 purchase orders at 50 units per order costing a total of £250 for an output of 250 units)	1.00
Production	(0.75 machine hours at £100 per machine hour)	75.00
Depreciation	(Asset cost over life cycle of 4 years = 16 quarters' depreciation at £8000 per quarter divided by life-cycle output of 5000 units)	25.60
Packing	(0.4 cubic metres at £20)	8.00
Distribution	(3 kg at £5)	15.00
Total cost		144.60

15.17 See 'Cost of quality', 'Just-in-time systems' and 'Activity-based management' in Chapter 15 for the answer to this question. You should also refer to 'Activity-based budgeting' in Chapter 10. All of the approaches seek to eliminate waste and therefore when the principles are applied to budget preparation there should be a move away from incremental budgeting to the resources that are required to meet budgeted demand. For an explanation of this point see 'Activity-based budgeting' in Chapter 10. Within the budgeting process a total quality ethos would result in a move towards a zero-defects policy when the budgets are prepared. There would be reduced budget allocations for internal and external failure costs and an increase in the allocation for prevention and appraisal costs.

The just-in-time philosophy would result in a substantial budgeted reduction in stocks and establishing physical targets that support JIT systems, such as manufacturing cycle efficiency and set-up times. See 'Operation processes' and 'Cycle time measures' in Chapter 16 for an explanation of some of the performance targets that are appropriate for JIT systems. The activity-based focus should result in the implementation of activity-based budgeting (see Chapter 10).

15.18 Benchmarking is a continuous process that involves comparing business processes and activities in an organization with those in other companies that represent world-class best practices in order to see how processes and activities can be improved. The comparison involves both financial and non-financial indicators.

Two different approaches are adopted in most organizations. Cost-driven bench-marking involves applying the principles of benchmarking from a distance and comparing some aspects of performance with those of competitors, usually using intermediaries such as consultants. The outcome of the exercise is cost reduction. The second approach involves process-driven benchmarking. It is a process involving the philosophy of continuous improvement. The focus is not necessarily on competitors but on a benchmarking partner. The aim is to obtain a better understanding of the processes and questions the reason why things take place, how they take place and how often they take place. The outcome should be superior performance through the strengthening of processes and business behaviour.

Inter-firm comparisons place much greater emphasis on the use of financial data and mostly involve comparisons at the company or strategic business unit level rather than at the business process or activity level. Inter-firm comparisons tend to compare data derived from published financial accounts whereas benchmarking also makes use of both internal and external data.

Benchmarking contributes to cost reduction by highlighting those areas where performance is inferior to competitors and where opportunities for cost reduction exist (e.g. elimination of non-value added activities or more efficient ways of carrying out activities).

Activity-based budgeting (ABB) is an extension of ABC applied to the preparation of budgets. It focuses on the costs of activities necessary to produce and sell products and services by assigning costs to separate activity cost pools. The cause and effect criterion based on cost drivers is used to establish budgets for each cost pool.

ABB involves the following stages:
1. Determining the budgeted cost (i.e. the cost driver rate) of performing each unit of activity for all major activities.
2. Determining the required resources for each individual activity to meet sales and production requirements.
3. Computing the budgeted cost for each activity.

Note that ABB focuses on budgets for the cost of activities rather than functional departments.

Zero-base budgeting tends to be used more as a one-off cost reduction programme. The emphasis is on functional responsibility areas, rather than individual activities, with the aim of justifying all costs from a zero base.

Activity analysis is required prior to implementing ABB. This process can help to identify non-value added activities that may be candidates for elimination or performing the activities in different ways with less resources. Activity performance measures can be established that enable the cost per unit of activity to be monitored and used as a basis for benchmarking. This information should highlight those activities where there is a potential for performing more efficiently by reducing resource consumption and future spending.

See 'Target costing' in Chapter 15 for an explanation of the objectives and workings of target costing.

Continuous cost improvement is a process whereby a firm gradually reduces costs without attempting to achieve a specific target. Target costing is emphasized more at a product's design and development stage whereas continuous cost improvement occurs throughout a product's life. The principles of target costing can also be applied to cost reduction exercises for existing products. Where this approach is applied there is little difference between the two methods. Both approaches clearly focus on reducing costs throughout a product's life cycle but target costing emphasizes cost reduction at the design and development stage. At this stage there is a greater potential for reducing costs throughout the product life cycle.

15.19 (a) The factors influencing the preferred costing system are different for every firm. The benefits from implementing ABC are likely to be influenced by the level of competition, the number of products sold, the diversity of the product range and the proportion of overheads and direct costs in the cost structure. Companies operating in a more competitive environment have a greater need for more accurate cost information, since competitors are more likely to take advantage of any errors arising from the use of distorted cost information generated by a traditional costing system. Where a company markets a small number of products special studies can be undertaken using the decision-relevant approach. Problems do not arise in determining which product or product combinations should be selected for undertaking special studies. Increased product diversity arising from the manufacture and sale of low-volume and high-volume products favours the use of ABC systems. As the level of diversity increases so does the level of distortion reported by traditional costing systems. Finally, organizations with a large proportion of overheads and a low proportion of direct costs are likely to benefit from ABC, because traditional costing systems can be relied upon only to report accurately direct product costs. Distorted product costs are likely to be reported where a large proportion of overheads are related to product variety rather than volume.

(b) For a more detailed answer to this question you should refer to 'Activity-based management' in Chapter 15. In particular, the answer should draw attention to the fact that ABM attaches costs to activities and identifies the cost drivers that cause the costs. Thus ABM provides a better understanding of what causes costs, and highlights ways of performing activities more efficiently by reducing cost driver transactions.

Costs can therefore be managed more effectively in the long run. Activities can be analysed into value added and non-value added activities and by highlighting the costs of non-value added activities attention is drawn to areas where there is an opportunity for cost reduction, without reducing the products' service potentials to customers.

Finally, the cost of unused activity capacity is reported for each activity, thus drawing attention to where capacity can be reduced or utilized more effectively to expand future profitability.

(c) See 'Target Costing' in Chapter 15 for the answer to this question.

Chapter 16

16.15 (a)

	Original budget based on 120 000 gross hours	Standard hours based on actual gross hours	Actual hours	Variance (hours)	Variance (£) at £75 per hour
Gross hours	120 000	132 000	132 000		
Contract negotiation	4 800 (4%)	5 280 (4%)	9 240 (7%)	3 960A	297 000A
Remedial advice	2 400 (2%)	2 640 (2%)	7 920 (6%)	5 280A	396 000A
Other non-chargeable	12 000 (10%)	13 200 (10%)	22 440 (17%)	9 240A	693 000A
Chargeable hours	100 800 (84%)	110 880 (84%)	92 400 (70%)	18 480A	1 386 000A

There was a capacity gain over budget of 10 080 (110 880 − 100 800) hours at a client value of £756 000 (10 080 hours at £75) but because all of this was not converted into actual chargeable hours there was a net fall in chargeable hours compared with the original budget of 8400 (100 800 − 92 400) hours at a client value of £630 000.

(b) *Financial performance*

Profit statement and financial ratios for year ending 30 April

	Budget (£000)	Actual (£000)
Revenue from client contracts (chargeable hours × £75)	7560	6930
Costs:		
Consultant salaries	1800	1980
Sundry operating costs	3500	4100
	5300	6080
Net profit	2260	850
Capital employed	6500	6500
Financial ratios:		
Net profit: Turnover	29.9%	12.3%
Turnover: Capital employed	1.16 times	1.07 times
Net profit: Capital employed	34.8%	13.1%

The above figures indicate a poor financial performance for the year. The statement in (a) indicates an increase in gross hours from 120 000 to 132 000 hours providing the potential for 110 880 chargeable hours compared with the budget of 100 800 hours. This should have increased fee income by £756 000 (10 080 × £75). However, of the potential 110 880 hours there were only 92 400 chargeable hours resulting in a shortfall of 18 480 hours at a lost fee income of £1 386 000. The difference between these two monetary figures of £630 000 represents the difference between budgeted and actual revenues.

Competitiveness

Competitiveness should be measured in terms of market share and sales growth. Sales are less than budget but the offer of free remedial advice to clients presumably represents the allocation of staff time to improve longer term competitiveness even though this has had an adverse impact on short-term profit.

Competitiveness may also be measured in terms of the relative success/failure in obtaining business from clients. The data shows that the budgeted uptake from clients is 40% for new systems and 75% for existing systems compared with actuals of 35% and 80% respectively. For new systems worked on there is a 16.7% increase compared with the budget whereas for existing systems advice actual is 4% less than budget.

Quality

The data indicate that client complaints were four times the budgeted level and that the number of clients requiring remedial advice was 75 compared with a budgeted level of 48. These items should be investigated.

Flexibility

Flexibility relates to the responsiveness to customer enquiries. For BS Ltd this relates to its ability to cope with changes in volume, delivery speed and the employment of staff who are able to meet changing customer demands. The company has retained 60 consultants in order to increase its flexibility in meeting demand. The data given show a change in the mix of consultancy specialists that may reflect an attempt to respond to changes in the marketing mix. The ratio of new systems to existing systems advice has changed and this may indicate a flexible response to market demands.

Resource utilization

The budget was based on chargeable hours of 84% of gross hours but the actual percentage was 70% (see part (a)). There was an increased level of remedial advice (6% of gross hours compared with 2% in the budget) and this may represent an investment with the aim of stimulating future demand.

Innovation

Innovation relates to the ability of the organization to provide new and better quality services. The company has established an innovative feature by allowing free remedial advice after completion of a contract. In the short term this is adversely affecting financial performance but it may have a beneficial long-term impact. The answer to part (a) indicates that remedial advice exceeded the adjusted budget by 5280 hours. This should be investigated to establish whether or not this was a deliberate policy decision.

Other points

Only budgeted data were given in the question. Ideally, external benchmarks ought to be established and the trend monitored over several periods rather than focusing only on a single period.

16.16 (a) The key areas of performance referred to in the question are listed in Exhibit 16.5 – financial, competitiveness, quality of service, flexibility, resource utilization and innovation.

Financial

- There has been a continuous growth in sales turnover during the period – increasing by 50% in 1999, 10% in 2000 and 35% in 2001.
- Profits have increased at a higher rate than sales turnover – 84% in 1999, 104% in 2000 and 31% in 2001.
- Profit margins (profit/sales) have increased from 14% in 1998 to 31% in 2001.

Competitiveness

Market share (total turnover/total turnover of all restaurants) has increased from 9.2% in 1998 to 17.5% in 2001.The proposals submitted to cater for special events has increased from 2 in 1998 to 38 in 2002. This has also been accompanied by an increase in the percentage of contracts won which has increased over the years (20% in 1998, 29% in 1999, 52% in 2000 and 66% in 2001). Although all of the above measures suggest good performance in terms of this dimension the average service delay at peak times increased significantly in 2001. This area requires investigating.

Quality of service

The increasing number of regular customers attending weekly suggests that they are satisfied with the quality of service. Other factors pointing to a high level quality of service are the increase in complementary letters from satisfied customers. Conversely the number of letters of complaints and reported cases of food poisoning have not diminished over the years. Therefore the performance measures do not enable a definitive assessment to be made on the level of quality of service.

Innovation/flexibility

Each year the restaurant has attempted to introduce a significant number of new meals. There has also an increase each year in the number of special theme evenings introduced and the turnover from special events has increased significantly over the years. These measures suggest that the restaurant has been fairly successful in terms of this dimension.

Resource utilization

The total meals served have increased each year. Idle time and annual operating hours with no customers have also decreased significantly each year. There has also been an increase in the average number of customers at peak times. The value of food wasted has varied over the years but was at the lowest level in 2001. All of the measures suggest that the restaurant has been particularly successful in terms of this dimension.

(b) *Financial*

Details of the value of business assets are required to measure profitability (e.g. return on investment). This is important because the seating capacity has been increased. This may have resulted in an additional investment in assets and there is a need to ascertain whether an adequate return has been generated. Analysis of expenditure by different categories (e.g. food, drinks, wages, etc.) is required to compare the trend in financial ratios (e.g. expense categories as a percentage of sales) and with other restaurants.

Competitiveness

Comparison with other restaurants should be made in respect of the measures described in (a) such as percentage of seats occupied and average service delay at peak times.

Quality of service

Consider using mystery shoppers (i.e. employment of outsiders) to visit this and competitor restaurants to assess the quality of service relative to competitors and to also identify areas for improvement.

Innovation/flexibility

Information relating to the expertise of the staff and their ability to perform multi-skill activities is required to assess the ability of the restaurant to cope with future demands.

Resource utilization

Data on the number of employees per customer served, percentage of tables occupied at peak and non-peak times would draw attention to areas where there may be a need to improve resource utilization.

16.17 (a) See 'The balanced scorecard' in Chapter 16 for the answer to this question. In particular, the answer should describe the four different perspectives of the balanced scorecard, the assumed cause-and-effect relationships and also provide illustrations of performance measures applicable to CM Ltd.

(b) See 'Benchmarking' in Chapter 16 for the answer to this question. The answer should stress the need to identify important activities or processes that may be common to other organizations (e.g. dispatching, invoicing or ordering activities) and to compare these activities with an organization that is considered to be a world leader in undertaking these activities.

16.18 See 'Cost of quality' in Chapter 15 and 'Quality measures' in the section relating to the balanced scorecard in Chapter 16 for the answer to this question. The answer could also draw off some of the content relating to performance measurement in service organizations described in Chapter 16 (note in particular the determinants of quality of service in Exhibit 16.5). The answer should also stress the need to monitor quality internally and externally. Internal controls and performance measures should be implemented as described in Chapters 15 and 16 so as to ensure that only products that meet customer quality requirements are despatched. To monitor quality externally customer feedback should be obtained and comparisons made with competitors. With service organizations the quality of the service can be assessed by using methods such as mystery shoppers. You should refer to Chapter 16 for a more detailed description of how quality can be monitored in service organizations.

16.19 (a) (i) Efficiency measures focus on the relationship between outputs and inputs. Optimum efficiency levels are achieved by maximizing the output from a given input or minimizing the resources used in order to achieve a particular output. Measures of effectiveness attempt to measure the extent to which the outputs of an organization achieve the latter's goals. An organization can be efficient but not effective. For example, it can use resources efficiently but fail to achieve its goals.

In organizations with a profit motive, effectiveness can be measured by return on investment. Inputs and outputs can be measured. Outputs represent the quality and amount of service offered. In profit-orientated organizations output can be measured in terms of sales revenues. This provides a useful proxy measure of the quality and amount of services offered. In non-profit-making organizations outputs cannot be easily measured in monetary terms. Consequently, it is difficult to state the objectives in quantitative terms and thus measure the extent to which objectives are being achieved.

If it is not possible to produce a statement of a particular objective in measurable terms, the objectives should be stated with sufficient clarity that there is some way of judging whether or not they have been achieved. However, the focus will tend to be on subjective judgements rather than quantitative measures of effectiveness. Because of the difficulty in measuring outputs, efficiency measures tend to focus entirely on input measures such as the amount of spending on services or the cost per unit of input.

(ii) Similar problems to those of measuring effectiveness and efficiency in nonprofit-making organizations arise in measuring the performance of non-manufacturing activities in profit-orientated organizations. This is because it is extremely difficult to measure the output of non-manufacturing activities.

(b) (i) *Adherence to appointment times*
1. Percentage meeting appointment times.
2. Percentage within 15 minutes of appointment time.
3. Percentage more than 15 minutes late.
4. Average delay in meeting appointments.

Ability to contact and make appointments
It is not possible to obtain data on all those patients who have had difficulty in contacting the clinic to make appointments. However, an indication of the difficulties can be obtained by asking a sample of patients at periodic intervals to indicate on a scale (from no difficulty to considerable difficulty) the difficulty they experienced when making appointments. The number of complaints received and the average time taken to establish telephone contact with the clinic could also provide an indication of the difficulty patients experience when making appointments.

Monitoring programme
1. Comparisons with programmes of other clinics located in different regions.
2. Questionnaires asking respondents to indicate the extent to which they are aware of monitoring facilities currently offered.
3. Responses on level of satisfaction from patients registered on the programme.
4. Percentage of population undertaking the programme.

(ii) Combining the measures into a 'quality of care' measure requires that weights be attached to each selected performance measure. The sum of the performance measures multiplied by the weights would represent an overall performance measure. The problems with this approach are that the weights are set subjectively, and there is a danger that staff will focus on those performance measures with the higher weighting and pay little attention to those with the lower weighting.

INDEX